SINGLE-PLAYER AND COOPERATIVE COVER

THE CAMPAIGN

MULTIPLAYER COVERAGE

GAMEPLAY

ARSENAL

UNLOCKS AND EXTRAS

CALL OF DUTY® MW3

Visit www.bradygames.com to access a free single-player strategy video

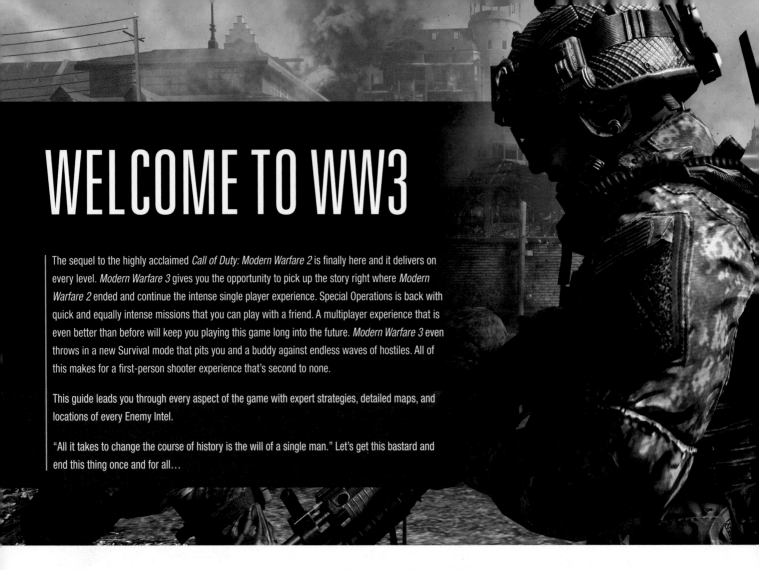

WELCOME TO WW3

The sequel to the highly acclaimed *Call of Duty: Modern Warfare 2* is finally here and it delivers on every level. *Modern Warfare 3* gives you the opportunity to pick up the story right where *Modern Warfare 2* ended and continue the intense single player experience. Special Operations is back with quick and equally intense missions that you can play with a friend. A multiplayer experience that is even better than before will keep you playing this game long into the future. *Modern Warfare 3* even throws in a new Survival mode that pits you and a buddy against endless waves of hostiles. All of this makes for a first-person shooter experience that's second to none.

This guide leads you through every aspect of the game with expert strategies, detailed maps, and locations of every Enemy Intel.

"All it takes to change the course of history is the will of a single man." Let's get this bastard and end this thing once and for all...

SPECIALIZED TRAINING

Call of Duty: Modern Warfare 3, like all other games in the *Call of Duty* series, is a first-person shooter (FPS). This means you play most of the game looking through the eyes of the main character as he fights his way through the campaign's many scenarios.

This section of the guide is for users new to first-person shooters, or those who haven't played an FPS in a few years.

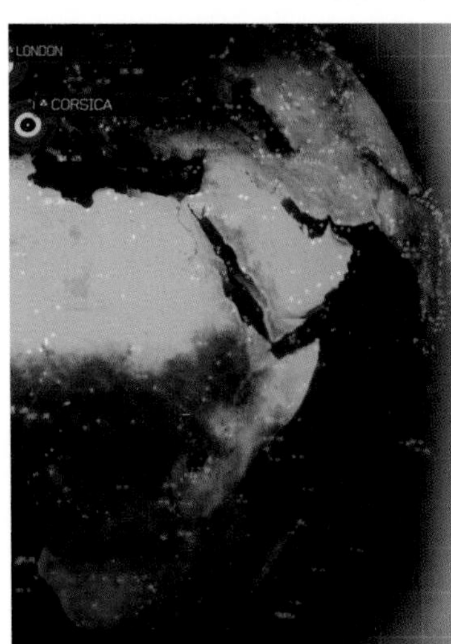

READ THE USER MANUAL

This chapter's purpose is to supplement—*not replace*—the in-game tutorials and the user's manual that comes with the game. Our primary goal is to expand on the information those sources already provide. The discussions in this chapter—and in this guide as a whole—assume that you've read the user manual, understand the basic controls, and grasp the bare essentials of playing the game.

GAME MODES

There are three ways to experience *Modern Warfare 3*.

SPECIAL OPS

Playing solo or co-op, rank up to unlock weapons, tactical support, levels, and more in Survival mode and in a variety of challenging Missions.

CAMPAIGN

Pick up the story where *Modern Warfare 2* ended, and continue the single-player experience.

MULTIPLAYER

Rank up, unlock new weapons, perks, pointstreaks, and much more, online and locally.

GAME DIFFICULTY

In Campaign mode, you can choose from four difficulties:

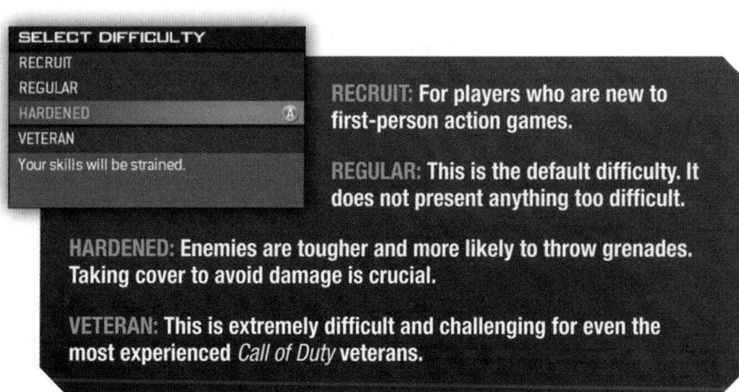

RECRUIT: For players who are new to first-person action games.

REGULAR: This is the default difficulty. It does not present anything too difficult.

HARDENED: Enemies are tougher and more likely to throw grenades. Taking cover to avoid damage is crucial.

VETERAN: This is extremely difficult and challenging for even the most experienced *Call of Duty* veterans.

HEALTH

There is no health meter or number to represent how much health you have. Your well-being is represented by blood splatter on the screen. A red arc shows up when you are hit. This arc represents the direction from which the attack originates.

As you continue getting hit, the blood splatter gets thicker until the words "You Are Hurt. Get to Cover!" show up onscreen. Move behind cover and the screen clears, showing that you are recovering.

TAKING COVER

In *Modern Warfare 3*, it's very important to take cover to avoid taking too much damage. Crouch down and move behind a wall, counter, rubble, or any object that can give some level of protection from incoming fire.

Most weapon fire penetrates softer objects such as wood, plaster walls, and cubicle walls. Use this to your advantage when enemies employ these as cover, but beware: their bullets penetrate these substances, too.

BASIC LOADOUT

At the start of each campaign level, you are given a particular weapon loadout. Usually it consists of two guns, four Flashbangs, and four Frag Grenades. Enemies drop their weapons when they're killed, giving you the opportunity to switch your guns often.

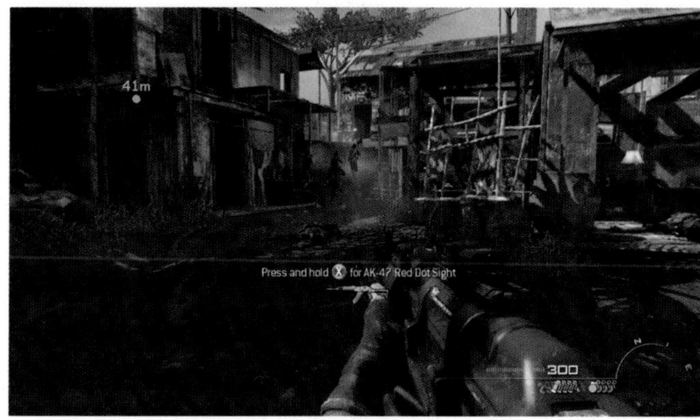

SHOOT FROM THE HIP

Whenever your weapon is ready to fire, a crosshair appears in the middle of the screen. This represents the spread of your weapon when you fire it from the hip or fire without targeting.

Firing in this manner is less accurate than aiming down the sights (ADS), so it's better to limit hip-firing to close-range weapons such as shotguns and machine pistols. This method is also a quicker way to fire. Long-range weapons, such as the sniper rifle, are very inaccurate when fired this way.

AIM DOWN THE SIGHT (ADS)

Aiming down the sight greatly improves the accuracy of your shots. It's the preferred way to fire your gun. It gives you a view of your weapon as you line up the shot with its sights. If a scope is attached to the weapon, then you only see through those optics. It may offer you the ability to zoom in on your target, giving you even better accuracy from long distances.

RELOADING

A number, along with some hash marks, appear in the screen's lower right corner. The marks represent how many rounds are left in your currently equipped weapon. The number shows how much ammo you possess for the gun.

To reload your weapon, press the Use button. Depending on which weapon is selected, the time required to reload can vary. It's always a good idea to duck behind cover when you reload, and sometimes it's better to switch to your other weapon if it reloads faster.

MELEE

You always have a combat knife equipped. If you can get close to an enemy, press in on the Right Analog Stick to knife the foe. To stay undetected, move behind a hostile target and melee him. With good timing, you can take down dogs and hyenas with the knife. Melee the animal just before it reaches you.

GRENADES

You use two types of grenades in the campaign: Flashbangs and Frag Grenades. Frag Grenades detonate explosively, causing damage to any target. Flashbangs are used to disorient and stun enemies.

Besides using Frag Grenades for blowing up things, you can also use them to flush enemies out from behind cover. This causes them to scatter, putting them out in the open for you to take down. Also note that you can "cook" grenades, allowing you to time your throws to detonate in midair, or to leave minimal time for foes to flee the target area. Simply hold the button, and the grenade's fuse starts; release the button to complete the throw. Don't cook the grenade too long, or it'll detonate in your hand!

Toss a Flashbang into a room to stun hostiles inside before you enter. You can then go in and pick off the disoriented foes.

GRENADE DANGER INDICATOR

The Grenade Danger Indicator pops up when a grenade lands near your location. A small arrow points to where it sits. Move away from it to avoid taking too much damage. If you're quick, move over to it, pick it up, and toss it back at the sender. Be careful though, as it can go off in your hands.

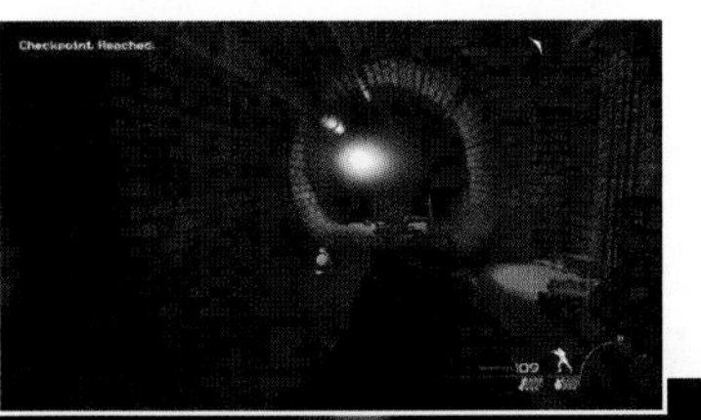

If you're against a strong barrier, such as concrete, and the icon indicates that the grenade is on the other side, duck behind cover to safely avoid the blast.

SPRINT

Pushing in on the Left Analog Stick causes your character to run faster. Sprint between pieces of cover to become a tougher target to hit.

WEAPONS

Modern Warfare 3 features seven types of guns, each with its own pros and cons. Each weapon has specific attributes, including accuracy, damage, range, fire rate, and mobility.

BREACHING

Several points in the campaign require you to breach a doorway. When you breach, you temporarily yield control of your character's movement, allowing you to focus entirely on firing your weapon. When a breach event starts, the game enters slow motion, giving you more time to shoot at enemies in the next room.

USE BUTTON

You employ the Use button (X/Square) when you perform many actions in the campaign. This includes planting explosives, using a turret, picking up Intel, and much more. Text appears onscreen when an item can be used.

DOWNED BUT NOT OUT ENEMIES

If you knock down an enemy and he doesn't die, he may try to crawl away or pull out his handgun. Be sure enemies are completely out before you change targets.

ACT 1

ACT I

BLACK TUESDAY

DELTA FORCE | 10:18 AUGUST 17 | MANHATTAN, NEW YORK

OPERATIVE SGT. DEREK "FROST" WESTBROOK, DELTA FORCE

SUPPORT SANDMAN, GRINCH, TRUCK

OBJECTIVES

DESTROY THE ENEMY JAMMING TOWER IN MANHATTAN.

- A FIGHT YOUR WAY TO THE STOCK EXCHANGE.
- B FLANK THE RUSSIANS ON WALL STREET.
- C FIGHT YOUR WAY TO THE STOCK EXCHANGE.
- D RALLY WITH YOUR SQUAD IN THE LOBBY.
- E GET TO THE STOCK EXCHANGE ROOF.
- F PLANT A THERMITE CHARGE ON THE JAMMER.
- F DETONATE THE THERMITE CHARGE.
- G USE THE PREDATOR TO TAKE OUT ENEMY FORCES.
- G USE THE PREDATOR TO TAKE OUT THE ENEMY HIND.
- H BOARD THE HELICOPTER.
- I SHOOT DOWN ENEMY HELICOPTERS.

ACHIEVEMENT/TROPHY

BACK IN THE FIGHT

The first Achievement or Trophy is earned by simply starting a Single Player Campaign on any difficulty.

The Russians are using electronic countermeasures to jam the satellite signal. A jamming tower is located on the roof of the Stock Exchange and until it is destroyed, there is no radio contact.

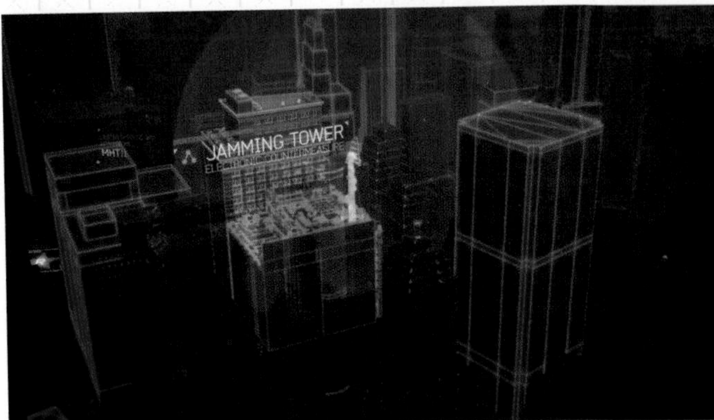

A Delta Force unit, call sign "Metal," is sent in to get this done. As they approach the area, their transport is overturned, so the group will have to huff it the rest of the way. Frost is equipped with an M4A1 and XM25, along with some Flashbangs and Frag Grenades.

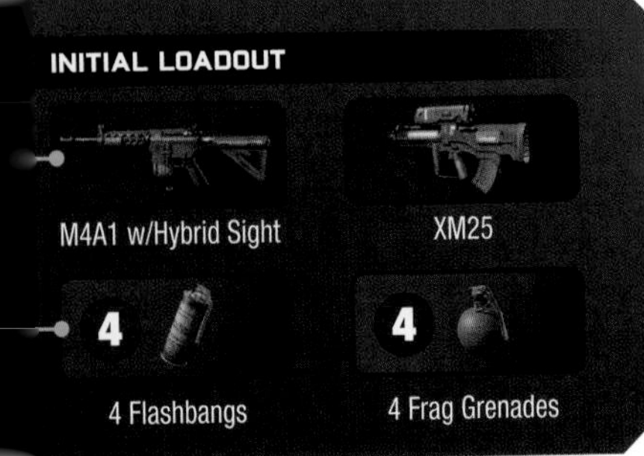

INITIAL LOADOUT
M4A1 w/Hybrid Sight
XM25
4
4 Flashbangs
4
4 Frag Grenades

"GET SWITCHED ON! WE GOTTA MOVE NOW!"

M4A1

CLIP SIZE	30
RANGE	MEDIUM TO LONG
WEAPON TYPE	ASSAULT RIFLE

The M4A1, the weapon with which you start this mission, is incredibly versatile. It fires deadly rounds at medium to long range.

This one is equipped with the Hybrid Sight attachment that gives you two options for the scope. Press Left on the D-Pad to switch to a scope with a bigger zoom.

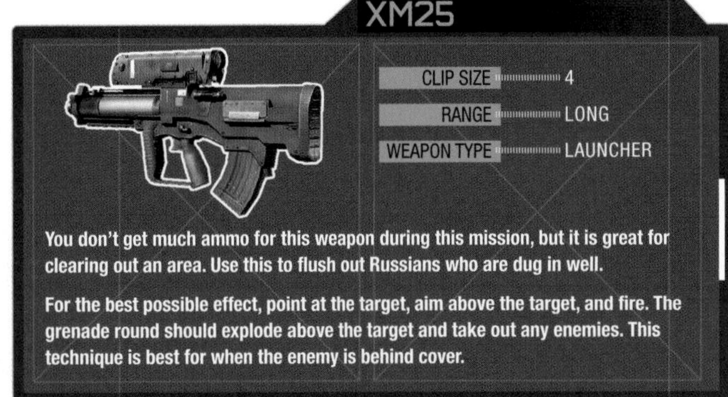

XM25

CLIP SIZE	4
RANGE	LONG
WEAPON TYPE	LAUNCHER

You don't get much ammo for this weapon during this mission, but it is great for clearing out an area. Use this to flush out Russians who are dug in well.

For the best possible effect, point at the target, aim above the target, and fire. The grenade round should explode above the target and take out any enemies. This technique is best for when the enemy is behind cover.

A OBJECTIVE

FIGHT YOUR WAY TO THE STOCK EXCHANGE

There is much resistance along the way from the Russians, so stay on your toes and stay behind cover whenever possible. Follow Sandman and Grinch to the fight ahead. Take cover behind the Samaritan and pop out to fire on a couple foes.

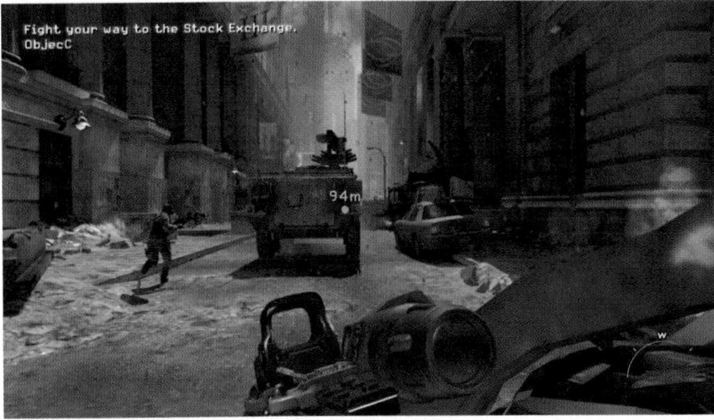

TACTICS

SNAP TO A NEARBY TARGET

Use the Aim Assist to your advantage by placing your cursor near the enemies ahead and aiming down the sight. With Aim Assist enabled, the cursor will snap to a nearby target. Release the aim after taking one out and press it again to move to the next guy. This is not available in Multiplayer, so if you would rather not get used to it, it can be disabled in the Options.

Quickly move from behind the vehicle to the planters and on to the closed stand on the left. Continue to pick off the enemies as they rush in from the next street. Recover your health by ducking behind cover whenever necessary and watch out for the Grenade icon.

GRENADE DANGER INDICATOR

The Grenade Danger Indicator pops up when the enemy has tossed a grenade near your location. A small arrow indicates the direction where it sits. Move away from it to avoid taking too much damage.

If you are quick, move over to it, pick it up, and toss it back at the sender. Be careful though, as it can go off in your hands.

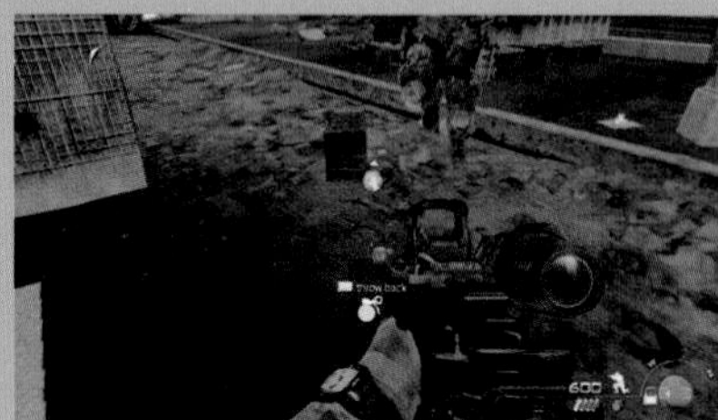

If you are against a strong barrier, such as concrete, and the icon indicates that the grenade is on the other side, duck behind the cover to safely avoid the blast.

YOU ARE HURT. GET TO COVER!

Blood splatter indicates when the player is being hurt and when you are low on health, and the phrase "You Are Hurt. Get to Cover!" appears on screen. Immediately get behind something or duck behind a barrier to recover your health. Once the screen starts to clear up, continue your onslaught.

Enemies will continue to pour into the firefight for a while, so keep eliminating them as they do. Once the coast is clear, approach the ramp barrier and a Russian armored vehicle rolls in with a mounted gun. Dodge behind cover and take him out first. Be careful, as it doesn't take much time for him to rip you apart.

There are a few more enemies left once this guy is taken care of. You may need to approach the vehicle to find the last enemy taking cover behind it. There is a plethora of weapons lying around if you are ready for a change. The M4A1 has a nice scope attachment, but so does the AK-47 if you find one with an ACOG. There may be a PKP Pecheneg that gives you a fully automatic with a huge clip. The reload is awfully slow, so be sure to keep it full.

AK-47

CLIP SIZE	30
RANGE	MEDIUM TO LONG
WEAPON TYPE	ASSAULT RIFLE

The AK-47 has an excellent medium to long range and is an extremely popular assault rifle from the Soviet Union. It can be matched up with several attachments, such as the GP-25 Grenade Launcher, ACOG Scope, Red Dot Sight, and Suppressed.

P90 / RED DOT SIGHT

CLIP SIZE	50
RANGE	MEDIUM
WEAPON TYPE	SUBMACHINE GUN

The P90 is a fully automatic weapon with a decent-sized magazine. You can find them with the Red Dot Sight and Holographic Attachments.

PKP PECHENEG

CLIP SIZE 100
RANGE LONG
WEAPON TYPE LIGHT MACHINE GUN

The PKP is a fully automatic, belt-fed machine gun with a large magazine. The high rate of fire will eat through the 100-bullet clip quickly, but the reload is very slow.

"FRIENDLIES! WATCH YOUR FIRE!"

The friendly vehicles, Firefly and Frolic, roll through the intersection, pointing you in the direction of the Stock Exchange. Take cover at the corner of the building on the right as more troops climb over the rubble down the street. Fire on them as you make your way down the sidewalk, over the barrier, and into the lobby of the 15 Broad building.

TACTICS

NO MAP WITHOUT SATELLITE COMMUNICATION

Until the jamming tower is taken care of, there is no communication with the satellite. Because of this, the map at the pause screen only shows the relative direction of your next objectives. Don't worry though; it is a pretty straightforward path to your destination.

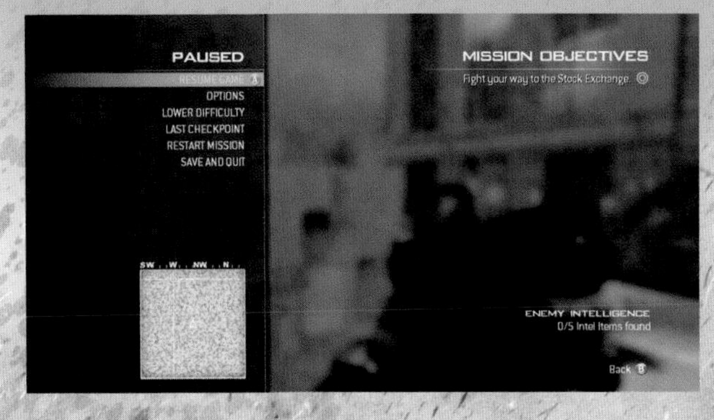

B OBJECTIVE

FLANK THE RUSSIANS ON WALL STREET

Your next objective is to flank the enemy by cutting through the building. Follow your squad up the stairs to room 130 where Sandman joins your side. Bust through the door and immediately look up the makeshift ramp to find two soldiers. Quickly take them down before climbing up to the next floor.

SPAS-12

CLIP SIZE	7
RANGE	SHORT
WEAPON TYPE	SHOTGUN

The SPAS-12 Shotgun is a great weapon in close quarters, but very ineffective from any distance. Grab this for your secondary weapon if you have a good medium- to long-range rifle. The Foregrip attachment gives you better aim with the gun.

Look down the right side of the wall and take down the enemy in the far room. Two more have you in their sights from the floor above. Follow Sandman around the right side of the crashed helicopter and through the bedroom to get the last two.

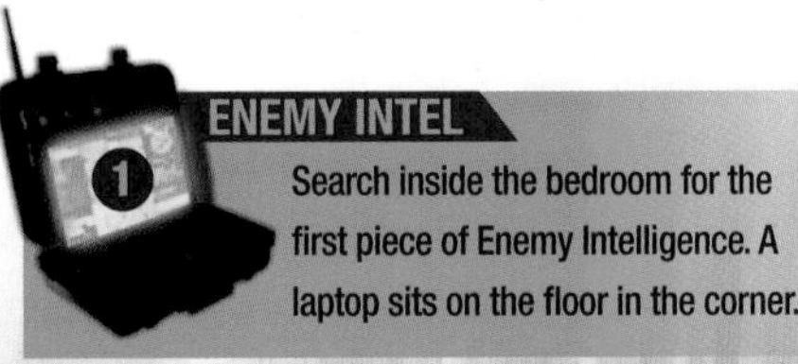

ENEMY INTEL

Search inside the bedroom for the first piece of Enemy Intelligence. A laptop sits on the floor in the corner.

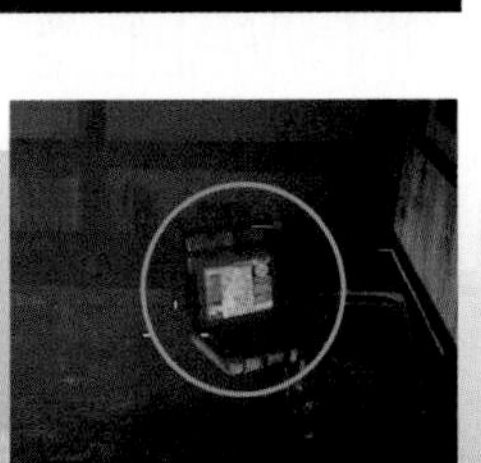

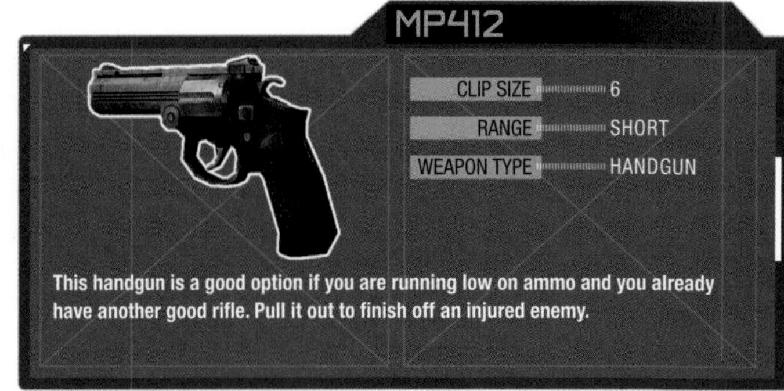

MP412

CLIP SIZE	6
RANGE	SHORT
WEAPON TYPE	HANDGUN

This handgun is a good option if you are running low on ammo and you already have another good rifle. Pull it out to finish off an injured enemy.

TACTICS

RUSSIANS ON WALL STREET

As you cut across this floor, watch out for the soldiers on Wall Street below. Don't linger out in the open, as they will fire on Frost.

Follow your partner down the stairwell to the exit. Once Sandman opens the door, toss a Flashbang into the alley to blind the two foes and quickly take them down with your assault rifle.

"SHOOTERS IN THE STORE BELOW. SWITCH 'EM OFF?"

Another staircase takes the squad into a small office behind a department store. Peer over the balcony and quickly take down the three soldiers below. There is one on each side of the room, and another ducks behind a counter in the middle.

"THE RUSSIANS HAVE IT LOCKED DOWN. THEY'RE KICKING OUR ASS! WE CAN'T GET THROUGH."

At this point, Grinch stays behind to overlook the floor while the rest of the squad takes them on below. As you head down the steps, feel free to spray bullets into the building entrance, as Russians are easy targets, but take cover below behind something sturdy before taking too much damage.

ENEMY INTEL

2

A piece of Intelligence sits on the counter under the staircase in the back of the store.

They will continue to file into the store, so target them quickly. The jewelry counters allow you to crouch and shoot through the glass tops, but you are also an easy target. There are pillars that provide better cover in the middle and back of the room. Dodge from one side to the other as you pick off the rest of the soldiers.

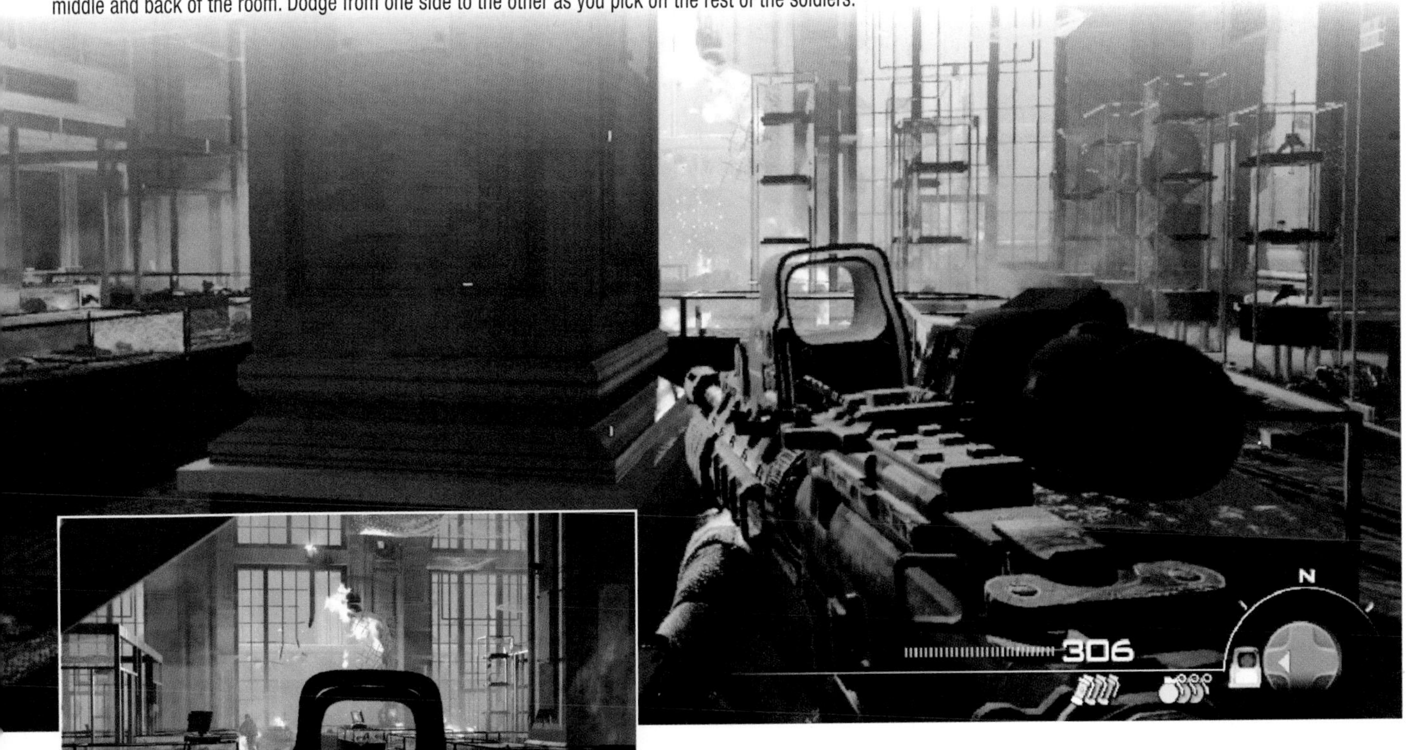

INTRO
BASICS
CAMPAIGN
SPECIAL OPS
ACHIEVEMENTS
MP GAMEPLAY
MP ARSENAL
MP MAPS
EXTRAS

C OBJECTIVE

FIGHT YOUR WAY TO THE STOCK EXCHANGE

Exit to the street where the Russians have the Stock Exchange entrance locked down. Take cover behind the rubble and switch over to your XM25. Launch a couple explosives over the barriers to flush out the enemy and then take them down.

Watch out when you hop over the barriers as enemies may flank you from the top of the steps on the right. Pick off each soldier who hides up there and then take cover behind one of those pillars. This gives you a good view of the Stock Exchange entrance.

D OBJECTIVE

RALLY WITH YOUR SQUAD IN THE LOBBY

Take out the guy who mans the mounted gun and then look out for anyone with an RPG. Make your way across the street as you take them down. Cut wide to the left to flank anyone who hides behind the truck and then enter the lobby. Reload your ammo at the ammo crates inside.

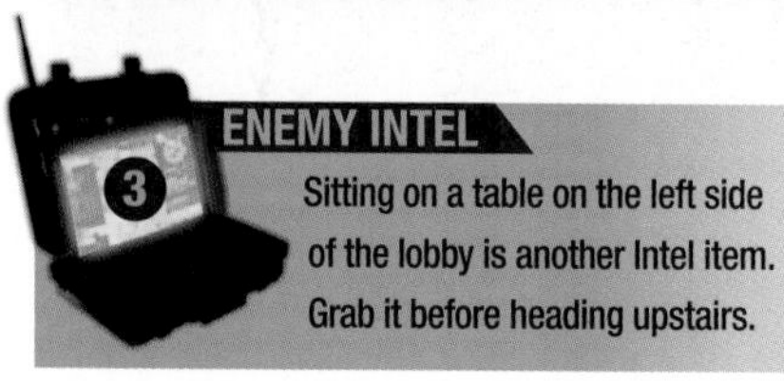

ENEMY INTEL

3 Sitting on a table on the left side of the lobby is another Intel item. Grab it before heading upstairs.

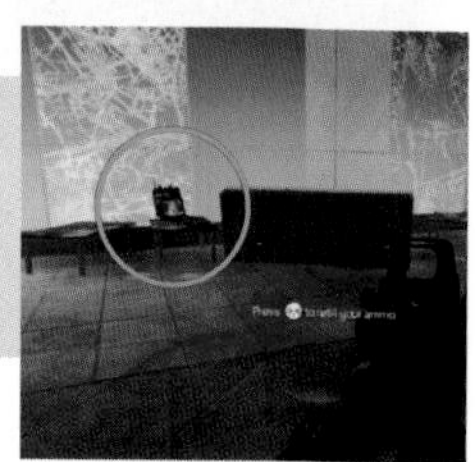

OBJECTIVE

GET TO THE STOCK EXCHANGE ROOF

Follow your squad mates up the escalator to reach the Stock Exchange. Quickly aim through the windows to take down a couple Russians who are easy fodder in the middle of the floor.

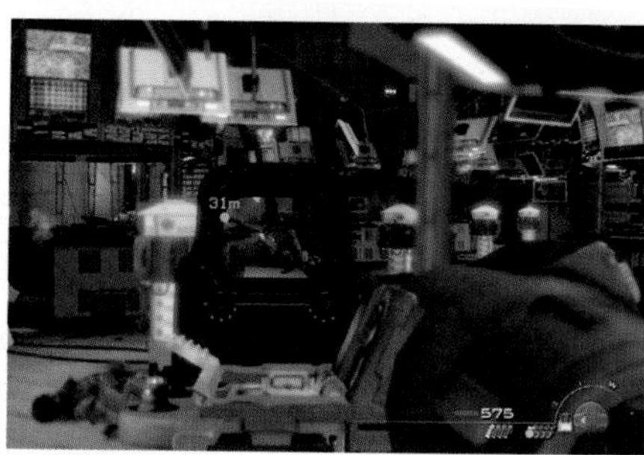

Make your way around the left side of the counters and clear out this side of the room. Now focus your attention toward the middle and then the back until your team runs for the stairs on the other side.

ENEMY INTEL

4

Sitting on the counter in the southwest corner of the Stock Exchange floor is the fourth Intel item.

Climb to the Stock Exchange balcony and pause for a moment. Look across the room where four Russian soldiers run across the far balcony. Take them down before hopping over the rail and continuing your climb.

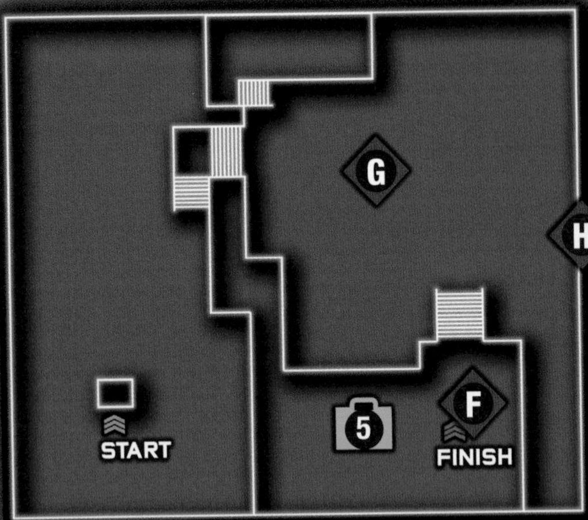

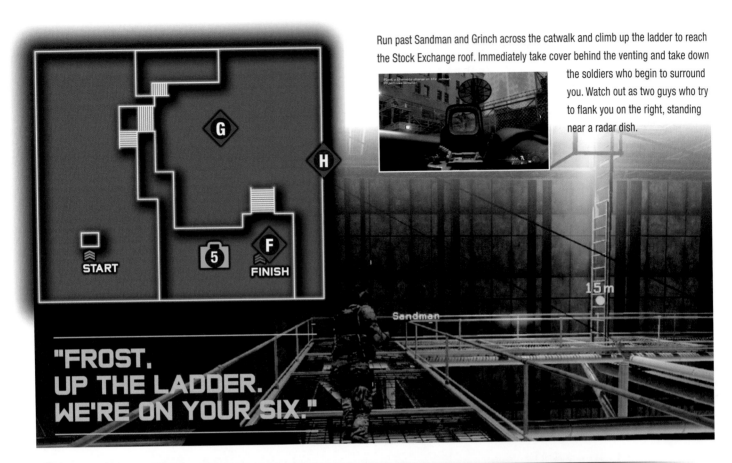

Run past Sandman and Grinch across the catwalk and climb up the ladder to reach the Stock Exchange roof. Immediately take cover behind the venting and take down the soldiers who begin to surround you. Watch out as two guys who try to flank you on the right, standing near a radar dish.

"FROST.
UP THE LADDER.
WE'RE ON YOUR SIX."

PLANT A THERMITE CHARGE ON THE JAMMER

Once they are all defeated, follow the steps to the second tier of the roof and duck behind the crates. Several men guard the tower, so eliminate them before venturing out into the open.

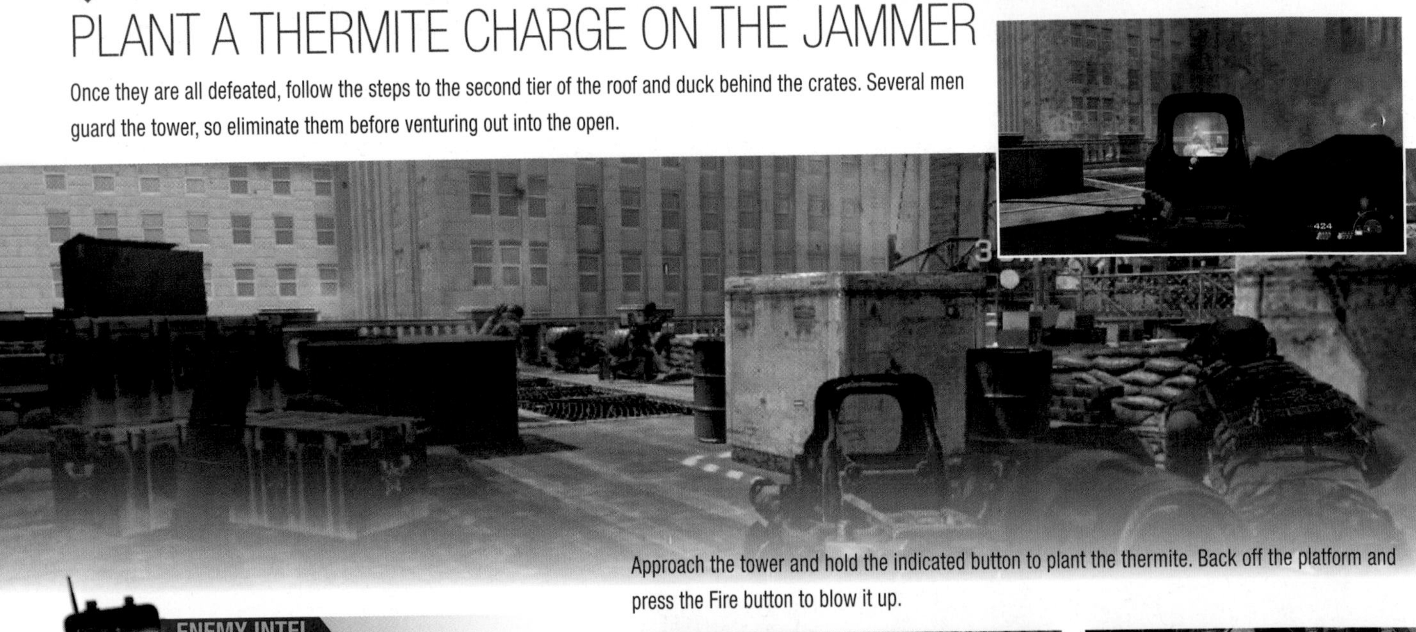

Approach the tower and hold the indicated button to plant the thermite. Back off the platform and press the Fire button to blow it up.

ENEMY INTEL

Before planting the explosive, search the folding tables on the right to find the final piece of Intel.

G OBJECTIVE

USE THE PREDATOR TO TAKE OUT THE ENEMY HIND

After the tower falls, four enemies appear on the rooftop across the street and there are more to the left. Pick them off from afar or use the Predator to launch a rocket their way. Then, use the Predator on the Hind helicopter that shows up. This clears the way for the helicopter.

TACTICS

THE PREDATOR

To use the Predator, press Right on the D-Pad to open the computer up. Aim in the general area of your target and fire the rocket. Use the right control stick to guide it to the destination and hold the Boost button to get it there faster. You are vulnerable as you open it up, so take cover behind the crates and fire quickly.

H OBJECTIVE

BOARD THE HELICOPTER

Run toward the helicopter and jump inside to man its turret. Use it to mow down the soldiers on the rooftop. After passing the next street, two enemy helicopters appear beside you. Put as many bullets as you can into them as the helicopter pursues them.

I OBJECTIVE

SHOOT DOWN ENEMY HELICOPTERS

TACTICS

AUDIO CUES

Listen to your squad while you take on these helicopters, as they will tell you where to look for them and when they have been taken down.

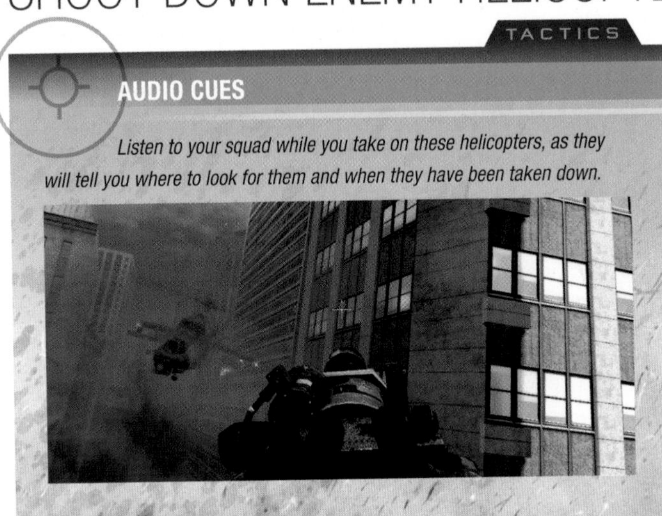

Don't relax after the two have been eliminated'. Another one shows up. Continue to fire on it, even when it ducks behind a building. After a short game of cat and mouse, it finally goes down and the first mission is complete.

ACHIEVEMENT/TROPHY

THIS IS MY BOOMSTICK

Thirty kills with the XM25 gets you this achievement. Launch the grenades into groups of enemies, such as at the doorway when you are fighting your way out of the store. Keep the weapon with you throughout the mission and use the ammo crates to refill the gun.

ACHIEVEMENT/TROPHY

TOO BIG TO FAIL

Get this Achievement/Trophy after you destroy the Jamming Tower and complete Black Tuesday on any difficulty.

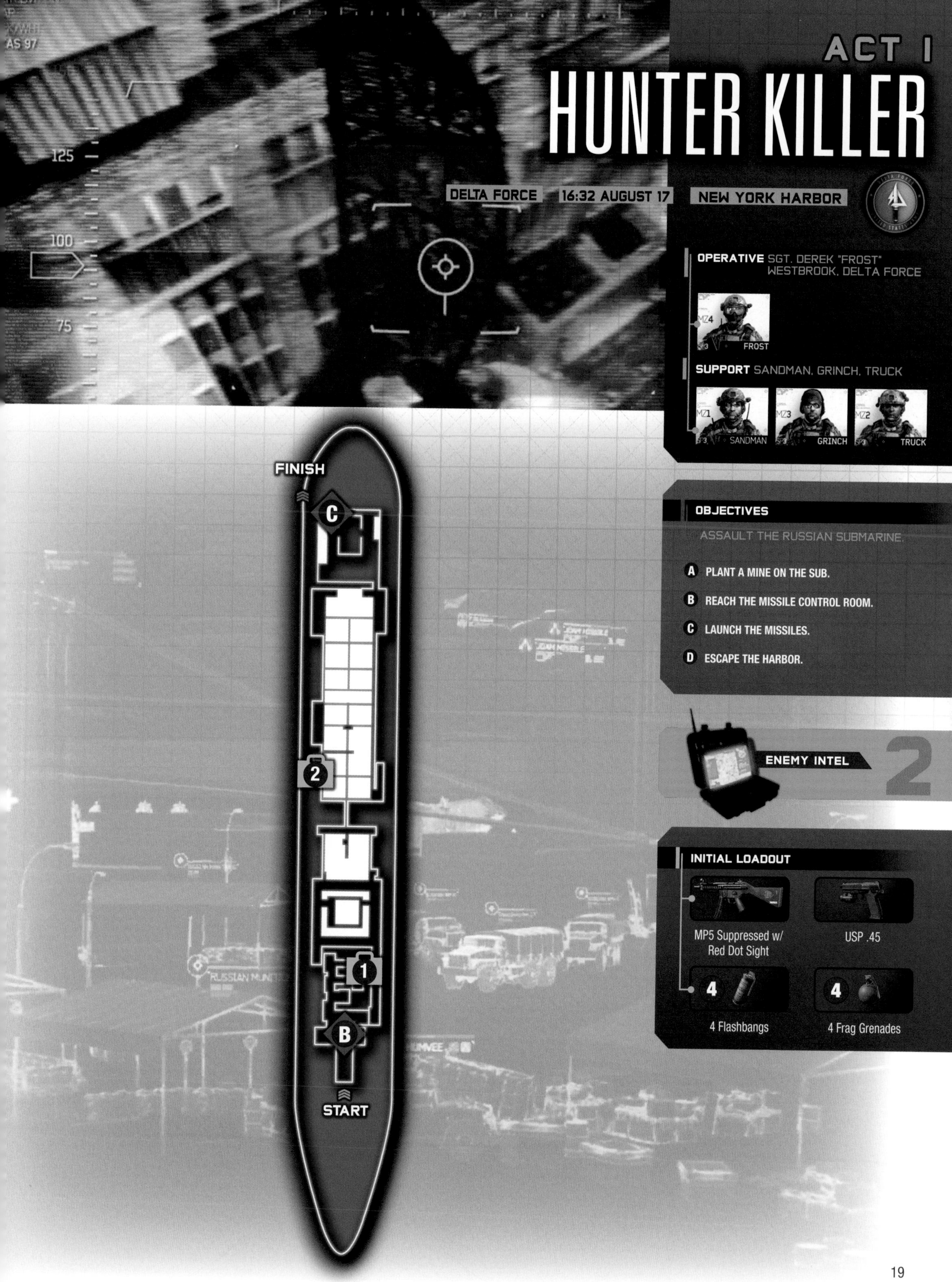
ACT I
HUNTER KILLER
DELTA FORCE
16:32 AUGUST 17
NEW YORK HARBOR
OPERATIVE SGT. DEREK "FROST" WESTBROOK, DELTA FORCE
FROST
SUPPORT SANDMAN, GRINCH, TRUCK
SANDMAN
GRINCH
TRUCK
FINISH
START
OBJECTIVES
ASSAULT THE RUSSIAN SUBMARINE.
A PLANT A MINE ON THE SUB.
B REACH THE MISSILE CONTROL ROOM.
C LAUNCH THE MISSILES.
D ESCAPE THE HARBOR.
ENEMY INTEL 2
INITIAL LOADOUT
MP5 Suppressed w/ Red Dot Sight
USP .45
4 Flashbangs
4 Frag Grenades

The Russian Oscar II Submarine sits in New York Harbor and contains enough cruise missiles to take out most of the Eastern Seaboard. It is up to Delta Force to infiltrate the vessel and turn their missiles against them.

A OBJECTIVE

PLANT A MINE ON THE SUB

Hold tight as Sandman opens up an entry point for the team. Once he is through, use your diver propulsion vehicle to follow the rest of the squad through the Brooklyn Battery Tunnel.

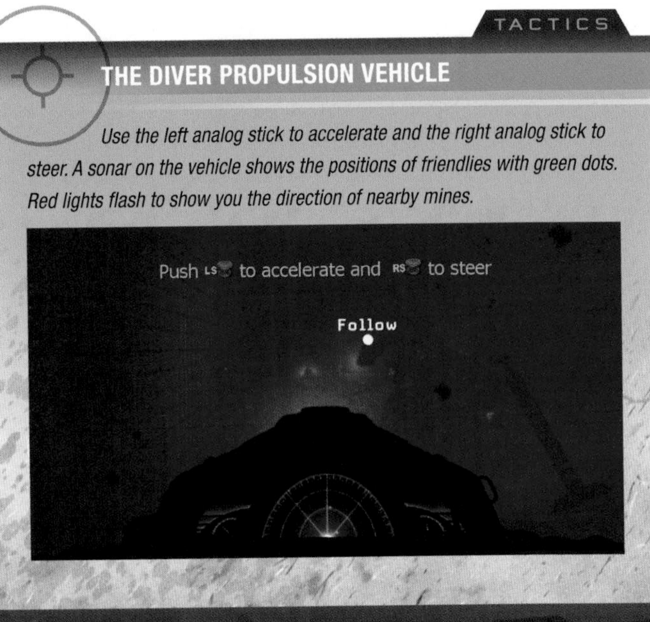
Push LS to accelerate and RS to steer
Follow

TACTICS

THE DIVER PROPULSION VEHICLE

Use the left analog stick to accelerate and the right analog stick to steer. A sonar on the vehicle shows the positions of friendlies with green dots. Red lights flash to show you the direction of nearby mines.

Continue to follow close behind as you meet up with the SEAL Team. Wind your way around the pipes while keeping your eyes peeled for mines. A red light flashes around the perimeter of the sonar when a mine is nearby. The location of the red light shows the direction of the mine.

Avoid these mines as you follow the soldiers under a low pipe. On the other side, the watercrafts are powered down as the submarine passes overhead. Once it has passed, approach the rudder and hold the indicated button to plant the explosives. This causes the sub to surface, and the team does the same.

10m
Press and hold X to plant the explosives.

B OBJECTIVE

REACH THE MISSILE CONTROL ROOM

Follow the guys up the back of the vessel as Russians emerge from the rear hatch. Take them down along with a couple more approaching from the far end. Follow Sandman as he climbs down the ladder.

MP5

CLIP SIZE	30
RANGE	MEDIUM
WEAPON TYPE	SUBMACHINE GUN

The MP5 is a fully automatic, close-range submachine gun with a decent fire rate. This one is suppressed and has a red dot sight. This works well down in the sub, as all the fighting is close combat.

USP .45

CLIP SIZE	12
RANGE	MEDIUM
WEAPON TYPE	HANDGUN

This handgun is a semi-automatic, single-fire weapon with good accuracy and low damage. Pull this out instead of taking time to reload your other weapon.

Follow Sandman into the bunkroom with your gun raised. Eliminate the two enemies in the other doorway. Head down the stairs to rejoin your partner.

"ALRIGHT FROST. SWEEP AND CLEAR. ALL UNKNOWNS ARE HOSTILE."

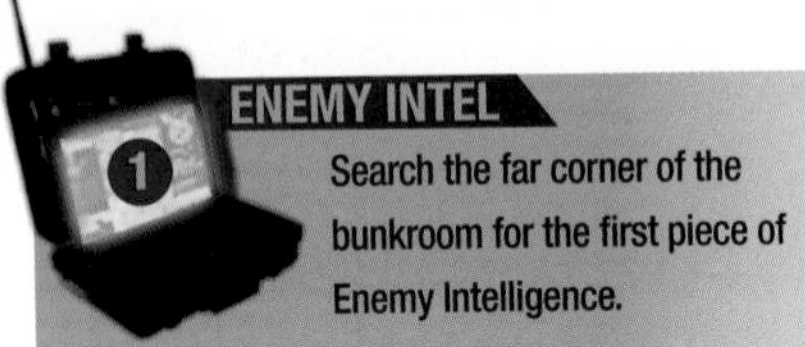

ENEMY INTEL

1 Search the far corner of the bunkroom for the first piece of Enemy Intelligence.

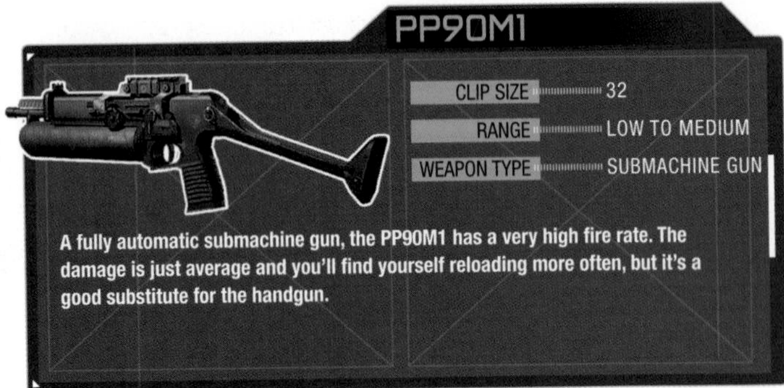

PP90M1

CLIP SIZE	32
RANGE	LOW TO MEDIUM
WEAPON TYPE	SUBMACHINE GUN

A fully automatic submachine gun, the PP90M1 has a very high fire rate. The damage is just average and you'll find yourself reloading more often, but it's a good substitute for the handgun.

Around the corner, take out the guy just inside the reactor room and another in the far corridor. Follow orders and take the left side. Shoot down any Russians who come down the steps before you follow the path and rendezvous with Sandman.

At the next steps, take out any enemies you can get a bead on before you proceed through the open door. You can see where most of them are by their laser sights. They often crouch around a corner. Approach slowly and take them out once you have a shot.

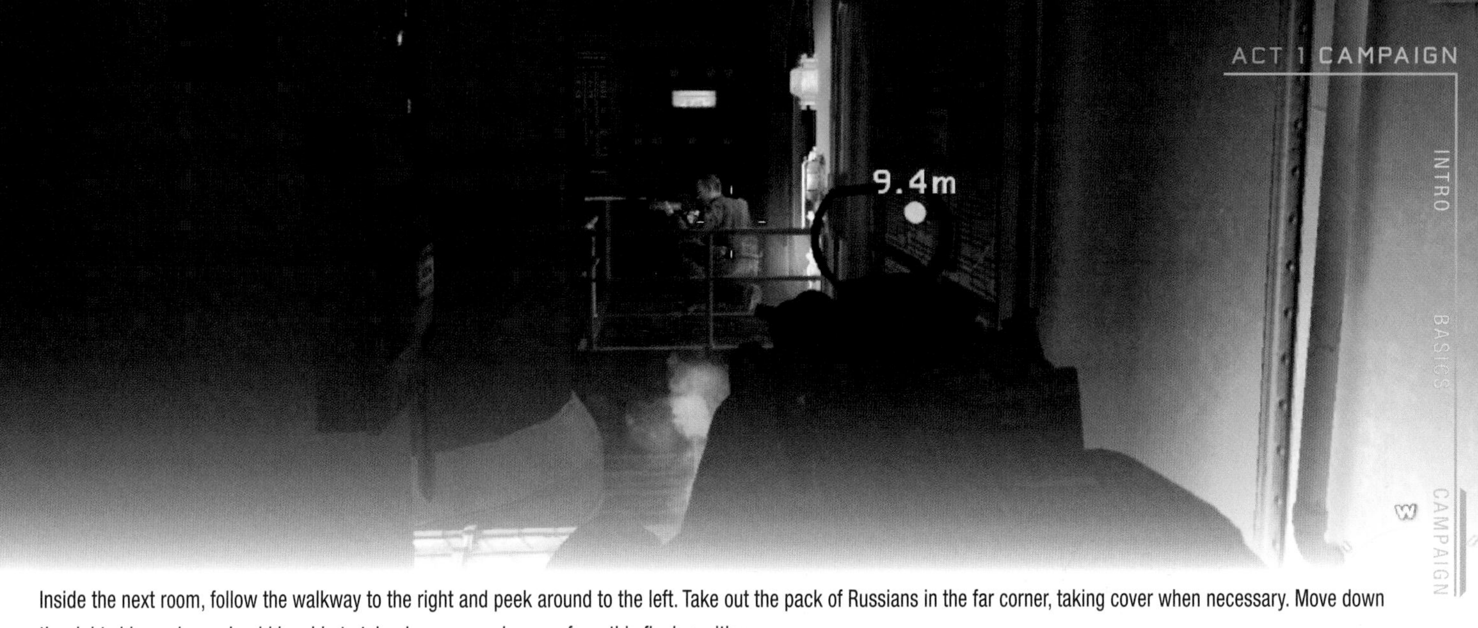

Inside the next room, follow the walkway to the right and peek around to the left. Take out the pack of Russians in the far corner, taking cover when necessary. Move down the right side, and you should be able to take down a couple more from this flank position.

"WE HAVE TO GET TO THE BRIDGE."

Cross over to the left path and take cover next to the doorway. Eliminate anyone you can from this position. Run up the nearby stairs and take cover next to the doorway.

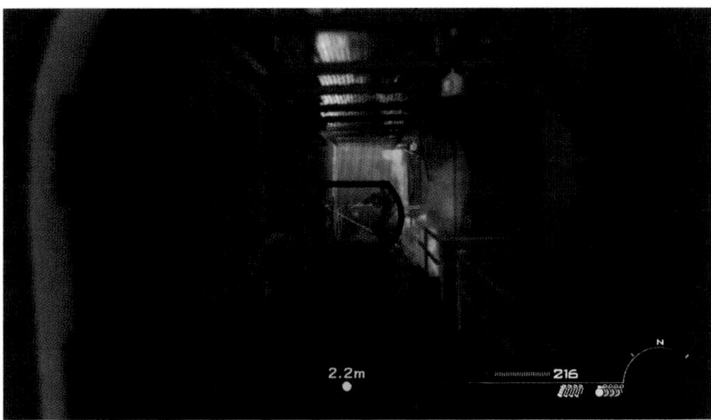

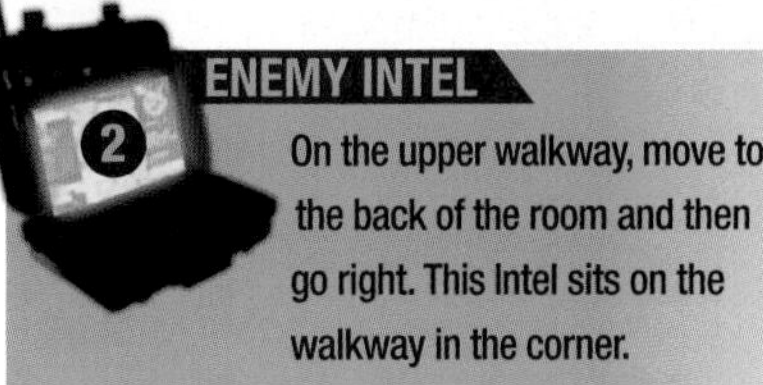

ENEMY INTEL

2 On the upper walkway, move to the back of the room and then go right. This Intel sits on the walkway in the corner.

TACTICS

WATCH OUT ABOVE AND BELOW

Watch out for Russians who fire on your position from above, or from below when you are on the upper walkways. Take out these guys by shooting through the grated walkway.

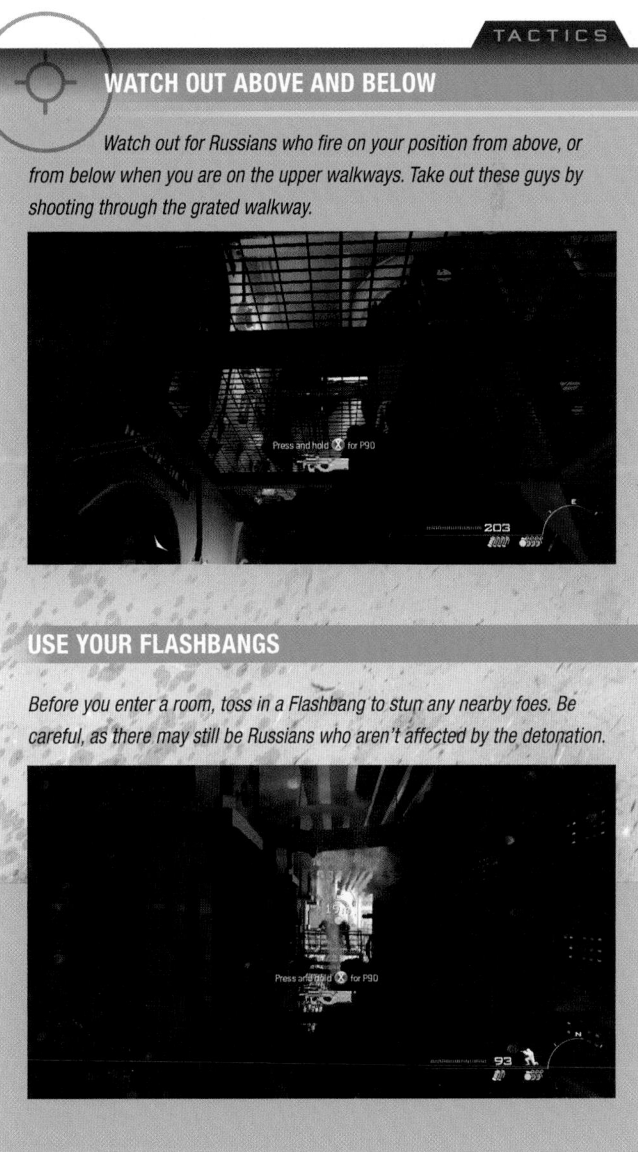

USE YOUR FLASHBANGS

Before you enter a room, toss in a Flashbang to stun any nearby foes. Be careful, as there may still be Russians who aren't affected by the detonation.

At the door, take out anyone you can, and then carefully enter the next room. Peek around the corners and pick off each foe as you make your way to the far right corner. If someone gives you trouble, try backing out of the room and entering the other door, or going downstairs to take him out.

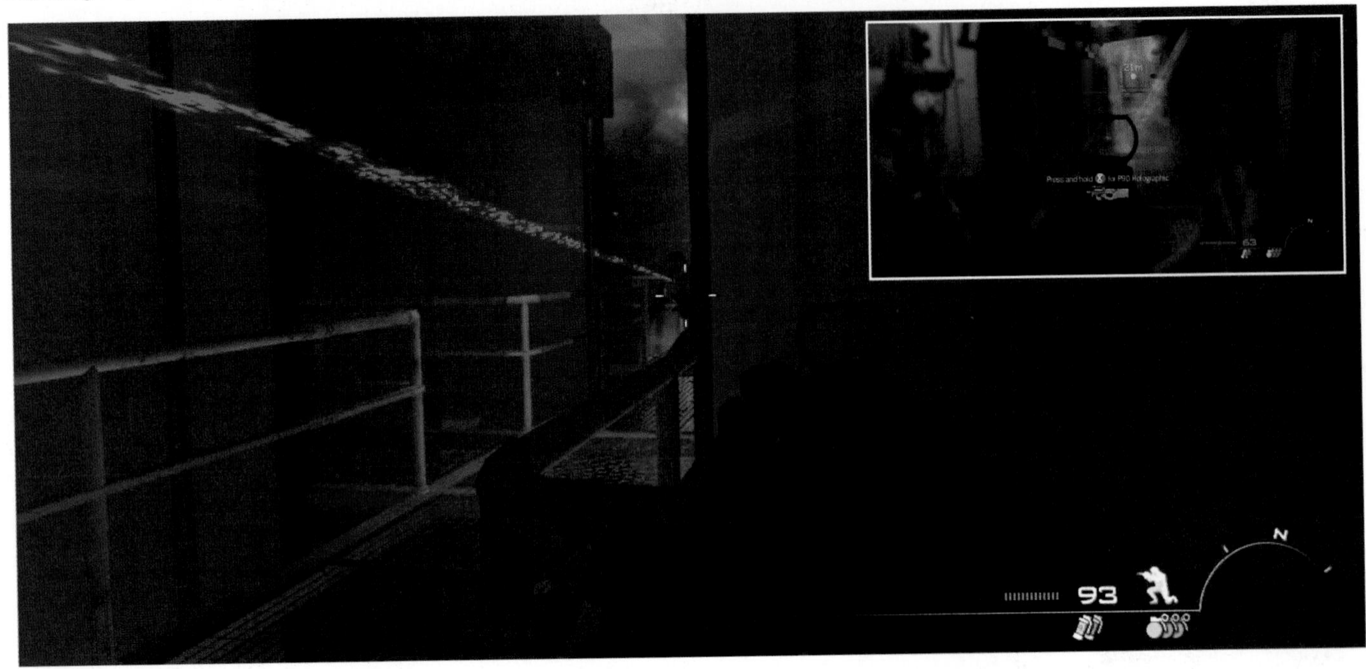

"PUT A KICKER CHARGE ON THE DOOR."

BREACH

Sandman waits at the door to the missile control room. Place the kicker charge, and he adds the rest. For roughly 10 seconds after the door blows, time slows considerably. Use this opportunity to eliminate any threats inside. Immediately target the enemy who lunges at you with a knife. Then you can take out the other four in any order.

STRIKER

CLIP SIZE	12
RANGE	LOW TO MEDIUM
WEAPON TYPE	SHOTGUN

The Striker is a semi-automatic, single-fire shotgun that's great for the submarine's close quarters. The accuracy is pretty poor, but it does a good job on the Russians at short range.

G18

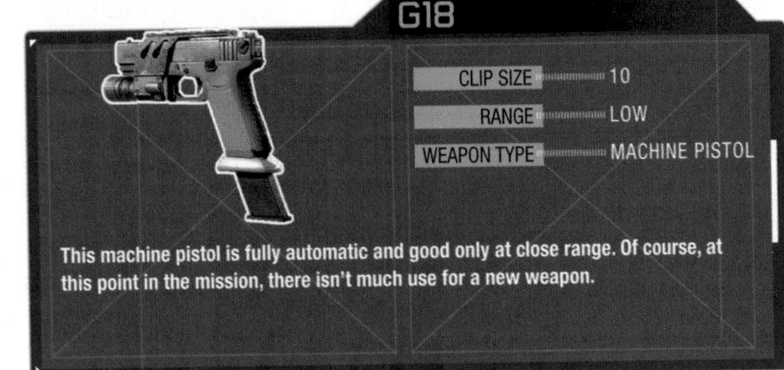

CLIP SIZE	10
RANGE	LOW
WEAPON TYPE	MACHINE PISTOL

This machine pistol is fully automatic and good only at close range. Of course, at this point in the mission, there isn't much use for a new weapon.

C OBJECTIVE

LAUNCH THE MISSILES

Clear out any remaining Russians before you approach the console in the far corner. When Sandman is ready, hold the indicated button to use it. Once you're done in here, quickly head up the ladder and through the hatch.

D OBJECTIVE

ESCAPE THE HARBOR

Run northwest toward the objective marker and hop into the zodiac. Immediately accelerate and follow the other boat as closely as possible.

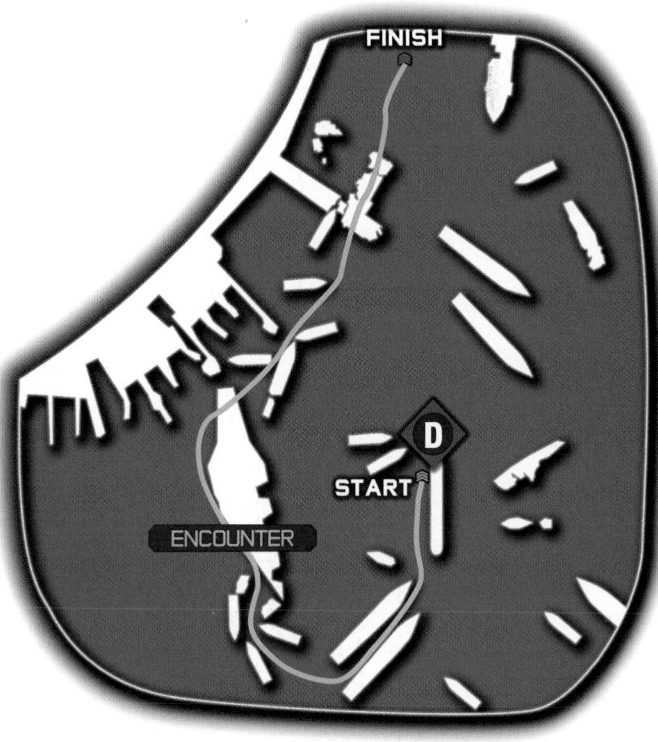

"GUN IT!"

Keep your eyes ahead on the other boat, and avoid the obstacles along the way. When the Russian ship pulls up beside you, quickly target the mines that conveniently sit in the back, and fire away.

ACHIEVEMENT/TROPHY

WET WORK

Take back New York Harbor by completing the Hunter Killer mission to earn the Wet Work Achievement/Trophy.

ZODIAC BOAT

Hold Right Trigger/R2 to accelerate, and use the analog stick to steer. Keep the accelerator pinned to keep up with the other boat.

Continue to follow your squad mates as you cut under the end of an aircraft carrier. Waves nearly push you off the path, but keep the boat pointed at the Follow marker. Cut under the bridge and over the makeshift ramp. Guide the boat into the helicopter transport that waits in the harbor.

ACHIEVEMENT/TROPHY

THE BIG APPLE

Complete Black Tuesday and Hunter Killer on Veteran difficulty.

ACT I
PERSONA NON GRATA
TASK FORCE 141
09:51 AUGUST 17
HIMACHAL PRADESH, INDIA
TASK FORCE
DISAVOWED
141
OPERATIVE YURI, TASK FORCE 141–DISAVOWED
SUPPORT PRICE, NIKOLAI, SOAP
OBJECTIVES
EVACUATE SOAP FROM THE MOUNTAIN SAFE HOUSE.
A DEFEND SOAP.
B HELP SOAP.
C FOLLOW CAPTAIN PRICE.
D GET TO THE WEAPONS CACHE.
E TAKE CONTROL OF UGV.
F CLEAR OUT AREA AROUND HELICOPTER.
G GET TO THE HELICOPTER.
ENEMY INTEL 4
INITIAL LOADOUT
AK-47 w/Red Dot Sight
Desert Eagle
4 Flashbangs
4 Frag Grenades
1
2
3
4
A
B
C
D
E
F
G
START
FINISH

"WE NEED TO GET SOAP TO THE CHOPPER."

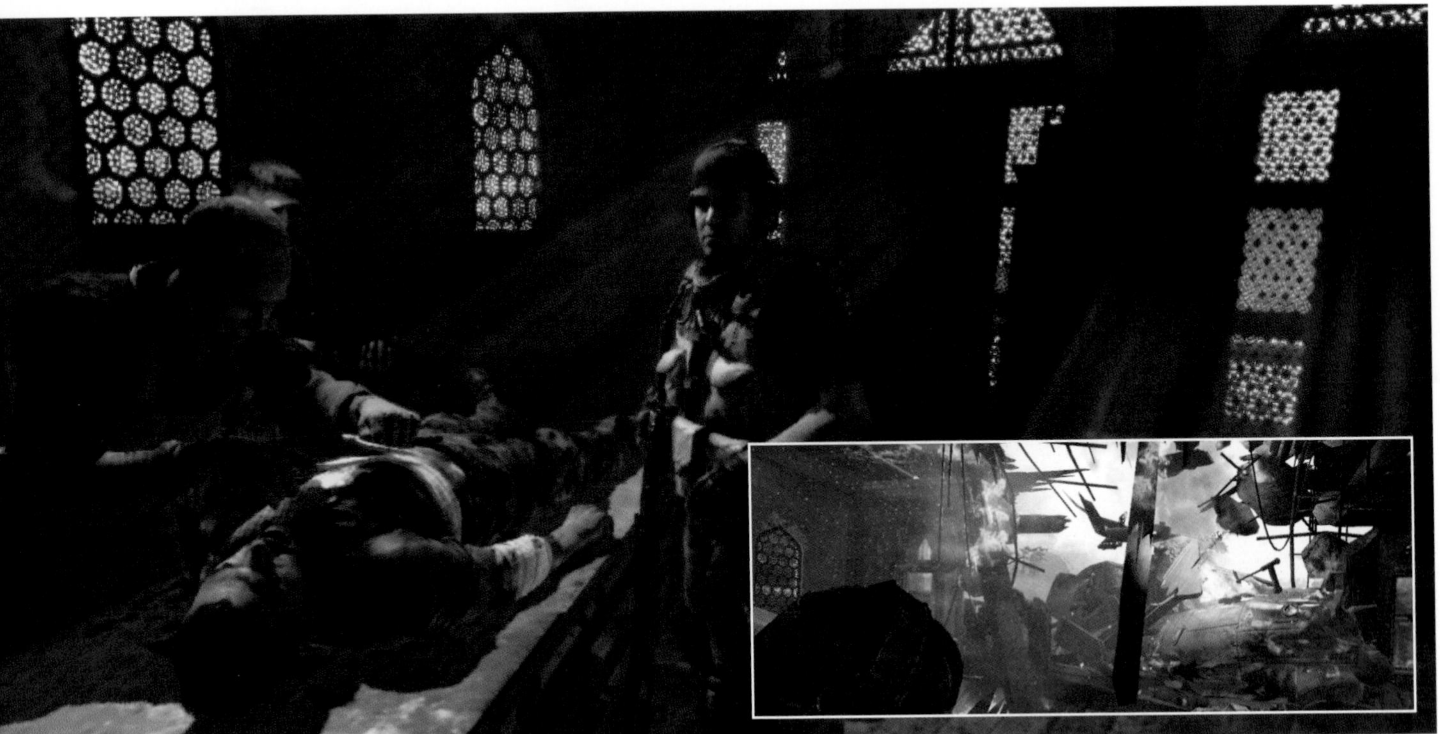

You assume the role of Yuri, an ex-Spetsnaz soldier who works for Nikolai. Soap is in bad shape and Makarov has found the safe house. It's time to go. A hole has been blown into the side of the house. Help Price fend off the attack.

DESERT EAGLE
CLIP SIZE 7
RANGE MEDIUM TO LONG
WEAPON TYPE HANDGUN
As a semi-automatic, single-fire handgun, the Desert Eagle inflicts great damage compared to other similar handguns. However, its accuracy makes it less effective from farther away.

A OBJECTIVE

DEFEND SOAP

Crouch behind the railing on the right balcony. It doesn't offer much protection, but you present a smaller target this way. Aim your gun at the doorway on the other end of the courtyard, and mow down the enemies as they make their way through.

MG36
CLIP SIZE 45
RANGE MEDIUM TO LONG
WEAPON TYPE LIGHT MACHINE GUN
The MG36 is a fully automatic light machine gun with an ample drum magazine. It possesses good damage, range, and fire rate, making it a nice option for this initial gunfight. You should switch back to the AK-47 before you move out, as the light machine gun will slow you down.

Watch out for enemy troops on the side balconies. Back away as you reload to limit the damage you take. Once the area is clear and your objective is complete, move back into the room.

B OBJECTIVE

HELP SOAP

Nikolai calls for your help, so approach the right side of Soap. Hold the indicated button to give Soap a shot. This calms him down as Makarov's men breach the room.

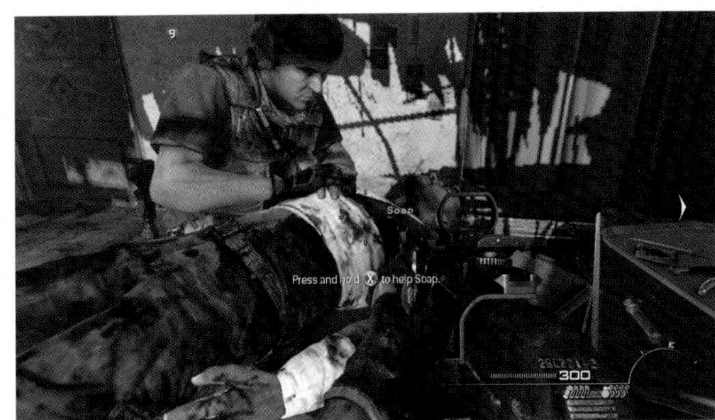

C OBJECTIVE

FOLLOW CAPTAIN PRICE

Follow Price into the hallway and help him take down the enemies who enter at the other end. Run down the stairs and out into the courtyard. Take cover behind a pillar and help eliminate the remaining foes.

ENEMY INTEL

1 Once the courtyard is clear, search an alcove on the north side of the courtyard to find Intel sitting on top of a crate.

D OBJECTIVE

GET TO THE WEAPONS CACHE

A UGV is stored at a weapons cache on the other side of town, and it would greatly help the team get to the chopper. Follow Price out to the street, but hold off on firing until the civilians have passed. Just behind them, take out Makarov's men.

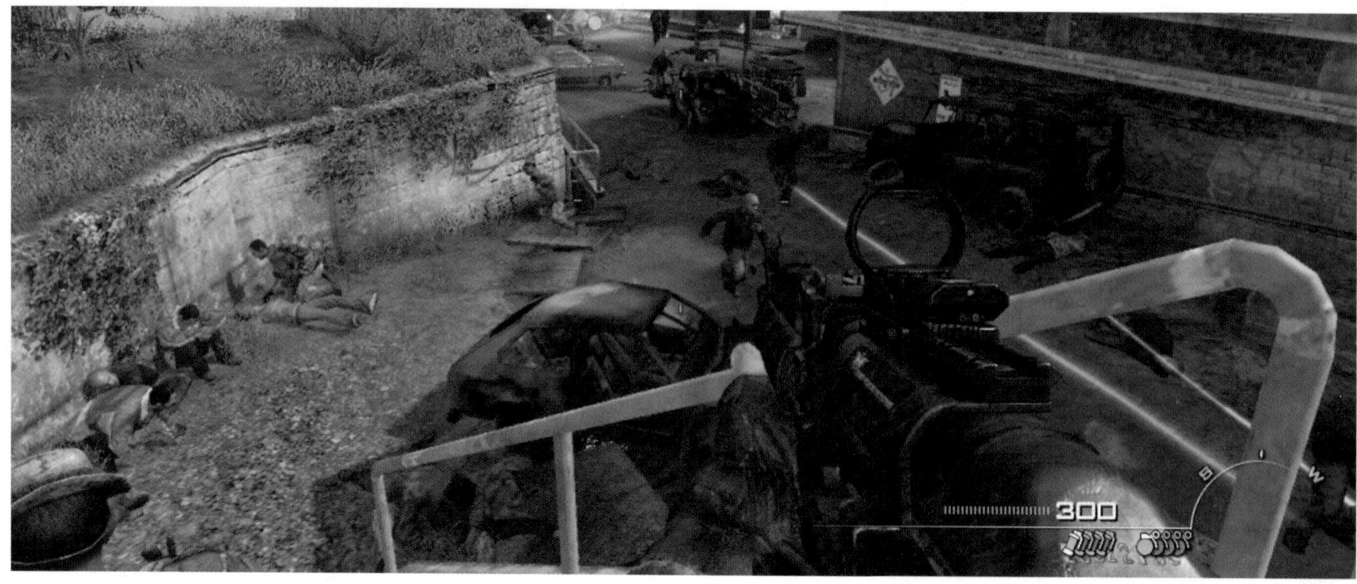

"YURI, WATCH THE BALCONIES!"

Take cover behind the vehicles and fire on the enemies down the street. Eliminate anyone on the balconies first. A guy jumps on the minigun on the balcony at the end of the street, so be sure to knock him off quickly.

Once the street is clear, run up the steps on the right side and enter the house. Run down the steps and use the window to flank any remaining enemies on the street.

ENEMY INTEL

2

Enter the house located across the alley from the Trekking Trade. Search the back bedroom for another piece of Intelligence.

Cut through the first floor of the building while you take pot shots at Makarov's men out in the street. Exit on the other side to rejoin your team.

Take cover in the alley and thin out the opposition at the intersection. Watch for anyone peeking out the upstairs windows. Once you have an opening, continue down the street toward the objective marker.

TACTICS

FLANKING POSITION

Take advantage of flanking positions in the alley and from windows as Makarov's men run down the street. Take them down as they pass.

Cut down another alley toward your destination, where a gate stops any progress. A big group of Makarov's men fire on your location from the other side. Follow Price into the building on the right and out the other side.

Continue to follow him into another building and through an access door on the floor. The weapons cache and the aforementioned UGV are below.

ENEMY INTEL

3

Look behind the UGV to spot another computer with Enemy Intel.

E OBJECTIVE

TAKE CONTROL OF UGV

Access the computer next to the door to take control of the unmanned ground vehicle. Price opens the door for you to guide the vehicle outside.

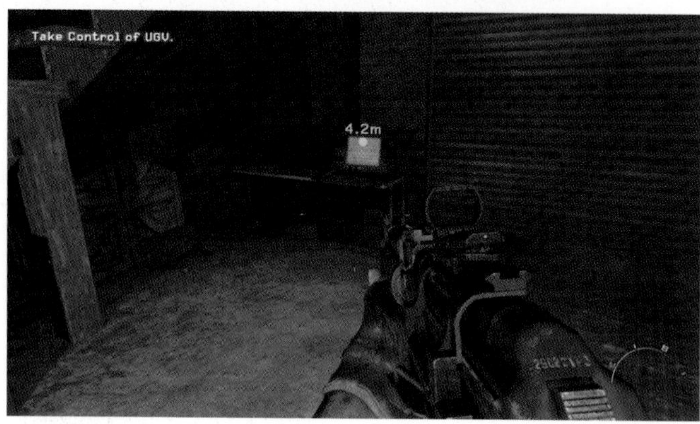

"CONTROLS ARE GOING TO BE IN RUSSIAN. YURI, YOU'RE UP."

TACTICS

CONTROLLING THE UGV

Use the analog sticks to move and look around. The Left Trigger/L2 zooms, the Right Trigger/R2 shoots the minigun, and Right Bumper/R1 fires grenades.

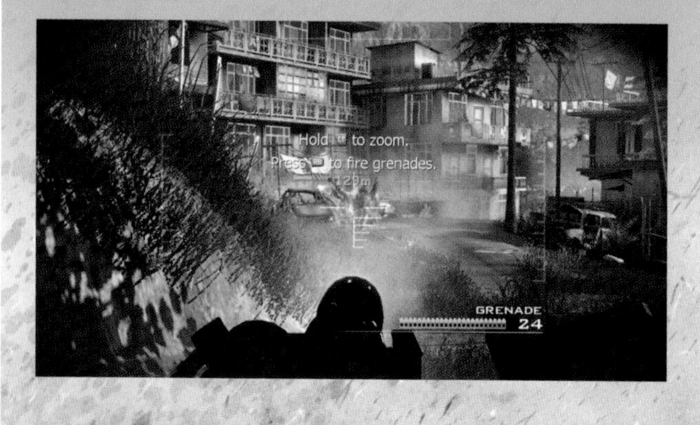

F OBJECTIVE

CLEAR OUT AREA AROUND HELICOPTER

Clear out anyone you see, including the helicopters above. You are limited to 24 grenades, but the path is short, so use them up as you proceed ahead. If you're going for all of the Achievements/Trophies, save grenades for the choppers. Follow the path down the hill and to the left, sweeping from side to side to avoid missing anyone.

Launch a couple grenades onto the balconies above to clear them, and then focus your gunfire on the three choppers that arrive. Stay on the path as you continue to your destination.

At the objective marker, spend some time protecting the helicopter as more enemies join the fight. Knock down the enemy chopper as soon as it pops in. This onslaught continues until an airstrike finally takes out the UGV.

ACHIEVEMENT/TROPHY

WHAT GOES UP...

Destroy all of the choppers with only the UGV's grenade launcher to score this Achievement/Trophy.

G OBJECTIVE

GET TO THE HELICOPTER

Now Yuri must meet up with the others at the helicopter. Sprint along the same path you took with the UGV.

ENEMY INTEL

45 Before you run too far, stop at the playground on the left and grab the Intel that sits on top of the slide. Secure it from below.

Sprint the entire way down the path as shells explode all around. A rooftop gives way, and you must guide Yuri around the collapsing house as he slides down the hill. This completes the escape from the safe house.

ACHIEVEMENT/TROPHY

CARPE DIEM

Earn another Achievement/Trophy after you escape the mountain safe house and complete Persona Non Grata on any difficulty.

ACT 1

TURBULENCE

FSO | 18:30 OCTOBER 3 | RUSSIAN PRESIDENT'S AIRPLANE, IL-96-300PU—"COMMAND POINT"

OPERATIVE ANDREI HARKOV. RUSSIAN FSO AGENT

SUPPORT CMDR. LEONID PUDOVKIN

OBJECTIVES

PROTECT THE RUSSIAN PEACE DELEGATION EN ROUTE TO HAMBURG.

- **A** ESCORT THE PRESIDENT.
- **B** MOVE TO GUARD POSITION.
- **C** LEAD THE PRESIDENT TO SAFETY.
- **D** SECURE THE PRESIDENT'S DAUGHTER.
- **E** LEAD THE PRESIDENT TO THE SAFE ROOM.
- **F** FOLLOW THE COMMANDER.
- **G** SECURE THE PRESIDENT.

ENEMY INTEL 2

INITIAL LOADOUT

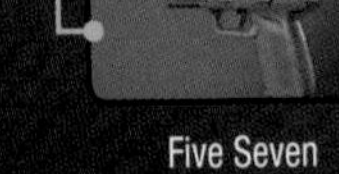

Five Seven

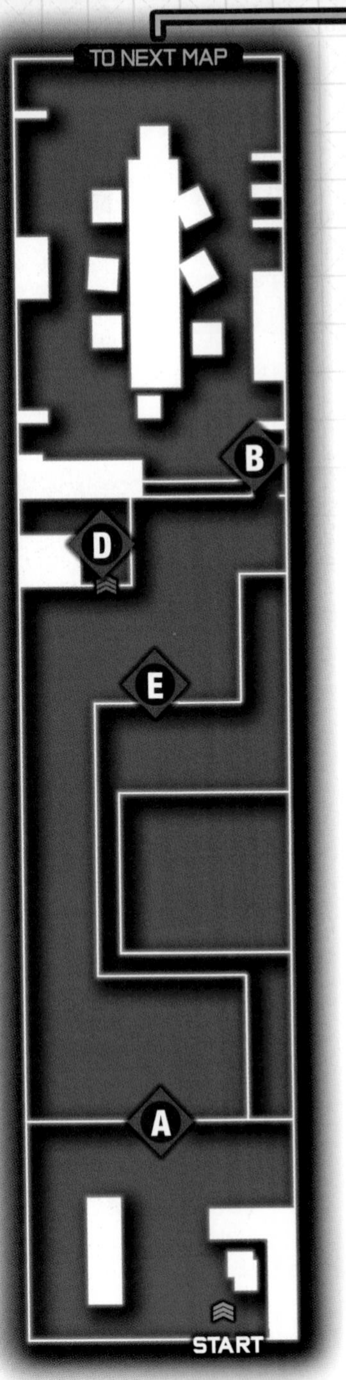

"TEAM ONE, REMAIN WITH THE PRESIDENT UNTIL TOUCHDOWN."

The Russian President Vorshevsky is headed to Hamburg for a peace conference aboard an Il-96-300PU aircraft, also known as "Command Point." It's up to Russian FSO Agents, including Andrei Harkov, to protect the delegation.

FIVE SEVEN
CLIP SIZE 15
RANGE MEDIUM
WEAPON TYPE HANDGUN
The Five Seven is a semi-automatic, single-fire handgun. It's a great option for a secondary weapon, but you may want to pick up a fully automatic weapon to go along with it when you get the opportunity.

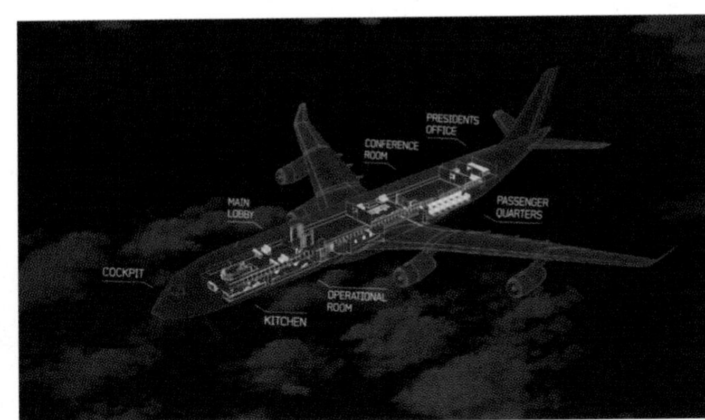

A OBJECTIVE

ESCORT THE PRESIDENT

You start out in the president's office as his daughter enters, reminding him of his meeting in the conference room. Commander Leonid Pudovkin falls in behind them, and you should do the same.

"GENTLEMEN, WE HAVE ONLY TWO CHOICES. PEACE OR WAR. LIFE OR DEATH."

B OBJECTIVE

MOVE TO GUARD POSITION

Follow them into the room and take your position in the right corner. The meeting barely gets started when gunfire is heard from elsewhere in the plane. Make your way to the opposite door as the antagonists breach the door. Take out the men who enter the room.

C OBJECTIVE

LEAD THE PRESIDENT TO SAFETY

You must take the president to a secure, safe location, so lead the way out the door. Grab the dropped AK-74u to complement your handgun.

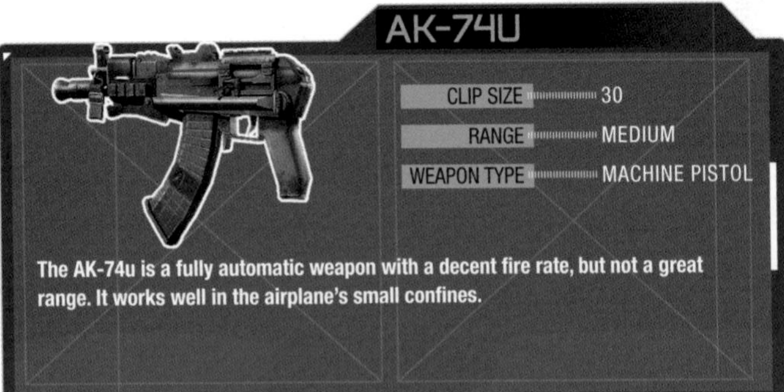

AK-74U

CLIP SIZE	30
RANGE	MEDIUM
WEAPON TYPE	MACHINE PISTOL

The AK-74u is a fully automatic weapon with a decent fire rate, but not a great range. It works well in the airplane's small confines.

TACTICS

TURBULENCE

The plane starts hitting some rough patches, so you get tossed around a bit. As long as your gun is up, you can still shoot. Be careful, as you may be jostled from side to side, putting you out in the open or possibly changing your target.

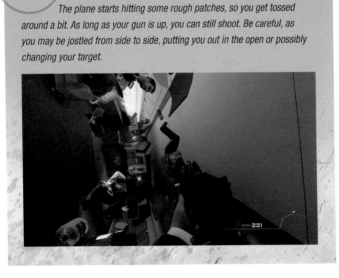

In the main lobby, you experience a period of weightlessness. Continue taking down the hijackers whenever you have control of your gun. Once the room is clear, you get a new objective to secure the president's daughter.

ACHIEVEMENT/TROPHY

FLIGHT ATTENDANT

Kill all five enemies during this zero-g sequence to score another Achievement/Trophy.

OBJECTIVE

SECURE THE PRESIDENT'S DAUGHTER

Head down the stairs and duck into the kitchen. Take cover at the doorway as you take out some of the foes in the next room.

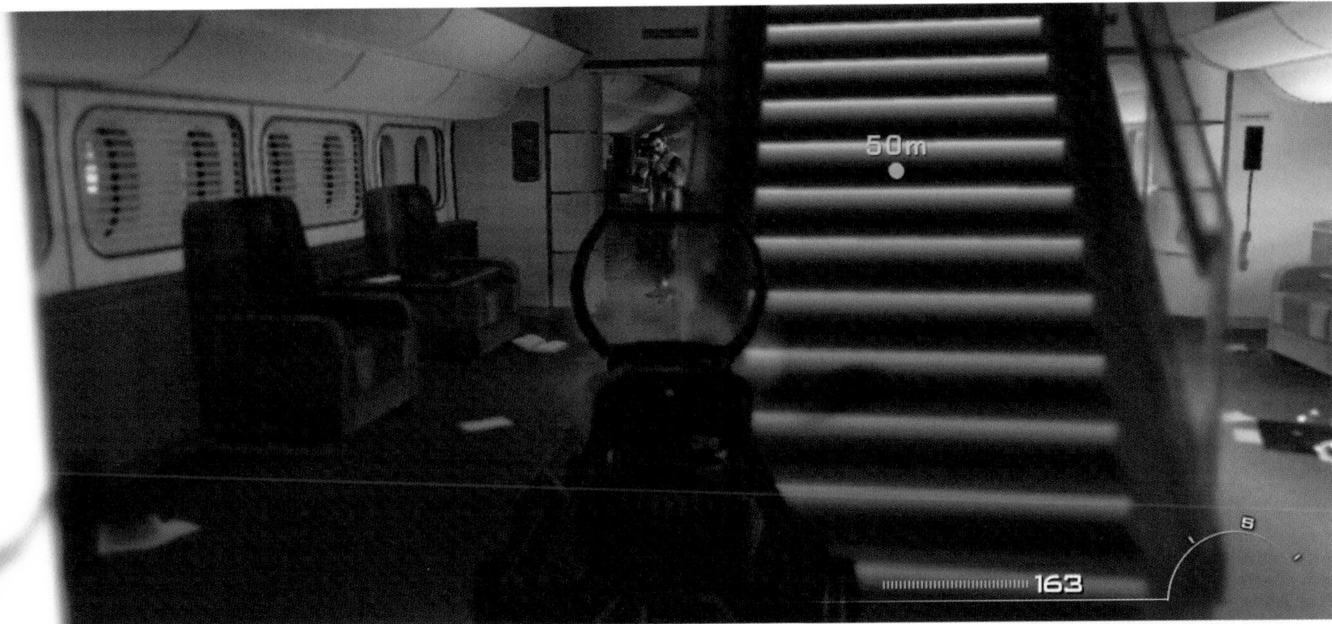

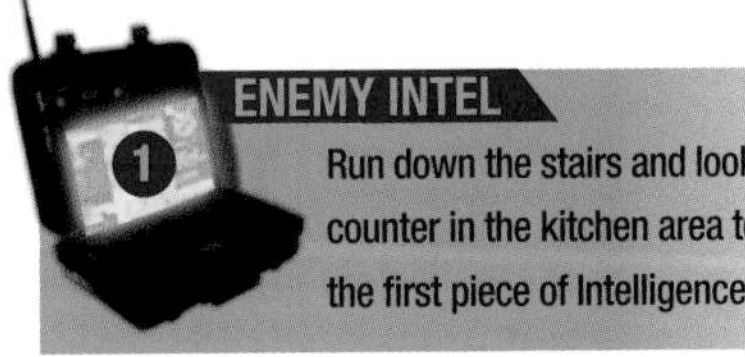

ENEMY INTEL

Run down the stairs and look on the counter in the kitchen area to find the first piece of Intelligence.

FMG9

CLIP SIZE	32
RANGE	LOW TO MEDIUM
WEAPON TYPE	MACHINE PISTOL

The FMG9 is a machine pistol with a decent clip size and acceptable range. Its high fire rate makes it a good secondary weapon for this mission.

After you clear out a few foes, sprint up to the next doorway and eliminate more of the hijackers in the next room. Crouch down and carefully make your way around the tables and chairs. Take down any remaining enemies as you continue ahead.

Watch out, as a couple of hijackers jump you at the next doorway. Keep pressing forward through the operations room and into the cargo area. Pick off the few guys who are holed up inside with the president's daughter.

OBJECTIVE

LEAD THE PRESIDENT TO THE SAFE ROOM

Now that the president is back together with his daughter, you must get them to the safe room. Move into the passenger quarters, but things go terribly wrong.

OBJECTIVE

FOLLOW THE COMMANDER

Follow Cmdr. Pudovkin through the plane wreckage, to the right, and over a log.

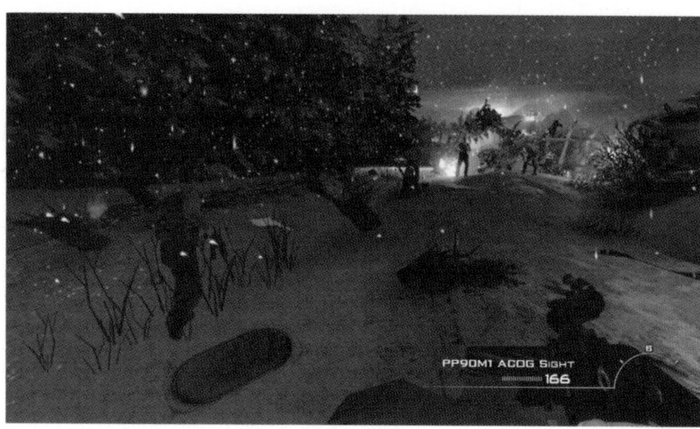

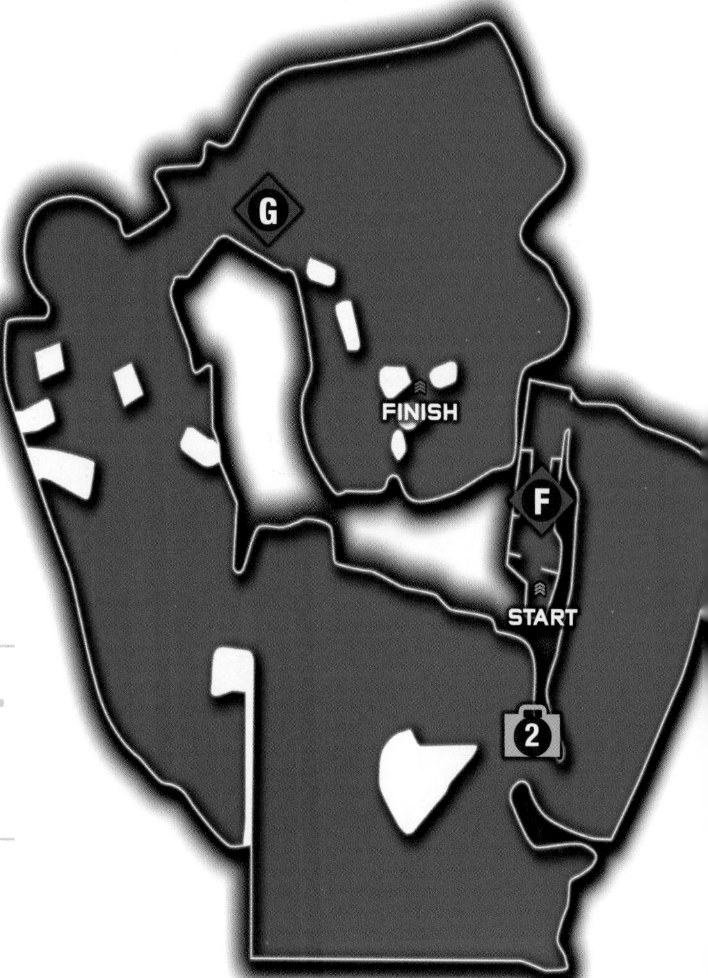

"COME ON, AGENT HARKOV. WE HAVE TO FIND THE PRESIDENT."

AA-12 SHOTGUN

CLIP SIZE	8
RANGE	LOW
WEAPON TYPE	SHOTGUN

The fully automatic AA-12 is great in close combat, as it delivers high damage and a high fire rate. However, its limited ammo and accuracy make it a poor choice in this gunfight.

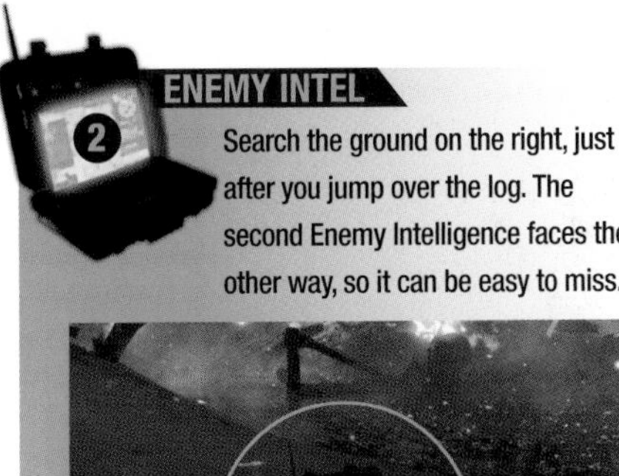

ENEMY INTEL

2 Search the ground on the right, just after you jump over the log. The second Enemy Intelligence faces the other way, so it can be easy to miss.

Continue behind the commander as you come upon more of Makarov's men. Take cover behind some wreckage and start firing at the bad guys. At this point, you gain a Flashbang and four Frag Grenades.

Use the grenades to flush out those who are hiding, and take them out. Keep pushing forward as you eliminate the threat. Eventually you reach a gate in the far corner, where the last of Makarov's men make a stand.

G OBJECTIVE

SECURE THE PRESIDENT

Enter the wooded area to find the rest of the airplane and the president. A helicopter lands to take him away. Approach it and open the door. This ends the mission.

ACHIEVEMENT/TROPHY

FREQUENT FLYER

Defend the Russian president and complete the Turbulence mission to earn this Achievement/Trophy.

ACT I

BACK ON THE GRID

TASK FORCE 141 | 18:27 OCTOBER 5 | SIERRA LEONE, AFRICA

OPERATIVE YURI, TASK FORCE 141–DISAVOWED

SUPPORT PRICE, SOAP

OBJECTIVES

INTERCEPT MAKAROV'S CARGO SHIPMENT IN SIERRA LEONE.

- **A** FOLLOW CAPTAIN PRICE.
- **B** PROVIDE OVERWATCH FOR PRICE AND SOAP.
- **C** REGROUP WITH CAPTAIN PRICE.
- **D** COMMANDEER THE TECHNICAL.
- **E** FOLLOW CAPTAIN PRICE.
- **F** USE THE MORTAR.
- **G** GET TO THE CHURCH.
- **H** SECURE THE CARGO.

FINISH

START

ENEMY INTEL 3

INITIAL LOADOUT

AK-47 Suppressed w/RedDot Sight

M14 EBR Scoped, Suppressed

4 Flashbangs

4 Frag Grenades

"KEEP IT SILENT. LET'S MOVE."

Makarov is using a local paramilitary group to move shipments through Sierra Leone. Price, Soap, and Yuri go in to intercept the cargo. The Sherbro River will allow them to get in close.

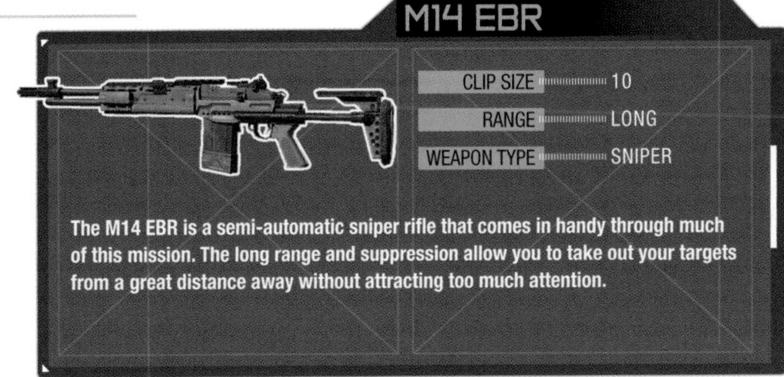

M14 EBR

CLIP SIZE	10
RANGE	LONG
WEAPON TYPE	SNIPER

The M14 EBR is a semi-automatic sniper rifle that comes in handy through much of this mission. The long range and suppression allow you to take out your targets from a great distance away without attracting too much attention.

A OBJECTIVE

FOLLOW CAPTAIN PRICE

Follow Price and Soap until you reach the road. Members of the militia approach, so crouch down and hide in the foliage. One guy is dropped off to patrol as the rest take off. Let Soap take care of him.

Continue to stay close behind Price as you travel down a dirt road. Eventually you reach a village where two guys are wrestling. Quickly use your sniper rifle to take down both of them.

At the next clearing, a villager is about to be set ablaze. Switch to your AK-47 and clear out the group of militia. Keep moving with Price and Soap.

"DON'T DO ANYTHING STUPID, LADS."

The crew reaches another big group of foes. Crouch down in the grass and let all of them pass—there are too many to confront. Wait for Price to move, and follow close behind.

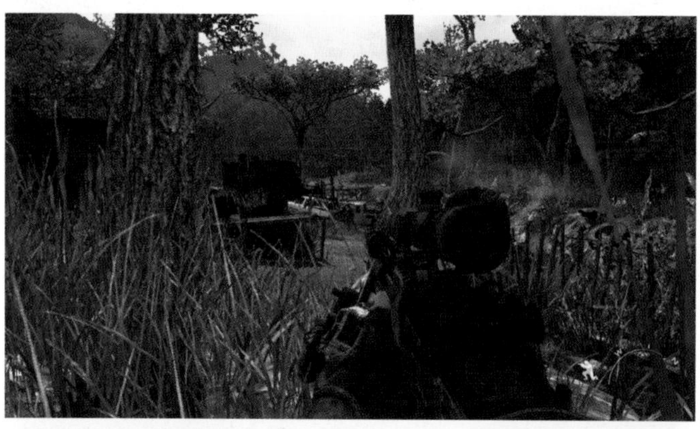

Sprint when they sprint, and when they get down on the side of the road, do the same. Another convoy passes by, so don't attract any attention. Once you get the "all clear," get up and sprint into the hut ahead.

"DROP THEM."

Wait there as a couple of militia men pass. When Price gives the all clear, follow him outside, where two men stand guard on the bridge ahead. Wait for a truck to pass on the nearby road, and then take down one of the guys with your sniper rifle. Price knocks down the other. Run up to the bridge as your partners move the bodies out of sight.

Once again, follow the captain further into the village. When he stops, pause as he takes out a lone militia man.

B OBJECTIVE

PROVIDE OVERWATCH FOR PRICE AND SOAP

Cut through another building and climb the ladder ahead. Price and Soap move on up to the factory, while Yuri stays back and provides overwatch. When you reach the roof, melee attack the guy sitting in the chair to take him out.

Find your partners below and watch out for any enemies who approach. Captain Price will let you know when this happens. First are two guys just up ahead. Zoom in on them with your sniper rifle, hold in the left stick to steady yourself, and squeeze the trigger to eliminate the threat.

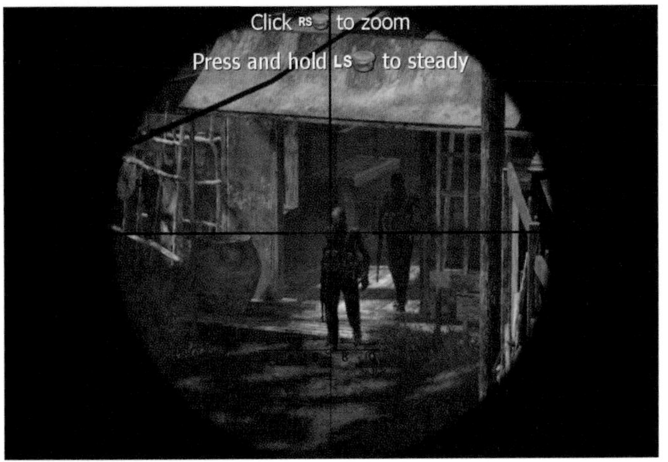

Take out two more who advance from the west (your left), and then a couple who patrol just in front of the factory. At this point your teammates breach the building.

C OBJECTIVE

REGROUP WITH CAPTAIN PRICE

Price lets you know that your group is compromised, and more of the militia advance on your position. Switch to your assault rifle and hop down to the road below. Eliminate as many foes as possible as you run toward the factory.

FAD

CLIP SIZE	30
RANGE	MEDIUM TO LONG
WEAPON TYPE	ASSAULT RIFLE

The FAD assault rifle is a fully automatic, all-purpose weapon with great range and fire rate. Pick it up if you want to swap out your sniper rifle for another automatic.

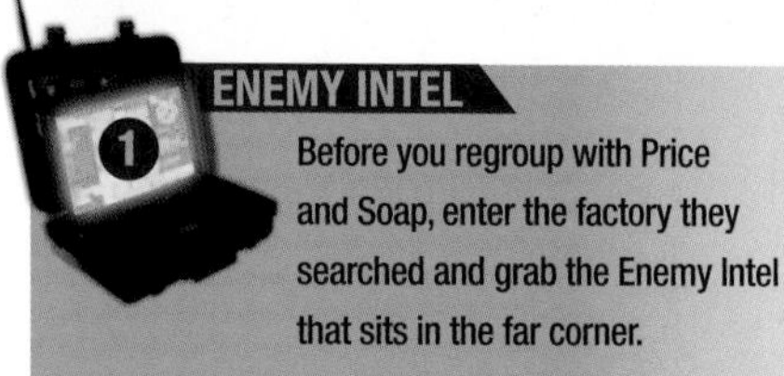

ENEMY INTEL

1 Before you regroup with Price and Soap, enter the factory they searched and grab the Enemy Intel that sits in the far corner.

TACTICS

FLANK

Use open structures and the alley on the right side to get a better position on the enemy. This allows you to surprise some of the men while they concentrate on Price and Soap.

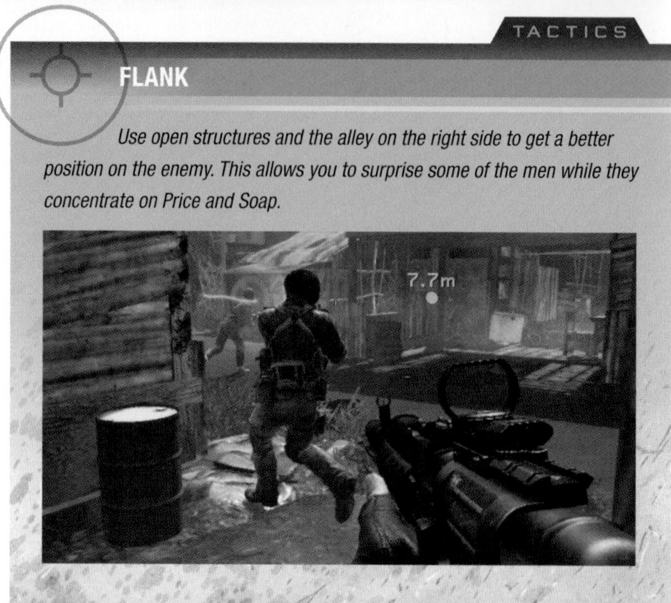

Meet up with Price at the corner. Then advance down the street to the left. Take cover along the way to fire at the enemy ahead. Watch behind you as militia men may approach from all sides.

MODEL 1887

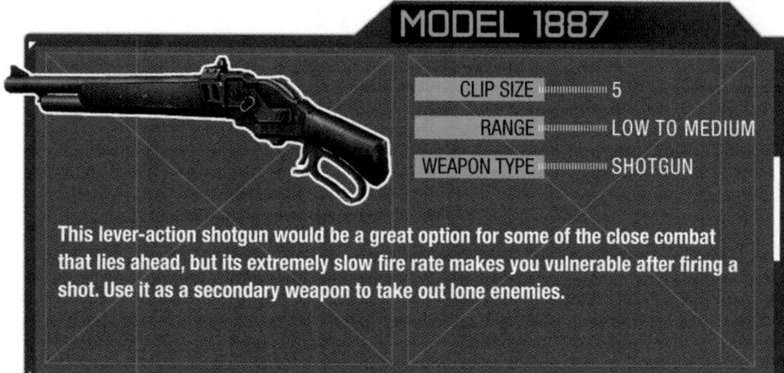

CLIP SIZE	5
RANGE	LOW TO MEDIUM
WEAPON TYPE	SHOTGUN

This lever-action shotgun would be a great option for some of the close combat that lies ahead, but its extremely slow fire rate makes you vulnerable after firing a shot. Use it as a secondary weapon to take out lone enemies.

As you run down the street to the southwest, look for a stove that sits in front of a shack. The second piece of Intelligence sits on a box inside that building.

Soap finds a path through a couple structures and up a ladder. Follow him up, and drop off the other side. Immediately take cover behind the stack of wood, and fire at the enemies across the road.

D OBJECTIVE

COMMANDEER THE TECHNICAL

A pickup truck pulls up just in front of you. Take out the guy who mans a .50 caliber mounted gun on the back. Then take up his position. Start out by obliterating another truck that rolls down the hill. The explosion thins the group around it.

Now, follow orders from Captain Price as he shouts out where the enemies are. The first are on the rooftops to the right. Then sweep to the left, taking out the guys on the hill ahead, and then more militia on the left side. Another truck shows up at the top of the hill, and more guys fire from the right.

E OBJECTIVE

FOLLOW CAPTAIN PRICE

After you take out more of their men, a mortar strikes nearby, knocking you off the gun. As you get up, you spot a big group of militia advancing on your position. Immediately follow Price and Soap as they flee to the north.

"THE WHOLE MILITIA IS HEADED STRAIGHT FOR US!"

Keep sprinting to keep up with them as they cut in and out of buildings and up a ladder. After jumping down onto a rooftop, Yuri breaks through to the ground below.

For the moment, you are on your own. Immediately, a foe attacks, so take him down, along with another farther up the path. Sprint that way to rejoin your team.

F OBJECTIVE

USE THE MORTAR

The militia is firing mortars from a tower just to the right. Take cover and shoot down the enemies inside. Run around the buildings and eliminate anyone still standing on the rooftops. Continue up the steps to find the mortar.

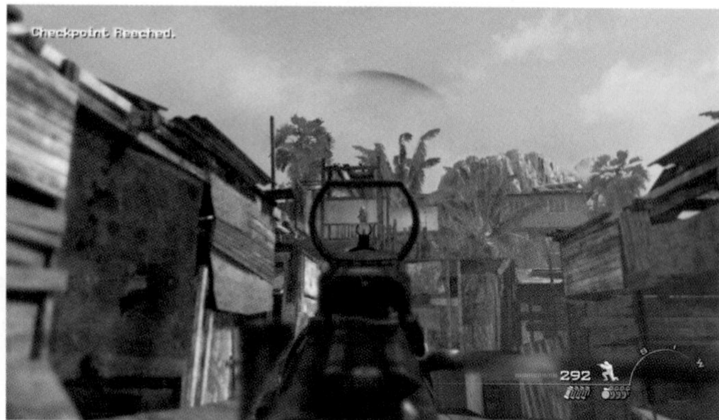

TACTICS

USING THE MORTAR

Hold the indicated button to use the mortar. A white reticle shows up on the ground ahead, marking where the mortar will land. Aim with the analog stick and launch a mortar via the usual Fire button.

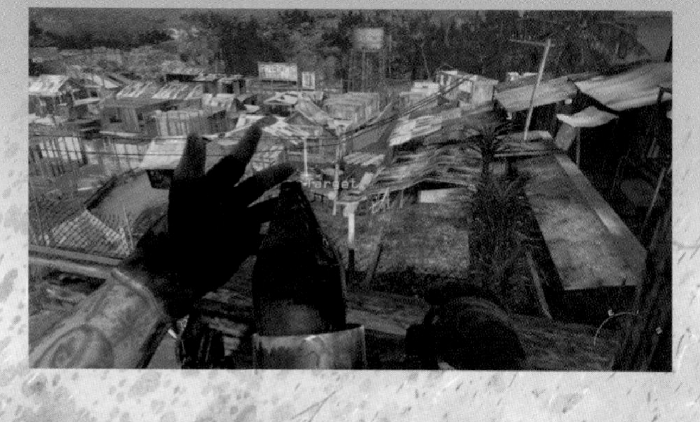

"THEN LET'S GIVE THEM A PROPER WELCOME."

Four targets that you must destroy with mortar fire arrive. First, a truck drives in on the right. Line up your reticle on the truck when it comes to a stop, and fire away. When two more appear on the left, eliminate them the same way. The second truck drives further into the area before stopping. Finally, a group of militia men march in on the right. You must be quick, because rockets coming your way from one of the rooftops. Once you take care of these targets, hop off the tower behind you.

ACHIEVEMENT/TROPHY

FOR WHOM THE SHELL TOLLS

Destroy all targets during the mortar sequence with only four shells in "Back on the Grid."

OBJECTIVE

GET TO THE CHURCH

Follow Soap through a pipe and directly into another firefight. You must work your way down the street, but militia men fire from all sides and from the rooftops above. Take cover and advance whenever possible. Knock down the guys on the rooftops first.

Follow your crew through the big warehouse, shooting anyone who gets in the way. At the next road, they fire from windows on the second floor. The fight gets intense, with enemies firing from nearly all sides.

"THEY'RE MOVING THE CARGO. WE'RE OUT OF TIME. GET TO THE CHURCH, NOW!"

Work your way from left to right, taking down anyone you see. Be sure to duck behind cover before you take too much damage. Check the rooftops and windows first as you advance up the path. After Price gives the all clear, move up to a door on the left.

Follow Soap through the building and back outside. Here you can see the church in the distance. Eliminate the adversaries to the left before you head up the hill. Be aware: more come out of the shops on the right.

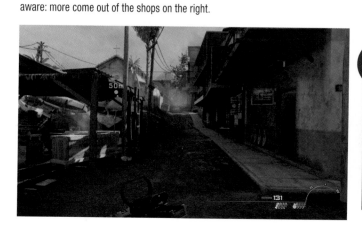

As you approach the church, the doors fly open and more foes fire from inside. Watch out for the hyena that attacks. It runs at you quickly, so backpedal a little and take it down. You can also kill it with a well-timed swipe of the knife. Clear out the rest of the enemies in the church and enter.

ENEMY INTEL

Search the back of the church to find this mission's final Intel on a table.

OBJECTIVE

SECURE THE CARGO

BREACH

Join Price and Soap at the side door. Breach the door, and a hyena immediately grabs hold. Use your free arm to take out the two militia men on the right, and then Yuri finishes off the animal.

ACHIEVEMENT/TROPHY

UP TO NO GOOD

Infiltrate the village and complete "Back on the Grid" on any difficulty for this award.

ACHIEVEMENT/TROPHY

OUT OF THE FRYING PAN...

Complete "Persona Non Grata," "Turbulence," and "Back on the Grid" on Veteran difficulty for another Achievement/Trophy.

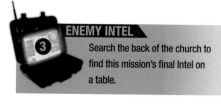

ACT I

MIND THE GAP

22ND SAS REGIMENT | 04:11 OCTOBER 6 | CANARY WHARF, LONDON

OPERATIVE SGT. MARCUS BURNS, 22ND SAS REGIMENT

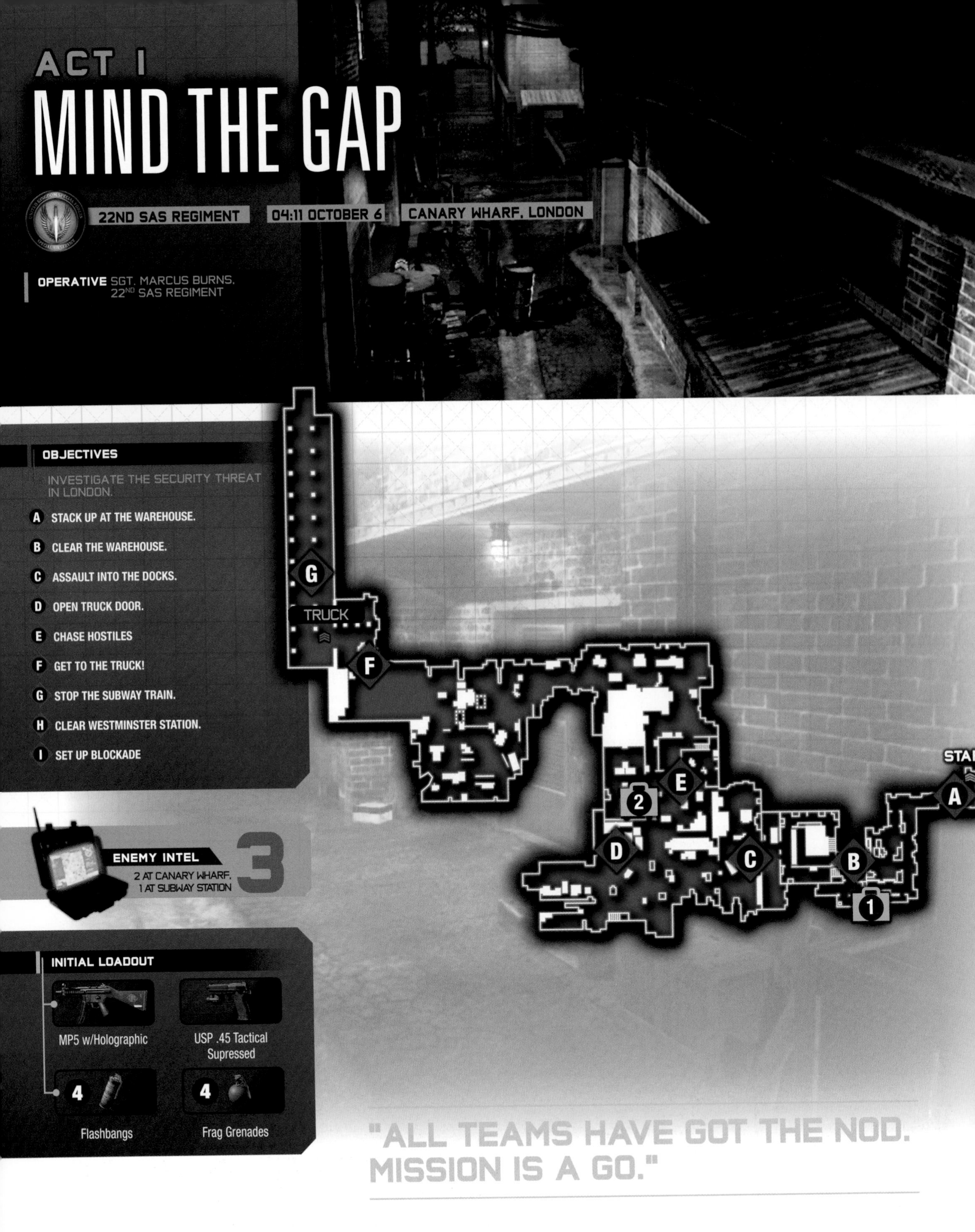

OBJECTIVES

INVESTIGATE THE SECURITY THREAT IN LONDON.

- **A** STACK UP AT THE WAREHOUSE.
- **B** CLEAR THE WAREHOUSE.
- **C** ASSAULT INTO THE DOCKS.
- **D** OPEN TRUCK DOOR.
- **E** CHASE HOSTILES
- **F** GET TO THE TRUCK!
- **G** STOP THE SUBWAY TRAIN.
- **H** CLEAR WESTMINSTER STATION.
- **I** SET UP BLOCKADE

ENEMY INTEL 3

2 AT CANARY WHARF, 1 AT SUBWAY STATION

INITIAL LOADOUT

- MP5 w/Holographic
- USP .45 Tactical Supressed
- 4 Flashbangs
- 4 Frag Grenades

"ALL TEAMS HAVE GOT THE NOD. MISSION IS A GO."

The French have intercepted a message concerning a suspicious shipment headed to London. Special Air Service of the United Kingdom Special Forces has been tasked with investigating this threat.

TACTICS

DISTURBING CONTENT NOTICE

At the start of this mission, you are asked if you want to skip some disturbing or offensive content. If you say yes, the final part of this level is left out. You are not penalized in terms of Achievements/Trophies or game completion.

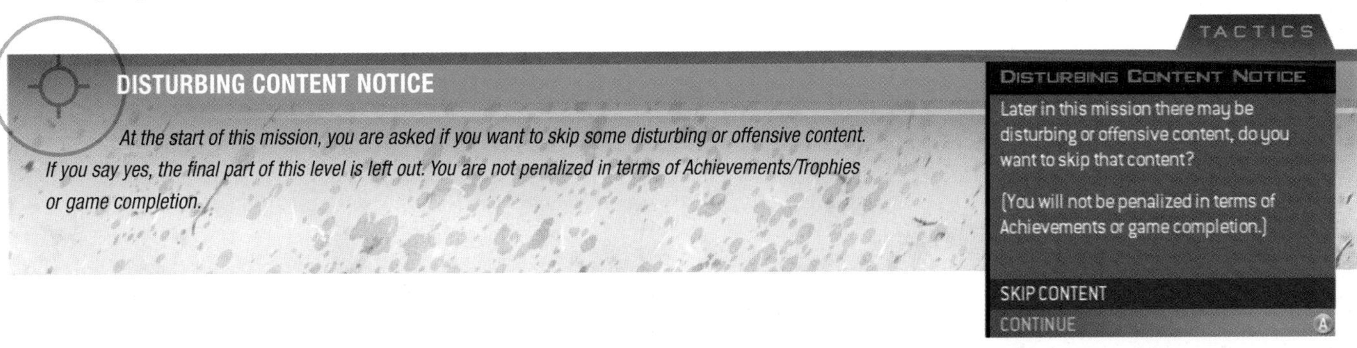

Disturbing Content Notice
Later in this mission there may be disturbing or offensive content, do you want to skip that content?
(You will not be penalized in terms of Achievements or game completion.)
SKIP CONTENT
CONTINUE

A OBJECTIVE

STACK UP AT THE WAREHOUSE

Your team is sent down to the docks at Canary Wharf to check out a truck suspected of being a threat. You must clear a couple of warehouses before securing the truck, though. Run into the alley and wait for a lone worker to emerge from a door. Take him down or let one of the other guys do it.

Enter that door and eliminate two more men who are on break. Return to the alley and wait for the other team to take care of another threat. Turn right and kill the pair of foes ahead. Join your partners at the door, and Corporal Griffin cuts the lock.

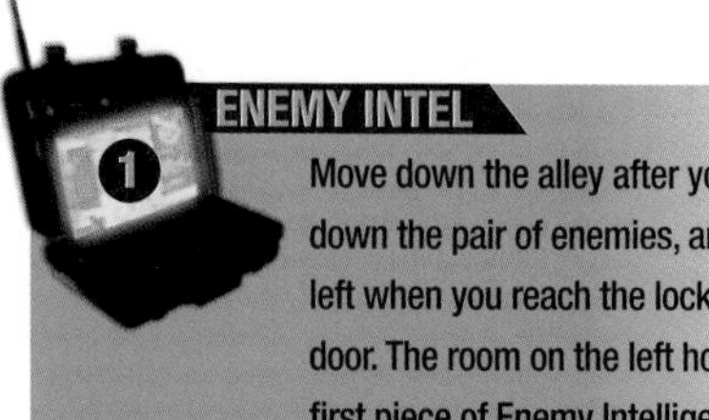

ENEMY INTEL

Move down the alley after you take down the pair of enemies, and turn left when you reach the locked door. The room on the left holds the first piece of Enemy Intelligence.

OBJECTIVE

CLEAR THE WAREHOUSE

Enter the building and run up the stairs. Move to the right side of the hall and knife an enemy who stands right at the corner. Peek around the next corner and take down a couple more workers.

Proceed up to the top floor as Special Forces take down two more foes. Knock out one of the windows ahead, and slide down the roof to the street below.

C OBJECTIVE

ASSAULT INTO THE DOCKS

Take cover behind a cargo container as you fire on the enemies ahead. Wait for them to blow their cover, and take them down. Move forward with your team as the enemy is eliminated.

TACTICS

FLUSH THEM OUT WITH GRENADES

Do not forget about your grenades. You can use them to flush out hiding enemies. Toss a Frag their way and mow them down as they flee. You should also be aware of incoming grenades. Return these to their rightful owners or run for cover.

D OBJECTIVE

OPEN TRUCK DOOR

Once the all clear is given, move up to the Charity Worldwide truck and open the rear doors.

E OBJECTIVE

CHASE HOSTILES

Run around the truck and hop onto the ledge. Eliminate the enemies who immediately start to run around the corner. Take cover at the corner and clear out the area ahead.

ENEMY INTEL

2

After you check the truck and clear out the enemies, run along the side of the building to the stairs. Climb them to the walkway above. Turn left and follow it up more steps and into an open doorway. The Intel rests on a table next to the windows.

Cut through the brick building with the stairs out front. More enemies wait for you on the other side. Finish them off from the doorway. You receive some air support from a friendly chopper that makes a run down the road ahead.

Drop down to the street and take cover behind a concrete barrier as you fight off the enemies. Make your way from cover to cover, being sure to check the other side of the road.

As you reach a stack of beams, the chopper makes another run, knocking loose some large pipes, which eliminate a big group of enemies. Cut through an open cargo container around the corner, and use it for cover against more foes to the right.

Keep more cover between you and the enemies by moving around the area's perimeter.

F OBJECTIVE

GET TO THE TRUCK!

Fight your way to a stack of barrels, where you receive an order to head for the truck. Quickly run down the hill toward the truck. You can lose the subway train immediately if you don't reach the truck quickly enough.

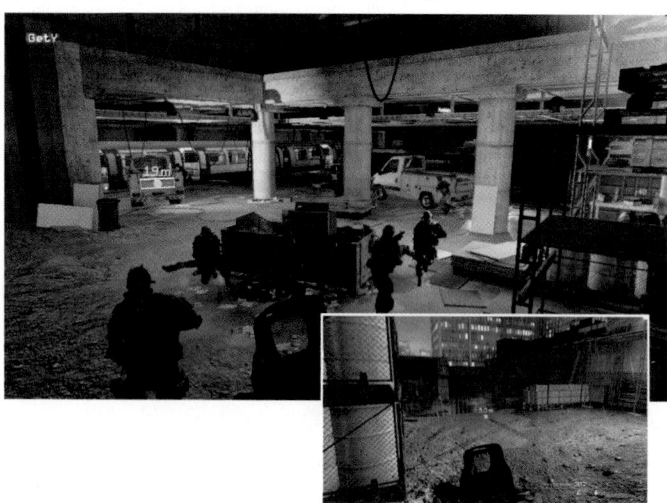

G OBJECTIVE

STOP THE SUBWAY TRAIN

Two trucks take off after the train. Sgt. Burns sits in the back of the second one. Watch for enemies inside the train—shoot at them. Continue to lay down fire whenever you have a shot, especially into the open doors. The truck moves back and forth a lot, continually making it difficult to get a good shot.

Be careful when the train passes through a station with civilians waiting on the platform. Hold your fire when another train cuts between the truck and your target. Eventually the train crashes and your truck goes down, too.

"BURNS, YOU ALRIGHT"?"

OBJECTIVE

CLEAR WESTMINSTER STATION

Sgt. Burns regains consciousness amid the wreckage. Follow Sgt. Wallcroft through a train car and into Westminster Station. Take down the enemies waiting there to welcome you. One foe fires from the top of the stairs on the left.

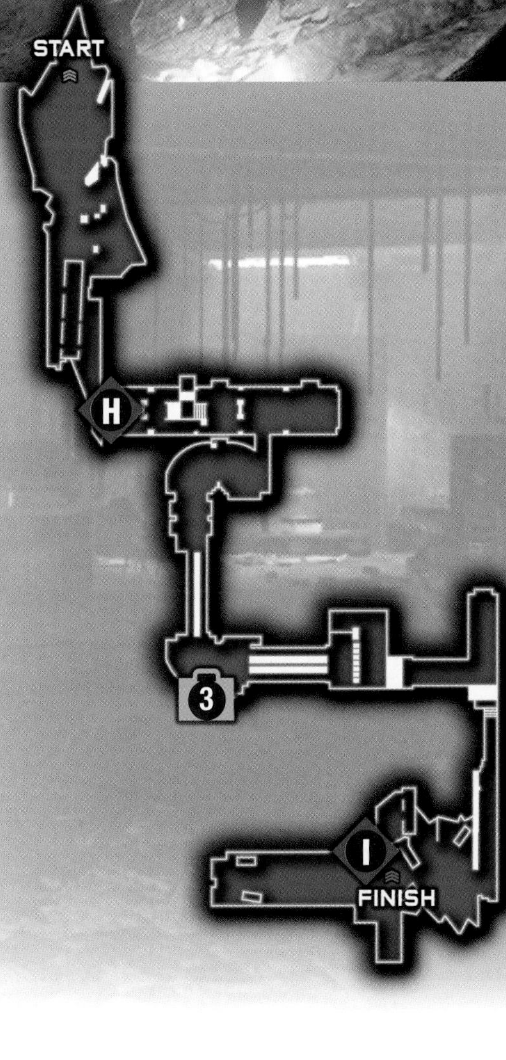

TACTICS

WATCH OUT FOR CIVILIANS

Watch out for civilians as you run and gun through the subway station.

Fight your way down through the station, using whatever you can as cover. Dart into the opening on the right, and fight off more foes around the corner. Watch out: they take cover behind nearly everything.

Approach the escalator and take down the foes who fire from above. Watch out for grenades that roll down the steps. Once it's clear, run upstairs and kill the guys around the newsstand.

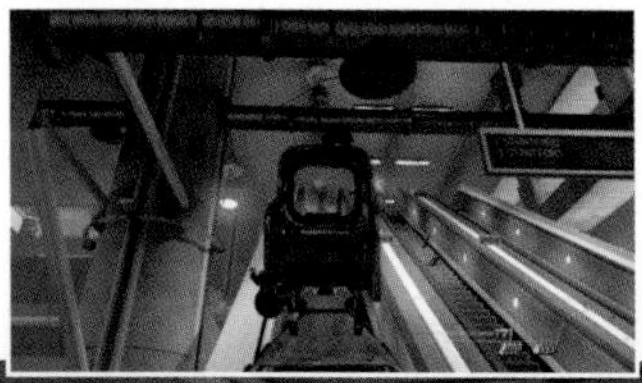

ENEMY INTEL

3

After you go up the escalator, search behind the counter of the newsstand to find the Intel.

"THE TRUCK WILL BE HERE ANY SECOND."

Go up another escalator and kill the men who fire from the turnstiles. Hop over them and run down the corridor to meet your backup. Exit the station to the right.

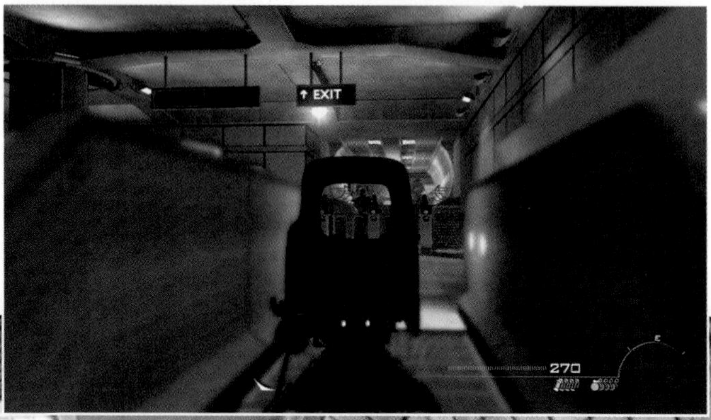

OBJECTIVE

SET UP BLOCKADE

More troops are dropped off topside as they try to set up a blockade. Run toward all of the commotion and wait for the truck to show up.

TACTICS

POSSIBLE DISTURBING CONTENT

If you chose to skip the offensive content at the beginning of this mission, then the following sequence is skipped. To avoid spoilers, we refrain from describing it here.

ACHIEVEMENT/TROPHY

ONE-WAY TICKET

Complete "Mind the Gap" by making it to Westminster to earn this Achievement/Trophy.

ACT 2

ACT II
GOALPOST

DELTA FORCE | 13:01 OCTOBER 6 | HAMBURG, GERMANY

OPERATIVE SGT. DEREK "FROST" WESTBROOK, DELTA FORCE

FROST

SUPPORT SANDMAN

SANDMAN

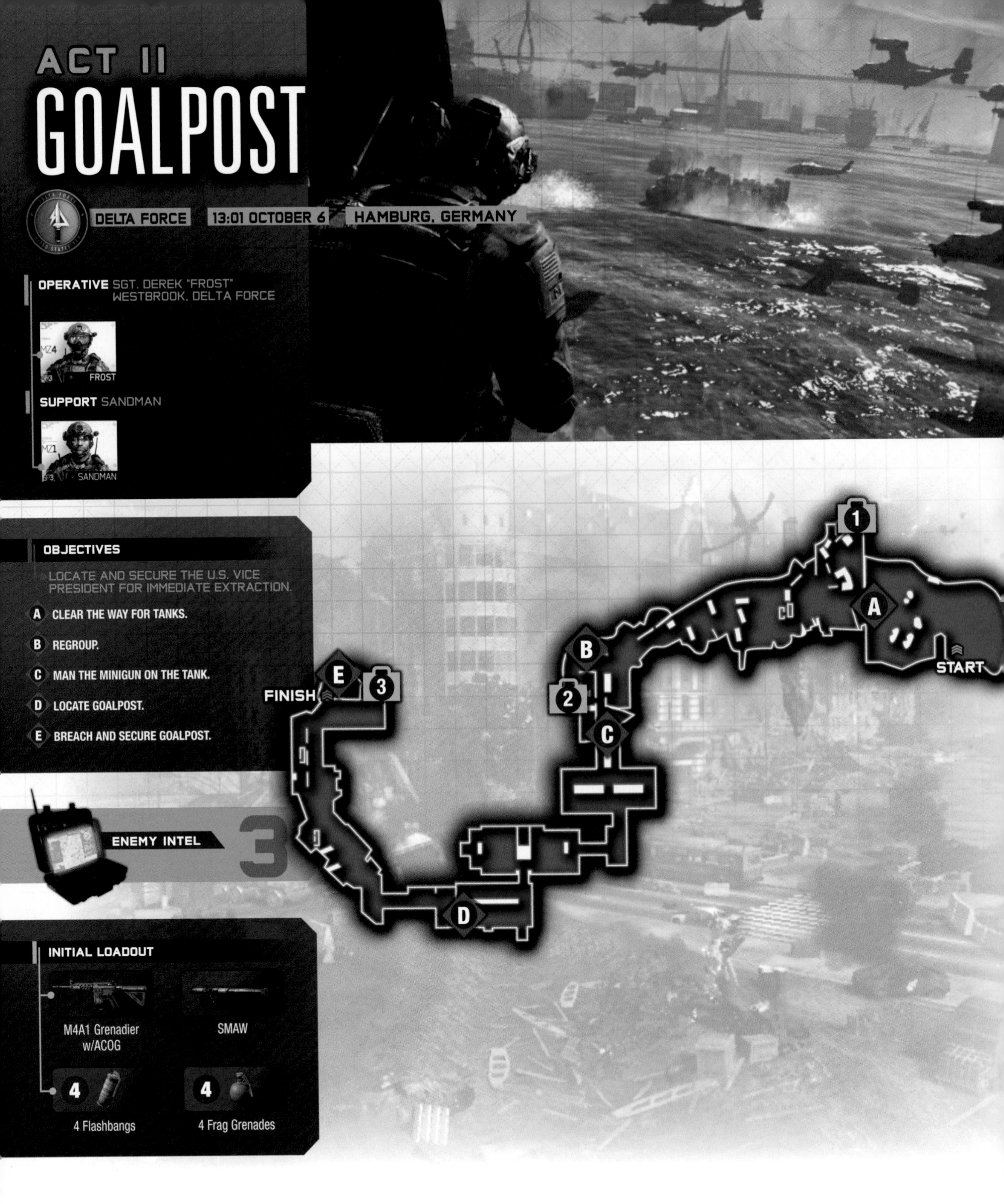

OBJECTIVES

LOCATE AND SECURE THE U.S. VICE PRESIDENT FOR IMMEDIATE EXTRACTION.

- **A** CLEAR THE WAY FOR TANKS.
- **B** REGROUP.
- **C** MAN THE MINIGUN ON THE TANK.
- **D** LOCATE GOALPOST.
- **E** BREACH AND SECURE GOALPOST.

ENEMY INTEL 3

INITIAL LOADOUT

- M4A1 Grenadier w/ACOG
- SMAW
- 4 Flashbangs
- 4 Frag Grenades

Your team has been rerouted for Hamburg, where the vice president has been taken hostage. You are dropped off at the beach, and your first objective is to clear a path for the tanks.

"THE CONVOY NEVER MADE IT TO THE EXTRACTION POINT."

SMAW

CLIP SIZE	1
RANGE	MEDIUM
WEAPON TYPE	LAUNCHER

The SMAW is a free-fire or vehicle-lock-on rocket launcher. This weapon comes in handy against the various Russian vehicles.

A OBJECTIVE

CLEAR THE WAY FOR TANKS

Sprint up to the wall on the left and move into the opening as smoke is deployed. Work your way over to the right side, watching out for Russians along the way. Use the concrete barriers to clear out the area around the crashed airplane.

ENEMY INTEL

1 Once the area is clear, enter the wreckage of the plane and make your way up to the front, where a piece of Enemy Intel is ready to be secured.

Run up the right side to another brick wall. Take out any enemy forces you can from that position, and then hop over the wall. Keep advancing forward from cover to cover, eliminating any threats you encounter.

TACTICS

HELP OUT

As you clear the enemies on the right side, occasionally look to the other side of the path to see if you have a good flanking position on more Russians. This helps your team advance along the street. Use the SMAW to cripple any tanks.

As you approach the corner, enter the gap in the wall and eliminate the enemies on the rubble mound and up on the bridge. Continue moving around the perimeter, crouching down to remain relatively hidden behind the short wall.

RPG-7

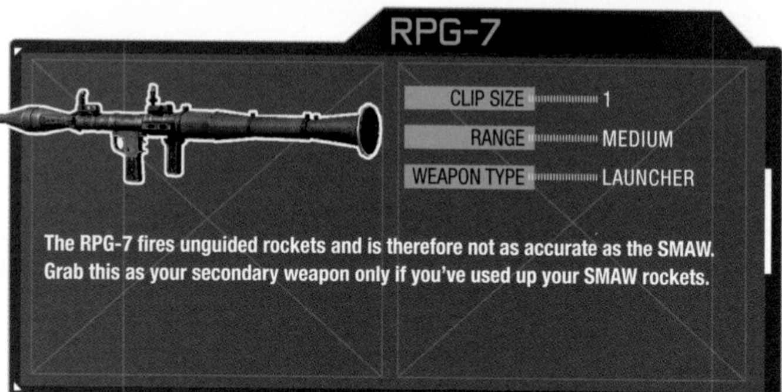

CLIP SIZE	1
RANGE	MEDIUM
WEAPON TYPE	LAUNCHER

The RPG-7 fires unguided rockets and is therefore not as accurate as the SMAW. Grab this as your secondary weapon only if you've used up your SMAW rockets.

As you proceed to the end of the wall, watch out for enemies across the road. Several Russians spill out from the south. Pick them off as they run for cover.

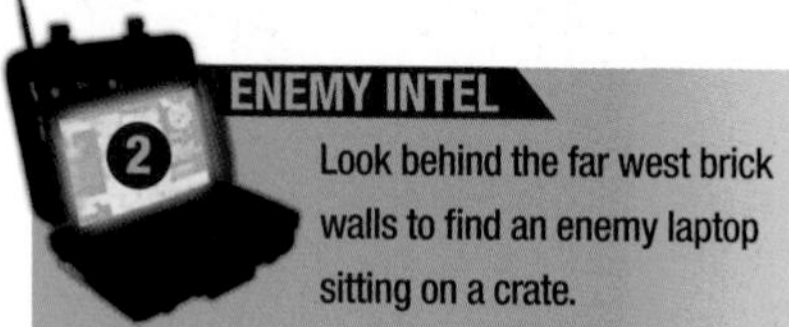

ENEMY INTEL

2

Look behind the far west brick walls to find an enemy laptop sitting on a crate.

B OBJECTIVE

REGROUP

"THE ONLY WAY THROUGH IS IN THAT PARKING GARAGE AND OUT THE OTHER SIDE."

As you move to the south, the enemies ahead are too focused on the tank to notice you, so kill them. Once the area is clear, regroup with your team at the tank.

C OBJECTIVE

MAN THE MINIGUN ON THE TANK

A sniper takes out the gunner on the back of the tank. Hop aboard to man the minigun. Once the tank starts to move forward, fire on the Russians along the sides of the road.

At the intersection, shoot down the enemies who attempt to flee back into the parking garage. The tank rolls through the structure. Fire at any Russians you see, and blow up the vehicles they hide behind.

TACTICS

LOOK OUT BEHIND YOU

Sweep all the way around, because it's easy to miss one guy. He will continue to pick away at your health from behind.

Your tank waits for Rhino One to pass and then enters another section of the garage. Destroy the jeep that approaches from the right. Then take out more Russians up ahead by causing the nearby cars to explode.

D OBJECTIVE

LOCATE GOALPOST

The tank crashes through the floor and lands on a lower level. The crew has to hoof it from here. Move forward and take cover behind a concrete barrier as another truck arrives. If you have any rockets, launch one to take care of it. Otherwise, fight your way through and exit the garage.

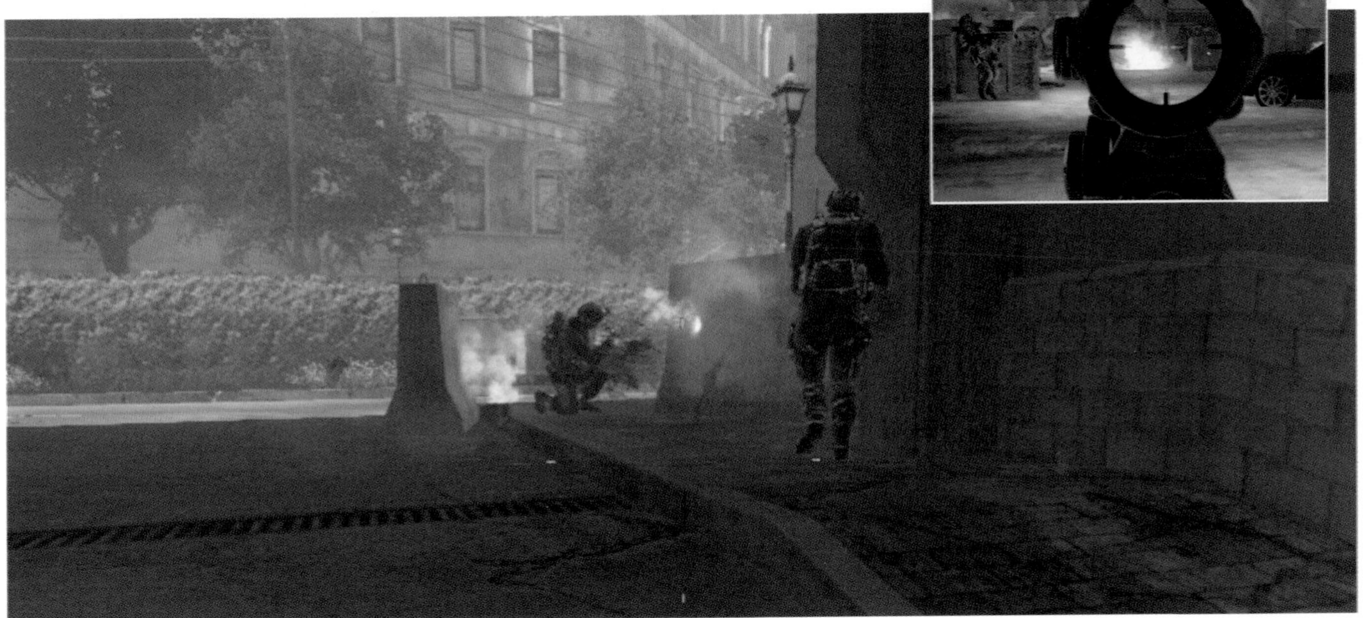

"ISR HAS SPOTTED THE CONVOY HALF A KLICK FROM YOUR POSITION."

Fight your way along the right side of the street, moving between cover whenever possible. Rhino One crashes through the wall, so use that opportunity to move up alongside them.

Once the sidewalk is clear, hop through the bank window on the right. Watch out, as a couple of Russians are just inside. Fight your way through the offices until you can't go any further.

TACTICS

WEAK WALLS

The cubicle walls and desks inside the building don't provide as much cover as the brick walls and concrete barriers outside. Use them to your advantage, but be careful when you're trying to heal up behind one of these objects.

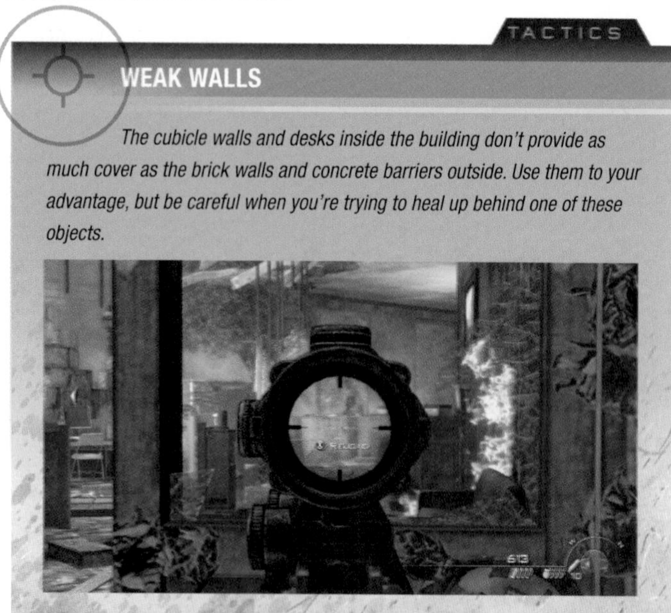

SCAR-L
CLIP SIZE 30
RANGE MEDIUM TO LONG
WEAPON TYPE ASSAULT RIFLE
The M16A4 assault rifle has a three-round burst with good accuracy, range, fire rate, and damage. This makes it a great option as your primary weapon.
The SCAR-L is another fully automatic, all-purpose weapon. It suffers from a slow reload time. If you're ready to abandon your rocket launcher, pick up this as your secondary.

Exit back out to the street and continue to fight your way to the north. Slowly work your way around the corner until you find the convoy at a dead end. Dart into the office building on the left.

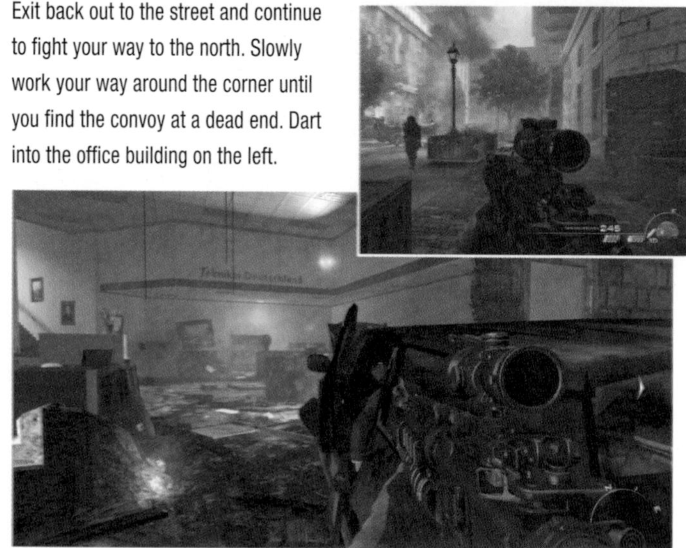

ENEMY INTEL

3 Search the cubicles along the east wall for a laptop that sits on one of the desks.

"CHECK THE AREA FOR ANY SIGN OF THE DELEGATES."

E OBJECTIVE

BREACH AND SECURE GOALPOST

BREACH

Follow the squad up the stairs as someone flees through the doorway ahead. Be sure your weapon is reloaded, and then breach the room. Your first target should be the man standing to the right, the one who is about to execute the hostage. Then go for the Russian who lunges toward you from the left. Clean up the room by eliminating the two in the back.

Exit out to the balcony to reach the extraction point.

ACHIEVEMENT/TROPHY

WELCOME TO WW3

Save the U.S. vice president by completing "Goalpost" on any difficulty to earn this Achievement/Trophy.

ACT II
RETURN TO SENDER
TASK FORCE 141
09:30 OCTOBER 8
BOOSAASO, SOMALIA
OPERATIVE YURI, TASK FORCE 141 - DISAVOWED
SUPPORT PRICE, NIKOLAI, SOAP
OBJECTIVES
STORM THE SOMALI COMPOUND AND PICK UP MAKAROV'S TRAIL.
A CAPTURE AND INTERROGATE WARAABE.
B MOVE TO LZ.
C HEAD TO THE SECONDARY LZ.
D FIND NIKOLAI'S CRASHED CHOPPER.
E RESCUE NIKOLAI.
ENEMY INTEL
3
INITIAL LOADOUT
M4A1 Grenadier w/ACOG
Desert Eagle
4
Flashbangs
4
Frag Grenades
LZ 2
LZ
START
A
B
C
1
2
3

Soap

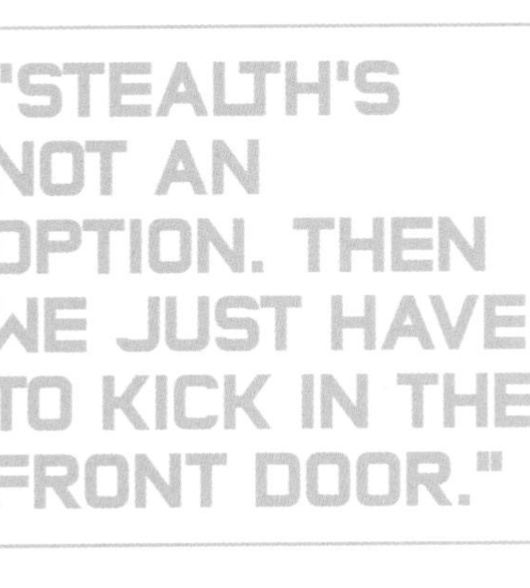
"STEALTH'S NOT AN OPTION. THEN WE JUST HAVE TO KICK IN THE FRONT DOOR."

INTRO
BASICS
CAMPAIGN
SPECIAL OPS
ACHIEVEMENTS
MP GAMEPLAY
MP ARSENAL
MP MAPS
EXTRAS

A delivery freighter has been traced to an outfit in Boosaaso, Somalia, run by a dangerous man named Waraabe. Price, Soap, and Yuri charge in to find out what he knows.

A OBJECTIVE

CAPTURE AND INTERROGATE WARAABE

A sandstorm is moving into the area, so this operation must be completed quickly. Stealth is out the door, so don't worry about making some noise. As soon as your gun is up, start picking off Waraabe's men at the gate.

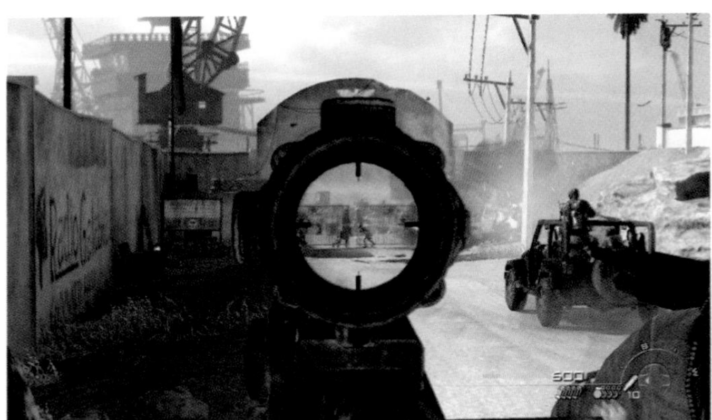

Once you're on the ground, move up to the concrete dock on the left and fire at the locals who surround you. They aren't the most skilled enemies you face, but they can do some damage in large numbers. Your M4A1 has a grenade attachment, so use it.

When Nikolai moves the chopper into position, you have an opportunity to use the remote chopper turret. Get behind some cover and press Right to bring up the computer screen. Take out as many targets as you can. You have to wait a while for Nikolai to get back into position. You know the turret is ready when the helicopter icon shows up next to the D-pad in the lower-right corner. You are also told when it's available.

Press to use remote chopper turret.

REMOTE CHOPPER TURRET

Watch out as you activate the remote turret, because you're still vulnerable. Once the screen is up, press Forward or Backward to adjust the zoom. Press the Fire button to shoot at targets. Hostile targets are shown with a red box around them. The screen shuts down when the chopper moves out of range.

ACHIEVEMENT/TROPHY

KILL BOX

You can earn a bonus Achievement/Trophy by killing 20 enemies in a single run with the remote chopper turret. You get a few opportunities to do this throughout this mission.

"TARGET BUILDING IN SIGHT!"

Watch out for mortars as you advance toward the buildings. When you hear that a technical is headed your way, spot the trucks as they come down the hill, and then take out the gunners on the backs.

Follow Price as he runs toward the target. When you reach the blue building on the left, enter through the doorway and go up the stairs. Eliminate any hostiles that occupy the upstairs, and then move to the balcony. From here, you can lay down some cover fire so your team can advance. Take cover inside whenever necessary.

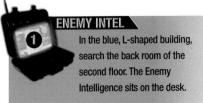

DRAGUNOV
CLIP SIZE 10
RANGE LONG
WEAPON TYPE SNIPER RIFLE
The Dragunov is a nice semi-automatic sniper rifle, and it couldn't be sitting in a better spot. Use it to take out enemies on the rooftops across the road.

ENEMY INTEL

1 In the blue, L-shaped building, search the back room of the second floor. The Enemy Intelligence sits on the desk.

Use the remote chopper turret whenever it becomes available. It's the easiest way to clear a path to your destination. Target the machine guns and rocket launchers as the chopper circles the area.

When you reach the next checkpoint, head down the stairs and join your team at the entrance to the west building. Follow them inside and up the steps. At the top floor, you spot more hostiles, so take them down. Eliminate those who guard the target room.

"YURI, SOAP— LET'S FIND THIS BASTARD."

BREACH

Approach the office door, reload your weapon, and plant the explosives. Target the middle guy first, as he's the closest threat. Take out the right two next, followed by the left. Be sure to leave the target that is marked by the word "Capture" alive for interrogating.

ENEMY INTEL

A desk in the southwest corner of the breached office holds another piece of Enemy Intelligence.

B OBJECTIVE

MOVE TO LZ

You have what you came for, so head for the landing zone. Exit to the north and run up the hill. The chopper should be waiting just around the corner.

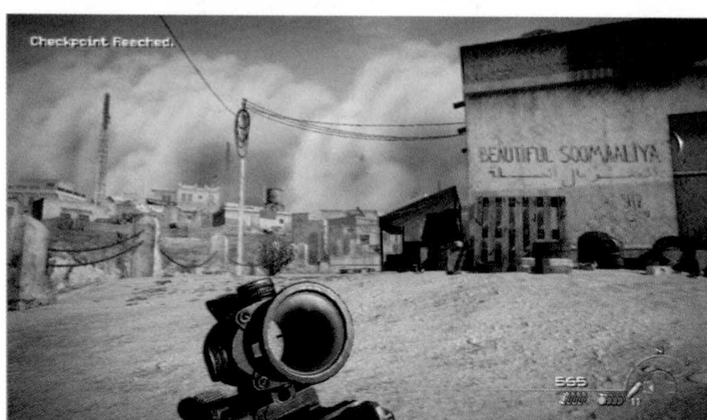

The locals are ready for you, making it too dangerous to land. Shoot the foes up on the roof and second floor first, and then move in.

C OBJECTIVE

HEAD TO THE SECONDARY LZ

Nikolai moves on to a new landing area, but with the sandstorm coming, you have limited time to get there. Once you pass the next intersection, you have three minutes to reach him.

Quickly advance down the street, taking out the gunner on the back of a truck that enters from the right. Again, watch out for enemies on the rooftops as you run to the east.

Cut to the left of a pile of bricks to avoid a burning car that rolls down the hill. Take cover on the left side as more of Waraabe's loyal men continue fighting. Eliminate the ones on the rooftop and balcony first, and then clear out the rest.

"WE'VE GOT TO PUSH THROUGH TO THE SECONDARY LANDING ZONE BEFORE THE STORM HITS. LET'S MOVE!"

ENEMY INTEL

3

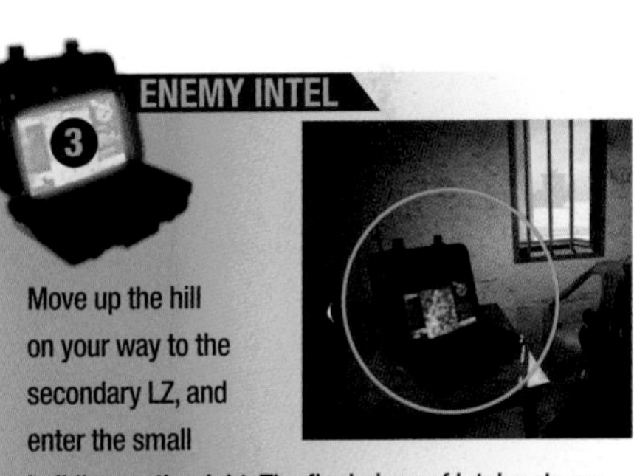

Move up the hill on your way to the secondary LZ, and enter the small building on the right. The final piece of Intel rests on a table inside.

Run up the hill and into a construction site. The sandstorm is just ahead, so you must hurry, although the timer is now off. Run inside the partially built building and gun down the enemies inside. Run up the steps to where a few more take cover behind the supplies. When the second floor is clear, run up the final steps to the top.

Again, it's too dangerous to land, so use the remote chopper turret to clear the area of hostiles. A rocket hits the helicopter and sends Nikolai out of control. Immediately run the opposite direction and jump over to the rope. Slide down to the ground below, where the sandstorm has caught up with you.

OBJECTIVE

FIND NIKOLAI'S CRASHED CHOPPER

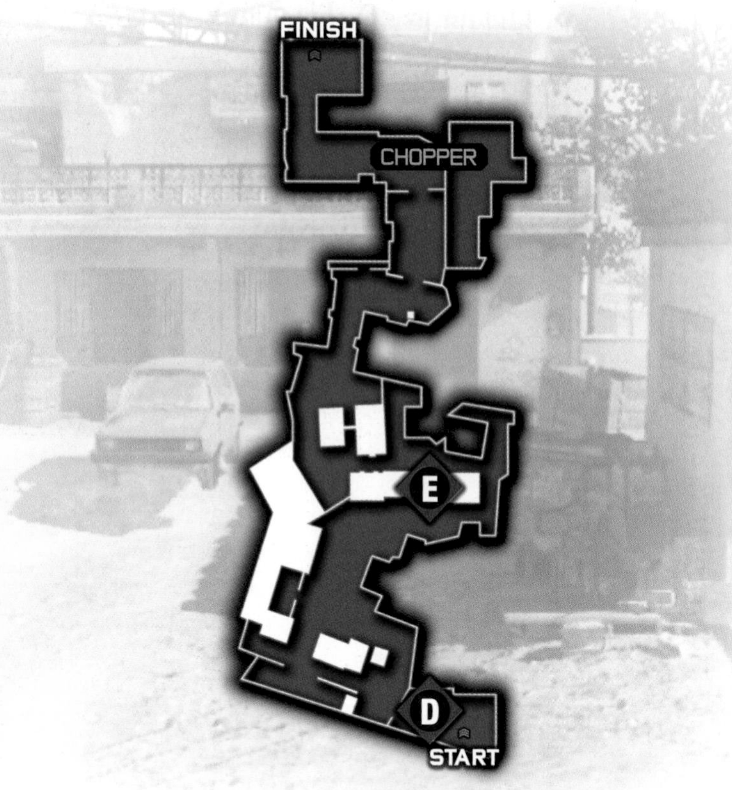

Follow Price into the darkness. A short way in, you run into some enemies. Target the silhouettes and gun them down. At the next street, a group of men pass. Eliminate them and then continue behind the captain.

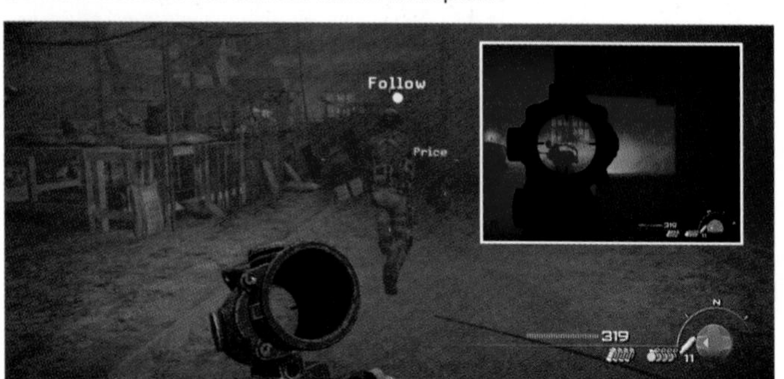

E

OBJECTIVE

RESCUE NIKOLAI

Two more groups of hostiles get in the way before you spot Nikolai's chopper. Run to Nikolai's position, where the enemy has him pinned down. When Captain Price instructs you to grab Yuri, run over to him and throw him over your shoulder.

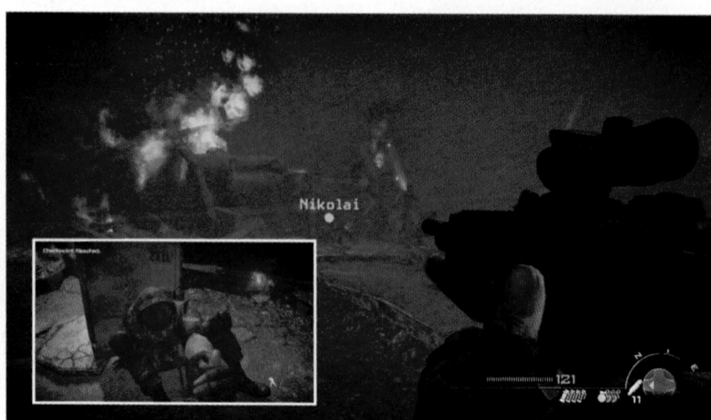

Follow the team through the village and down the hill. Hop into the jeep to make the getaway.

ACHIEVEMENT/TROPHY

SANDSTORM!

Get this Achievement/Trophy after you assault the shipping company and complete "Return to Sender" on any difficulty.

ACHIEVEMENT/TROPHY

PAYBACK

You can earn another Achievement/Trophy by completing "Mind the Gap," "Goalpost," and "Return to Sender" on Veteran difficulty.

ACT II
BAG AND DRAG

DELTA FORCE | 14:10 OCTOBER 9 | MONTMARTRE HILL, PARIS

OPERATIVE SGT. DEREK "FROST" WESTBROOK, DELTA FORCE

FROST

SUPPORT SANDMAN, GRINCH

SANDMAN | GRINCH

OBJECTIVES

CAPTURE VOLK ALIVE IN PARIS.

- **A** RENDEZVOUS WITH THE GIGN SQUAD.
- **B** FOLLOW THE GIGN LEADER.
- **C** USE THE AIR SUPPORT MARKER TO DESTROY THE BTR.
- **D** FOLLOW THE GIGN LEADER THROUGH THE CATACOMBS.
- **E** CAPTURE VOLK.
- **F** GET IN THE VAN.

ENEMY INTEL 4

INITIAL LOADOUT

SCAR-L w/ACOG Sight	USP .45
4 Flashbangs	4 Frag Grenades

"THE AIR IS STILL DIRTY FROM THE CHEMICAL ATTACK. KEEP YOUR MASKS ON."

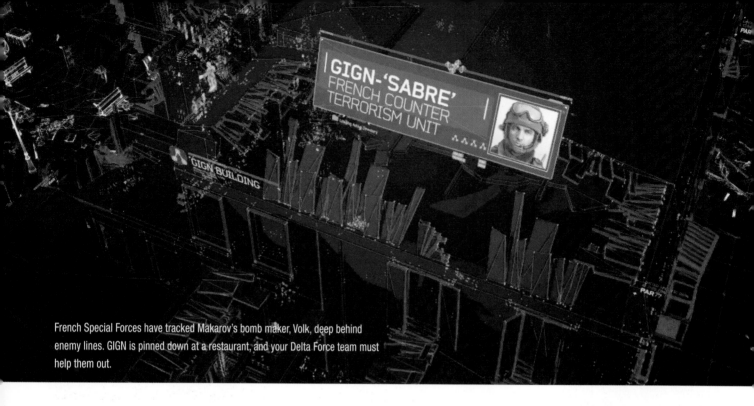

French Special Forces have tracked Makarov's bomb maker, Volk, deep behind enemy lines. GIGN is pinned down at a restaurant, and your Delta Force team must help them out.

OBJECTIVE

RENDEZVOUS WITH THE GIGN SQUAD

The chopper drops you off on a Paris rooftop, along with Sandman and Grinch. You must fight your way to the GIGN squad. Follow Sandman through an apartment to a hole in the wall.

He removes a piece of debris that reveals a path along a narrow ledge. Sidle into the next room, and then continue behind your team until you reach a window across from the bookstore.

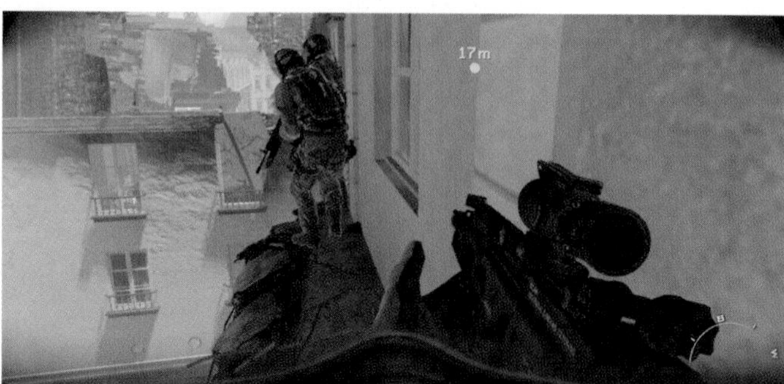

The opposition fires at you from inside. Drop down to the street and take cover next to the door. There are men on both levels. Take out anyone you can see above, and then move inside.

Fight your way to the stairs ahead and proceed up them. Once you hear that the top floor is clear, head down the other stairs.

ENEMY INTEL
1
Before you return downstairs in the bookstore, search between the two bookcases on the west wall. An enemy laptop sits on the windowsill.

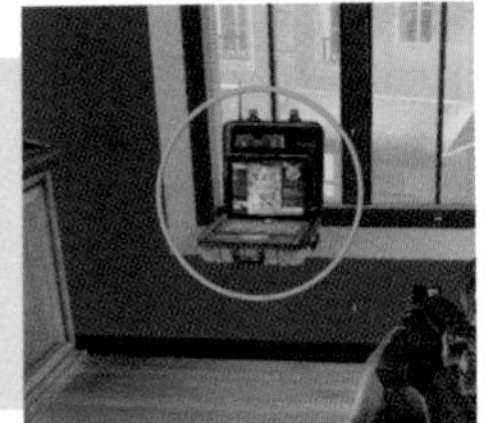

Watch out—more foes may be occupying the lower level. Once it's clear, proceed to the exit in the southeast corner. Here, you meet up with the GIGN squad.

B OBJECTIVE

FOLLOW THE GIGN LEADER

Run down the alley and enter the open door at the back of the restaurant. GIGN informs your team that Volk launched the chemical attack from the catacombs. Follow the GIGN leader into the restaurant.

"THE RUSSIANS LAUNCHED THE CHEMICAL ATTACK FROM A STAGING GROUND IN THE CATACOMBS. WE'RE BETTING VOLK IS STILL THERE."

This assault rifle is a decent all-purpose weapon. Its poor accuracy is offset by high damage.

Eliminate the enemies in front of the building and then take cover in the street. Shoot down anyone you can from that position, including the RPG at the top of the steps.

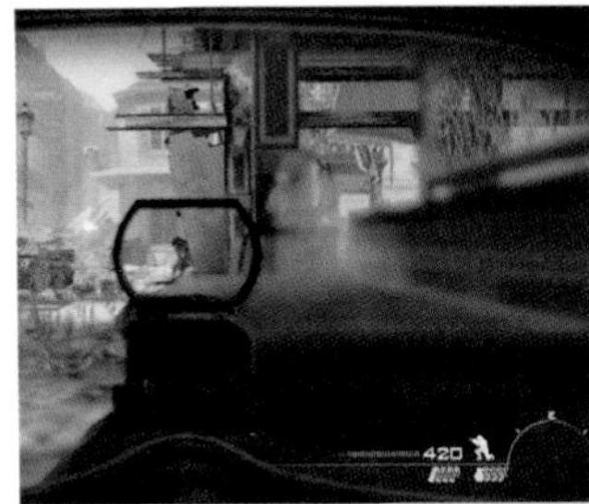

Cross the road and enter the building. Peek out the north door and eliminate any hostiles at the café across the alley. Enter the back door and move up to the front.

ENEMY INTEL

2 In the back room of the café, Enemy Intelligence sits out in the open.

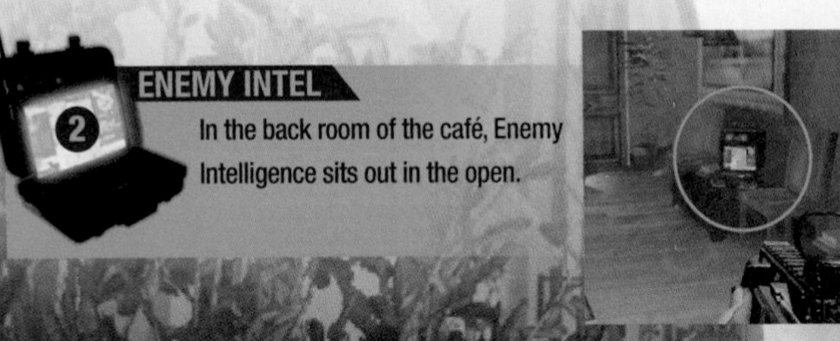

P99
CLIP SIZE 5
RANGE MEDIUM
WEAPON TYPE HANDGUN

This semi-automatic handgun is very similar to the USP .45 except with a smaller magazine.

Fire at the men across the path and then at the top of the steps. Once it's clear, follow the GIGN squad up and into a doorway on the right. Take out the soldiers on the balcony across the alley.

"WE GOT BAD GUYS INBOUND...LOOKS LIKE MOSCOW DOWN THERE."

Follow the squad back down to the street and around the corner. From the top of the next staircase, you spot a convoy of Russian soldiers below. Press Right on the D-pad to select your air support marker. Then toss it in the middle of them. This summons air support that wipes out all of them.

C OBJECTIVE

USE THE AIR SUPPORT MARKER TO DESTROY THE BTR

As the smoke clears, head down and around the corner. Move up to the top step next to the newsstand. When you see the BTR enter from the alley across the way, toss another air support marker nearby to wipe it out. This obliterates the enemies in that area, but soldiers remain on the left and right, so be aware.

ACHIEVEMENT/TROPHY

DANGER CLOSE

Earn the Danger Close Achievement/Trophy by taking down a chopper with an AC-130 Smoke Grenade. Once you see the Russian chopper arrive and drop off some troops, toss the air support marker underneath it. The AC-130 should take down the helicopter during its run.

Dive behind cover and take care of anyone left. Be careful if you hide behind a car. If it catches on fire, it will explode. Warhammer gets ready for another air support run if you want to drop another marker in the far corner, but be sure to get out of the way if you do so.

D OBJECTIVE

FOLLOW THE GIGN LEADER THROUGH THE CATACOMBS

Once the area is clear, follow the GIGN leader to the catacombs entrance and climb inside. Because the toxin levels are safe, gas masks are removed. The following section is very dark, and only Sabre has a light, so stick close by.

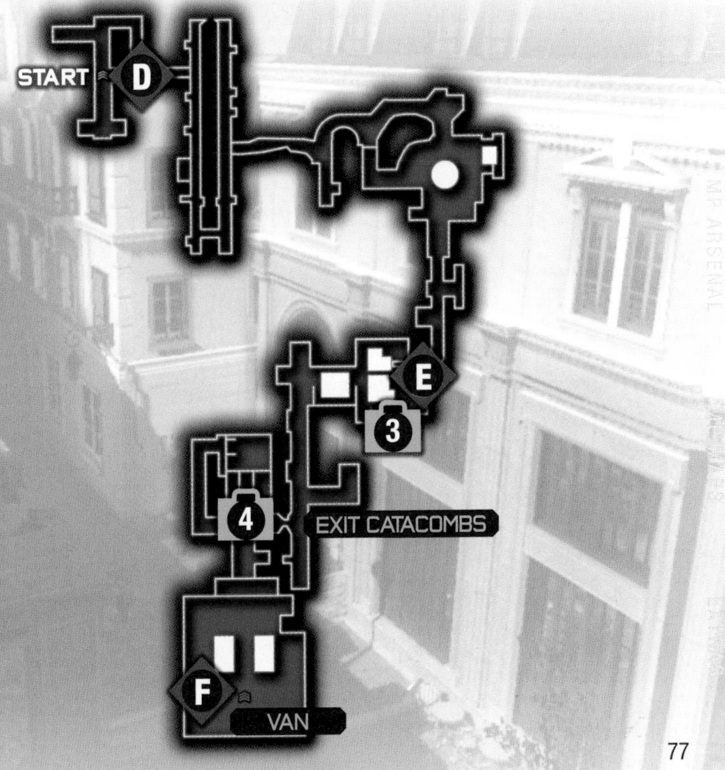

Follow him down the steps, over a bridge, and through a door. Stay close behind the GIGN guys as they snake through some tight areas. Be ready when Sabre reaches a gate on the left. An enemy breaks down the gate on him. Quickly take out the foe.

E OBJECTIVE

CAPTURE VOLK

Take down another guy ahead just before a Flashbang is thrown. Volk is inside the room on the right, surrounded by his men. Quickly take down the soldiers before you pursue Volk.

ENEMY INTEL

3 Before you go after Volk, look in the corner to the south to find this mission's third Intel.

Quickly run up the steps into a long corridor. Fight through a few of Volk's men to a ladder that exits the catacombs. Continue in hot pursuit of Volk back to the outdoors.

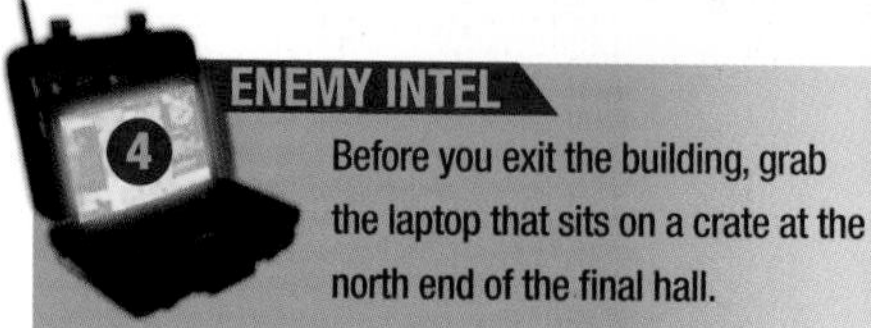

ENEMY INTEL

4 Before you exit the building, grab the laptop that sits on a crate at the north end of the final hall.

OBJECTIVE

GET IN THE VAN

As you run outside, you spot Volk getting into a gray sedan. Sprint to the blue van and get in. Once you're inside, immediately lay down fire on the soldiers ahead.

"FROST, I NEED YOU BACK HERE, NOW."

When you move to the back of the van, pick up the L86 LSW light machine gun. A tank chases your vehicle down a set of steps. At this point, fire at anything that moves.

L86 LSW

CLIP SIZE	100
RANGE	MEDIUM TO LONG
WEAPON TYPE	LIGHT MACHINE GUN

The L86 LSW light machine gun has a large magazine and a quick reload time. This makes it great for laying down constant gunfire on the pursuing enemies.

Aim at the drivers of the trucks, and then focus on the chopper to the left. After a brief shortcut, you jump back to the front seat. You now have a shot at Volk's sedan, so take it out with the machine gun.

The van slams into the side of the vehicle and time slows down. Take out the two guys in the back seat to end the chase.

ACHIEVEMENT/TROPHY

BACK SEAT DRIVER

Track down Volk and complete "Bag and Drag" to get this award.

ACT II

IRON LADY

DELTA FORCE | 07:42 OCTOBER 9 | PARIS, FRANCE

OPERATIVE SGT. DEREK "FROST" WESTBROOK, DELTA FORCE

SUPPORT SANDMAN, GRINCH, TRUCK, GATOR

OBJECTIVES

ESCORT VOLK TO THE EXTRACTION POINT.

- **A** GET TO THE OSPREY.
- **B** CLEAR ENEMIES AT THE ROUNDABOUT.
- **C** CLEAR ENEMIES ON THE STREET.
- **D** DESTROY THE BUILDING WITH RPGS.
- **E** SHOOT AT THE COURTYARD BUILDING THAT CONTAINS ENEMY FORCES.
- **F** GO UPSTAIRS AND FLANK THE MG NEST.
- **G** MARK THE TANK AC-130 TARGET WITH THE AIR-SUPPORT STROBE.
- **H** ESCORT FRIENDLIES TO THE LZ.
- **I** DESTROY THE TANKS ON THE BRIDGE.
- **J** TAKE OUT ENEMY TANKS WITH THE JAVELIN.
- **K** PUSH TO THE LANDING ZONE FOR EXTRACTION.
- **L** DEFEND THE LZ UNTIL EVAC ARRIVES.
- **M** BOARD THE CHOPPER.

ENEMY INTEL 2

INITIAL LOADOUT

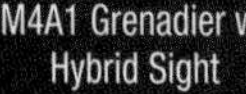

M4A1 Grenadier w/ Hybrid Sight

USP .45

4 Frag Grenades

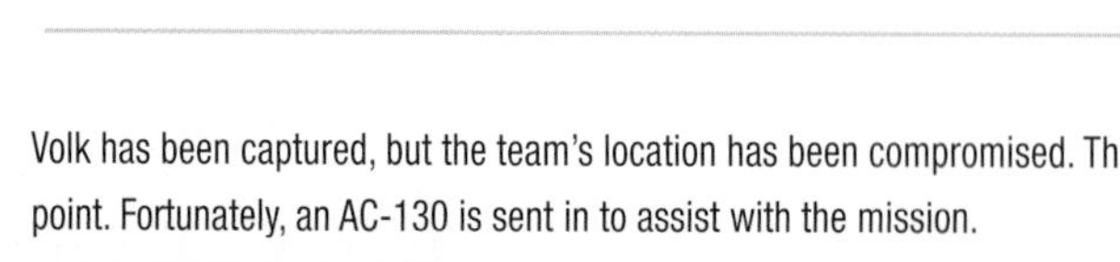

Volk has been captured, but the team's location has been compromised. They have to fight their way to the extraction point. Fortunately, an AC-130 is sent in to assist with the mission.

A OBJECTIVE

GET TO THE OSPREY

An Osprey hovers at the end of the street, waiting to extract the team and Volk. Run toward the aircraft until it is shot out of the air. Move to the left side of the path to avoid the crash.

B OBJECTIVE

CLEAR ENEMIES AT THE ROUNDABOUT

You now man the guns on the AC-130. You can choose from three weapons: a 105mm Howitzer, a 40mm auto-cannon, and a 25mm Vulcan cannon. With its big blast radius, the 105mm cannon is effective against vehicle targets. The 40mm auto-cannon has a decent fire rate and creates a small explosion on impact. The 25mm cannon is a fully automatic Gatling gun that's good for smaller targets and when firing close to your team.

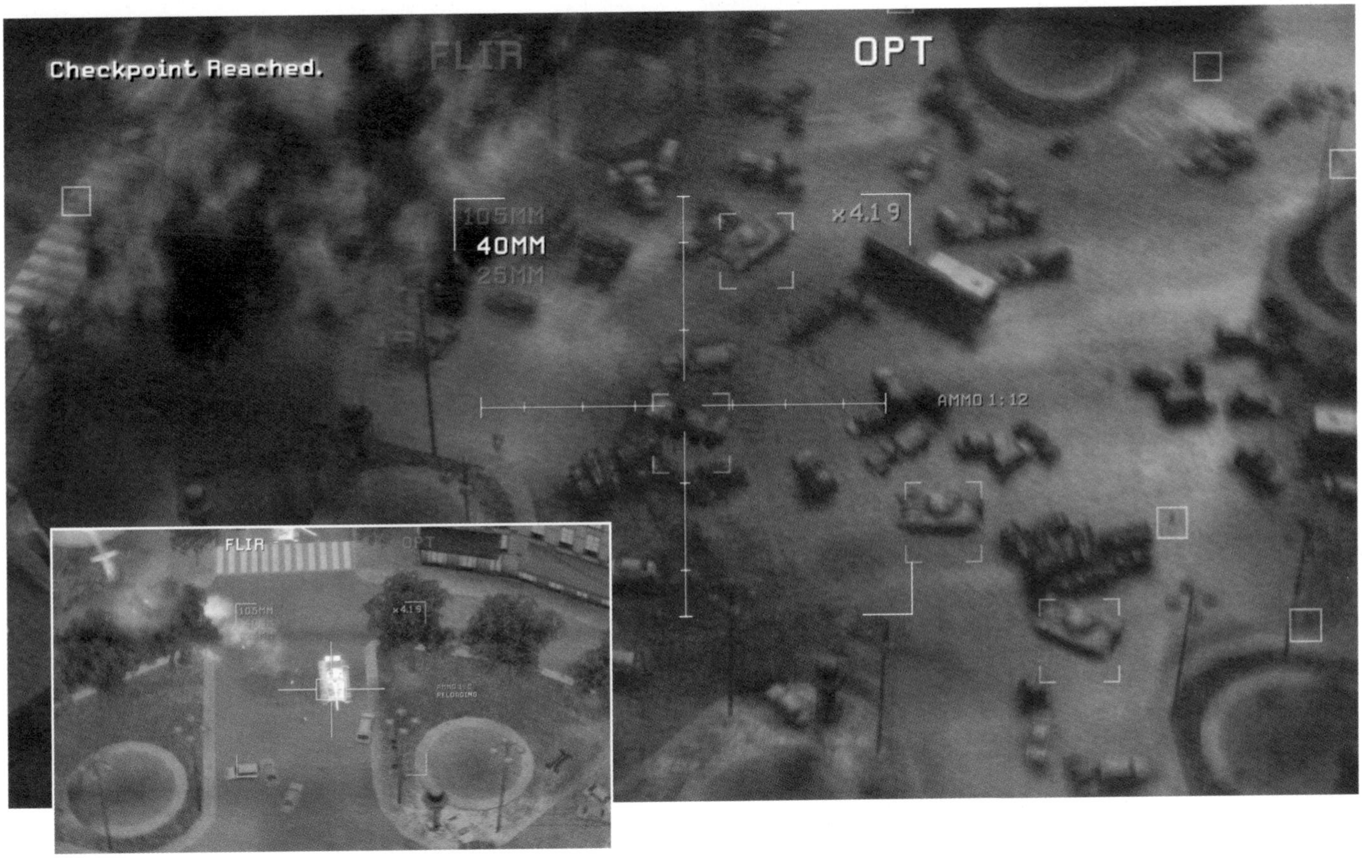

TACTICS

THE AC-130'S WEAPONS

Press X/Square to switch between FLIR (Infrared) and enhanced imaging. In FLIR, the targets are white and marked by squares in the enhanced imaging option. The Y/Triangle button switches between the three weapons. Use the left analog stick to zoom in and out.

Destroy the tanks and helicopters at the roundabout by using the AC-130's three cannons. Once you destroy the targets, an ally finishes off the rest with a bombing run.

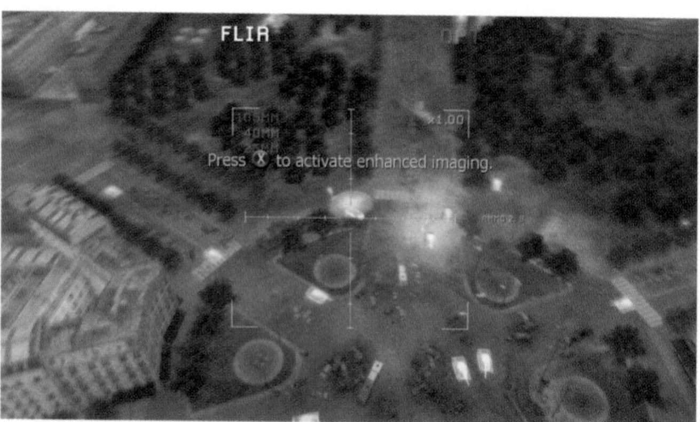

TACTICS

DON'T FIRE ON THE BUILDINGS

Avoid firing at the buildings, as civilians may still be inside. If you accidently hit one, you will be warned.

C OBJECTIVE

CLEAR ENEMIES ON THE STREET

The plane moves to the other side of Metal Zero One, where more hostiles advance on their location. They are located at the left end of the street. Use the 25mm on the nearby enemy forces first. They are marked with the blue smoke.

Next, the blue smoke marks enemies at the intersection. Take care of them with the bigger weapons.

D OBJECTIVE

DESTROY THE BUILDING WITH RPGS

The building just ahead of Metal Zero One hides some enemies with RPGs. You now have the go-ahead to fire on this specific building. Look for the spot with satellites on top and smoke trails coming out the side. Send a shot from the 105mm cannon to eliminate them.

E OBJECTIVE

SHOOT AT THE COURTYARD BUILDING THAT CONTAINS ENEMY FORCES

After a scare from an incoming missile, look for the courtyard below. Fire a shot to clear out some of the hostiles.

F OBJECTIVE

GO UPSTAIRS AND FLANK THE MG NEST

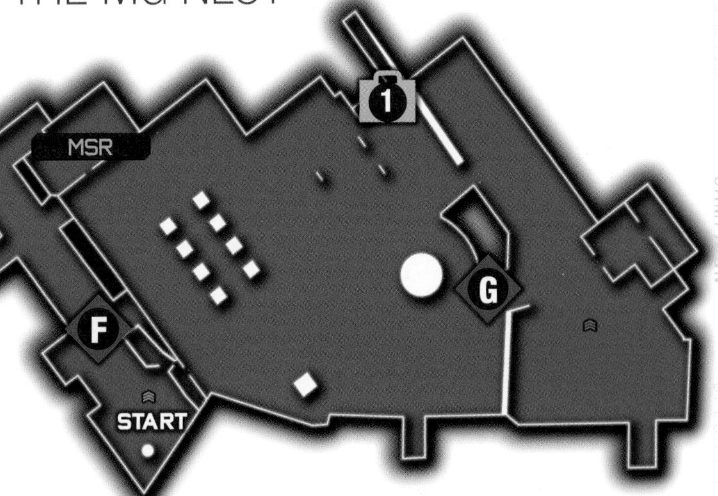

Now, back as Frost, run up the stairs to the left and take cover in the hallway. Eliminate the two enemies, and then proceed down the hall. Enter the open doorway around the corner.

MSR

CLIP SIZE	5
RANGE	LONG
WEAPON TYPE	SNIPER RIFLE

The MSR is a high-powered, bolt-action sniper rifle. It has great accuracy and damage. It works well on the enemies in the courtyard. Press the left analog stick to steady your aim.

Grab the MSR sniper rifle that sits next to the door, and use it on the machine gun operator first. Pick off more enemy forces with this long-range weapon while you enjoy a good vantage point.

Press and hold LS to steady
Press and hold X for M4A1 Grenadier w/ Red Dot Sight
22

After you use up the ammo in the MSR, grab your M4A1 and hop down to rejoin your crew. Continue to take out the enemies around the courtyard.

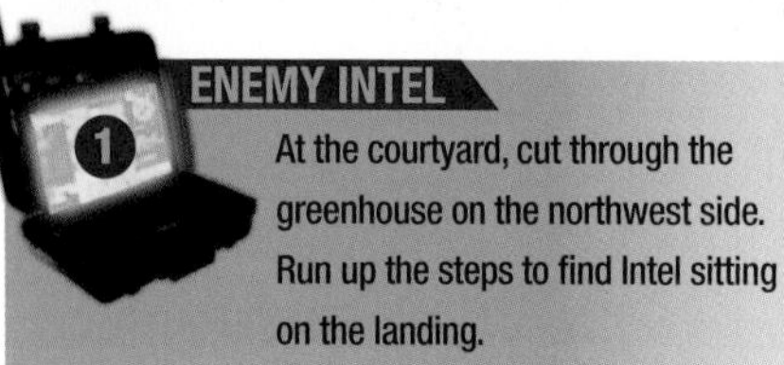

ENEMY INTEL

At the courtyard, cut through the greenhouse on the northwest side. Run up the steps to find Intel sitting on the landing.

Run up the structure in the middle of the yard, and man the machine gun on the other side. First, scan the balconies and take out any Russians who occupy them. Then, concentrate your fire on the ground forces.

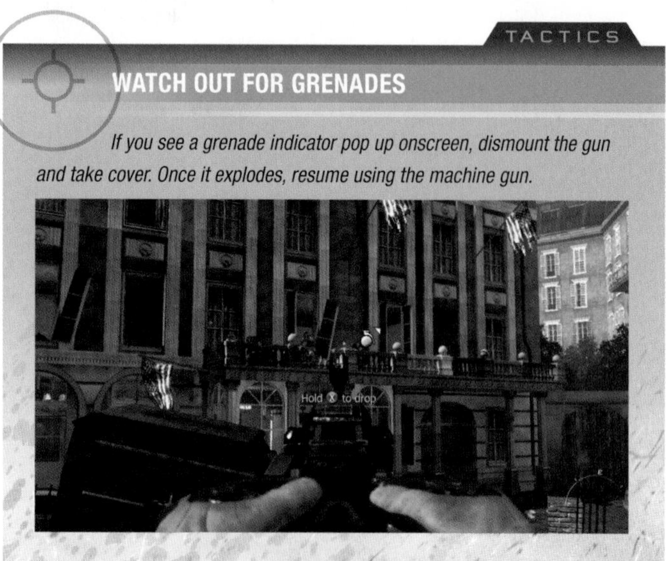

TACTICS

WATCH OUT FOR GRENADES

If you see a grenade indicator pop up onscreen, dismount the gun and take cover. Once it explodes, resume using the machine gun.

G OBJECTIVE

MARK THE TANK AC-130 TARGET WITH THE AIR-SUPPORT STROBE

"TALK TO ME, WARHAMMER. WHERE ARE YOU?"

When the tank breaks through the wall, drop the machine gun and switch to the air support marker. Toss it at the vehicle, and let the AC-130 do the rest.

H OBJECTIVE

ESCORT FRIENDLIES TO THE LZ

Metal Zero One is now ready to move to the landing zone. It's up to you in the AC-130 to get them there safely. Two friendly vehicles show up at the roundabout; be careful not to fire on them. Immediately start firing at the enemy forces that arrive. As before, don't fire at the buildings.

One member of the crew jumps on the .50 caliber gun on the back of a truck, and a camera shows you what he sees. Use the 25mm cannon to get the hostiles off their tail.

More trucks, choppers, and tanks try to stop them from reaching the landing zone. Watch for anyone to get close to the friendlies, and take them down.

ACHIEVEMENT/TROPHY

MÉNAGE À TROIS

Any time during this mission, you can earn an Achievement/Trophy by destroying three tanks in one shot with the 105mm gun. A great time for this is during the chase after making a couple of hard lefts. Three tanks sit at the bottom of the intersection. Use the 105mm Howitzer on them to earn the award.

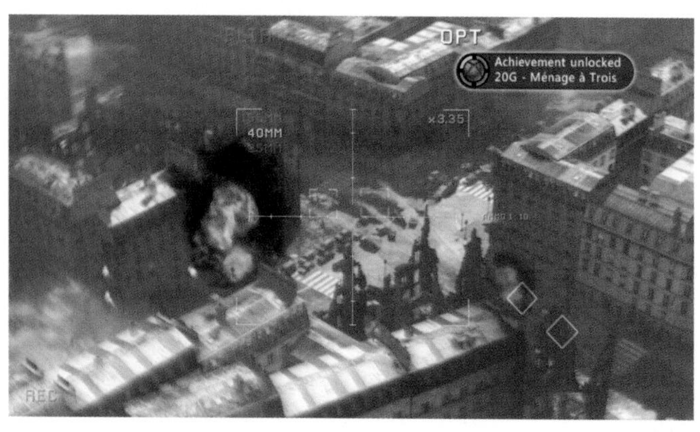

When the trucks reach the water, two choppers harass them. Switch to the 25mm cannon and knock them out of the air. Two more replace them, so dispatch them as well.

I OBJECTIVE

DESTROY THE TANKS ON THE BRIDGE

The trucks come to a stop at the bridge when tanks block the path. Launch one last shot at them before you resume controlling Frost.

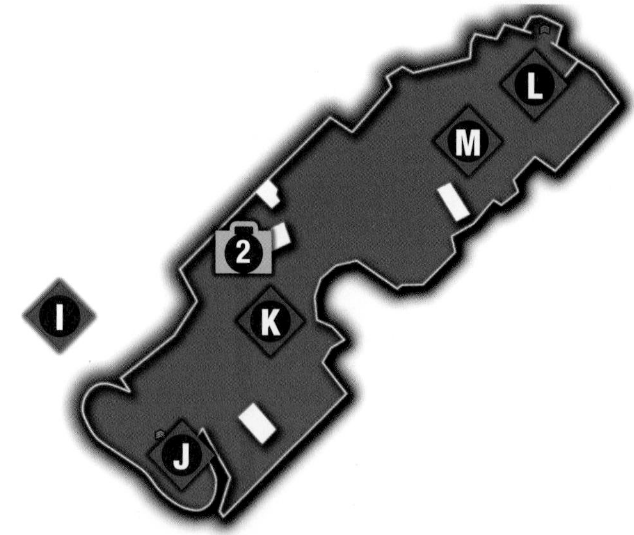

J OBJECTIVE

TAKE OUT ENEMY TANKS WITH THE JAVELIN

Hop out of the truck and pick up the Javelin that sits on the ground. Step behind cover and target one of the tanks. Once the weapon locks on, fire away. Do the same for the other tank.

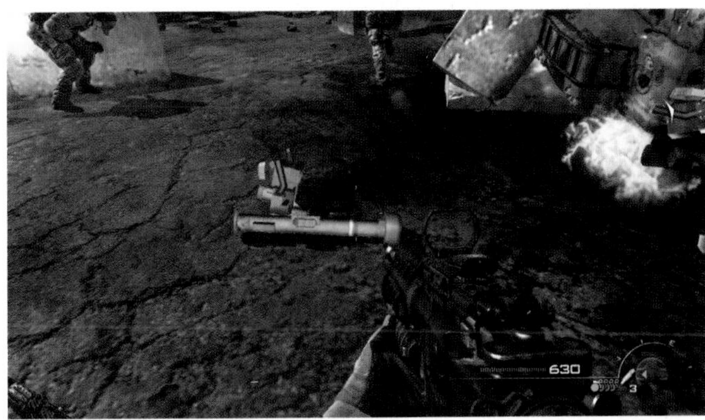

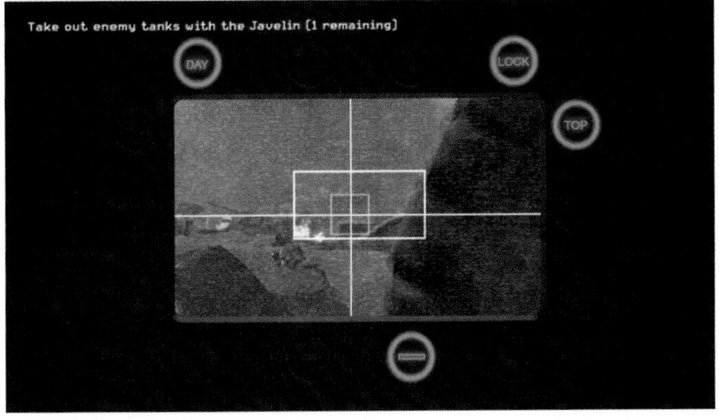

"FINISH OFF THOSE TANKS!"

JAVELIN

CLIP SIZE	1
RANGE	MEDIUM
WEAPON TYPE	LAUNCHER

The Javelin is a lock-on guided missile. When you aim the weapon, a screen pops up showing targets as green boxes. Move the white reticle over the box and wait for it to lock on. This is indicated by a horizontal line and a vertical line crossing at the target. Press the Fire button to send the missile. You can stay behind cover as you do this.

K OBJECTIVE

PUSH TO THE LANDING ZONE FOR EXTRACTION

ENEMY INTEL

2

After you destroy the tanks and before you move to the landing zone, enter the bus on the left side of the bridge. Another enemy laptop lies in the back.

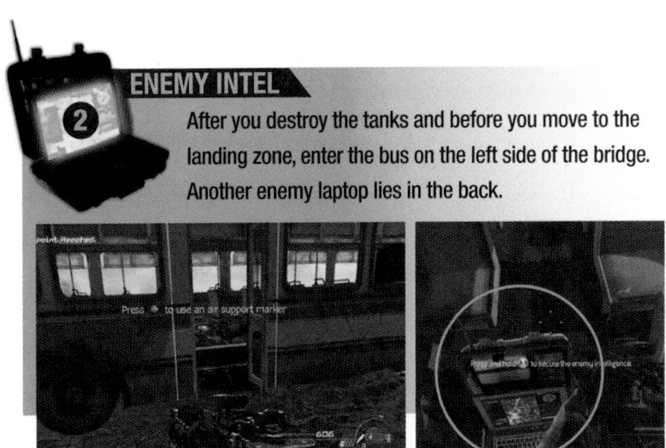

Switch back to your assault rifle and fight your way up the bridge. An air support marker becomes available as the AC-130 gets into position. Save it until you reach the LZ.

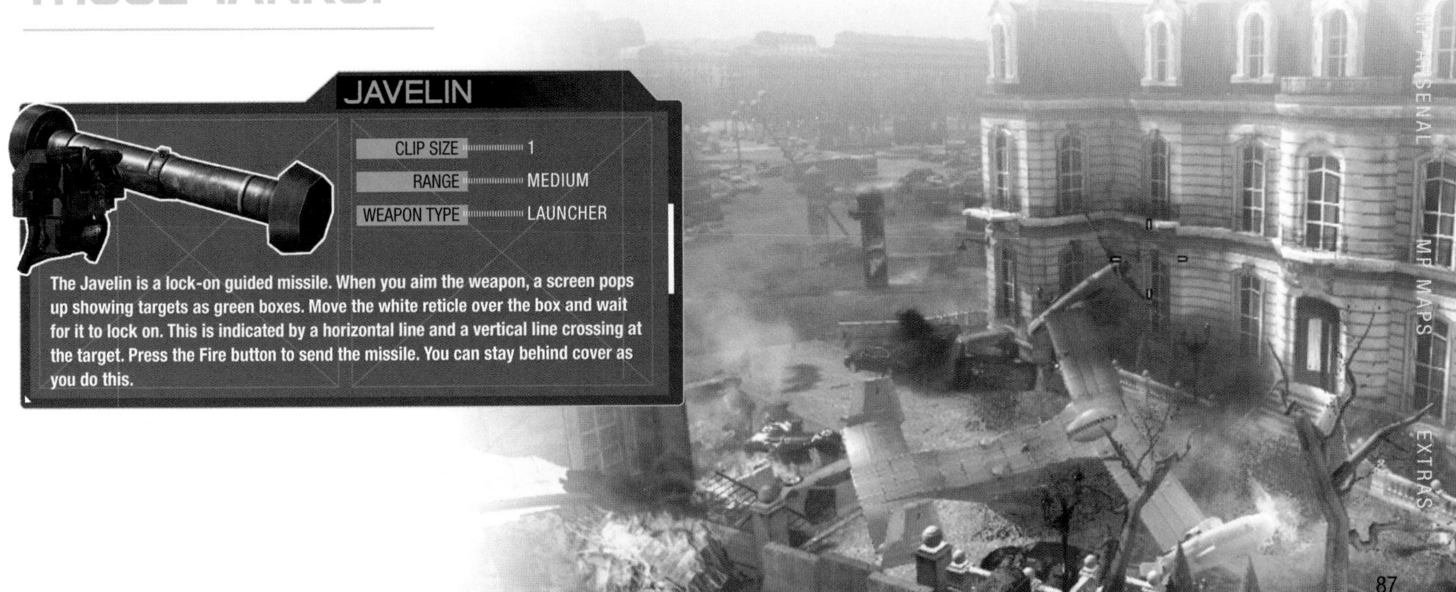

OBJECTIVE

DEFEND THE LZ UNTIL EVAC ARRIVES

Once you reach that spot, you are instructed to hold your position. Run up to the barrier and throw the grenade as far as you can. Continue to take down any advancing enemies until the AC-130 becomes available again.

M OBJECTIVE

BOARD THE CHOPPER

Keep this up until the chopper arrives. Approach the left side and sit next to Sandman.

ACHIEVEMENT/TROPHY

WE'LL ALWAYS HAVE PARIS

Escape Paris with Volk and complete "Iron Lady" on any difficulty to earn an Achievement/Trophy.

ACHIEVEMENT/TROPHY

CITY OF LIGHTS

Complete "Bag and Drag" and "Iron Lady" on Veteran difficulty to earn this Achievement/Trophy.

ACT II
EYE OF THE STORM

TASK FORCE 141 | 21:36 OCTOBER 10 | PRAGUE, CZECH REPUBLIC

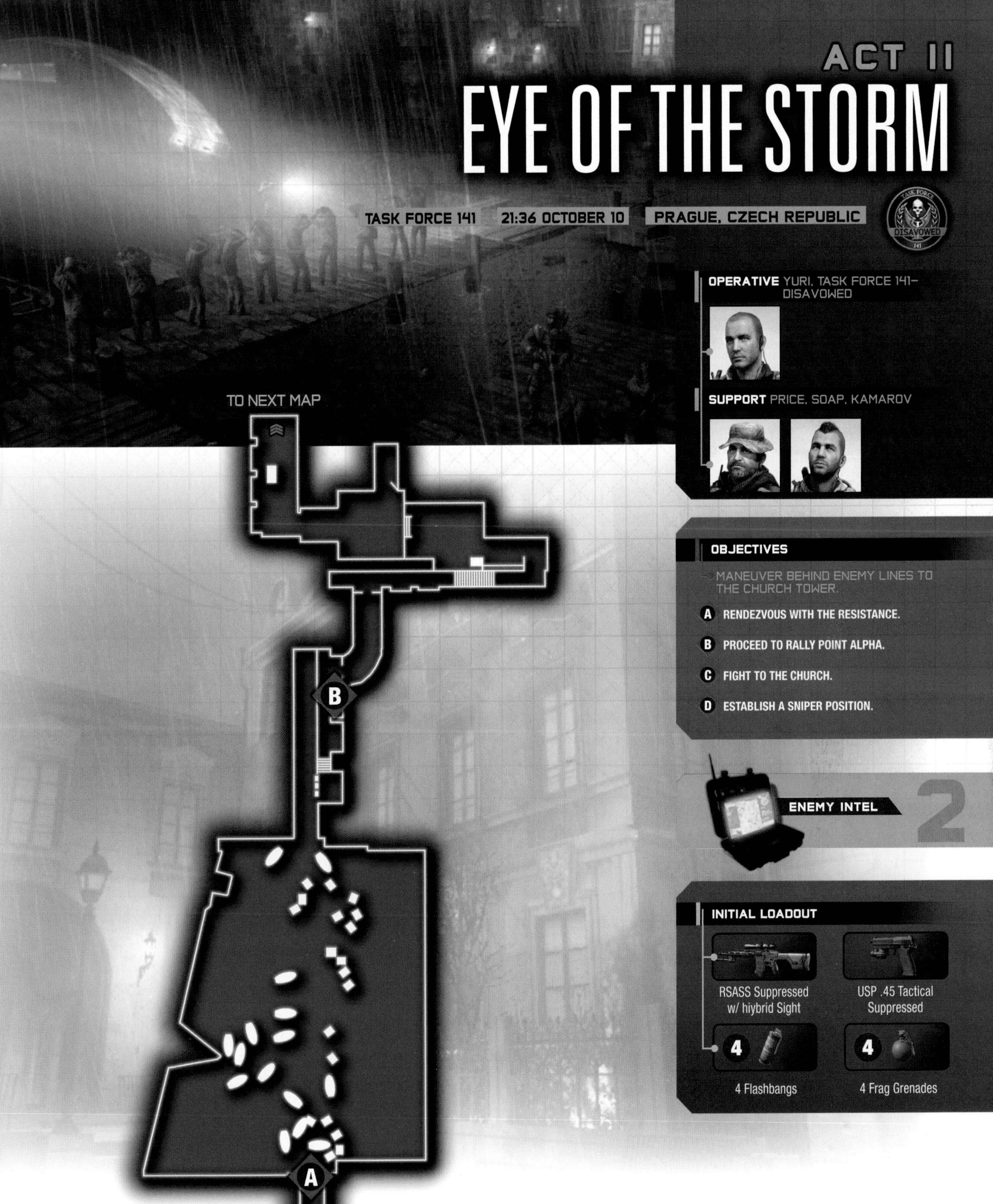

OPERATIVE YURI, TASK FORCE 141–DISAVOWED

SUPPORT PRICE, SOAP, KAMAROV

OBJECTIVES

- MANEUVER BEHIND ENEMY LINES TO THE CHURCH TOWER.

A. RENDEZVOUS WITH THE RESISTANCE.

B. PROCEED TO RALLY POINT ALPHA.

C. FIGHT TO THE CHURCH.

D. ESTABLISH A SNIPER POSITION.

ENEMY INTEL

2

INITIAL LOADOUT

RSASS Suppressed w/ hiybrid Sight

USP .45 Tactical Suppressed

4 Flashbangs

4 Frag Grenades

"WELCOME TO PRAGUE, GENTS."

According to information from Volk, we now know that Makarov is meeting with his top advisors at Hotel Lustig in Prague. Price and Kamarov will infiltrate the hotel while Yuri and Soap provide overwatch at the church tower. We'll have to get help from the resistance to reach our destination.

RSASS
CLIP SIZE 20
RANGE LONG
WEAPON TYPE SNIPER RIFLE
The RSASS sniper rifle is semi-automatic, with great accuracy and damage. This one is suppressed with a hybrid sight, so it can be used for long-range sniping and in the heat of battle.

A OBJECTIVE

RENDEZVOUS WITH THE RESISTANCE

The path ahead goes right under Russian soldiers who have captured a few of the resistance. You have to move quickly but quietly. Follow closely behind Price and Soap through the murky water. Price puts up his hand if he wants you to stop, so keep an eye on him.

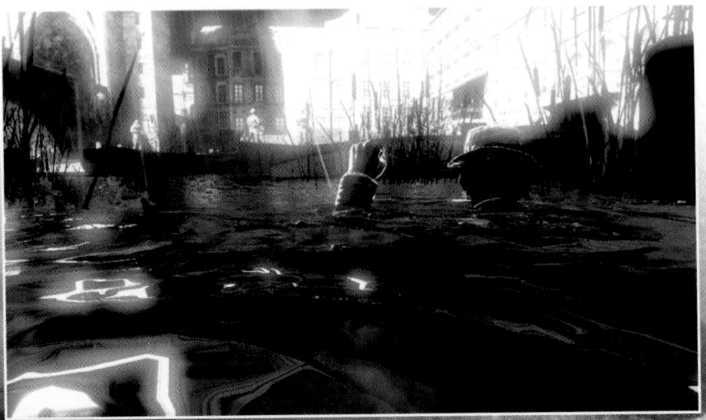

Wade through the water and under the docks until Price stops you. Wait for the guards to pass, and then continue following him to the rendezvous point.

B OBJECTIVE

PROCEED TO RALLY POINT ALPHA

At this point, Soap and Yuri split off. Follow Soap through the tunnels until you're back outside. Crouch down at the archway and wait for some of the guards ahead to split off. When Soap gives you the go-ahead, snipe the two men on the roof, and he takes care of the rest.

Follow Soap to the right and stop when he does. Wait for two Russians to enter the street and then take one down—again, Soap handles the other. Quickly cross the road, sticking close to your partner.

ENEMY INTEL 1

After you take out the two guards and cross the street, grab the laptop that sits on the counter in the hotel lobby.

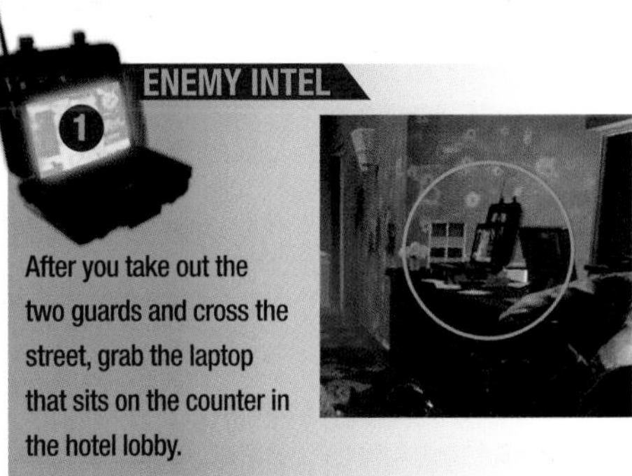

"WATCH YOUR MOVEMENT ON THE STREET. KEEP YOUR EYES HIGH. SNIPERS ARE EVERYWHERE."

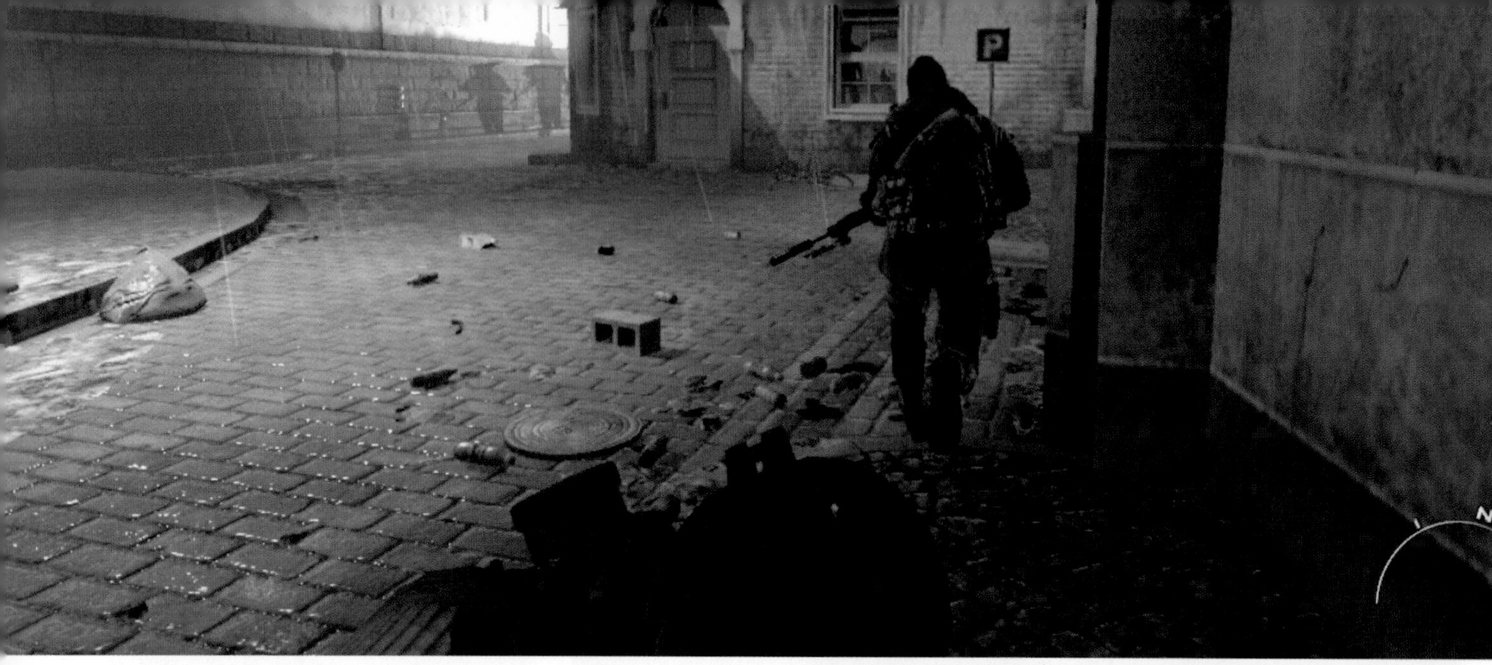

Pause inside the hotel lobby while Soap checks in with the others. Then, follow him out the other door. Sprint down the street when you spot an enemy convoy.

Inside the building, go prone and crawl alongside the windows. A couple of Russians enter the building, but keep moving. When one of them moves to the window, stop and wait for him to clear the immediate area. Pause again as you round the corner, and wait for two more guys to move past. It may be tempting to take them on, but you don't want to attract any attention at this point.

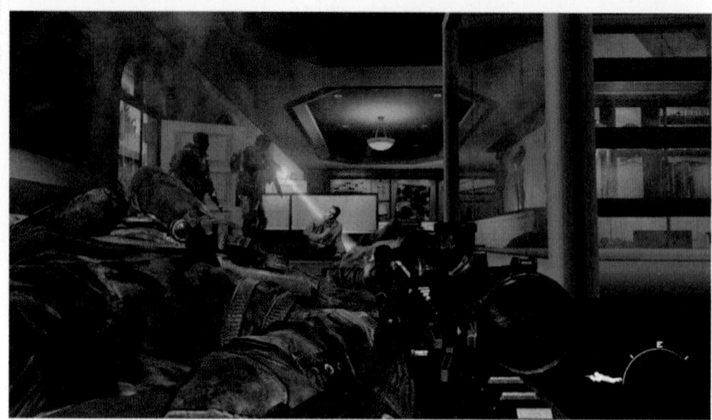

Once the entryway is clear, crawl to the open door. On Soap's command, get up and move to the left. Do what he does as he takes cover, and then follow him over the fence.

Let Soap take care of a lone soldier and then crouch up to the fencing. Wait out of sight while Soap checks in with the resistance. Two Russian snipers show up on the west rooftop. Aim your rifle their way just as they are taken out by some friendlies.

C OBJECTIVE

FIGHT TO THE CHURCH

Switch to your short-range scope by pressing Left on the D-pad. When the resistance makes their move, run around to the left and take cover behind the statue.

ENEMY INTEL

2

A piece of Enemy Intelligence sits on a table south of the statue. It's located under a Prague umbrella.

"GET TO COVER! THEY ARE BRINGING IN ARMOR!"

Lay down some cover fire as Soap moves forward, and then fight your way to his side. Continue to fight off the Russians until Soap informs you of an incoming tank. Hop up the ledge and grab the RPG-7. Use it to destroy the tank that enters from the north.

FINISH

D

FROM PREVIOUS MAP

Follow Soap to the left and through a gate. Keep close to him as he goes down a hall and up the stairs. Sprint through the chaos of the second floor and down another flight of stairs.

Exit through the door and immediately duck behind the planter. First, snipe the two soldiers who man the machine guns to the west. Then, clear out a few more of the enemy troops and they retreat around the corner.

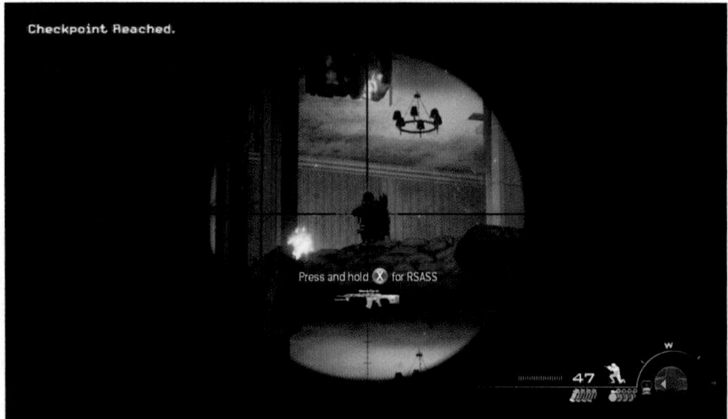

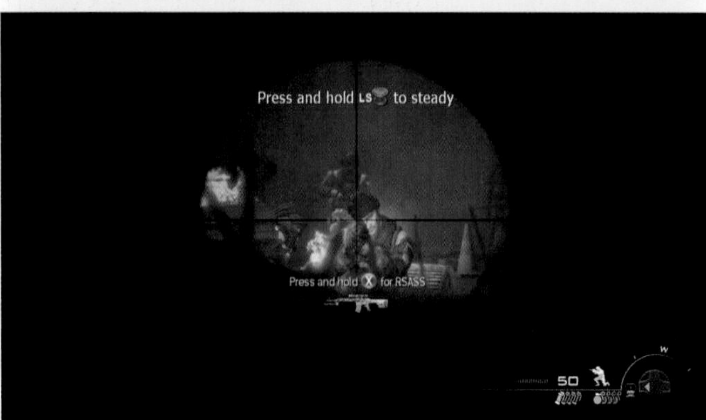

"WE'RE GETTING OUT OF THIS COURTYARD."

Join the friendly fighters as they head down the street, but move to the left sidewalk. Sprint to the statue and follow Soap through a window on the left.

Continue to follow Soap through the gallery, across the street, and into the next building. Stop alongside him behind the pillar while enemy forces move past the window.

Pause again in the next room and wait for Soap's "Go." After he takes down a guy with his grenade, duck behind the counter ahead and eliminate the soldiers who enter the building.

Once the room is clear, follow Soap back out to the street. Sprint down the sidewalk and go prone behind a pickup truck as a Russian convoy rolls past. After the tank crushes the truck, get up and sprint across the street to the church.

D OBJECTIVE

ESTABLISH A SNIPER POSITION

Follow Soap through the church and onto the scaffolding ahead. It's a few hours until the meeting—plenty of time to get ready at the sniper position.

ACHIEVEMENT/TROPHY

VIVE LA RÉVOLUTION!

Complete "Eye of the Storm" by reaching the church on any difficulty.

ACT II
BLOOD BROTHERS

TASK FORCE 141 | 07:01 OCTOBER 11 | PRAGUE, CZECH REPUBLIC

OPERATIVE YURI, TASK FORCE 141—DISAVOWED

SUPPORT PRICE, SOAP

OBJECTIVES

TAKE DOWN MAKAROV AT THE HOTEL LUSTIG.

- **A** ELIMINATE THREATS ON THE BALCONY.
- **B** FOLLOW PRICE.
- **C** PROTECT SOAP.
- **D** ESCAPE.

ENEMY INTEL

1

INITIAL LOADOUT

M4A1 Grenadier w/Red Dot Sight	Desert Eagle
4 Flashbangs	4 Frag Grenades

Yuri and Soap are set up in the church tower, while Kamarov has infiltrated the hotel and Price is ready to join him. For this part of the level, you see only through the scope of your RSASS sniper rifle.

"YOU SEEM TO KNOW A LOT ABOUT MAKAROV."

A OBJECTIVE

ELIMINATE THREATS ON THE BALCONY

Makarov's convoy arrives at the hotel. You can get a good look at him in his armored vehicle, but you can't do anything yet. Look above the balcony around the front statue to spot Price.

Now move your aim to the balcony and find the guard who moves to the right. Wait for the two guards to line up, and then take them out together. Continue to eliminate the hostiles.

The curtain comes down, giving you access to more enemies inside. Once you take care of them, Price moves in further, but he's greeted with a big surprise.

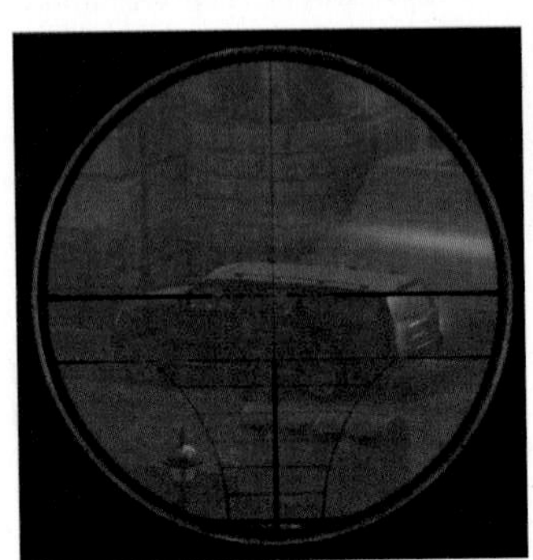

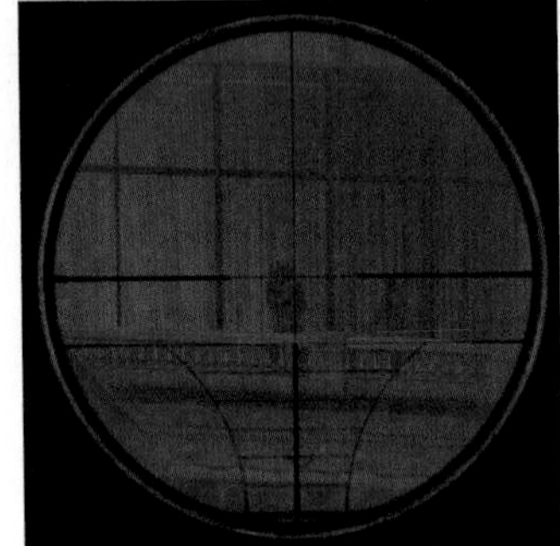

B OBJECTIVE

FOLLOW PRICE

When Price meets up with you on the street below, pick up Soap and follow him to the northwest. Stay right behind Price, and you'll be okay.

"IT'S NOT SAFE HERE. WE HAVE TO MOVE."

Cut through the opening that Price created, and continue through the building and out to a back alley. Set Soap down next to the dumpster, and Price trades with you. Now you have point.

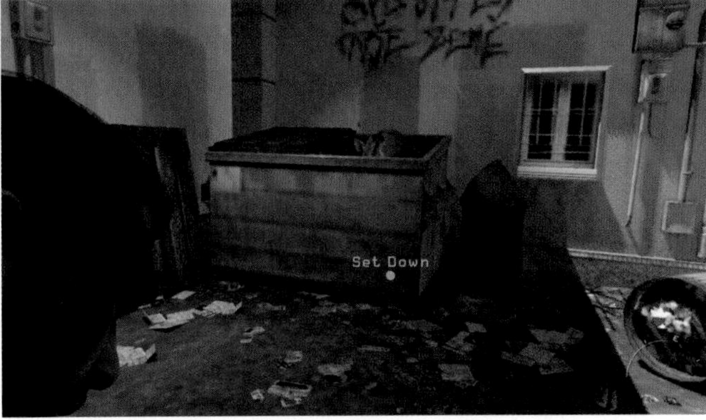

C OBJECTIVE

PROTECT SOAP

Move around Price and Soap, and enter the office. Take out the guys in the gallery, along with two more to the right.

ENEMY INTEL

1

Search the northeast corner of the gallery for the first piece of Enemy Intel.

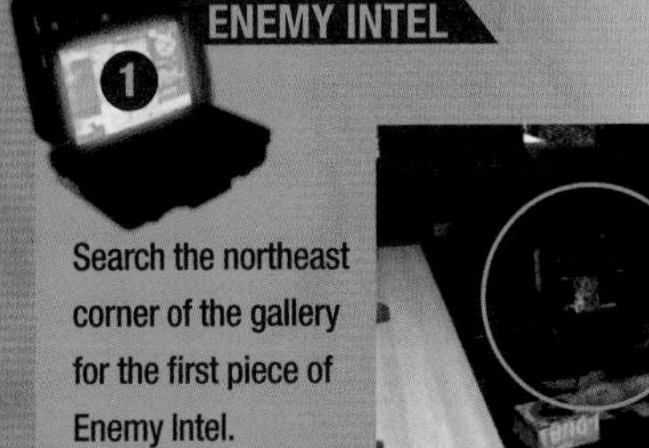

More men show up out on the street. Take out a couple of them, follow Price to the statue, and take cover. Watch for enemies to the south and east. A sniper gets a bead on you from the second story to the east.

Price warns you of more on the roof to the south. Fire at them as he escapes behind you, and then follow suit. Cut through the building to the next street. Take cover and eliminate a few more of Makarov's men who advance from the west.

Fight your way through the archway, taking down every foe who approaches, and move into the shop on the left. Dive behind a counter and fend off the attack from the west.

"HEAD FOR THAT BUILDING TO THE NORTHWEST!"

Once the coast is clear, flee across the street and onto the basketball court. Turn around and protect Price and Soap from the advancing troops.

Keep backing up as you fight until you drop off the other side. Join your team behind the planter and defend your position. Keep an eye out on all sides.

TACTICS

USE YOUR GRENADES

Don't forget about your grenades. Use them to keep the enemy at bay. Also use the grenade attachment of your M4A1 if it's available.

D OBJECTIVE

ESCAPE

When you reach the next checkpoint, resistance fighters join in. Price picks up Soap again and moves to the doorway, so cover them. Follow them inside, and help Soap when you're instructed to do so. It's too dangerous there[md]follow Price through the pub and into a back doorway.

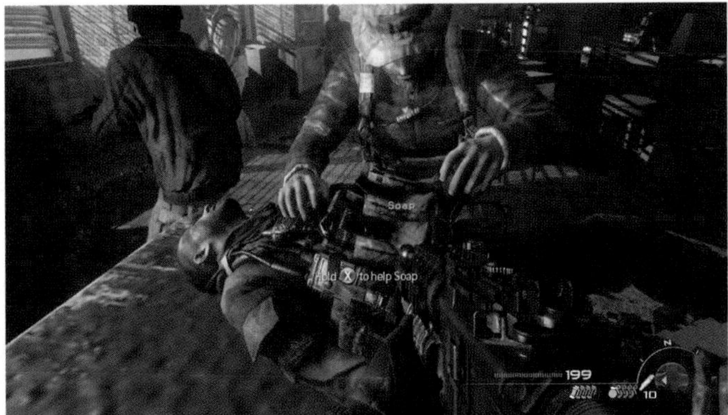

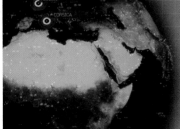

SPOILER-FREE

To avoid revealing significant plot events, we've intentionally refrained from describing the next sequence. Abide by any onscreen prompts through the following scenes to complete the mission.

ACHIEVEMENT/TROPHY

REQUIEM

Finish "Blood Brothers" and escape the city to earn an Achievement/Trophy.

ACT 3

ACT III

STRONGHOLD

TASK FORCE 141 | 22:48 OCTOBER 12 | PRAGUE, CZECH REPUBLIC

OPERATIVE YURI, TASK FORCE 141–DISAVOWED

SUPPORT PRICE

OBJECTIVES

- INFILTRATE THE CASTLE TO DISCOVER MAKAROV'S LOCATION.
- A FIND A WAY INTO THE CASTLE.
- B TAKE OUT THE GUARD BY THE ROAD WITHOUT BEING DETECTED.
- C PLANT C4 UNDER THE PLATFORM.
- D FIND THE COMM STATION.
- E PLANT C4 ON THE BRIDGE.
- F TIME THE BLAST WITH THE SOUND OF THUNDER.
- G ESCAPE THE CASTLE.
- H DETONATE THE C4 UNDER THE BRIDGE.
- I PARACHUTE TO SAFETY.

ENEMY INTEL 2

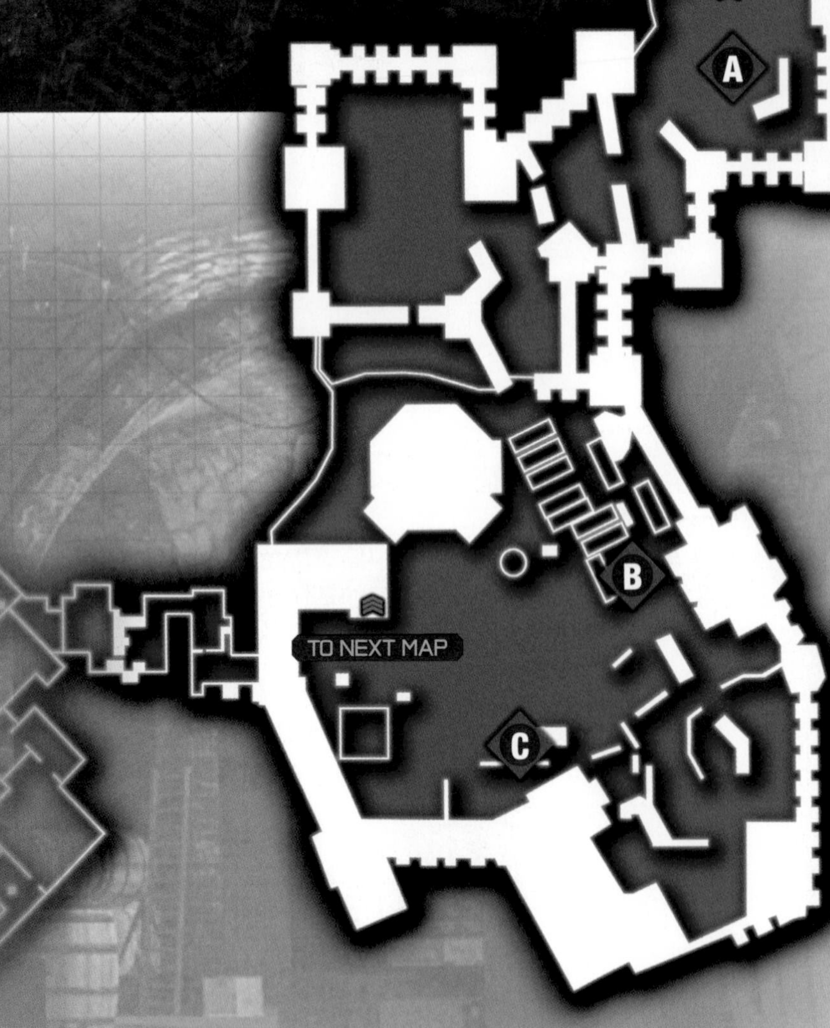

INITIAL LOADOUT

MP5 Suppressed w/Red Dot Sight

P99 Tactical

4 Flashbangs

4 Frag Grenades

NIGHT VISION

"THE PLACE IS A FORTRESS–ONLY ONE WAY IN OR OUT."

Makarov used to cache weapons at an old castle in Prague, so Price and Yuri are going to infiltrate it. If Makarov isn't there, then at least they might find out where he is.

A OBJECTIVE

FIND A WAY INTO THE CASTLE

Upon landing at the castle grounds, turn off your night vision goggles and crouch behind the stone wall. Stay out of the guard's light. Get up when Captain Price does, and follow him to a pile of rocks.

Follow Captain Price down behind some trucks. When Price moves, stay close behind. When he stops, stop. Go past the line of vehicles and then crawl under the last two.

B OBJECTIVE

TAKE OUT THE GUARD BY THE ROAD WITHOUT BEING DETECTED

Pause for the two guards to pass, and then move out. Sneak up behind the enemy with his back turned, and melee attack to take him down. After your partner hides the body, follow him up the steps, and then crawl under the platform.

C OBJECTIVE

PLANT C4 UNDER THE PLATFORM

Crawl alongside Captain Price until you see one of the guards' lights. Remain still until he passes, and then continue forward. Under the platform, an icon shows where to plant some C4. Press the designated button to do so and then move on.

When the captain moves, get up and lay low behind a couple barrels. Follow him to the security office door. Let him handle the guards inside, and follow him in.

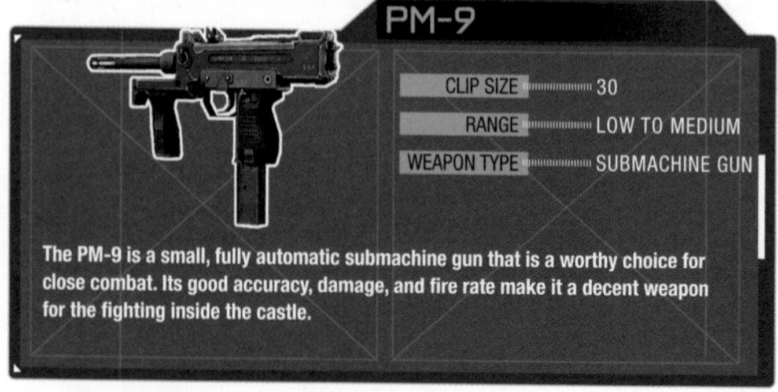

PM-9

CLIP SIZE	30
RANGE	LOW TO MEDIUM
WEAPON TYPE	SUBMACHINE GUN

The PM-9 is a small, fully automatic submachine gun that is a worthy choice for close combat. Its good accuracy, damage, and fire rate make it a decent weapon for the fighting inside the castle.

"YEAH, WELL, WE JUST HAVE TO KNOCK ON THE DOOR."

D OBJECTIVE

FIND THE COMM STATION

Stick with Price when he enters the castle. Turn on your night vision as you descend into the dungeon. Once the lights are killed, run down the corridor and take care of the guards along the way. Knifing works on the lone foes, but you may run into a small group at the other end.

Checkpoint Reached.
330

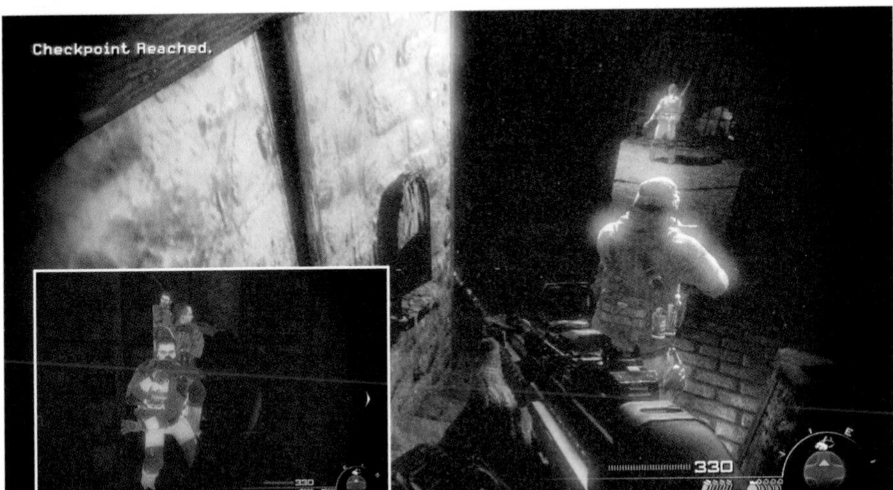

Clear out the area, and then head east at the next hallway. When the enemy tosses out some flares, switch off the night vision and fire at the enemies in the next room. Use the doorway and the crates ahead for cover. Watch out, as some guards fire on you from below.

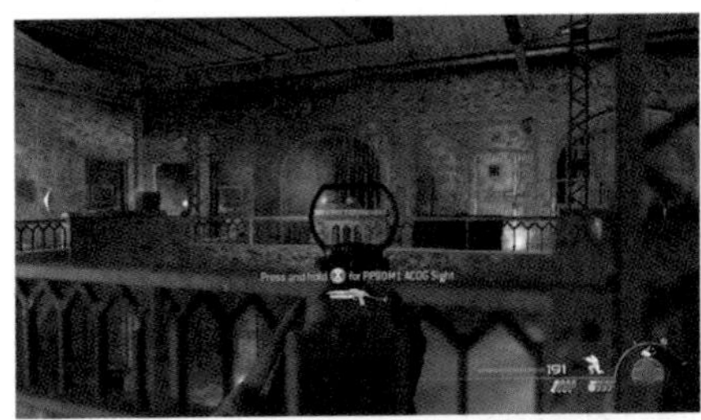

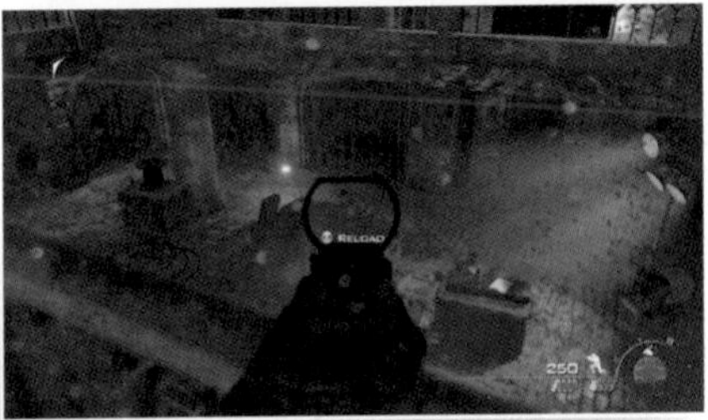

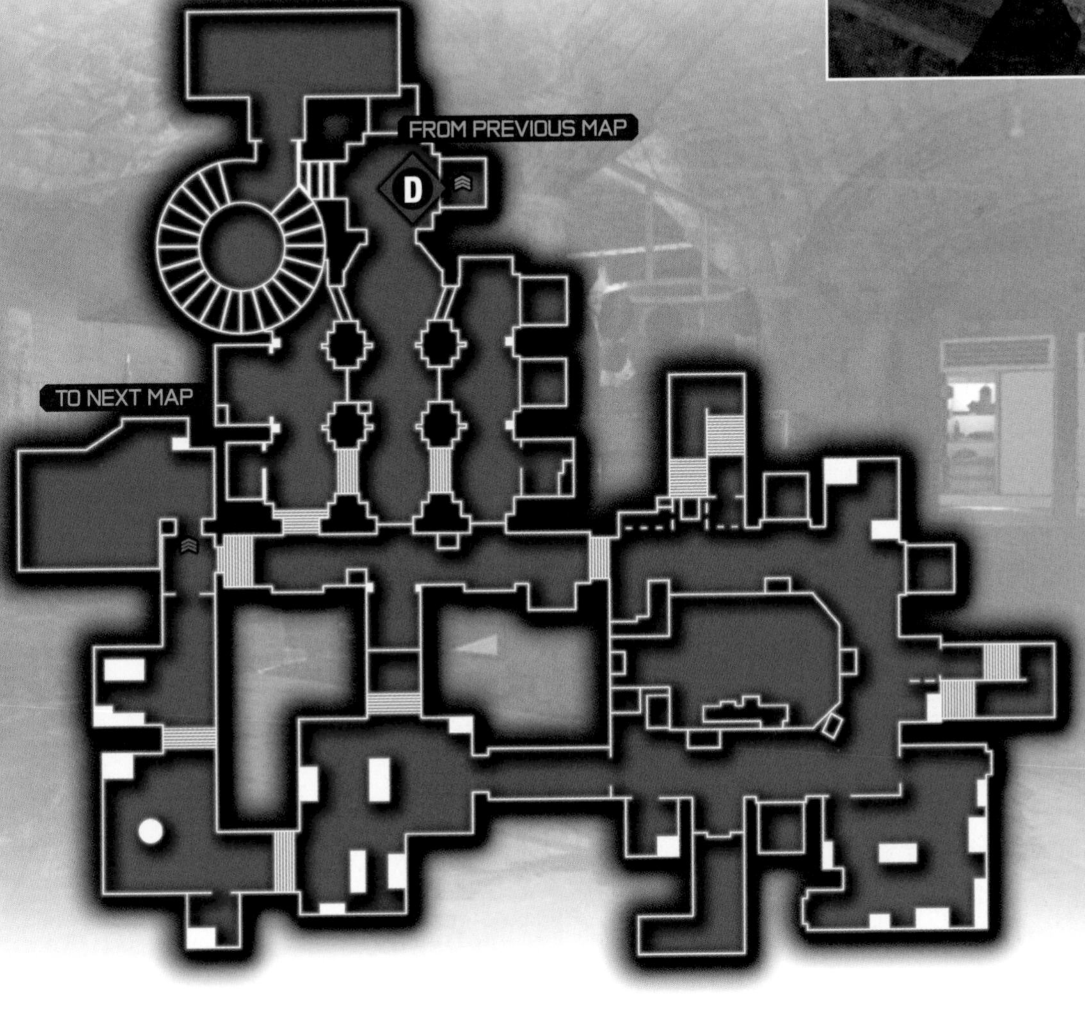

FROM PREVIOUS MAP
D
TO NEXT MAP

More of Makarov's men enter from the southeast and southwest; stay put until you take care of them all. Toss a grenade into the office in the corner to flush anyone out of there. Once it's clear, move into the southwest room and take down the guy inside.

TACTICS

WATCH YOUR BACK

Be careful as you move through the castle, as guards may approach from behind.

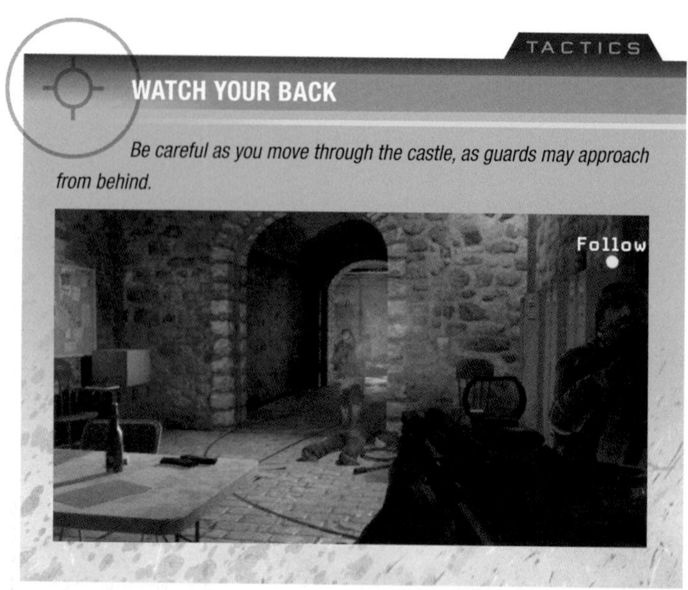

"YOU'RE ON POINT. GO!"

E OBJECTIVE

PLANT C4 ON THE BRIDGE

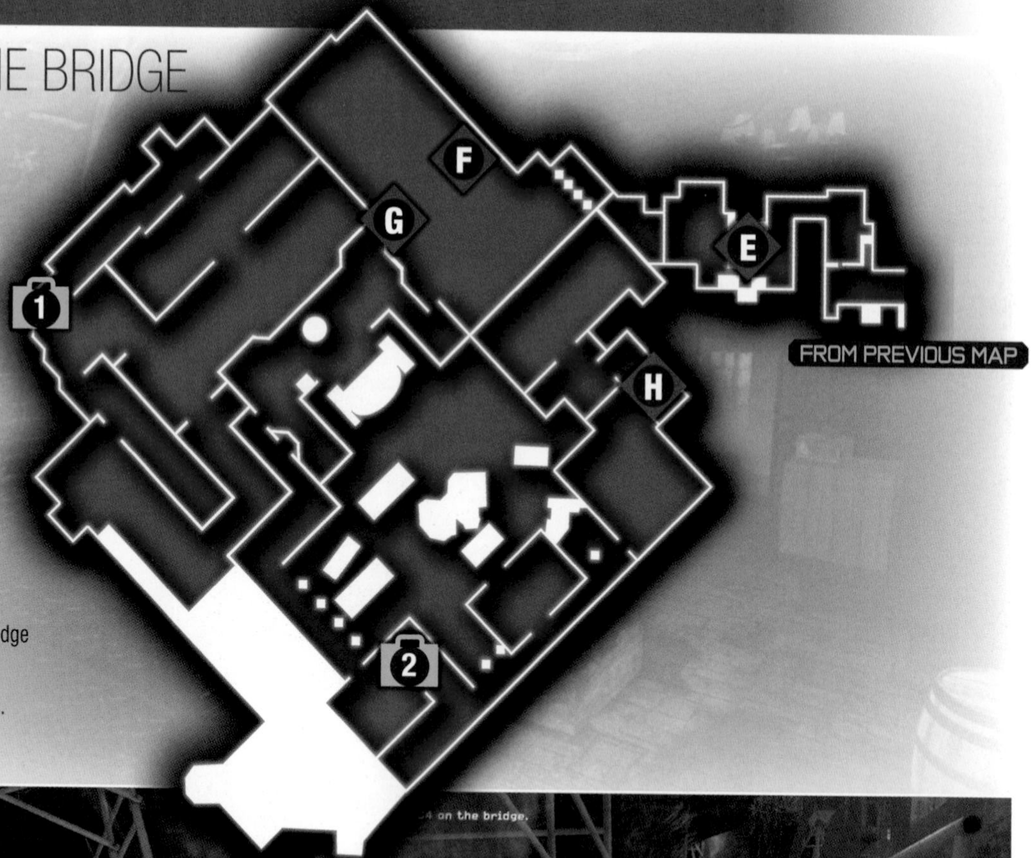

FROM PREVIOUS MAP

Stay on the path as it goes north, and then wait for Price to open the next door. Follow him outside and up the scaffolding. The bridge above is the only way out, so the support column makes a great place for explosives. Plant some C4 in the indicated location.

Sidle along the narrow ledge. Continue following your partner across the scaffolding, up another ladder, and back into the castle.

"THIS WHOLE THING LOOKS LIKE IT'S ABOUT TO COLLAPSE. TAKE IT SLOW."

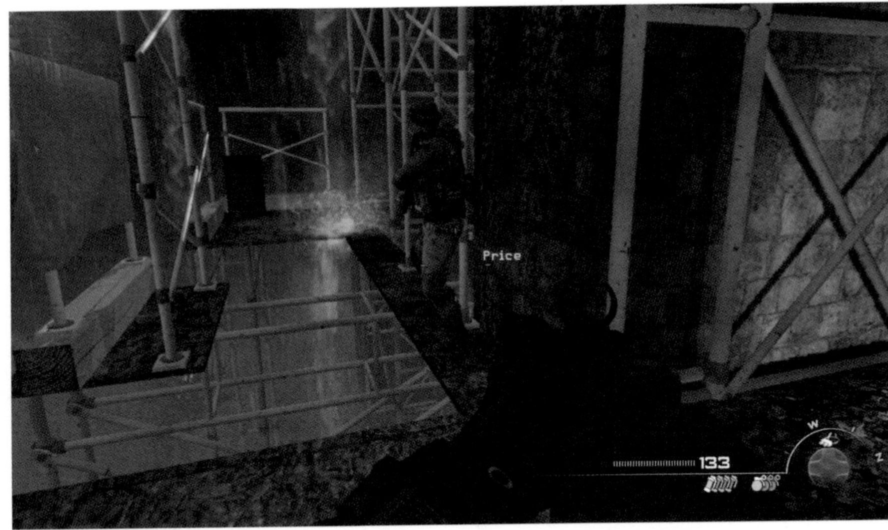

F OBJECTIVE

TIME THE BLAST WITH THE SOUND OF THUNDER

Just down the hall, Captain Price decides that the best path to the control center is through the wall, and he sets up some explosives. You are the trigger man. When Price says, "Go," press the Fire button to take out a huge chunk of the wall.

Follow him inside and climb up until you reach your destination. Here, you find what you came for, so now it's time to go. Not a minute too soon, either, because the guards have discovered your mess.

G OBJECTIVE

ESCAPE THE CASTLE

Captain Price and Yuri fall into the kitchen below. Fight your way out of the room, but watch out—a guard has shoved a cart in your direction. Finish him off and run up the steps.

Price runs into the wine cellar through the right door. Enter the left door and take cover inside the office. Eliminate the soldiers in the cellar and jump through the window.

Once you're outside, when your partner yells "Flashbang," turn back to the doorway to avoid the blast. Take down the guard who appears on the steps, and then climb to the next floor.

Stick with Price as he runs back inside and around the corner. Eliminate the troops on the far end, and then duck through the left doorway. At the next door, finish off the rest of the enemies in the room.

ENEMY INTEL

After you clear out the big room, run through the left side and into the open doorway. A laptop sits on the equipment ahead.

"YURI, DON'T SLOW DOWN NOW. SORT THEM OUT."

If necessary, restock on grenades to the right of the Intel, and then follow Price into the next room.

Take out the men who attempt to flee, and then set up at the door or window. Pick off the enemies who hide behind the crates before you go outside. Run to the wall ahead to find an RPG-7. Use it on the chopper above, and then switch to the RSASS sniper rifle that also leans against the wall.

Snipe Makarov's men who stand on the walkway across the courtyard. Run through the doorway to the right and take down a soldier who waits ahead. Now you can focus your attention on protecting Price, who has moved down to the courtyard.

Use the sniper rifle to clear a path for him. After you kill a few of their men, turn around and proceed along the path. When more enemy forces get in your way, finish them.

Once the walkway is clear, check on Price again and clear out more enemies if necessary. Move into the southernmost building ahead.

ENEMY INTEL

Inside the room south of the courtyard, look for a laptop sitting on a crate.

H OBJECTIVE

DETONATE THE C4 UNDER THE BRIDGE

Run down the next walkway and into another house, where you rejoin the captain. Step outside and squeeze the Fire button once you have the C4 detonator in your hand. This takes out part of the bridge.

Join Price in the next room and hop out the window. Run across what's left of the bridge. Duck behind the crates on the right and fend off Makarov's men.

"DETONATING THE C4, NOW!"

I OBJECTIVE

PARACHUTE TO SAFETY

Follow Price to the vehicle and climb into the back seat. Continue to take out anyone you can while he drives the two of you off the castle grounds. After you crash through the fence, hold the Use button to deploy your reserve chute.

ACHIEVEMENT/TROPHY

STORM THE CASTLE

Discover Makarov's next move by completing "Stronghold" on any difficulty and earn another Achievement/Trophy.

ACHIEVEMENT/TROPHY

THE DARKEST HOUR

Complete "Eye of the Storm," "Blood Brothers," and "Stronghold" on Veteran difficulty to earn this award.

ACT III

SCORCHED EARTH

DELTA FORCE | 10:18 OCTOBER 13 | BERLIN, GERMANY

OPERATIVE SGT. DEREK "FROST" WESTBROOK, DELTA FORCE

FROST

SUPPORT SANDMAN, GRINCH, TRUCK

SANDMAN GRINCH TRUCK

OBJECTIVES

REACH THE RUSSIAN PRESIDENT'S DAUGHTER BEFORE MAKAROV'S MEN GET TO HER.

- **A** GET TO OVERWATCH TO PROVIDE SNIPER SUPPORT.
- **B** PROVIDE SNIPER COVER FOR GRANITE TEAM.
- **B** DESTROY THE RUSSIAN TANKS USING THE A-10.
- **C** RAPPEL DOWN THE BUILDING.
- **D** GET TO THE BRIDGE.
- **E** DESTROY THE RUSSIAN TANK USING THE RPG.
- **F** ADVANCE WITH THE GERMAN TANKS.
- **G** GET TO THE HOTEL.
- **H** GET TO THE ROOF.

ENEMY INTEL 5

INITIAL LOADOUT

- ACR Hybrid Sight
- M14 EBR Scoped
- 4 Flashbangs
- 4 Frag Grenades

"BERLIN'S GETTING RIPPED APART DOWN THERE."

The Russian president's daughter has been found in a hotel in Berlin. Metal Zero One is tasked with providing cover for Granite Team while they go in and get her.

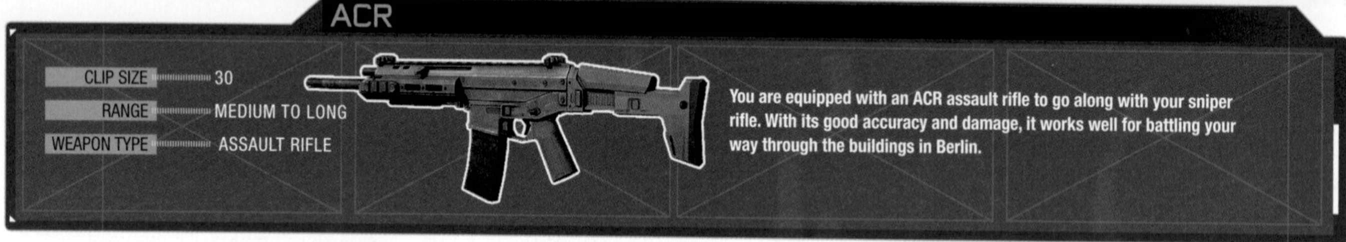

ACR
CLIP SIZE 30
RANGE MEDIUM TO LONG
WEAPON TYPE ASSAULT RIFLE
You are equipped with an ACR assault rifle to go along with your sniper rifle. With its good accuracy and damage, it works well for battling your way through the buildings in Berlin.

A OBJECTIVE

GET TO OVERWATCH TO PROVIDE SNIPER SUPPORT

After a brief glimpse into the immediate future, Metal Zero One is en route to the building where they will provide overwatch. As soon as you are dropped off on the roof, start picking off the enemy troops who emerge from the building.

When the area is clear, hop over the vents and enter the open door ahead. Run up the steps and allow Sandman to take down the first enemy. Move to the right around the floor's perimeter, keeping an eye out for hostiles within the cubicles.

ENEMY INTEL

1 Enter the northwest cubicle to find the first piece of Intelligence on the southern desk.

Run up the ramp to the next floor and take cover behind the cubicle walls. Clear out the bad guys as you make your way up the left side, keeping an eye out for grenade danger indicators.

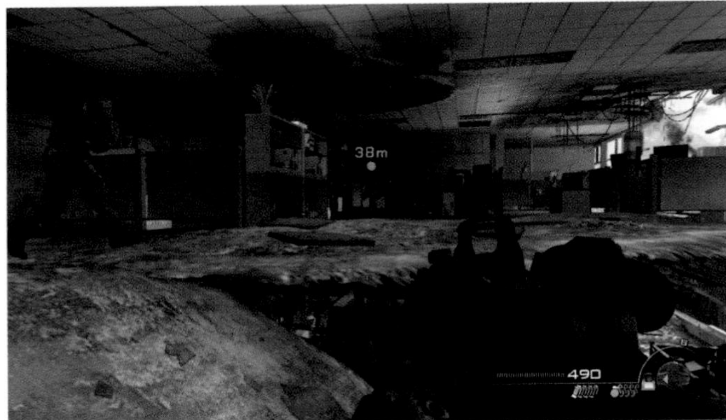

"SECURE THIS AREA FAST!"

Enter the stairwell and climb to the roof. Sandbags provide protection as you eliminate the hostiles. Once the coast is clear, proceed to the northwest corner.

B OBJECTIVE

PROVIDE SNIPER COVER FOR GRANITE TEAM

Pull out your M14 EBR sniper rifle and find your targets in the scope. Take down all of them to create a safe landing zone for Granite Team.

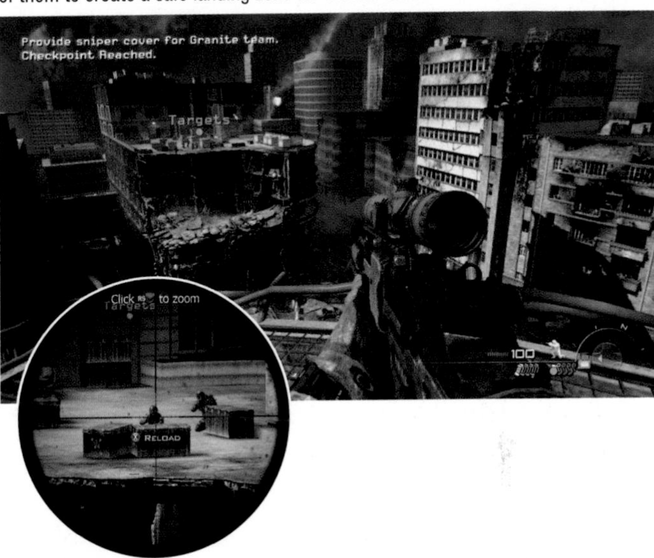

After they exit the chopper, aim at the open door to the left of their position. Eliminate the new threat that emerges from inside. Now that the roof is clear, Granite Team continues their operation.

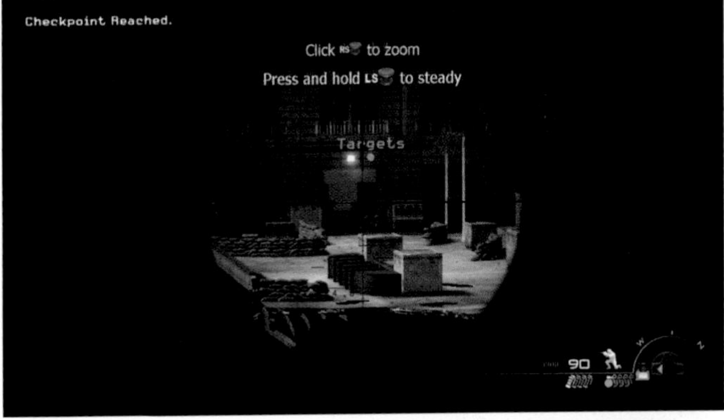

TACTICS

USING THE SNIPER RIFLE

Don't forget that you can click the right analog stick to zoom in and out. Press and hold the left analog stick to hold your breath and steady the aim.

B OBJECTIVE

DESTROY THE RUSSIAN TANKS USING THE A-10

Russian tanks roll in from the east and fire on Granite's position. Provide coordinates for the A-10 so that the strafing run goes through the tank.

TACTICS

SELECTING COORDINATES

When an A-10 is ready for a strafing run, select the targeting binoculars by pressing Right on the D-pad. Press the Fire button to place the cursor where you want to start. Use the right stick to move another cursor to where you want the attack to end. Press the Fire button to set the second point.

Two more tanks roll into view and continue moving. Set coordinates so that the line runs through both vehicles and a little ways down the street. If the strafing run doesn't destroy both tanks, you do get another run to finish the job.

ACHIEVEMENT/TROPHY

NEIN

Earn an Achievement/Trophy by killing nine enemies with an A-10 strafing run. For the first strafing run, enemy troops run from the far sidewalk into the roundabout. Set coordinates through the cars that provide cover for many of them.

C OBJECTIVE

RAPPEL DOWN THE BUILDING

Granite Team moves in and runs into some trouble. Get up from your position and run over to the southeast side of the building.

"ARMOR IS DOWN. GRANITE: YOU'RE GOOD TO GO."

ENEMY INTEL

2 Before you rappel down the building, move to the steps near the roof's east corner. An enemy laptop is hidden behind the fence.

Join the team close to the roof's south corner and find the rappel point. Press the Use button to hook up and descend the building. Head south down the path.

OBJECTIVE

GET TO THE BRIDGE

Move through the parking lot and enter the door in the corner. Climb the steps and take cover behind the car ahead.

ENEMY INTEL

3 After you rappel down the building, run to the south and enter the bookstore on the right. The third Intel sits on the right side of the counter.

E OBJECTIVE

DESTROY THE RUSSIAN TANK USING THE RPG

Grab the RPG and send a rocket into the Russian tank down the street. Switch back to your original weapon and fight your way down the left sidewalk.

F OBJECTIVE

ADVANCE WITH THE GERMAN TANKS

Squeeze through the narrow opening and fall in behind the tanks. Enemy troops litter both sides of the street ahead, so advance cautiously. Move up to the left side of the right-hand tank, and stay with it as it rolls forward.

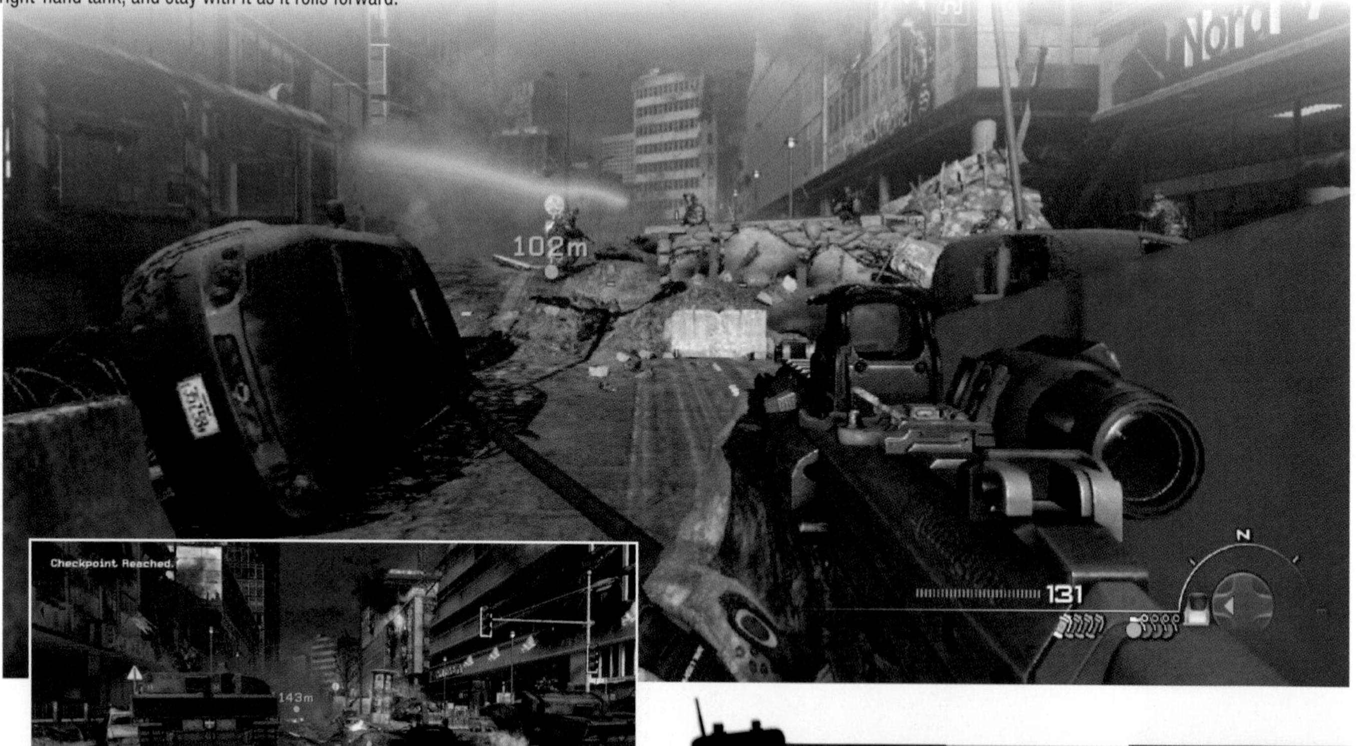

ENEMY INTEL

4

After you pass the bus that sits in the middle of the street, run over to the left sidewalk and enter the small room closest to the bridge. A piece of Enemy Intelligence sits on a crate in the corner.

Advance up the street with your team until an explosion knocks you off your feet.

G OBJECTIVE

GET TO THE HOTEL

When you recover, follow Sandman through the rubble and collapsing building. You eventually exit back outside, and Sandman informs you that the hotel is just ahead.

Russian soldiers advance from the hotel. Dive behind some rubble and take them down. Once the area is clear, enter the hotel.

"WE'VE GOT TO GET THE HELL OUT OF THE KILL ZONE."

GET TO THE ROOF

Fight your way through the bar and down into the lobby. Quickly move to the far corner and enter the stairwell.

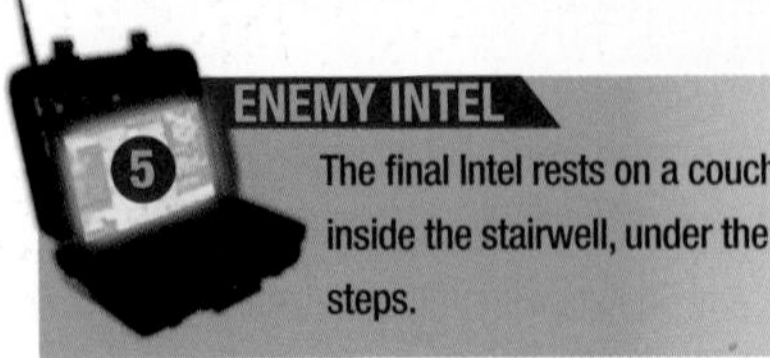

ENEMY INTEL

The final Intel rests on a couch inside the stairwell, under the steps.

Follow Sandman up to the third floor and run to the door at the end of the hall. Take down the enemies who get in your way.

BREACH

As Sandman goes to open the door, an explosion knocks him into you. Yuri grabs Sandman's handgun, so quickly take down the two hostiles who stand in the opening. Run into the room, but it is too late.

ACHIEVEMENT/TROPHY

BAD FIRST DATE

Find the girl in "Scorched Earth" on any difficulty to get this award.

ACT III

DOWN THE RABBIT HOLE

DELTA FORCE / TASK FORCE 141 | 11:08 OCTOBER 14 | EASTERN SIBERIA, RUSSIA

OPERATIVE YURI, DELTA FORCE/ TASK FORCE 141–DISAVOWED

SUPPORT PRICE, SANDMAN, GRINCH, TRUCK

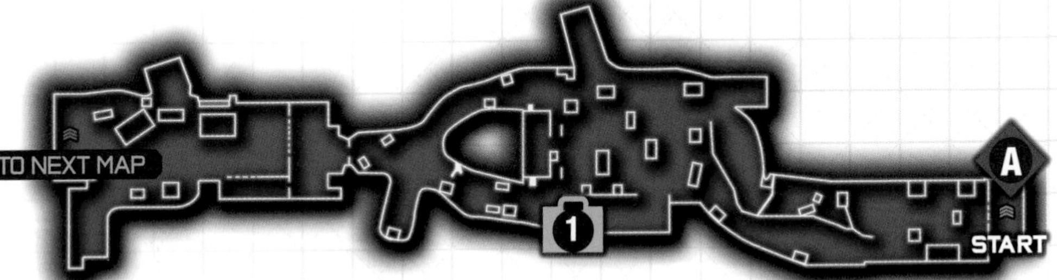

OBJECTIVES

RESCUE THE RUSSIAN PRESIDENT.

- **A** FIND AND RESCUE PRESIDENT VORSHEVSKY.
- **B** ESCAPE WITH THE PRESIDENT.

ENEMY INTEL 2

"ONCE WE GET BOOTS ON THE GROUND, IT IS GOING TO GET LIVELY."

The helicopter has taken the Russian president's daughter to a diamond mine in Siberia. It's only a matter of time before he gives up the launch codes. Delta Force and Task Force 141 are going in as a joint operation.

INITIAL LOADOUT

G36C w/Red Dot Sight

M4A1 w/ACOG

4 Flashbangs

4 Frag Grenades

NIGHT VISION

 OBJECTIVE

FIND AND RESCUE PRESIDENT VORSHEVSKY

Yuri joins members of Metal Zero One in the mineshaft. The elevator comes to a stop and a few of Makarov's men are there to welcome you. Quickly eliminate them before the team plummets to the bottom level.

Immediately flip on your night vision and lay down fire on the enemies ahead. Take cover if you are wounded, and then climb out of the car. Guys pour out of a tunnel ahead and from above. Once you take care of them, follow Sandman through the right path.

Turn off the night vision, as there is plenty of light in this next area. Climb partway up the ramp so you are not vulnerable to anyone on the floor. Aim up to the catwalk above and knock out the snipers.

Move out to the floor and dive behind the machinery. You can also take cover inside the office on the left. Kill the two foes wielding RPGs on the upper platform first. Clear out any remaining troops below.

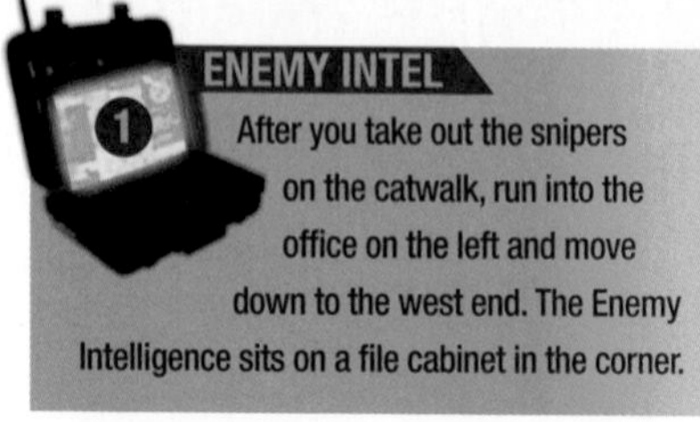

ENEMY INTEL

After you take out the snipers on the catwalk, run into the office on the left and move down to the west end. The Enemy Intelligence sits on a file cabinet in the corner.

The team again splits up through two tunnels; follow Sandman to the right. You converge on a few more bad guys at the other end. Take care of them and then wait for Truck to cut his way through the locking mechanism on the next door.

Follow Price through the door, where more of Makarov's men flee to cover. Shoot them down as they run.

Move into the left side of the office and take cover next to the window. Use this angle to get at the enemies on the right. Watch out: an RPG is set up further down. Join your team at the other window to get at any remaining Russian troops.

When the level is clear, your crew heads out. Run into the stairwell on the left. Two foes wait at the landing, so be ready to drop them. Continue to the third floor.

"OVERLORD, THIS IS SANDMAN. WE'RE AT THE BOTTOM OF THE MINE. WE'RE GOING TO NEED AIR SUPPORT."

TO NEXT MAP

FROM PREVIOUS MAP

"UAV IS ON STATION WITH A FULL LOAD OF AGMS, READY FOR TARGETS."

Follow the captain through the door that leads out to the mine. Four RPGs are ready to take down your air support. Quickly take them out, then fire down at the troops below. Use grenades or a dropped RPG-7 to speed up the fight.

Once the area is clear, hop over the right rail and slide down to the ground. More friendlies arrive to help.

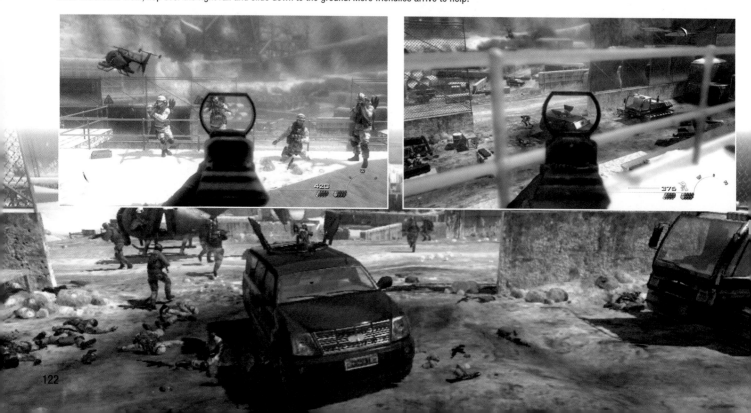

Move up to the concrete barriers ahead and take cover. When the Predator comes online, press Right on the D-pad to bring up the targeting screen. Aim the missile away from your team and into a group of hostiles.

TACTICS

PREDATOR UAV

Whenever the Predator becomes available, use it to thin out enemy forces. Control it the same way you did in the first mission, Black Tuesday. Aim in the general area of your target and fire the rocket. Use the right control stick to guide it to the destination, and hold the Boost button to get it there faster. You are vulnerable when you access the targeting screen, so be sure you are well protected.

Work your way into the construction site and eliminate any remaining enemies. More of Makarov's men drop in as you proceed. Move from cover to cover, sweeping through the grounds.

"VIPER 6, WE'RE MOVING TO THE CONSTRUCTION YARD. WATCH YOUR FIRE."

Cut through the big pipes to reach the next checkpoint. Run up the ramp and into the structure to get a flanking position on a few enemies inside and out. Then, move back outside and duck behind more concrete barriers. Look out for RPGs and take them down first. As the site clears out, move up with your team.

As you turn the corner and spot your destination, dive behind cover. Your air support obliterates many of the enemy troops. Now you can advance inside with your squad.

BREACH

Move down the corridor, taking out any helpless foes along the way. Breach the door, but don't fire any shots. Alena Vorshevsky is tied up inside.

"THEY TOOK HER FATHER DEEPER INTO THE MINE. THEN THAT'S WHERE WE'RE GOING."

Once the president's daughter is rescued, follow Sandman through the next door and down the hill, dropping the two enemies ahead. Move to the left side and fire at the enemy troops who cross the bridge below.

Finish off any stragglers as you run down to the bridge. Hook up at the rappel point and descend deeper into the mine. The president is being taken away just ahead, but you have to deal with the surrounding troops first.

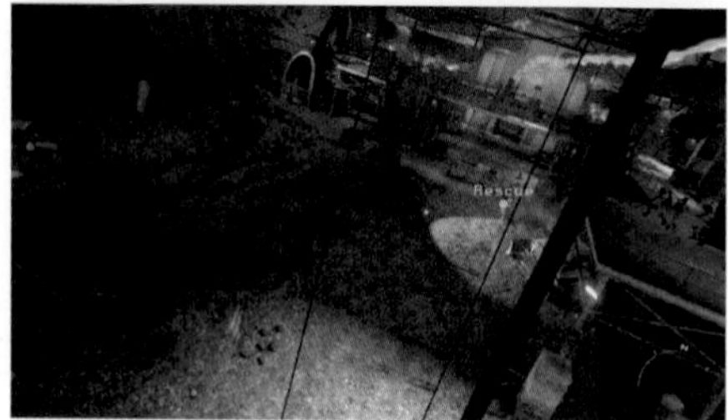

Several men line the walkway overhead, including some with RPGs. Take cover on the left side and eliminate them first. Push forward and clear out the remaining foes.

BREACH

The door that leads to the president is impenetrable. Follow Price up the steps. He wants to set up charges in a circle, allowing the team to breach the room from above. Reload your weapon and then hold the Use button at the highlighted spot. At this point, you drop down with the ceiling. One of the men grabs the president—shoot him in the head first. Then you can take out the other four as you continue to fall.

B OBJECTIVE

ESCAPE WITH THE PRESIDENT

Quickly move up the ramp and run for the machine gun ahead. Use it to spray bullets at the attackers. They fire from the walkway above and from behind cover below. Some men advance on your position. Keep scanning the room, firing the weapon as you do. Also look to the sides of the walkway, as an enemy appears on each side in an attempt to flank you.

ENEMY INTEL

Before you leave with the president, go to the south side of the room. The second Intel rests on a barrel.

"LOOKS LIKE OUR RIDE'S HERE."

Drop the gun and take cover if you start taking too much damage. When you hear the command to go, follow your team toward the landing zone.

When you regain control of a gun, protect Sandman, Truck, and Grinch by shooting down any advancing foes. After a short fight, the helicopter makes its escape out of the mine.

ACHIEVEMENT/TROPHY

DIAMOND IN THE ROUGH

Complete "Down the Rabbit Hole" on any difficulty by rescuing the Russian president.

ACT III
DUST TO DUST

TASK FORCE 141 | 22:14 JANUARY 21 | ARABIAN PENINSULA

OPERATIVE CAPTAIN PRICE, TASK FORCE 141

SUPPORT YURI

OBJECTIVE

A KILL MAKAROV.

ENEMY INTEL 3

INITIAL LOADOUT

PKP Pecheneg w/Red Dot Sight

M4A1 Grenadier w/ACOG

4 Flashbangs

4 Frag Grenades

JUGGERNAUT SUIT

"...ALL IT TAKES TO CHANGE THE COURSE OF HISTORY IS THE WILL OF A SINGLE MAN."

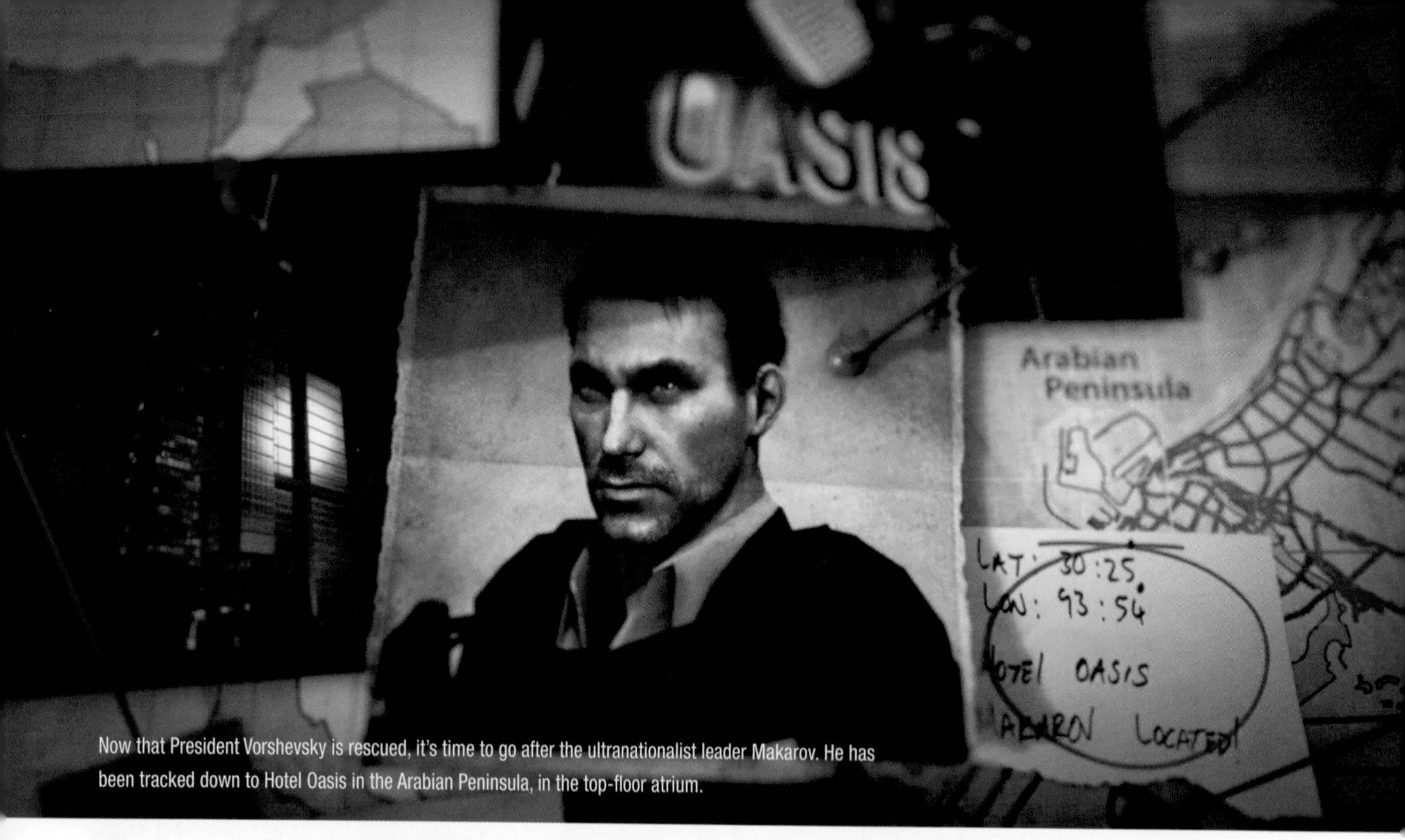

Now that President Vorshevsky is rescued, it's time to go after the ultranationalist leader Makarov. He has been tracked down to Hotel Oasis in the Arabian Peninsula, in the top-floor atrium.

A OBJECTIVE

KILL MAKAROV

Yuri and Price, equipped with Juggernaut suits, plan to fight their way to the top of the hotel and finish this thing once and for all. You play as Captain Price this time.

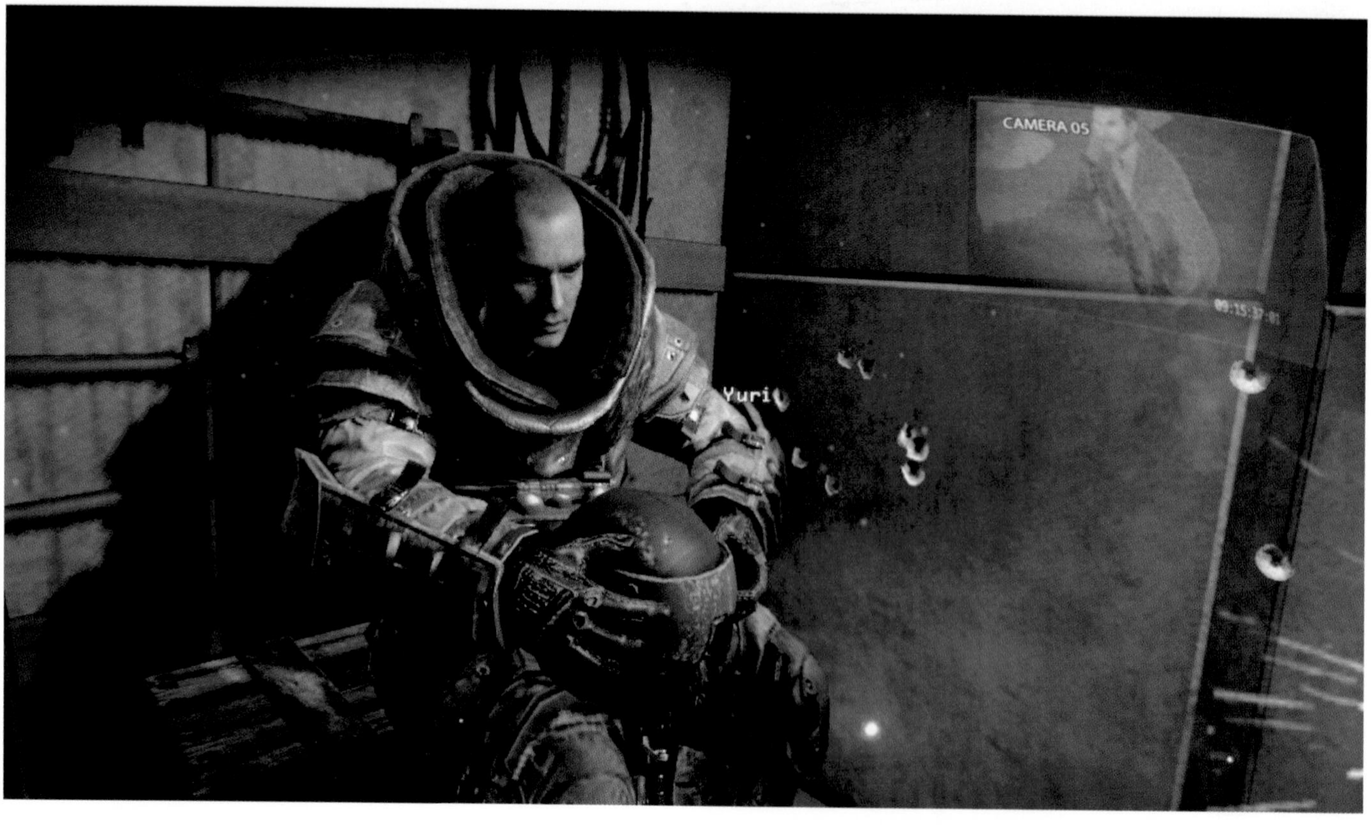

TACTICS

EXTRA PROTECTION

The Juggernaut suit provides an extra layer of armor that facilitates a more straightforward attack. You still take damage, but it takes longer for the enemy to knock you down.

Several of Makarov's men meet you as soon as you touch the street. Pull out the PKP Pecheneg light machine gun and mow them down. The high rate of fire eats away at the enemy quickly. Be aware that the reload time leaves you vulnerable for a short period.

TACTICS

WEAPONRY

Price is also equipped with an M4A1 with grenade launcher attachment and the usual assortment of grenades. Don't be afraid to use everything you have to reach Makarov quickly.

"DON'T LET UP!"

Destroy the cars in this outside area to dispatch a few enemies at a time. As you approach the fountain, take out the RPGs that fire from the second floor.

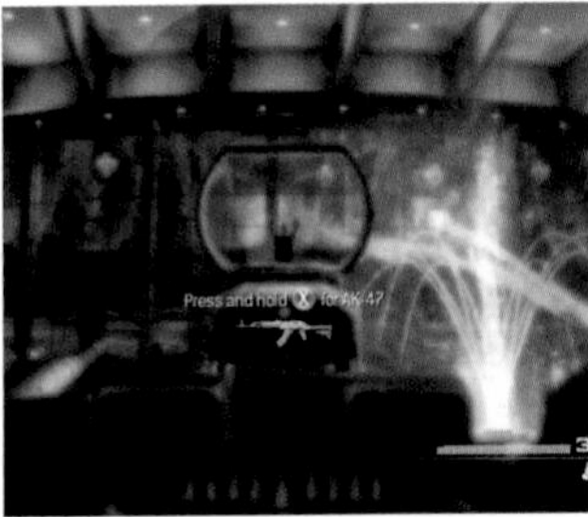

Around the other side, civilians spill out of the hotel. Hold your fire until you're in the hotel lobby. Hostiles run down the escalators to greet you, with more watching from the floor above. Push up the steps and toward the back of the building.

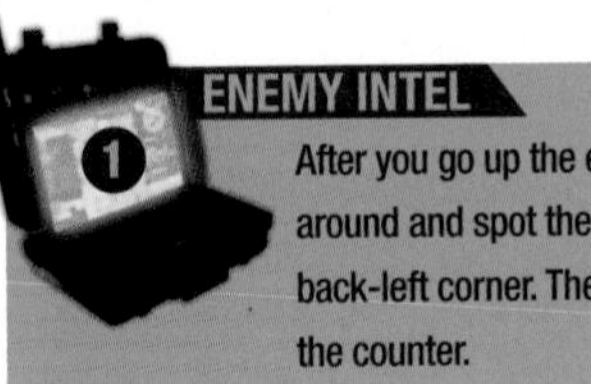

ENEMY INTEL

1 After you go up the escalator, turn around and spot the bar in the back-left corner. The Intel sits on the counter.

When the right elevator opens up for you, join Yuri inside. A chopper attacks your position. Use the light machine gun to light it up. It crashes into the elevators, shattering your helmet. The suits are not much help now.

"THE LIFT'S UP AHEAD. PRICE, OVER HERE."

Yuri calls for another lift from Nikolai. When it arrives, run and jump over to it. Makarov is now headed to his chopper in an attempt to escape. You have four minutes to reach him.

FROM PREVIOUS MAP

TO NEXT MAP

"HE'S NOT GETTING AWAY!"

The elevator drops you off at the top-floor restaurant. You no longer have the extra armor, so take cover whenever you can. Switch to your assault rifle and push around the room's perimeter. Makarov's loyal men wait around every corner and behind every chair.

ENEMY INTEL
2
Follow Yuri into the poker room, where a laptop sits on the table.

ENEMY INTEL
3
Just past the entrance to the restaurant, a laptop sits on the bar to the right.

When you enter the restaurant, the helicopter flies past the window as Makarov exits the room. You have to hurry now.

Walk further into the restaurant, and the chopper destroys it with a slew of rockets. This causes Price to slide toward his doom. Press the indicated button to hold on when you're prompted to do so.

"DON'T LET HIM GET AWAY!"

Move to the north through the rubble and up the stairs. Once you're outside, you spot Makarov climbing into the chopper. Sprint toward him.

Be sure to sprint all the way there, or you won't make it. As you step on the rail, jump toward the aircraft. Price grabs hold of the landing skid.

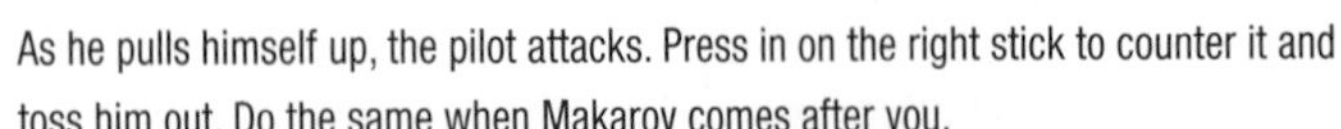
As he pulls himself up, the pilot attacks. Press in on the right stick to counter it and toss him out. Do the same when Makarov comes after you.

Once you're back on the roof, press the buttons when you're prompted to avenge Soap and complete the campaign.

ACHIEVEMENT/TROPHY

THIS IS THE END

Complete "Scorched Earth," "Down the Rabbit Hole," and "Dust to Dust" on Veteran difficulty.

ACHIEVEMENT/TROPHY

WHO DARES WINS

Complete the campaign on any difficulty.

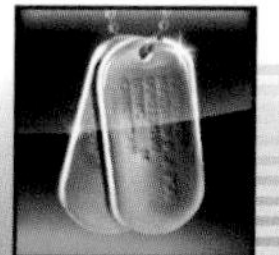

ACHIEVEMENT/TROPHY

THE BEST OF THE BEST

Complete the campaign on Hardened or Veteran difficulty.

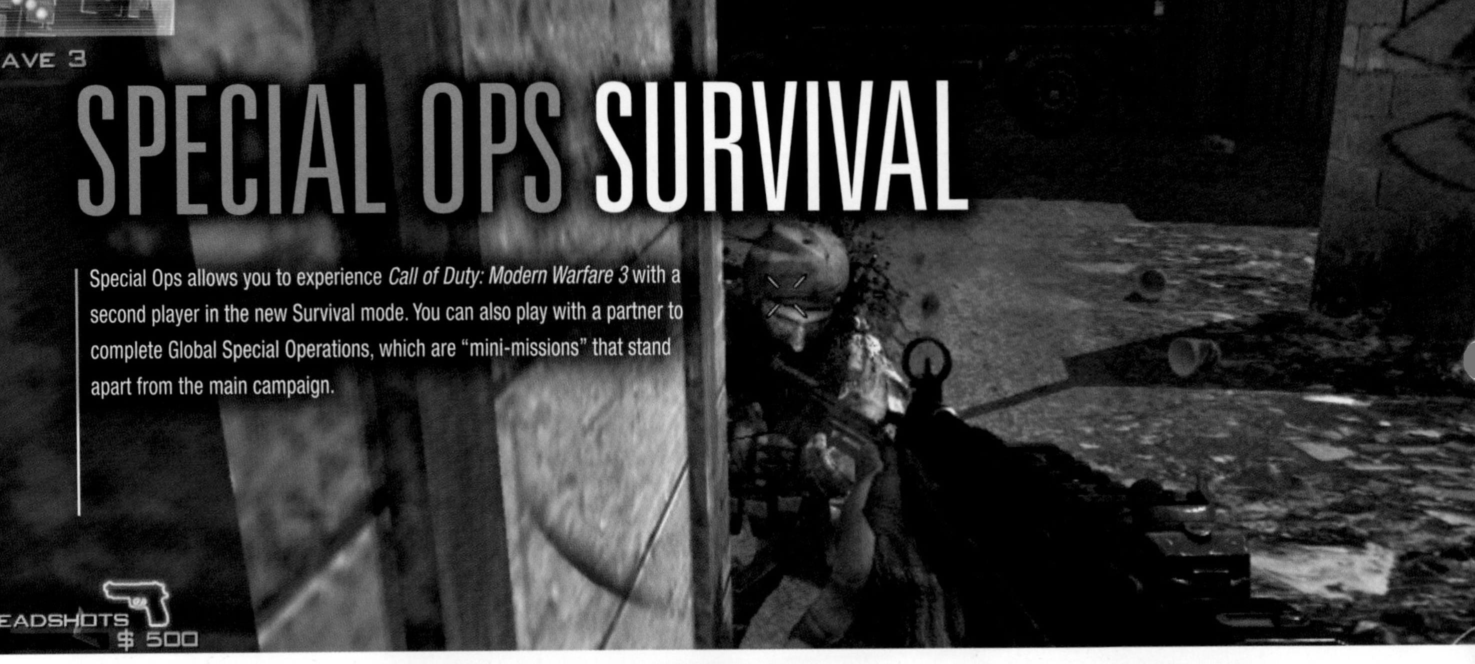

SPECIAL OPS SURVIVAL

Special Ops allows you to experience *Call of Duty: Modern Warfare 3* with a second player in the new Survival mode. You can also play with a partner to complete Global Special Operations, which are "mini-missions" that stand apart from the main campaign.

The following chapter provides all the necessary information and strategies to get you through Special Ops mode, including maps for each Survival level and Special Ops mission.

Survival mode pits you against countless waves of enemies. You can play it solo or with two players. It takes place on the same 16 maps that appear in multiplayer. Only four are unlocked from the start, and the rest become available as you level up in Special Ops.

You earn experience points for each game of Survival you complete. This allows you to increase in rank just as you can in multiplayer, though these ranks are kept separate. Leveling up opens new maps in Survival and new missions in Global Special Operations. It also allows you to use new weapons and equipment in Survival mode.

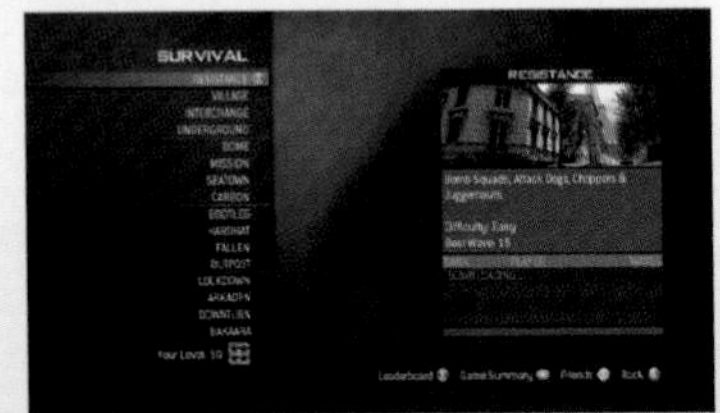

The enemies get tougher as you fight through the waves. They start out as standard foes, such as Russian dock workers, and progress to Juggernauts. The next page provides a look at the different types.

ACHIEVEMENT/TROPHY

UNSTOPPABLE

Reach Wave 15 in each mission of Special Ops Survival mode.

THE HUD

In Survival mode, the heads-up-display (HUD) gives you all the information you need to make your way through the enemy waves. The mini-map appears in the top-left corner. This shows you where you and your partner are, along with any incoming enemies—they show up as red dots. Your current Wave progress appears below the map.

The two mini-challenges and your current money balance appear in the lower-left corner. The lower-right corner shows you how many grenades you have, along with your ammo supply. The number indicates how many rounds you have in reserve, while the dashes represent the bullets in the weapon.

The D-pad indicates whether you have an item in the equipment slot. After you purchase an item from the Air Support Armory, an icon appears to the right of the D-pad. If you have Self Revive and/or Armor, they appear in the middle of the lower screen.

Armory icons appear on your HUD—they show you where to buy your supplies. A gun icon represents the Weapon Armory, a grenade signifies the Equipment Armory, and a jet denotes the Air Support Armory. An arrow beside each icon indicates the direction in which to look for the corresponding armory.

THE ENEMIES

STANDARD FOES

These are the regular enemies who just carry a gun and come straight for the player. This includes the following as they increase in difficulty:

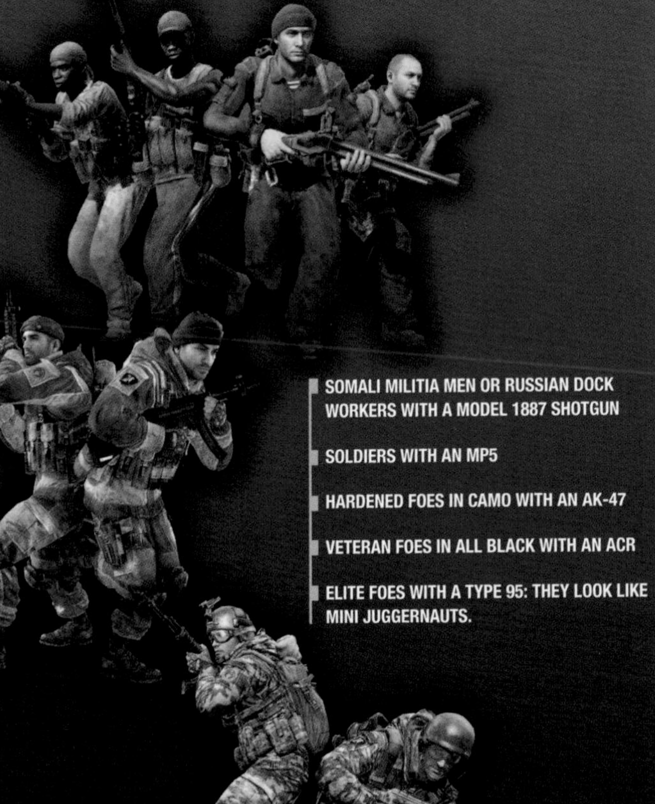

- SOMALI MILITIA MEN OR RUSSIAN DOCK WORKERS WITH A MODEL 1887 SHOTGUN
- SOLDIERS WITH AN MP5
- HARDENED FOES IN CAMO WITH AN AK-47
- VETERAN FOES IN ALL BLACK WITH AN ACR
- ELITE FOES WITH A TYPE 95: THEY LOOK LIKE MINI JUGGERNAUTS.

SPECIAL AIs

Special AIs perform special actions, such as the following:

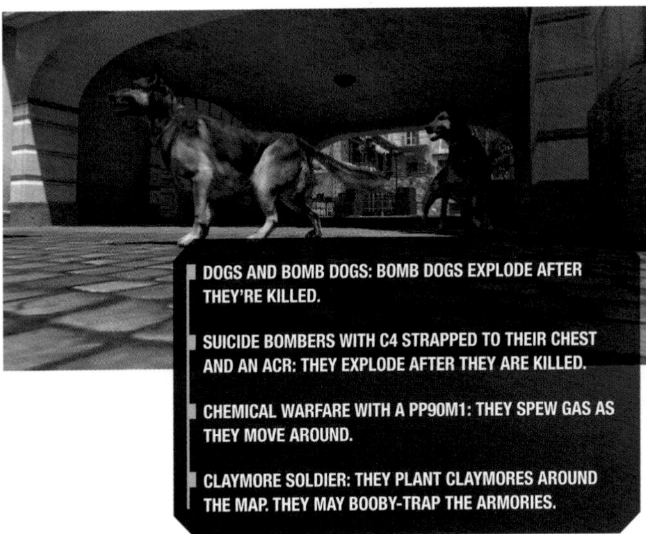

- DOGS AND BOMB DOGS: BOMB DOGS EXPLODE AFTER THEY'RE KILLED.
- SUICIDE BOMBERS WITH C4 STRAPPED TO THEIR CHEST AND AN ACR: THEY EXPLODE AFTER THEY ARE KILLED.
- CHEMICAL WARFARE WITH A PP90M1: THEY SPEW GAS AS THEY MOVE AROUND.
- CLAYMORE SOLDIER: THEY PLANT CLAYMORES AROUND THE MAP. THEY MAY BOOBY-TRAP THE ARMORIES.

CHOPPERS

Choppers are equipped with a machine gun and are introduced in Wave 6.

JUGGERNAUTS

These are the tough guys in the game, as they require some major firepower to take down.

- RREGULAR JUGGERNAUT
- RIOT SHIELD JUGGERNAUT: HE WILL DROP THE SHIELD AND TURN INTO A REGULAR JUGGERNAUT.
- ARMORED JUGGERNAUT

EARNING MONEY

You earn is earned as you play through a Survival game. You can use this currency to purchase new weapons and equipment. Your money always starts out at 0 for Wave 1, and it's displayed at the screen's bottom-left corner. Each time you kill an enemy, money is added to your account—the tougher the foe, the more money you earn.

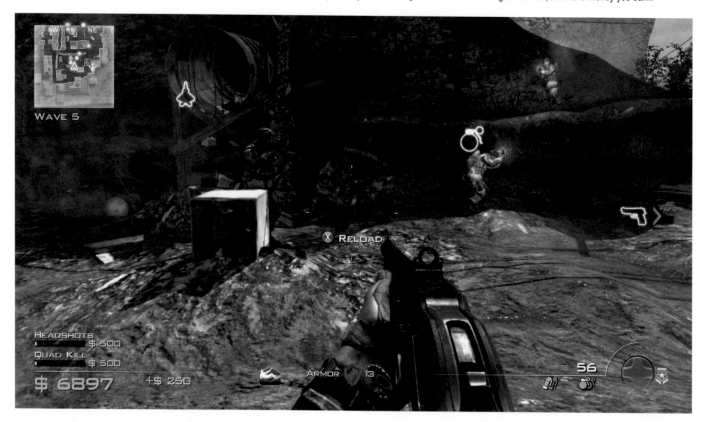

At the end of each wave, you earn a Wave Bonus, dependent on your combat performance. Six factors contribute to this: time taken, current wave, number of kills, headshots, accuracy, and damage taken. The better you perform, the more money you earn.

The final way to earn money is with streaks. Two random streaks appear above your money in the screen's bottom-left corner. Killing enemies in specific ways fills the progress bar. Once it's full, you earn $500. If you continue the streak, you can earn $1000, and so on. The possible streaks are described in the chart to the right:

STREAK	DESCRIPTION
Kill Streak	Increases with each kill. Resets when damaged.
Quad Kill	Take out four enemies with one grenade. Does not reset.
Rampage	Increases with each kill. Slowly goes down when not killing.
Knife Streak	Increases with each knife kill. Does not reset.
Headshot	Increases with each headshot. Does not reset.
Flash Kill	Increases with each blinded-by-Flashbang kill. Does not reset.

The streaks change and reset with each wave.

THE ARMORIES

After you finish off the first three Waves, you gain access to three armories. This is where you use your money to get new weapons and equipment. Not everything is available when you first play Survival mode. You unlock certain items as you level up. When you access an armory, you can share money with your teammate, $500 at a time. The following tables show what level is required to purchase each item and how much it costs.

WEAPON ARMORY

Complete the first to open the first armory. This allows you to purchase new weapons and upgrade your current ones. Have the weapon you want to replace in your hands when you make a purchase.

WEAPON ARMORY Lv. 50
Refills ammo for your primary weapons.
REFILL BULLET AMMO $750
HANDGUNS
MACHINE PISTOLS
ASSAULT RIFLES
SUB MACHINE GUNS
LIGHT MACHINE GUNS
SNIPER RIFLES
SHOTGUNS
$5143 SHARE $500 Back

HANDGUNS

WEAPON	LEVEL	COST	DESCRIPTION
Five Seven	1	250	Semi-automatic (single fire).
USP .45	1	250	Semi-automatic (single fire).
MP412	2	250	Revolver.
Desert Eagle	11	250	Semi-automatic (single fire).
.44 Magnum	20	250	Revolver.
P99	40	250	Semi-automatic (single fire).

MACHINE PISTOLS

WEAPON	LEVEL	COST	DESCRIPTION
G18	1	1500	Fully automatic, close range.
Skorpion	3	1500	Fully automatic, close range.
MP9	17	1500	Fully automatic, close range.
FMG9	37	1500	Fully automatic, close range.

ASSAULT RIFLES

WEAPON	LEVEL	COST	DESCRIPTION
M4A1 (m4short)	1	3000	Fully automatic, all-purpose weapon.
M16A4	1	3000	3-round burst.
SCAR-L	5	3000	Fully automatic, all-purpose weapon.
ACR 6.8	14	3000	Fully automatic, all-purpose weapon.
AK-47	24	3000	Fully automatic, all-purpose weapon.
FAD	32	3000	Fully automatic, all-purpose weapon.
G36C	39	3000	Fully automatic, all-purpose weapon.
CM901	43	3000	Fully automatic, all-purpose weapon.
MK14	47	3000	Semi-automatic (single fire).
TYPE95	50	3000	3-round burst.

SUBMACHINE GUNS

WEAPON	LEVEL	COST	DESCRIPTION
MP5	1	2000	Fully automatic, close range.
UMP45	4	2000	Fully automatic, close range.
MP7	13	2000	Fully automatic, close range.
PM-9 (M9 Beretta)	23	2000	Fully automatic, close range.
PP90M1	38	2000	Fully automatic, high fire rate.
P90	46	2000	Fully automatic, large magazines.

LIGHT MACHINE GUNS

WEAPON	LEVEL	COST	DESCRIPTION
M60E4	12	7000	Fully automatic, large magazines.
PKP Pecheneg	18	7000	Fully automatic, large magazines.
MK46	34	7000	Fully automatic, large magazines.
L86 LSW	41	7000	Fully automatic, large magazines.
MG36	48	7000	Fully automatic, large magazines.

SNIPER RIFLES

WEAPON	LEVEL	COST	DESCRIPTION
MSR	7	2000	Bolt action.
Dragunov	16	2000	Semi-automatic (single fire).
RSASS	29	2000	Semi-automatic (single fire).
L118A (weapon_l96a1)	35	2000	Bolt action.
AS50	42	2000	Semi-automatic (single fire).
Barrett .50Cal	49	2000	Semi-automatic (single fire).

SHOTGUNS

WEAPON	LEVEL	COST	DESCRIPTION
Model 1887	1	2000	Lever-action.
USAS 12	6	2000	Fully automatic, low ammo.
SPAS-12	16	2000	Pump action.
KSG 12	26	2000	Double barrel.
Striker	33	4000	Semi-automatic (single fire).
AA-12	44	5000	Fully automatic, low ammo.

WEAPON UPGRADES

WEAPON UPGRADE	LEVEL	COST	DESCRIPTION
Holographic Sight	1	1000	Holographic sight.
Red Dot Sight	7	750	Precision sight.
Grip	19	1250	Vertical foregrip for reduced recoil.
M203 Grenade Launcher	28	1500	Undermounted grenade launcher.
GP25 Grenade Launcher	28	1500	Undermounted grenade launcher.
M320 Grenade Launcher	28	1500	Undermounted grenade launcher.
ACOG Scope	30	1250	Enhanced zoom ACOG scope.
Shotgun Attachment	45	1500	Undermounted shotgun attachment.

EQUIPMENT ARMORY

After you finish the second wave, the Equipment Armory opens. This gives you access to explosives, armor, and other equipment. Items that have to be used, such as the sentry guns, take up your equipment slot (press Right on the D-pad). You can have only one item in this slot at a time.

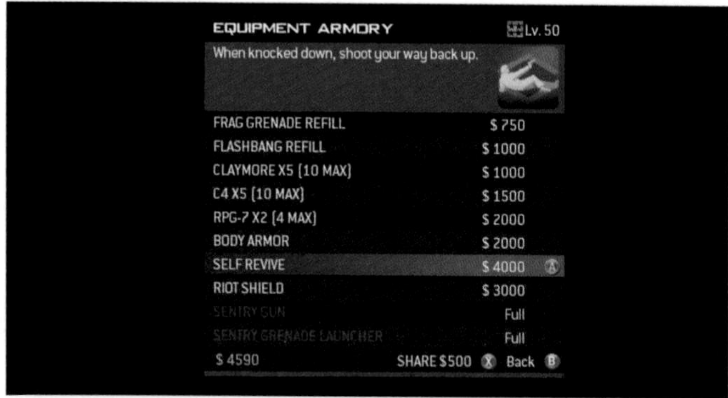

EQUIPMENT	LEVEL	COST	DESCRIPTION
Frag Grenade Refill	1	750	Refills Frags up to 4.
Flashbang Refill	1	1000	Refills Flashbangs up to 4.
Claymore x5 (10 Max)	2	1000	Directional anti-personnel mine set off by an enemy entering its proximity.
C4 x5 (10 Max)	3	1500	Charge of plastic explosives, set off manually with a detonator.
RPG-7 x2 (4 Max)	27	2000	RPG-7 x2.
Body Armor	10	2000	250 Armor hit points.
Self Revive	13	4000	When you're knocked down, shoot your way back up.
Sentry Gun	17	3000	Mini-gun mounted sentry.
Sentry Grenade Launcher	31	4000	Grenade launcher mounted sentry.
Riot Shield	37	3000	Bullet resistant.

AIR SUPPORT ARMORY

Use this armory to call in Predator missiles, friendly support, and perk air drops. All of these occupy the equipment slot until you use them. The Delta Squad and Riot Shield Squad call in extra troops to help you fight off the enemies. See the chart at the top of the next column.

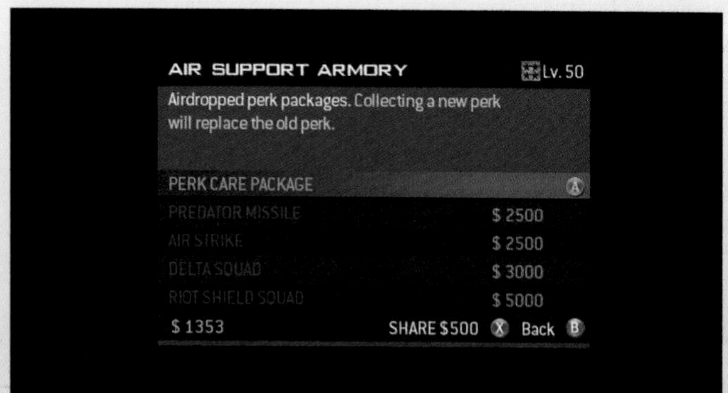

AIR SUPPORT	LEVEL	COST	DESCRIPTION
Predator Missile	1	2500	Missile from UCAV.
Air Strike	4	2500	Precision Air Strike on selected location.
Delta Squad	14	3000	Delta Force allies dropped in via chopper.
Riot Shield Squad	21	5000	Riot Shield allies dropped in via chopper.
Quickdraw	1	3000	Faster aiming.
Steady Aim	8	3000	Increased hip fire accuracy.
Stalker	22	4000	Move faster while aiming.
Extreme Conditioning	36	4000	Sprint for longer distances.
Sleight of Hand	50	5000	Faster reloading.

BLEEDING OUT AND SELF REVIVE

In two player, if a player is knocked down (but not out) or bleeding out, the second player can revive him. A timer counts down from 1:30. Each instance after that, the timer decreases until it reaches the minimum of 0:30. You can crawl over to your teammate, who can then revive you. The other player receives a message of "Teammate Down," along with a timer. Approach the downed player and hold the Use button until he recovers.

If you have Self Revive and are knocked down, you can still use your handgun. Taking down an enemy before time runs out gets you on your feet immediately.

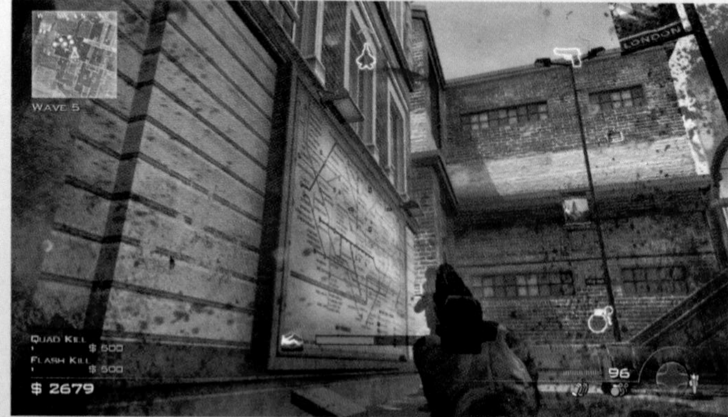

You start out with the Revive perk in the first twelve maps. For the final four, you must purchase it once it's available.

TIPS AND STRATEGIES

There are many ways to play through Survival mode, but the following tips, useful information, and strategies may help.

- THE MAPS IN SURVIVAL MODE ARE THE SAME AS IN MULTIPLAYER, SO IT'S A GOOD PLACE TO LEARN YOUR WAY AROUND.
- THE ENEMIES YOU SEE ON EACH WAVE AND THE PLACES FROM WHICH THEY EMERGE ARE ALWAYS THE SAME. MEMORIZING THIS INFORMATION CAN HELP YOU PREPARE FOR WHAT'S COMING.
- DO NOT PURCHASE ANYTHING THROUGH THE EARLY WAVES. BUILD UP A NICE NEST EGG SO YOU CAN SPLURGE ON THE GOOD STUFF LATER. PICK UP THE ENEMIES' DROPPED WEAPONS TO RESTOCK YOUR AMMO. THE HANDGUN AND KNIFE ARE ALL YOU NEED FOR THE FIRST WAVES.
- LEAVING ONE ENEMY ALIVE ALLOWS YOU TO COLLECT ANY DROPPED AMMUNITION.
- ENEMIES MOVE FASTER AS YOU PROGRESS THROUGH THE WAVES. EVENTUALLY, IT SEEMS LIKE THEY ARE INSTANTLY ON TOP OF YOU. BE PREPARED.
- FLASHBANGS ARE VERY POWERFUL IN SURVIVAL. THEY ARE CHEAP, AND THEY STUN ALL GROUND TROOPS, INCLUDING JUGGERNAUTS.
- USE SENTRY GUNS TO DEFEND YOUR POSITION. BE CAREFUL ON THE CHOPPER WAVES, AS THEY CAN RIP THROUGH THE SENTRIES. SENTRIES ARE MOVABLE AFTER PLACEMENT, SO GRAB THEM AND MOVE THEM INSIDE BEFORE CHOPPERS ARRIVE.
- SENTRY GUNS BECOME LESS EFFECTIVE IN LATER WAVES, AS THEY ARE DESTROYED VERY QUICKLY.
- SET UP TWO SENTRY GUNS CROSSING EACH OTHER AT 90 DEGREES TO COVER A LARGE AREA.
- THE AIR STRIKE GRENADE IS STICKY, SO YOU CAN STICK IT TO A CHOPPER.
- LIGHT MACHINE GUNS ARE EXTREMELY GOOD AGAINST THE CHOPPERS. TWO RPG ROCKETS ALSO WORK WELL.
- THE PREDATOR MISSILE IS VERY EFFECTIVE AGAINST JUGGERNAUTS. C4 IS ALSO GREAT AGAINST THEM.
- RIOT SHIELD SQUADS CAN GIVE YOU AN EXTRA LAYER OF DEFENSE.
- DELTA SQUADS AND RIOT SHIELD SQUADS WORK WELL AS DISTRACTIONS.
- IF YOU LIKE THE IDEA OF RELOADING LESS OFTEN, SAVE UP FOR TWO LIGHT MACHINE GUNS.
- YOU CAN ALWAYS SEE THE AIRPLANE THAT PROVIDES THE AIR STRIKES. WATCH IT TO SEE WHERE THE ATTACK WILL TAKE PLACE.
- USE AIR STRIKES IN OPEN AREAS FOR A MORE EFFECTIVE ATTACK.
- THE RIOT SHIELD IS EFFECTIVE AT PROVIDING DEFENSE, BUT IT WILL BREAK.
- DO NOT MELEE CHEMICAL WARFARE ENEMIES, AS DOING SO STUNS YOU.
- MOVING THROUGH CHEMICAL MINES SLOWS YOU DOWN.
- AFTER YOU REACH LEVEL 50, YOU GET ACCESS TO THE SLEIGHT OF HAND PERK. THIS IS ONE OF THE BEST ITEMS TO PURCHASE.
- DON'T FORGET THAT YOU CAN SHARE MONEY AT THE ARMORIES. DO THIS TO PURCHASE THE MORE EXPENSIVE ITEMS.
- HANG OUT NEAR THE EQUIPMENT ARMORY SO YOU CAN ACCESS THE EXPLOSIVES AND BODY ARMOR EASILY.
- THERE ARE MANY GOOD LOCATIONS FOR BOTTLENECKING OR CREATING CHOKEPOINTS. PICK ONE WITH A NICE EXIT, SUCH AS A WINDOW.
- USE A RIOT SHIELD TO GET CLOSE TO A DOWNED TEAMMATE, AND THEN DROP IT TO REVIVE.
- SET UP CLAYMORES IN A LOOP AND RUN AWAY FROM THE ENEMY MOB.

THE MAPS

The maps are divided into four tiers that get tougher as you progress. The first four maps are Easy difficulty, the next four are Regular, and so on. The enemies you see and your initial loadout are the same throughout each tier.

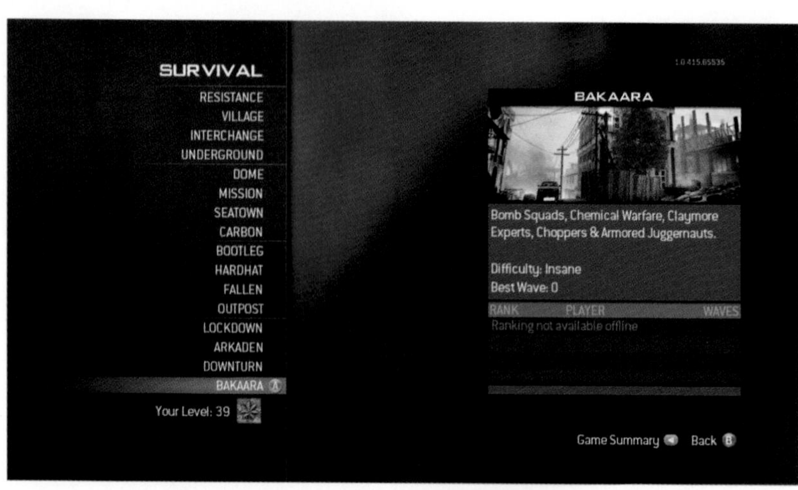

RESISTANCE

DIFFICULTY:	EASY
UNLOCKED AT LEVEL:	ALREADY UNLOCKED
ENEMIES:	BOMB SQUADS, ATTACK DOGS, CHOPPERS, AND JUGGERNAUTS.

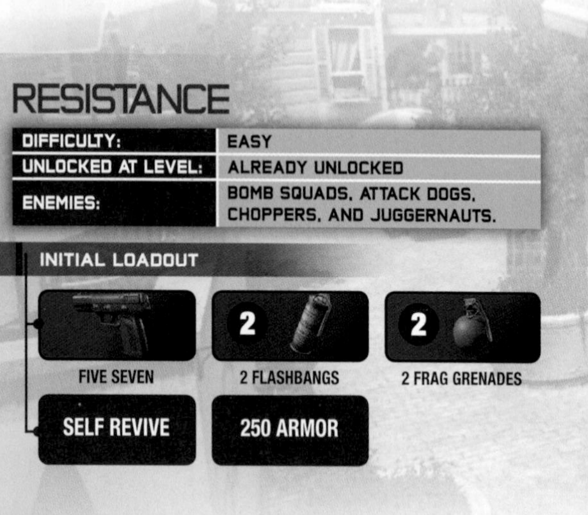

VILLAGE

DIFFICULTY:	EASY
UNLOCKED AT LEVEL:	ALREADY UNLOCKED
ENEMIES:	BOMB SQUADS, ATTACK DOGS, CHOPPERS, AND JUGGERNAUTS.

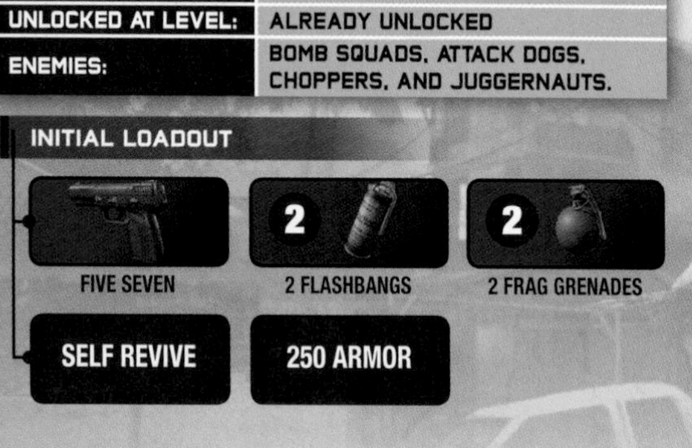

INTERCHANGE

DIFFICULTY:	EASY
UNLOCKED AT LEVEL:	ALREADY UNLOCKED
ENEMIES:	BOMB SQUADS, ATTACK DOGS, CHOPPERS, AND JUGGERNAUTS.

INITIAL LOADOUT

FIVE SEVEN

2 FLASHBANGS

2 FRAG GRENADES

SELF REVIVE

250 ARMOR

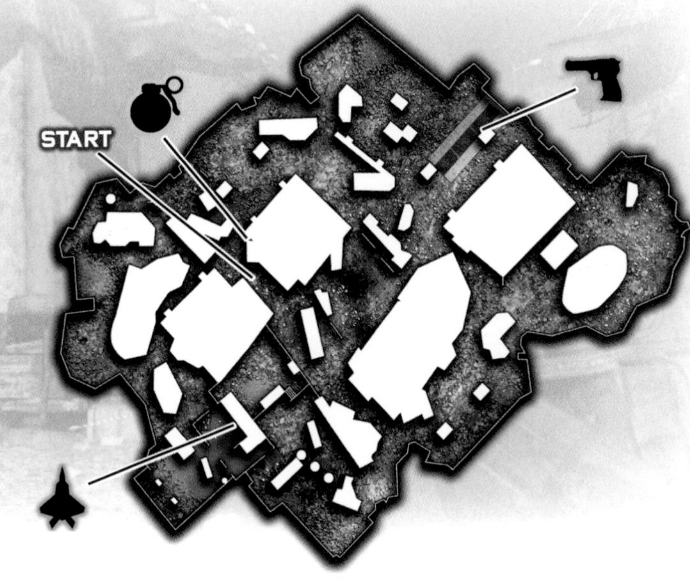

UNDERGROUND

DIFFICULTY:	EASY
UNLOCKED AT LEVEL:	ALREADY UNLOCKED
ENEMIES:	BOMB SQUADS, ATTACK DOGS, CHOPPERS, AND JUGGERNAUTS.

INITIAL LOADOUT

FIVE SEVEN

2 FLASHBANGS

2 FRAG GRENADES

SELF REVIVE

250 ARMOR

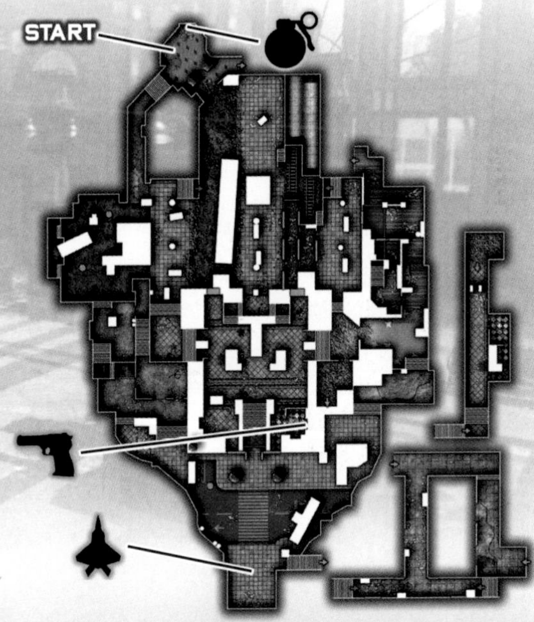

DOME

DIFFICULTY:	REGULAR
UNLOCKED AT LEVEL:	8
ENEMIES:	BOMB SQUADS, CHEMICAL WARFARE, CHOPPERS, AND RIOT SHIELD JUGGERNAUTS.

INITIAL LOADOUT

USP .45

2 FLASHBANGS

2 FRAG GRENADES

SELF REVIVE

250 ARMOR

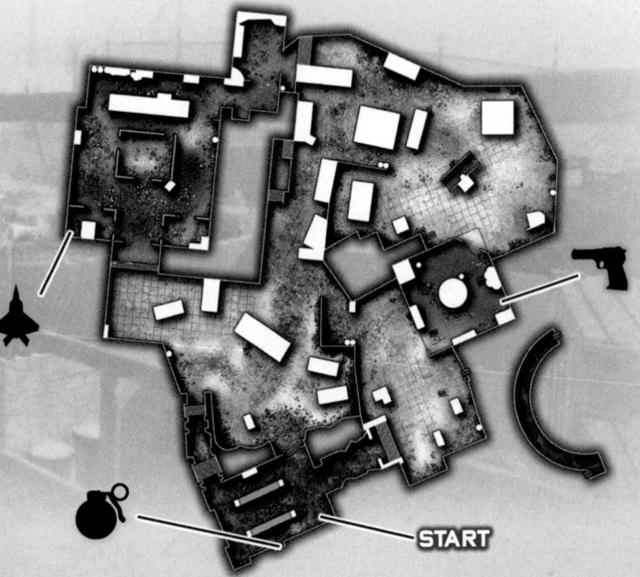

MISSION

DIFFICULTY:	REGULAR
UNLOCKED AT LEVEL:	8
ENEMIES:	BOMB SQUADS, CHEMICAL WARFARE, CHOPPERS, AND RIOT SHIELD JUGGERNAUTS.

INITIAL LOADOUT

USP .45

2 FLASHBANGS

2 FRAG GRENADES

SELF REVIVE

250 ARMOR

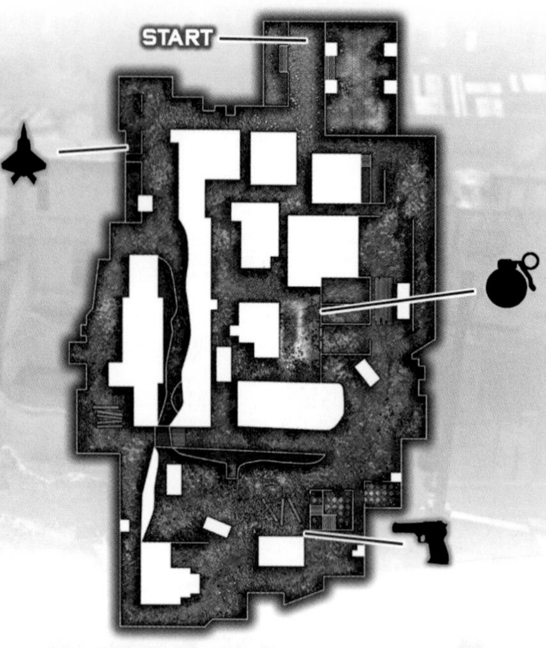

SEATOWN

DIFFICULTY:	REGULAR
UNLOCKED AT LEVEL:	8
ENEMIES:	BOMB SQUADS, CHEMICAL WARFARE, CHOPPERS, AND RIOT SHIELD JUGGERNAUTS.

INITIAL LOADOUT

USP .45

2 FLASHBANGS

2 FRAG GRENADES

SELF REVIVE

250 ARMOR

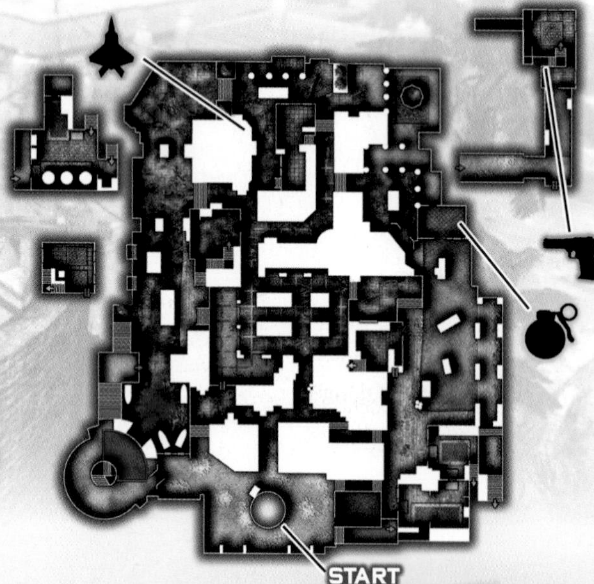

CARBON

DIFFICULTY:	REGULAR
UNLOCKED AT LEVEL:	8
ENEMIES:	BOMB SQUADS, CHEMICAL WARFARE, CHOPPERS, AND RIOT SHIELD JUGGERNAUTS.

INITIAL LOADOUT

USP .45

2 FLASHBANGS

2 FRAG GRENADES

SELF REVIVE

250 ARMOR

BOOTLEG

DIFFICULTY:	HARD
UNLOCKED AT LEVEL:	15
ENEMIES:	BOMB SQUADS, CLAYMORE EXPERTS, CHOPPERS, AND RIOT SHIELD JUGGERNAUTS.

INITIAL LOADOUT

MP412

2 FLASHBANGS

SELF REVIVE

250 ARMOR

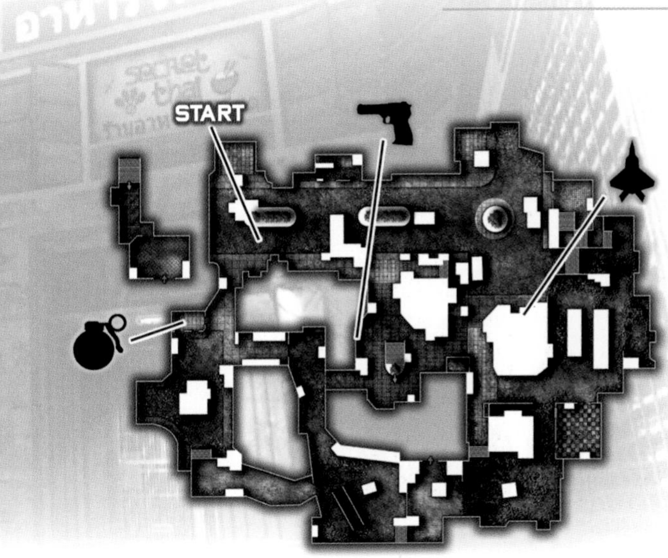

HARDHAT

DIFFICULTY:	HARD
UNLOCKED AT LEVEL:	15
ENEMIES:	BOMB SQUADS, CLAYMORE EXPERTS, CHOPPERS, AND RIOT SHIELD JUGGERNAUTS.

INITIAL LOADOUT

MP412

2 FLASHBANGS

SELF REVIVE

250 ARMOR

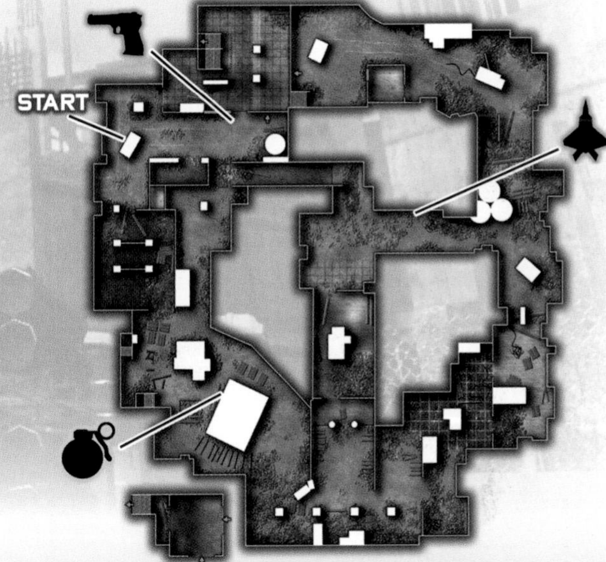

FALLEN

DIFFICULTY:	HARD
UNLOCKED AT LEVEL:	15
ENEMIES:	BOMB SQUADS, CLAYMORE EXPERTS, CHOPPERS, AND RIOT SHIELD JUGGERNAUTS.

INITIAL LOADOUT

MP412

2 FLASHBANGS

SELF REVIVE

250 ARMOR

OUTPOST

DIFFICULTY:	HARD
UNLOCKED AT LEVEL:	15
ENEMIES:	BOMB SQUADS, CLAYMORE EXPERTS, CHOPPERS, AND RIOT SHIELD JUGGERNAUTS.

INITIAL LOADOUT

MP412

2

2 FLASHBANGS

SELF REVIVE

250 ARMOR

LOCKDOWN

DIFFICULTY:	INSANE
UNLOCKED AT LEVEL:	25
ENEMIES:	BOMB SQUADS, CHEMICAL WARFARE, CLAYMORE EXPERTS, CHOPPERS, AND ARMORED JUGGERNAUTS.

INITIAL LOADOUT

M16A4 W/RED DOT SIGHT

SELF REVIVE

250 ARMOR

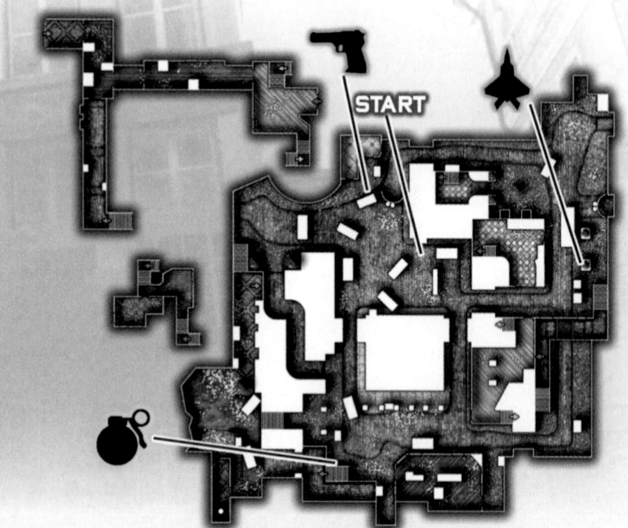

ARKADEN

DIFFICULTY:	INSANE
UNLOCKED AT LEVEL:	25
ENEMIES:	BOMB SQUADS, CHEMICAL WARFARE, CLAYMORE EXPERTS, CHOPPERS, AND ARMORED JUGGERNAUTS.

INITIAL LOADOUT

M16A4 W/RED DOT SIGHT

SELF REVIVE

250 ARMOR

DOWNTURN

DIFFICULTY:	INSANE
UNLOCKED AT LEVEL:	25
ENEMIES:	BOMB SQUADS, CHEMICAL WARFARE, CLAYMORE EXPERTS, CHOPPERS, AND ARMORED JUGGERNAUTS.

INITIAL LOADOUT

M16A4 W/RED DOT SIGHT

SELF REVIVE

250 ARMOR

BAKAARA

DIFFICULTY:	INSANE
UNLOCKED AT LEVEL:	25
ENEMIES:	BOMB SQUADS, CHEMICAL WARFARE, CLAYMORE EXPERTS, CHOPPERS, AND ARMORED JUGGERNAUTS.

INITIAL LOADOUT

M16A4 W/RED DOT SIGHT

SELF REVIVE

250 ARMOR

SPECIAL OPS MISSIONS

The Global Special Operations give you an opportunity to play alongside another player in short missions. Nearly all of these missions take place in locations you see in the campaign. Four are already unlocked, and you access the rest as you level up in Special Ops.

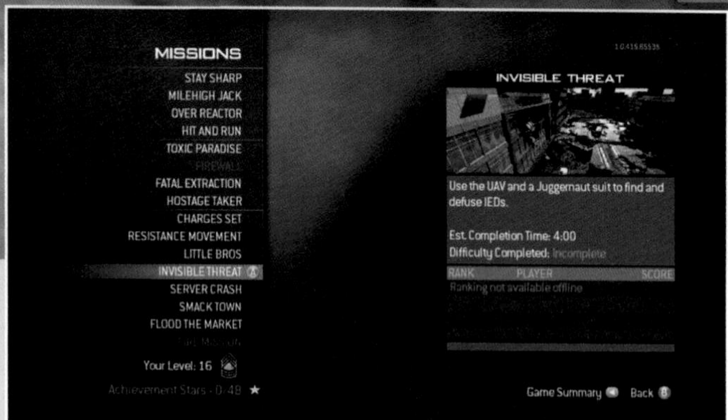

Each mission has a primary objective, and most have secondary objectives within them. You must achieve the former to complete the mission, but optional objectives boost your score if you achieve them.

MISSION SUCCESS!

		Points
Difficulty	Regular	10000
Time	5:54.0	3916
Kills	66	1650
Turrets Active	2	350
Hyena Knife Kills	7	525
Score		16441

Play Again Ⓨ Return to Special OPS Ⓑ

Besides the two obstacle course missions, your score is always based on the difficulty, your completion time, and the number of kills. On top of that, bonus factors also affect your score, such as accuracy, specific types of kills, and rescuing hostages.

After you complete a mission, you are given 1 to 3 stars depending on your performance. In the two obstacle course missions, this is totally dependent on time. For the rest of the missions, it depends on difficulty: one star for Regular difficulty, two for Hardened, and three for Veteran.

ACHIEVEMENT/TROPHY

OVERACHIEVER

Earn 48 stars (3 per mission) in Special Ops Mission Mode.

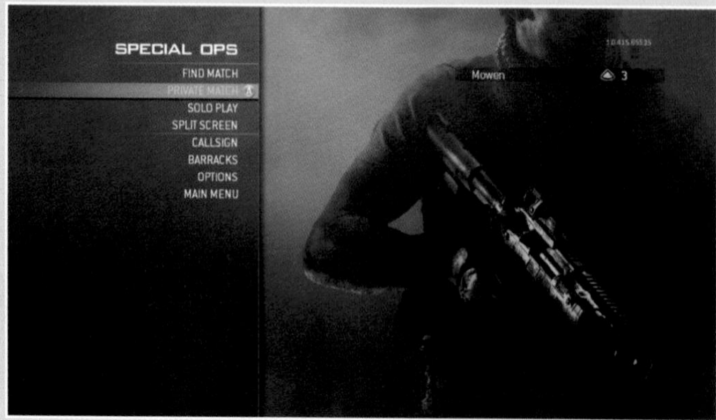

You can play these mini-missions solo (except for two), two-player split-screen, or online with another player.

In the case of two players, if one player is downed (but not out) or bleeding out, the second player can revive him. When you're downed, you can still use your handgun as a timer counts down from 1:30. Taking down an enemy during this period gets you on your feet immediately. Otherwise, you must wait for your partner. The other player receives a message of "Teammate Down," along with a timer. Approach the downed player and hold the Use button until he recovers.

MISSION 1 STAY SHARP

UNLOCKED AT LEVEL	ALREADY UNLOCKED
EST. COMPLETION TIME	0:45
LOCATION	SHOOTING RANGE/ OBSTACLE COURSE

OBJECTIVE

TEST YOUR SKILLS ON THE OBSTACLE COURSE.

MISSION SCORE

- COURSE TIME
- ENEMIES HIT
- CIVILIANS HIT

INITIAL LOADOUT

ACR 6.8

USP .45

OBJECTIVE

TAKE OUT ALL OF THE ENEMY TARGETS, AND DO IT FAST

The first mission tests your weapon skills on an obstacle course. A nearby table provides a selection of handguns and automatic weapons. If you're comfortable with the assault rifles, grab the M16A4, M4A1, or AK-47 off the table to replace your handgun. Your completion time determines how many stars you earn. Finish within 28 seconds for 3 stars, 40 seconds for 2 stars, and simply finish for 1 star.

From the start, the left route takes you to a shooting range, but you want to go to the right to start the course. The clock starts once you or your partner crosses the white line, so make sure you're ready.

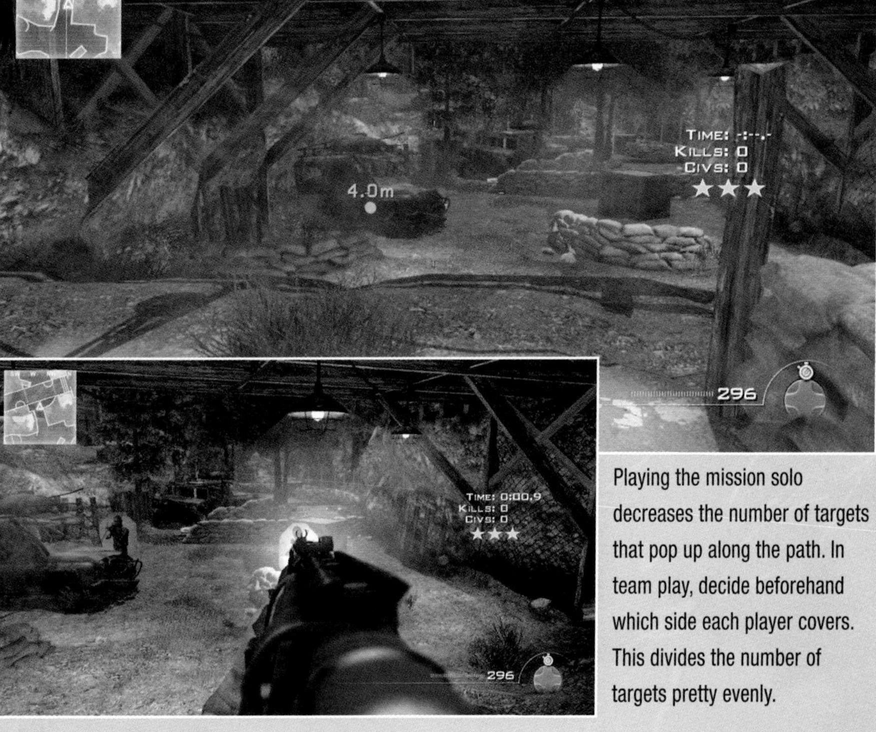

Playing the mission solo decreases the number of targets that pop up along the path. In team play, decide beforehand which side each player covers. This divides the number of targets pretty evenly.

A few civilian targets are thrown in, so be careful. If you hit a civilian, a star is immediately taken away and points are deducted from your score.

Once a set of targets is downed, sprint to the next spot. Move quickly through the first building, but stay alert for an enemy that pops out. Quickly knife him as you speed through. At the home stretch, two moving dog targets join the mix.

Pass through the final door and shoot the enemies surrounding Sandman, who stands behind the desk. Be careful, because a civilian stands on the left. With two players, try switching sides. Have the right-hand player shoot to the left and vice versa—every second counts.

MISSION 2
MILEHIGH JACK

UNLOCKED AT LEVEL	ALREADY UNLOCKED
EST. COMPLETION TIME	2:30
LOCATION	RUSSIAN PRESIDENT'S AIRPLANE, IL-96-300PU—"COMMAND POINT"

OBJECTIVE

CAPTURE PRESIDENT VORSCHEVSKY FOR MAKAROV BY HIJACKING HIS PLANE.

MISSION SCORE

- DIFFICULTY
- TIME
- KILLS
- ACCURACY
- DAMAGE TAKEN

INITIAL LOADOUT

- AK-47 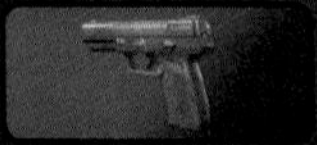
- FIVE SEVEN 
- 4 FLASHBANGS

OBJECTIVE

FIND THE PRESIDENT TO TAKE HIM HOSTAGE

For Milehigh Jack, you assume the role of the hijackers from the Turbulence mission in the campaign. This mission starts on the lower level as you breach the cargo area.

You have 2:25 in team play and 3:30 in solo to capture the president. Push to the bathrooms and toss a Flashbang into the lobby ahead. This gives you a little extra time while your adversaries are stunned.

After you take down the guy at the top of the steps, throw another Flashbang upstairs and then move up. Have the front player crouch down at the top of the steps so the second player can shoot over the top.

OBJECTIVE

CAPTURE THE PRESIDENT

Fight your way to the meeting room door and get ready to breach. A lone guard is in the far right corner, and the rest are congregated in the back left. Have the player on the left eliminate the foe on the right and then join his partner in assaulting the group.

Be careful not to shoot the president, who is crouched behind the table. Anyone else is fair game. Once the room is clear, move in and capture the head honcho.

MISSION 3
OVER REACTOR

UNLOCKED AT LEVEL	ALREADY UNLOCKED
EST. COMPLETION TIME	6:00
LOCATION	SUBMARINE, NEW YORK HARBOR

OBJECTIVE

STOP THE RUSSIAN SUBMARINE FROM HAVING A NUCLEAR MELTDOWN.

MISSION SCORE

- DIFFICULTY
- TIME
- KILLS
- SMOKE KILLS

INITIAL LOADOUT

- AA-12 SHOTGUN
- MP7 
- 4 FLASHBANGS 
- 4 GRENADES 

START

VALVE

EXIT

OBJECTIVE

INFILTRATE THE RUSSIAN SUB

The Russians have rigged a sub in New York Harbor for a nuclear meltdown, and you are dropped on board to avert the catastrophe. Two soldiers emerge from the smokescreen ahead. Try to take them down before they come out.

TACTICS

SMOKE KILLS

There's an added incentive to take down the Russians in the smoke. Each kill in the smoke adds points to your score. Another opportunity arises at the end of this mission, too.

OBJECTIVE

GET TO THE NUCLEAR REACTOR

Disarm the thermite attached to the hatch and then climb in. A five-minute timer starts counting down to the point of meltdown. You must reach the reactor before the timer hits zero.

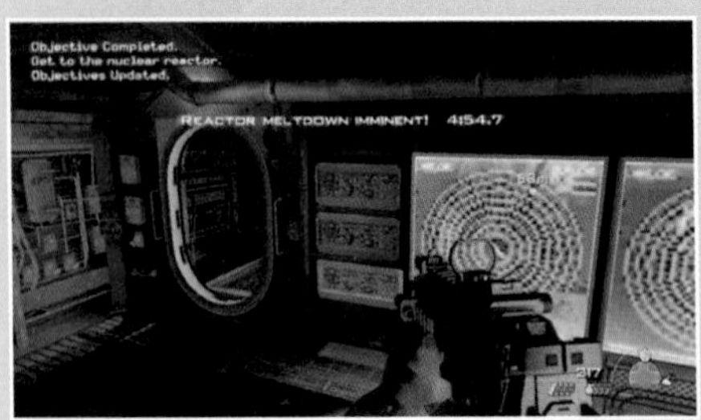

Turn on your night vision as you fight your way through the first compartment. This makes the enemies easier to spot.

With two players, one should go up and the other should go down. This makes reviving more difficult, since you have to run up or down the stairs to reach your partner, but it allows you to watch each other's back easily.

Meet up below and then split up, one left and the other right. Push into the reactor room and have one player use the valve to shut down the reactor. The other player should keep watch out in the hallway.

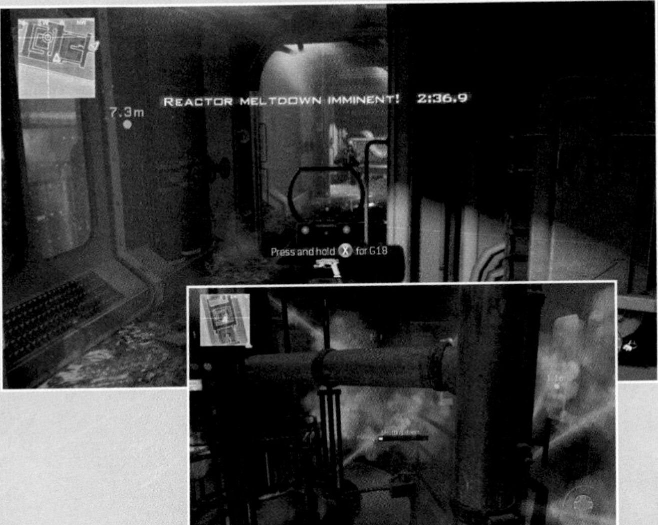

OBJECTIVE

FIND A WAY OFF THE SUB

Continue up the steps and through the bunkroom. Climb up the ladder to exit the sub.

OBJECTIVE

GET TO THE EXTRACTION POINT

Use the crates for cover as more Russians are dropped on top of the submarine. Once you eliminate that group, split up and move toward the extraction point.

The enemy troops put up a smokescreen, so use your thermal goggles to see them coming. Fight your way through to the helicopter.

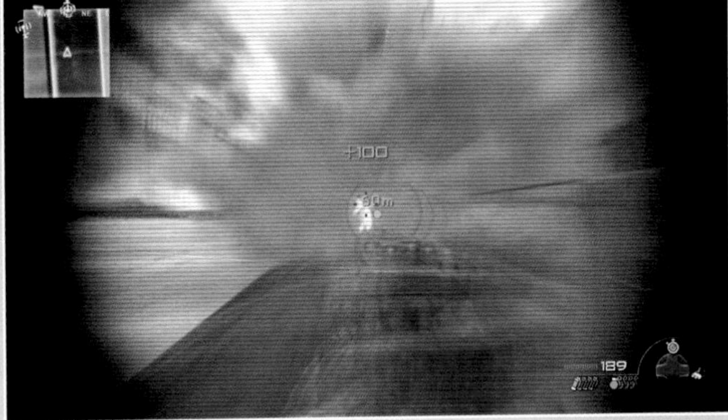

MISSION 4
HIT AND RUN

UNLOCKED AT LEVEL	ALREADY UNLOCKED
EST. COMPLETION TIME	4:30
LOCATION	BOOSAASO, SOMALIA

OBJECTIVE

LOCAL STRONGMEN ARE HOLDING OUR EMBASSY STAFF FOR RANSOM. WE DON'T NEGOTIATE WITH TERRORISTS.

MISSION SCORE

- DIFFICULTY
- TIME
- KILLS
- TIME TO KILL HELICOPTER

INITIAL LOADOUT

- MP5
- DRAGUNOV
- 4 FLASHBANGS
- 4 GRENADES

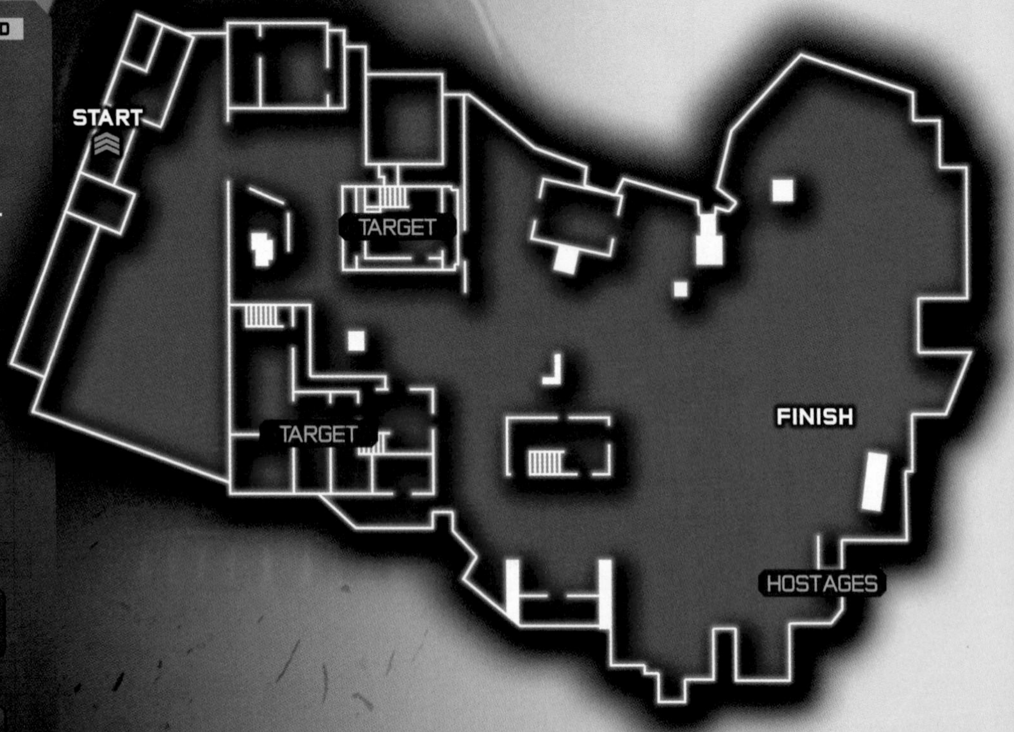

START

TARGET

TARGET

FINISH

HOSTAGES

OBJECTIVE

ELIMINATE COLONEL FARHAN. ELIMINATE CAPTAIN MAHAD

Your first objective is to take out two local strongmen, Colonel Farhan and Captain Mahad, who are holding the embassy staff as hostages. You start on a balcony on the area's west side. One target is held up in the building to the east with the Somali flag. The other is in the L-shaped building southeast of your position. The hostages are in a shipping container at the far docks.

Eliminate Colonel Farhan
Eliminate Captain Mahad
Objectives Updated.
46m
51m

Start by sniping the two RPG users on the roof ahead. Continue to thin out the enemy forces from the balcony until two Little Birds approach from the east.

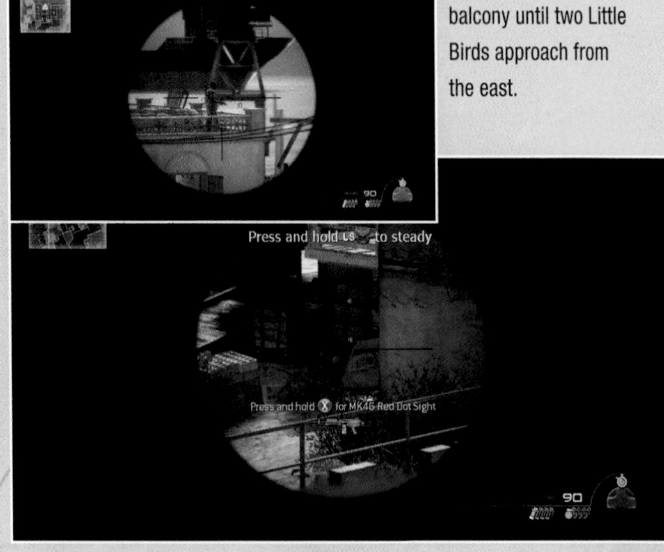

Press and hold LS to steady
Press and hold X for MK46 Red Dot Sight

One player should grab the Stinger, and the other can use the PKP Pecheneg to rip through the choppers as quickly as possible. The faster you dispose of them, the higher your "Time to Kill Heli" score bonus.

Get off the balcony and head for your targets. It's easier to move through the buildings as a team. To speed things up, send one player to the right building and the other to the left.

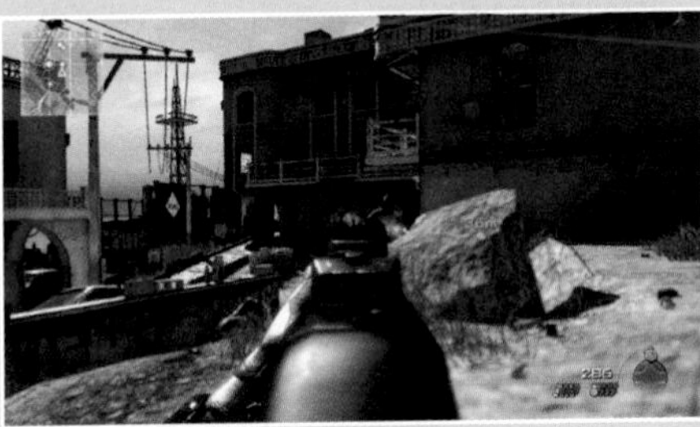

TACTICS

DON'T PUT HOSTAGES IN HARM'S WAY

Be careful when you shoot near the hostages. If you shoot the container they are in, the mission fails immediately. Have the player who moves up the left side take out anyone in front of the box.

OBJECTIVE

SIGNAL THE RESCUE CHOPPERS WITH A SMOKE GRENADE

Move in and free the hostages. Grab a PKP Pecheneg light machine gun off the ground first and make sure it's loaded. Now you must throw the Smoke Grenade to signal your location.

OBJECTIVE

RESCUE THE HOSTAGES

Once both targets are down, meet up back on the north side. Have the player with the sniper rifle climb the small northeast building and take out the guys around the storage containers. The other player can then move up the left side and get a flanking position.

OBJECTIVE

DEFEND THE AREA UNTIL EXFIL ARRIVES

A horde of Somali fighters enters from the north—mow them down with your machine gun. Fight them off as another chopper approaches from the east. Defend the area until the 1:30 timer reaches zero and the friendly helicopter arrives.

TACTICS

STRIKE!

As your helicopter arrives, the enemy retreats. This is a great opportunity to earn the Strike! Achievement/Trophy. Toss a Frag Grenade into the group before you board your ride.

MISSION 5
TOXIC PARADISE

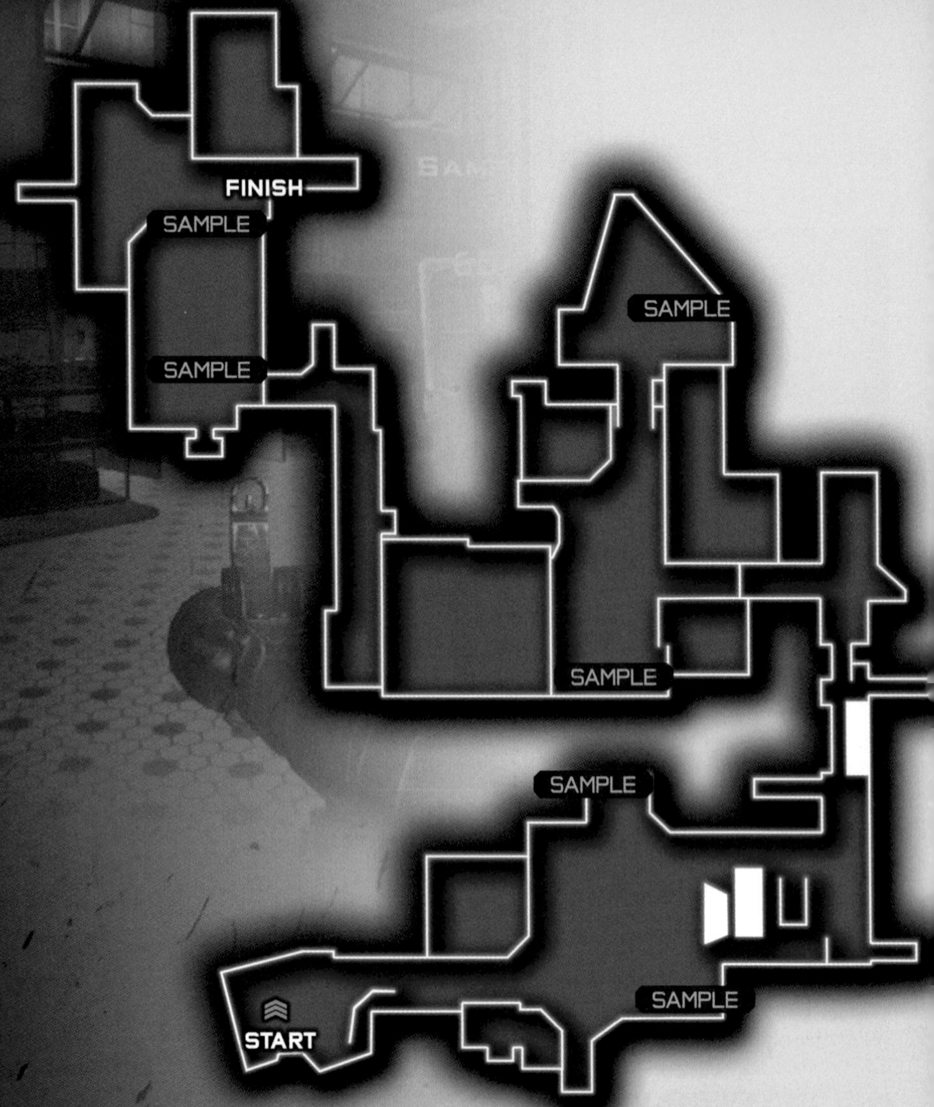

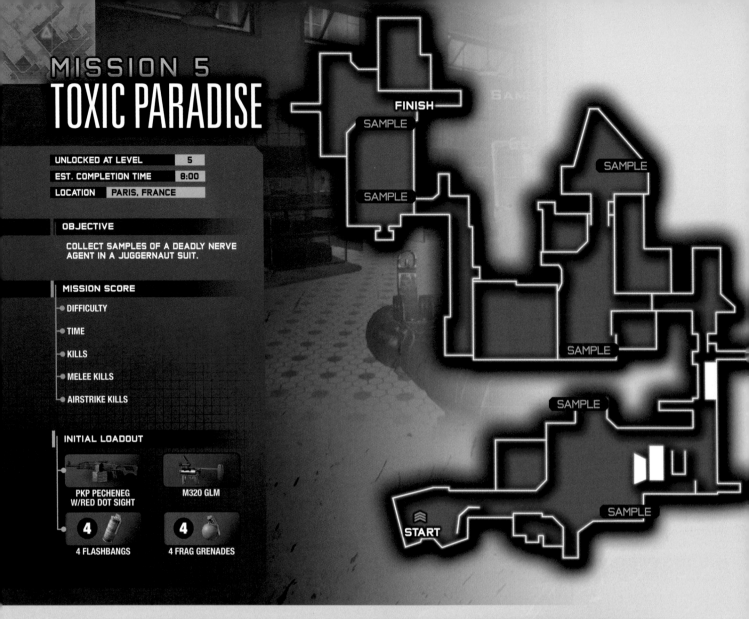

UNLOCKED AT LEVEL	5
EST. COMPLETION TIME	8:00
LOCATION	PARIS, FRANCE

OBJECTIVE

COLLECT SAMPLES OF A DEADLY NERVE AGENT IN A JUGGERNAUT SUIT.

MISSION SCORE

- DIFFICULTY
- TIME
- KILLS
- MELEE KILLS
- AIRSTRIKE KILLS

INITIAL LOADOUT

- PKP PECHENEG W/RED DOT SIGHT
- M320 GLM 
- 4 FLASHBANGS 
- 4 FRAG GRENADES 

OBJECTIVE

COLLECT 1ST AND 2ND CHEMICAL SAMPLES

The chemical attack is over, but there is still a need for proof of contamination. You must retrieve chemical samples from six spots. Both players are equipped in a Juggernaut armor suit to endure that extra damage. Each player also has an air support marker. Use this to clear out a big group of enemies. A few minutes after one run, the airplane will be ready for another.

Split up down the road. One player should cut through the pub on the left, and the other move through the shops on the right. Any time you enter a large, open area, cross your fire and watch over the other player's blind spots.

Once an area is clear, the left player should move up and collect the first sample. Then he can protect player two as he grabs the second.

OBJECTIVE

COLLECT 3RD CHEMICAL SAMPLE

Watch out for airstrikes behind the newsstand. You know they're coming by the red smoke. As you climb the stairs, toss your air strike marker onto the landing to eliminate the threat above. Refill your ammo at the ammo crates on the right side.

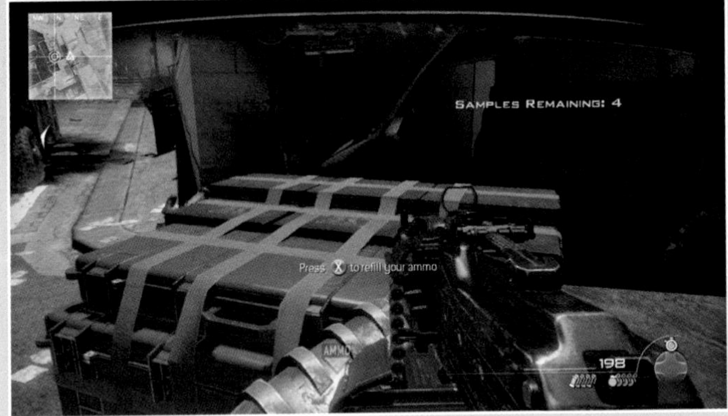

Climb the ladder into the burning building, and clear it out as you move north toward the next sample. One player provides overwatch as the other collects the sample. Remember that you can still look around while you do this, so rotate toward the stairs to watch your flank.

OBJECTIVE

COLLECT 4TH CHEMICAL SAMPLE

Toss a couple of air support markers into the area below to clear it out a little. The fourth sample sits on the far side behind the newsstand. One player should pick up a dropped RPG-7 before you proceed.

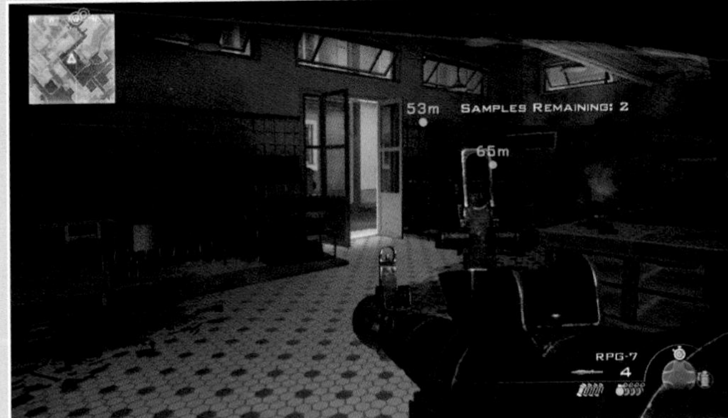

OBJECTIVE

COLLECT 5TH CHEMICAL SAMPLE

Another weapon crate is in the back of the restaurant, so fill up. Just outside, a Juggernaut marches down the alley, accompanied by a soldier. Toss a Smoke Grenade out the door and hightail it back into the eatery.

Back your way through the building as you launch rockets and grenades into the armored enemy. Once you defeat it, trade out the RPG for an automatic weapon, and run down the alley.

At the other end, you enter the bookstore. Climb the stairs to find the fifth sample near the edge of the balcony.

OBJECTIVE

COLLECT 6TH CHEMICAL SAMPLE

The final sample sits in between the two exits on the other side of the shop. After you collect it, call in an airstrike outside the left door, and then run into the next building.

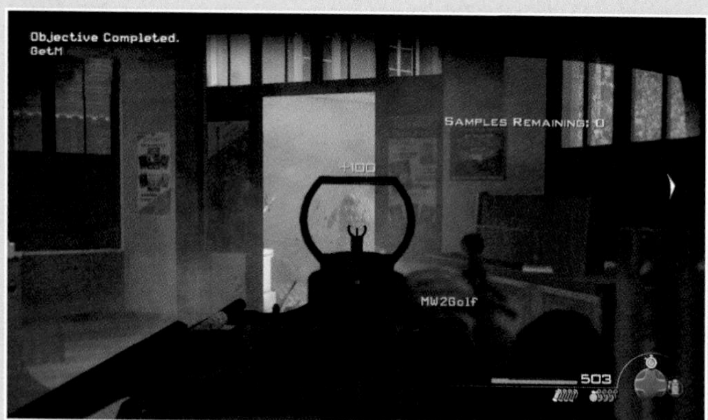

OBJECTIVE

GET TO EXTRACT LZ

Toss a grenade through the opening in the wall. When the first floor is clear, run up the stairs and fight your way to the extraction point.

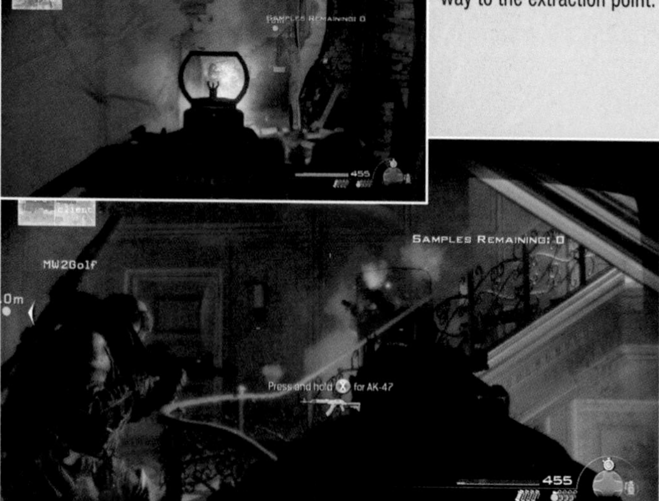

MISSION 6
FIREWALL

UNLOCKED AT LEVEL	5
EST. COMPLETION TIME	4:00
LOCATION	CANARY WHARF, LONDON

OBJECTIVE

HACK INTO ENEMY SECURITY SENTRIES AND REACH THE SUBWAY IN TIME.

MISSION SCORE

- DIFFICULTY
- TIME
- KILLS

INITIAL LOADOUT

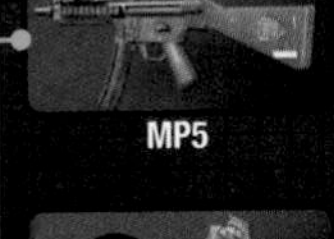

MP5

USP .45 TACTICAL SUPPRESSED

4 FLASHBANGS

4 FRAG GRENADES

NIGHT VISION GOGGLES

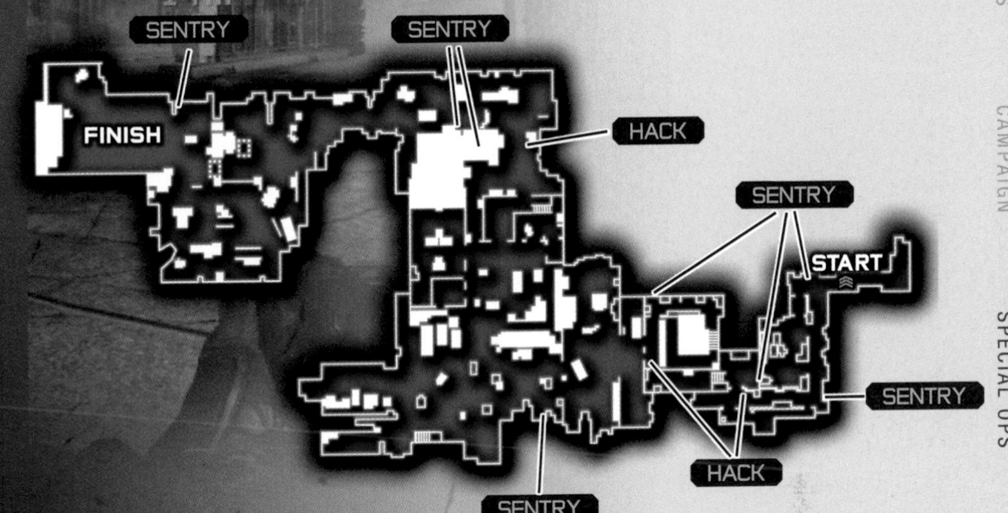

OBJECTIVE

GET TO THE EXTRACTION POINT. HACK DEFENSE SYSTEM ALONG THE WAY

This mission is accessible only with two players. The first player must reach the extraction point within four minutes, hacking the defense system along the way. The other player has control of the sentry camera system, which gives him access to several sentry guns.

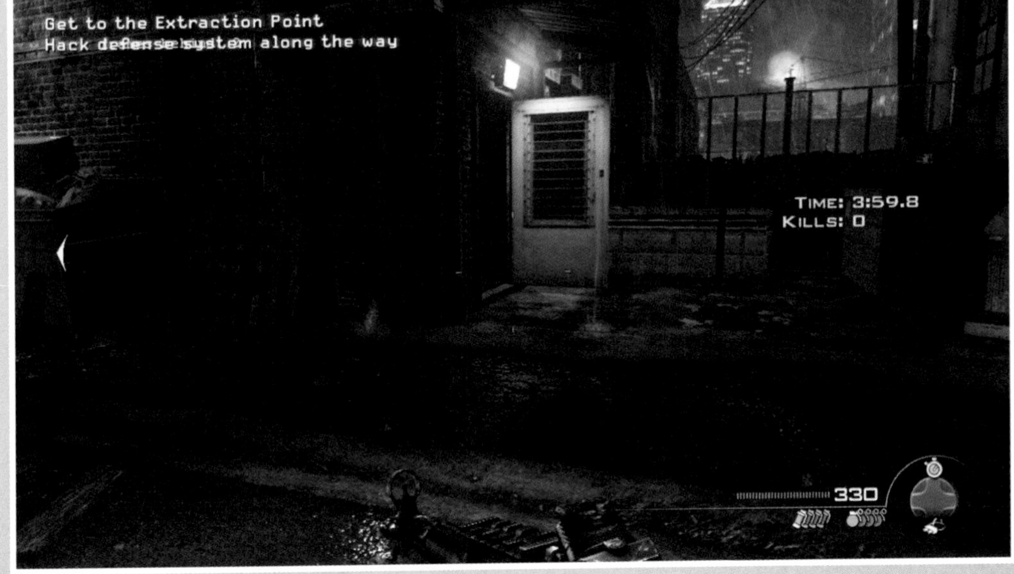

HACK DEFENSE SYSTEM 1

The first player's path is the same one you use in the beginning of the "Mind the Gap" mission to reach the subway. The other player uses the sentries to protect him. Although the first player is the one putting his life on the line, the second player enjoys a much higher kill count.

Through the beginning alleys, duck inside the buildings while the sentry clears out the path. At the doors to the warehouse, hack the computer to gain access.

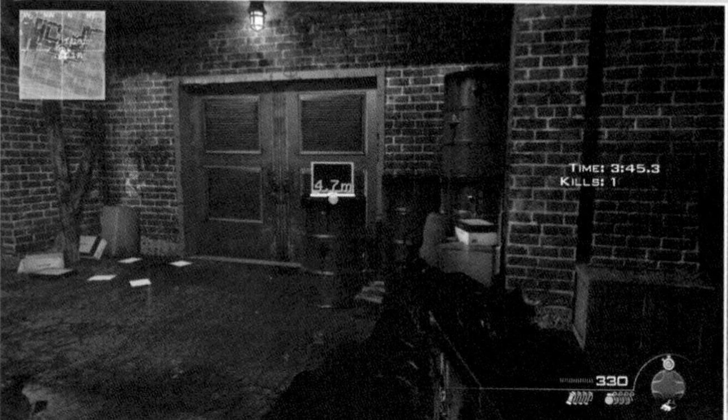

HACK DEFENSE SYSTEM 2

Let the turrets clear out the inside as you climb to the top floor. After the first player runs past the windows on the second floor, the turret should look to the right as more enemies approach from behind.

The next floor is not visible to the camera system, so the first player is on his own. Take down the two foes there, and hack into the defense system at another laptop.

HACK DEFENSE SYSTEM 3

Burst through the window and slide into the dock yard. The second player has a wide area to look after here. Rotate to the left and take down the two choppers that drop off more guards.

Run through the gate toward your partner and then past the forklift on the right to find the third computer. Hack it and hop down to the street. A sentry camera on the street and another at the extraction point help you complete this mission.

MISSION 7
FATAL EXTRACTION

UNLOCKED AT LEVEL	5
EST. COMPLETION TIME	5:30
LOCATION	SIERRA LEONE, AFRICA

OBJECTIVE

INTERCEPT ENEMY INTEL TO LOCATE AND ELIMINATE THE HIGH-VALUE TARGET.

MISSION SCORE

- DIFFICULTY
- TIME
- KILLS
- TURRETS ACTIVE
- HYENA KNIFE KILLS

INITIAL LOADOUT

M4A1 W/HYBRID SIGHT

4 FLASHBANGS

4 SEMTEX

MORTAR

START

OBJECTIVE

INTERCEPT ENEMY INTEL

This mission starts in the Sierra Leone church where you ended a cargo search in the campaign. If you don't like your initial loadout, a nice selection of weapons lies on the floor for your consideration.

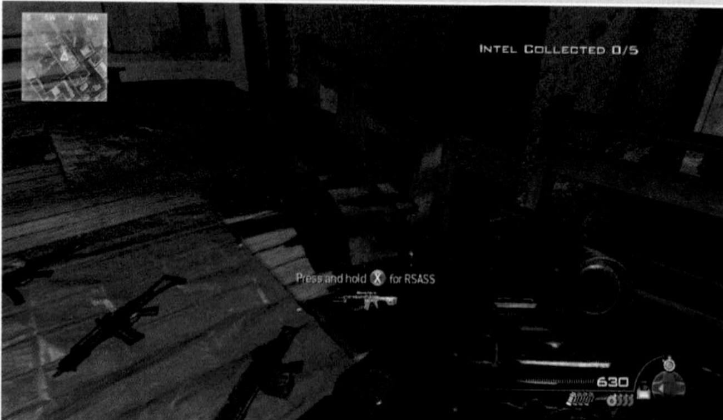

In an attempt to keep things low-key, the locals deliver paper communications by hand. Your first objective is to collect five pieces of this Intel. When you kill someone with the Intel, you hear that Intel has been dropped or is on the ground, and an objective marker appears at its location. Move to the Intel and hold the Use button to pick it up.

From the start, go after the enemies on the roof and balcony to the right. Watch out for sentry guns that are placed throughout the village. One sits just northwest of the church, and another sits on a patio to the east.

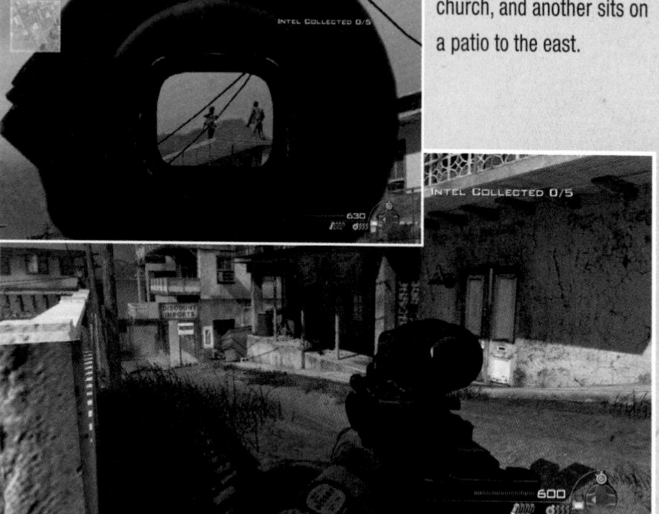

TACTICS

TURRETS ACTIVE

You can easily disable the turrets with gunfire or a swipe of the knife, if you can get to them without drawing their fire. However, you receive bonus points for each turret that remains active.

Watch out for hyenas as they attack you head-on. Knife them just before they reach you to score another bonus.

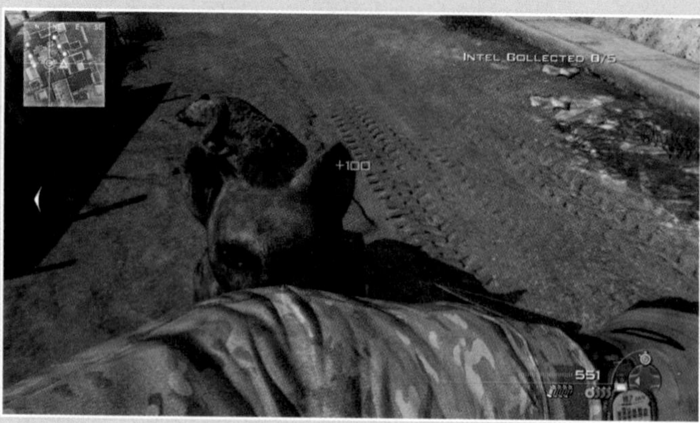

Fight your way to each dropped Intel, being extra cautious of enemies shooting from above. If Intel is dropped on the north balcony, use the stairs inside the pharmacy.

The final two pieces of Intel drop around the warehouse. Once you collect them, head east, cut through the pipe, and climb up to the platform.

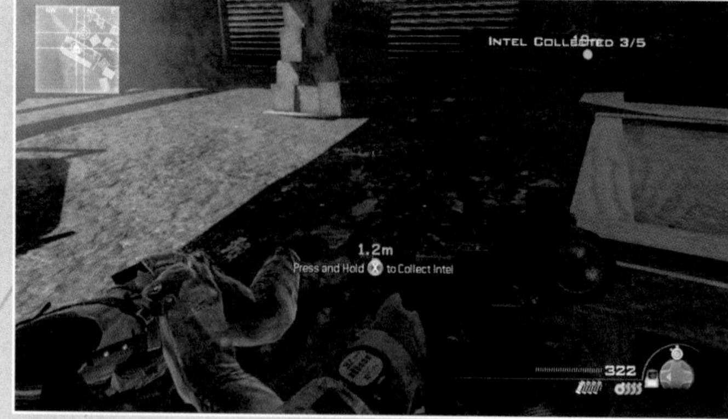

OBJECTIVE

LOCATE THE ENEMY SAFE HOUSE. PAINT THE SAFE HOUSE FOR AN AIR STRIKE

Defend that position until two safe houses are identified—or one if you're playing solo. Press Right on the D-pad to paint the target for air strike. Press the Fire button to confirm. The mission ends once the safe house or houses are destroyed.

MISSION 8

HOSTAGE TAKER

UNLOCKED AT LEVEL	5
EST. COMPLETION TIME	3:00
LOCATION	HAMBURG TARMAC

OBJECTIVE

USE STEALTH TO SAVE THE PRESIDENT'S DAUGHTER BEFORE MAKAROV'S MEN FIND HER.

MISSION SCORE

- DIFFICULTY
- TIME
- KILLS
- TIME SEEN
- HOSTAGES RESCUED

INITIAL LOADOUT

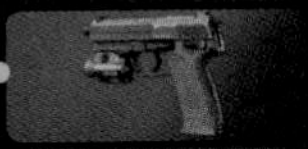

- USP .45 TACTICAL SUPPRESSED
- FRAG GRENADE 

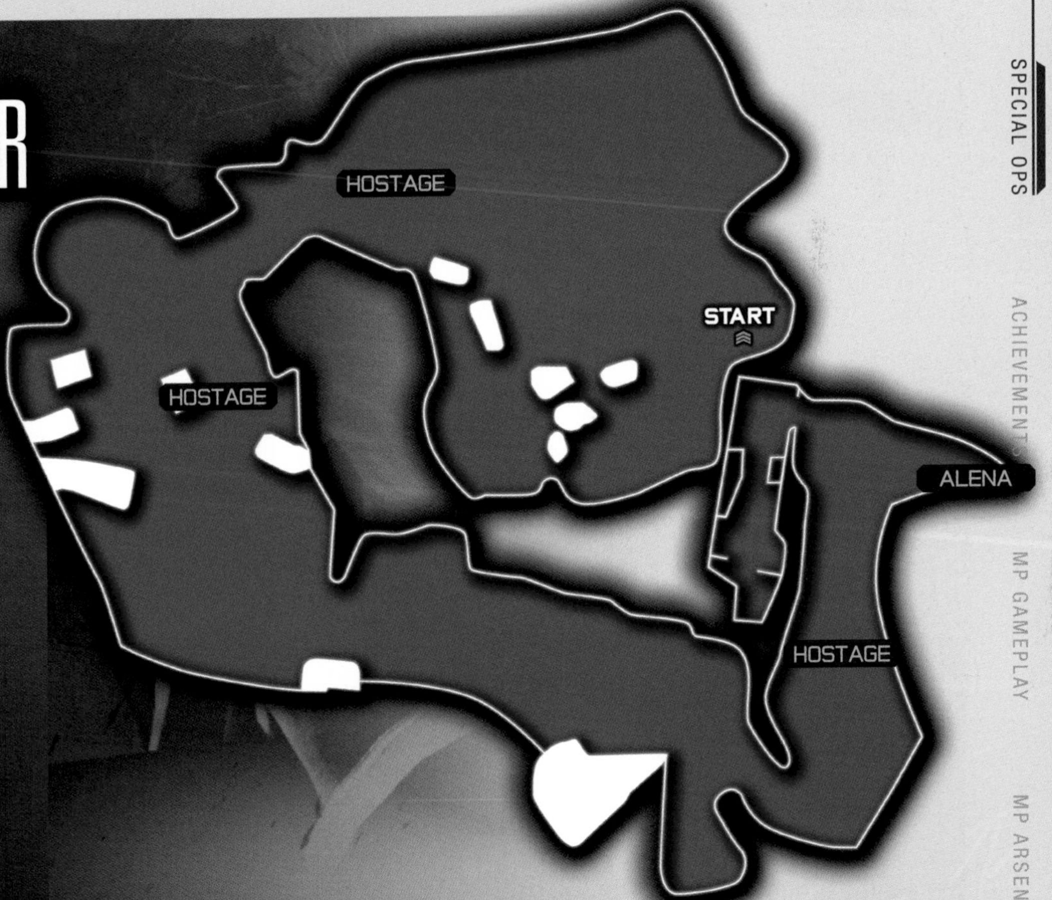

HOSTAGE
START
HOSTAGE
ALENA
HOSTAGE

OBJECTIVE

SECURE THE PRESIDENT'S DAUGHTER

Makarov's men search the plane wreckage for the president's daughter, and they take hostages along the way. Stealth is extremely important during this mission, as your adversaries will kill the hostages if they detect you coming. There are three hostages and, if they are killed, you only lose this bonus score. You can still complete the mission.

Move through the first area, taking out each enemy with your knife until you reach the first hostage. Use your suppressed handgun to take out the man standing over him. Then approach the hostage and hold the Use button to save him.

TACTICS

TIME SEEN

You receive a bonus based on the amount of time that the enemy sees you. In two-player, these times are separate. As long as the enemy is alerted to your position, the time tally increases and your bonus decreases.

OBJECTIVE

DISABLE THE HELICOPTER

Stay out of the helicopter's search light to avoid detection. If it sees you, the chopper can be disabled. Grab a dropped AK-74u and knock the 'copter out of the air. You can also take cover out of its light until it moves away. The mini-map displays the helicopter's location.

Continue moving stealthily between the vehicles, where another hostage is held. Take out the surrounding enemies, and then eliminate the hostage-taker.

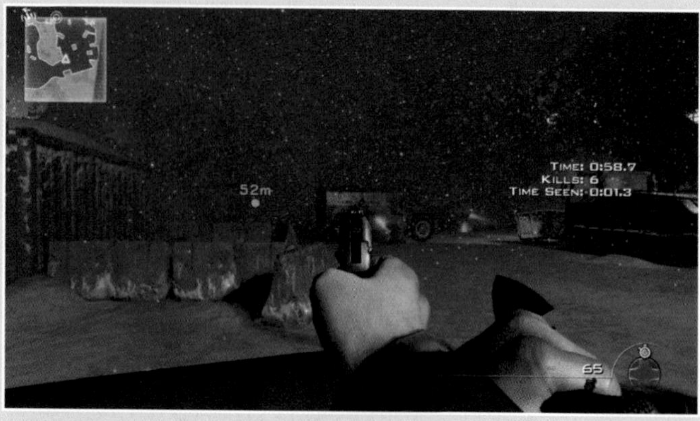

Continue along the tarmac, quietly taking out the enemies. The last hostage is held near the main wreckage.

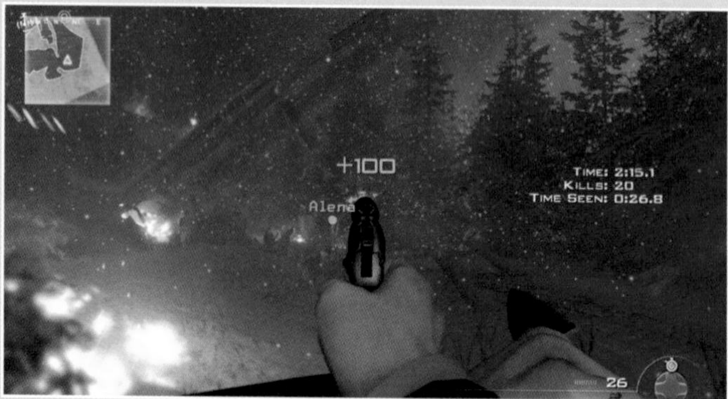

When you reach Alena's location, two of Makarov's men are there. If one of them is holding her, take down the other guy first. Then wait for an opening as Alena struggles with her captor. Take him down to complete the mission.

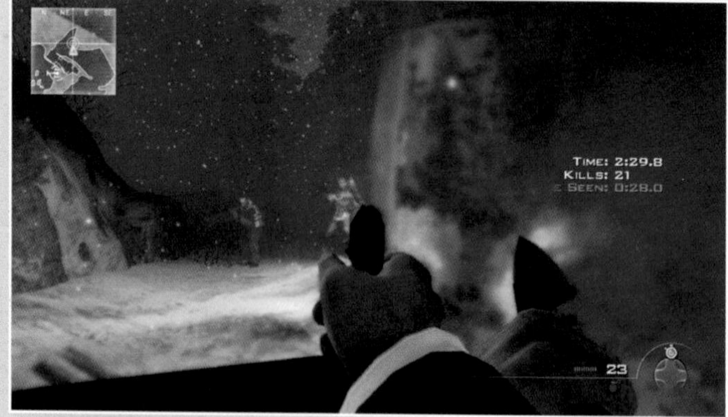

MISSION 9
CHARGES SET

UNLOCKED AT LEVEL	10
EST. COMPLETION TIME	0:45
LOCATION	SHOOTING RANGE/ OBSTACLE COURSE

OBJECTIVE

ANOTHER ROUND ON THE OBSTACLE COURSE WITH NEW WEAPONS, MORE TANGOS, AND EXPLOSIVE BREACHING.

MISSION SCORE

- COURSE TIME
- ENEMIES HIT
- CIVILIANS HIT

INITIAL LOADOUT

MP5

USP .45

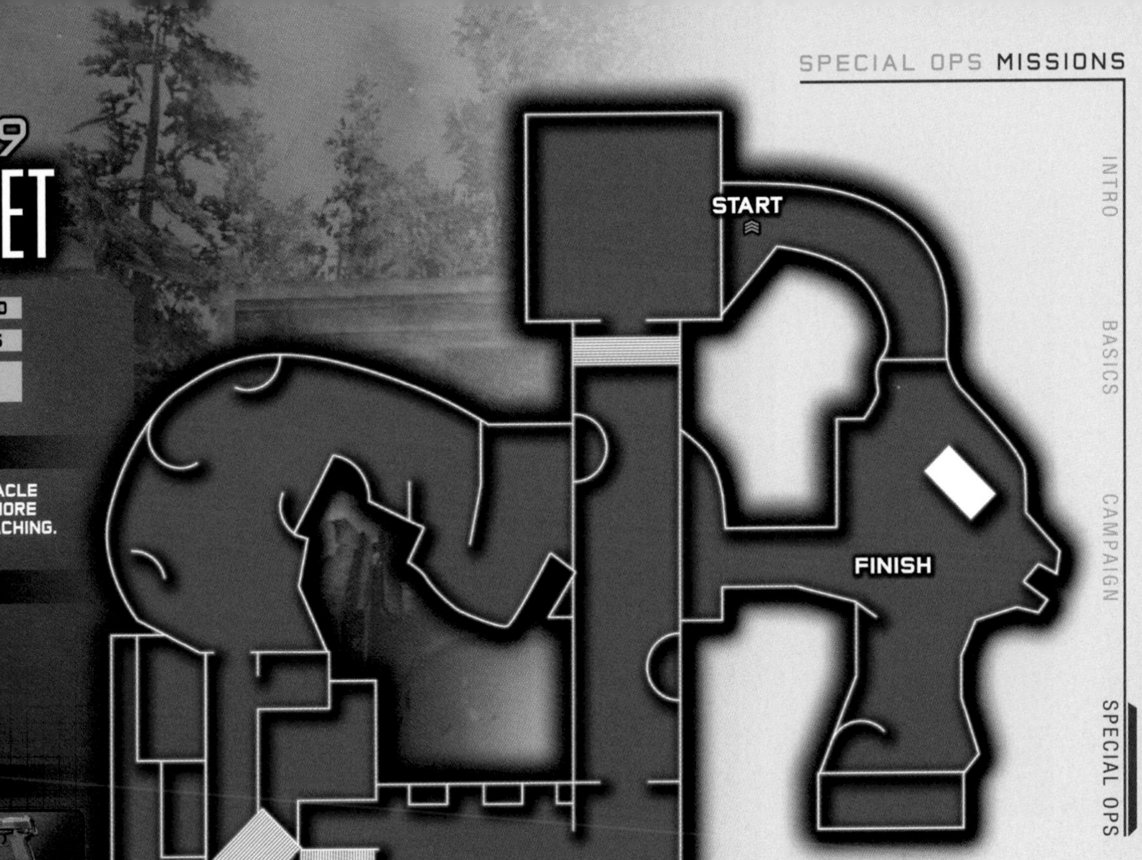

OBJECTIVE

USE EXPLOSIVES TO BREACH AND CLEAR ALL ENEMY TARGETS

Charges Set puts you back on the obstacle course from the first mission. This time, you run it in the opposite direction and breach through a couple doors. Complete it within 33 seconds for 3 stars, 45 seconds for 2 stars, and simply finish for 1 star.

As before, you can choose from several weapons on the folding table if you don't like the initial loadout.

Start by breaching the door. Have the left player take down the right targets, and vice versa. Watch out, as two civilians are inside.

When you're outside, have the left player take the left side and the right player take the right side, except for the two phases in which the targets appear above.

Then, divide the targets as high and low. This can save valuable seconds along the way.

Breach the second room and eliminate the targets the same way as before.

Run down the stairs and be ready for another target to pop out directly in front of you. Knife it along the way.

Quickly complete the rest of the course just as before, and sprint to the finish.

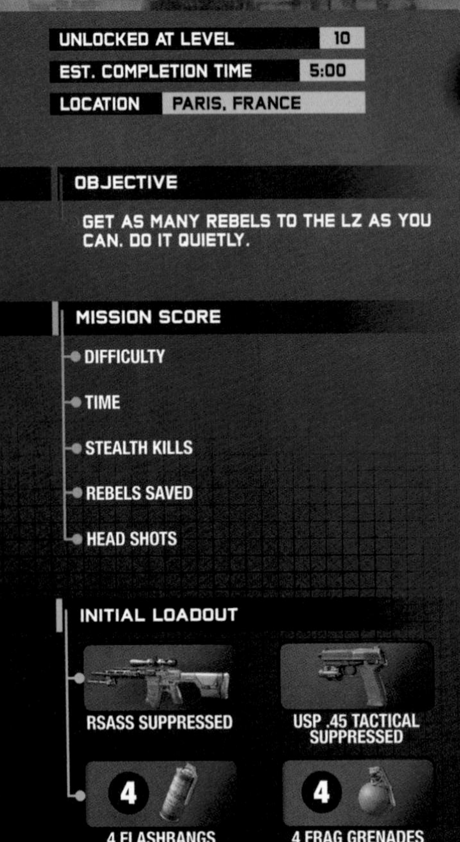

OBJECTIVE

COLLECT REBELS ON YOUR WAY TO THE EXTRACTION POINT

In order to repay the resistance for their help in the "Eye of the Storm" mission, you must get as many rebels to the landing zone as you can. Seven are held captive along the path ahead. If either player is detected, the captors will kill them.

If you miss when you shoot one of the soldiers, you have a short time to take him out before you're detected. This amount of time gets shorter with higher difficulties.

> **TACTICS**
>
> **REBELS SAVED**
>
> *Your primary objective is to get the rebels to the landing zone, but saving the rebels only adds points to your score. You can complete the mission without saving a single member of the resistance, though they did help the team reach the church tower.*

REBEL 1

From the start, have one player step outside to the right to get a better angle. The other player should remain at the opening. Two soldiers escort the first rebel just down the street—look for their lights. Coordinate which player takes each guard, and take them down. Watch out, as two more guards are nearby on the street.

Press and hold LS to steady

> **TACTICS**
>
> **STEALTH KILLS AND HEAD SHOTS**
>
> *Only stealth kills count toward your final score. If you are detected, taking down an enemy does not score anything. Eliminating the guards with head shots gives you another score boost.*

REBEL 2

Before you free the first rebel, step up to the gallery entrance on the right. Take down the two enemies inside, and rescue the rebel who hides behind the counter.

REBEL 3

Return to the street and free the first guy. As you approach the intersection, a dog and two guards chase the third rebel. Immediately take down the dog and then the two enemies to save him.

REBEL 4

Always watch out for the soldiers, and take them down from a distance. You usually find them in pairs. When the route turns to the left, watch out for two soldiers who exit the building to the east. Once you take care of them, look for another rebel hidden in the shadows to the south.

REBEL 5

Switch to your handgun as you cut through the apartment building. You can take down most of the soldiers inside with your knife. Use your suppressed USP .45 on the two that stand together.

REBEL 6

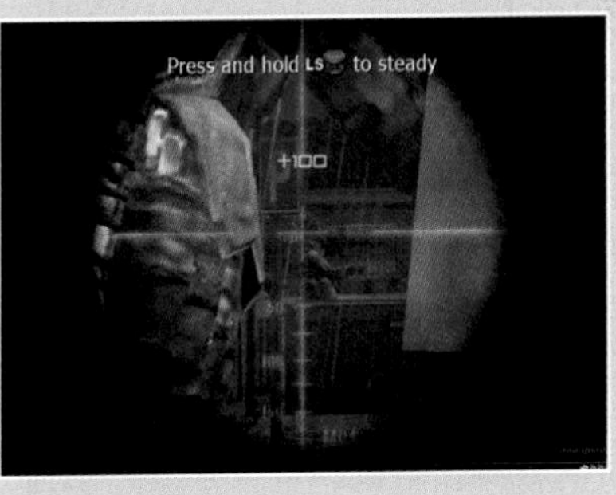
Press and hold LS to steady
+100

After you exit the building and dispatch the guys just outside, carefully approach the fountain. Eliminate the two soldiers to the right, and then the two who hold the next rebel on the left side.

REBEL 7

After you hop the fence and take care of the guards ahead, enter the building to the southeast. Another rebel is just inside to the right. The extraction point is just to the south, but you should still be careful. If you are detected, you will lose the rebels who follow. A dog and a few more guards stand between you and the truck.

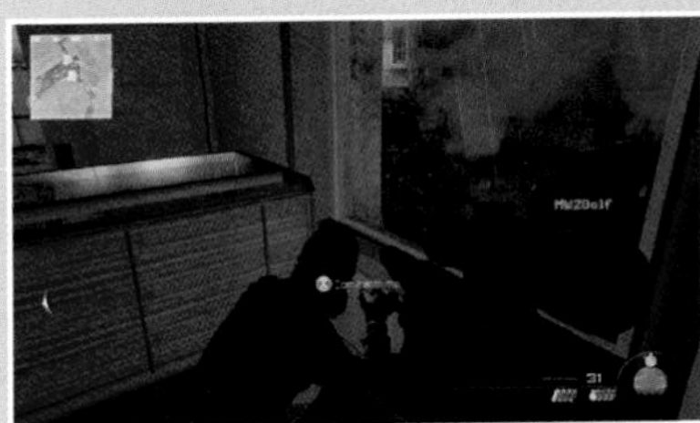

MISSION 11
LITTLE BROS

UNLOCKED AT LEVEL	10
EST. COMPLETION TIME	5:30
LOCATION	BERLIN, GERMANY

OBJECTIVE

DESTROY SENSITIVE DATA BEFORE THE RUSSIANS GET THEIR HANDS ON IT.

MISSION SCORE

- DIFFICULTY
- TIME
- KILLS
- KILLS RETREATING FROM PARKWAY
- ENEMIES KILLED WITH BOMB

INITIAL LOADOUT

- SCAR-L ACOG SIGHT
- MP5 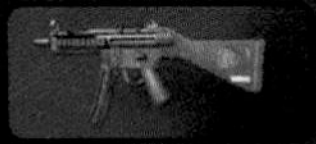 
- 4 FLASHBANGS 
- 4 FRAG GRENADES

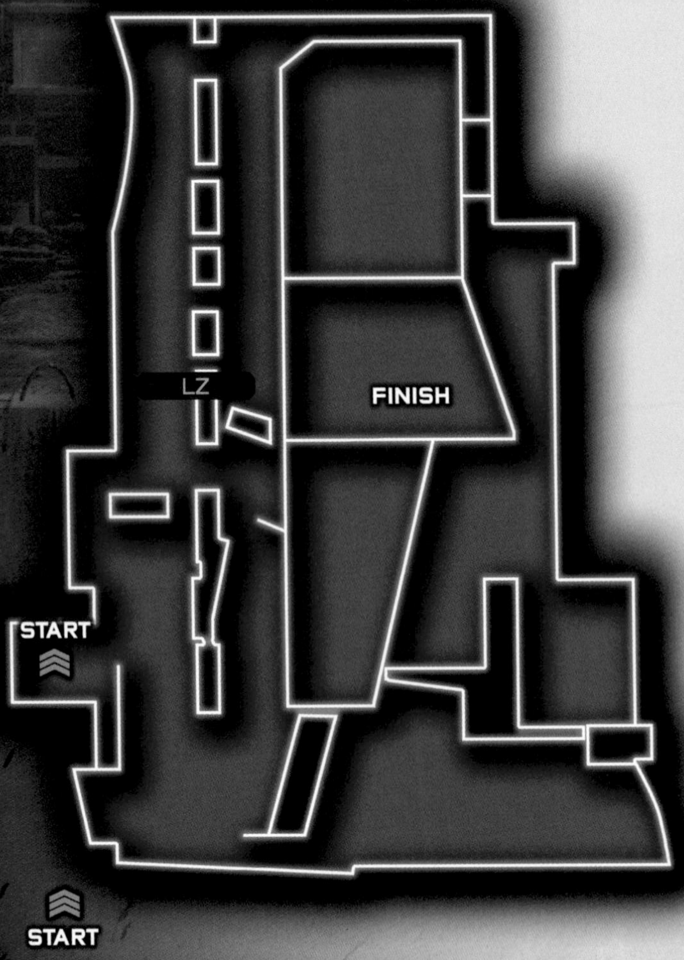

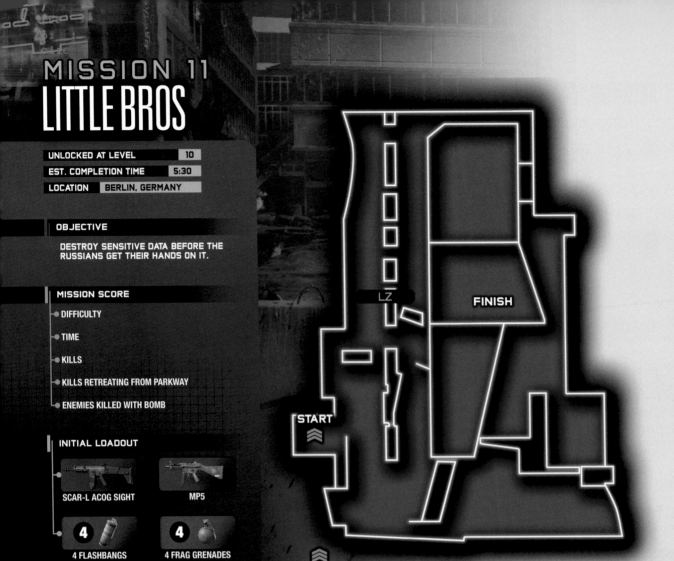

LZ

FINISH

START

START

OBJECTIVE

RENDEZVOUS WITH BRAVO TEAM

There are two distinct roles in Little Bros, but you can play this one in solo play. The first player starts on the street, and the second begins on a chopper.

The player on the street has 30 seconds until help arrives. Take cover on the street and eliminate the enemy soldiers as they arrive. The other player starts with a SMAW on the helicopter. Use it to destroy the three tanks on the bridge. Switch to your SCAR-L and help out your partner on the street. The helicopter does not land unless the area is free of enemies.

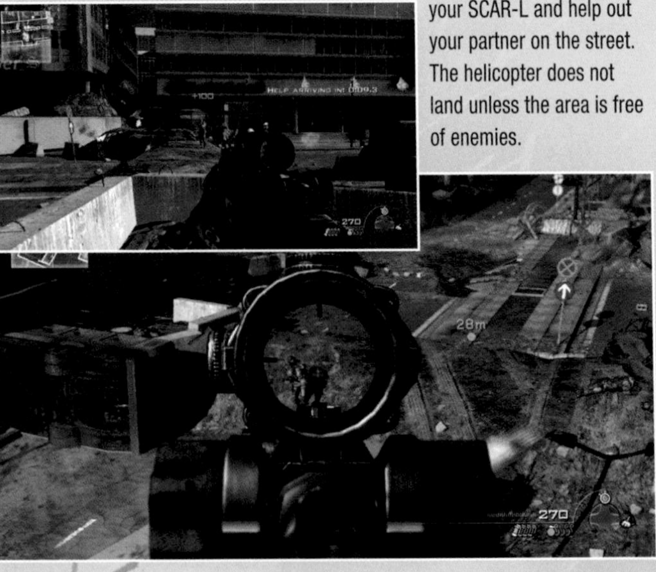

OBJECTIVE

INFILTRATE THE INTELLIGENCE BUILDING

Continue to fire at the soldiers on the street as the chopper carries both players to the roof. This time, player one stays on the aircraft to give support to player two, who gets out of the helicopter.

As the support, the helicopter moves you around the building so you almost always have a view of your teammate. Take out as many foes as you can. When the opposition puts up a smokescreen, turn on your thermal goggles to get a better view.

Fight your way to the stairwell and down into the office building. Continue around the perimeter, turning on your thermal goggles to spot the hostiles.

OBJECTIVE

FIND AND ARM THE BOMB

As you move down the ramp to the lower floor, your partner joins you. Make your way to the middle of the cubicles to find the bomb. Hold the Use button to arm it.

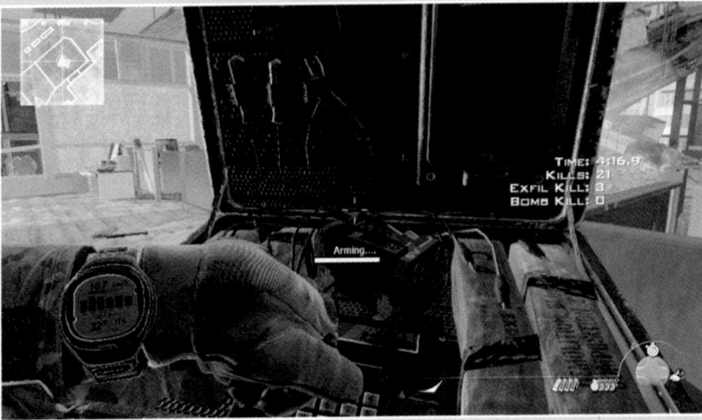

OBJECTIVE

MEET THE RESCUE TEAM AT THE EXTRACTION POINT

Team up on the rest of the enemies that get in your way as you proceed to the extraction point.

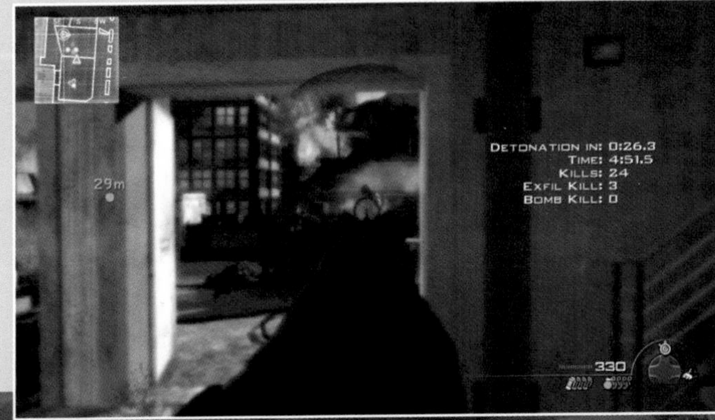

MISSION 12

INVISIBLE THREAT

UNLOCKED AT LEVEL	10
EST. COMPLETION TIME	4:00
LOCATION	BERLIN, GERMANY

OBJECTIVE

USE THE UAV AND A JUGGERNAUT SUIT TO FIND AND DEFUSE IEDs.

MISSION SCORE

- DIFFICULTY
- TIME
- KILLS
- EXPLOSIVE KILLS (50)
- MELEE KILLS (50)

INITIAL LOADOUT

- L86 LSW
- 4 FLASHBANGS 
- 4 FRAG GRENADES 

START

START

OBJECTIVE

DEFUSE ALL OF THE IEDs ON THE PARKWAY

Eight IEDs are scattered throughout the parkway in Berlin. It's up to Metal Zero Four to defuse them. When there are two players, one is located on the roof with a sniper rifle and remote control of a UAV carrying a Predator missile. The other player is on the street in a bomb disposal suit. When you play solo, you're in the bomb disposal suit and have remote control of the UAV, thus giving you both jobs.

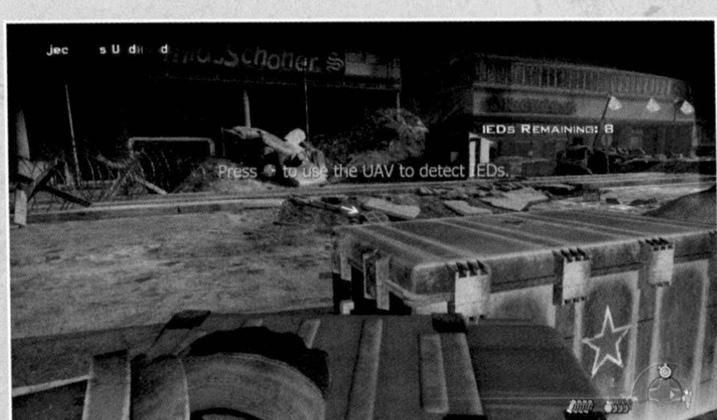

Press Right on the D-pad to have the UAV detect IEDs. This identifies their locations on the street. Then press the Fire button to send a missile toward the rightmost IEDs. This clears out any enemies in the area.

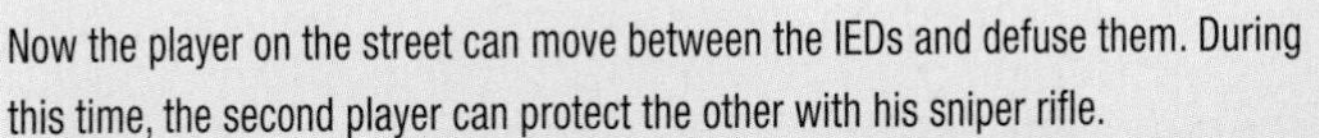

Now the player on the street can move between the IEDs and defuse them. During this time, the second player can protect the other with his sniper rifle.

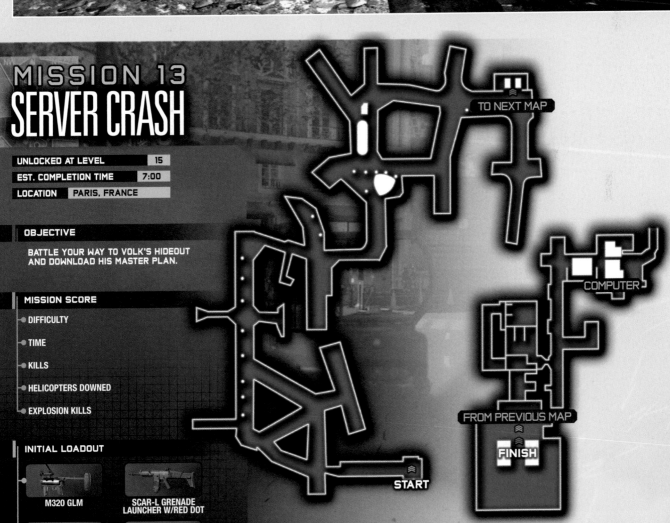

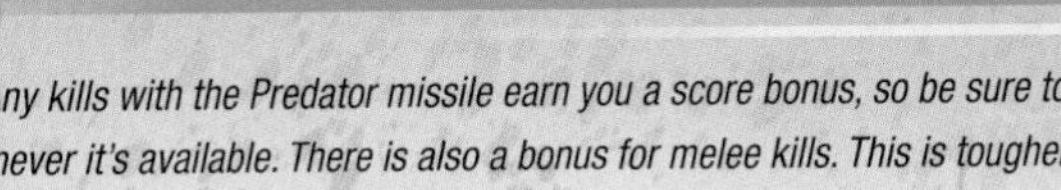

TACTICS

EXPLOSIVE KILLS AND MELEE KILLS

Any kills with the Predator missile earn you a score bonus, so be sure to use it whenever it's available. There is also a bonus for melee kills. This is tougher because the soldier in the bomb disposal suit has to perform them.

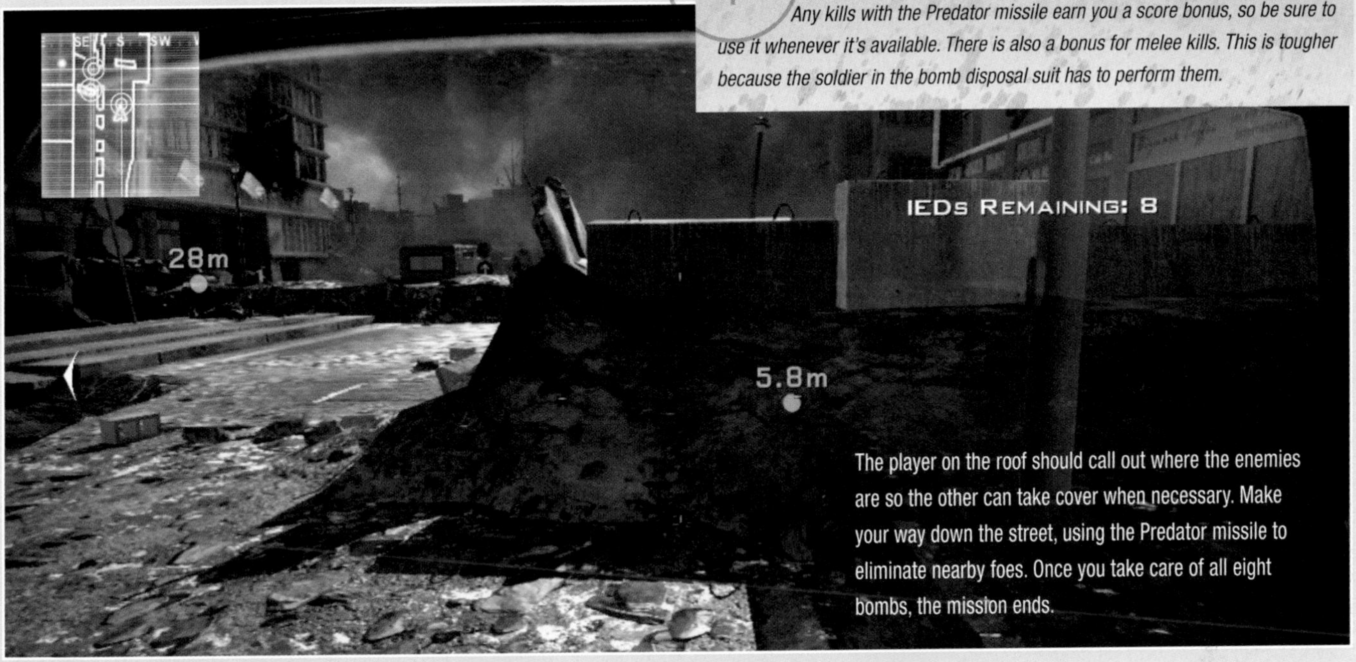

IEDs REMAINING: 8

28m

5.8m

The player on the roof should call out where the enemies are so the other can take cover when necessary. Make your way down the street, using the Predator missile to eliminate nearby foes. Once you take care of all eight bombs, the mission ends.

MISSION 13
SERVER CRASH

UNLOCKED AT LEVEL	15
EST. COMPLETION TIME	7:00
LOCATION	PARIS, FRANCE

OBJECTIVE

BATTLE YOUR WAY TO VOLK'S HIDEOUT AND DOWNLOAD HIS MASTER PLAN.

MISSION SCORE

- DIFFICULTY
- TIME
- KILLS
- HELICOPTERS DOWNED
- EXPLOSION KILLS

INITIAL LOADOUT

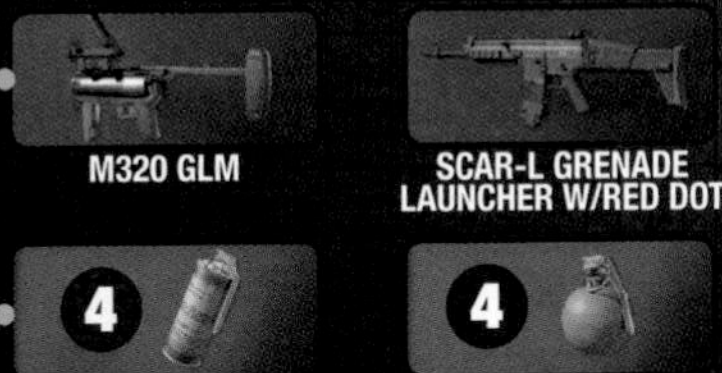

- M320 GLM
- SCAR-L GRENADE LAUNCHER W/RED DOT
- 4 FLASHBANGS
- 4 FRAG GRENADES

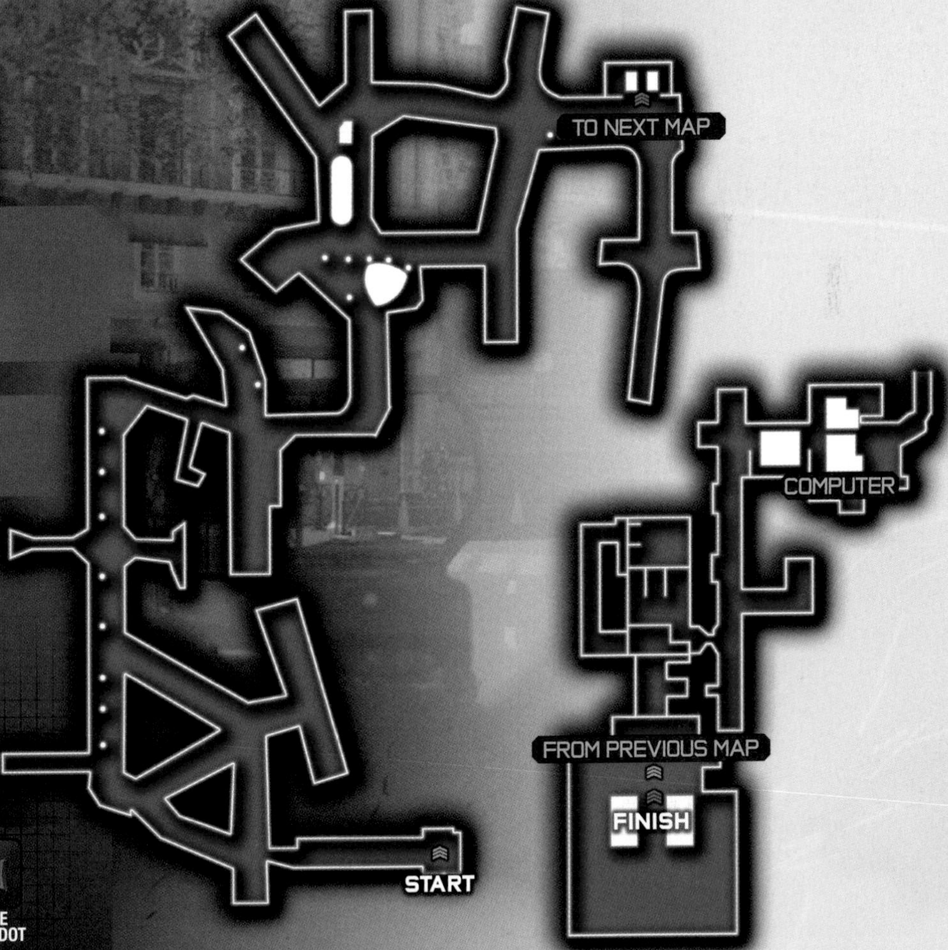

TO NEXT MAP

COMPUTER

FROM PREVIOUS MAP

FINISH

START

OBJECTIVE

SURVIVE THE ESCORT

Volk is planning something big, so you're sent into his hideout to download his plan. You start on the back of a jeep with plenty of firepower, a grenade launcher, and an assault rifle equipped with a grenade launcher.

TACTICS

HELICOPTERS DOWNED AND EXPLOSION KILLS

You have plenty of grenades, and you're rewarded each time you take someone down with them. You also get a score bonus for taking down choppers. They fly next to you as you drive along the water, and two more fly overhead as you go up the steps.

During the drive to the hideout, use your grenade launchers to take out the enemy troops and vehicles along the way. Pull out the SCAR-L assault rifle to shoot down the choppers. When the escort ends, jump out and enter the building.

OBJECTIVE

CONNECT THE DSM TO VOLK'S COMPUTER NETWORK

Fight your way down into the catacombs. Follow the long corridor to the stairs, and continue down them to find the computer. Attach the DSM to the network by pressing the Use button.

OBJECTIVE

PROTECT THE DSM UNTIL THE TRANSFER IS COMPLETE

Now you have to protect the computer until the files are copied. There's an entrance on the east and west. Have each player set up in opposite corners and protect an opening.

OBJECTIVE

RETRIEVE THE DSM

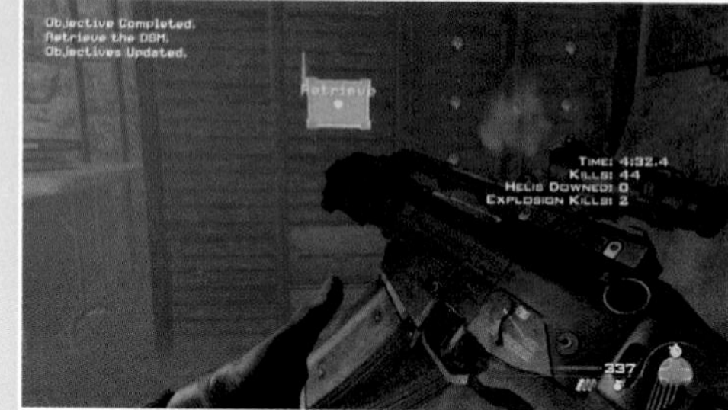

Once the transfer is complete, grab the DSM and head back up the stairs.

OBJECTIVE

ESCAPE WITH THE INTEL

In the long corridor, a Juggernaut heads your way. Use Flashbangs to stun it, and eat away at its health with whatever grenades you have left.

Fight your way out of the building by retracing your steps back outside. Get into the jeep to complete the mission.

MISSION 14
SMACK TOWN

UNLOCKED AT LEVEL	15
EST. COMPLETION TIME	8:00
LOCATION	BOOSAASO, SOMALIA

OBJECTIVE

RELIEVE THE LOCAL MILITIA OF THEIR CONTRABAND.

MISSION SCORE

- DIFFICULTY
- TIME
- KILLS
- HELICOPTERS DOWNED
- EXPLOSION KILLS

INITIAL LOADOUT

- PKP PECHENEG RED DOT SIGHT
- M4A1 GRENADIER W/RED DOT SIGHT  
- 4 FLASHBANGS 
- 4 FRAG GRENADES

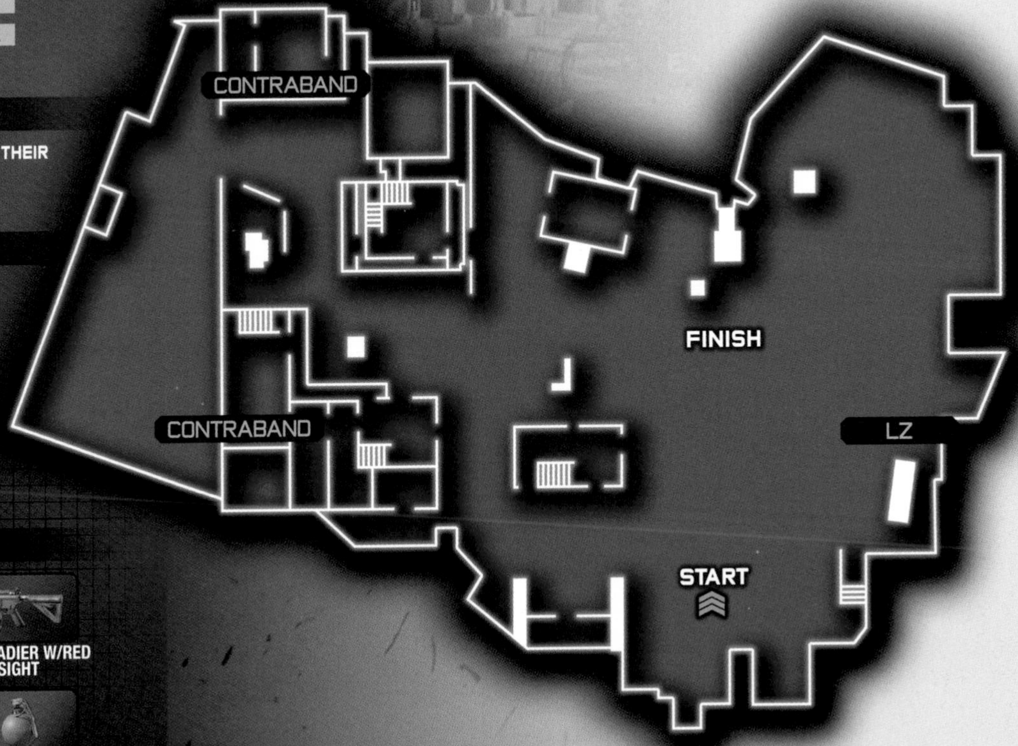

CONTRABAND
CONTRABAND
FINISH
LZ
START

INTRO
BASICS
CAMPAIGN
SPECIAL OPS
ACHIEVEMENTS
MP GAMEPLAY
MP ARSENAL
MP MAPS
EXTRAS

OBJECTIVE

LOCATE CRASH SITE BRAVO

Smack Town takes you back to Somalia, where the local militia has gathered some contraband. Team Bravo was sent in to take care of it, but they haven't been heard from.

You start on a chopper heading toward Bravo's last known location. Immediately take out the truck that drives up the middle of the village. Continue to fire at the militia as your team reports the whereabouts of the lost squad. As more enemies enter the area, blow up the truck to thin their number.

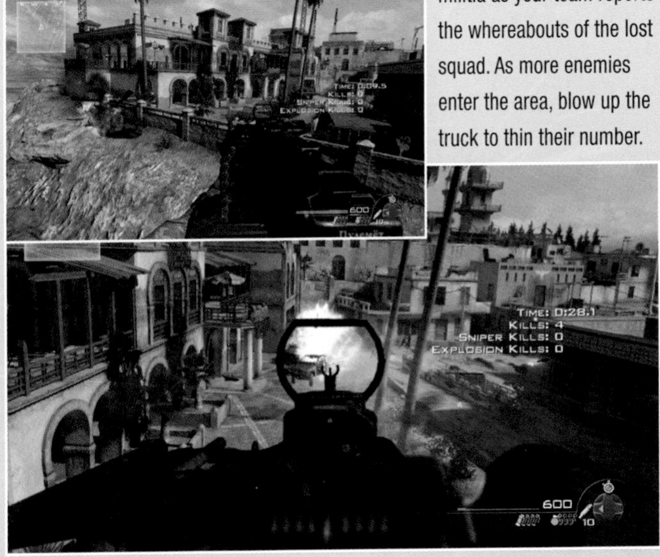

OBJECTIVE

FIND A SAFE LZ AND PROCEED ON FOOT

The chopper circles around the buildings, giving you a better shot at the militia. Use your grenade launcher to take out the enemies on the roofs. There's an added bonus for killing them with explosives.

OBJECTIVE

LOCATE AND DESTROY ALL NARCOTICS

After you circle around twice, you come to a stop on the east side. Have one player stay in the chopper, as the other goes down to the docks. Move into the blue, L-shaped building and climb to the second floor. The first pallet of narcotics is in the back room. Place the C4, move a safe distance away, and blow it up. Exit down the steps and run north to the next building. Climb up to the roof and plant more C4 on the second contraband.

OBJECTIVE

GET TO THE EXTRACTION POINT

Once you take care of the narcotics, run to the east where a helicopter waits for you.

INTRO
BASICS
CAMPAIGN
SPECIAL OPS
ACHIEVEMENTS
MP GAMEPLAY
MP ARSENAL
MP MAPS
EXTRAS

MISSION 15
FLOOD THE MARKET

UNLOCKED AT LEVEL	15
EST. COMPLETION TIME	8:30
LOCATION	MANHATTAN

OBJECTIVE

FIND THE ENCRYPTION CODES IN THE STOCK EXCHANGE AND UPLOAD THEM TO CENTOCOM.

MISSION SCORE

- DIFFICULTY
- TIME
- KILLS
- XM25 KILLS

INITIAL LOADOUT

- M4A1 W/HYBRID SCOPE
- XM25
- 4 FLASHBANGS
- 4 FRAG GRENADES

START

FINISH

OBJECTIVE

FIND THE RUSSIAN ENCRYPTION CODES

Flood the Market occurs in the same place where the campaign starts: Manhattan. You start in the department store just down the street from the stock market. Russian encryption codes are located on the stock exchange floor—three in solo play and five in two player.

Head out to the street and equip the XM25. Launch a couple explosives over the barricades to thin out the Russians. There's a score bonus for every kill you make with the XM25.

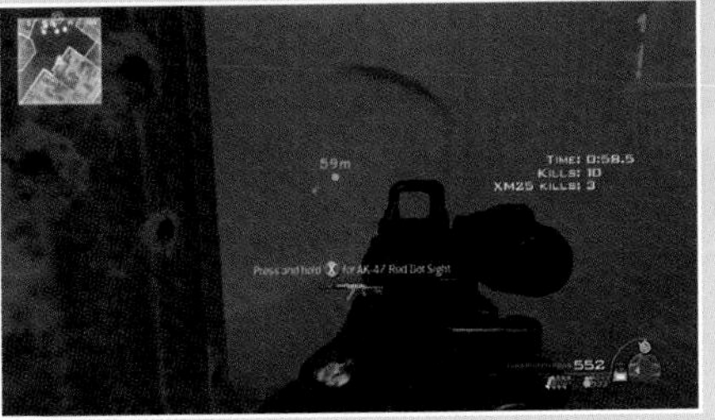

Watch out for the enemy's grenades, as they release a poisonous gas that eats away at your health.

Climb up the steps on the right to get a good view of the street. Pick off anyone you can from there before you proceed. Keep an eye out for the two dogs that attack. Knife them as they lunge your way.

Crouch down and work your way around the stock exchange floor. The encryption codes are marked on the map, and they appear as objective markers on your HUD.

Run around the area's perimeter as you fight your way into the stock exchange building. Refill your weapons in the lobby, and then take the escalator to the second floor.

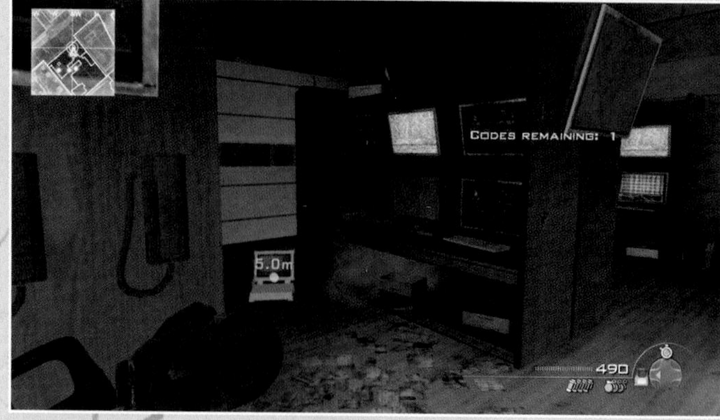

OBJECTIVE

UPLOAD THE ENCRYPTION CODES TO CENTCOM

Once you collect all the codes, head for the southwest corner and climb up to the roof, just as you did in the first mission of the campaign.

Fight your way to the tower in the southeast corner, and start uploading the encryption codes.

OBJECTIVE

RESTART THE UPLOAD (IF NECESSARY)

You must stay on the eastern half of the roof, or the upload will stall. If this happens, return to the tower and restart the upload. Be careful, as the Russians may have tossed poisonous gas in the area. You can either wait it out or access the computer from the side.

OBJECTIVE

DEFEND THE COMMUNICATION TOWER

Take cover and defend your location until the upload is complete. Enemies fire from the roof across the street and from the other side of your building.

MISSION 16
FIRE MISSION

UNLOCKED AT LEVEL	15
EST. COMPLETION TIME	2:30
LOCATION	EASTERN SIBERIA, RUSSIA

OBJECTIVE

DISABLE ENEMY ANTI-AIR DEFENSE AND INFILTRATE THEIR BASE WITH AC-130 SUPPORT.

MISSION SCORE

- DIFFICULTY
- TIME
- KILLS

INITIAL LOADOUT

- M4A1 W/ACOG 
- 4 FLASHBANGS 
- 4 FRAG GRENADES

FINISH

OVER-RIDE SECURITY

DISABLE DEFENSES

PLANT C-4

START

OBJECTIVE

PLANT C4 ON THE CONSTRUCTION SITE BASEMENT DOOR

The final mission in Special Ops is available for two players only. One player fights his way through the construction site and completes the objectives. The other player mans the guns on an AC-130 high above.

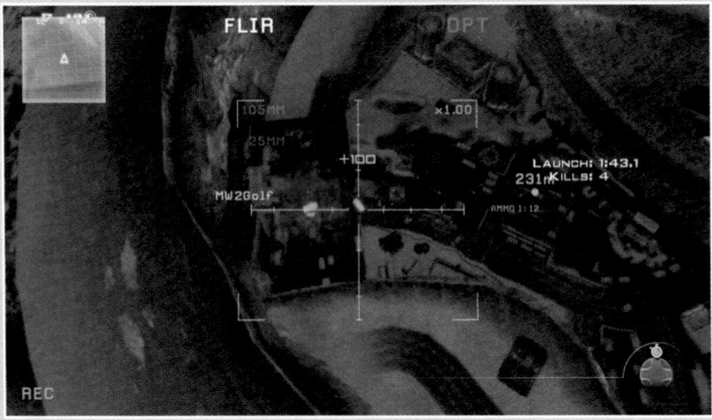

As the gunner, use the 25mm cannon when you fire near your partner. Employ the bigger weapons on targets that are a safe distance away. Remember that you can press the Use button to switch between the two views, FLIR (Infrared) and enhanced imaging. This should be familiar to you if you played through the "Iron Lady" mission in the campaign.

As the soldier on the ground, quickly make your way to the construction site. A timer counts down from 1:50, which is when the anti-air defenses are to attack the AC-130. Move around the left side of the site, hop over the rail, and place the C4 on the door.

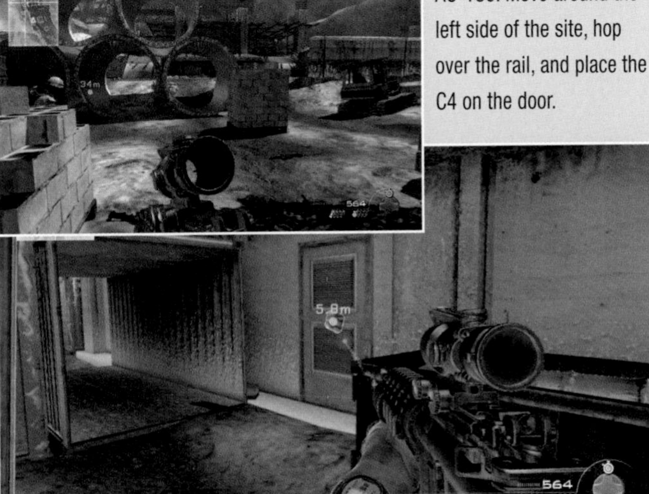

OBJECTIVE

PREVENT ANTI-AIR DEFENSES FROM ATTACKING THE AC-130

Sprint into the basement and take out the three enemies inside. Immediately access the laptop on the table and disable the anti-air defenses.

OBJECTIVE

OVERRIDE THE SECURITY LOCK ON THE MAIN ENTRANCE

A new timer starts to count down from 1:15, so hurry back outside and run up the steps to the northwest. Enter the trailer and use the computer inside to unlock the main entrance.

OBJECTIVE

INFILTRATE THROUGH THE MAIN ENTRANCE

As the AC-130 gunner hammers the final destination, sprint to the north and into the building.

ACHIEVEMENTS AND TROPHIES

There are 50 Achievements/Trophies in *Modern Warfare 3*. It is not easy to get them all, especially the Survival mode awards. All Achievements/Trophies are earned in Campaign or Special Ops.

CAMPAIGN

The following are earned by completing the story mode. Finish the campaign on Veteran to earn them all.

For the Big Apple, you must select New Game on Veteran difficulty and then complete the first two missions to earn it. You do not get credit if you skip the prologue.

NAME	DESCRIPTION
BACK IN THE FIGHT	START THE SINGLE-PLAYER CAMPAIGN ON ANY DIFFICULTY.
TOO BIG TO FAIL	DESTROY THE JAMMING TOWER. COMPLETE "BLACK TUESDAY" ON ANY DIFFICULTY.
WET WORK	TAKE BACK NEW YORK HARBOR. COMPLETE "HUNTER KILLER" ON ANY DIFFICULTY.
CARPE DIEM	ESCAPE THE MOUNTAIN SAFE HOUSE. COMPLETE "PERSONA NON GRATA" ON ANY DIFFICULTY.
FREQUENT FLYER	DEFEND THE RUSSIAN PRESIDENT. COMPLETE "TURBULENCE" ON ANY DIFFICULTY.
UP TO NO GOOD	INFILTRATE THE VILLAGE. COMPLETE "BACK ON THE GRID" ON ANY DIFFICULTY.
ONE WAY TICKET	MAKE IT TO WESTMINSTER. COMPLETE "MIND THE GAP" ON ANY DIFFICULTY.
WELCOME TO WW3	SAVE THE U.S. VICE PRESIDENT. COMPLETE "GOALPOST" ON ANY DIFFICULTY.
SANDSTORM!	ASSAULT THE SHIPPING COMPANY. COMPLETE "RETURN TO SENDER" ON ANY DIFFICULTY.
BACK SEAT DRIVER	TRACK DOWN VOLK. COMPLETE "BAG AND DRAG" ON ANY DIFFICULTY.
WE'LL ALWAYS HAVE PARIS	ESCAPE PARIS WITH VOLK. COMPLETE "IRON LADY" ON ANY DIFFICULTY.
VIVE LA RÉVOLUTION!	REACH THE CHURCH. COMPLETE "EYE OF THE STORM" ON ANY DIFFICULTY.

NAME	DESCRIPTION
REQUIEM	ESCAPE THE CITY. COMPLETE "BLOOD BROTHERS" ON ANY DIFFICULTY.
STORM THE CASTLE	DISCOVER MAKAROV'S NEXT MOVE. COMPLETE "STRONGHOLD" ON ANY DIFFICULTY.
BAD FIRST DATE	FIND THE GIRL. COMPLETE "SCORCHED EARTH" ON ANY DIFFICULTY.
DIAMOND IN THE ROUGH	RESCUE THE RUSSIAN PRESIDENT. COMPLETE "DOWN THE RABBIT HOLE" ON ANY DIFFICULTY.
THE BIG APPLE	COMPLETE "BLACK TUESDAY" AND "HUNTER KILLER" ON VETERAN DIFFICULTY.
OUT OF THE FRYING PAN...	COMPLETE "PERSONA NON GRATA", "TURBULENCE", AND "BACK ON THE GRID" ON VETERAN DIFFICULTY.
PAYBACK	COMPLETE "MIND THE GAP", "GOALPOST", AND "RETURN TO SENDER" ON VETERAN DIFFICULTY.
CITY OF LIGHTS	COMPLETE "BAG AND DRAG" AND "IRON LADY" ON VETERAN DIFFICULTY.
THE DARKEST HOUR	COMPLETE "EYE OF THE STORM", "BLOOD BROTHERS", AND "STRONGHOLD" ON VETERAN DIFFICULTY.
THIS IS THE END	COMPLETE "SCORCHED EARTH", "DOWN THE RABBIT HOLE", AND "DUST TO DUST" ON VETERAN DIFFICULTY.
WHO DARES WINS	COMPLETE THE CAMPAIGN ON ANY DIFFICULTY.
THE BEST OF THE BEST	COMPLETE THE CAMPAIGN ON HARDENED OR VETERAN DIFFICULTY.

CAMPAIGN SKILL

Some of the campaign missions have a bonus Achievement/Trophy for completing a specific task.

THIS IS MY BOOMSTICK

KILL 30 ENEMIES WITH THE XM25 IN "BLACK TUESDAY."

Launch grenades with the XM25 into groups of enemies, such as at the doorway when you are fighting your way out of the store. Keep the weapon with you throughout the mission, and use the ammo crates to refill the gun.

WHAT GOES UP...

DESTROY ALL THE CHOPPERS WITH ONLY THE UGV'S GRENADE LAUNCHER IN "PERSONA NON GRATA."

While you clear out the path to the helicopter, use only the UGV's grenades on the enemy choppers.

FLIGHT ATTENDANT

KILL ALL 5 ENEMIES DURING THE ZERO-G SEQUENCE IN "TURBULENCE."

As you fight through the airplane's main lobby, you are knocked around and then experience a period of weightlessness. Carefully take out all five hijackers who also float around the room.

KILL BOX

KILL 20 ENEMIES WITH THE CHOPPER GUNNER IN A SINGLE RUN IN "RETURN TO SENDER."

There are several times that you gain access to remote chopper turret. You need to be quick and accurate to take out 20 enemies in one run.

DANGER CLOSE

TAKE DOWN A CHOPPER WITH AN AC-130 SMOKE GRENADE IN "BAG AND DRAG."

Once you see the Russian chopper show up and drop off some troops, toss the air support marker underneath it. The AC-130 should take down the helicopter during its run.

FOR WHOM THE SHELL TOLLS

DESTROY ALL TARGETS DURING THE MORTAR SEQUENCE WITH ONLY 4 SHELLS IN "BACK ON THE GRID."

You must take out four targets with mortars before continuing the mission. First, a truck drives in on the right. Line up your reticle on the truck when it comes to a stop, and fire away. Two more appear on the left; eliminate them the same way. The second truck drives further into the area before stopping. Finally, a group of militia men march in on the right.

MÉNAGE À TROIS

DESTROY 3 TANKS WITH A SINGLE 105MM SHOT IN "IRON LADY."

A great time for this is during the chase after making a couple hard lefts. Three tanks sit at the bottom of the intersection. Use the 105mm Howitzer on them to earn the award.

NEIN

KILL 9 ENEMIES WITH A-10 STRAFING RUNS IN "SCORCHED EARTH."

For the first strafing run, there are enemy troops who run from the far sidewalk into the roundabout. Set coordinates through the cars that provide cover for many of them.

COLLECTING INTEL

Collect all of the Intel Items in the campaign to earn these two awards. Refer to our campaign chapter for locations.

INFORMANT

COLLECT 22 INTEL ITEMS.

SCOUT LEADER

COLLECT 46 INTEL ITEMS.

SPECIAL OPS

The rest of the Achievements/Trophies are earned in Special Ops mode.

BRAG RAGS

EARN 1 STAR IN SPECIAL OPS MISSION MODE.

TACTICIAN

EARN 1 STAR IN EACH MISSION OF SPECIAL OPS MISSION MODE.

OVERACHIEVER

EARN 48 STARS IN SPECIAL OPS MISSION MODE.

STRIKE!

KILL 5 ENEMIES WITH A SINGLE GRENADE IN SINGLE-PLAYER OR SPECIAL OPS.

In the Special Ops mission "Hit and Run," toss a grenade as the locals flee just before Exfil arrives.

JACK THE RIPPER

MELEE 5 ENEMIES IN A ROW IN SINGLE-PLAYER OR SPECIAL OPS.

Move through the shadows in the Special Ops mission "Hostage Taker." Take out the first five enemies with the knife to earn this one. There are other good opportunities in the campaign, as well.

50/50

COMPLETE A SPECIAL OPS MISSION MODE GAME WITH THE SAME NUMBER OF KILLS AS YOUR PARTNER.

BIRDIE

DOWN 2 ENEMY HELICOPTERS WITHOUT GETTING HIT IN A SPECIAL OPS SURVIVAL GAME.

Grab a Predator and RPG before the first Helicopter wave (Wave 6). Take out the first with the Predator, and then step out and eliminate the second.

SERRATED EDGE

FINISH A JUGGERNAUT WITH A KNIFE IN SPECIAL OPS.

In Survival, shoot a Juggernaut in the head to weaken it, and then finish it off with the knife.

ARMS DEALER

BUY ALL ITEMS FROM THE SURVIVAL WEAPON ARMORY.

DEFENSE SPENDING

BUY ALL ITEMS FROM THE SURVIVAL EQUIPMENT ARMORY.

DANGER ZONE

BUY ALL ITEMS FROM THE SURVIVAL AIR SUPPORT ARMORY.

GET RICH OR DIE TRYING

HAVE $50,000 CURRENT BALANCE IN A SPECIAL OPS SURVIVAL GAME.

I LIVE

SURVIVE 1 WAVE IN A SPECIAL OPS SURVIVAL GAME.

SURVIVOR

REACH WAVE 10 IN EACH MISSION OF SPECIAL OPS SURVIVAL MODE.

UNSTOPPABLE

REACH WAVE 15 IN EACH MISSION OF SPECIAL OPS SURVIVAL MODE.

NO ASSISTANCE REQUIRED

COMPLETE A SPECIAL OPS MISSION MODE GAME ON HARDENED OR VETERAN WITH NO PLAYER GETTING DOWNED.

PLATINUM TROPHY ON PLAYSTATION 3

ALL IN

EARN ALL AVAILABLE TROPHIES FOR *MODERN WARFARE 3.*

INTRODUCTION

WELCOME BACK, SOLDIER.

Call of Duty: Modern Warfare 3 multiplayer is the culmination of years of gameplay experiments, design refinement, and responses to fan feedback. Taking all the good of the previous games and mixing it with new features and additions, multiplayer is fast and intense, with the best features polished, improved, and expanded.

As *Modern Warfare* has evolved, it has become increasingly complex, with more weapons, equipment, pointstreaks, perks, and attachments—and now proficiencies are added to the mix. This guide is intended to give you useful, practical advice on every possible loadout choice, as well as fundamental gameplay tips and clean, highly detailed maps of every level in multiplayer.

With 80 (or 800!) levels of warfare ahead of you, we've written this guide to help you on your way, and to make sure you have fun with the fantastic multiplayer features.

- The *Gameplay* chapters focus on multiplayer fundamentals. A small section is dedicated returning players, highlighting some of the more radical changes from previous *Call of Duty* multiplayer.
- *Arsenal* sections comprise the meat of the multiplayer guide, with information and advice on every item you can add to a character loadout—and there are a lot of items!
- The *Maps* and *Modes* chapters provide highly detailed maps, as well as overviews of the basic game modes, including modes that are new to *Modern Warfare 3*.
- *Unlocks* and *Extras* are the wrap-up sections, with unlock tables and other odds and ends stowed away safely.

FIELD GUIDE

BASIC TRAINING. FEELING GREEN? BRUSH UP!

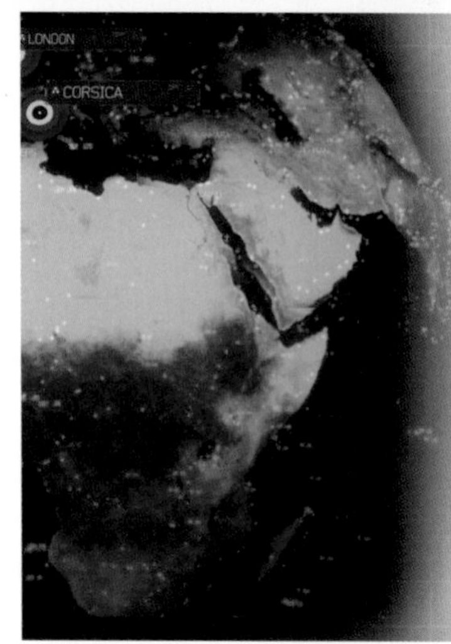

READ THE USER MANUAL

This chapter's purpose is to supplement—*not replace*—the in-game tutorials and the user's manual that comes with the game. Our primary goal is to expand on the information those sources already provide. The discussions in this chapter—and in this guide as a whole—assume that you've read the user manual, understand the basic controls, and grasp the bare essentials of playing the game.

GAME CONCEPTS

MOVEMENT

While it seems fundamental, movement is a critically important skill to master. Here's a brief primer on some key topics.

MOBILITY

Carrying heavy weaponry slows your movement speed. Note that, unlike past *Call of Duty* titles, this time around, the heaviest *carried* weapon slows your speed, not the heaviest weapon *in your hands.*

Put a bit more thought into grabbing random Launchers or LMGs you find on the battlefield. You don't want to slow down a fast run-and-gun SMG character class!

- **SMGs, Pistols, and Shotguns have the highest mobility.**
- **Assault Rifles are next.**
- **Sniper Rifles and the Riot Shield are slower, and the AR50 and Barrett .50 are slower still.**
- **LMGs and heavy Launchers are the slowest.**

Heavy weapons also have an impact on the length of your sprint, so you are slower *and* you cover less ground.

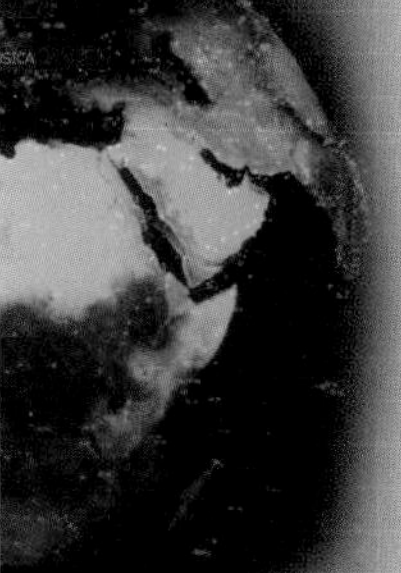

PRONE IMPROVEMENTS

Prone now provides a *very* significant bonus to accuracy when you use an LMG or a Sniper Rifle.

CROUCHING AND PRONE

Crouching or going prone improves your aim and reduces your silhouette, and it allows you to better exploit low cover. Both positions are important; use them often while you're on the battlefield.

SPRINTING

Sprinting increases your movement speed, but it also makes you louder and more noticeable as you move across the battlefield. Use sprint to move quickly from cover to cover, or to cross open areas. *Don't* use sprint constantly in enemy territory or for running around dangerous corners. Sprinting into an enemy who is already ADS in your general direction is all but certain death.

MANTLING

Mantling is the act of pulling yourself up over a ledge, window, or other low obstruction. Using mantling well gives you greater flexibility in your paths through a level, as you can pull yourself over low walls and into buildings through windows.

Be aware that performing a mantle drops your weapon, so don't mantle into rooms with known enemy presence if you can avoid it! The Pro version of Extreme Conditioning doubles your mantle speed, reducing your window of vulnerability and speeding your movement even more.

JUMPING

Jumping is most useful to aid your mantling efforts. It is not a commonly used action on the field, partly because it severely degrades your accuracy, and partly because it makes you loud and conspicuous. Jumping is also sharply limited; after your first full-strength jump, successive jumps are much lower and weaker until you give yourself time to recover.

COMBAT

Combat is the heart and soul of *Call of Duty: Modern Warfare 3.* The following advice will give you an edge.

AIM DOWN SIGHTS (ADS)

Aiming down sights (ADS) is the act of raising your gun into position and aiming carefully down the gun's barrel. At any distance beyond close range, ADS should be your standard engagement method with any weapon, barring very specific setups (typically Steady Aim with SMGs).

Note that while you aim down sights, your movement speed is reduced. It's useful for making careful aim adjustments at a distance. But it can be a hindrance at shorter distance, where a fast-moving SMG or Shotgun user firing from the hip can outmaneuver you easily.

Weapons raise at different speeds, and some attachments (and perks) can affect ADS times.

- SMGs, Shotguns, Pistols and MPs have fast (.2s) ADS times.
- Assault Rifles have normal ADS times (.3s).
- LMGs and Snipers have slow ADS times (.4s).
- Certain optics can slow your ADS speed.
- The Quickdraw perk halves ADS time.
- The Stalker perk allows full-speed movement while ADS.

HIP-FIRE

Hip-fire is the act of shooting without using ADS. Very inaccurate, hip-fire is best used with weapons that have tight hip-fire spreads, at close to close-medium distance. The Steady Aim perk improves hip-fire spreads by 35 percent, a near-necessity for using hip-fire spray at anything beyond short range.

- SMGs, Shotguns, Pistols, and MPs have the best hip-fire accuracy.
- ARs are in the middle.
- LMGs and Snipers have very poor hip-fire accuracy.

ACCURACY

Your accuracy with your weapon is critically important, and knowing what improves or impairs your aim is crucial.

- Standing still, crouching, going prone, using a Grip, holding your breath, and the Steady Aim perk all improve your accuracy.
- Moving, firing (especially full auto), jumping, and getting shot all reduce your accuracy.
- The Rapid Fire attachment greatly reduces accuracy in exchange for increased rate of fire.

For fully automatic weapons, you should generally use full auto only at close range when hip-fired; out to close-medium if hip-fired with Steady Aim; and out to medium when ADS. At any greater distance, full auto is usually far too inaccurate to down targets efficiently. Instead, use short trigger pulls to fire two or three bullets at a time in rapid succession.

PENETRATION

High-powered weapons can often shoot straight *through* walls and other cover, even seemingly impenetrable hard cover.

- LMGs and Sniper Rifles have the best penetration.
- Assault Rifles are in the middle.
- Shotguns, SMGs, Pistols, and MPs have poor penetration. Exceptions to this include the Magnum pistols and the UMP .45 SMG).
- The Impact proficiency maximizes penetration values for a primary weapon.

Shooting enemies successfully through cover takes practice, but it's a worthwhile skill to learn. Spend some time with an LMG or an AR using Impact, and experiment with tagging enemies through cover.

Damage through cover is always lower than your base damage value, so downing a target behind hard cover takes more hits than it would in the open. Note that the damage you deal through cover is also affected by the angle at which you strike the surface. Hitting straight-on provides the best penetration and damage, while a sharp angle reduces damage.

EXPLOSIONS

Vehicles of all kinds, and occasionally barrels of oil or fuel, can be destroyed to cause an explosion that's fatal to anyone nearby. But be careful: these explosions can easily kill you or, in the case of a burning vehicle, kill your teammates!

You can use these environmental hazards to good effect by detonating them with any explosive weapon: Frag Grenades, Semtex, C4, even a carefully placed Bouncing Betty or Claymore. The explosion of a vehicle is powerful, and it instantly kills any enemy near it. You can also shoot to detonate them, but be aware that this consumes a lot of your magazine for anything other than an LMG. It also gives away your location.

BURNING VEHICLES

Exercise caution near any burning vehicle. Once they're on fire, they burn down until they explode, detonating with their usual explosive ferocity. Because there is no good way to tell whether a vehicle is about to blow, keep your distance or hurry the explosion with a few bullets.

MELEE

Knife strikes are an instantly lethal and stealthy way to dispatch enemies at close range. If you manage to sneak up behind enemies, it's often a good idea to take them out with a knife if you aren't using a Silencer on your weapon. Melee hits with the Riot Shield are *not* instantly lethal; it takes two shield bashes to down someone.

You can improve your melee effectiveness with the Steady Aim Pro perk, which reduces melee recovery time. The Melee proficiency for the Riot Shield speeds melee attacks.

EQUIPMENT

Equipment is vital to your success on the battlefield. Experiment with *all* types of lethal and tactical equipment in all game modes, and on all maps. Smoke isn't especially useful in an FFA match, but it's crucial in objective modes when you need cover. A Portable Radar isn't very exciting if you're running and gunning, but it can be a powerful defensive tool if you're guarding an area or an objective.

STRIKE PACKAGES

Assault and Support Pointstreaks are critically important in all modes—especially objective modes. Experiment with different sets of Pointstreaks, figure out what level of streak you can *reliably* achieve, and target your choices around that level. There's no harm in going for the gold every now and then, but running 12/15/17 isn't a great idea for even the best player if you want to support your team!

Specialist is indeed a special package: it's at its strongest when you are a highly skilled, very aggressive player. Experiment with it in FFA, Mercenary playlists, Ground War on offense, and objective modes on offense.

HEAD-UP DISPLAY (HUD)

Using your HUD well can give you a distinct advantage in battle. Following are some quick tips:

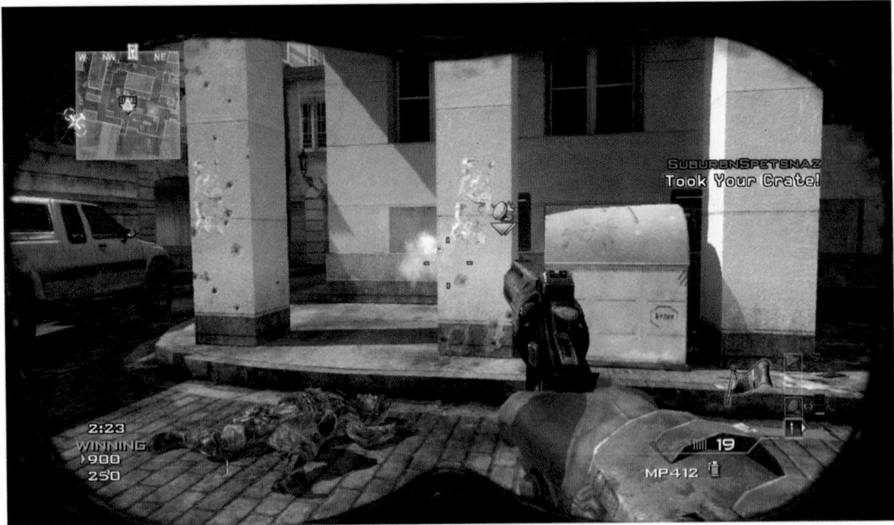

KILLCAM

When an enemy kills you in non-Hardcore modes, you instantly get a playback from that player's perspective, showing your last few seconds of life. This camera can give you valuable insight into where the enemy was located, how he was moving, and what he was using. If you're a newer player, get in the habit of watching almost every killcam. It's extremely useful to learn what experienced players use, where they hide, and how they move through a map.

Even as an experienced player, you can use killcams to check on an unusual death, or to help locate a long-range sniper. Bear in mind that, due to the realities of Internet latency, what you see on a killcam is what the *other* player saw. It may not always match up with what *you* saw. This is simply a fact of online gaming!

MAIN MAP

Bring up the Main menu to view an enlarged, full-size map of the level.

This is useful both when you're new to the levels and getting your bearings, *and* whenever you have any type of UAV in the air. If you're in a relatively safe location, get in the habit of quickly bringing up the main map just as a UAV goes online. This snapshot of all enemy positions can give you a great read on where the enemy team is clustered, or where they're headed, allowing you to respond appropriately. Remember that players using the Assassin perk do not show up on the map, so don't assume you're completely safe!

The main map also lets you see any enemies firing their weapons. They show up as red dots regardless of their positions, so you can use the main map to track enemies even without a UAV.

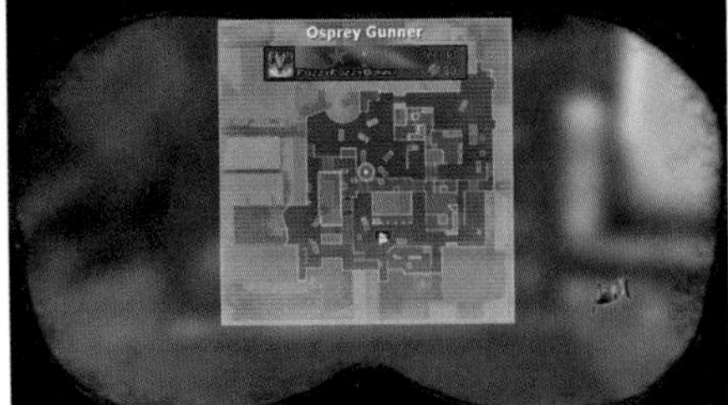

MINIMAP

Your minimap in the upper left corner is always active and provides you with a quick view of your immediate surroundings. This helps you navigate unfamiliar terrain more easily. Once you know the maps cold, your minimap is still vital, as it relays friendly positions, enemy red dots, and locators from UAVs, AUAVS, Recon, or Portable Radar detection. Keep half an eye on the minimap at all times; knowing where you are in relation to your teammates and the enemy team is vital.

HIT MARKERS

Any time you deal damage to an enemy, your crosshairs briefly flare and you hear a distinct sound effect: this is a hit marker. Hit markers are useful if you're on target at extreme distance, if you're hitting an enemy through a wall or other hard cover, or if a grenade you toss into a room locates an enemy. Use hit markers to confirm enemy presence and respond appropriately. You can also 'scout' ahead of or behind yourself with grenades or Claymores.

INFO MARKERS

Numerous onscreen indicators appear during a match—especially an objective match. As an example, in Headquarters or Domination, you can always see the position of the current HQ or which team controls any given Domination point. In Domination, you can also see if a point is being captured if it's flashing.

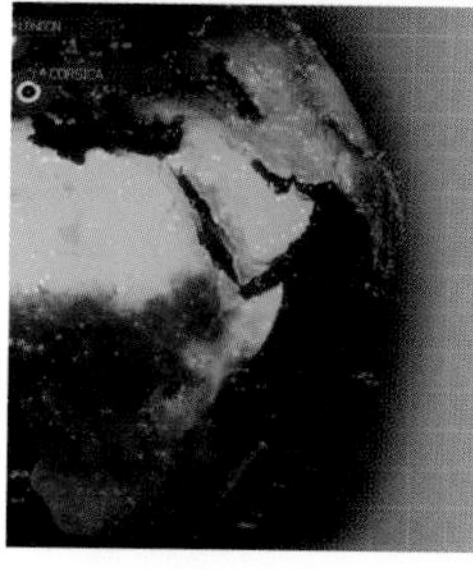

SNEAKY CAPS

An old Domination trick that still works: When a player steps on a hostile Domination point, a voiceover normally alerts the enemy team that their point is being captured. However, if you step onto a *second* enemy point as soon as the first voiceover starts playing, no second voiceover is triggered. Unless the enemy team has sharp players who note the info marker flashing, or spot you directly, you can 'sneak' a Domination point by coordinating a 'tag' of one point while you steal another.

Teammates who fall in battle are also marked on your HUD with a skull. This marker can be almost as useful as a minimap red dot for confirming enemy locations. Pay attention to your HUD indicators. It takes practice to absorb all of the information while still scanning for enemies and fighting, but it gives you an edge in battle once you can!

CUSTOMIZATION

If you're a new player, customizing your five initial loadouts (or more, once you unlock more slots via Prestige) can be a daunting task. A good starting point is to set up one configuration for each of the five weapon classes: SMG, Shotgun, AR, LMG, and Sniper. Then cycle through new weapons, equipment, and perks as you unlock them. Don't forget to play with the Riot Shield in objective modes, as well!

Create configurations for run-and-gun aggression, defensive camping, objective capturing, all-around utility, team support, lone-wolf play, and so on. Often, multiple builds can be useful in the same game, such as switching between defense and offense in an objective mode.

ANTI-AIR

Always, *always* have at least one build with an anti-air Launcher and either Blind Eye or a Scrambler. You need the ability to take down heavy enemy air power quickly, and you can't always rely on your teammates to do so. Don't let a Pave Low destroy your team—take it down! And don't forget: shooting down enemy air support also rewards you with points toward your Pointstreak.

In time, favorite combinations begin to emerge, but it's important to explore all the options before you settle on any one configuration.

SPECIAL TACTICS

Finally, here are some quick tips on a variety of subjects. Pay attention: any one of these can save your life many times over!

COVER

In *Call of Duty: Modern Warfare 3,* cover is life. The more obstructions between you and the guy with his gun trained on your head, the better. Hard cover can sponge up all but the heaviest bullet impacts, can block launchers completely, and can prevent you from being spotted in the first place. Soft cover or low cover may not block line of sight totally, but it can still soak up some errant shots. It also provides you with limited protection when you sprint from place to place.

While you learn the new maps, pay attention to areas that have abundant, line-of-sight-blocking cover, as well as the areas that have little to no cover. Mentally mark those as dangerous to move through—but good to protect!

FULL-AUTO AND HIP-FIRE

Use full-auto fire only when you're fighting at close range; at longer distance, use burst fire (emulate the M16 and the Type 95). Hip-fire is most useful up close and personal. SMGs, Shotguns, and dual-wielded MPs benefit the most from hip-fire due to their high movement speed and lethality at short range. Bring Steady Aim if you expect to hip-fire often, and abuse the combination of mobility and accuracy!

DANGEROUS ACTIONS

Reloading, throwing grenades, using Equipment, and using Pointstreaks all take time. They take just enough time that, if you perform these actions in dangerous territory, odds are an enemy will kill you while you're still pushing buttons or fumbling with a magazine. Get into the habit of ducking behind some cover before you perform any of these tasks. Note also that all of these actions have distinct sound effects. Very alert enemies can locate you solely from the sound of a UAV activation or a grenade toss!

STAY ALERT

When you down an enemy, *especially* with a non-Silenced weapon, expect one of his buddies to come investigate. Be prepared for the backup. Don't stay in the open, reloading. Instead, find some nearby cover or move on quickly.

Remember that when you down enemies, they can hear you firing, see the death marker from their teammate, see the red dot on the minimap, see the tracers from your shots, and so on. All of this can attract the attention of nearby enemies. Just remember: *there are always two!*

If you're skilled or lucky enough to get into a flanking position, where you see the enemy team sprint past you unaware, wait and check the back to make sure a straggler isn't bringing up the rear before you jump out and perform your best action-movie massacre on them! Nothing is more frustrating than coming up behind three oblivious enemies and getting shot in the back by the fourth because you didn't check.

LOCATING ENEMIES

- **HEAR THEM:** Use Sitrep Pro or Dead Silence to help with locating nearby enemies.
- **SEE THEM:** Use HUD indicators, minimap dots, teammate deaths, or simple experience to get your eyes and your sights in the right position to spot enemies. Use Thermal Scopes, controlled aerial Pointstreaks, or the Recon Drone to call targets.
- **FIND THEM:** UAV, AUAV, Recon, Sitrep, and Marksman, all can help you locate enemies.

RUN, RUN, RUN

Sprint is very, very dangerous. It is important, but easy to abuse. Try to play a few matches without sprinting at all (on small to medium maps—we aren't that cruel).

See how it affects your situational awareness, and how often you get the drop on loud, sprinting enemy players with their guns down. Combining quick sprints with careful movement is vital to success in every game mode.

KEY EQUIPMENT

- **BOUNCING BETTIES, CLAYMORES, C4:** Powerful defensive tools. Block chokepoints, guard objectives, protect your back when camping.
- **FLASH AND CONCUSSION GRENADES:** Disable enemies before engaging them.
- **SCRAMBLER, TROPHY SYSTEM:** Protect a defensive position, or use the Scrambler outside an enemy position before attacking.
- **EMP GRENADE:** Disable enemy equipment and instantly destroy expensive Pointstreaks. The EMP Grenade does not kill enemy helicopters, but it will keep them from firing for a few seconds.
- **TACTICAL INSERTION:** Absolutely vital in HQ, Demolition on offense, CTF on offense, and occasionally other objective modes on medium to large maps. Use it!
- **PORTABLE RADAR:** Powerful on defense.
- **SMOKE GRENADE:** Vital on offense and sometimes defense in objective modes. Create cover in an area that lacks it, cover a bomb plant or defuse, or distract the enemy team by smoking an area you *don't* plan to traverse.
- **ANTI-AIR LAUNCHERS:** Never let the enemy rule the skies: deny their air support.

FOR RETURNING VETERANS

ANOTHER TOUR. HEAR THE CALL ONE MORE TIME.

This section provides a quick summary of some major and minor changes in *Call of Duty: Modern Warfare 3* for those familiar with the series.

WEAPON CHANGES

With the removal of Stopping Power, weapons have been rebalanced across the board, with new damage values and fire rates. Generally, weapons are just as lethal at shorter range as they were with Stopping Power, but they require an extra shot or two at longer range.

ACCURACY TWEAKS

Recoil is more noticeable on most weapons. All weapons now have some level of sway, meaning that long-range shooting requires better aim and more careful trigger control.

EXPERIENCE SYSTEM

Weapons can earn experience points and gain levels. All weapons, perks, and Pointstreaks are still acquired by earning levels, but a new system unlocks attachments and the new proficiencies. Each weapon in your arsenal earns experience when you use it, in the same way that *you* earn experience. As you level up each specific weapon, you unlock the attachments and proficiencies for that weapon.

STRIKE PACKAGES

Choose a Strike Package loadout to quickly customize your Pointstreak rewards. Pointstreaks have been reorganized into three categories, known as Strike Packages.

- **ASSAULT STREAKS** are primarily offensive in nature.
- **SUPPORT STREAKS** are primarily defensive or team-play oriented.
- **SPECIALIST STREAKS** are dedicated entirely to improving your personal power with bonus perks.

POINTSTREAKS

Complete objectives or shoot down air support to earn Pointstreaks! In the past, Pointstreaks could be earned only by killing other players, or by killing them with a Pointstreak reward. Points can now be earned for completing objectives in any objective mode, and for shooting down air support in any mode. This rewards players for tackling objectives and shooting down anything from a UAV to a Pave Low.

MODES

New Modes: Team Defender, Kill Confirmed

Team Defender and Kill Confirmed have been added as standard modes. Additionally, you can play several new alternate modes in private matches, and you can save your custom game mode settings to your online vault to be shared with friends.

EXPLOSIVES

Explosives have been weakened across the board. Expect less effective explosive bombardment in objective modes. Scavenger no longer resupplies explosives.

PRONE ENHANCEMENT

LMGs and Sniper Rifles now benefit greatly from the prone position. While you're prone, recoil is *greatly* reduced, granting significantly improved accuracy with bursts of LMG fire, and almost no recoil whatsoever when firing semi-auto Sniper Rifles.

LMG TWEAKS

Light Machine Guns now have damage falloff at a distance, just as all other non-Sniper Rifle weapons do. LMGs still have high base damage and long range, so they are still the second most powerful ranged weapons in the game. LMGs can also now take the Rapid-Fire attachment, trading some control for better time to kill.

RECOVER EQUIPMENT

All types of deployed Equipment can be recovered.

RECOVERABLE EQUIPMENT

CLAYMORE	C4	BOUNCING BETTY
TACTICAL INSERTION	TROPHY SYSTEM	PORTABLE RADAR

You can move several Pointstreaks from place to place.

MOVEABLE POINTSTREAKS

SENTRY GUN	I.M.S.	SAM TURRET	REMOTE SENTRY

WEAPON SHIFTS

SMGs cannot be dual wielded, and Shotguns cannot be taken as secondary weapons.

PERK CHANGES

Perks have been significantly overhauled. Stopping Power and Danger Close have been removed. Many other perks have been removed, altered, or reorganized. See the Perks section for more details.

CUSTOMIZE

ELITE OPERATORS ARE GRANTED TOTAL DISCRETION WHEN CHOOSING THEIR LOADOUTS.

CREATE A CLASS

Not sure what you want to make? Use the following build-a-class guide to construct your own class.

1. Determine the purpose of the class. Offense? Defense? Flag Running? Point Capture? Long range combat? CQC?

2. Pick a primary weapon. Match up the range band of the weapon with the size of the map, the needs of the mode, and your intended role.

    - **SNIPER RIFLES AND LMGS:** Long range, point coverage
    - **ASSAULT RIFLES:** Medium range, all purpose
    - **SMGS AND SHOTGUNS:** Close-medium range or close quarters, fast movement
    - **RIOT SHIELD:** Objective defense

3. Select Attachments and a Proficiency. These are highly personal choices. Make your primary weapon as comfortable as possible. Emphasize strengths or minimize weaknesses.

4. Pick a secondary weapon. Complement your primary weapon to give yourself another option in firefights.

    - **PISTOLS:** Useful backup weapon for Sniper Rifles or LMGs; also strong with rapid-fire weapons as a quick-switch finisher when you run dry.
    - **MACHINE PISTOLS:** Rapid-fire CQC weaponry; a powerful close-range backup option for Burst ARs and the MK14, LMGs, and Sniper Rifles.
    - **LAUNCHERS:** Weaken groups of enemies, tag campers and enemies inside rooms, take down enemy air support.

5. Choose Lethal Equipment. This additional weaponry broadens your options in different situations.

    - **EXPLOSIVES:** Take Frag Grenades or Semtex based on the distance from which you expect to engage—Frag for longer distances, Semtex for shorter ones.
    - **THROWING KNIFE:** Take the Throwing Knife for a stealthy ranged kill option. Can also be used while sprinting or reloading as a quick attack. Resupplies with Scavenger.
    - **BOUNCING BETTIES/CLAYMORES:** Use these to cover your back or protect an objective.
    - **C4:** Use C4 to cover an objective or a second route within your field of view when covering an area. Double tap reload to quickly detonate.

6. Choose Tactical Equipment. Complement your combat role.

    - **FLASHBANG:** Blind enemies inside rooms; airburst over outdoor objectives to blind all nearby enemies.
    - **CONCUSSION:** Stagger enemies in the open; stun enemies inside rooms and flank
    - **EMP:** Shut down enemy equipment around objectives with ease; destroy low-flying air support.
    - **SMOKE:** Cover key objectives while on offense; create cover in the open to bypass enemy overwatch.
    - **TROPHY SYSTEM:** Protect yourself from explosives while defending objectives or while inside a room.
    - **SCRAMBLER:** Protect yourself and teammates from air support; blind enemies near an objective on offense or defense. Plant outside a small building before assaulting it.
    - **PORTABLE RADAR:** Detect incoming enemies while on defense; plant near an objective or building on offense before assaulting it. Toss atop buildings or other cover to conceal it from enemy eyes.
    - **TACTICAL INSERTION:** Vital in objective modes on large maps. Very useful for CTF flag running, Demolition offense, Headquarters.

7. Choose your perks. Create a perk combination that suits your chosen battlefield role.

    - **PERK SLOT 1:** Strong utility perks. Tag enemy positions, reload rapid-fire weapons quickly, defend against air support, sprint long distances, or constantly refill your ammo.
    - **PERK SLOT 2:** Powerful perks that heavily influence your build. Double speed ADS, near immunity to explosives, faster Pointstreaks, invisibility, or dual primary weapons.
    - **PERK SLOT 3:** Supplementary perks that augment your abilities. Spot enemies at long range, move quickly while ADS, spot all enemy equipment, improve your hip-fire, or move silently.

8. Select a Strike Package and Death Streak.

    - **ASSAULT:** High-powered offensive Pointstreaks. High streaks are demanding, requiring extremely strong offensive play or cautious defensive play to achieve.
    - **SUPPORT:** Fantastic teamplay rewards; enhance your entire team's effectiveness. Streak continues even if you die. Ideal for aggressive play in objective modes with a high death toll.
    - **SPECIALIST:** Lone wolf power. Enhance your combat abilities to their absolute peak. Strongest for skilled players who can disrupt an enemy team's backline solo.
    - **DEATH STREAKS:** Minimize the pain. Choose a Death Streak that best fits the game mode and role you expect to play.

9. Go forth and kick ass.

CUSTOM CLASSES BY WEAPON TYPE

CLASS TWEAKING

For all builds, swapping out weapons within the same *weapon class* maintains the overall intent of any given build. If you don't have the FAD or ACR 6.8 unlocked, no problem—substitute the M4A1 or the G36C. No Type 95? Use the M16. No Stinger? Use the SMAW.

Perks are more important, and are usually crucial for the build to function effectively. Most attachments and Proficiencies are less critical, though a Silencer is very important in stealth builds. Equipment and Death Streaks aren't vital to the build's intent, either, though Equipment is more important for some of the builds.

Finally, Assault and Support Strike Packages are built to show you useful combinations and options. Unlock your favorites that work well together. Specialist is an exception, because several builds are created to maximize its potential.

THE EVIL GAMER

WEAPON TYPE	ASSAULT RIFLE
PRIMARY WEAPON	AK-47
ATTACHMENT	GRENADE LAUNCHER
PROFICIENCY	KICK
SECONDARY WEAPON	AA-12
ATTACHMENT	EXTENDED MAGS
	EQUIPMENT
LETHAL	SEMTEX
TACTICAL	CONCUSSION GRENADE
PERK 1	SCAVENGER
PERK 2	OVERKILL
PERK 3	SITREP
STRIKE PACKAGE	ASSAULT
POINTSTREAK 1	PREDATOR MISSILE
POINTSTREAK 2	REAPER
POINTSTREAK 3	AC-130
DEATH STREAK	FINAL STAND

An aggressive build, Overkill gives you access to a powerful medium-range weapon with the AK-47 and a lethal close-range AA-12 for clearing rooms. Use the Grenade Launcher, Semtex, and Concussion Grenades to assault enemy positions.

Scavenger is taken to keep you rolling with constant ammo resupply, while Sitrep both protects you from enemy equipment and helps locate targets to eliminate. Sitrep Pro gives you superior reactions to nearby enemies.

This offensive Assault package is built to rain down hellfire on the enemy team. Use your expendable supplies to rack up kills for the Predator, and if you chain into a Reaper, your AC-130 is all but guaranteed. The 1-2 punch of a Reaper followed by an AC-130 is both lethal and demoralizing for the enemy team.

Exercise restraint to reach your Predator. Aim for a multi-kill over a pile of dog tags, get your Reaper, then hole up in a safe location to bombard the enemy and unlock the Osprey Gunner to tear the enemy team apart.

THE SANDY

WEAPON TYPE	SHOTGUN
PRIMARY WEAPON	SPAS-12
ATTACHMENT	EXTENDED MAGS
PROFICIENCY	RANGE
SECONDARY WEAPON	FIVE SEVEN
ATTACHMENT	TACTICAL KNIFE
	EQUIPMENT
LETHAL	SEMTEX
TACTICAL	CONCUSSION GRENADE
PERK 1	EXTREME CONDITIONING
PERK 2	ASSASSIN
PERK 3	STEADY AIM
STRIKE PACKAGE	ASSAULT
POINTSTREAK 1	PREDATOR MISSILE
POINTSTREAK 2	AH-6 OVERWATCH
POINTSTREAK 3	PAVE LOW
DEATH STREAK	FINAL STAND

(The Sandy continues next page.)

THE SANDY (CONTINUED)

A challenging class, The Sandy is built to get into range with the SPAS-12 (no matter the size of the map) and take down enemies in one shot. A backup Five Seven with Tactical Knife gives a super-fast stab with Steady Aim Pro.

Extreme Conditioning and Assassin combine to give you the mobility and stealth needed to close the distance, while Steady Aim is vital for hip-firing the SPAS on the move.

This Assault streak gives you a Predator to bump your streak up, and an AH-6 and Pave Low to provide constant air support while you continue to clean up on the ground with the SPAS.

THE HUTCH

WEAPON TYPE	SNIPER RIFLE
PRIMARY WEAPON	BARRETT .50
ATTACHMENT	VARIABLE ZOOM SCOPE
PROFICIENCY	SPEED
SECONDARY WEAPON	.44 MAGNUM
ATTACHMENT	TACTICAL KNIFE
	EQUIPMENT
LETHAL	SEMTEX
TACTICAL	CONCUSSION GRENADE
PERK 1	EXTREME CONDITIONING
PERK 2	QUICKDRAW
PERK 3	DEAD SILENCE
STRIKE PACKAGE	SPECIALIST
PERK REWARD 1	ASSASSIN
PERK REWARD 2	BLIND EYE
PERK REWARD 3	SITREP
DEATH STREAK	FINAL STAND

A mobile sniper build, the Hutch is meant to be used while staying in motion around the map, not camping in one location. Use Quickdraw to perform instantly lethal shots at medium to long range, and the Magnum as a super-fast quickswitch backup in close-range situations.

Extreme Conditioning and Dead Silence give you needed mobility, allowing you to run farther, mantle quicker, fall anywhere, and stay quiet while doing so. Quickdraw is taken instead of the usual Overkill to give immediate access to Barrett usage.

The follow-up perks grant you immediate stealth protection, followed by Sitrep to highlight enemy locations before you become a one-man army with full perk unlocks.

NO NUKES FOR YOU

WEAPON TYPE	LIGHT MACHINE GUN
PRIMARY WEAPON	PKP PECHENEG
ATTACHMENT	GRIP
PROFICIENCY	KICK
SECONDARY WEAPON	STINGER
ATTACHMENT	NONE
	EQUIPMENT
LETHAL	BOUNCING BETTY
TACTICAL	PORTABLE RADAR
PERK 1	BLIND EYE
PERK 2	BLAST SHIELD
PERK 3	MARKSMAN
STRIKE PACKAGE	ASSAULT
POINTSTREAK 1	I.M.S.
POINTSTREAK 2	ASSAULT DRONE
POINTSTREAK 3	JUGGERNAUT
DEATH STREAK	FINAL STAND

Built to lock down entire areas around objectives and completely deny the enemy air support, this build uses the PKP customized for maximum recoil reduction to ensure accurate long-range fire, and a Stinger for dedicated anti-air coverage. Your Bouncing Betty and Portable Radar guard your back.

Blind Eye conceals you from anti-air allowing you to utilize your Stinger against heavy air support, while Blind Eye Pro allows you to easily shoot down UAVs and light air support with your PKP. Blast Shield protects you from enemies trying to root you out, and Marksman allows you to spot enemies at long ranges more easily.

This Assault package is designed to assist you in locking down an area. Use your I.M.S. to guard your back or to cover an objective. Unlock the Assault Drone and clean house on the enemy team as they try to push against an area you control. Finish with Juggernaut and move out into the open with your new LMG blazing.

CHIEF GRUNT

WEAPON TYPE	SUB MACHINE GUN
PRIMARY WEAPON	MP7
ATTACHMENT	EXTENDED MAGS
PROFICIENCY	FOCUS
SECONDARY WEAPON	MP9
ATTACHMENT	AKIMBO
	EQUIPMENT
LETHAL	BOUNCING BETTY
TACTICAL	FLASH GRENADE
PERK 1	SLEIGHT OF HAND
PERK 2	ASSASSIN
PERK 3	STEADY AIM
STRIKE PACKAGE	SUPPORT
POINTSTREAK 1	UAV
POINTSTREAK 2	COUNTER-UAV
POINTSTREAK 3	ADVANCED UAV
DEATH STREAK	JUICED

Designed to support your team while hounding the enemy team's flanks at close range, the MP7 has predictable recoil, allowing you to spray from the hip at close range or tap out accurate fire at a distance. Akimbo MP9s give you even more close-range firepower.

Sleight of Hand lets you reload your rapidly firing weapons quickly, while Assassin gives you the coverage to close with the enemy team, and Steady Aim combined with Focus on your MP7 gives you a huge edge in CQC engagements.

Support is taken to give your team (and you!) constant aerial recon. Because close-range attack is risky, even death can't stop your Pointstreaks from rolling on, guaranteeing coverage no matter how many you kill on each assault.

ONE OR MORE SHOTS, ONE KILL

WEAPON TYPE	SNIPER RIFLE
PRIMARY WEAPON	RSASS
ATTACHMENT	THERMAL SCOPE, SILENCER
PROFICIENCY	ATTACHMENT
SECONDARY WEAPON	MP9
ATTACHMENT	SILENCER
	EQUIPMENT
LETHAL	CLAYMORE
TACTICAL	SMOKE GRENADE
PERK 1	BLIND EYE
PERK 2	ASSASSIN
PERK 3	SITREP
STRIKE PACKAGE	ASSAULT
POINTSTREAK 1	I.M.S.
POINTSTREAK 2	ATTACK HELICOPTER
POINTSTREAK 3	PAVE LOW
DEATH STREAK	JUICED

A completely stealthy long-range assassin build, the Thermal Silenced RSASS provides a stable and quick-firing sniper rifle that can easily pick out targets with Thermal behind any cover or in any shadow. Aim for two quick shots to down your prey. Use two nasty tricks with this build: First, when you score a kill, stay in the scope. Your prey has a very difficult time locating you from a purely Thermal killcam! Second, toss a Smoke Grenade on an objective or chokepoint as bait, then use the Thermal to pierce the veil and take down your target.

Blind Eye and Assassin provide the core of a stealth build, while Sitrep gives you an edge for locating enemies, as well as an early audio warning if an enemy comes near your position.

The I.M.S., along with your Claymore, guards your back, while the Attack Helicopter and Pave Low provide fire and forget Pointstreaks so you can continue your deadly silent overwatch on the battlefield.

CUSTOM CLASSES BY MODE

THE NOMAD

MODE	FREE FOR ALL
PRIMARY WEAPON	FAD
ATTACHMENT	SILENCER
PROFICIENCY	IMPACT
SECONDARY WEAPON	P99
ATTACHMENT	EXTENDED MAGS
	EQUIPMENT
LETHAL	SEMTEX
TACTICAL	CONCUSSION GRENADE
PERK 1	BLIND EYE
PERK 2	QUICKDRAW
PERK 3	STALKER
STRIKE PACKAGE	ASSAULT
POINTSTREAK 1	UAV
POINTSTREAK 2	ATTACK HELICOPTER
POINTSTREAK 3	AH-6 OVERWATCH
DEATH STREAK	DEAD MAN'S HAND

This class is built for running and gunning while alone in the desert of free-for-all. The FAD is an all-around good AR with stable firing characteristics and a high rate of fire. The P99 with extended mags is a strong secondary with plenty of ammo when the mag in your FAD is drained and you need to finish off your target. The common Semtex/Concussion Equipment combo provides the damage and utility for a mobile class.

For perks, Blind Eye protects you from the inevitable onslaught of air support. Quickdraw provides an ADS boost—important for frequent target engagement while moving around the map. Additionally, the pro version reduces grenade toss time, bringing your weapon to the ready faster. The ADS movement speed boost provided by Stalker is an excellent addition for the frantic pace of an FFA game.

The Assault Strike Package Pointstreaks are bog standard and provide eyes on the enemy and unmanned helicopters to rake in the kills while you concentrate on ground combat and looping your streaks.

THE CRYPT

MODE	TEAM DEATHMATCH
PRIMARY WEAPON	M4A1
ATTACHMENT	RED DOT SIGHT, GRENADE LAUNCHER
PROFICIENCY	ATTACHMENT
SECONDARY WEAPON	FMG9
ATTACHMENT	SILENCER
	EQUIPMENT
LETHAL	FRAG
TACTICAL	EMP GRENADE
PERK 1	RECON
PERK 2	HARDLINE
PERK 3	STALKER
STRIKE PACKAGE	SUPPORT
POINTSTREAK 1	COUNTER-UAV
POINTSTREAK 2	AIRDROP TRAP
POINTSTREAK 3	EMP
DEATH STREAK	REVENGE

The Crypt is built for the true battlefield enthusiast. The versatility of the M4A1 makes up for its somewhat lower damage numbers and covers nearly all engagement scenarios when paired with a Machine Pistol like the FMG9. Adding a Grenade Launcher takes care of mass engagements from a distance and adding a Silencer to the FMG9 provides some stealth when caught away from teammates behind enemy lines. The EMP Grenade is useful for ruining a would-be devastating Pointstreak as it can take out several dangerous air assault vehicles, and any enemy equipment.

The Recon perk assists your team with directional radar information when you hit an enemy which is useful for quick target acquisition by any nearby allies. When paired with a Support Strike Package, Hardline can provide the help your team needs to stay in the lead.

For the Strike Package, take a counter-UAV to cripple enemy radar and an EMP to completely shut down their Pointstreak support and radar. The airdrop trap is an evil addition that can result in enemy casualties when greed gets the better of them—and extra easy kills if placed carefully.

MAP ROBOT

MODE	SEARCH AND DESTROY
PRIMARY WEAPON	ACR 6.8
ATTACHMENT	HYBRID SIGHT
PROFICIENCY	STABILITY
SECONDARY WEAPON	SKORPION
ATTACHMENT	AKIMBO
	EQUIPMENT
LETHAL	FRAG
TACTICAL	PORTABLE RADAR
PERK 1	BLIND EYE
PERK 2	QUICKDRAW
PERK 3	SITREP
STRIKE PACKAGE	SUPPORT
POINTSTREAK 1	UAV
POINTSTREAK 2	BALLISTIC VESTS
POINTSTREAK 3	SAM TURRET
DEATH STREAK	FINAL STAND

The Map Robot is a generalist and is wary of any specialized offensive equipment, preferring to focus on shooting guys with guns. The addition of a Hybrid Sight on the ACR extends its utility to medium-long fire-fights without sacrificing the solid performance of a Red Dot Sight entirely. Switch to the dual Skorpions when you close the distance to dominate enemies at short range. The Portable Radar can be a strong piece of equipment in S&D, both protecting a bomb site from flanking and providing quick insight into the enemies' defenses.

Blind Eye provides protection from enemy air support, immunity to sentries, and invisibility to Thermal and a good number of controlled Pointstreaks. Quickdraw helps to nullify the ADS penalty of the Hybrid scope, while Sitrep aids in locating defending campers and hearing incoming enemies.

The Support package is chosen to minimize the loss from death, granting your team radar coverage, extra armor, and a SAM to shut down enemy air support.

THE SILENT DELIVERY MAN

MODE	SABOTAGE
PRIMARY WEAPON	P90
ATTACHMENT	EXTENDED MAGS, SILENCER
PROFICIENCY	ATTACHMENT
SECONDARY WEAPON	USP .45
ATTACHMENT	SILENCER
	EQUIPMENT
LETHAL	C4
TACTICAL	EMP GRENADE
PERK 1	BLIND EYE
PERK 2	ASSASSIN
PERK 3	DEAD SILENCE
STRIKE PACKAGE	ASSAULT
POINTSTREAK 1	PREDATOR MISSILE
POINTSTREAK 2	PRECISION AIRSTRIKE
POINTSTREAK 3	STRAFE RUN
DEATH STREAK	DEAD MAN'S HAND

Equally effective at bomb running or retrieving, this full-stealth build preys upon your enemies' reliance on radar and equipment for bomb defense. The P90's high fire rate combined with extended mags allows you to dispatch two or three enemies without reloading. A quick switch to a silenced UMP .45 can finish off any remaining prey. An EMP Grenade can disable any defensive equipment before an assault on the bomb site.

Blind Eye, Assassin, and Dead Silence are the standard full-stealth assortment of perks. Outside of physically sighting you and communicating your location to teammates, your enemies should have no Intel on your location.

Using an Assault Strike Package with three heavy damage, targeted strike Pointstreaks allows you to swing from bomb defense to offense quickly, decimating any bomb defense that may exist before making the move to the bomb site.

THE TECHMARINE

MODE	DOMINATION
PRIMARY WEAPON	M60E4
ATTACHMENT	GRIP
PROFICIENCY	STABILITY
SECONDARY WEAPON	XM25
ATTACHMENT	N/A
EQUIPMENT	
LETHAL	BOUNCING BETTY
TACTICAL	TROPHY SYSTEM
PERK 1	RECON
PERK 2	HARDLINE
PERK 3	SITREP
STRIKE PACKAGE	SUPPORT
POINTSTREAK 1	UAV
POINTSTREAK 2	SAM TURRET
POINTSTREAK 3	ESCORT AIRDROP
DEATH STREAK	FINAL STAND

This is a purpose-built point defense class, capable of setting up shop at a domination point and denying enemy advancement. When properly positioned to cover an area, the M60E4 lays down a wall of lead that only the most tactical of flankers can disrupt. You can set the airburst distance for the XM25 for distance kills or as a CQC-in-a-pinch weapon. Bouncing Betties provide perimeter protection and notification of a breach, while the Trophy System can stop an offensive explosive, giving you time to react and adjust fire to the incoming threat.

Recon allows you to essentially "paint" incoming forces for your team, lighting them up on the radar as they advance. Hardline ensures that all of your hard work mowing down defenders is constantly rewarded and provides a slightly shorter path to the Escort Airdrop.

The UAV and SAM turret come early, providing general information and Pointstreak defense, but the truly powerful reward is the Escort Airdrop. When dropped over a domination point, it showers your team with gifts from the hovering mechanical god while providing cover fire for the unwrapping of the packages.

THE DUCK-BLOCK

MODE	HEADQUARTERS
PRIMARY WEAPON	RIOT SHIELD
ATTACHMENT	N/A
PROFICIENCY	SPEED
SECONDARY WEAPON	G18
ATTACHMENT	AKIMBO
EQUIPMENT	
LETHAL	C4
TACTICAL	TROPHY SYSTEM
PERK 1	SCAVENGER
PERK 2	BLAST SHIELD
PERK 3	STEADY AIM
STRIKE PACKAGE	SUPPORT
POINTSTREAK 1	BALLISTIC VESTS
POINTSTREAK 2	REMOTE SENTRY
POINTSTREAK 3	JUGGERNAUT RECON
DEATH STREAK	FINAL STAND

This class is for the defensive player whose objective is to secure HQ points at any cost. The Riot Shield provides the player victory through attrition as the enemy team unleashes their offensive power with a greatly reduced effect. The Akimbo G18s provide good close-combat power once you hear the tell-tale clicking of attackers reloading after dumping their entire mag into your shield. The speed proficiency boosts mobility for long runs to moving HQ sites, and the C4 can be used to set traps for incoming offensive assaults. Take a Trophy System to protect against the first rounds of incoming ordnance before hunkering down behind your bulletproof glass for the slow burn to victory.

Scavenger provides you with ammo replenishment for the long periods between deaths that are the objective of this defensive loadout. Blast Shield provides added protection from grenades and explosives when capturing or destroying an HQ point. Steady Aim helps with the stability of Akimbo G18s and the Pro version speeds melee recovery when shield-bashing enemies.

What would a defensive build be without a Support Strike Package? Ballistic Vests help the entire team stay alive for point capture or assault. The remote sentry can be set up for point defense and used from a prone position—and your riot shield may protect you from incidental fire while you're out of commission! Finally, the Juggernaut Recon reward ascends the Duck-Block player to the highest levels of defensive distraction, a straight upgrade to an improved version of the same build!

SIEGEBREAKER

MODE	HEADQUARTERS ALTERNATE
PRIMARY WEAPON	PP90M1
ATTACHMENT	RAPID-FIRE
PROFICIENCY	KICK
SECONDARY WEAPON	M320 GLM
ATTACHMENT	NONE
	EQUIPMENT
LETHAL	FRAG
TACTICAL	TACTICAL INSERTION
PERK 1	RECON
PERK 2	BLAST SHIELD
PERK 3	SITREP
STRIKE PACKAGE	SUPPORT
POINTSTREAK 1	BALLISTIC VESTS
POINTSTREAK 2	RECON DRONE
POINTSTREAK 3	EMP
DEATH STREAK	JUICED

Custom made for cracking defenses in Headquarters, the Siegebreaker uses Tac Inserts to respawn near HQ when on the assault, while the PP90M1 provides devastating close-range firepower to clear a room.

Recon allows your Frag Grenades and the M320 to light up enemies inside an HQ, giving your team instant positional info on all enemies within. Blast Shield and Sitrep both give you an edge while attacking or defending the Headquarters.

This support setup is extremely helpful for tackling HQ points. Use Ballistic Vests just before an assault or after you have secured the point. The Recon Drone lets you give near-perfect Intel on an enemy team within an HQ, while scrambling their radar by hovering near the HQ. Finally, the EMP shuts down the enemy team's HUD, crippling their ability to respond to the shifting HQ position.

THE RAZVEDCHIK

MODE	CAPTURE THE FLAG
PRIMARY WEAPON	MP5
ATTACHMENT	RAPID FIRE
PROFICIENCY	FOCUS
SECONDARY WEAPON	MP9
ATTACHMENT	EXTENDED MAGS
	EQUIPMENT
LETHAL	THROWING KNIFE
TACTICAL	TACTICAL INSERTION
PERK 1	EXTREME CONDITIONING
PERK 2	ASSASSIN
PERK 3	STEADY AIM
STRIKE PACKAGE	ASSAULT
POINTSTREAK 1	UAV
POINTSTREAK 2	ATTACK HELICOPTER
POINTSTREAK 3	PAVE LOW
DEATH STREAK	JUICED

This scout class is all about mobility. Primary SMG and secondary Machine Pistol allow you to quickly dispatch your enemies from close range as you speed into their base, while a Throwing Knife can be used to silently and quickly take out an attacker. Tactical Insertions are a must-have on offense in CTF for quick flag runs.

For perks, Extreme Conditioning allows you to sprint quickly across the map, with Assassin and Steady Aim to improve your odds of avoiding or surviving an engagement while running.

The UAV, Attack Helicopter, and Pave Low Pointstreaks are devastating to a defense or to pursuing attackers, and their unmanned nature allows you to continue flag-running while still wreaking havoc.

TIER-1 ASSAULT

MODE	DEMOLITION
PRIMARY WEAPON	STRIKER
ATTACHMENT	GRIP
PROFICIENCY	RANGE
SECONDARY WEAPON	TYPE 95
ATTACHMENT	RED DOT SIGHT
	EQUIPMENT
LETHAL	SEMTEX
TACTICAL	SMOKE GRENADE
PERK 1	EXTREME CONDITIONING
PERK 2	OVERKILL
PERK 3	STEADY AIM
STRIKE PACKAGE	SPECIALIST
POINTSTREAK 1	SLEIGHT OF HAND
POINTSTREAK 2	ASSASSIN
POINTSTREAK 3	BLIND EYE
DEATH STREAK	MARTYRDOM

Using both an automatic shotgun and a burst-fire AR, this build is meant for assaulting the demolition site and clearing out defenders. The Striker with a Range Proficiency can be used to quickly clear a room or small area. Use Smoke Grenades for bomb planting to prevent snipers or LMG cover fire from directly targeting the bomb planter.

Extreme Conditioning and Steady Aim provide the mobility and hip-fire accuracy necessary for deadly shotgun assault. Since this loadout uses a Specialist Strike Package, initial perk choices are only important as a means to get to a full perk unlock.

Sleight of Hand, Blind Eye, and Assassin grant direct lethality and survivability boosts, easily propelling you toward the full perk unlock at eight kills.

THE COLLECTOR

MODE	KILL CONFIRMED
PRIMARY WEAPON	CM901
ATTACHMENT	RED DOT SIGHT
PROFICIENCY	KICK
SECONDARY WEAPON	MP412
ATTACHMENT	AKIMBO
	EQUIPMENT
LETHAL	FRAG
TACTICAL	CONCUSSION GRENADE
PERK 1	SCAVENGER
PERK 2	QUICKDRAW
PERK 3	STALKER
STRIKE PACKAGE	ASSAULT
POINTSTREAK 1	PREDATOR MISSILE
POINTSTREAK 2	REAPER
POINTSTREAK 3	OSPREY GUNNER
DEATH STREAK	REVENGE

The CM901 benefits from a recoil reduction and is a hard-hitting assault rifle. Akimbo MP412s offer good CQC power. The Collector is a lethal deathmatch build with choices centered around the clustered nature of Kill Confirmed battles.

Because you're eliminating enemies and collecting their tags, you might as well get some ammo while you're there with Scavenger! Scavenger is vital for fueling your long run to the Osprey Gunner.

Exercise restraint to reach your Predator, aim for a multi-kill over a pile of dogtags, get your Reaper, then hole up in a safe location to bombard the enemy and unlock the Osprey Gunner to tear the enemy team apart.

THE HERO

MODE	TEAM DEFENDER
PRIMARY WEAPON	SCAR-L
ATTACHMENT	HEARTBEAT SENSOR
PROFICIENCY	IMPACT
SECONDARY WEAPON	.44 MAGNUM
ATTACHMENT	TACTICAL KNIFE
	EQUIPMENT
LETHAL	SEMTEX
TACTICAL	FLASH
PERK 1	RECON
PERK 2	QUICKDRAW
PERK 3	STALKER
STRIKE PACKAGE	SUPPORT
POINTSTREAK 1	COUNTER-UAV
POINTSTREAK 2	BALLISTIC VESTS
POINTSTREAK 3	ADVANCED UAV
DEATH STREAK	REVENGE

Team defender is all about the health of the team and the protection of the target. The jack of all trades utility of a well-balanced AR like the SCAR-L and a hard-hitting secondary for kill finishing fit well into this role. Take advantage of Impact to drill enemies through cover and tag them with Recon.

Recon lets your team know where all of the threats are without constant communication—most importantly letting your flag carrier know about incoming enemies. Quickdraw and Stalker offer balanced offensive and defensive power so that you are ready for the flow of combat roles, as in Team Defender.

Counter-UAV and Advanced UAV shut down the enemy team's situational Intel and boost your team's. Ballistic Vests provide a health edge for your team to assist with protection of your team's asset or assaulting the enemy asset. Finding a place to deploy them that fits with the shifting nature of Team Defender can be challenging. Just place them and hope for the best while defending the area from enemy takeover.

MULTIPLAYER ARSENAL

THE TOOLS OF THE ELITE SOLDIER. USE THEM WELL.

WEAPONS

AS A HIGHLY TRAINED SPECIAL OPERATIVE, YOU ARE SKILLED WITH ALL FORMS OF WEAPONRY.

The weapons you use determine your role on the battlefield, from fast-moving SMG assault to long-range Sniper support.

Mastery of all weapon types is essential to the flexible combatant. Whether the mission is urban search and destroy or open-field battle, having the skill and confidence to choose the correct weapon and utilize it effectively is a vital talent. Commit these weapon briefings to memory and train relentlessly with all types of weaponry.

A WORD ABOUT STATISTICS

We have included very detailed breakdowns of the weapons in *Call of Duty: Modern Warfare 3* this time around. While there is value in knowing the minutiae of weapon breakdowns in each weapon class, here a few points to keep in mind:

- **Infinity Ward may change these numbers with patches down the line. If any weapon proves to be wildly over- or underpowered, expect it to change.**
- **Most of the differences within a given weapon class *are* minute. A great deal of weapon selection is personal preference. One gun might have a better damage range but more pronounced recoil, while another reloads faster and has a quicker fire rate but less effective range.**
- **Finally, recoil is a powerful balancing feature. The combination of recoil patterns, recentering speed, sway, and rate of fire all combine to create a unique feel to each weapon. If you can't hit your target, it doesn't matter how good the weapon looks on paper!**

Playing well and choosing an appropriate weapon class for the map and mode influences your success more than numbers in a table. Use the stats in this chapter to fine-tune your choices between a few favorite guns. Don't let them blind you to the benefits of other weapons!

PRIMARY WEAPONS

ASSAULT RIFLES

ALL-PURPOSE FLEXIBLE WEAPONS, EFFECTIVE IN A WIDE RANGE OF ENGAGEMENTS.

PROS
ACCURATE AND EFFECTIVE AT MANY RANGES
BURST, SEMI-AUTOMATIC, AND AUTOMATIC FIRE TYPES
WIDE VARIETY OF ATTACHMENTS
GOOD PENETRATION
CONS

COMBAT ROLE	ALL-PURPOSE WEAPON
PREFERRED MAP TYPE	MEDIUM TO LARGE, WITH MIXED TERRAIN
OPTIMAL RANGE BAND	CLOSE-MEDIUM TO MEDIUM-LONG

ASSAULT RIFLE TYPES

Assault Rifles come in three types:

- **FULLY AUTOMATIC**
- **BURST-FIRE (M16 AND TYPE 95)**
- **SEMI-AUTOMATIC (MK14 ONLY)**

Of the three types, the fully automatic is the most common and the easiest to use for a beginner. Full-auto rifles are easy to use at medium range, and can still be effective at short range when fired from the hip, or at long range with careful trigger control.

Burst-fire rifles and the MK14 are generally more effective at medium to long range, where their superior accuracy gives you an edge. As a counter-balance, they are somewhat worse at short range, where they lack the full-auto "spray and pray" of the other ARs.

SHORT, CONTROLLED BURSTS

Use fully automatic weapons at long distance by performing quick two- to three-round bursts in rapid succession. With practice, you can use a full-auto rifle almost like the burst-fire weapons, giving you greatly improved accuracy at a distance.

ASSAULT RIFLE CUSTOMIZATION

Assault Rifles have a wide range of attachments and can be configured for greater effectiveness at any range band.

This gives you the flexibility to customize your favorite AR for the specific map and mode you are playing.

ASSAULT RIFLE PROFILES

ALL ASSAULT RIFLES HAVE *MEDIUM* PENETRATION.

DAMAGE DATA

WEAPON NAME	MIN DAMAGE	DAMAGE	ROUNDS PER MINUTE	MAX DAMAGE RANGE	MIN DAMAGE RANGE	HEADSHOT MULTIPLIER	HEADSHOT MIN	HEADSHOT MAX
ACR 6.8	30	45	705	1000	1500	1.4	42	63
AK-47	25	49	689	1250	1800	1.4	35	69
CM901	25	49	666	800	1900	1.4	35	69
FAD	24	30	1000	800	1000	1.7	41	51
G36C	25	40	769	900	1600	1.4	35	56
M4A1	20	42	780	800	1400	1.4	28	59
SCAR-L	20	35	750	1200	1800	1.5	30	52
BURST-FIRE	—	—	—	—	—	—	—	—
M16A4	25	45	780	1000	2000	1.4	35	63
TYPE 95	20	55	1000	800	2000	1.4	28	77
SEMI-AUTOMATIC	—	—	—	—	—	—	—	—
MK14	49	75	545	1000	2000	1.4	69	105

RECOIL DATA

ACR 6.8
RECENTER SPEED 1350

AK-47
RECENTER SPEED 1400

CM901
RECENTER SPEED 1450

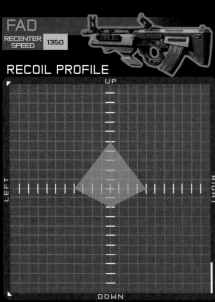

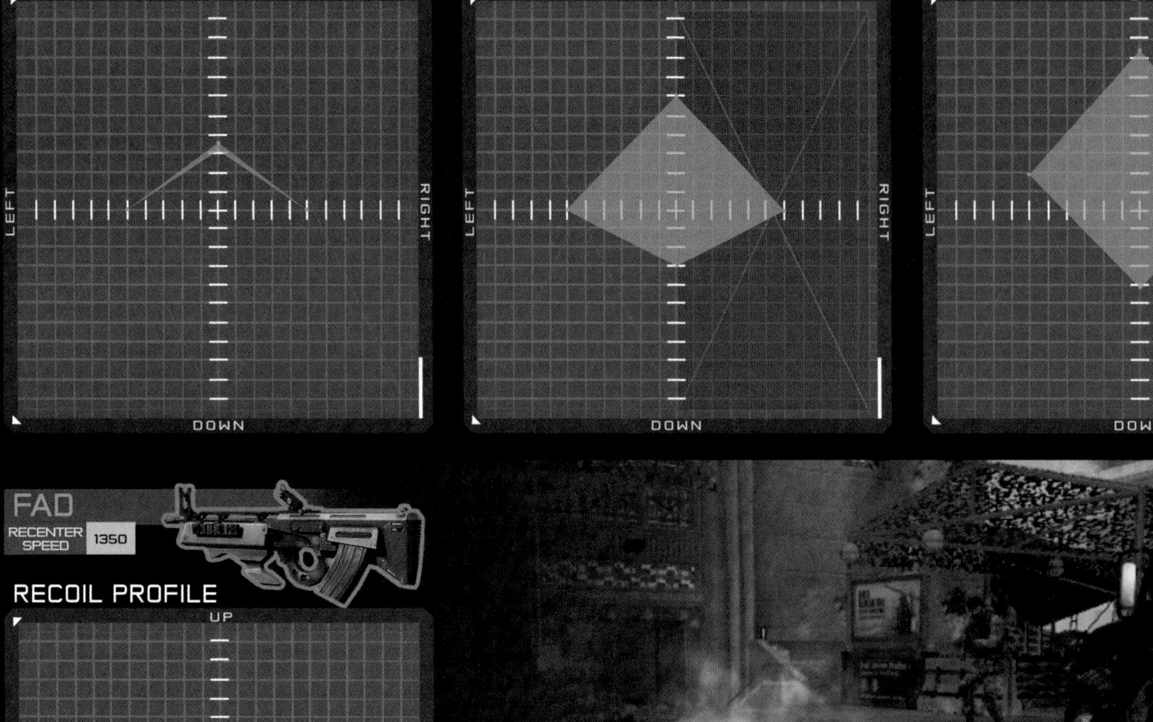

FAD
RECENTER SPEED 1350

RECOIL PROFILE
UP
LEFT
RIGHT
DOWN

G36C

RECENTER SPEED 1600

RECOIL PROFILE

UP LEFT RIGHT DOWN

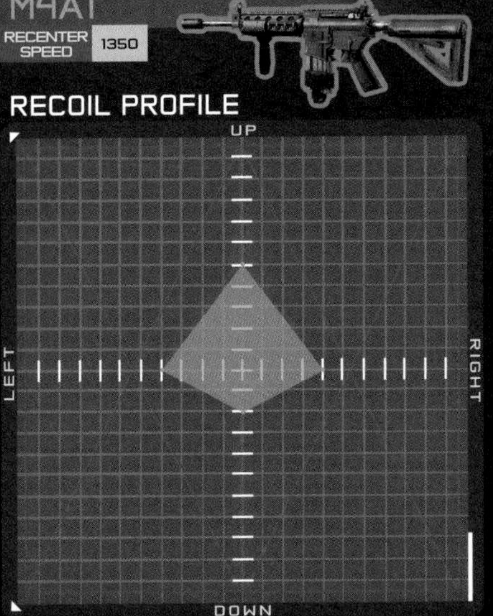

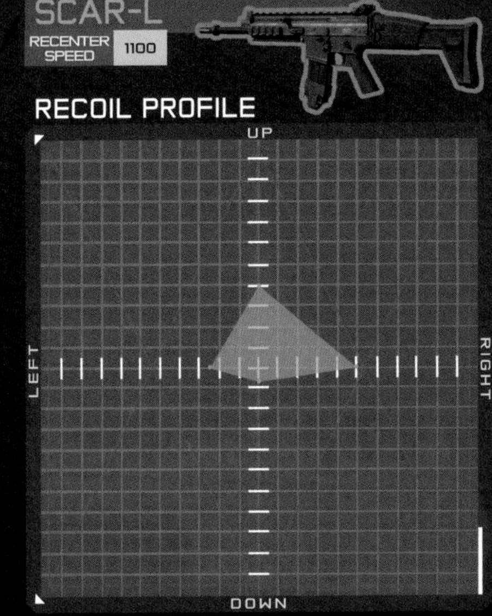

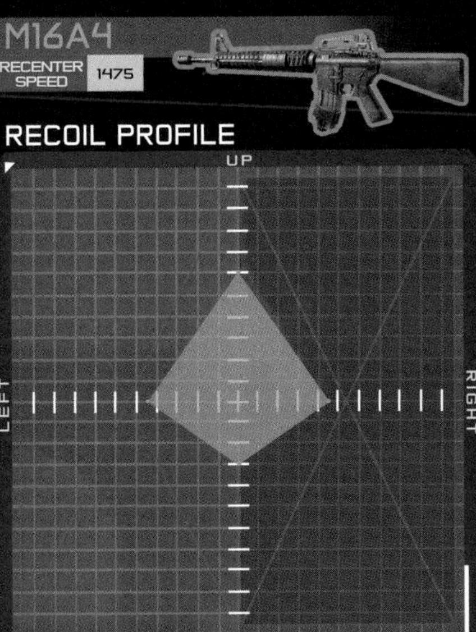

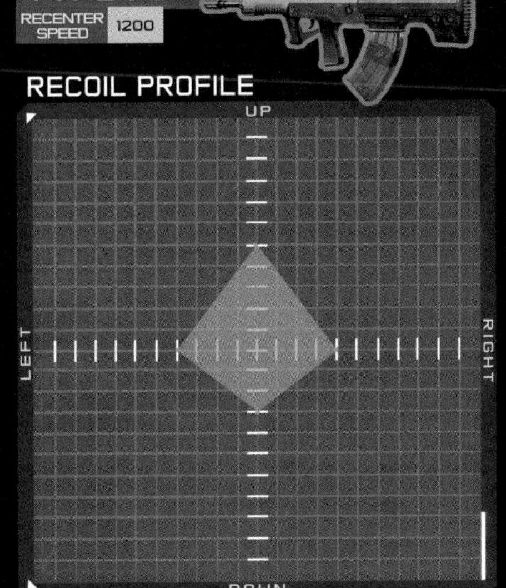

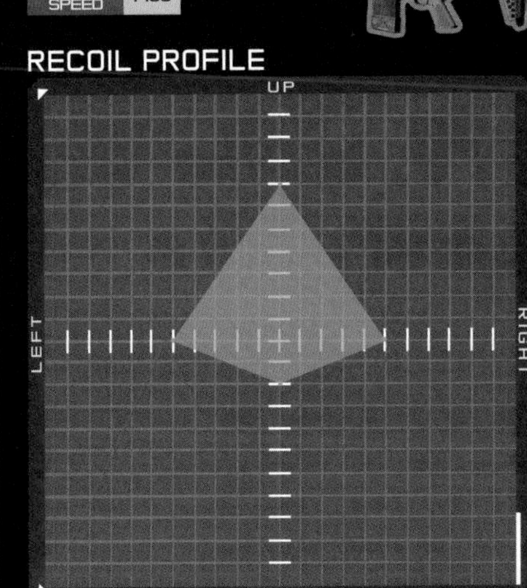

EASE OF USE DATA

WEAPON NAME	RELOAD TIME	RELOAD TIME (FROM EMPTY)	RELOAD TIME (AMMO ADDED)	DROP TIME	RAISE TIME
ACR 6.8	1.9	2.5	1.1	0.6	0.75
AK-47	2.5	3.25	1.75	0.6	1.15
CM901	2.33	2.7	1.1	0.45	0.75
FAD	3.2	3.56	1.5	0.66	1.1
G36C	2.433	3.466	1.5	0.3	0.5
M4A1	2.03	2.36	1.1	0.45	0.75
SCAR-L	2.4	2.68	1.1	0.45	0.75
BURST-FIRE	—	—	—	—	—
M16A4	2.03	2.36	1.1	0.45	0.75
TYPE 95	2.76	3.3	2.06	0.83	0.83
SEMI-AUTOMATIC	—	—	—	—	—
MK14	2.67	3.5	1.9	0.45	1.13

AMMO DATA

WEAPON NAME	STARTING AMMO	MAX AMMO	MAGAZINE SIZE
ACR 6.8	90	180	30
AK-47	90	180	30
CM901	90	180	30
FAD	120	240	40
G36C	90	180	30
M16A4	90	180	30
M4A1	90	180	30
MK14	60	120	20
SCAR-L	90	180	30
TYPE 95	90	180	30

HIGHLY MOBILE CQC WEAPONS WITH HIGH RATES OF FIRE AND GOOD HIP-FIRE ACCURACY.

PROS
EXCELLENT MOBILITY
GOOD HIP-FIRE ACCURACY
HIGH RATE OF FIRE
HIGH DAMAGE AT CLOSE RANGE
CONS
POOR ACCURACY AND DAMAGE AT A DISTANCE
LOW PENETRATION

COMBAT ROLE	CLOSE QUARTERS COMBAT
PREFERRED MAP TYPE	SMALL TO MEDIUM, FAVORING MIXED AND URBAN TERRAIN
OPTIMAL RANGE BAND	CLOSE TO MEDIUM

ASSAULT SPECIALIST

SMGs are the weapon of choice for short-range firefights and any objective mode that demands mobility. They feature high movement speed, fast aim-down-sight (ADS) times, high rates of fire, and good hip-fire accuracy. SMGs are ideal for fast, aggressive assaults on objective targets, or for flanking maneuvers on the enemy team.

SMGs are built to win close-range engagements. Take advantage of this strength by forcing short-range firefights—you don't want to be competing at a distance with close-range weapons.

SUBMACHINE GUN TYPES

All SMGs are automatic fire, and all have very similar statistical profiles. Choosing your favorite SMG is two parts personal preference and one part hard numbers.

Experiment with the different SMGs to test their recoil patterns—all are balanced with different rates of fire, damage, and recoil. Some SMGs are stable enough to be used comfortably at medium range with a proper sight fitted and careful trigger control. Others are best used at short range, especially if you have the Rapid-Fire attachment equipped.

SUBMACHINE GUN CUSTOMIZATION

If you're using an SMG specialized for close range only, consider taking the Overkill perk, or taking a Launcher or pistol to have the ability to fight at a distance. SMGs can be fitted with optics to enhance their effectiveness at distance, but carefully consider the map and game mode you're playing before you attempt to use one in this way. The best-case scenario for this setup is in games that have plenty of close-range engagements but a few medium-range lines of fire that are critical for the game mode.

SUBMACHINE GUN PROFILES

ALL SMGS HAVE *LOW* PENETRATION, EXCEPT THE UMP45, WHICH HAS *HIGH* PENETRATION.

DAMAGE DATA

WEAPON NAME	MIN DAMAGE	DAMAGE	ROUNDS PER MINUTE	MAX DAMAGE RANGE	MIN DAMAGE RANGE	HEADSHOT MULTIPLIER	HEADSHOT MIN	HEADSHOT MAX
MP5	20	42	800	600	800	1.5	30	63
MP7	20	35	895	500	750	1.5	30	52
P90	20	42	857	600	750	1.5	30	63
PM-9	20	35	1090	400	600	1.5	30	52
PP90M1	17	42	1000	600	750	1.5	26	63
UMP45	17	49	750	600	900	1.5	26	74

RECOIL DATA

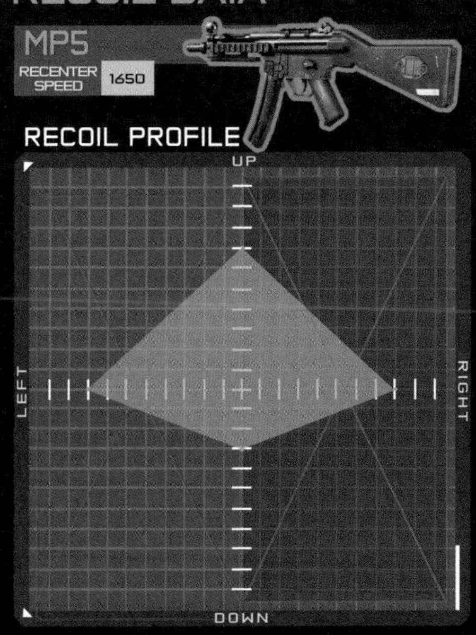

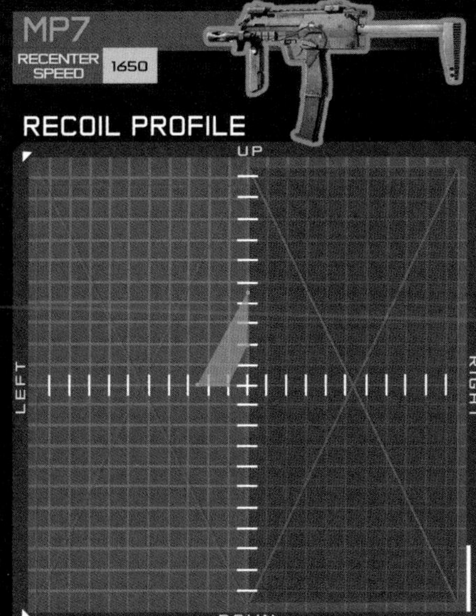

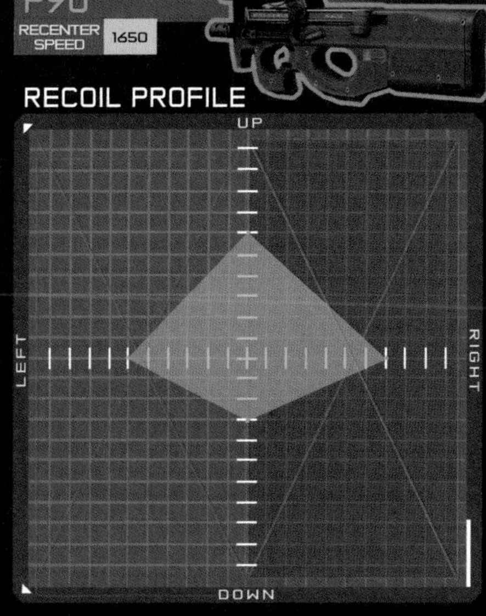

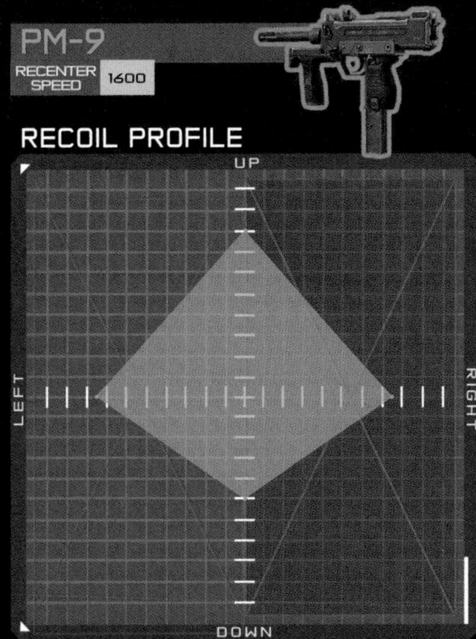

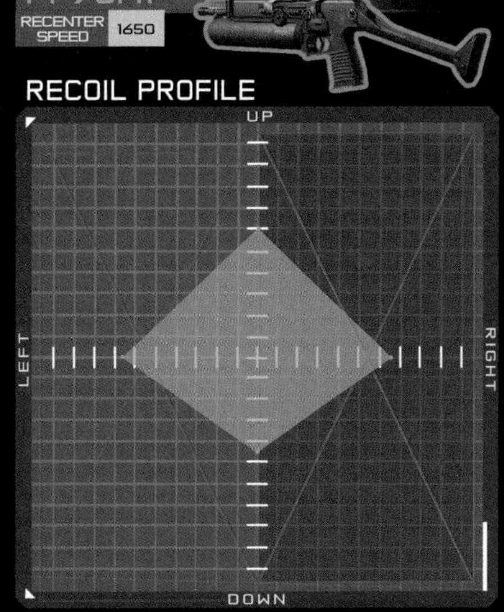

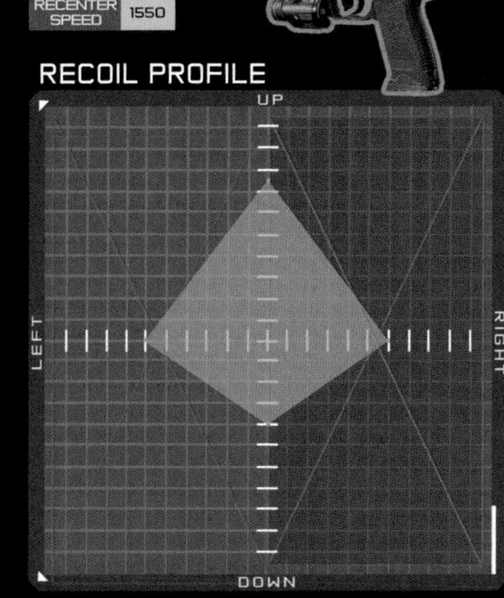

EASE OF USE DATA

WEAPON NAME	RELOAD TIME	RELOAD TIME (FROM EMPTY)	RELOAD TIME (AMMO ADDED)	DROP TIME	RAISE TIME
MP5	2.53	3.03	1.77	0.5	0.83
MP7	3	3.63	2.167	0.42	0.8
P90	2.76	3.5	1.77	0.8	0.76
PM-9	3	4.13	2.2	0.42	1.233
PP90M1	3.03	3.97	2.06	0.66	1.333
UMP45	2.5	3.03	1.8	0.8	0.76

AMMO DATA

WEAPON NAME	STARTING AMMO	MAX AMMO	MAGAZINE SIZE
MP5	90	180	30
MP7	120	240	40
P90	150	300	50
PM-9	96	192	32
PP90M1	108	216	36
UMP45	96	192	32

LIGHT MACHINE GUNS

POWERFUL MACHINE GUNS, IDEAL FOR MEDIUM- TO LONG-RANGE SUPPRESSION AND DEFENSIVE LOCKDOWN.

PROS
HIGH DAMAGE, GOOD PENETRATION
LARGE MAGAZINES
EXTREMELY STABLE WHEN PRONE
EFFECTIVE AGAINST CERTAIN AIR SUPPORT
CONS
POOR MOBILITY AND ADS SPEEDS
POOR HIP-FIRE ACCURACY
LOUD AND VERY VISIBLE WHEN FIRED FULL-AUTO

COMBAT ROLE	SUPPRESSION AND LONG-RANGE ENGAGEMENT
PREFERRED MAP TYPE	MEDIUM AND LARGE WITH GOOD SIGHT LINES WHILE PRONE
OPTIMAL RANGE BAND	MEDIUM TO LONG

SUPPRESSIVE FIREPOWER

LMGs are the heavy hitters of your arsenal. With large magazines, high damage and great penetration, they can be used to cover an area extremely effectively. Consider LMGs to be the inverse of SMGs. While SMGs excel at close-range rapid assault, LMGs excel at locking down an area defensively.

LMGs are poor on offense due to the slowest movement speed of all weapons, terrible hip-fire spreads, the slowest ADS speed, and their very loud and distinctive reports and muzzle flashes (though a Silencer can help with the last problem).

Treat LMGs as a form of specialist Sniper Rifle, and you won't be far off the mark. Think about the map in terms of lines of fire and areas with lots of cover that you can exploit. Constantly change your angle when you cover an area or objective, and you can cause serious pain for anyone trying to enter your zone of control.

SHOOTING THE SKY

LMGs are particularly well suited for taking down UAVs, CUAVs, and the various low-flying support helicopters.

With the Blind Eye Pro perk, an LMG can take down even the heavily armored Pave Low almost as efficiently as an anti-air launcher. Be wary of doing so unless you're sure the area from which you're firing is secure. Spraying bullets into the air with an LMG tends to attract attention...

LIGHT MACHINE GUN TYPES

All LMGs fulfill the same battlefield role, but there are some differences in rates of fire and recoil patterns. Also, two LMGs load via large canister magazines rather than belt-fed ammo boxes. As a consequence, they have *vastly* quicker reload times, which can be a factor in some situations.

RELOAD AT YOUR OWN RISK

Don't let the urge to play action movie hero get to you. Spraying on full-auto is a bad idea for many reasons, not the least of which is that the reload time on an LMG is the longest in the game.

Conserving ammo allows you to cover an area without reloading. Because a lot of players are used to seeing a spray of fire and then attacking when they expect a reload, you can catch them dead in your sights when they come into the open.

LIGHT MACHINE GUN CUSTOMIZATION

LMGs benefit significantly from the Grip attachment, as it allows you to better manage their heavy recoil, especially on maps or modes where prone use is difficult. It's possible to use a Silencer on LMGs, which can help reduce their otherwise easily recognizable muzzle flash and loud noise.

BIPOD STABILITY

When prone, LMGs have massively reduced recoil. Whenever you can, go prone while you cover an area!

LIGHT MACHINE GUN PROFILES

ALL LMGS HAVE *HIGH* PENETRATION.

DAMAGE FALLOFF

LMGs now suffer damage falloff. This is new to *Modern Warfare 3*—take note!

DAMAGE DATA

WEAPON NAME	MIN DAMAGE	DAMAGE	ROUNDS PER MINUTE	MAX DAMAGE RANGE	MIN DAMAGE RANGE	HEADSHOT MULTIPLIER	HEADSHOT MIN	HEADSHOT MAX
M60E4	30	50	600	700	1500	1.4	42	70
MG36	25	40	769	900	1600	1.4	35	56
MK46	25	40	857	750	1500	1.4	35	56
PKP PECHENEG	25	40	705	1200	1600	1.4	35	56
L86 LSW	20	38	800	850	1500	1.4	28	53

RECOIL DATA

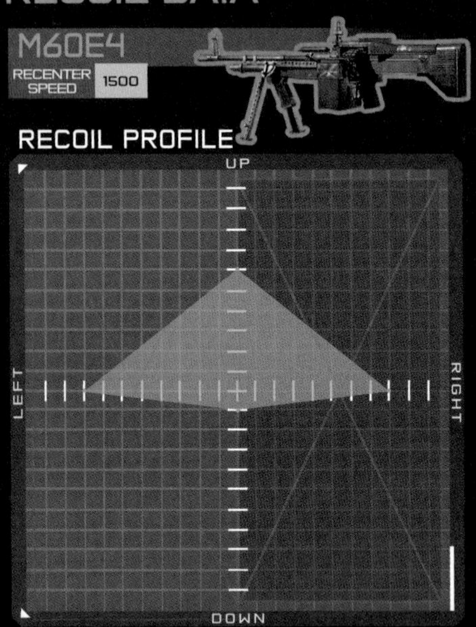

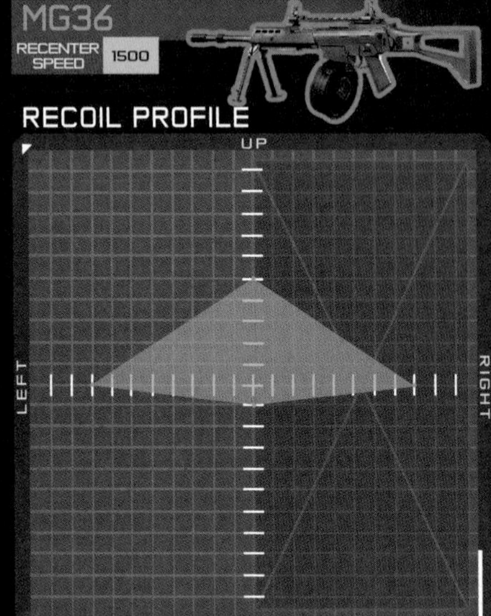

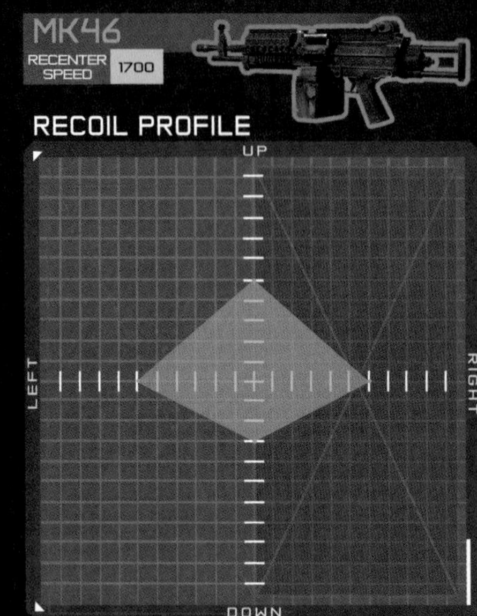

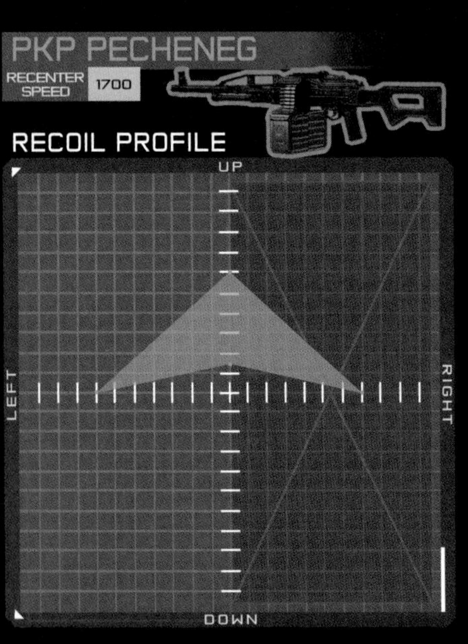

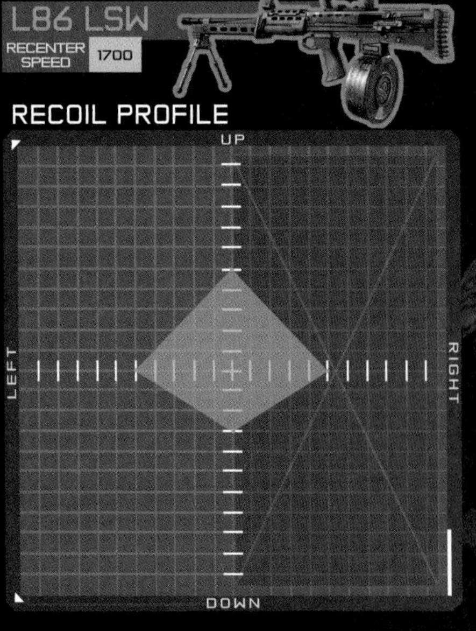

EASE OF USE DATA

WEAPON NAME	RELOAD TIME	RELOAD TIME (FROM EMPTY)	RELOAD TIME (AMMO ADDED)	DROP TIME	RAISE TIME
M60E4	9.3	9.3	6.8	0.533	0.83
MG36	3.73	4.53	4	0.533	0.83
MK46	8.67	8.67	7.13	0.6	1.25
PKP PECHENEG	8.06	8.66	6.13	0.6	1.36
L86 LSW	3.76	3.76	3	0.75	1.03

AMMO DATA

WEAPON NAME	STARTING AMMO	MAX AMMO	MAGAZINE SIZE
M60E4	200	300	100
MG36	200	300	100
MK46	200	300	100
PKP PECHENEG	200	300	100
L86 LSW	200	300	100

SNIPER RIFLES

TOOLS OF THE PRECISION MARKSMAN, SNIPER RIFLES ARE LETHAL AT EXTREME RANGE.

PROS
ONE-SHOT KILLS
EFFECTIVE AT EXTREME RANGE
CONS
POOR WEAPONS AT SHORTER RANGE
DEMAND HIGH ACCURACY TO BE EFFECTIVE

COMBAT ROLE	LONG-RANGE ENGAGEMENTS AND AREA DENIAL
PREFERRED MAP TYPE	MEDIUM AND LARGE MAPS WITH LONG LINES OF FIRE
OPTIMAL RANGE BAND	MEDIUM-LONG TO LONG

ONE SHOT, ONE KILL

Capable of instantly dispatching a target at ultra-long range, Sniper Rifles are the perfect weapons for covering long lanes of fire. By moving quickly from location to location on open maps with a lot of cover, or by locking down the approach to an objective, you can make it extremely difficult for the enemy team to get close to you or an objective.

With practice, you can use Sniper Rifles effectively at medium range by performing quick scoped shots. However, at that distance, enemy Assault Rifles have a much easier time targeting you.

Sniper Rifles require a unique skill set to use well, and they can be unwelcoming if you're new to the game. Try the semi-automatic rifles when you're learning. They're much more forgiving of missed shots than the bolt-action rifles. And don't discount the psychological impact of a Sniper Rifle. Many players *hate* being sniped. They will go out of their way to hunt you down, ignoring objectives or focusing on revenge to the exclusion of easier targets. Exploit this behavior whenever you can!

When you ADS with a Sniper Rifle scope, your view suffers very significant sway—enough that aiming at long-range targets becomes difficult. To steady your aim, you can hold your breath. You can do this only for a few seconds, and releasing it causes your view to sway wildly for a moment, long enough to lose a target if you release at the wrong time.

Get in the habit of scanning for targets at medium range, without scoping. Scope at longer range when you spot movement. In both situations, quickly hold your breath and take the shot. You can improve your results against medium-range targets by scoping and holding your breath simultaneously, and taking the shot the instant you're on target. If you're new to sniping, the Marksman perk can help. It gives you long-range target acquisition and the ability to hold your breath longer if necessary.

SNIPER RIFLE TYPES

There are two types of Sniper Rifle. Bolt-action rifles have high damage but lower rates of fire, while semi-automatic rifles deal less damage and require more accurate aim but can fire more quickly. Both types can be highly effective. Experiment with each rifle to learn its recoil pattern, and choose your favorite based on its killshot profile—the various rifles have different multipliers for different areas of your target.

SNIPER RIFLE CUSTOMIZATION

Sniper Rifles are heavily influenced by the optics you use on them. Default sights, Variable Zoom scopes, Thermals, and ACOGs all provide a very different sniping feel, and each is appropriate for different maps and modes.

A Silencer also has a dramatic impact on Sniper Rifle performance. Unlike other weapon types, where a Silencer reduces the minimum and maximum damage ranges, on Sniper Rifles, the Silencer outright reduces the damage, requiring a more accurate shot or a greater number of shots to kill.

BIPOD STABILITY

Like LMGs, Sniper Rifles have greatly improved control when you fire them prone. This is especially noticeable with the semi-auto rifles. Take advantage of this feature by engaging moving targets at very long range in any area where you can go prone with a good line of sight.

SNIPER RIFLE PROFILES

ALL SNIPER RIFLES HAVE *HIGH* PENETRATION. THE BARRETT .50CAL AND THE AS50 BOTH HAVE SLOWER MOVEMENT SPEED THAN OTHER SNIPER RIFLES. THE L118A IS A BOLT-ACTION RIFLE, AND THE AS50 HAS A SHARPLY LIMITED FIRE RATE.

DAMAGE DATA

WEAPON NAME	DAMAGE	ROUNDS PER MINUTE	HEADSHOT MULTIPLIER	NECK MULTIPLIER	UPPER TORSO MULTIPLIER	LOWER TORSO MULTIPLIER	KILLSHOT FROM
AS50	98	200	1.5	1.1	1.1	1	UPPER TORSO AND UP
BARRETT .50CAL	98	1200	1.5	1.5	1.5	1.1	LOWER TORSO AND UP
DRAGUNOV	70	1200	1.5	1.1	1.1	1	HEADSHOT ONLY
L118A	98	225	1.5	1.5	1.5	1.1	LOWER TORSO AND UP
MSR	98	1200	1.5	1.5	1.5	1.1	LOWER TORSO AND UP
RSASS	70	1200	1.5	1.5	1.5	1.1	UPPER TORSO AND UP

RECOIL DATA

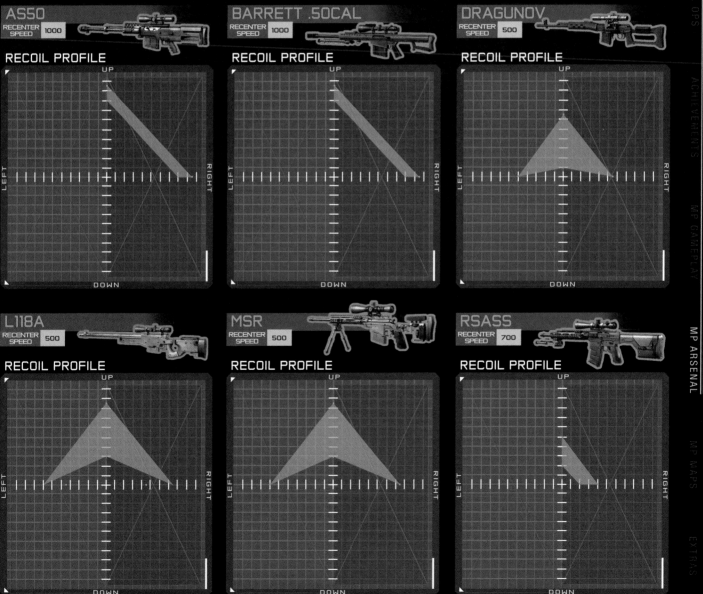

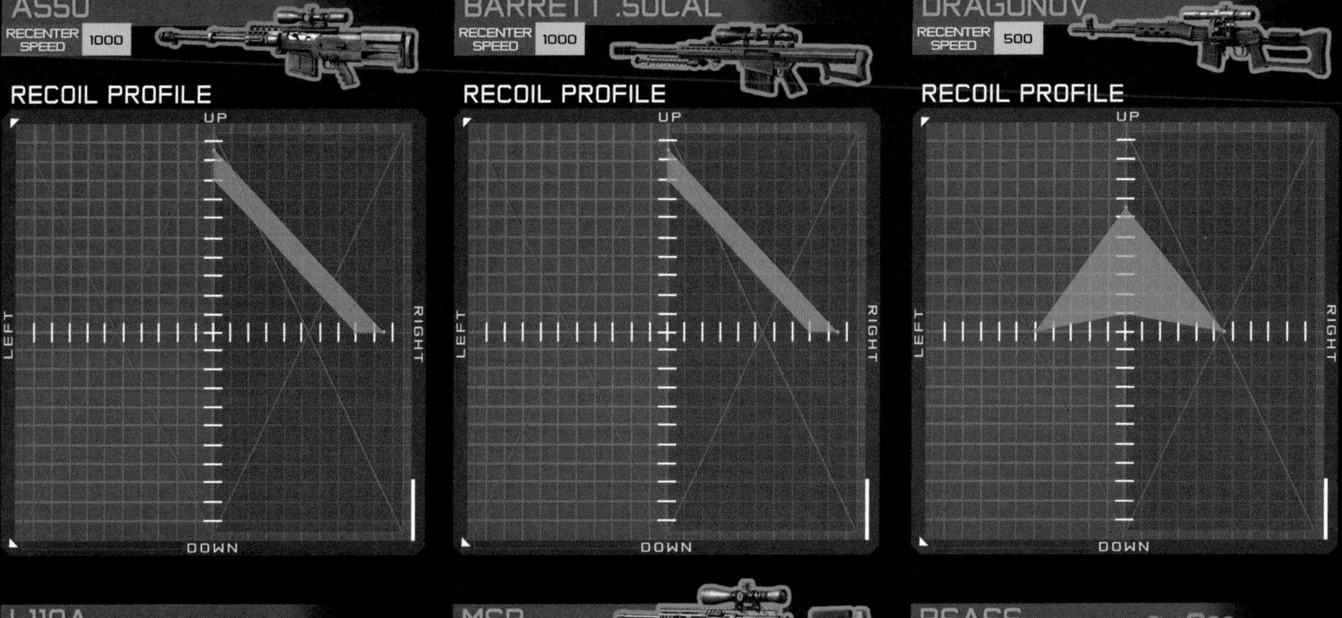

L118A

RECENTER SPEED 500

RECOIL PROFILE

UP

LEFT

RIGHT

DOWN

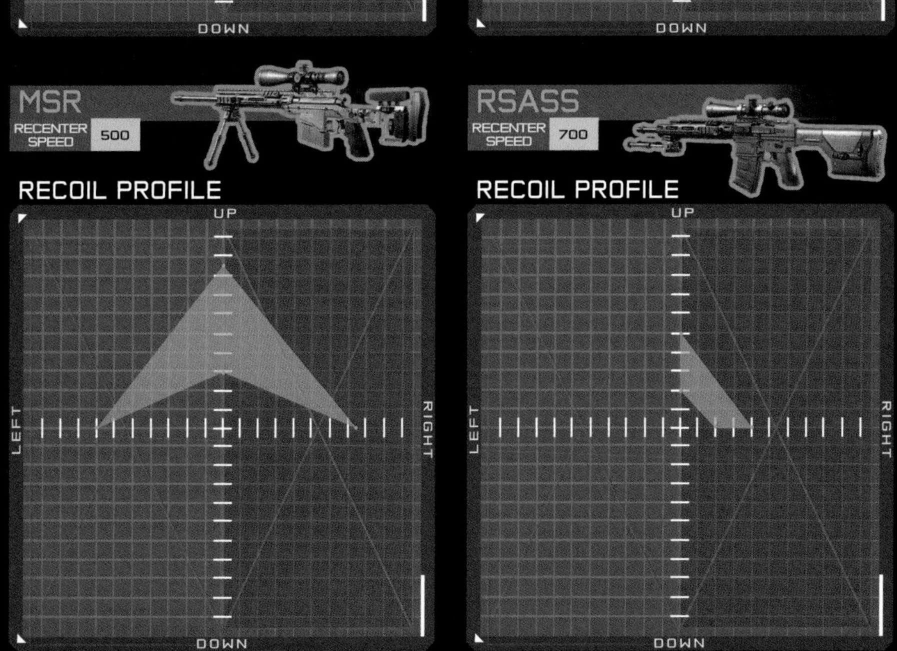

EASE OF USE DATA

WEAPON NAME	RELOAD TIME	RELOAD TIME (FROM EMPTY)	RELOAD TIME (AMMO ADDED)	DROP TIME	RAISE TIME
AS50	3.56	4.46	0	0.93	1.23
BARRETT .50CAL	3.917	4.25	2.8	0.7	1
DRAGUNOV	2.75	3.55	1.75	0.85	1.15
L118A	3.03	4.3	2.8	0.8	1.25
MSR	2.268	3.867	2.8	0.8	1
RSASS	2.7	2.93	2.4	0.55	0.9

AMMO DATA

WEAPON NAME	STARTING AMMO	MAX AMMO	MAGAZINE SIZE
AS50	15	30	5
BARRETT .50CAL	30	60	10
DRAGUNOV	30	60	10
L118A	20	40	5
MSR	20	40	5
RSASS	40	80	20

SHOTGUNS

DEVASTATING WEAPONS IN SHORT-RANGE URBAN ENGAGEMENTS.

PROS
ONE-SHOT KILLS AT CLOSE RANGE
HIGH MOBILITY
GOOD HIP-FIRE ACCURACY
CONS
EFFECTIVE AT SHORT RANGE ONLY
LIMITED AMMUNITION ON SEMI-AUTO VARIANTS
SLOW RE-FIRE RATE ON PUMP-ACTION VARIANTS
SLOW RELOAD TIMES

COMBAT ROLE	ROOM CLEARING
PREFERRED MAP TYPE	SMALL TO MEDIUM WITH HIGH URBAN DENSITY
OPTIMAL RANGE BAND	SHORT RANGE

ROOM SWEEPERS

Shotguns are lethal close-range weapons, ideal for clearing rooms and patrolling urban areas with sharp corners and short engagement distances. Shotguns are devastating at close range, but they are literally useless at a distance. Unlike other weapons, which simply suffer reduced damage at long range, shotgun pellets simply vanish past their minimum damage range.

This also means that the Range proficiency and the Silencer attachment are both important for shotguns, for different reasons. Range increases the shotgun's actual effective distance. Meanwhile, in exchange for quieting a shotgun's report, a Silencer *decreases* the maximum distance that you can inflict *any* damage with a shotgun.

Despite their limitations, shotguns are extremely powerful, as they can take down targets in one shot. The automatic versions can often down multiple enemies at close range with little difficulty.

SHOTGUN TYPES

The two types of shotguns are pump-action and automatic. Pump-action shotguns (lever action in the case of the 1887) deal more damage per shot but have much slower re-fire rates. This means that an inaccurate first shot may not leave you any chance for a second shot. On the other hand, automatic shotguns can lay down an impressive wall of lead in a short amount of time. They are especially lethal around indoor objectives, and they're powerful defending narrow chokepoints.

SHOTGUN CUSTOMIZATION

Shotguns benefit relatively little from most attachments, though a Grip on the automatic variants and Extended Mags can be helpful. We don't recommend a Silencer for most maps, because, while other weapons lose some *maximum* damage range, shotguns lose range *period*. Given that they're already short-range weapons, this can limit them nearly to knifing distance.

SHOTGUN PROFILES

ALL SHOTGUNS HAVE *LOW* PENETRATION. SHOTGUNS DO NOT DEAL BONUS HEADSHOT DAMAGE.

DAMAGE DATA

WEAPON NAME	MIN DAMAGE	DAMAGE	ROUNDS PER MINUTE	MAX DAMAGE RANGE	MIN DAMAGE RANGE	NUM PELLETS	MIN TOTAL DAMAGE	MAX TOTAL DAMAGE
AA-12	5	15	400	250	450	8	40	120
KSG 12	15	28	163	400	600	6	90	168
MODEL 1887	20	30	240	300	700	8	160	240
SPAS-12	5	25	127	400	700	8	40	200
STRIKER	15	25	352	300	600	6	90	150
USAS 12	5	25	139	400	700	6	30	150

RECOIL DATA

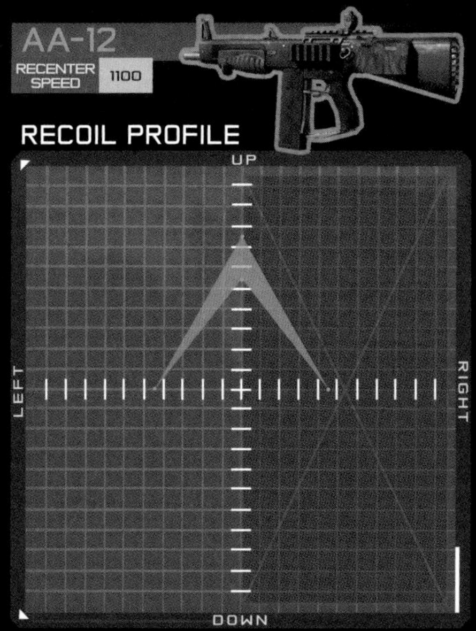

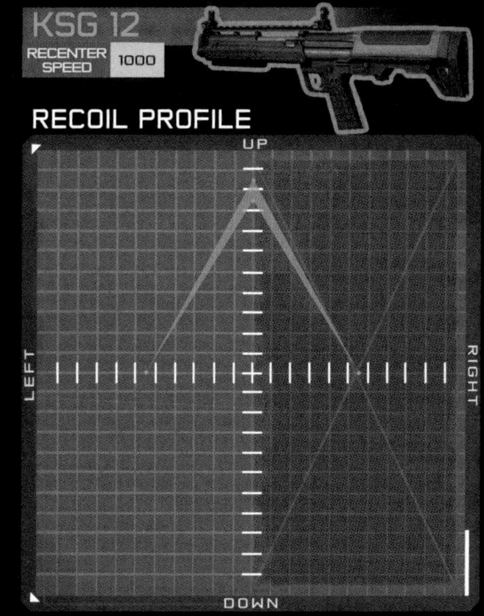

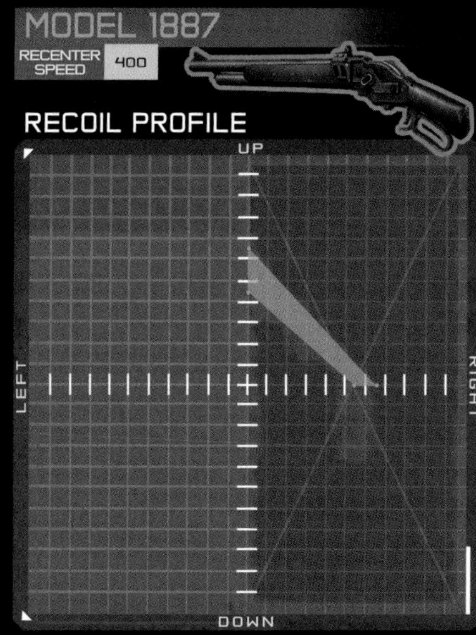

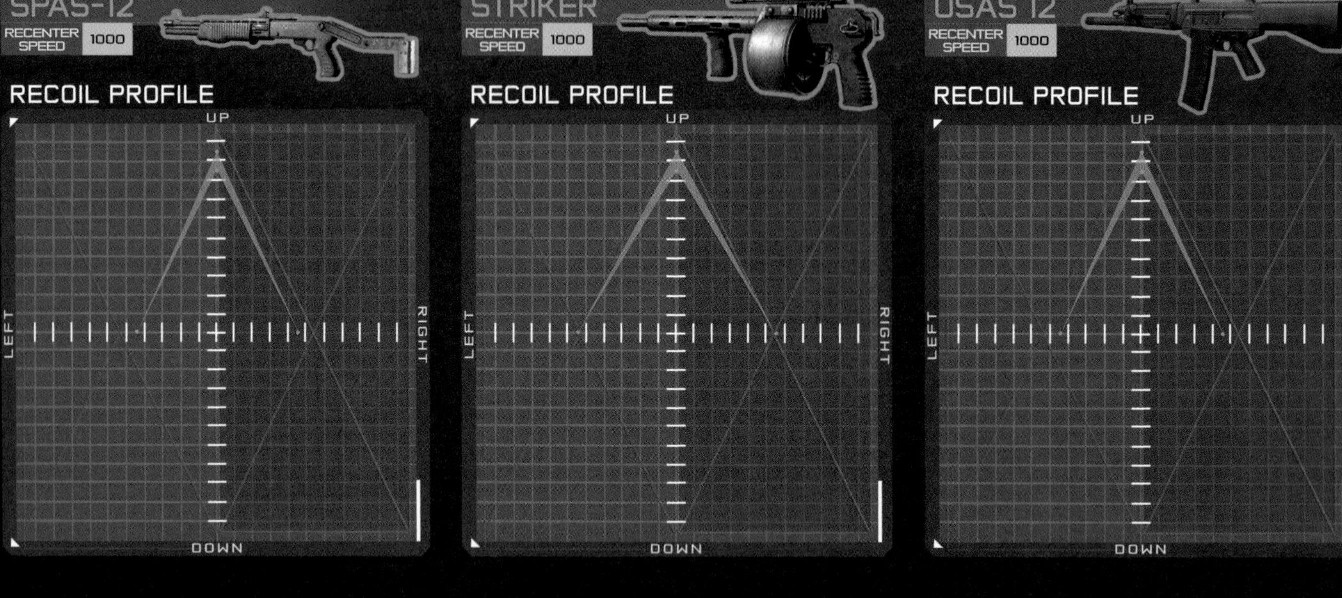

EASE OF USE DATA

WEAPON NAME	RELOAD TIME	RELOAD TIME (FROM EMPTY)	RELOAD TIME (AMMO ADDED)	DROP TIME	RAISE TIME
AA-12	2.75	3.583	2	0.6	1
KSG 12	0.66	0.66	0	0.83	0.96
MODEL 1887	0.65	0.85	0.6	0.75	1.233
SPAS-12	0.667	0.667	1	0.83	1.075
STRIKER	0.666	0.666	0.3	0.83	1
USAS 12	3.2	3.93	0	0.93	1.16

AMMO DATA

WEAPON NAME	STARTING AMMO	MAX AMMO	MAGAZINE SIZE
AA-12	16	32	8
KSG 12	36	60	12
MODEL 1887	28	56	7
SPAS-12	32	64	8
STRIKER	36	60	12
USAS 12	36	56	6

RIOT SHIELD

A PROTECTIVE SHIELD TO GUARD YOURSELF AND TEAMMATES, BLOCK HALLWAYS, AND DEFEND OBJECTIVES.

A ONE-MAN WALL

The Riot Shield is an unusual 'weapon,' an almost purely defensive tool that's effective in certain objective modes. We don't recommend it for general deathmatch modes. However, in objective modes the Riot Shield can be valuable in blocking an access route or providing cover from long-range fire while you claim an objective.

When you stand with the Riot Shield, it blocks you from most incoming frontal fire, but shots can still hit your feet. If you are crouched, you can deflect almost all incoming fire.

When a Riot Shield is placed on your back via weapon switching, it blocks shots from the rear, just as if you were using it from the front. This can occasionally save your life! It's actually possible to survive an I.M.S. strike by going prone with a Riot Shield on your back!

You can perform melee strikes with the Riot Shield, but unlike the knife, it takes two hits from the shield to down a target. Of course, if your target is ineffectually spraying at you from short range, go for it! As a general rule, the Riot Shield is most effective when organized teammates can exploit it. Such players can use the added cover and distraction that a shield user provides to claim an objective or flank an enemy position.

SECONDARY WEAPONS

MACHINE PISTOLS

RAPID-FIRE SECONDARY WEAPONS, IDEAL FOR CLOSE-RANGE ENGAGEMENTS.

PROS
HIGH RATES OF FIRE
CAN BE DUAL-WIELDED
CONS
HEAVY RECOIL
VERY LOW DAMAGE AT RANGE

COMBAT ROLE	CLOSE-RANGE BACKUP WEAPON

CLOSE-QUARTERS BACKUP

Machine Pistols make excellent secondary weapons when you carry Sniper Rifles, LMGs, and burst and semi-auto ARs. Because Machine Pistols are essentially 'mini' SMGs, they help fill the role of a CQC weapon at ranges where those weapons are not as effective.

Machine Pistols have very high rates of fire and good damage at short distance. But they also have extreme recoil and deal poor damage at a distance. This makes them perfect for a quick swap at short range, or to clear a room, but not so great for taking out a target even at medium range.

MACHINE PISTOL CUSTOMIZATION

Machine Pistols can be dual-wielded, giving you extreme close-range firepower, at the cost of negating your medium-range ability. A Machine Pistol with a Silencer is also an effective stealth tool if your primary weapon is unsuppressed and you're in hostile territory.

MACHINE PISTOL PROFILES

ALL MACHINE PISTOLS HAVE *LOW* PENETRATION.

DAMAGE DATA

WEAPON NAME	MIN DAMAGE	DAMAGE	ROUNDS PER MINUTE	MAX DAMAGE RANGE	MIN DAMAGE RANGE	HEADSHOT MULTIPLIER	HEADSHOT MIN	HEADSHOT MAX
FMG9	20	40	1034	400	700	1.4	28	56
G18	17	42	1000	300	500	1.4	24	59
MP9	19	33	895	1000	1600	2	38	66
SKORPION	20	30	857	900	1500	2	40	60

RECOIL DATA

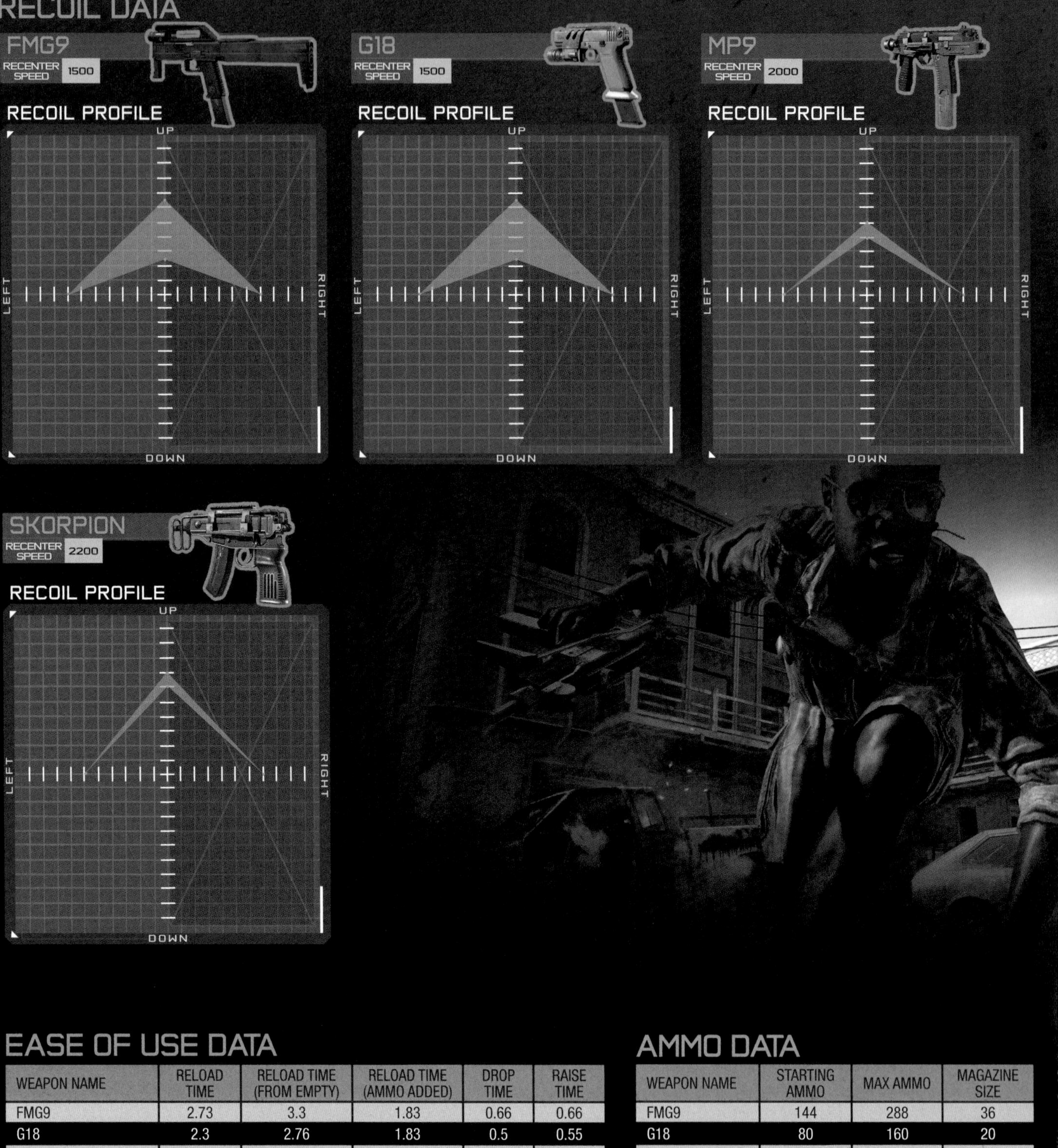

EASE OF USE DATA

WEAPON NAME	RELOAD TIME	RELOAD TIME (FROM EMPTY)	RELOAD TIME (AMMO ADDED)	DROP TIME	RAISE TIME
FMG9	2.73	3.3	1.83	0.66	0.66
G18	2.3	2.76	1.83	0.5	0.55
MP9	2.1	2.933	1.33	0.42	0.8
SKORPION	2.43	3.23	1.77	0.42	0.66

AMMO DATA

WEAPON NAME	STARTING AMMO	MAX AMMO	MAGAZINE SIZE
FMG9	144	288	36
G18	80	160	20
MP9	128	256	32
SKORPION	80	160	20

FAST-SWITCHING SECONDARY WEAPONS, BEST USED TO FINISH A DAMAGED ENEMY WHEN YOUR PRIMARY MAGAZINE IS EMP .

PROS
QUICK SWITCH TIMES
ACCURATE

CONS
SEMI-AUTOMATIC ONLY
LOW DAMAGE AT RANGE
HIGH-CALIBER PISTOLS HAVE LIMITED AMMUNITION

COMBAT ROLE	FAST-SWAP BACKUP WEAPON

QUICK SWITCHING BACKUP

Pistols are accurate semi-automatic weapons that pack a punch at close range and have very quick switch times. This allows you to switch out your primary weapon when you dump a magazine, and finish off wounded targets before they can reload. Because of this trait, Pistols are ideal backup weapons for SMGs or LRs, as they can help you to come out on top in a close-range engagement when your ammo runs dry.

HIGH-CALIBER PISTOLS

The three heavy-impact Pistols, the .44 Magnum, Desert Eagle and MP412, have smaller ammo capacity and harsh recoil (particularly the Desert Eagle). However, you can use all three somewhat effectively for Pistol 'sniping' at a distance. With careful aim, you can inflict solid damage on a stationary or slow-moving target. This can be helpful if your primary weapon is poorly suited to long-range combat, or you simply need a backup distance weapon in a pinch.

PISTOL CUSTOMIZATION

Dual-wielded Pistols are very similar to dual-wielded Machine Pistols, with the advantage of quicker switch times and higher initial damage at very close range. Against a foe that's even slightly damaged, four of the Pistols can take out the target instantly if both initial shots are on the mark. Pistols can also use the Tactical Knife attachment, a unique perk that gives you a knife with a quicker stab and a faster recovery, ideal for short-range stealth kills.

ALL LOW-CALIBER PISTOLS HAVE *LOW* PENETRATION; THE .44 MAGNUM, DESERT EAGLE, AND MP412 HAVE *MEDIUM* PENETRATION.

DAMAGE DATA

WEAPON NAME	MIN DAMAGE	DAMAGE	ROUNDS PER MINUTE	MAX DAMAGE RANGE	MIN DAMAGE RANGE	HEADSHOT MULTIPLIER	HEADSHOT MIN	HEADSHOT MAX
.44 MAGNUM	17	49	750	500	1250	1.4	24	69
DESERT EAGLE	25	49	750	350	1200	1.4	35	69
FIVE SEVEN	17	36	1000	550	800	1.4	24	50
MP412	17	49	750	500	1250	1.4	24	69
P99	17	49	1200	550	800	1.4	24	69
USP .45	17	40	750	450	1000	1.4	24	56

RECOIL DATA

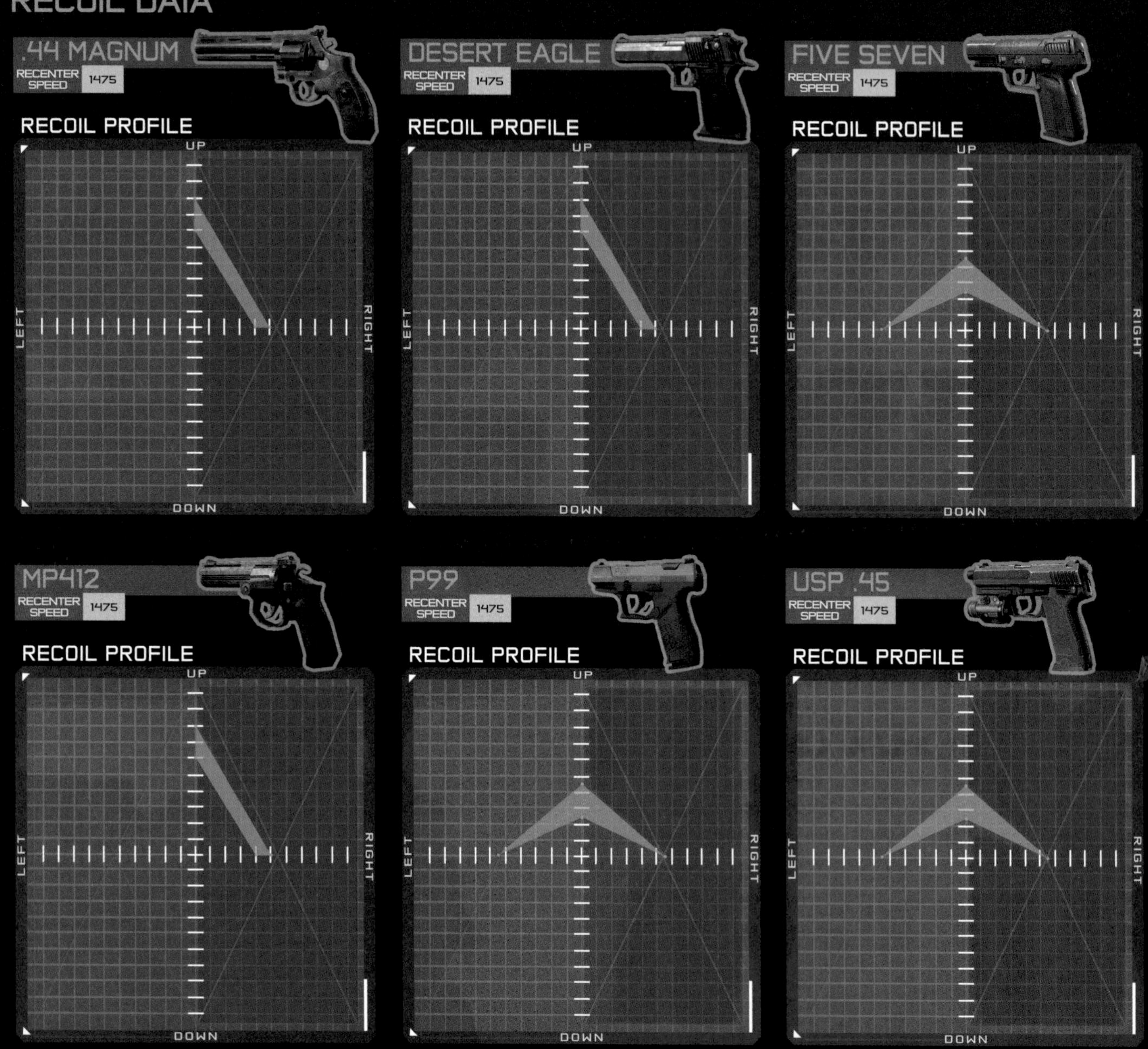

WEAPON NAME	RELOAD TIME	RELOAD TIME (FROM EMPTY)	RELOAD TIME (AMMO ADDED)	DROP TIME	RAISE TIME
.44 MAGNUM	3	3	1.43	0.45	0.55
DESERT EAGLE	1.96	2.1	1.43	0.45	0.55
FIVE SEVEN	1.8	2.5	0.1	0.46	0.46
MP412	4.16	4.16	3.2	0.45	0.55
P99	1.83	2.1	1.23	0.533	0.566
USP .45	1.625	1.917	1.2	0.45	0.55

WEAPON NAME	STARTING AMMO	MAX AMMO	MAGAZINE SIZE
.44 MAGNUM	36	64	6
DESERT EAGLE	24	48	8
FIVE SEVEN	48	96	16
MP412	36	64	6
P99	36	72	12
USP .45	36	72	12

LAUNCHERS

ANTI-AIR AND EXPLOSIVE WEAPONRY FOR DESTROYING ENEMY AIR SUPPORT, CLEARING OBJECTIVES, AND ELIMINATING CAMPERS.

PROS
EFFECTIVE AT CLEARING OBJECTIVES OR SMALL ROOMS
EFFECTIVE AGAINST LARGE GROUPS
CONS
LIMITED AMMUNITION
SLOW FIRE RATES
REQUIRE DIRECT HITS FOR LETHAL SHOTS

COMBAT ROLE	ANTI-AIR, AREA DENIAL

EXPLOSIVE DAMAGE

Explosives have been greatly weakened in Modern Warfare 3...to the relief of every player who has ever sat on a Domination or HQ point. However, it's important to note their damage behavior. Any damage you take from an explosive weapon will be at least the minimum damage. This means that if you even graze a player with a grenade or launcher explosive, you can dispatch him with only a few shots. If you see a hit marker from an explosive, you can be certain your target is weak!

OUT WITH A BANG

Launchers are special weapons designed to take out air support, dispatch large groups of clumped-up enemies, and dig campers out of small rooms. You can use the SMAW and Javelin as anti-air or anti-ground, while the Stinger is anti-air only. The RPG is strong enough to work for anti-air, but it's an unguided projectile, making it difficult to use against most air support. The M320 and XM25 are primarily anti-infantry, though you *can* shoot at low-flying air support, albeit ineffectively.

The SMAW and RPG-7 serve dual purposes. The SMAW has an advantage in anti-air due to its lock-on capability. The RPG-7 has the infantry edge thanks to its two shots versus the SMAW's one. The SMAW is much more accurate when fired against infantry. However, the RPG has a bad tendency to drift off target at anything greater than short range.

XM25 USAGE

The XM25 is a very unusual weapon, firing a projectile that automatically airbursts when it reaches a target range. To set the distance, ADS the weapon and then select a target range. Then, any projectiles you fire from the weapon automatically detonate at the selected range.

There are a few ways to exploit this. One is to target a doorway, window, or objective area and lob grenades that detonate on target every time. Another is to intentionally set the range extremely short and use the XM25 as a perverse short-range explosive 'shotgun.'

Be warned—the XM25 deals very low damage for an explosive weapon. And it has a tiny blast radius, so don't expect a single hit to kill, especially at a distance with glancing hits.

Be careful with the larger anti-air Launchers. The RPG, SMAW, and especially the Javelin and Stinger have very noticeable silhouettes at a distance. They can give away your presence where you would otherwise be hidden behind cover. This makes the dedicated anti-air Launchers a poor choice for aggressive run-and-gun or stealth builds. You don't want a Stinger poking out behind cover, giving you away!

The Javelin is generally a poor anti-infantry weapon, but you can use it to effectively bomb objective areas in the open. Just be careful where you fire it; the projectile arcs forward and straight up before coming down. Don't hit a ceiling in front of you!

The Stinger makes up for its inability to be used against infantry with the best anti-air capability, boasting two shots and a rapid, strong target lock.

AIR DENIAL

Air support is extremely important in every mode of *Modern Warfare 3*, and therefore air *denial* is just as important, if not more so. Always, *always* keep a build around that has at least one dedicated anti-air weapon. The SMAW or Javelin work, but the Stinger is ideal for a purely anti-air role. Once you unlock it, the Blind Eye perk works hand-in-hand with anti-air Launchers to protect you against aircraft until you can destroy them, though you can also use a Scrambler for the same purpose.

AIR DENIAL REWARDS

Beyond the immediate tactical benefit of shooting down enemy UAVs, CUAVs, helicopters, and other air support, remember that shooting down any air support earns you points toward your Pointstreaks. Over the course of a match, if you're aggressive about shooting down air support, you can rack up quite an impressive amount of bonus Pointstreak points, not counting the benefits to your team!

ANTI-AIR BUILDS

Always retain a loadout with at least a Stinger, SMAW, or Javelin. The Blind Eye perk or a Scrambler is also crucial. You need a way to dispatch enemy air support quickly. Never let an enemy Pave Low or Osprey rule the skies uncontested!

LAUNCHER PROFILES

DAMAGE DATA

DAMAGE FROM EXPLOSIVES REACHES ITS MAXIMUM AT THE CENTER OF THE BLAST. DAMAGE DECREASES IN A LINEAR MANNER TO THE MINIMUM DAMAGE VALUE AT THE EDGE OF THE BLAST RADIUS.

WEAPON NAME	EXPLOSION MINIMUM DAMAGE	EXPLOSION MAXIMUM DAMAGE	BLAST RADIUS
JAVELIN	50	300	23
M320 GLM	25	110	7.6
RPG-7	49	135	6.5
SMAW	55	115	10
STINGER	55	155	10
XM25	35	55	3.8

RECOIL DATA

RECOIL IS ESSENTIALLY IRRELEVANT FOR LAUNCHERS, EXCEPT THE XM25, WHICH HAS EXTREME VERTICAL KICK WHEN IT'S FIRED RAPIDLY.

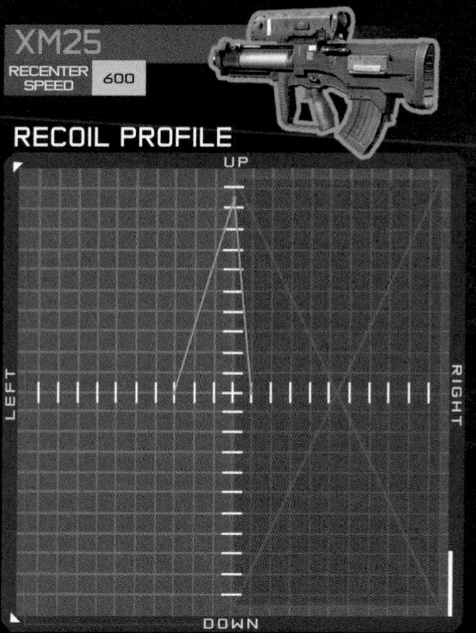

EASE OF USE DATA

LAUNCHERS DO NOT HAVE A 'FROM EMPTY' RELOAD TIME; THEY ALWAYS RELOAD AT THE SAME SPEED.

WEAPON NAME	RELOAD TIME	RELOAD TIME (AMMO ADDED)	DROP TIME	RAISE TIME
JAVELIN	3	2.5	0.75	1.4
M320 GLM	2.63	0	0.6	0.866
RPG-7	3.292	1.17	0.467	0.73
SMAW	3	2.3	0.66	1
STINGER	3	2	0.7	1
XM25	4.33	0	0.5	1.06

AMMO DATA

WEAPON NAME	STARTING AMMO	MAX AMMO	MAGAZINE SIZE
JAVELIN	1	1	1
M320 GLM	2	1	1
RPG-7	2	1	1
SMAW	1	1	1
STINGER	2	1	1
XM25	6	6	4

ATTACHMENTS

CUSTOMIZE AND ENHANCE YOUR WEAPON WITH SPECIAL MODIFICATIONS.

Attachments modify your weapon to suit your personal preferences, as well as the map or game mode you're playing. Once unlocked, any weapon (other than a Launcher) can have one attachment equipped. With the Attachment Proficiency, it's possible to equip a second attachment, increasing your tactical options.

OPTICS

IRON SIGHTS

ASSAULT RIFLES	SMGs	LMGs	SHOTGUNS	MACHINE PISTOLS

Iron sights are often difficult for newer players to use, but they do have some advantages over specialized optics. Iron sights do not obscure your view in the same way that attached optics do, and some optics can even increase your ADS times.

However, not all iron sights are created equal. Some weapons have very clear, very functional iron sights that are easy to use, even at a distance. Others are considerably bulkier, and may make using the weapon at a distance much more difficult.

Spend time experimenting with iron sights. It's important to become comfortable with them, because skipping an optical attachment allows you to use other attachments, many of which are very effective. With that said, when you're starting out, an Assault Rifle fitted with a Red Dot Sight is the baseline weapon of choice to learn with!

RED DOT SIGHT AND HOLOGRAPHIC SIGHT

ASSAULT RIFLES	SMGs	LMGs	SHOTGUNS	MACHINE PISTOLS

The RDS and Holo sights are very simple sights that provide a single red dot or a custom crosshair as your targeting reticle.

These sights are useful for any weapon that has uncomfortable iron sights, and are especially useful on ARs, which benefit from the increased ease of target acquisition at longer ranges. If you select no special custom reticle, you are given the simple red dot by default.

CUSTOM RETICLES

The standard reticle for the Red Dot Sight or Holographic Sight is a simple red dot. However, it is possible to modify your RDS with a custom reticle.

Experiment with these custom optics using different weapons, as some allow for easier target acquisition at close range, while less obtrusive reticles are easier to use at long range.

ACOG SIGHT

ASSAULT RIFLES	SMGs	LMGs	SNIPER RIFLES

The ACOG (Advanced Combat Optical Gunsight) provides enhanced zoom at the cost of slightly slower ADS times on ARs and SMGs. The ACOG is useful on ARs, LMGs, and Sniper Rifles for increasing their effective range (in the case of ARs and LMGs) or for allowing quick medium-range shots (in the case of Sniper Rifles).

Taking an ACOG on the SMGs is generally not a great option, as they have extreme damage falloff, meaning that even though you can see your target at a distance, actually eliminating it is more difficult than the other options. ACOG sights vary by gun manufacturer, so different weapons have slightly different ACOG sights.

HYBRID SIGHT

ASSAULT RIFLES

The Hybrid Sight is a specialized optical attachment only available to Assault Rifles. Essentially, it provides the benefits of a Red Dot Sight and an ACOG. You have one and then you add the other, giving you the best of both worlds—the qualities of an RDS for mid-range, and the benefits of an ACOG for medium-long range.

The downsides to the Hybrid sight are twofold. First, it slows your ADS time slightly, making it a worse option for medium-range combat against other ARs using irons or simple optics. Second, the necessity to toggle between sights can leave you using the wrong sight at the wrong time—or worse, get you killed mid-switch.

With those weaknesses in mind, if you diligently switch sights before you get into firefights so that you have the right type ready most of the time, the Hybrid can treat you well. Consider using Quickdraw to nullify the ADS sight time penalty.

HAMR SCOPE

SMGs

The SMG version of the Hybrid Sight, the HAMR (High Accuracy Multi-Range) sight allows you to toggle between a Red Dot and an ACOG-equivalent scope. Note that the HAMR has an even harsher ADS speed penalty than the Hybrid, so be sure to pair it with Steady Aim (and don't sight at close to close-medium range) or Quickdraw (to nullify the ADS time penalty).

THERMAL

ASSAULT RIFLES	SNIPER RIFLES

Thermal scopes are unique and powerful zooming sights that give you the same zoom as an ACOG, but light up warm bodies in bright white. This makes targeting enemies at a distance in cover or in darkened areas extremely easy, so consider making use of a Thermal sight on maps that have abundant cover and poor lighting conditions.

The Thermal sight has a few weaknesses that balance its power. First, as with the ACOG, it penalizes ADS times for ARs and SMGs by a significant amount (more than double the ACOG penalty). Second, the Thermal sight requires you to steady your aim by holding your breath, just as if you were using a Sniper Rifle sight.

Note that Thermal sights can pierce clouds of smoke from Smoke Grenades, which can be a powerful tactic for covering an objective area.

VARIABLE ZOOM SCOPE

SNIPER RIFLES

The VZS is a normal Sniper Rifle scope that allows you to switch between different zoom magnifications. This is especially useful on larger maps, where you may need to take shots at medium ranges, or at extreme ranges, where the enhanced zoom offered by the Variable scope comes into play.

As it has no disadvantages compared to a regular Sniper scope, consider taking it as your 'default' scope if you aren't planning on using a different attachment on medium and large maps.

WEAPON EXTENSIONS

SHOTGUN

ASSAULT RIFLES

WEAPON NAME	MIN DAMAGE	DAMAGE	MAX DAMAGE RANGE	MIN DAMAGE RANGE	NUM PELLETS	MIN TOTAL DAMAGE	MAX TOTAL DAMAGE
SHOTGUN ATTACHMENT	5	25	500	650	6	30	150

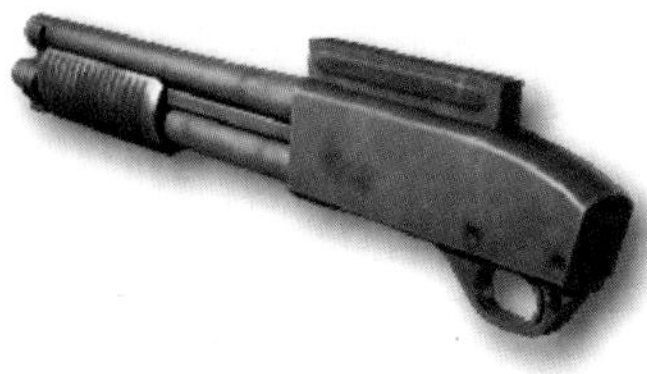

The Shotgun attachment adds an underslung 'master key' to your Assault Rifle. This attachment is very useful on automatic ARs and the MK14, as it gives you a powerful close-range option when you are entering close quarters areas or highly congested short-range engagement areas near objectives.

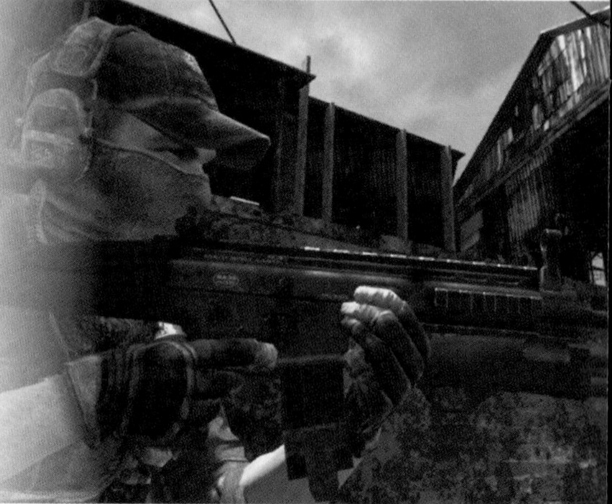

While this Shotgun attachment lacks the punch of a true Shotgun, it is preferable to the close-range spray and pray AR engagement.

The most important point to remember about the Shotgun attachment is that you have to use it. Unless you remember to switch to it before you get into a situation where you need it, you might as well not be using it at all! Switch before entering rooms or areas where CQC is expected.

GRENADE LAUNCHER

ASSAULT RIFLES

The Grenade Launcher attachment is functionally identical to the M320 GLM grenade launcher, and as such, it is a powerful and useful tool for clearing rooms or objectives.

Because getting a killshot with a single grenade is more difficult in *Modern Warfare 3*, it is more effective to use this in concert with a partner. Launch a grenade just as your teammate is about to assault an objective point or clear a room. You only get two shots with the Grenade Launcher attachment, and you cannot get reloads, so make those shots count.

Depending on the nationality of your weapon, you may equip a GP25, M320, or M203 underslung Grenade Launcher. All have the same damage output, with slightly different reloading animations.

WEAPON MODS

SILENCER

ASSAULT RIFLES	SMGs	LMGs	SNIPER RIFLES	SHOTGUNS

The Silencer is a very powerful attachment. While it reduces your effective range by lowering your minimum and maximum damage ranges by 25 percent, it also removes your Red Dot from the radar in non-Hardcore modes, and reduces the sound and muzzle flash of your weapon.

As a result, the Silencer is absolutely vital on any stealthy build. Used properly, it can keep you alive in enemy territory, especially in concert with the stealth perks.

In general, the Silencer is most useful on the ARs and (especially) SMGs, weapons which work well when playing a mobile and aggressive build. It can also be very helpful on an LMG or Sniper Rifle if you are willing to trade damage in exchange for being much harder to locate.

We don't recommend using a Silencer on Shotguns, as the range reduction lowers the actual range that your Shotgun can deal damage, not just the damage falloff. However, if you insist, Shotguns do have SMG-equivalent mobility, so you can use one in enemy territory if the map allows for close-range engagements.

RAPID FIRE

ASSAULT RIFLES (M16A4 AND TYPE 95 ONLY)	SMGs	LMGs

Rapid Fire is a unique attachment that increases Rate of Fire by 20 percent. On the two Burst-fire ARs, it essentially increases the odds of a single burst killshot at medium and longer ranges, especially on mobile targets running perpendicular to your view. The quicker burst is more likely to land all three shots on target.

For SMGs and LMGs, however, Rapid Fire simply gives them a nasty increase in RoF, and therefore potentially lowers their time to kill. In both weapons, Rapid Fire causes greatly increased recoil, which makes SMGs more lethal at close range, but much harder to use at a distance.

On LMGs, Rapid Fire can be useful when carefully burst-firing, especially on weapons with low cyclic rates. Using an LMG with Rapid Fire on full-auto is a great way to put a lot of bullets into a nearby wall, but not so great at actually downing targets at range.

EXTENDED MAGS

ASSAULT RIFLES	SMGs	LMGs	SNIPER RIFLES
SHOTGUNS	MACHINE PISTOLS	HANDGUNS	

Extended Mags increases the ammo available in your magazine by 50 percent. This is especially useful on automatic Shotguns, SMGs, Machine Pistols, and Handguns—all weapons that suffer from rapidly depleted magazines. On ARs, they are nice, but there are typically better attachment options, and LMGs and Sniper Rifles rarely need to make use of them.

GRIP

LMGS	SHOTGUNS

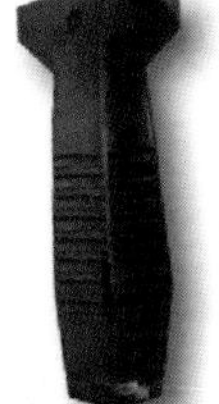

The Grip is a specialized attachment that reduces view kick (visible recoil) by 10 percent and improves recentering speed by 25 percent.

On Automatic Shotguns, the Grip can make them a bit more controllable on full-auto, but the Grip is most useful on the LMGs, where the increased control helps mitigate the harsh recoil. Note that because LMGs have an inherent accuracy bonus when prone, the Grip is most useful when you are firing the LMG from the hip or while crouched. It has relatively little impact when you are prone.

Decide whether you need a Grip based on the map you are playing, and the role you are assuming. A Grip is more useful if you are mobile, or if the map or mode is unfriendly to prone setup.

UPGRADES

AKIMBO

MACHINE PISTOLS | HANDGUNS

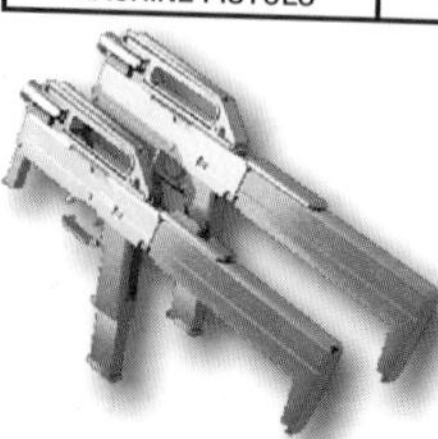

Available only to Machine Pistol and Handgun secondaries, Akimbo lets you dual wield your weapon of choice. Akimbo weapons have maximum base hip-fire spread, you cannot ADS, and they drain ammo at a ferocious rate.

In exchange, you gain essentially halved time to kill at close ranges, doubling your lethality in a short-range engagement.

Taking Akimbo MPs or pistols can be effective if your primary weapon is more useful at medium range or longer. This gives you a powerful close-range option that can take out almost any enemy before they can eliminate you. Steady Aim makes Akimbo weapons considerably more accurate, enough so that you can take down targets out to close-medium range with solid trigger control.

TACTICAL KNIFE

HANDGUNS

The Tactical Knife is a specialized pistol 'attachment.' When equipped with a Tactical Knife, your pistol and knife are held in the Harries grip, with the knife offhand supporting your pistol hand from below. The advantage to this setup in-game is faster knifing and faster recovery from a stab, whether it's a hit or a miss. This can save your life in a surprise encounter, and gives you the fastest possible stealth knife kills.

HEARTBEAT SENSOR

ASSAULT RIFLES | LMGs | SNIPER RIFLES

The Heartbeat Sensor is a specialized attachment that scans an arc in front of you every few seconds for hostile players. Note that because the Sensor scans slowly and has a limited frontal arc, it is very easy to miss a nearby hostile if you are constantly shifting your aim around.

The Sensor is most effective when you are holed up on defense, watching an area with hard cover that your Sensor can penetrate, or on offense where you can use the Sensor to scan a building or dense cover for targets.

Be very careful about losing focus on your surroundings when using the Sensor. Paying too much attention to it on defense can get you killed if an enemy with Assassin comes at you!

Instead of constantly watching the sensor, listen for the 'ping' of detected enemies, then check quickly to see where they are. Remember that because they are likely on the move, they may not be where the sensor last spotted them.

PRIMARY WEAPON ATTACHMENTS

ASSAULT RIFLES

ASSAULT RIFLE ATTACHMENTS

RED DOT SIGHT | SILENCER | GRENADE LAUNCHER | ACOG SCOPE | RAPID FIRE | HEARTBEAT SENSOR

HYBRID SIGHT | SHOTGUN | HOLOGRAPHIC SIGHT | EXTENDED MAGS | THERMAL

ONLY THE M16A4 AND TYPE 95 HAVE ACCESS TO RAPID FIRE.

SUBMACHINE GUNS

SUBMACHINE GUN ATTACHMENTS

RED DOT SIGHT

SILENCER

RAPID FIRE

ACOG SCOPE

HAMR SCOPE

HOLOGRAPHIC SIGHT

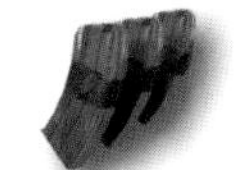
EXTENDED MAGS

THERMAL

LIGHT MACHINE GUNS

LMG ATTACHMENTS

RED DOT SIGHT

SILENCER

GRIP

ACOG SCOPE

RAPID FIRE

HEARTBEAT SENSOR

HOLOGRAPHIC SIGHT

EXTENDED MAGS

THERMAL

THE PKP PECHENEG CANNOT USE THE HEARTBEAT SENSOR.

SNIPER RIFLES

SNIPER RIFLE ATTACHMENTS

ACOG SCOPE

SILENCER

THERMAL

EXTENDED MAGS

HEARTBEAT SENSOR

VARIABLE ZOOM SCOPE

SHOTGUNS

SHOTGUN ATTACHMENTS

GRIP

SILENCER

RED DOT SIGHT

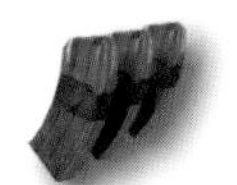
EXTENDED MAGS

HOLOGRAPHIC SIGHT

EXTENDED MAGS

THE MODEL 1887 CANNOT USE ATTACHMENTS, OR THE 2 ATTACHMENTS PROFICIENCY.

SECONDARY WEAPON ATTACHMENTS

MACHINE PISTOLS

MACHINE PISTOL ATTACHMENTS

SILENCER

AKIMBO

RED DOT SIGHT

HOLOGRAPHIC SIGHT

EXTENDED MAGS

HANDGUNS

HANDGUN ATTACHMENTS

SILENCER

AKIMBO

TACTICAL KNIFE

EXTENDED MAGS

THE M412, .44 MAGNUM AND DESERT EAGLE CANNOT USE SILENCERS OR EXTENDED MAGS.

LAUNCHERS

LAUNCHERS DO NOT HAVE ATTACHMENTS.

PROFICIENCIES

LONG HOURS OF PRACTICE GRANT YOU AN EDGE WITH YOUR CHOSEN WEAPON.

Proficiencies are special upgrades available only on your primary weapons (secondary weapons do not gain Proficiencies). When unlocked by leveling up your weapons, you can then activate a Proficiency on top of any Attachment equipped to the weapon. Each Proficiency offers a slight upgrade to your weapons' performance, improving your effectiveness with your favored weaponry.

FULLY PROFICIENT

Reaching eight kills with the Specialist Strike Package unlocks all perks—and it also unlocks almost all Proficiencies. This hidden upgrade makes you considerably more dangerous with any primary weapon you use. Take advantage of it!

PROFICIENCY BRIEFING

KICK

ASSAULT RIFLES | SMGs | LMGs | SNIPER RIFLES | SHOTGUNS

Kick reduces recoil by 20 percent, allowing for steadier full-auto and faster recovery from shots.

FOCUS

ASSAULT RIFLES | SMGs | LMGs | SNIPER RIFLES | SHOTGUNS

Reduces visual recoil by 50 percent when you are hit. Focus is very effective for SMGs and Shotguns. It is also helpful for ARs, as it can keep your shots on target when you enter a heads-up one-on-one firefight.

IMPACT

ASSAULT RIFLES | LMGs | SNIPER RIFLES

Impact grants maximized penetration for any weapon. This is especially powerful on Assault Rifles and SMGs, as LMGs already have strong penetration, and Sniper Rifles are difficult to use for intentional walling shots.

BREATH

ASSAULT RIFLES

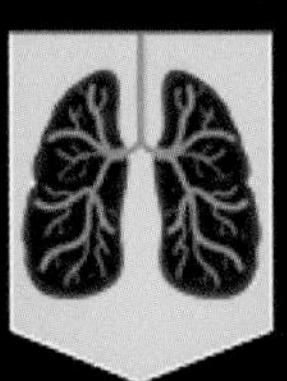

Allows you to remove the slight sway from Assault Rifles by holding your breath. Very situational, most useful with the Type 95, M16A4 or MK14 with a long-range sight fitted. Breath can be used with automatics, as well, for careful long-range burst-fired shots, though the benefit is small.

ATTACHMENT

ASSAULT RIFLES | SMGs | LMGs | SNIPER RIFLES | SHOTGUNS

Allows the use of two attachments. It is a solid all-around Proficiency, useful in many situations. This Proficiency is also notably useful for stealth builds, as it allows you to use a Silencer alongside any other Attachment. The Attachment Proficiency is also helpful if you are still getting comfortable with iron sights, as it allows you to take an optical

STABILITY

ASSAULT RIFLES | SMGs | LMGs | SNIPER RIFLES

Reduces idle weapon sway by 25 percent. Consider this to be an 'automatic' Breath for long-range combat. It is most useful on LMGs, as they need the enhanced accuracy for long-range shots, though ARs also benefit from it.

MELEE

SHOTGUNS | RIOT SHIELD

Grants 35 percent faster melee recovery. Melee can be useful if you are stalking targets with a stealth Shotgun build. With the Riot Shield, it allows you to take down targets much more quickly at close range.

DAMAGE

SHOTGUNS

Provides a significant 40 percent Damage boost. Damage is strong on the Shotguns that already have solid range, and very important for the pump-action Shotguns that may not get a second shot.

SPEED

LMGs | SNIPER RIFLES | RIOT SHIELD

Improves movement speed by 10 percent, or one step up on the mobility scale. Speed is an important upgrade for LMGs and the Riot Shield. It is less critical for Sniper Rifles, excepting the Barrett and AS50, which are heavier and slower than other Sniper Rifles.

RANGE

SMGs | SHOTGUNS

Offers a 25 percent boosted effective range. This is very useful on Shotguns, particularly the automatic variants. Some SMGs can benefit from this upgrade, as well, especially if you are intent on using medium-range optics.

PRIMARY WEAPONS

ASSAULT RIFLE

ASSAULT RIFLE PROFICIENCIES

KICK | IMPACT | ATTACHMENT | FOCUS | BREATH | STABILITY

SNIPER RIFLES

SNIPER RIFLE PROFICIENCIES

KICK | IMPACT | ATTACHMENT | FOCUS | SPEED | STABILITY

SUBMACHINE GUNS

SUBMACHINE GUN PROFICIENCIES

KICK | RANGE | ATTACHMENT | FOCUS | MELEE | STABILITY

SHOTGUNS

SHOTGUN PROFICIENCIES

KICK | FOCUS | ATTACHMENT | MELEE | RANGE | DAMAGE

LIGHT MACHINE GUNS

LIGHT MACHINE GUN PROFICIENCIES

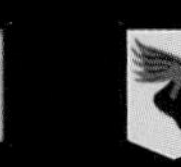

KICK | IMPACT | ATTACHMENT | FOCUS | SPEED | STABILITY

RIOT SHIELD

RIOT SHIELD PROFICIENCIES

MELEE | SPEED

SECONDARY WEAPONS

SECONDARY WEAPONS DO NOT HAVE PROFICIENCIES.

EQUIPMENT

HI-TECH EQUIPMENT AND SPECIALIZED EXPLOSIVES GRANT YOU AN EDGE IN BATTLE.

You are allowed to carry one Lethal and one Tactical option into battle. Flash and Concussion grenades each give you two grenades, while all other Lethal and Tactical gear gives you only a single item. Note that Scavenger does *not* resupply Lethal equipment other than the Throwing Knife, so use your Lethal choices wisely.

All of the placeable Tactical equipment can be picked up and then redeployed. This also applies to Bouncing Betties, Claymores, and C4. Throwing Knives can be retrieved from walls or bodies, assuming you can find them.

LETHAL

LETHAL EQUIPMENT CAN CLEAR A ROOM OR GUARD YOUR BACK.

FRAG

A BASIC HAND GRENADE THAT CAN BE 'COOKED' TO AIRBURST, OR THROWN AROUND CORNERS.

EXPLOSION MINIMUM DAMAGE	EXPLOSION MAXIMUM DAMAGE	BLAST RADIUS
55	130	6.5

Frag Grenades have a three-and-a-half-second fuse, and can be 'cooked' by holding the Grenade button for up to three seconds before throwing it. Doing so allows you to airburst Frag Grenades, turning them into lethal targeted explosives, ideal for fishing campers out of windows or bombing an objective point precisely.

COOK 'EM

Frag Grenades have a 3.5-second fuse, and you can easily time your throws by watching your reticle. While you cook the grenade, the reticle pulses once per second, so you can throw it at 1, 2, or 3 seconds for different airburst distances.

Because Frag Grenades can also be thrown without cooking, you can bounce them off walls or ceilings, or roll them around corners, allowing you to attack a target indirectly. At the very least, Frag Grenades can flush a target out of hiding. And remember, if a target is even *grazed* by the explosion, know that you can down it in just a few shots.

HOT POTATO

You can pick up and throw a Frag Grenade that has landed near you. You have very little time to do this, though, so make a snap decision—either throw the grenade or get away fast! There is always a risk of picking up a grenade that has been slightly cooked, causing it to blow up in your hand or almost immediately after you throw it. However, every now and then, you can score the ultimate in humiliating kills, tossing a Frag straight back at its owner and killing him!

SEMTEX

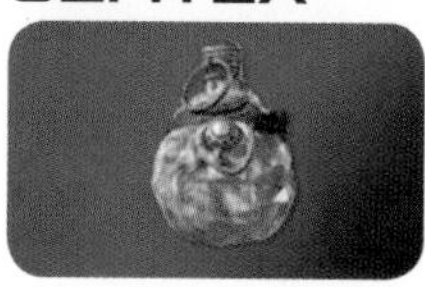

A STICKY EXPLOSIVE WITH A SHORT FUSE AND LIMITED THROWING RANGE.

EXPLOSION MINIMUM DAMAGE	EXPLOSION MAXIMUM DAMAGE	BLAST RADIUS
55	130	6.5

Semtex has explosive power identical to the Frag Grenade, but it trades the ability to be cooked or rolled around corners for a shorter fuse time and the ability to stick to any target. You can stick Semtex to walls, floors, ceilings, objectives...even other players!

STUCK!

Toss a Semtex on a friendly teammate sprinting into a room to create a mobile bomb. Just don't try this in Hardcore...

Semtex is a good choice for any mobile or offensive build, as you can toss it immediately for an instant threat. Meanwhile, Frag Grenades take a few seconds to either cook or detonate. Semtex explodes more quickly, and the ability to stick it to a target lets you control the explosion center's exact location. Note that Semtex can't be thrown nearly as far as Frag Grenades. So, if you're on a larger map or you anticipate the need for a longer throw, use Frags instead.

THROWING KNIFE

A STEALTHY AND LETHAL ALTERNATIVE TO HANDHELD EXPLOSIVES.

The throwing knife is an instantly lethal thrown blade that can be retrieved after embedding itself in an object—or another player!

The throwing knife is difficult to use well, but it is stealthy, can be recovered (and resupplied with Scavenger, unlike all other Equipment), and can also be thrown instantly while you're reloading or otherwise unable to fight.

BOUNCING BETTY

A 360-DEGREE PROXIMITY MINE.

EXPLOSION MINIMUM DAMAGE	EXPLOSION MAXIMUM DAMAGE	BLAST RADIUS
70	100	6.5

The Bouncing Betty is a new class of proximity explosive. When it's triggered, it launches itself into the air and detonates, causing an explosive blast in a 360-degree radius.

It's possible to duck or go prone to avoid half or all of the explosion. So, pay careful attention to the sound the Betty makes when it trips, and you might save yourself from the blast. Compared to the Claymore, the Bouncing Betty is easier to use. You can place it in more locations with the certainty of a lethal explosion. However, an alert enemy can dodge it, making it weaker against skilled players.

WATCH MY BACK

Bouncing Betties and Claymores are the tools of choice for guarding your back when you're camping an area defensively, or covering an objective. While neither is as effective as a teammate, sometimes you must set up shop without a friendly to cover you. In those instances, either explosive can be a life-saver. Even if they don't kill a hostile, an explosion can alert you to their presence.

Bear in mind that the Stalker perk renders both triggers nearly totally ineffective, so don't trust them blindly!

CLAYMORE

A PROXIMITY MINE WITH A FRONTAL EXPLOSION ARC.

EXPLOSION MINIMUM DAMAGE	EXPLOSION MAXIMUM DAMAGE	BLAST RADIUS
50	200	6.5 (FRONTAL ARC)

Claymores are frontal-cone proximity explosives, detonating at ankle level. Proper placement of Claymores is vital for full effectiveness.

When you use a Claymore to cover a doorway or other narrow entrance, place it facing away from the doorway. That is to say, you want your target to walk through the doorway, trip the Claymore, and have the blast project from the door into the room, killing the foe while he moves into the Claymore's blast zone. If you face the Claymore directly toward the doorway or opening, sprinting enemies may trip the Claymore and be past the blast cone before it can take them out.

You can jump to avoid some Claymore damage. However, unless you clear the frontal blast arc, you can't dodge the damage entirely, unlike a Bouncing Betty. Because Claymores deal more maximum damage, they are lethal out to about twice the range of a Bouncing Betty. But they lack the full 360-degree coverage that a Betty provides.

C4

A MANUALLY DETONATED, HIGH-POWER EXPLOSIVE.

EXPLOSION MINIMUM DAMAGE	EXPLOSION MAXIMUM DAMAGE	BLAST RADIUS
50	200	6.5

C4 is a manually triggered explosive that can be attached to any wall, ceiling, or convenient vehicle. It's very useful in objective modes where you know where your enemies will be. It's less useful for guarding your back, due to the need to trigger it manually. You can detonate C4 by shooting it, using the detonator via the Fire button, or by double-tapping the Reload button.

C4 has the strongest blast of all Lethal explosives, and it's especially deadly when attached to a vehicle—the resulting blast is guaranteed to take out any enemies in the vicinity.

Use C4 on Domination points, Headquarters, and on Search & Destroy and Demolition bomb targets. On some maps, use C4 on chokepoints that you're already monitoring. By having C4 down one route and your gun aimed at another, you can effectively guard two routes.

DOM BOMBS

Domination is particularly friendly to C4. Since you receive a visual and aural cue when a point is being overtaken, you can detonate C4 to take out an enemy without even watching the location.

When you place C4, try to attach it to a ceiling, wall, or other surface that's difficult to spot. Placing it on the ground in a Domination point is very common, but canny enemies will simply shoot it or detonate it with an explosive.

QUICK DETONATION

Double-tapping the Reload button is the fastest way to detonate your C4. Plus, it allows you to use your gun while still having the option to trigger the blast.

TACTICAL

TACTICAL EQUIPMENT GRANTS YOU SPECIAL COMBAT CAPABILITIES.

EQUIPMENT DISABLING

Flash, Concussion, and EMP grenades can all be used to temporarily or permanently disable deployed equipment. Claymores, C4, and Bouncing Betties are all shut down when a Flashbang or Stun grenade strikes them. Sentries are disabled, and all sorts of deployed equipment can be outright destroyed by an EMP Grenade blast.

Be aware that the disabling effect of Flash and Concussion grenades is temporary, so make sure you clear the area of any dangerous explosives or other deployed equipment before the effect wears off.

FLASH GRENADE

BLINDING AND INCAPACITATING SUPPORT GRENADES.

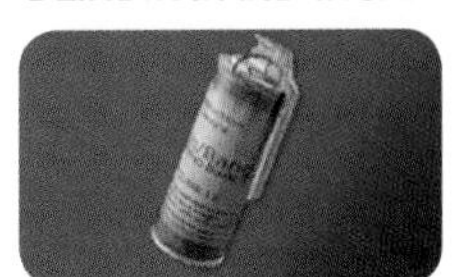

Flash Grenades are powerful support tools, disabling enemies with a blinding flash of light that stops sprinting and causes total visual impairment if the grenade goes off with the target looking directly at it.

Flash grenades have a 1.5-second fuse, and do not have a contact fuse. This means they can be "cooked" and airbursted. A full-contact blind lasts for 5.5 seconds. This is especially nasty near objectives in the open, because airbursting the Flashbang near the target is all but guaranteed to blind anyone looking at the objective area. If the objective is inside, you can simply throw the Flashbang into the room.

Be careful about using Flashbang hit markers as a guarantee that your targets are blinded. Flashbangs fully blind only if the explosion is near your target *and* the target is facing directly toward it. Enemies at a distance facing slightly away from the grenade may receive just a very slight flash. If you sprint in assuming they are blind, expect to eat a bullet.

ROOM CLEARING

Flashbangs, along with their cousin the Concussion Grenade, are ideal for room sweeping. The standard tactic is to throw in the grenade and time your assault to enter the room *immediately* after the grenade detonates.

While this sounds nice in theory, there are a few problems in practice. Flashbangs don't necessarily thwart enemies who are already in ADS facing the doorway you enter. Even if they're blinded, they can simply hold the trigger to spray a perfectly accurate wall of lead at the entrance. The other problem is that an alert enemy who sees the grenade enter the room through an opening will be prepared for your assault from that direction.

Often, a better tactic is to throw the grenade in one opening and then assault through a second entrance. This gives you the best possible chance of engaging a blinded enemy firing in the wrong direction.

CONCUSSION GRENADE

SLOWS MOVEMENT/TURNING SPEED, ADDS SWAY, STOPS SPRINT.

Concussion Grenades are powerful stun weapons that stagger enemies caught in the blast radius. It slows their movement and causes their aim to sway wildly. A direct hit results in a 5.5-second stun. Concussion Grenades work best with mobile character loadouts on targets in the open. If you tag an enemy and then hit him from the side or rear while he cannot turn from the stun, you have an easy kill.

Concussion Grenades have a short fuse, but they do not detonate until they hit the ground. This means you can throw them a long way, but they cannot be airbursted. Generally, throwing "Hail Marys" with Concussion Grenades is a waste of resources. But if you need to stop a flag runner or to stagger enemies around an objective point, it can be useful.

Like Flashbangs, Concussion Grenades stop enemies from sprinting. Unlike Flashbangs, their stun effect is noticeable even if they catch a target at the edge of the blast radius. You can't be sure when a target is blinded, but you can be sure when a target is stunned and turns slowly.

SCRAMBLER

THE SCRAMBLER IS A DEPLOYED PIECE OF EQUIPMENT THAT SETS UP A SMALL FIELD OF RADAR-BLOCKING INTERFERENCE.

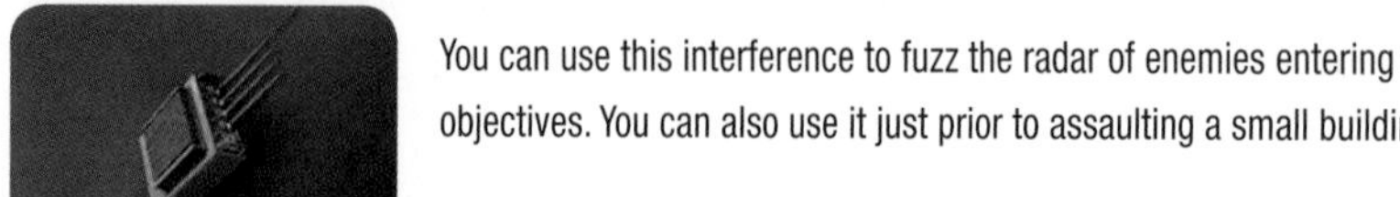

You can use this interference to fuzz the radar of enemies entering small buildings or located near objectives. You can also use it just prior to assaulting a small building or room.

Scramblers have an additional, very useful trait: when you stand inside the Scrambler's radius, it essentially acts as the Blind Eye perk—you are invisible to air support. Note that you are *not* invisible to UAV or immune to CUAV use, so don't try to 'hide out' in a Scrambler field. Be aware that camping out near a deployed Scrambler can be risky if you're trying to be stealthy. The very presence of a Scrambler alerts any enemy that approaches.

EMP GRENADE

THE EMP GRENADE IS A POWERFUL NEW SUPPORT TOOL THAT CAN DISABLE AND DESTROY DEPLOYED EQUIPMENT.

The EMP Grenade has a 12-meter radius, a 10-second duration, and a 1-second fuse. It is so powerful that it can actually destroy low-flying air support, including the Osprey Gunner, Escort Airdrop, AH-6, and Pave Low. It works equally well against deployed I.M.S. systems, any type of Sentry gun, the Assault Drone, Recon Drone, and all other types of deployed equipment.

In addition to those powerful effects, it also disables affected players' HUDs, shutting off their radar and all other onscreen indicators (though not in Hardcore mode). EMP Grenades also inflict a bit of a Flashbang effect targets hit with them, though not to the degree of an actual Flashbang Grenade. EMPs have a short fuse and *can* be airbursted. Throwing them over or near an objective is easy and effective, but you can't throw them particularly long distances.

SMOKE GRENADE

SMOKE GRENADES ARE VITAL SUPPORT TOOLS, CREATING TEMPORARY COVER WHEREVER YOU NEED IT.

Smoke is critically important in objective-based game modes, but less so in deathmatch modes. However, it can still be useful to create a screen for moving across a covered lane of fire. Note that Thermal sights can see through smoke clouds, so be wary of using Smoke to cover an objective assault if you know that an enemy with a Thermal scope has eyes on the objective. When you play objective game modes, keep a build with Smoke Grenades around at all times.

TROPHY SYSTEM

THE TROPHY SYSTEM INTERCEPTS INCOMING PROJECTILES OF ANY TYPE.

The Trophy System is a powerful new defensive tool. When deployed, it intercepts all incoming projectiles…*all.* As in, all types of grenades, including grenade launcher projectiles, C4, RPG rounds, SMAW and Javelin shots, Predator missiles, Reaper missiles, even AC130 cannon rounds!

The Trophy System has a range just shy of 10 meters, and can destroy only two incoming projectiles before shutting down. Gunfire or a grenade can easily disable it. Nevertheless, it's a vital new piece of equipment for objective-based game modes.

With the Blast Shield perk and a Trophy System deployed, you can often survive any indirect attempt to root you out of a Headquarters, off of a Domination point, or away from Demo bomb location. Even without Blast Shield, the Trophy System is still extremely powerful. It deploys quickly enough that you can even use it in the open to save yourself from an incoming Predator! Once the Trophy System is deployed, you can move it. So, if you secure an objective without using up its charges, you can always move it to a new location.

TACTICAL INSERTION

A VITAL TOOL IN OBJECTIVE-BASED GAME MODES, THE TACTICAL INSERTION ALLOWS YOU TO SET YOUR OWN SPAWN POINT.

In modes like Headquarters or Demolition, where you often spawn far from the objective, and in almost any objective mode on a larger map, Tactical Insertions allow your team to maintain offensive pressure. Carefully placed Tactical Insertions also allow you spring nasty surprises on unsuspecting defenders or campers in any mode. If you hide a Tactical Insertion in an area near the bulk of the enemy team, your respawn can yield a lot of enemy deaths once you glean their exact positions from your preceding death. Keep a character build with Tactical Insertion handy if you frequently play modes like Capture the Flag, Headquarters, or Demolition.

PORTABLE RADAR

THE PORTABLE RADAR SETS UP A SMALL AREA OF ENEMY DETECTION (ROUGHLY 21.5 METERS).

While it's active, it emits a radar 'ping' every two seconds that detects any enemies who lack the Assassin perk in its radius. Because the Portable Radar has a short range, a fast-moving enemy can traverse its detection area and be through before it sweeps the area again, so don't trust it as a perfect defensive tool.

RADAR PITCH

The noise that the Portable Radar makes when it picks up an enemy changes, based on the target's distance. This makes the Portable Radar useful even in Hardcore mode without a minimap active, as the audio ping still alerts you to a nearby enemy.

The Portable Radar is a powerful piece of equipment for defending fixed locations, notably near objectives. Place the Radar in an out-of-the-way corner near an objective, and you're alerted to enemies sneaking into the area around it.

SPECIAL RADAR

The Recon Juggernaut and the Assault Drone both have a built-in Portable Radar. Take advantage of it!

Portable Radar can also be effective with a long-range build, whether you're using a Sniper Rifle, an LMG, or an AR with a precision scope. Toss the Portable Radar on top of a building or in a dark corner where you set up shop, and place a Claymore or Bouncing Betty at any uncovered entrance. Be aware that enemies with some combination of Sitrep, Assassin, and Stalker can bypass these defenses, but they still allow you to create a respectable stronghold.

MULTIPLAYER PERKS

PERKS REPRESENT YOUR ELITE TRAINING, GRANTING ABILITIES ABOVE AND BEYOND THE COMMON BATTLEFIELD SOLDIER.

You can equip up to three perks, one from each perk category. Choose your perks carefully to complement your character loadout and the game mode you are playing. You unlock new perks via leveling. You unlock the Pro upgrades by completing challenges.

PRO PERK CHALLENGES

PERK 1 CHALLENGES

Recon	Paint enemies with Recon
Sleight of Hand	Get kills with Sleight of Hand set
Blind Eye	Destroy enemy Pointstreak rewards with Blind Eye set
Extreme Conditioning	Sprint with Extreme Conditioning set
Scavenger	Resupply using Scavenger

PERK 2 CHALLENGES

Quickdraw	Get kills within a few seconds of entering ADS
Blast Shield	Survive explosions with Blast Shield set
Hardline	Earn Pointstreaks with Hardline set
Assassin	Get kills while an enemy UAV is active
Overkill	Get kills with your second primary weapon

PERK 3 CHALLENGES

Marksman	Get kills while holding your breath
Stalker	Get kills while ADS with Stalker set
Sitrep	Destroy enemy devices (of any type) with Sitrep set
Steady Aim	Get hip-fire kills with Steady Aim set
Dead Silence	Get close-range kills

PERK 1

RECON

STANDARD	Highlights enemies struck with any explosive damage on the minimap for 12 seconds
PRO	Highlights enemies hit with bullets

Recon is a powerful team-play perk that highlights enemies damaged with explosions on the minimap with perfect directional and positional information, just as though you had an AUAV active. This means that any time you toss a Flashbang, Concussion, or Frag, or use a Launcher, you can light up an entire room of enemies, or highlight every enemy in the vicinity of an objective.

Recon Pro upgrades this effect to include your bullets. This can be particularly effective when you use the Impact proficiency or an LMG and deliberately target enemies through walls (especially easy near objectives). Beyond the powerful benefits of knowing how an enemy is covering a room, highlighting enemies through a wall also opens them up to easy elimination with further shots through the wall.

SLEIGHT OF HAND

STANDARD	Doubles reload speed
PRO	Doubles weapon switch speed

Sleight of Hand doubles reloading speed, greatly reducing the chances of getting caught mid-reload while on the move. It's also powerful with SMGs and MPs that have high fire rates and that drain their magazines quickly. The Pro upgrade doubles weapon switch times, allowing you to swap to a fast-raising secondary at lightning speed. This upgrade also combos extremely well with either the Overkill perk, or simply picking up a second primary weapon on the battlefield that complements your current main weapon. An Assault Rifle and Shotgun combo works quite nicely.

Sleight of Hand is best for aggressive character builds. Fast reloading is less important if you're playing defensively, where the chance of running into an enemy around a corner while you're in mid-reload isn't as great.

BLIND EYE

STANDARD	Cannot be spotted by air support or sentries, invisible to player-controlled Pointstreaks
PRO	Launchers lock on twice as fast, bullets deal 60% boosted armor-piercing damage against all air support and deployed Pointstreaks

Blind Eye grants immunity to all forms of air support, as well as invisibility to Thermal scopes, Recon Drones, Assault Drones, Sentry Guns, and the Remote Sentry. Note that a player controlling a Pointstreak can still target you—you simply lack the red targeting highlight of a player without Blind Eye.

Automated air support does not target you at all, although you can still die from collateral damage if you get too close to a targeted player that doesn't have Blind Eye!

Blind Eye Pro gives you powerful anti-air upgrades. It grants a 60-percent damage bonus to your shots, as well as armor piercing, which is necessary for damaging the heavy attack helicopters with bullets. On top of that effect, it also speeds up lock-ons with the Javelin and Stinger, exposing you to less danger when you shoot down air support. Note that the bullet damage increase is a risky upgrade, because firing wildly into the air is a great way to get shot. However, it does allow you to destroy all UAVs easily with an AR, and you can down helicopters extremely quickly with an LMG.

EXTREME CONDITIONING

STANDARD	Doubles sprint distance
PRO	Doubles mantling speed

Extreme Conditioning doubles the distance you can sprint, allowing you to move farther and faster than other players. This is especially noticeable when you use an SMG or Shotgun, which gives you full-speed mobility. It's less pronounced with a heavy LMG or Sniper Rifle. Extreme Conditioning can still be quite helpful with an LMG. It allows you to move between favorable positions much more quickly than without it.

It's also an important perk if you intend to use an LMG in an offensive manner in objective-based game modes. In such cases, reaching a target quickly is valuable. You can use it in other modes to outflank an enemy position quickly. However, be very careful with Extreme Conditioning; sprinting blindly around a map is a great way to get killed when you round a corner.

The Pro upgrade gives you 50 percent faster mantling speed, which increases your maneuverability even further. It minimizes your window of vulnerability when you climb into a room or over an obstacle.

SCAVENGER

STANDARD	Causes enemies to drop ammo backpacks to resupply magazines and throwing knives
PRO	Spawn with two extra magazines

Scavenger allows you to pick up ammo packs from downed enemies, replenishing ammo for your primary and secondary weapons. Scavenger does not replenish Launcher ammo or Lethal ammo of any sort, except Throwing Knives.

Scavenger is a valuable perk for builds using weapons with high fire rates, or builds that are stealthy or otherwise rely on a specific weapon, especially one with two attachments equipped. It's also useful for play styles that are defensive or typically suffer a low number of deaths per round.

The Pro upgrade grants you two extra magazines on your starting loadout, which isn't an extremely useful upgrade. However, it does give you more leeway to expend ammunition before you have to search out packs, which can expose you to danger. Standard and Pro are also useful for builds running Impact on ARs or LMGs with the intention to deliberately dump ammunition through hard cover and into buildings. This is noticeably more effective in concert with a teammate running Recon.

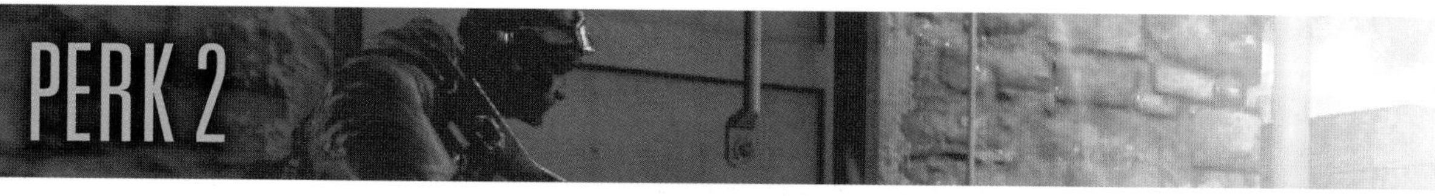

PERK 2

QUICKDRAW

STANDARD	Halves ADS time
PRO	Doubles the speed of equipment usage

Quickdraw is a very powerful perk for aggressive and mobile builds. It gives you an edge in any sort of midrange combat, allowing you to sight twice as fast. In any heads-up, one-on-one firefight, getting your sights on target first often means victory, and Quickdraw all but guarantees your sights come up faster. Quickdraw is a powerful perk on ARs for midrange combat. It's also strong on SMGs, partly because of the Pro benefit. If you plan to use a Sniper Rifle on the move, Quickdraw is vital for quickly scoping and downing targets.

The Pro upgrade is also very helpful, speeding up all Equipment usage by 50 percent. This means faster recovery from thrown grenades, and quicker Equipment deployment, which leaves you vulnerable for a shorter duration.

BLAST SHIELD

STANDARD	45% reduced damage from explosives
PRO	50% reduced blind or stun time

Blast Shield is a powerful defensive perk, reducing incoming explosive damage by 45 percent. This all but guarantees you can survive an explosion at anything but pointblank range. Blast Shield is extremely useful in certain objective modes, where you can expect to have explosives lobbed at you with great frequency. Blast Shield can often save you from Claymores, Bouncing Betties, and even heavy-duty Pointstreaks that cause explosive damage.

The Pro upgrade halves the duration and effect of Flashbangs and Concussion grenades. This is another powerful effect for defending an objective or protecting yourself from an assault when you're camping in a room.

HARDLINE

STANDARD	1 less point required for Pointstreak rewards
PRO	Two assists add a Pointstreak point. Death Streaks require one less death.

Hardline reduces by one the number of kills you need to reach a Pointstreak. The Pro upgrade allows two assists to count as a kill toward a Pointstreak. It also reduces by one the deaths needed to trigger a Death Streak. At first glance, Hardline might seem like a weak perk, but its power is not in going from 16 to 17 kills. Rather, it's most useful when you're running a Strike Package consisting of low-end Pointstreaks.

Over the course of a match, you can have a great many runs of three to five kills. With Hardline, those effectively become four to six kills. Consider the power of constant UAVs at two kills with an Assault package, or constant CUAV coverage and Ballistic Vest drops from Support.

The Pro upgrade is simply an added bonus. It helps take the edge off if you're one of those players who has a chronic problem with kill stealers. Don't bother with Hardline on a Specialist package. While it's nice to get your perks rolling after one kill, there are better initial choices than Hardline.

ASSASSIN

STANDARD	Undetectable by UAV, AUAV, Portable Radar, Thermal Sights, and Heartbeat Sensors
PRO	Immune to CUAV and EMP effects. No red name or crosshair when targeted.

Assassin is a powerful and vital perk for stealth builds. At base level, it renders you immune to UAV coverage. It also protects you from Portable Radar and Heartbeat Sensor scans, and hides you from Thermal scopes.

The Pro upgrade grants you immunity to CUAV and EMP effects—both the EMP Pointstreak and EMP Grenades. Even more powerful, it removes the red name and crosshair popup when an enemy aims at you.

Assassin Pro is a near-mandatory perk for aggressive stealthy builds. It's also very important in deathmatch modes where hiding from UAVs and CUAVs can earn you a lot of extra kills. The temporary confusion that the absence of a name or crosshair alert causes is icing on the cake. Note that Assassin Pro renders you immune to the effect of EMPs, but it does not save your active Pointstreaks from instant destruction by EMPs.

OVERKILL

STANDARD	Equip two primary weapons
PRO	One attachment on second weapon

Overkill allows you to carry a second primary weapon. The Pro upgrade allows you to take a single attachment for your second primary. Overkill can be very useful for running two weapons of differing range bands—typically an AR, LMG, or Sniper Rifle paired with a Shotgun. The AR/Shotgun build is especially dangerous on maps with mixed urban terrain. You can clean up in close quarters with a shotgun while retaining effective mid-range fighting power.

Note that you can simply pick up a secondary weapon in the field, but this carries all sorts of attendant risks. And there's no guarantee that you'll find the appropriate second weapon for your setup.

Taking Overkill on your Specialist Strike Package builds is very powerful. Overkill is the only perk that has no effect when activated by a full 8 Pointstreak as a Specialist. More critically, having two primary weapons gives you even more power when you unlock all Proficiencies.

PERK 3

MARKSMAN

STANDARD	Extends the range and arc where red enemy names appear
PRO	Doubles held breath duration

Marksman has a subtle effect, increasing the range and the arc at which you can spot the red names of enemies. This can greatly increase your lethality with ARs, LMGs, and Sniper Rifles. These weapons benefit from long-distance target acquisition. It can also save your life or your teammates' lives by spotting and calling targets early.

The Pro upgrade doubles held breath duration. This is mostly relevant to newer Snipers and has a minimal impact on the Breath proficiency.

STALKER

STANDARD	Full-speed movement while ADS
PRO	Adds a 2-second delay to Claymore, Bouncing Betty, and I.M.S. activation

Stalker is a powerful, game-changing perk, allowing you to move at full speed while ADS. This is especially lethal with SMGs and ARs, providing you the accuracy of ADS without the movement speed penalty. This can give you the edge in mid-range firefights.

One quirk for veteran players is that this perk can affect your aim a bit when you first begin using it. Because ADS normally slows your movement, you may have already adapted your aiming habits to the reduced speed—Stalker may require you to recalibrate those habits.

The Pro upgrade is a nice added bonus: it delays the activation of Claymores, Bouncing Betties, and the I.M.S. The delay is long enough for you to sprint out of range easily—very nice if you happen to pass through a doorway while ADS and trip a Claymore. One humorous but somewhat unfortunate side effect to this delay is that, on occasion, the belated trigger and blast can end up killing a teammate. Call out explosives!

SITREP

STANDARD	Detect enemy Equipment and deployed Pointstreaks
PRO	Louder enemy footsteps

Sitrep is a powerful perk in objective-based game modes, and it's a useful perk all around. While the perk is active, all enemy Equipment is visible with a red glow, even through walls! This also applies to grenades in the air or on the ground, making them very easy to spot and avoid. Not only does this provide near total protection from C4, Claymores, and Bouncing Betties, it also applies to deployed Pointstreaks. The perk also makes it extremely easy to shoot Equipment through walls, destroy it with grenades, or avoid it entirely.

Furthermore, Sitrep acts as a sort of visual radar. Very frequently, Equipment is located near the person who deployed it. This can give you an advantage over those who think their backs are covered. You can use Sitrep to warn teammates of Equipment locations. A single alert player who communicates well with Sitrep can nearly shut down an entire enemy team's Equipment edge in objective-based game modes.

The Pro upgrade increases the volume of enemy footsteps significantly. This is a very powerful upgrade if your audio system is up to par, or if you're wearing headphones. With Sitrep Pro, it's nearly impossible for anyone to sneak up on you without Dead Silence. It also allows you to pinpoint nearby enemy positions with greater accuracy.

STEADY AIM

BASE	Reduces hip-fire spread by 35%
PRO	Recover from melee attacks 40% quicker

Steady Aim reduces hip-fire spread by roughly 35 percent, significantly improving the accuracy of weapons fired without ADS. Steady Aim is a near mandatory perk for run-and-gun SMG and Shotgun builds. It allows you to fire from the hip at short range, eliminating the time it takes to ADS. It also gives you a speed and mobility advantage over any enemy trying to ADS against you. Steady Aim is helpful for any build running Akimbo MPs or Handguns, which have very poor accuracy beyond extremely short range without it.

Steady Aim Pro causes your knife lunges to recover 40 percent faster, which can save your life if you knife one enemy when a second is nearby. Steady Aim Pro with a Tactical Knife Pistol or a Melee-upgraded Shotgun or Riot Shield is also quite effective.

DEAD SILENCE

STANDARD	Silences movement, halves Recon duration
PRO	No falling damage

Dead Silence is another powerful stealth perk. It grants you silent movement and the slight bonus of halving the period in which Recon makes you visible on radar (down to six seconds from the normal 12).

Dead Silence is most effective on offensive builds that use silenced weapons and Assassin to stay completely off the radar and nearly undetectable outside direct visual contact.

Dead Silence is a strange perk in that its power is somewhat dependent on the skill of your opponents. Better players are more alert to sounds around them, but newer players are less likely to react to footsteps. So, to avoid 'wasting' a perk, assess its value with the playing conditions and the skill of your opponents in mind.

Dead Silence Pro adds the strange bonus of eliminating falling damage. This is useful primarily for granting you new ways to move through levels safely. It can let you survive otherwise fatal or heavily damaging jumps and escape angry pursuers with ease.

STRIKE PACKAGES

AS A SPECIALIST OPERATIVE, YOU HAVE THE AUTHORITY TO CALL IN POWERFUL AIR SUPPORT.

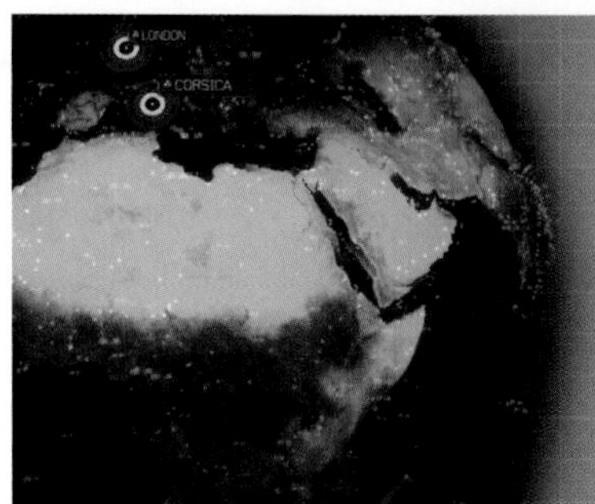

POINTSTREAK LOOPING

If you earn your final Pointstreak, you immediately reset to your first reward—you don't have to die to earn another streak reward!

THERE ARE THREE STRIKE PACKAGES:

ASSAULT IS OFFENSIVE, ORIENTED TOWARD SUPPRESSING THE ENEMY WITH POWERFUL AIR SUPPORT.

SUPPORT IS PRIMARILY DEFENSIVE AND SUPPORTIVE, PROVIDING REWARDS THAT BENEFIT YOU AND YOUR TEAM AS A WHOLE.

SPECIALIST IS THE LONE-WOLF STRIKE PACKAGE. KILLS EARN YOU MORE PERKS, WITH EIGHT KILLS UNLOCKING *ALL* PERKS AND ALMOST ALL PROFICIENCIES AS WELL.

Strike Packages allow you to choose from three different sets of Pointstreak rewards. Earn the required number of kills, and you unlock the ability to call in powerful support. Or, in the case of the Specialist package, unlock multiple perks for your own use.

Kills are not the only way to acquire rewards. You also earn points toward your streaks by completing any objective in objective-based game modes, and for shooting down enemy air support. Finally, the Hardline perk reduces by one the number of points required for any Pointstreak reward. Plus, Hardline Pro makes two assists count as a Pointstreak point.

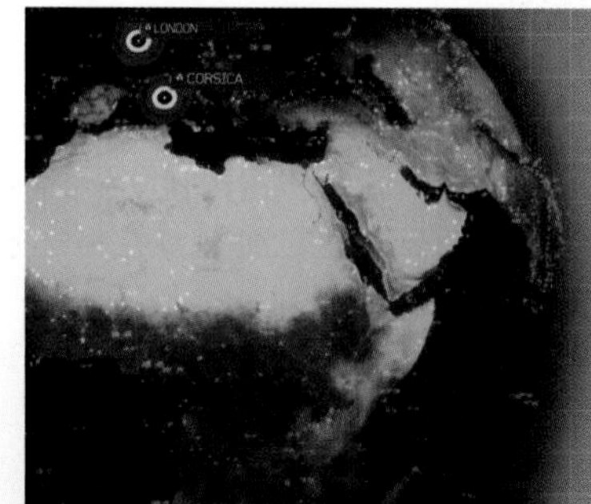

SPAWN PROTECTION

For five seconds after you respawn, you do not appear on the radar for controlled aerial Pointstreaks, and automatic Pointstreaks do not target you.

POINTSTREAK CHAINS

Kills inflicted by your active Pointstreak rewards *do* count toward your next Pointstreak.For example, if you have your Assault Package set to Predator/Attack Helicopter/Reaper, you can use the Predator to get two kills and immediately earn the chopper. Then, if the chopper gets two kills, you can immediately use the Reaper.

However, note that your *final* Pointstreak never gives you points toward your next chain. So, in the preceding example, once you earn your Reaper, the kills you acquire with it would not count toward your next Predator. If your setup is UAV/Reaper/Osprey Gunner, the Reaper would contribute kills toward the Osprey Gunner, but the Osprey would not help you earn the next UAV.

EACH OF THE THREE PACKAGES ACQUIRES REWARDS SLIGHTLY DIFFERENTLY:

ASSAULT STREAKS RESET IF YOU DIE. ALL REWARDS MUST BE EARNED WITHIN ONE LIFE.

SUPPORT STREAKS DO *NOT* RESET IF YOU DIE. REWARDS CAN BE EARNED OVER THE COURSE OF MULTIPLE SPAWNS.

SPECIALIST REWARDS ONE NEW PERK EVERY TWO KILLS, UP TO SIX KILLS. AT EIGHT KILLS, ALL PERKS AND NEARLY ALL PROFICIENCIES ARE UNLOCKED UNTIL YOU DIE. EVERY TWO KILLS PAST EIGHT REWARDS YOU WITH BONUS EXPERIENCE. ALL BENEFITS ARE LOST ON DEATH.

Assault and Support rewards that are earned are kept, regardless of death. In other words, if earn an AC-130 with an Assault Package but you die before you can use it, you can still use the AC-130 after you respawn. However, Pointstreak rewards used after you have died do *not* add to your next Pointstreak chain.

It's also possible to cycle through your Pointstreak rewards—each of your three slots can be used as you see fit. This can be very useful; as an example, conserve a UAV until you acquir a Precision Airstrike or Stealth Bomber, and then call it in to pick up targets. You could also sit on a CUAV before staging an offensive assault, and call in a helicopter to make locating your team and the 'copter much more difficult.

THE MOTHER OF ALL BOMBS

Can you score 25 unassisted kills—using only your weapon—with no Pointstreak assistance whatsoever?

ASSAULT

UAV: 3 POINTS

CONTROLLED?	NO
DEPLOYED?	NO
AIRDROPPED?	NO

The UAV is an aerial drone that provides radar sweeps of the area, giving you periodic positional updates of all enemies on the map. A good habit to get into when a UAV comes online is to check your main map quickly, noting the positions of enemies. This can give you a good feel for where the other team is clustered. Remember that players using Assassin are invisible to UAV sweeps, so don't get complacent when a UAV is active.

The UAV is a vital Pointstreak reward. Be sure to have it on at least one of your builds at all times. UAVs are critically important for staging an effective offense, and they're nearly as important on defense. UAVs last for 60 seconds, stay active on the map where they can be shot for 30 seconds, and each additional UAV activated adds five seconds to the UAV timer. UAVs do not have flares, and they're weak enough for small arms fire to destroy them.

UAV UPGRADES

UAVs normally perform slow radar sweeps, but if multiple UAVs are active at once, the sweeps can be improved. Deploying two UAVs doubles the sweep speed, but three UAVs trigger an Advanced UAV effect! The position and facing of all enemies appears on the map, just as if you're using an Advanced UAV.

CARE PACKAGE: 4 POINTS

CONTROLLED?	NO
DEPLOYED?	YES
AIRDROPPED?	YES

The Care Package gives you the chance to gamble with your Pointstreak rewards. When you activate it, you can throw down a smoke beacon for a support helicopter to fly in and drop a Care Package crate. The contents of that crate are random. You might luck out and score a high-end streak, but more likely, you'll earn a low-end reward.

Oh, and yes, falling packages can indeed crush you, your teammates, and enemies. Mind your head. On the other hand, don't call in Care Packages with hard cover overhead; packages can get stuck out of reach!

Note that players can shoot down the care package chopper, but doing so before it delivers its cargo simply makes it drop its payload immediately.

POINTSTREAK CHAINS

*Care Package rewards do **not** count toward your accumulation of Pointstreak points.*

INTELLIGENT MUNITIONS SYSTEM (IMS): 5 POINTS

CONTROLLED?	NO
DEPLOYED?	YES
AIRDROPPED?	YES

The Intelligent Munitions System is a super-powered proximity mine. Armed with four intelligent, seeking explosives that deploy when an enemy moves into range, the IMS is ideal for blocking chokepoints or defending objective areas. Deploy the IMS out of sight, around corners, inside doorways, and behind cover near objectives, and you are all but guaranteed to rack up several kills before the enemy deals with it.

You can move the IMS from place to place, although we don't recommend moving it long distances due to your vulnerability and visibility while you carry it. Should you die while you're carrying the IMS, it may deploy if you're in a location that allows it.

It *is* possible to dodge the IMS, though doing so is very difficult. When the IMS is triggered, its projectile launches into the air, rocketing toward its target at lightning speed. To survive, you need to put hard cover between you and the IMS *immediately*. This is usually possible only if you're already sprinting with a light weapon. Going prone with a Riot Shield on your back or facing the explosive directly can save you as well. But in general, the IMS is far harder to avoid than Claymores or Bouncing Betties. Blast Shield will *not* save you from a direct impact.

The best solution is simply to *shoot* the IMS. It's very vulnerable to bullet damage. However, it's relatively resistant to explosives. So, if the IMS is carefully positioned out of sight, destroying it with grenades can be difficult—unless you have an EMP Grenade, which can down it instantly.

PREDATOR MISSILE: 5 POINTS

CONTROLLED?	YES
DEPLOYED?	NO
AIRDROPPED?	NO

The classic Predator makes its return, and it's just as effective and lethal as before. You can steer the Predator to target highlighted enemies. Press the Fire button to activate its missile's thrusters, speeding its impact but reducing your fine movement control.

In multiplayer, *many* buildings have holes in their rooftops, so look around when you explore the maps—you can land Predators inside many structures. Because the blast from the Predator is large and powerful, it's possible to kill targets under hard cover by planting the Predator just inside a doorway or at the edge of cover.

When you have to escape an inbound Predator, try to find hard cover above *and* between you and the impact site. Remember that you can use the Trophy System to save yourself from a Predator if you're stuck in the open!

AGMS FOR AA

You can use the Predator to take out a great deal of air support or even ground-based Pointstreak support. Drop a Predator on a Pave Low, Assault Drone, or even a Juggernaut to eliminate a dangerous threat to your team!

Although it's difficult, it is possible to neutralize an AC-130 with a Predator if you get lucky and the angles line up properly.

SENTRY GUN: 5 POINTS

CONTROLLED?	NO
DEPLOYED?	YES
AIRDROPPED?	YES

The Sentry Gun is a deployable, movable automatic turret that acquires and fires at any enemy forces in its frontal arc. The Sentry turret is absolutely lethal on open ground, but somewhat less effective if there is a lot of hard cover in its line of fire.

The Sentry Gun Pointstreak must be airdropped in a Care Package, which makes it a poor streak to use on offensive or mobile builds. However, it is very powerful on defense for covering an objective or blocking off an approach route. You can bypass a Sentry entirely with the Blind Eye perk. In the absence of that option, you can also disable it with a Flash or Concussion Grenade, or destroy it completely with an EMP Grenade. A Scrambler *does* protect you from a Sentry, but running out in the open and dropping a Scrambler so you can shoot or bypass a Sentry usually isn't a safe tactic!

PRECISION AIRSTRIKE: 6 POINTS

CONTROLLED?	YES
DEPLOYED?	NO
AIRDROPPED?	NO

The Precision Airstrike calls in a manually targeted aerial assault that impacts a few seconds after you call it in, carpet-bombing a long, narrow stretch of the map. The Precision Airstrike can be tricky to use, because you have to anticipate where your opponents will be after you call in the strike *and* after they respond to the incoming airstrike warning. Consequently, the airstrike is most effective on open maps with little overhead cover, and in objective modes, where you can bomb areas that *must* be defended.

This makes the airstrike ideal for covering a Domination capture or a Demolition bomb plant. Any objective mode where players need to clear or cover an objective in the open gives added power to the Precision Airstrike. Try to save your airstrikes in objective modes for coordinated objective pushes. If possible, don't call one in without a UAV in the air to guide your strike for maximum damage.

ATTACK HELICOPTER: 7 POINTS

CONTROLLED?	NO
DEPLOYED?	NO
AIRDROPPED?	NO

The classic Attack Helicopter calls in a support chopper that patrols the map, gunning down enemy forces. The 'copter support sticks around until it is destroyed or its time in theater expires. This makes the Pointstreak's effectiveness almost entirely dependent on the enemy team's vigilance and speed in taking down aerial threats.

Assuming your chopper isn't blasted out of the sky on arrival, it's generally more effective on maps with a lot of open ground. Maps with a ton of hard cover give the chopper few angles for attack. Compared to guided or deployed Pointstreaks, the Attack Helicopter is nice because it is fire-and-forget. Once deployed, you can use the chopper's extra covering fire to aid you in offense or defense. The Attack Helicopter has one set of flares.

STRAFE RUN: 9 POINTS

CONTROLLED?	NO
DEPLOYED?	NO
AIRDROPPED?	NO

The Strafe Run Pointstreak calls in a massive double strafing run by *five* attack helicopters. You choose the initial direction and area of attack. Then the choppers fly in, sweep the map, turn a 180, and then sweep the map a second time before they depart. On open maps, these sweeps can be absolutely devastating. In any objective mode with a target in the open, you can use the Strafe Run to cover the objective effectively. The Strafe Run helicopters have *no* flares.

One very serious word of caution: While the Strafe Run is powerful, it has the potential to backfire badly. Normally, air support destroyed by an enemy gives a single point toward a Pointstreak.

However, every single helicopter in a Strafe Run counts as air support. As a result, the enemy team can gain up to *five* points toward Pointstreaks by destroying your Strafe Run force. Furthermore, two Stinger Missiles are enough to accomplish this task.

Pay attention to how aggressive the enemy team is about neutralizing air support. If they're shooting UAVs out of the sky with ARs and firing SMAWs and Stingers at any serious air support, don't use this Pointstreak on them!

AH-6 OVERWATCH: 9 POINTS

CONTROLLED?	NO
DEPLOYED?	NO
AIRDROPPED?	NO

The AH-6 Overwatch calls in a chopper to be your personal escort! While on overwatch, this chopper aggressively attacks any enemy that dares to shoot at you, and it follows you around the map like a loyal hound. The only downside to this personal escort is that it can give away your general position. This may not be in your best interest while you're on offense or if you're using a stealth build. Otherwise, the AH-6 is a nice supportive Pointstreak. It can also be very effective on defense for locking down an objective or a part of the map. This helicopter has one set of flares.

LOW-HANGING FRUIT

The AH-6 can be destroyed by a single EMP Grenade, because it flies low enough for the EMP blast to hit it.

REAPER: 9 POINTS

CONTROLLED?	YES
DEPLOYED?	NO
AIRDROPPED?	NO

The Reaper is a super-powered Predator. While orbits high above the battlefield, it allows you to fire and manually guide a very large supply of AGMs at the enemy team.As you paint a target location for the missile, be aware that you simultaneously create a gigantic, glowing red mark on the ground where you are aiming! Alert players scatter for cover when they're targeted. Whenever you can, try to guide the missile down near your target point by aiming on top of buildings or away from enemies—then swerve at the last second to nail your intended target.

Because you can guide the missiles, and your viewing angle on the map changes as the Reaper orbits the battlefield, you can occasionally slingshot AGMs directly into doorways or windows, dispatching targets who think they're safe from your rain of hellfire. Like the various attack helicopters, the Reaper has one set of flares.

ORBITAL RECON

One of the Reaper's strengths is that it provides a fantastic overview of the battlefield, and you can easily call targets for your teammates. Enemies tend to run for cover when they hear a Reaper in the sky. So again, call out enemy targets that you cannot reach. You can inflict almost as much damage on the enemy team by calling locations as you can by launching missiles.

ASSAULT DRONE: 10 POINTS

CONTROLLED?	YES
DEPLOYED?	YES
AIRDROPPED?	YES

The Assault Drone is an armored attack bot equipped with machine guns, rockets, and an integrated Portable Radar system. After you call in an Assault Drone drop with your Smoke Grenade, you can then deploy the Drone to the battlefield. You must operate the Assault Drone manually, so be sure to hide somewhere safe before you take control of it.

The Assault Drone is a perfect tool for breaking defensive stalemates and assaulting objectives. Lead the charge for your teammates, or simply set up shop near a known enemy position, and call out targets using your Radar sweeps. Be aware that the Drone shows up on enemy minimaps automatically, meaning there is no reason to be 'stealthy' with the Drone. The enemy team knows where it is at all times, unless you deploy a CUAV first.

While you use the Assault Drone, you have infinite ammo, but you must reload every 50 rounds or two rockets fired. Otherwise, you are unrestricted in your ability to roam the level and engage targets!

DRONE DESTRUCTION

The Assault Drone is resilient to gunfire and most explosives, but it is highly vulnerable to the EMP Grenade. Try to keep your distance from enemy forces if you know they're using EMPs, as they have a short effective range.

AC-130: 12 POINTS

CONTROLLED?	YES
DEPLOYED?	NO
AIRDROPPED?	NO

A devastating angel of death, the AC-130 Pointstreak calls in an orbiting gunship armed with 125mm and 40mm cannons, and 25mm guns. While it orbits the battlefield, enemy players are highlighted, and you can switch between normal and thermal views to spot players against different backgrounds more easily. When you use the AC-130, cycle rapidly between all three weapons to inflict maximum devastation on the enemy team. Fire a 125mm shot immediately, switch to the 40mm and fire four quick shots, and then switch to the 25mm to spray an area, and repeat.

Just like the Reaper, the AC-130 provides you with a perfect aerial view of the battlefield. Use this edge to call out targets to your teammates while you're in the air. You have unlimited ammunition, so it's important to dump as much high-powered ordnance on the battlefield as possible while you control the AC-130. The AC-130 has two sets of flares.

PAVE LOW: 12 POINTS

CONTROLLED?	NO
DEPLOYED?	NO
AIRDROPPED?	NO

The Pave Low calls in a powerful armored assault helicopter that sticks around even longer than the basic Attack Helicopter. In addition to its increased battlefield presence, it also attacks more accurately, frequently, and aggressively than the Attack Helicopter. It's also more heavily armored, being nearly impregnable to small-arms fire without Blind Eye Pro equipped.

The Pave Low does have the Achilles heel of having only one set of flares *and* being vulnerable to EMP Grenades on some maps due to its low flight path. Otherwise, the Pave Low is a straight upgrade to the Attack Helicopter, providing superior air support while it's on the field.

JUGGERNAUT: 15 POINTS

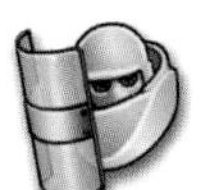

CONTROLLED?	YES
DEPLOYED?	NO
AIRDROPPED?	YES

The Juggernaut is an airdropped package that grants you a suit of powerful Juggernaut armor, an M60 and a USP, along with automatic access to the Scavenger perk, ensuring near-infinite ammo. While you're wear the Juggernaut armor, you show up on the enemy team's radar. In exchange, you're granted extremely rapid health regeneration—enough that taking you down requires concentrated effort from multiple enemies. Juggernaut is a powerful Pointstreak. It gives you the potential to roll the entire enemy team if they fail to coordinate and deal with the threat you present. The Assault package Juggernaut does *not* have a Portable Radar like the Support version.

While the Juggernaut is powerful, it does have a few weaknesses to exploit. First of all, it's *slow.* Canny opponents can simply keep their distance and stay behind hard cover to avoid you. This is a noticeable disadvantage on larger maps in objective modes. The Juggernaut is weak to RPG and SMAW fire. A direct shot can take out the Juggernaut instantly. If you spot a Juggernaut on the enemy team, immediately break out your SMAW or RPG!

OSPREY GUNNER: 17 POINTS

CONTROLLED?	YES
DEPLOYED?	NO
AIRDROPPED?	NO

Fans of the Chopper Gunner rejoice, haters of it despair: the Osprey Gunner takes the place of that lethal Pointstreak in *Call of Duty: Modern Warfare 3.* Calling in the Osprey Gunner puts you in command of a powerful VTOL aircraft armed with 25mm cannons and unlimited ammunition. The cannon fire is powerful enough to inflict splash damage on targets near the point of impact. Conveniently, targets are highlighted on your screen with red indicators.

When you call in the Osprey Gunner, you select an initial destination for the Osprey. When it arrives, it drops off three Assault Care Packages! Because the Osprey is momentarily immobile and vulnerable while it drops its payload, be sure to select a target zone carefully, and communicate with your team to provide cover for you.

Once the Osprey drops off the packages, it begins to move around the mission area automatically, giving you a range of targeting angles from with to dispatch the enemy team. As with other aerial Pointstreaks you can control, one of the Osprey's major strengths is the ability to call enemy target locations for your team. The Osprey has one set of flares.

DOWN THAT BIRD

The Osprey's vulnerability when it arrives on the map gives you a narrow window of opportunity to destroy it before it causes serious damage to your team. Quickly switch to a build with an anti-air launcher to dispatch it. If you have an EMP Grenade, it's possible to hit the Osprey when it comes near the ground to deposit its Care Package loadout.

Failing all of the above, stay inside hard cover, and avoid openings of any kind. The cannon fire can kill you with splash damage through a doorway.

SUPPORT

UAV: 4 POINTS

CONTROLLED?	NO
DEPLOYED?	NO
AIRDROPPED?	NO

Identical to the UAV from the Assault Package, the only difference for the Support streak is that it requires four kills instead of three. This compensates for Support's easier Pointstreak acquisition.

COUNTER-UAV: 5 POINTS

CONTROLLED?	NO
DEPLOYED?	NO
AIRDROPPED?	NO

The Counter-UAV (CUAV) is a powerful defensive Pointstreak. When you activate it, a jamming UAV blocks the enemy team's radar entirely. This powerful effect gives your entire team 'silencers' of a sort, disables enemy UAVs and AUAVs, and gives your team a window of opportunity to stage an assault while the enemy team is radar blind. The CUAV is strongest when you play objective modes with a team; it's weaker, though still useful, in deathmatch modes.

BALLISTIC VESTS: 5 POINTS

CONTROLLED?	NO
DEPLOYED?	YES
AIRDROPPED?	NO

Ballistic Vests is another powerful Support Pointstreak, giving you a package of Ballistic Vests that you can drop anywhere on the battlefield. Once deployed, anyone on your team can access the package. Using the package requires a few seconds, so be sure to place the vests out of sight or in a low-traffic area.

When you equip a vest, your screen has a noticeable yellow tint around the edges, and your health is doubled. Assaulting an enemy position while your entire team is equipped with vests provides a tremendous edge. The extra 'health' wears off completely once the vest is damaged, and you must acquire another vest to restore the defensive bonus. Always communicate with your team when you drop vests; they are powerful only if your team uses them!

AIRDROP TRAP: 5 POINTS

CONTROLLED?	NO
DEPLOYED?	YES
AIRDROPPED?	YES

The Airdrop Trap calls in a booby-trapped Care Package. To the enemy, it often appears as a high-end Pointstreak. Any greedy enemy who tries to steal the package triggers a high-powered explosion with a 10-meter radius. The blast inflicts 200 max/50 minimum damage, making it instantly lethal to any enemy players clustered around the package.

When you use the Airdrop Trap, you can almost assuredly catch the enemy team at least once. Smart opponents will then communicate that someone on your team is using Traps, making future success less likely. To disguise the Airdrop Trap, try to mix it in with real Care Packages, and drop it in an area that seems 'likely' for a real Care Package drop. If you repeatedly fling the target smoke on top of the enemy team and flee the area, don't expect to fool anyone. Make the enemy team work for it a bit to disguise its true nature.

SAM TURRET: 8 POINTS

CONTROLLED?	NO
DEPLOYED?	YES
AIRDROPPED?	YES

The SAM Turret is a useful defensive Pointstreak. When it's activated, you call in a package that delivers your SAM Turret. As a result, don't expect this streak to save you from an immediate aerial threat. Use it as a backup, not an instant answer. A good tactic is to drop the SAM Turret package, pick it up, and then save it until you need it. Assuming you earn more than one in a match, you can place one in a good location as insurance, and save the second for an emergency.

The SAM Turret fires relatively weak rockets. Multiple shots are required to down any high-powered air support, even the 'low end' Attack Helicopter. However, it is very strong against enemy UAVs of all sorts, including Counter, Advanced, and the Reaper. The SAM Turret does target Recon Drones as well! The SAM Turret has a 360-degree arc of fire, but terrain can block its shots, so place it in an elevated position with a clear line of sight to the sky, ideally in an out-of-the-way part of the map. Like the Sentry Guns, a single knife stab up close or gunfire from a distance can destroy the SAM Turret.

RECON DRONE: 10 POINTS

CONTROLLED?	YES
DEPLOYED?	YES
AIRDROPPED?	NO

The Recon Drone is a new and unique Support Pointstreak. You operate a tiny remote-controlled scout helicopter (think model helicopter size). This Recon Drone carries sophisticated targeting equipment that allows you to spot enemy troops as though you're in one of the high-powered aerial Pointstreaks. This makes calling out enemy locations for your team extremely easy.

As long as you hug cover and manipulate elevation wisely, you can be a difficult target for the enemy team to hit. Thus, you may enjoy a long run of intelligence gathering for your team, which can be powerful if you communicate well.

The Recon Drone has an additional trick up its sleeve: you can 'tag' any enemy in sight by 'shooting' the target. Once tagged, the foe appears on your entire team's radar, similar to the Recon perk or an AUAV. Additionally, the tag causes a quick blinding effect due to a camera flash, much like a glancing Flashbang effect. To exploit this to the fullest, don't tag a target you are following—you can report its location verbally. Instead, wait for a teammate to get near, then blind the target just as your teammate attacks, all but ensuring a kill.

Finally, the Recon Drone is equipped with a built-in Scrambler. This makes the Drone especially useful in objective modes. You can hover just outside a known defensive position and scramble the entire enemy team nearby. The triple utility of scouting, tagging, and scrambling makes the Recon Drone a superior Support streak. But its value depends entirely on your ability to communicate and your team's ability to work together.

ADVANCED UAV: 12 POINTS

CONTROLLED?	NO
DEPLOYED?	NO
AIRDROPPED?	NO

The Advanced UAV is a tremendously powerful Support Pointstreak. It calls in a 'super' UAV that provides perfect positional *and* directional radar locations for every enemy without the Assassin perk on the map. Thus, when this AUAV goes airborne, your team receives an overwhelming intelligence advantage, which it can ruthlessly exploit for a powerful assault.

Combine the launch of an AUAV with a CUAV, and you can shut down the enemy team, denying radar access while your team has near-perfect locational information. If you're running Support, strongly consider including this streak in your loadout.

REMOTE SENTRY: 12 POINTS

CONTROLLED?	YES
DEPLOYED?	YES
AIRDROPPED?	YES

The Remote Sentry is a radio-controlled Sentry Gun. Place it and then find a hidey hole nearby to activate it from safety. The Remote Sentry has many of the same strengths and weaknesses as the regular Sentry Gun, but it differs in two key ways.

First, you have to control it. This means you need to gain more advantage from the Remote Sentry than you would provide yourself, which is tough to accomplish. Second, the Remote Sentry does have full 360-degree rotation. Place it carefully, and you can gain an excellent vantage point on any incoming enemies, especially if teammates or equipment block other avenues of approach.

Blind Eye (or a Scrambler) makes targets 'invisible' to the Remote Sentry. However, since you have a ground-level view of the area, this rarely makes targeting more difficult, even without the red targeting indicators.

Experiment with the Remote Sentry on defense in objective modes. Properly supported, it can stall an enemy team nicely. But it can rarely achieve much when you place it carelessly or alone. Oh, and yes, you can shoot yourself with your own Remote Sentry...

C4 AND THE REMOTE SENTRY

A rare quirk involving the Remote Sentry is that double-tapping Reload at close range picks up the Remote Sentry—it also causes any C4 you've deployed to detonate. Be aware of this corner case if you happen to be using C4 alongside a Remote Sentry, and you can avoid an embarrassing accident.

STEALTH BOMBER: 14 POINTS

CONTROLLED?	YES
DEPLOYED?	NO
AIRDROPPED?	NO

The Stealth Bomber is a super-powered Precision Airstrike. You call a target location and direction, and a Stealth Bomber saturates your target location from end to end. The bomb blast radius and power is considerably greater than the Precision Airstrike. It kills anyone inside the area instantly. The bombing run's sheer force even staggers enemies under hard cover.

Use the Stealth Bomber in much the same way you would a regular airstrike. First get a UAV in the air to locate the enemy team, or use it to cover an objective push or defense. While the Stealth Bomber sweeps an area, it's very easy for teammates to secure an objective unless the enemy has perfect cover nearby.

EMP: 18 POINTS

CONTROLLED?	NO
DEPLOYED?	NO
AIRDROPPED?	NO

The EMP triggers a massive, high-altitude nuclear explosion. This creates an EMP shockwave that instantly downs all enemy air support, disables their HUD *completely*, and shuts down their radar, Pointstreaks, and even electronic optical sights! The EMP lasts for 60 seconds. For the duration, your team has a powerful advantage over the enemy team, but don't take the EMP as license to attack indiscriminately.

The blast is powerful and debilitating, but not much more than an AUAV/CUAV combo. A good player's aim isn't significantly impaired even if he's using optics. The EMP is still very useful and powerful, particularly for its ability to shut down any powerful enemy Pointstreak instantly. When you earn an EMP, hold onto it. Save it for a key offensive push or to destroy a high-end enemy Pointstreak.

JUGGERNAUT RECON: 18 POINTS

CONTROLLED?	YES
DEPLOYED?	YES
AIRDROPPED?	YES

The Juggernaut Recon is identical to the Assault Juggernaut in defensive strength and slow movement speed. It is airdropped onto the map, and once acquired, it equips you with Juggernaut armor. The difference is the loadout: the Juggernaut Recon comes with a Riot Shield and a USP, as well as permanent Portable Radar. This makes the Juggernaut Recon a very useful spearhead for a team push, or a *very* annoying defender at a chokepoint or near an objective.

Between the massive health and the Riot Shield, the Juggernaut Recon is difficult to take out even with a SMAW or RPG. If you play it well, the Juggernaut Recon can be just as devastating to an enemy team as the Assault Juggernaut's M60.

ESCORT AIRDROP: 18 POINTS

CONTROLLED?	YES
DEPLOYED?	NO
AIRDROPPED?	NO

The Escort Airdrop is the Support equivalent of the Assault's Osprey Gunner. Instead of controlling the VTOL helicopter, you can choose a target zone for a drop of *five* Support Care Packages. One has a high chance of being an Airdrop Trap every time.

Once the Escort Osprey is in position, it *stays* in position, covering its dropped prizes and mowing down any enemies foolish enough to approach the vicinity. Unlike the Osprey Gunner, which deals most of its damage *after* it drops, and is therefore best deployed in an out-of-the-way-area, the Escort Airdrop is best near (but not directly on) an objective or a very high traffic area.

Properly covered, the Escort Osprey can all but guarantee an objective's successful defense or assault. Or it can lock down an area of the map in a deathmatch mode. Although the enemy is likely to hide out while it's present, that predictability can give you easy target locations. Be sure to support the Escort Osprey. While it is powerful, it has blind spots. One fast enemy with an EMP Grenade can take it down in a single throw.

SPECIALIST

Specialist is a unique new Strike Package. Rather than a special set of Pointstreak rewards, Specialist instead rewards you with *perks*. Every two kills rewards you with a new perk, up to three perks. Should you score an eighth kill, you are rewarded with *every perk in the game*. On top of that, you are granted Impact, Speed, Stability, Focus, Kick, Range *and* Melee proficiencies for any primary weapon you use. Every two kills beyond the maximum awards you with bonus experience.

Specialist is a powerful Strike Package, but its strength is *entirely* dependent on your personal skill. It's ideal for talented lone wolf players, but it's also an inherently selfish Strike Package. It provides no radar coverage for your team, no air support, and no defenses. To make up for this, you *must* exploit the Specialist package's power to cause serious problems for the enemy team. This usually means playing aggressively rather than defensively.

ONE-MAN ARMY

Because of Specialist's perk unlocks, you have a tremendous stealth advantage, faster mobility, better accuracy, better range, quicker ADS, faster reloads, and near-perfect situational awareness. Nevertheless, you can still go down to a few bullets, so is powerful yet vulnerable. High risk, high reward. Feel like you have what it takes?

If you take Specialist, Overkill is a key initial perk to pick, as it gives you two primary weapons immediately. You would otherwise gain no benefit from 'earning' Overkill later. Hardline is an option, but you essentially trade a customized second primary weapon for a one-kill replacement perk and one fewer kill to reach the magic unlock number. A Silencer is also a good idea. Once you pair it with the total stealth package of a full unlock, you become nearly invisible to the enemy team. Only direct visual contact gives away your position, and sometimes not even then, due to Assassin Pro.

PREPPING FOR WAR

Choose your initial perks and the first three perk unlocks carefully. It's a good idea to select perks that give you immediate combat advantages rather than more subtle benefits.

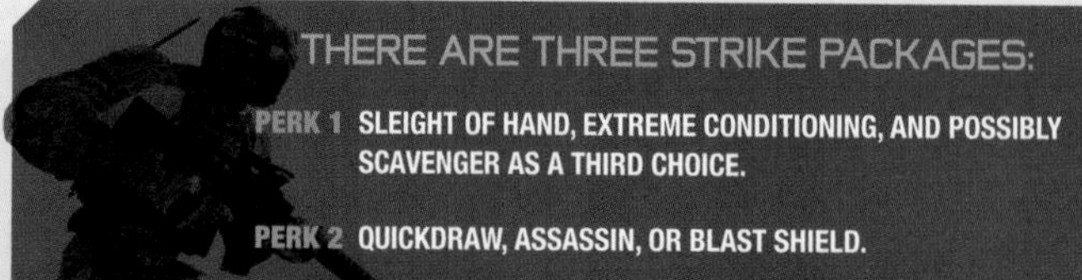

THERE ARE THREE STRIKE PACKAGES:
PERK 1 SLEIGHT OF HAND, EXTREME CONDITIONING, AND POSSIBLY SCAVENGER AS A THIRD CHOICE.
PERK 2 QUICKDRAW, ASSASSIN, OR BLAST SHIELD.
PERK 3 STALKER, STEADY AIM, DEAD SILENCE, AND POSSIBLY SITREP.

You can take the remaining perks (Recon, Blind Eye, Hardline, Overkill, Marksman, and Dead Silence) as part of your initial package, or you can wait to unlock them at eight kills. Of your three perk unlocks, take the ones that grant your loadout the most direct benefit for the first two. Choose the least critical as your third.

PRO SPECIALIST

Specialist uses whatever Pro or Standard perk unlocks you have available. If you intend to use this strike package often, be sure to unlock all Pro versions as quickly as possible to gain the maximum benefit!

DEATH STREAKS

KILL THE PAIN OF FAILURE WITH A DEATH STREAK.

Death Streaks are 'rewards' for consecutive deaths without any kills. While they're not exactly the type of reward you want to earn on a regular basis, Death Streaks can help dig you out of a hole if you're just having a bad day.

We consider Death Streaks the least important part of your loadout—we're planning for success here, not failure! So, don't agonize over the decision. You can pick one as much to annoy your killers as to help you get back into the game.

JUICED

4 DEATHS

Juiced grants a 25 percent speed bonus for a few seconds after respawning. While it's generally unimpressive, Juiced can be helpful in CTF, Headquarters, or Demolition on offense, when you need to get back to your target area quickly.

REVENGE

5 DEATHS

Revenge permanently highlights your last killer on your minimap. This can get you an easy revenge kill. Be careful not to let the allure of a marked target draw you out into the open for *other* enemies to shoot you.

FINAL STAND

4 DEATHS

Final Stand is one of the best Death Streaks in terms of 'efficiency.' When you're downed with Final Stand, you drop to your back, but you can still use your weapons and equipment. You can crawl in Final Stand, but be warned: doing so drops your weapon. And, if you move just as you fall into Final Stand, you give up the chance to retaliate immediately against your enemy.

If you manage to stay alive in Final Stand without getting shot, you eventually stand up to fight again—crawl to cover! This is particularly nice for preserving any streak you have going on an Assault or Specialist Strike Package. But obviously, you have to die a fair amount to get to this point. Final Stand is nice with Hardline, as it triggers after three deaths. This isn't an uncommon occurrence when you play offense in an objective mode, or when you have a bad day in Deathmatch.

MARTYRDOM

4 DEATHS

Martyrdom drops a live Frag Grenade where you die. Occasionally, you can catch your killer or his buddy with your death, but alert enemies can simply sprint away from your body.

DEAD MAN'S HAND

6 DEATHS

Dead Man's Hand drops you into a Last Stand pose, holding an armed C4 charge! You can detonate the C4 manually, or if the enemy is foolish enough to shoot you at close range, it detonates automatically. Either way, the blast is a full-strength C4 bomb. If you go down in close quarters, you can expect to take an enemy with you. Given its power, Dead Man's Hand appropriately requires the longest Death Streak.

HOLLOW POINTS

5 DEATHS

Hollow Points simply gives you more stopping power in the form of added bullet damage for *one* kill. Not an especially crucial Death Streak, as the others at least give you unique benefits. Hollow Points simply shaves a few shots off a kill.

MULTIPLAYER MAPS

KEY

	Team Spawn Points		Domination Flags		Ladder
	Bomb–Search & Destroy / Sabotage Modes		CTF Flags		Sabotage Plant Destinations
	Search & Destroy / Demolition Plant Site		Headquarters Point		Arrows are color-coded to match the levels to which they lead

OTO RECONNAISSANCE

e following chapter, reconnaissance photos accompany each multiplayer map. These photos include numbered pointers (1) in their upper-left corners.

se pointers match up with identical pointers placed on the Team Deathmatch maps. Each pointer's location on the map indicates where its corresponding onnaissance photo was taken. Likewise, the direction of each pointer shows which way the camera faced when the photo was taken.

Size Classification:	Large
Terrain Classification:	Urban
Engagement Profile:	Mixed
Conflict Between:	SAS and Inner Circle

TEAM DEATHMATCH

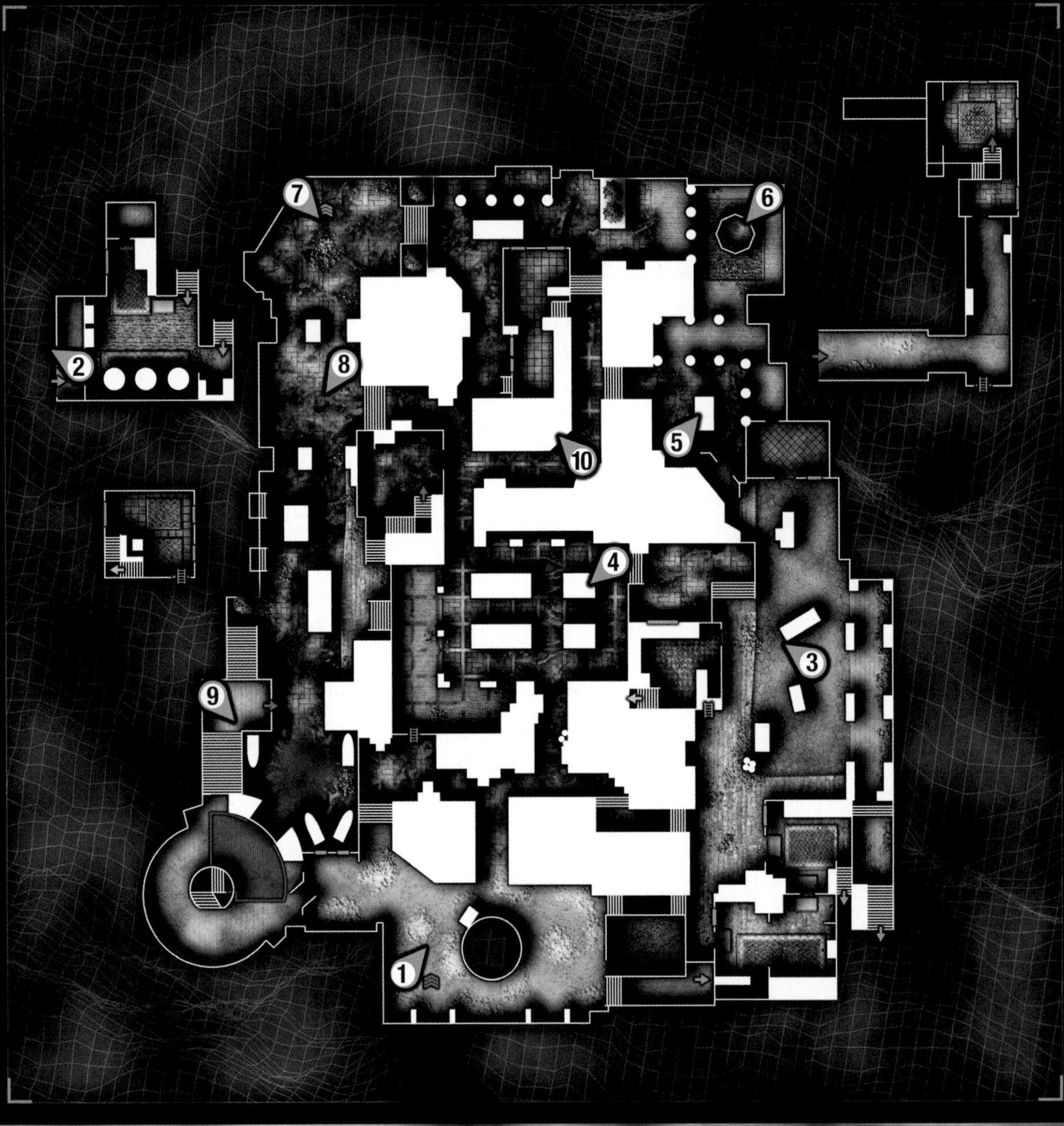

SABOTAGE

DEMOLITION

An old coastal fortress town in the Middle East, Seatown features a mix of open streets, confined alleys, and small buildings. This is an ideal map for flexible character builds and flexible play. You can move between all three types of engagements. Or, if you prefer, you can stick to one type of terrain as much as you wish. The alleys and the central market are dangerous areas—they attract high traffic due to their accessibility from all parts of the map. Move swiftly through these areas, and don't linger unless you're seeking conflict. The building interiors scattered about the map are powerful vantage points for controlling the east, west, and center of the map. Lock them down or deal with their inhabitants, but never ignore them.

DOMINATION

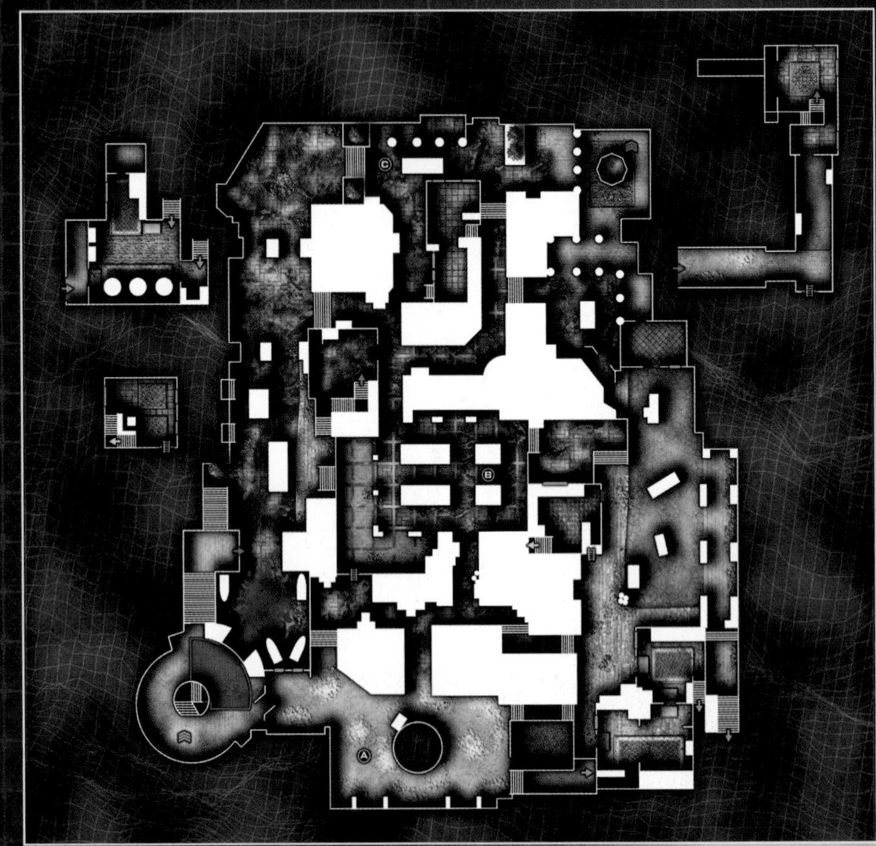

HEADQUARTERS

KEY

	Team Spawn Points
	Bomb–Search & Destroy / Sabotage Modes
A B	Search & Destroy / Demolition Plant Site
A B C	Domination Flags
	CTF Flags
	Headquarters Point
	Ladder
	Sabotage Plant Destinations
	Arrows are color-coded to match the levels to which they lead

CAPTURE THE FLAG

SEARCH & DESTROY

LOADOUT SUGGESTION

GHOST

A pure stealth build, silenced and quiet in every possible way. Abuse your invisibility to run up your Specialist streak.

PRIMARY WEAPON	SCAR-L	
ATTACHMENT	SILENCER	
PROFICIENCY	KICK	
SECONDARY WEAPON	P99	
ATTACHMENT	SILENCER	
EQUIPMENT		
LETHAL	BOUNCING BETTY	
TACTICAL	PORTABLE RADAR	
PERK 1	BLIND EYE	
PERK 2	ASSASSIN	
PERK 3	DEAD SILENCE	
STRIKE PACKAGE	SPECIALIST	
POINTSTREAK 1	QUICKDRAW	
POINTSTREAK 2	SLIGHT OF HAND	
POINTSTREAK 3	SITREP	
DEATH STREAK	REVENGE	

DOME

Size Classification:	Small
Terrain Classification:	Mixed
Engagement Profile:	CQC
Conflict Between:	Spetsnaz and Delta

TEAM DEATHMATCH

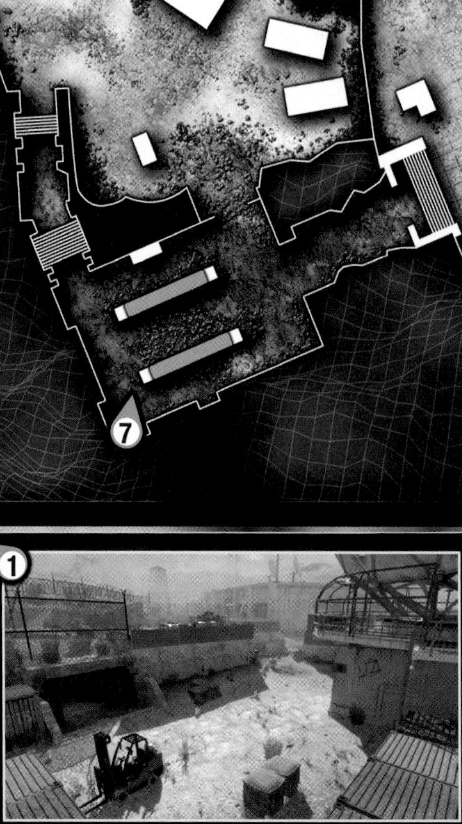

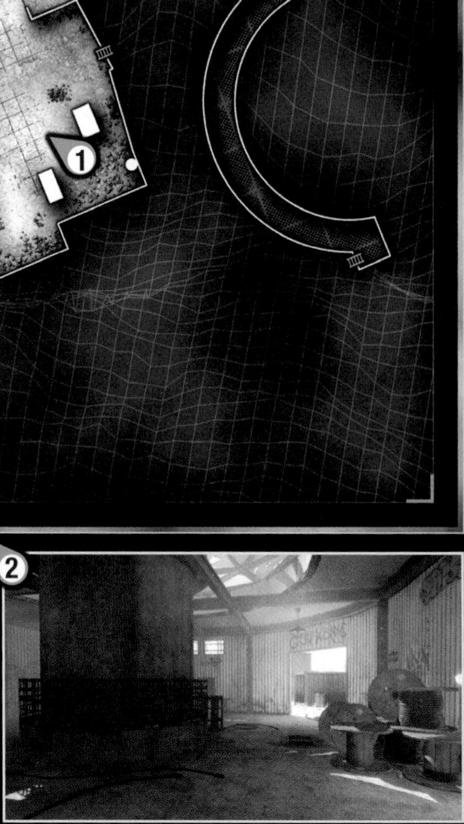

3

4

5

6

7

SABOTAGE

DEMOLITION

A tiny, derelict military outpost in the desert, Dome is a fast-paced, small-scale map. Despite its size, Dome has decent separation between the various parts of the map. Thus, you can exploit the cover and limited routes between areas to block off a section as 'yours' and kill anyone entering it.

In objective-based game modes, expect very messy, brutal confrontations—it isn't tough to fling grenades to any part of the map. Any assault will come via a few obvious routes, making for bloody firefights. The elevated catwalk outside the titular Dome is a bit of a trap. While it does have good line of sight to most of the map, you're badly exposed while you're up top. Get up, get a kill or two, and get down if you plan to use it at all. The ruined bunker and building interior are both dangerous to traverse, as both areas can easily accommodate corner campers. Use grenades to clear a path.

DOMINATION

HEADQUARTERS

KEY

	Team Spawn Points
	Bomb–Search & Destroy / Sabotage Modes
A B	Search & Destroy / Demolition Plant Site
A B C	Domination Flags
	CTF Flags
	Headquarters Point
	Ladder
	Sabotage Plant Destinations
	Arrows are color-coded to match the levels to which they lead

SEARCH & DESTROY

LOADOUT SUGGESTION

RUSH AND ASSAULT

Extreme close-range firepower combines with Focus to give you the edge in face-to-face firefights. Stick to the interior areas and chokepoints.

PRIMARY WEAPON	MP5	
ATTACHMENT	RAPID FIRE	
PROFICIENCY	FOCUS	
SECONDARY WEAPON	P99	
ATTACHMENT	EXTENDED MAGS	
EQUIPMENT		
LETHAL	THROWING KNIFE	
TACTICAL	CONCUSSION GRENADE	
PERK 1	SLIGHT OF HAND	
PERK 2	HARDLINE	
PERK 3	STEADY AIM	
STRIKE PACKAGE	SUPPORT	
POINTSTREAK 1	UAV	
POINTSTREAK 2	COUNTER UAV	
POINTSTREAK 3	AIRDROP TRAP	
DEATH STREAK	REVENGE	

ARKADEN

Size Classification:	Medium
Terrain Classification:	Urban
Engagement Profile:	CQC
Conflict Between:	Spetsnaz and SAS

TEAM DEATHMATCH

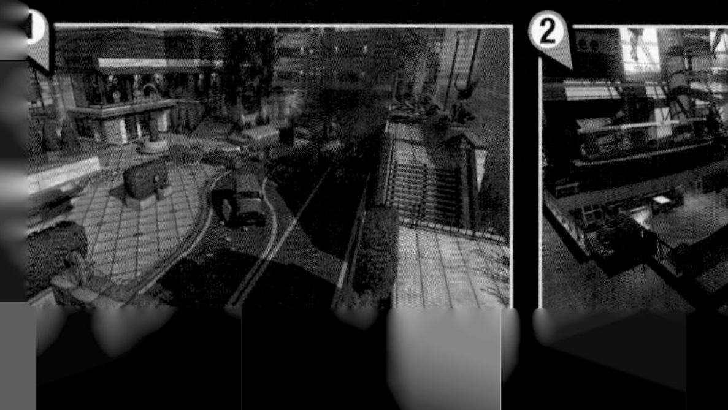

5

6

7

8

9

DEMOLITION

rkaden is a medium-size German mall. If you njoy tight, fast-paced combat in urban areas, his is the map for you. Arkaden offers swift ravel between the center and all parts of the nap. As a result, the central courtyard and the pper-floor mall interior see a *lot* of traffic. Be ery careful in the halls connecting the map's ast and west edges to the center. They have imited cover, which makes lingering in them xtremely dangerous.

Stay alert for campers on the east and west edges outside the mall. Both the front street and he rear loading bay have abundant cover and lenty of obscure locations for patient players o ambush travelers. On Arkaden, objective-based modes are intense, travel times are ow, and the narrow hallways and chokepoints create fearsome firefights. Exploit your tactical grenades and Equipment wisely to punch a hole in solid defenses.

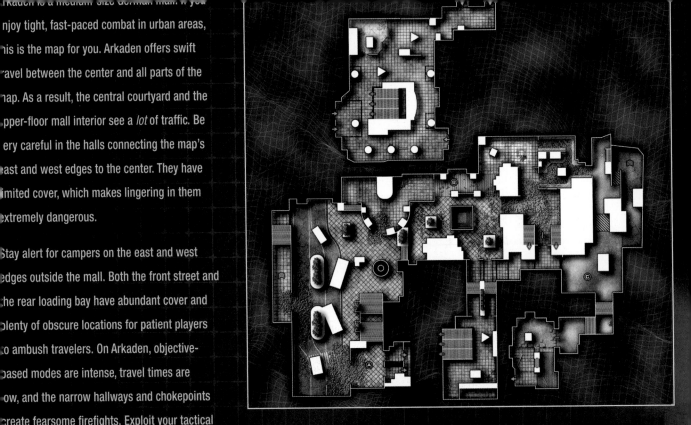

HEADQUARTERS

KEY

	Team Spawn Points
	Bomb–Search & Destroy / Sabotage Modes
A B	Search & Destroy / Demolition Plant Site
A B C	Domination Flags
	CTF Flags
	Headquarters Point
	Ladder
	Sabotage Plant Destinations
	Arrows are color-coded to match the levels to which they lead

CAPTURE THE FLAG

SEARCH & DESTROY

LOADOUT SUGGESTION

THE POOSE

Patrol the hallways with an ammo-overloaded, silenced P90. Break blockades with your RPG.

PRIMARY WEAPON	P90
ATTACHMENT	EXTENDED MAGS, SILENCER
PROFICIENCY	ATTACHMENT
SECONDARY WEAPON	RPG-7
ATTACHMENT	NONE
EQUIPMENT	
LETHAL	BOUNCING BETTY
TACTICAL	EMP GRENADE
PERK 1	SCAVENGER
PERK 2	HARDLINE
PERK 3	STEADY AIM
STRIKE PACKAGE	SUPPORT
POINTSTREAK 1	UAV
POINTSTREAK 2	BALLISTIC VESTS
POINTSTREAK 3	ADVANCED UAV
DEATH STREAK	REVENGE

BAKAARA

Size Classification:	Medium
Terrain Classification:	Open
Engagement Profile:	Mixed
Conflict Between:	Africa Militia and PMC

TEAM DEATHMATCH

1

2

DEMOLITION

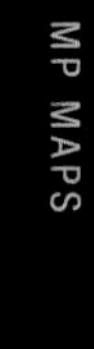

A helicopter crash in an African city is this map's focal point. Bakaara is an open urban level, with three long sightlines down each main path from the east to the west. Consequently, Bakaara is heaven for snipers and assault rifles outfitted for long-range combat.

The downed chopper in the eastern courtyard has the only usable turret on any multiplayer map. It's a bit of a booby prize, as you're dangerously exposed to flanking or a well-aimed bullet while you operate the turret. Don't hop on it unless you have teammates covering your flanks.

Objective modes demand control of the firing lanes nearest the objectives. Have shooters set up to monitor the nearest lanes continually. The accessible buildings scattered around the map have excellent overwatch to the streets, so expect players to hole up in them throughout the match. It *is* possible to use shorter-range weapons on Bakaara, but you must be acutely aware of enemy positions. Use the limited cover and the buildings' walls in the correct lane to shield you from unfriendly eyes.

KEY

	Team Spawn Points
	Bomb–Search & Destroy / Sabotage Modes
	Search & Destroy / Demolition Plant Site
Ⓐ Ⓑ Ⓒ	Domination Flags
	CTF Flags
	Headquarters Point
	Ladder
	Sabotage Plant Destinations
	Arrows are color-coded to match the levels to which they lead

CAPTURE THE FLAG

SEARCH & DESTROY

LOADOUT SUGGESTION

THE OPERATOR

Cover the long sightlines with your Mk14, using your Equipment and Pointstreaks to guard your back.

PRIMARY WEAPON	MK14	
ATTACHMENT	RED DOT SIGHT	
PROFICIENCY	STABILITY	
SECONDARY WEAPON	MP9	
ATTACHMENT	EXTENDED MAGS	
EQUIPMENT		
LETHAL	CLAYMORE	
TACTICAL	TROPHY SYSTEM	
PERK 1	BLIND EYE	
PERK 2	QUICKDRAW	
PERK 3	MARKSMAN	
STRIKE PACKAGE	ASSAULT	
POINTSTREAK 1	I.M.S.	
POINTSTREAK 2	AH-6 OVERWATCH	
POINTSTREAK 3	ASSAULT DRONE	
DEATH STREAK	FINAL STAND	

RESISTANCE

Size Classification:	Large
Terrain Classification:	Open
Engagement Profile:	Mixed
Conflict Between:	Spetsnaz and GIGN

TEAM DEATHMATCH

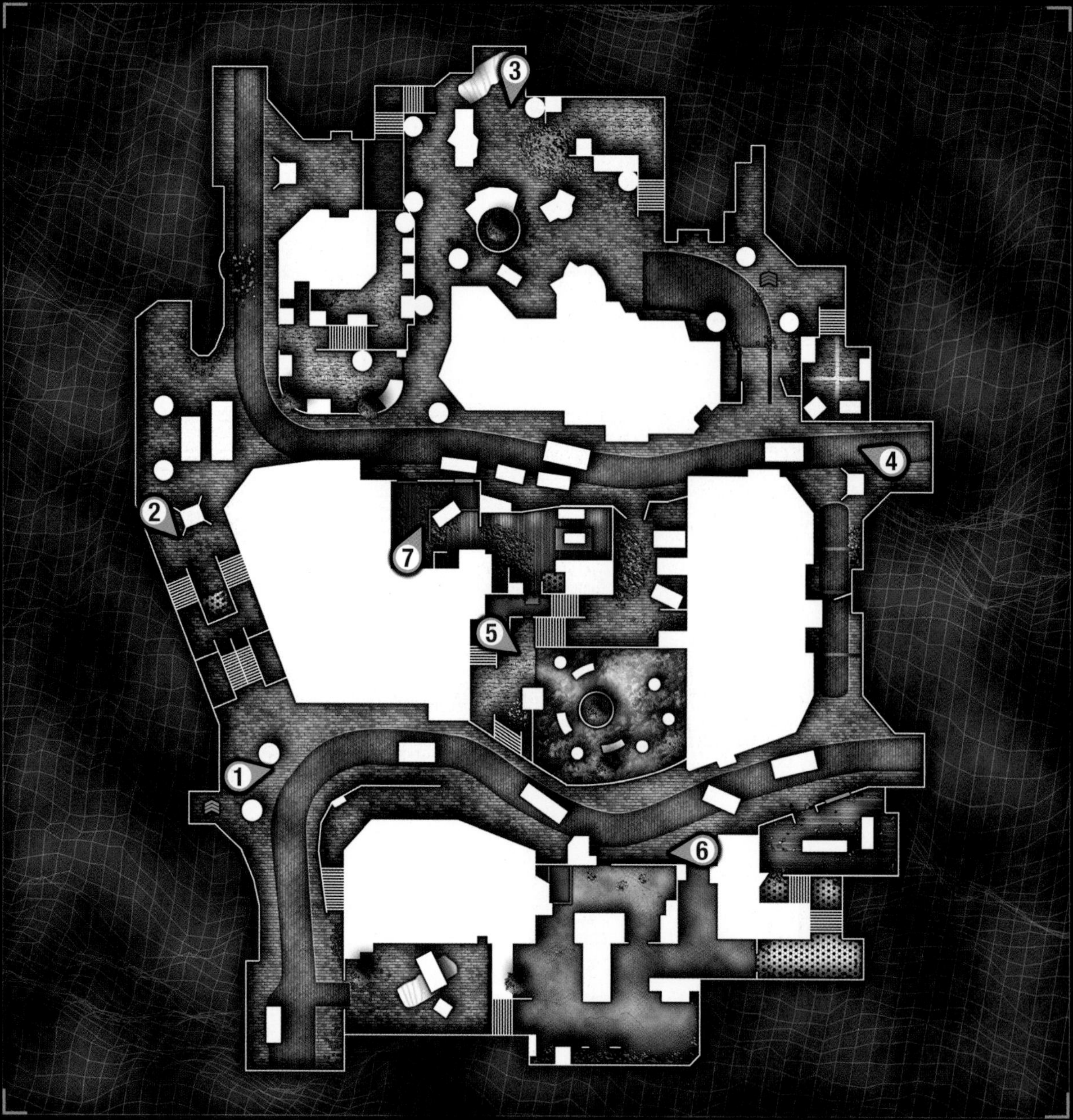

DEMOLITION

A downtown Parisian district, Resistance is a large and surprisingly open urban map. It features a steep elevation change from the raised southwest to the lower outdoor shopping plaza in the northeast. The open streets create clear and dangerous lines of fire across the map. Whenever you can, use the buildings to cross through the map's center or southeast portion.

In objective modes where you have to traverse the streets, be sure to bring Smoke Grenades to create cover when and where you need it. Otherwise, reaching your target can be a bloody task.

The southern vine trellis, the central fountain, and the northern plaza are all heavy conflict zones, although the center and north usually see more traffic. In the plaza to the north, the raised platforms—particularly the one on the west—all have superior elevation and line of sight to the surrounding streets. Control them, avoid them, or get shot from them!

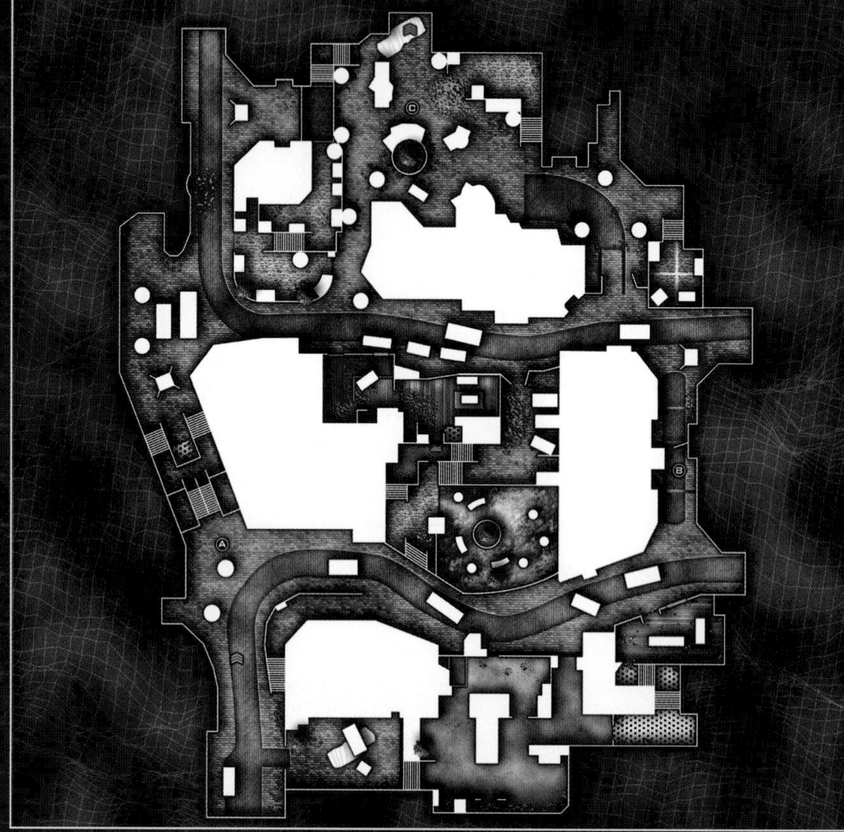

HEADQUARTERS

KEY

	Team Spawn Points
	Bomb–Search & Destroy / Sabotage Modes
A B	Search & Destroy / Demolition Plant Site
A B C	Domination Flags
	CTF Flags
	Headquarters Point
	Ladder
	Sabotage Plant Destinations
	Arrows are color-coded to match the levels to which they lead

SEARCH & DESTROY

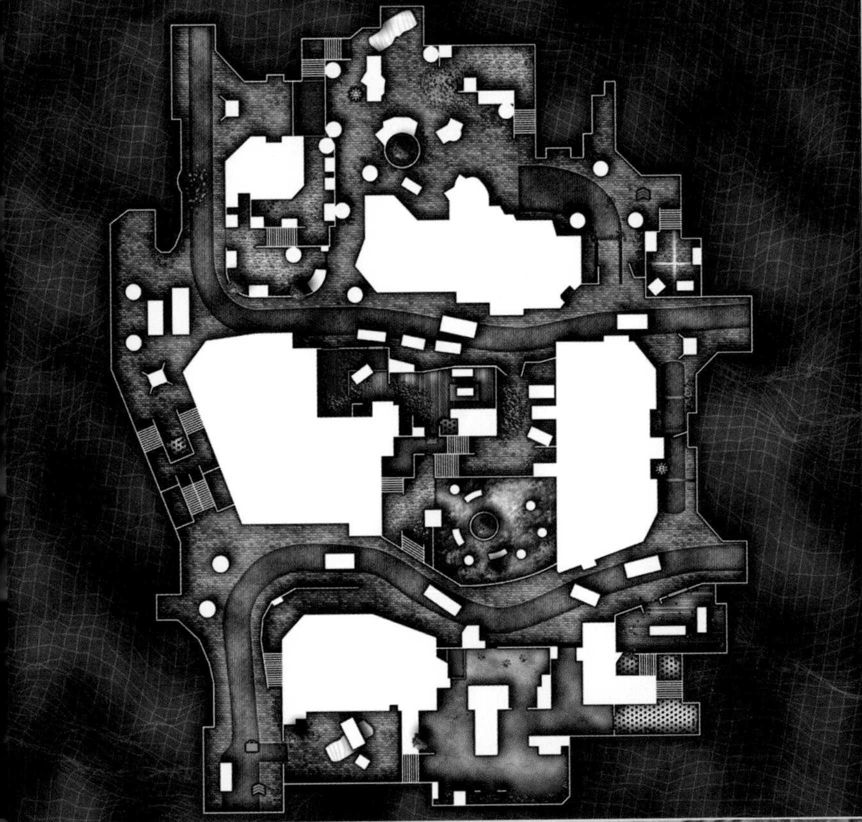

LOADOUT SUGGESTION

LETHALE

Control the streets with this surprisingly nimble LMG loadout.

PRIMARY WEAPON	L86 LSW
ATTACHMENT	GRIP
PROFICIENCY	RAPID FIRE
SECONDARY WEAPON	DESERT EAGLE
ATTACHMENT	TACTICAL KNIFE
EQUIPMENT	
LETHAL	C4
TACTICAL	TROPHY SYSTEM
PERK 1	EXTREME CONDITIONING
PERK 2	QUICKDRAW
PERK 3	STALKER
STRIKE PACKAGE	ASSAULT
POINTSTREAK 1	SENTRY GUN
POINTSTREAK 2	AH-6 OVERWATCH
POINTSTREAK 3	PAVE LOW
DEATH STREAK	JUICED

DOWNTURN

Size Classification:	Large
Terrain Classification:	Mixed
Engagement Profile:	Mixed
Conflict Between:	Spetsnaz and Delta

TEAM DEATHMATCH

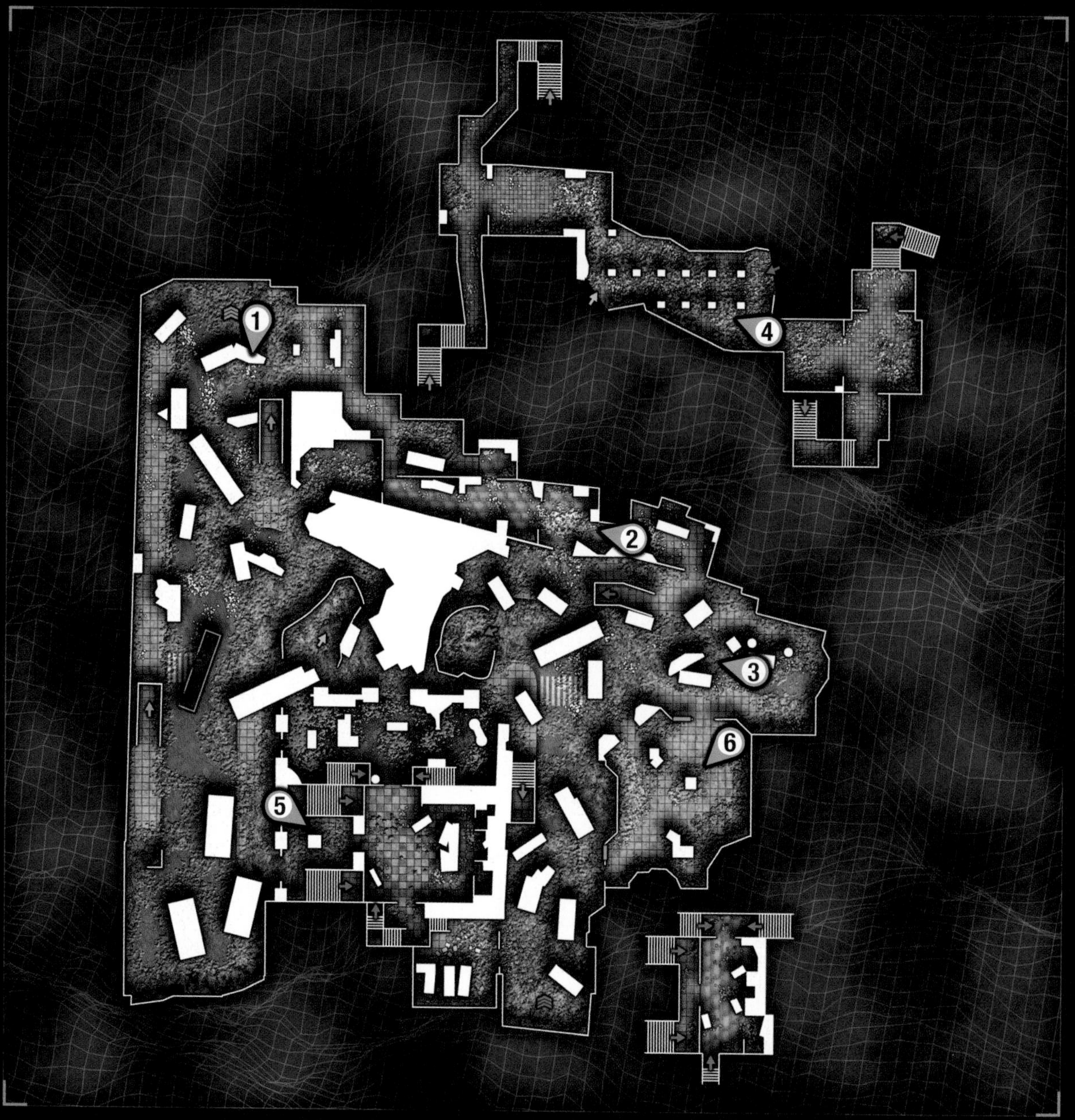

1

2

3

4

5

6

SABOTAGE

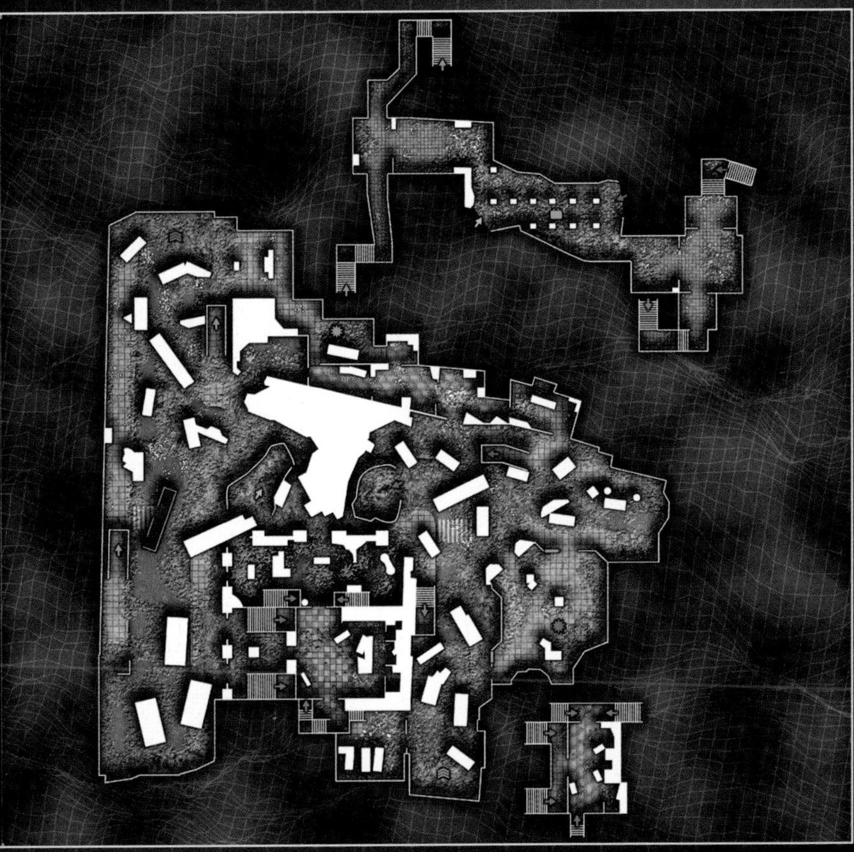

DEMOLITION

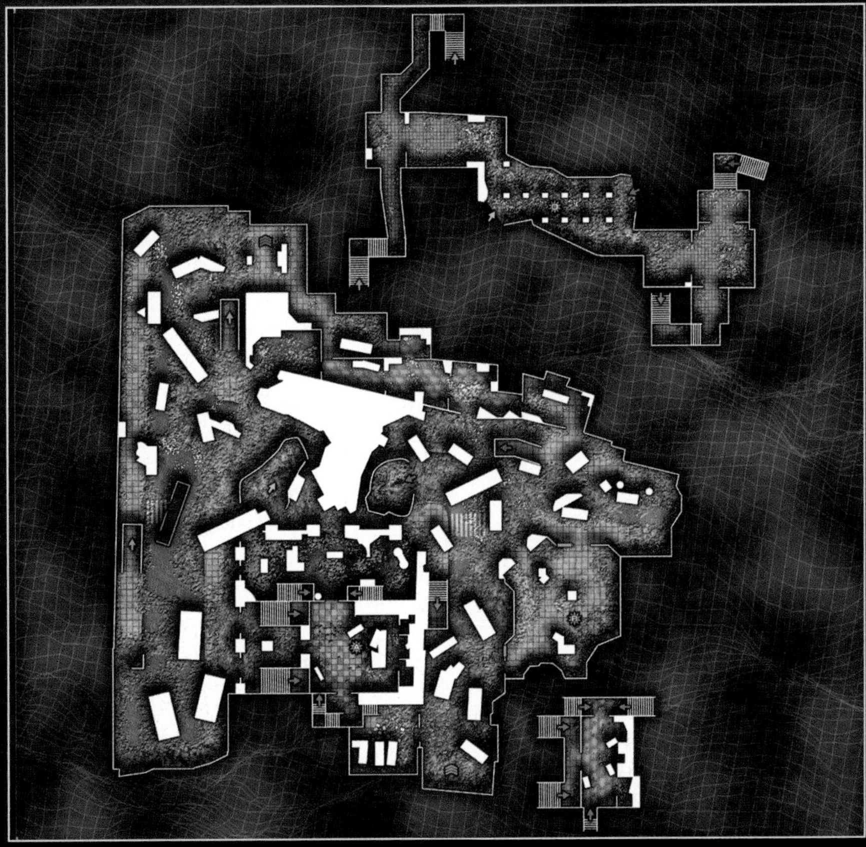

Downturn depicts the blasted-out streets of New York after the Russian invasion. It's a mixed urban map featuring large streets filled with cover and dense buildings, along with a sizable underground area. Downturn sees heavy conflict out on the streets and down below in the subway access tunnels. You can also expect significant engagements inside the two building complexes to the south and north.

Be extra careful if you have to pass through the large store in the southeast. It has the least cover of any area on the map. Similarly, watch out as you navigate the long, narrow path through the northern building. You make a distressingly easy shot for anyone covering the hall from the east or west.

The underground area has a ton of access points in the east, west, and from above in the center. It's also possible to walk above the tunnels, though you're somewhat exposed to fire on the main street. The streets themselves have considerable cover, but you still don't want to be caught stationary out in the open. Stay mobile and constantly scan for threats.

DOMINATION

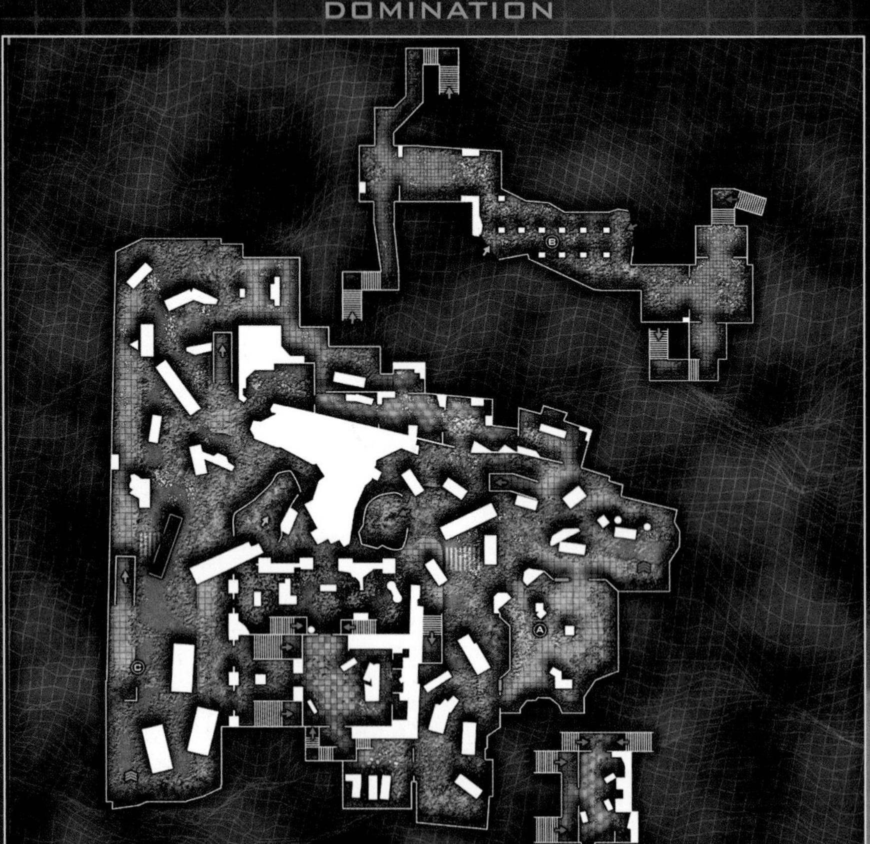

HEADQUARTERS

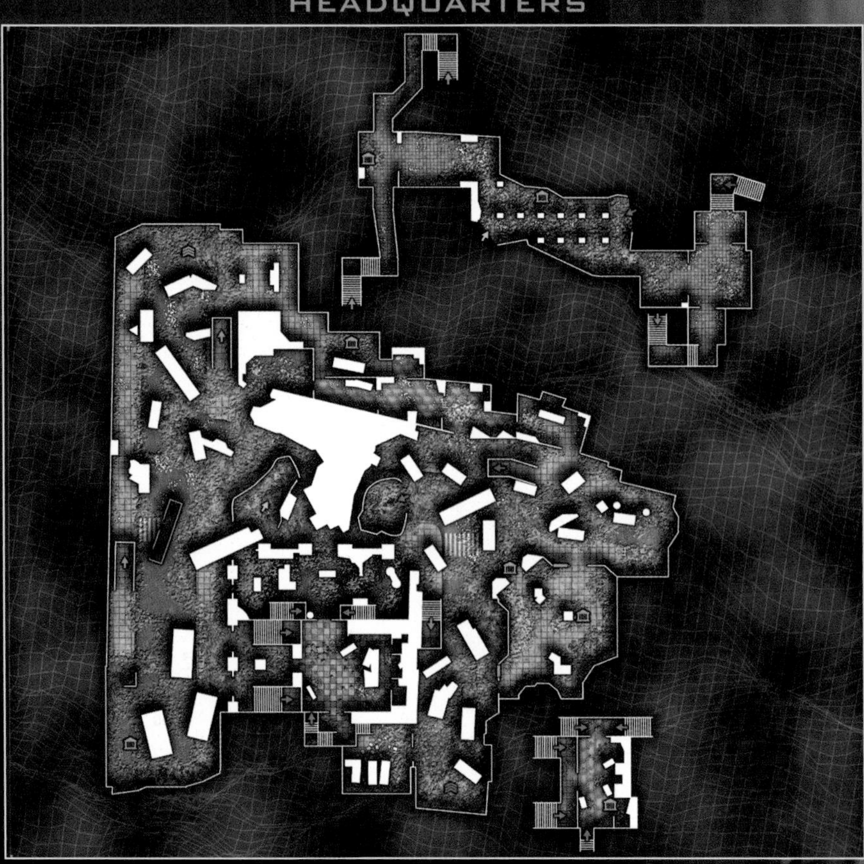

KEY

	Team Spawn Points
	Bomb–Search & Destroy / Sabotage Modes
A B	Search & Destroy / Demolition Plant Site
A B C	Domination Flags
	CTF Flags
	Headquarters Point
	Ladder
	Sabotage Plant Destinations
	Arrows are color-coded to match the levels to which they lead

CAPTURE THE FLAG

SEARCH & DESTROY

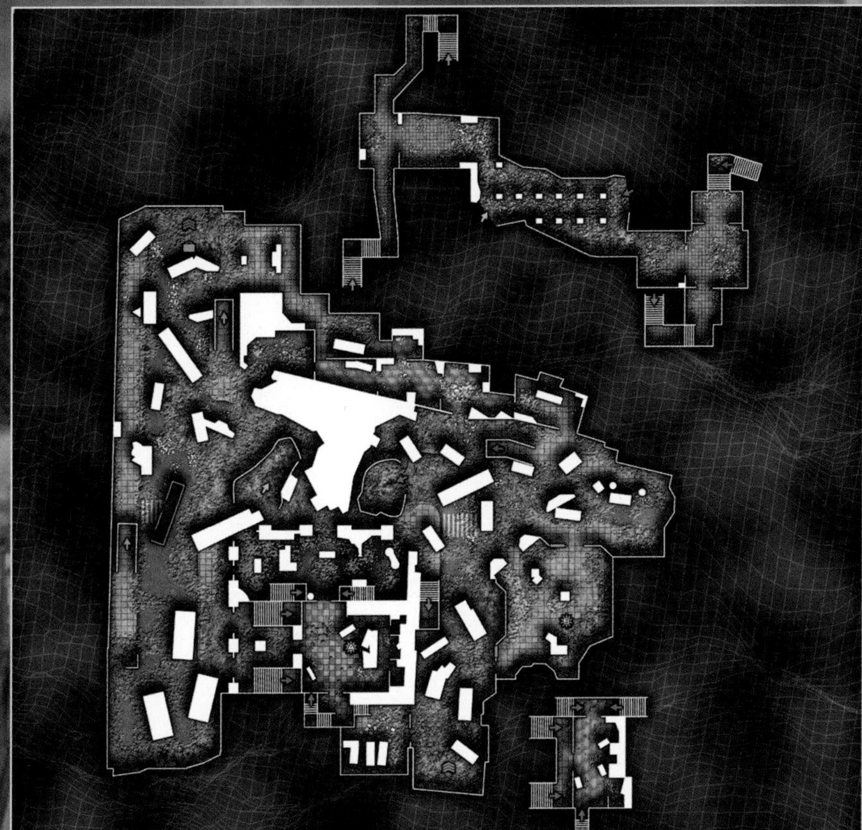

LOADOUT SUGGESTION

RF & E

A fast-moving sniper build, operate as though you're using a very lethal long-range assault rifle.

PRIMARY WEAPON	MSR	
ATTACHMENT	ACOG	
PROFICIENCY	SPEED	
SECONDARY WEAPON	G18	
ATTACHMENT	EXTENDED MAGS	
EQUIPMENT		
LETHAL	FRAG	
TACTICAL	SMOKE GRENADE	
PERK 1	EXTREME CONDITIONING	
PERK 2	QUICKDRAW	
PERK 3	STALKER	
STRIKE PACKAGE	ASSAULT	
POINTSTREAK 1	UAV	
POINTSTREAK 2	SENTRY GUN	
POINTSTREAK 3	ATTACK HELICOPTER	
DEATH STREAK	FINAL STAND	

BOOTLEG

Size Classification:	Medium
Terrain Classification:	Urban
Engagement Profile:	Mixed
Conflict Between:	Spetsnaz and PMC

TEAM DEATHMATCH

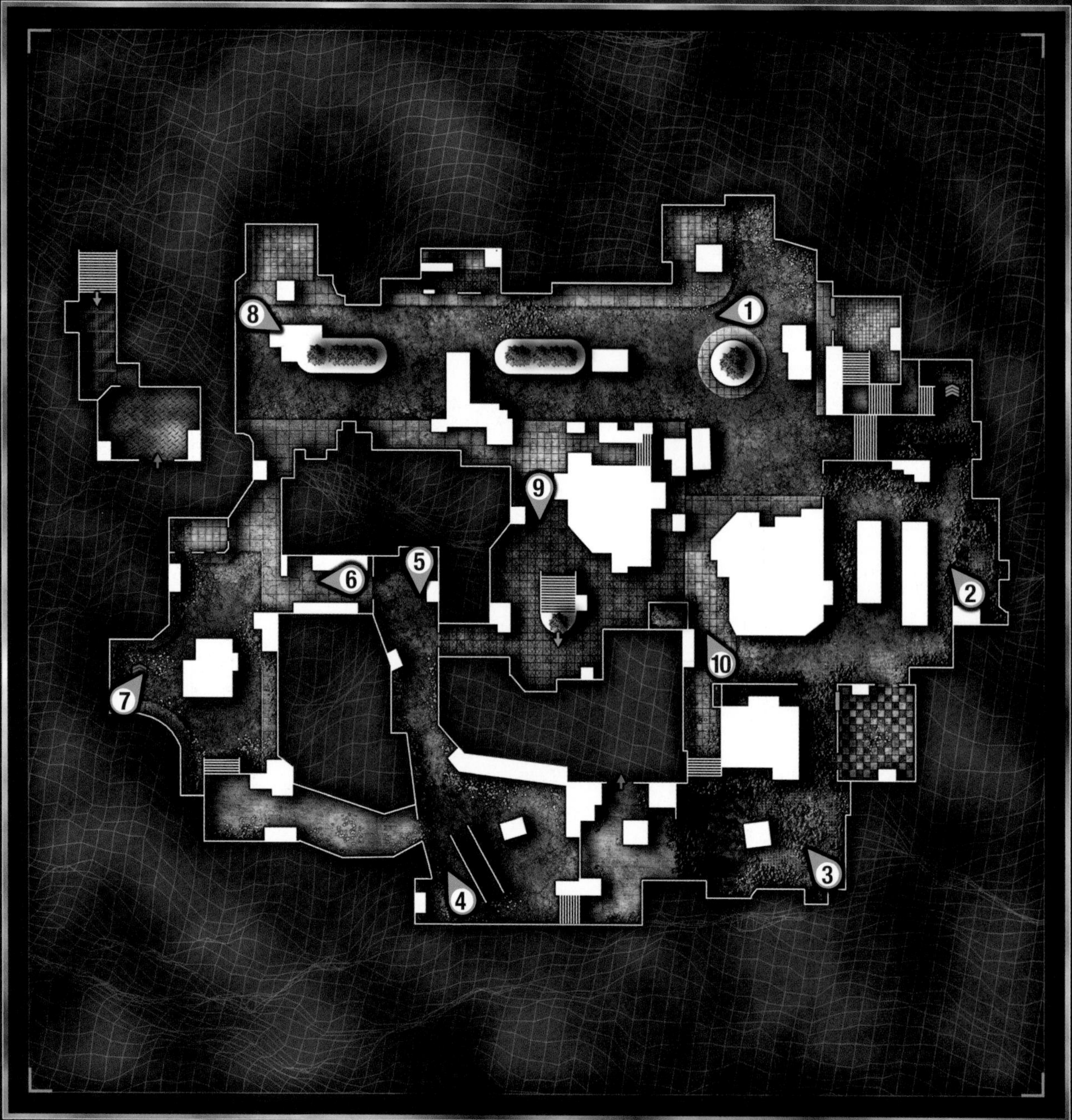

SABOTAGE

DEMOLITION

eg could be any one of a hundred small n cities, with its abundant neon and aped alleyways. Bootleg is a fast-paced, ium-size urban map. There are some tough kepoints and a lot of CQC in the interior s. The only lengthy firing lane of note is eath the freeway overpass on the map's h edge.

le the other outer areas around the east, t, and south appear more open, elevation nges and a considerable amount of cover ak up sight lines significantly. The map's erior is made up of several twisting alleys, of which can contain nasty enemy surprises und every corner. Bring a close-quarters apon and stay alert.

HEADQUARTERS

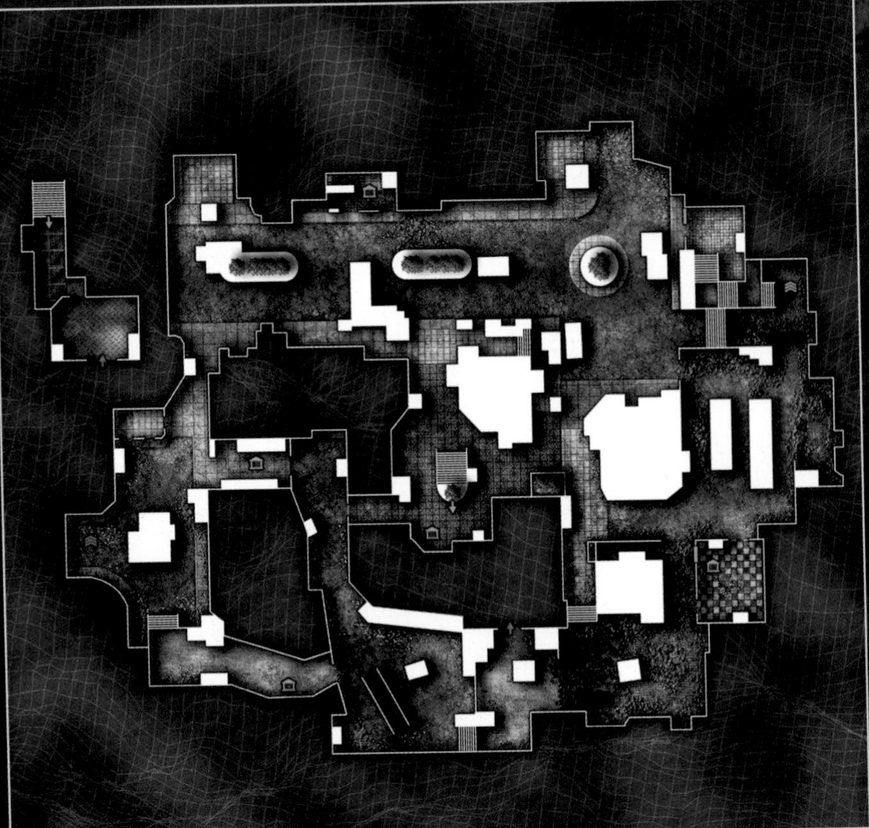

KEY

	Team Spawn Points
	Bomb–Search & Destroy / Sabotage Modes
	Search & Destroy / Demolition Plant Site
Ⓐ Ⓑ Ⓒ	Domination Flags
	CTF Flags
	Headquarters Point
	Ladder
	Sabotage Plant Destinations
	Arrows are color-coded to match the

CAPTURE THE FLAG

SEARCH & DESTROY

LOADOUT SUGGESTION

THE AGGRESSOR

Sweep the narrow alleyways with your shotgun, and the open areas with your rifle, staying invisible to radar with twin silencers.

PRIMARY WEAPON	KSG 12	
ATTACHMENT	SILENCER	
PROFICIENCY	RANGE	
SECONDARY WEAPON	M16A4	
ATTACHMENT	SILENCER	
EQUIPMENT		
LETHAL	SEMTEX	
TACTICAL	FLASH GRENADE	
PERK 1	EXTREME CONDITIONING	
PERK 2	OVERKILL	
PERK 3	STEADY AIM	
STRIKE PACKAGE	SPECIALIST	
POINTSTREAK 1	ASSASSIN	
POINTSTREAK 2	BLIND EYE	
POINTSTREAK 3	SITREP	
DEATH STREAK	HOLLOW POINTS	

CARBON

Size Classification:	Medium
Terrain Classification:	Mixed
Engagement Profile:	CQC
Conflict Between:	Africa Militia and PMC

TEAM DEATHMATCH

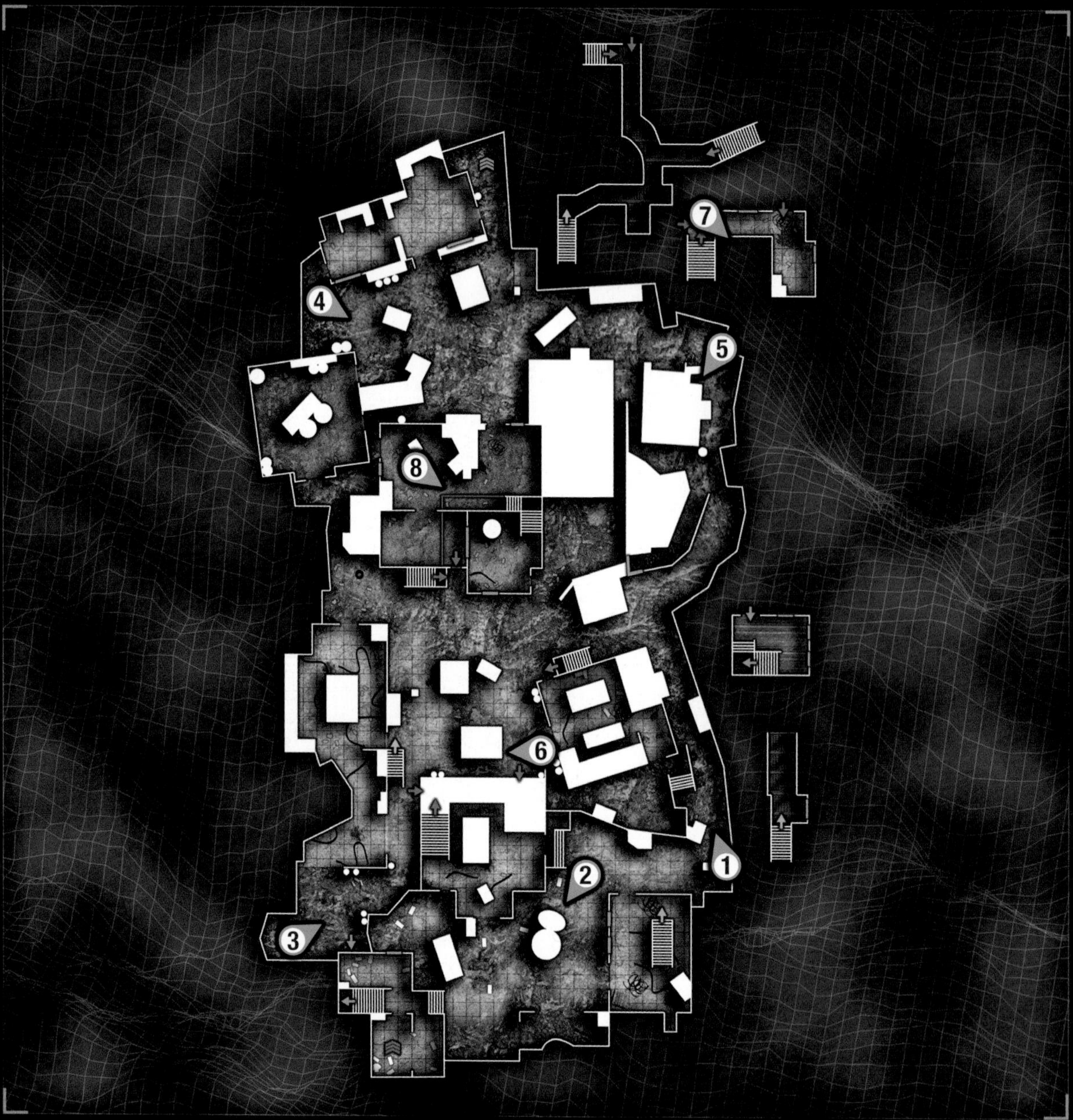

3

4

5

6

7

8

SABOTAGE

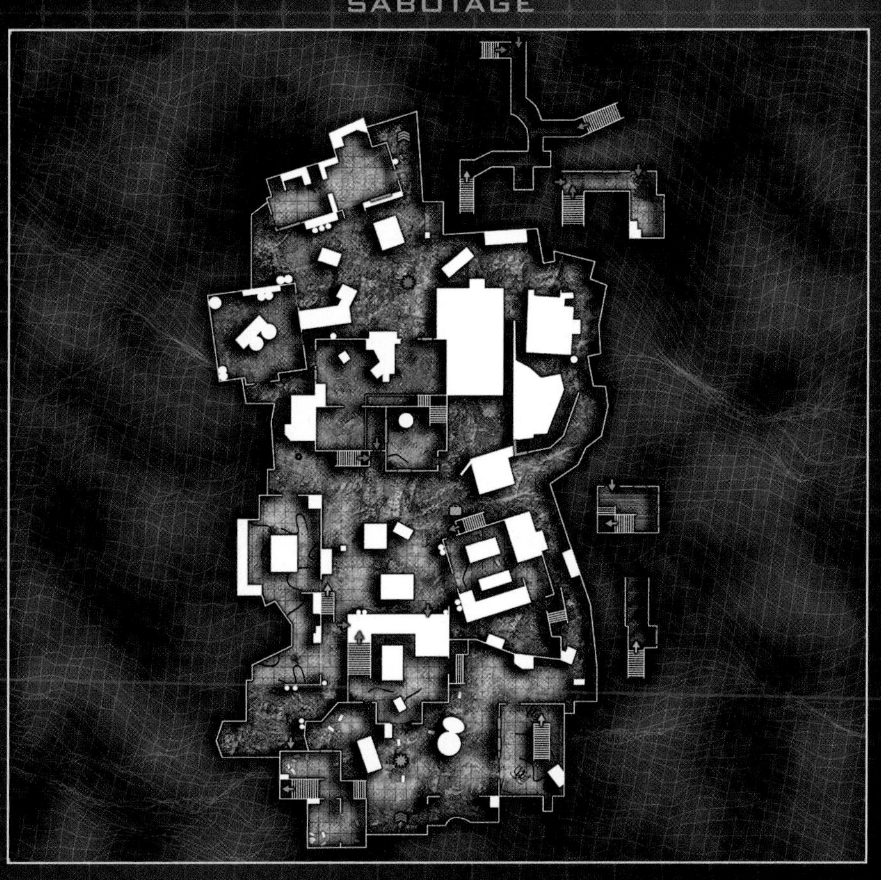

DEMOLITION

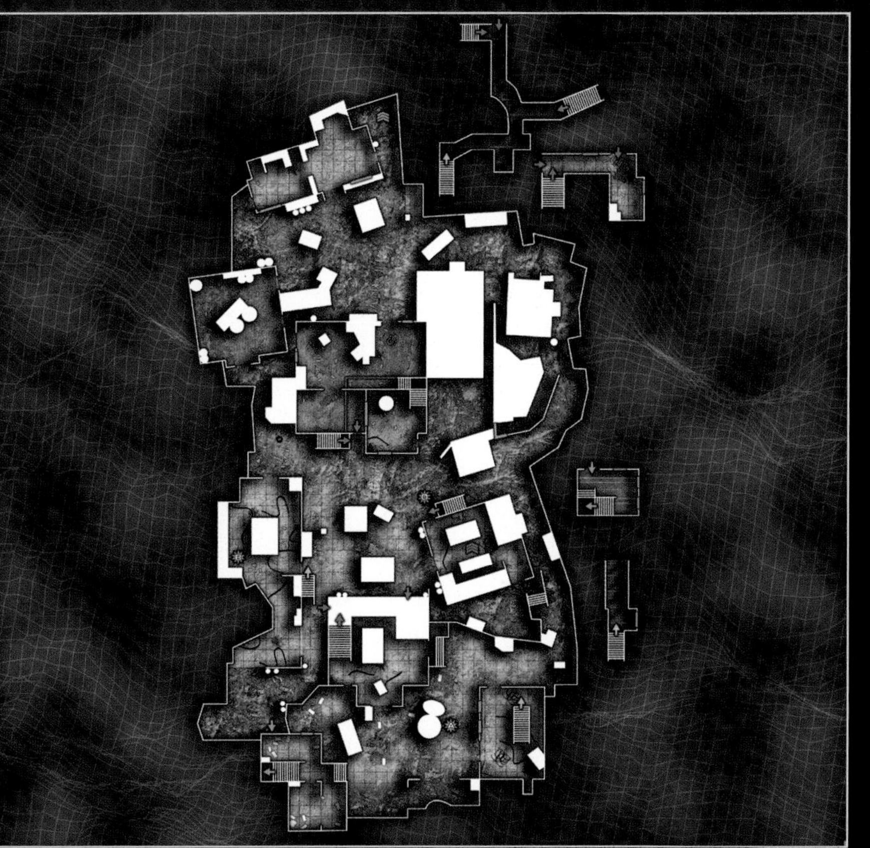

Carbon is a medium-large map set in a run-down African refinery. Carbon is one of the more complex maps in the game, and one of the more difficult. It's filled with accessible buildings from north to south, and nearly every point on the map has multiple entrances and exits. This makes covering your six devilishly difficult. The map slopes from a high to the north down to the lower south end, so elevation changes contribute to the challenge. Communicate constantly with your teammates, and choose your routes carefully in objective modes. The enemy team can hole up in almost any building and watch any route—but not all of them at once, or with perfect coverage. A large, raised catwalk is in the center of the map, but be wary of using it as an overwatch position, because it's dangerously exposed.

DOMINATION

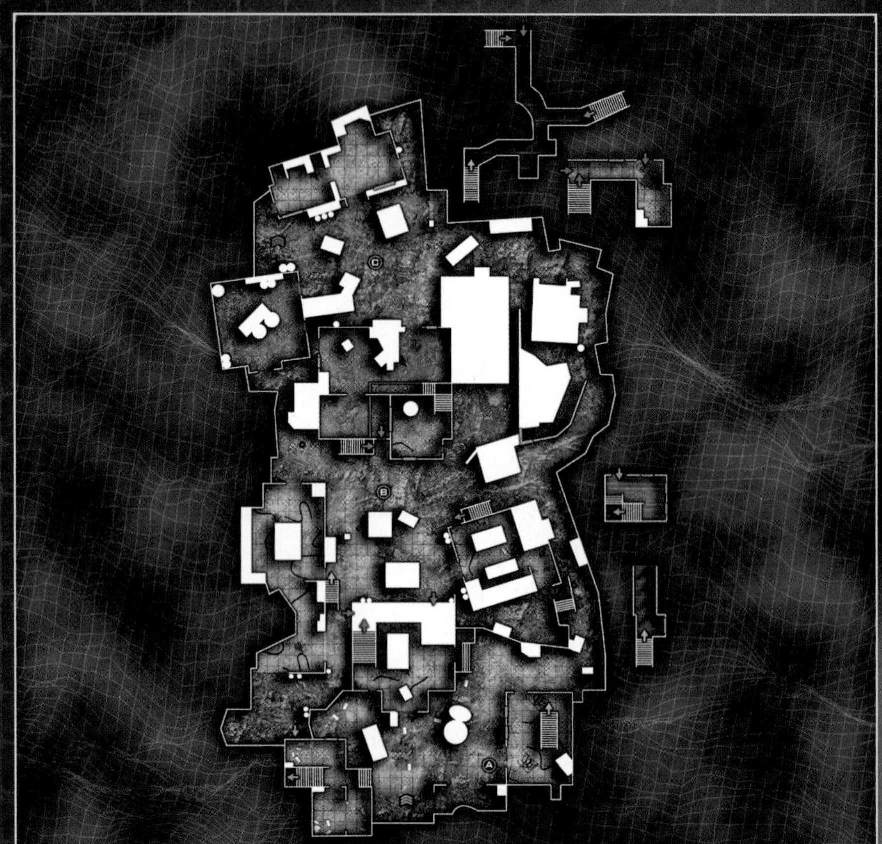

HEADQUARTERS

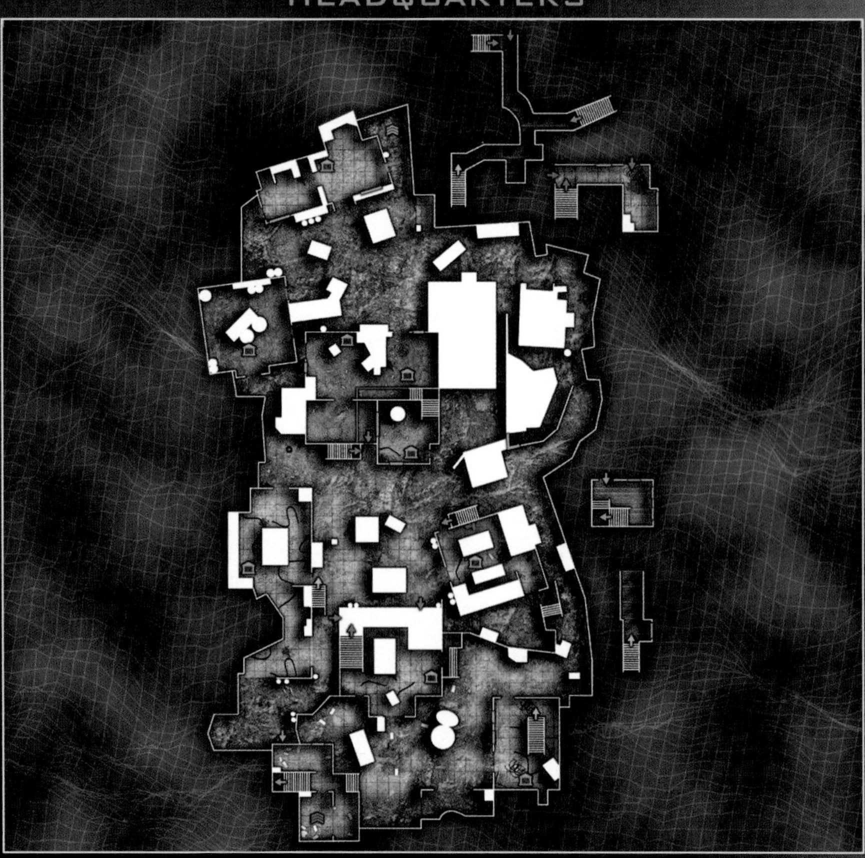

KEY

	Team Spawn Points
	Bomb–Search & Destroy / Sabotage Modes
	Search & Destroy / Demolition Plant Site
Ⓐ Ⓑ Ⓒ	Domination Flags
	CTF Flags
	Headquarters Point
	Ladder
	Sabotage Plant Destinations
	Arrows are color-coded to match the levels to which they lead

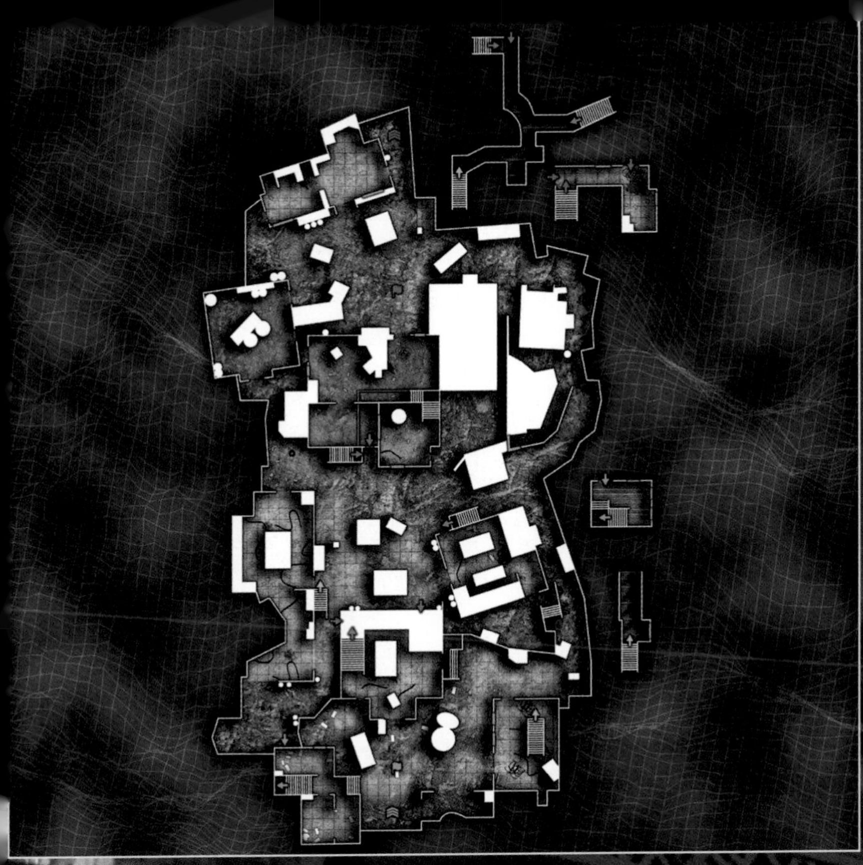

SEARCH & DESTROY

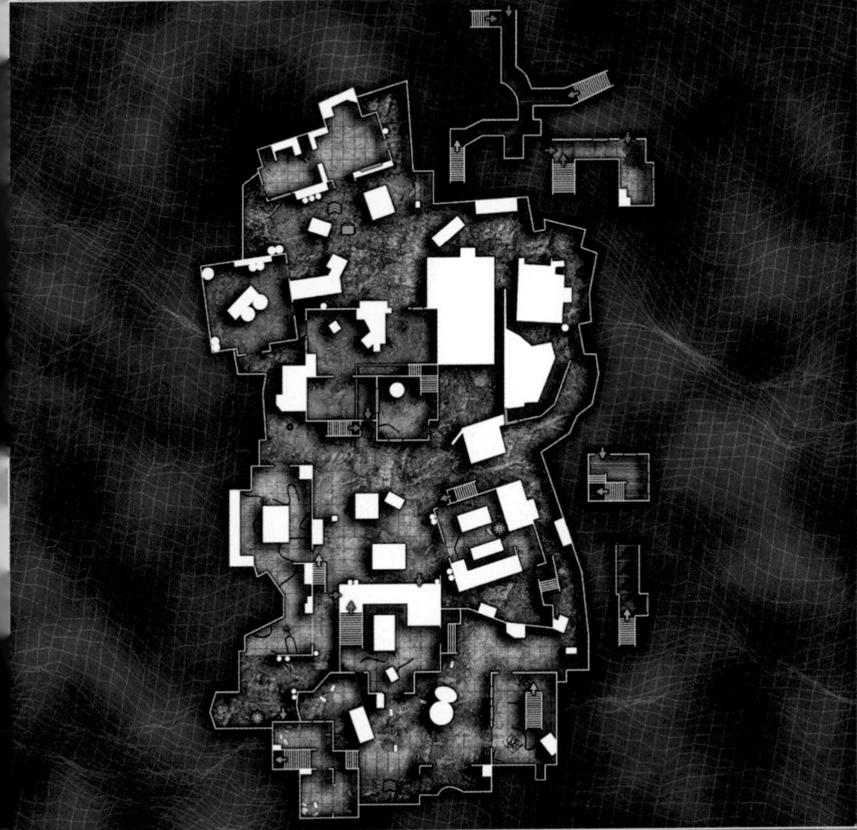

THUMPER

Drill enemies through walls with your Impact-enhanced rifle, and light them up with Recon and explosives.

PRIMARY WEAPON	ACR 6.8	
ATTACHMENT	HEARTBEAT SENSOR	
PROFICIENCY	IMPACT	
SECONDARY WEAPON	M320 GLM	
ATTACHMENT	NONE	
EQUIPMENT		
LETHAL	FRAG	
TACTICAL	PORTABLE RADAR	
PERK 1	RECON	
PERK 2	QUICKDRAW	
PERK 3	SITREP	
STRIKE PACKAGE	ASSAULT	
POINTSTREAK 1	UAV	
POINTSTREAK 2	I.M.S.	
POINTSTREAK 3	AH-6 OVERWATCH	
DEATH STREAK	DEAD MAN'S HAND	

HARDHAT

Size Classification:	Small
Terrain Classification:	Open
Engagement Profile:	CQC
Conflict Between:	Spetsnaz and Delta

TEAM DEATHMATCH

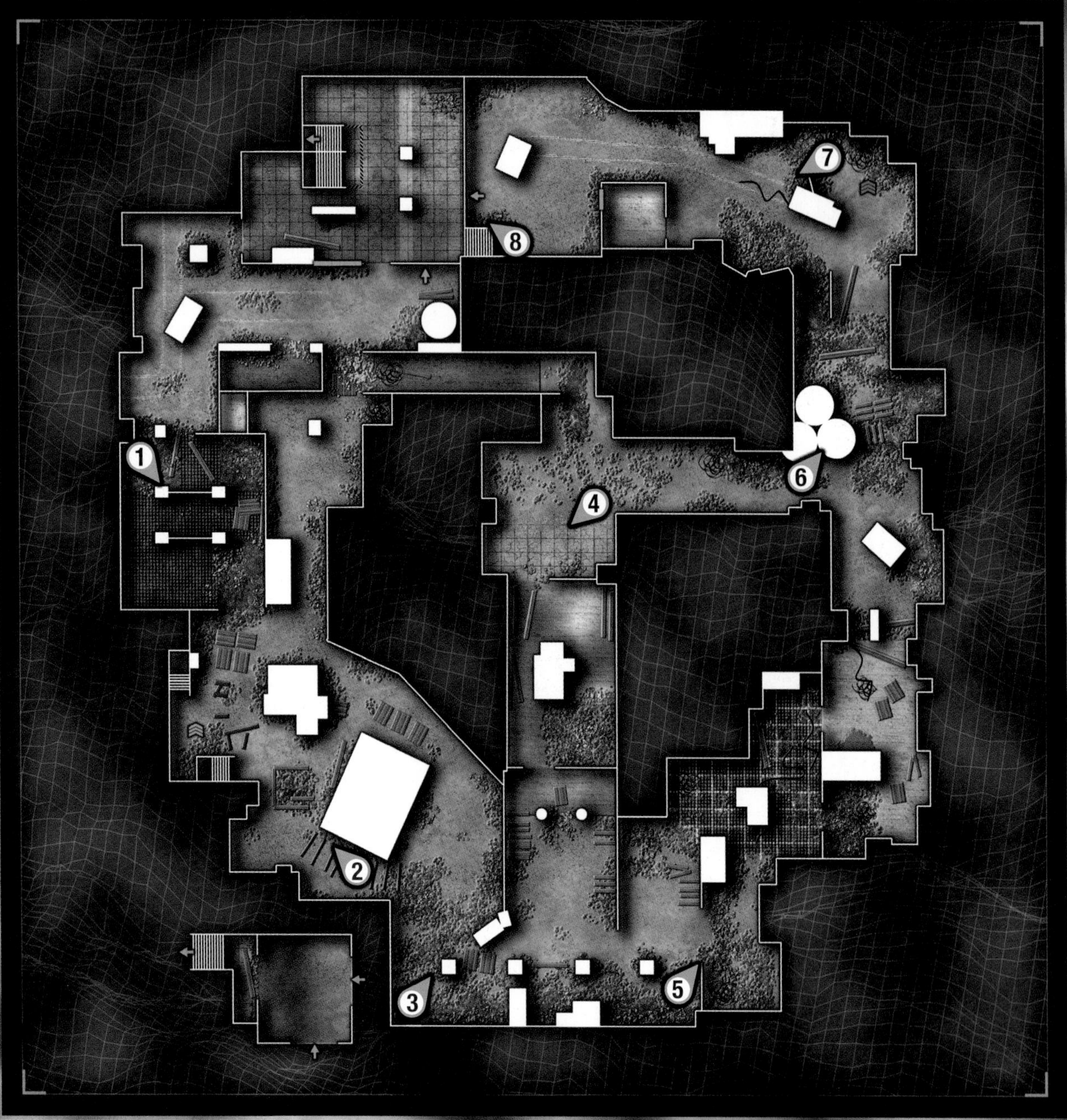

SABOTAGE

DEMOLITION

Set in an unfinished construction site, Hardhat is the smallest map in the game. Consequently, it makes for an intense match, with only three routes in and out of the central building. The remaining conflict takes place all around the level's outskirts.

Despite the small size, there are some surprising elevation changes, so watch out when you travel the outer edges. Height issues make several chokepoints even more dangerous. The 'safest' areas—if such can be said for any part of this level—are the northwest and southeast, where there's enough cover to conceal yourself from roaming packs of enemies.

In objective modes, all bets are off. Expect mayhem no matter where you turn. The hard chokepoints and limited alternate routes create killing grounds all over the map.

KEY

	Team Spawn Points
	Bomb–Search & Destroy / Sabotage Modes
A B	Search & Destroy / Demolition Plant Site
A B C	Domination Flags
	CTF Flags
	Headquarters Point
	Ladder
	Sabotage Plant Destinations
	Arrows are color-coded to match the levels to which they lead

DOMINATION

HEADQUARTERS

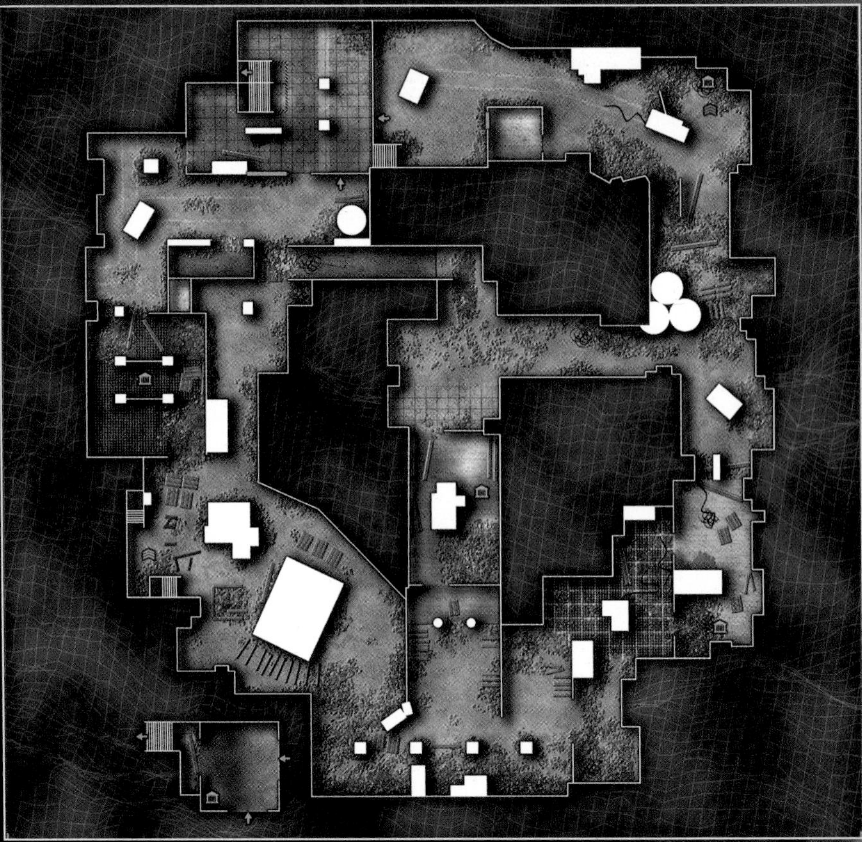

CAPTURE THE FLAG

SEARCH & DESTROY

LOADOUT SUGGESTION

MODERN WARRIOR

Drop the Riot Shield on your back to provide some rear bullet protection, and break out the 1887 to deliver the pain to the front.

PRIMARY WEAPON	RIOT SHIELD
ATTACHMENT	NONE
PROFICIENCY	SPEED
SECONDARY WEAPON	MODEL 1887
ATTACHMENT	NONE
EQUIPMENT	
LETHAL	SEMTEX
TACTICAL	EMP GRENADE
PERK 1	SLIGHT OF HAND
PERK 2	OVERKILL
PERK 3	STEADY AIM
STRIKE PACKAGE	ASSAULT
POINTSTREAK 1	UAV
POINTSTREAK 2	PRECISION AIRSTRIKE
POINTSTREAK 3	STRAFE RUN
DEATH STREAK	MARTYRDOM

LOCKDOWN

Size Classification:	Large
Terrain Classification:	Urban
Engagement Profile:	Long Range
Conflict Between:	Spetsnaz and Delta

TEAM DEATHMATCH

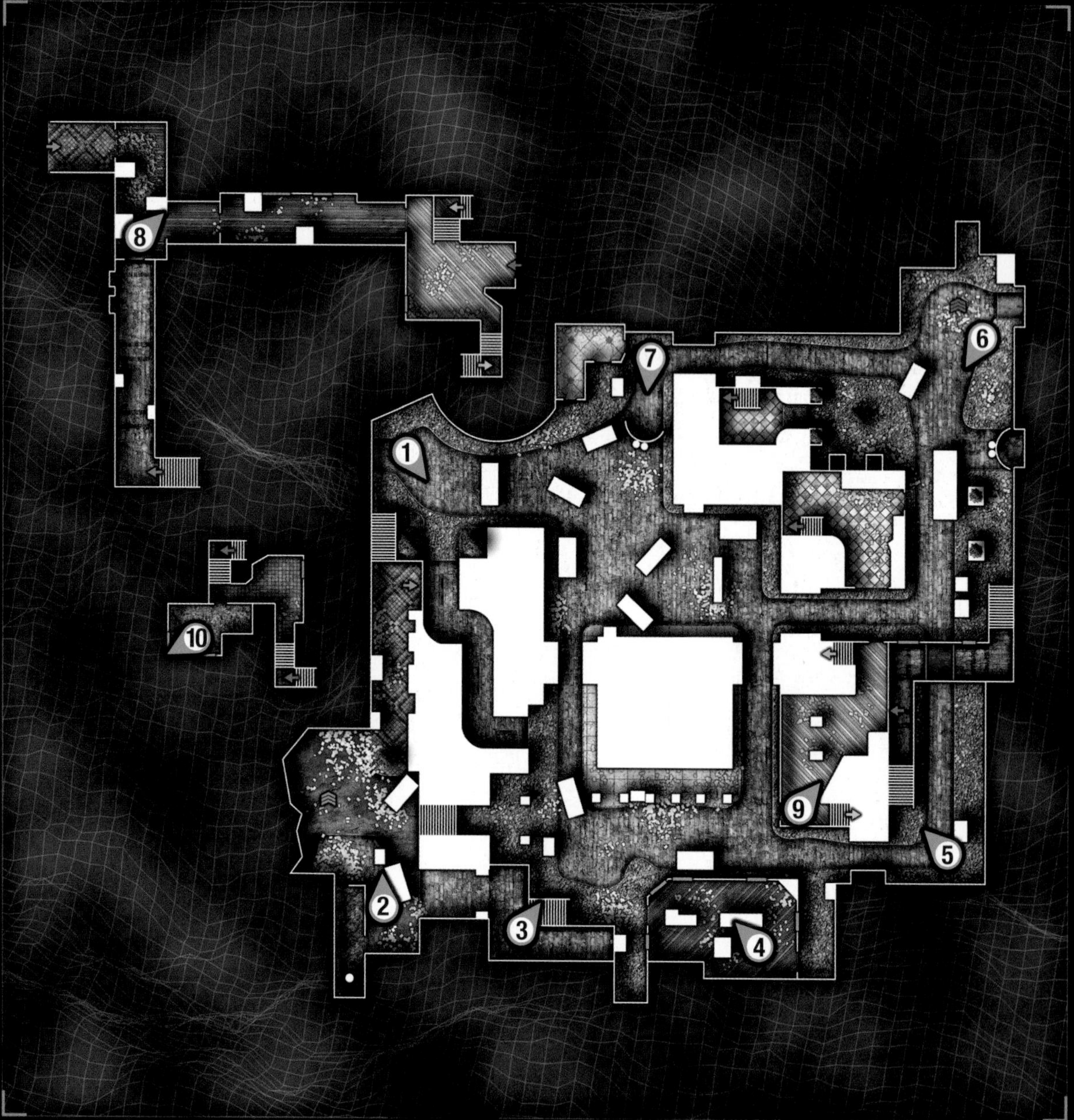

DEMOLITION

Lockdown is a very large map, set in the downtown of a European city. With its long sightlines and exposed streets, Lockdown is a heaven for snipers, light machine gunners, and long-range assault rifle users. All of the streets are dangerous, with little cover and numerous overlooks from nearby ledges or buildings. Move quickly and hug the walls when you travel through the streets.

The hall that passes through the map's center from east to west is extremely dangerous. While it has overwatch on some areas in the center, it's accessible at both ends from multiple areas, meaning it sees very high traffic.

In objective modes, there are usually multiple routes to any target area. But once you reach the target itself, there are usually only a few access points that defenders need to watch. So, prepare your assault with smoke and tactical grenades to clear a path. In deathmatch modes, the northeast buildings and southwest ledges and buildings are somewhat safer than the exposed streets or the dangerous central hall.

DOMINATION

HEADQUARTERS

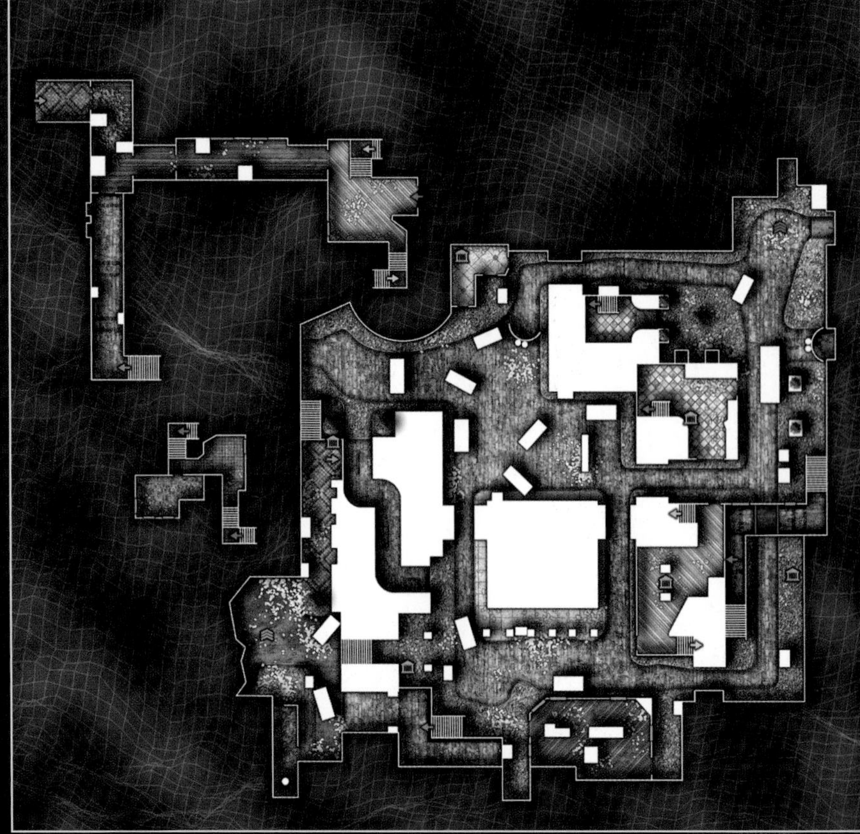

KEY

	Team Spawn Points
	Bomb–Search & Destroy / Sabotage Modes
A B	Search & Destroy / Demolition Plant Site
A B C	Domination Flags
	CTF Flags
	Headquarters Point
	Ladder
	Sabotage Plant Destinations
	Arrows are color-coded to match the levels to which they lead

CAPTURE THE FLAG

SEARCH & DESTROY

LOADOUT SUGGESTION

THE SLOW BLADE

Keep your distance and take down targets at range. Use your Stinger with Scrambler cover to eliminate any serious enemy air power.

PRIMARY WEAPON	TYPE 95	
ATTACHMENT	RAPID FIRE	
PROFICIENCY	STABILITY	
SECONDARY WEAPON	STINGER	
ATTACHMENT	NONE	
EQUIPMENT		
LETHAL	CLAYMORE	
TACTICAL	SCRAMBLER	
PERK 1	EXTREME CONDITIONING	
PERK 2	QUICKDRAW	
PERK 3	MARKSMAN	
STRIKE PACKAGE	SUPPORT	
POINTSTREAK 1	COUNTER UAV	
POINTSTREAK 2	STEALTH BOMBER	
POINTSTREAK 3	ESCORT AIRDROP	
DEATH STREAK	FINAL STAND	

VILLAGE

Size Classification:	Medium
Terrain Classification:	Open
Engagement Profile:	Mixed
Conflict Between:	Africa Militia and PMC

TEAM DEATHMATCH

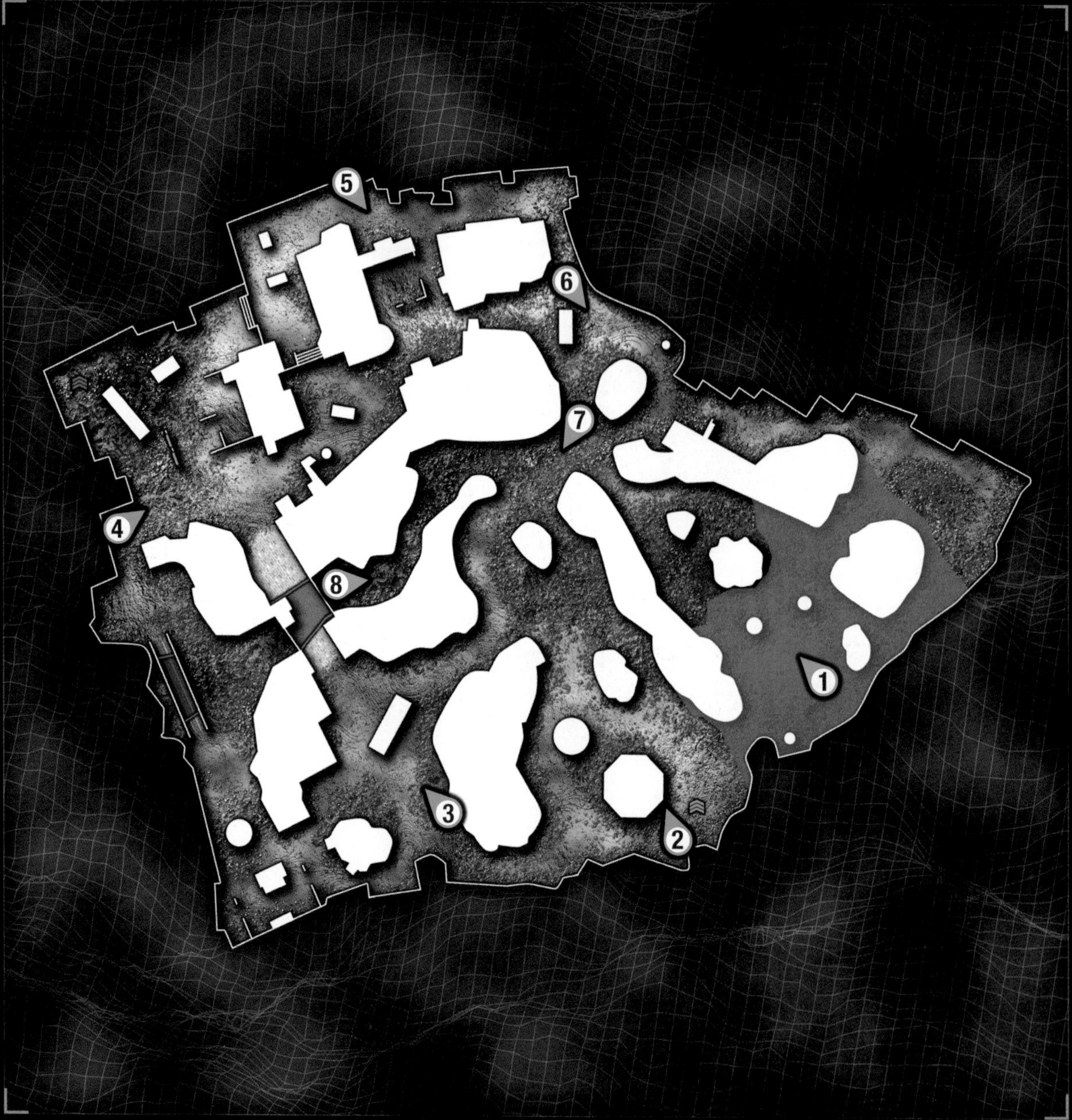

1 2 3 4 5 6 7 8

1

2

3

4

5

6

7

8

SABOTAGE

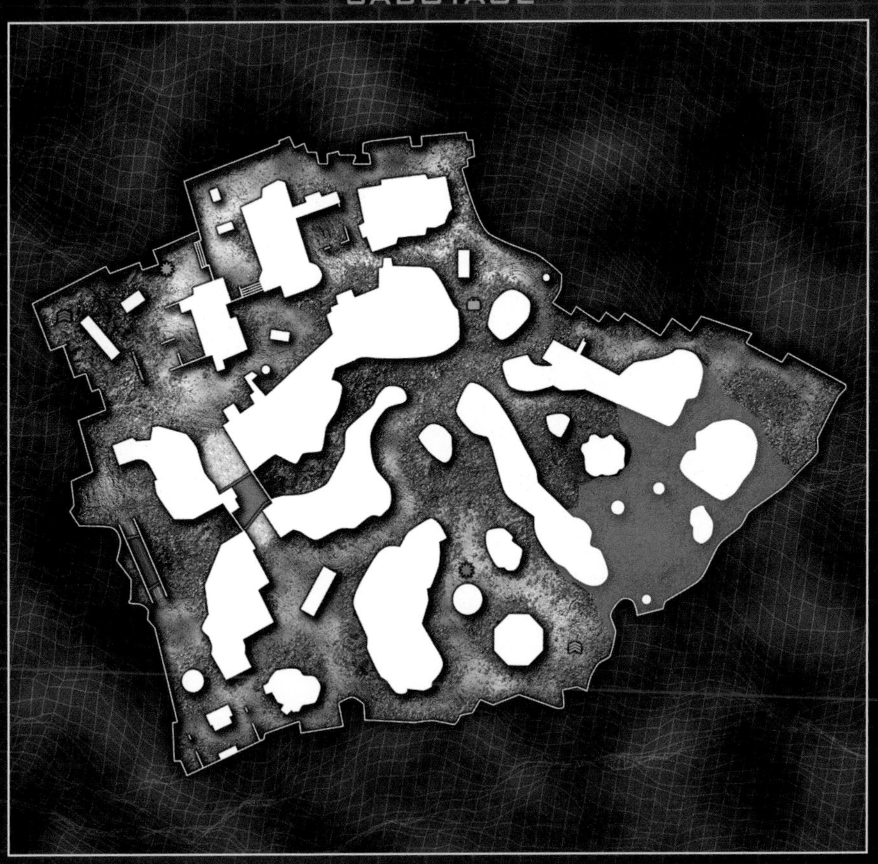

DEMOLITION

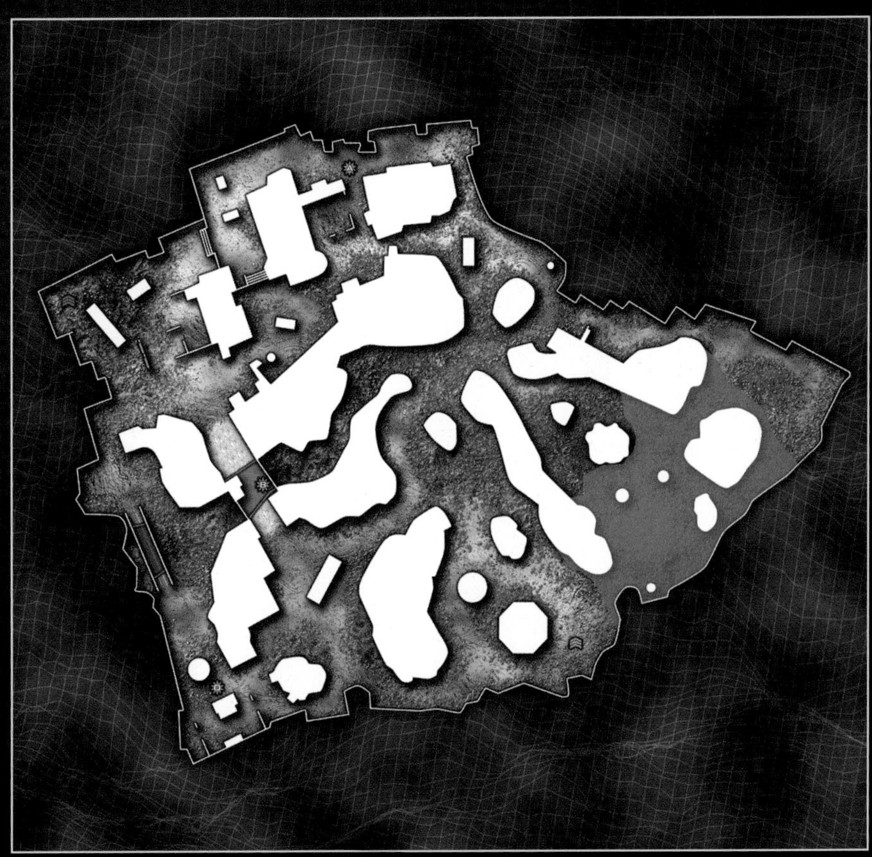

Village is set in an African shanty town. Half the map is inside the town's outskirts, and the other half is outside the town, near a cave complex and riverbed. Village plays significantly differently depending on what part of the map you occupy. The northern shanty town has lots of sharp corners and a fair amount of cover. The southern half has lots of open ground, elevation changes, and curving, organic turns.

Depending on your loadout, you can find success on this level by forcing engagements in one area. In objective modes, where you must assault certain locations, it pays to bring a flexible build. When you travel in the open areas near the cave, you're dangerously exposed from multiple directions, with little cover and few deceptive routes of escape.

DOMINATION

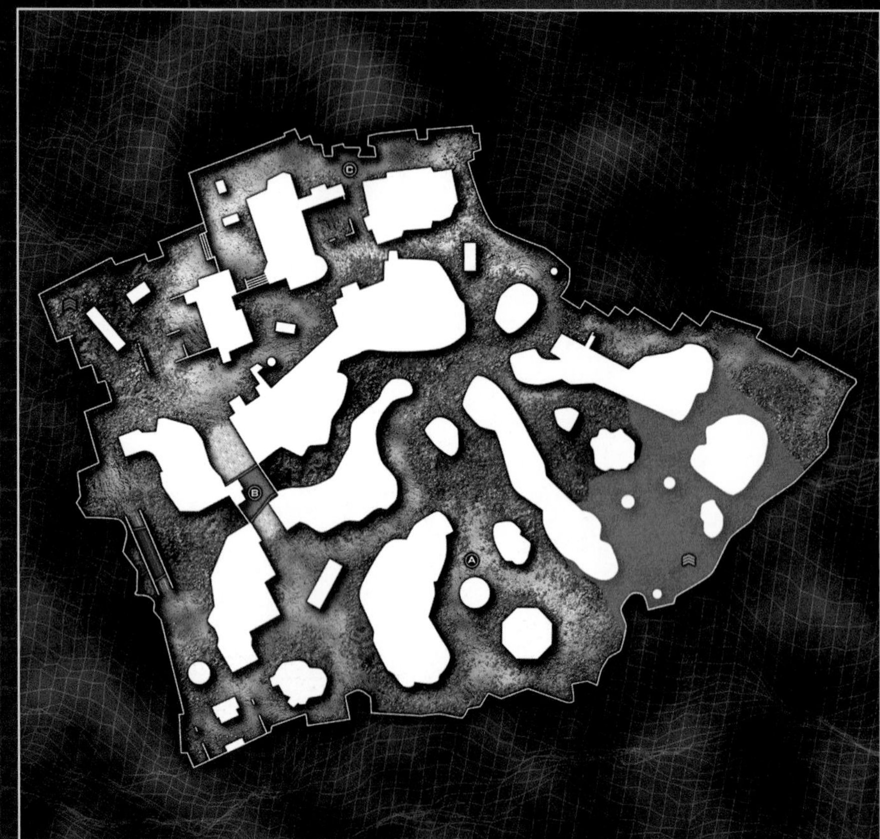

HEADQUARTERS

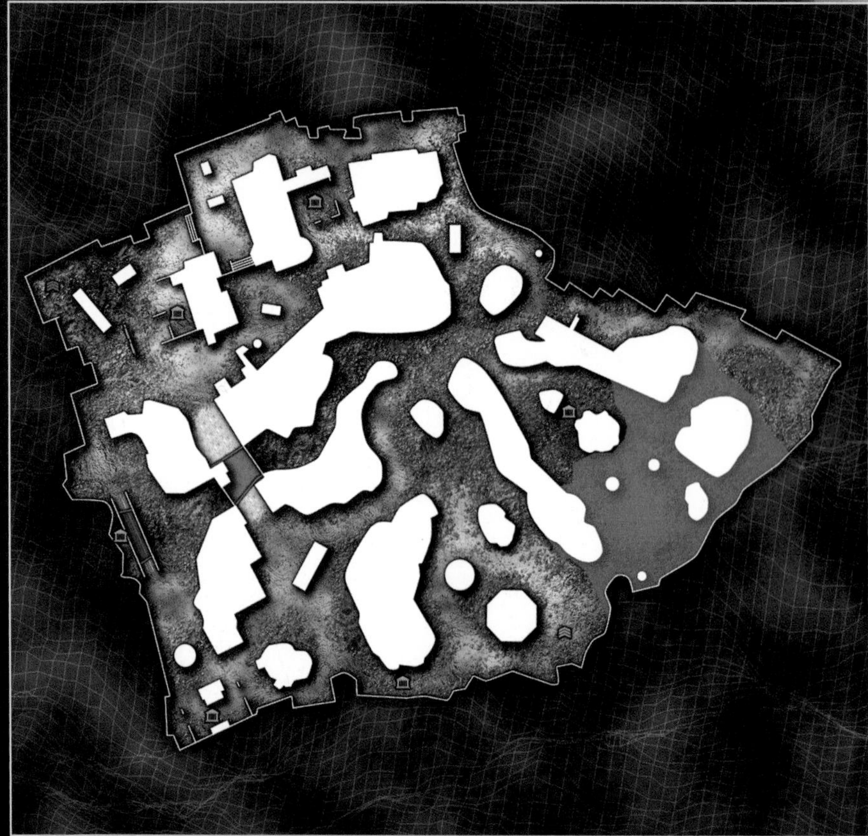

KEY

	Team Spawn Points
	Bomb–Search & Destroy / Sabotage Modes
	Search & Destroy / Demolition Plant Site
Ⓐ Ⓑ Ⓒ	Domination Flags
	CTF Flags
	Headquarters Point
	Ladder
	Sabotage Plant Destinations
	Arrows are color-coded to match the levels to which they lead

CAPTURE THE FLAG

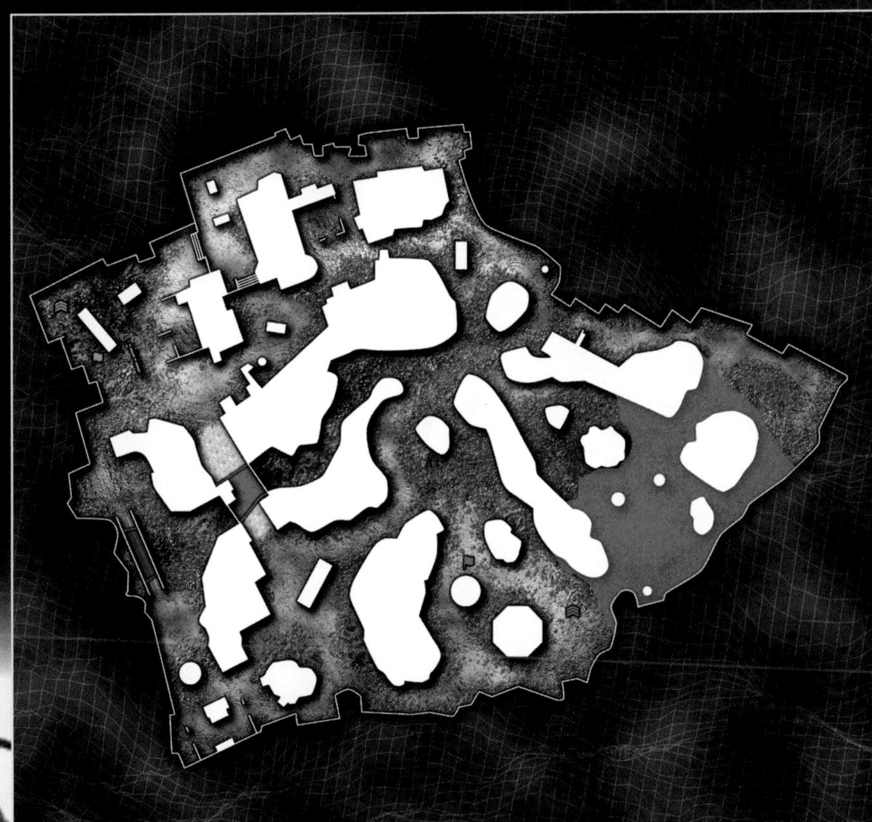

SEARCH & DESTROY

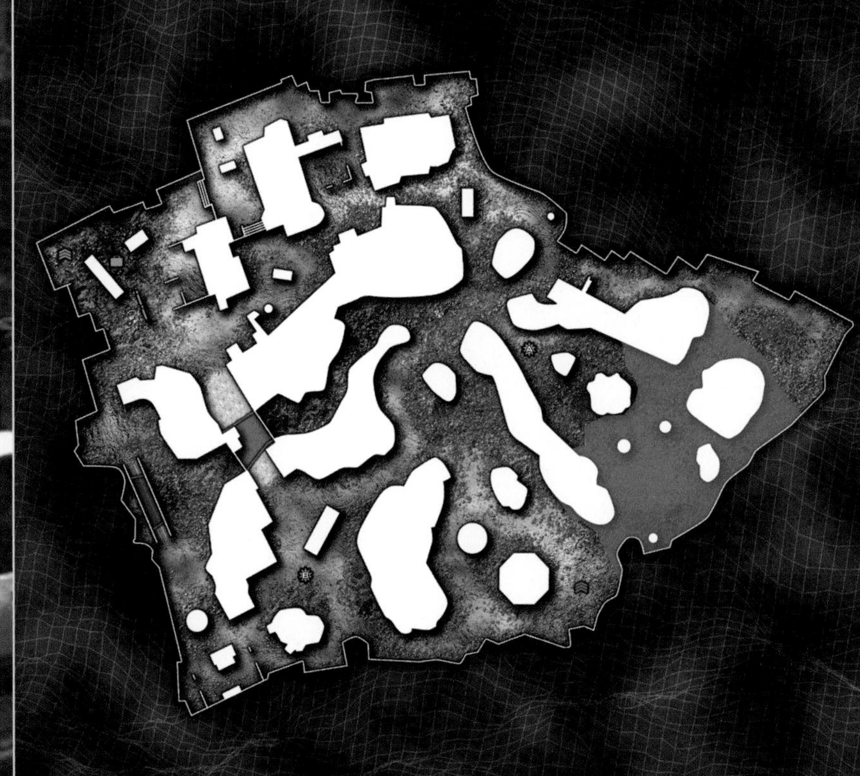

LOADOUT SUGGESTION

THE FITZY

Built for speed and efficiency, your perks give you an edge in any direct combat engagement. Use your silenced MP to dispatch targets in CQC without alerting nearby enemies.

PRIMARY WEAPON	M4A1
ATTACHMENT	HYBRID SIGHT
PROFICIENCY	KICK
SECONDARY WEAPON	FMG9
ATTACHMENT	SILENCER
EQUIPMENT	
LETHAL	FRAG GRENADE
TACTICAL	FLASH GRENADE
PERK 1	SLIGHT OF HAND
PERK 2	QUICKDRAW
PERK 3	STALKER
STRIKE PACKAGE	ASSAULT
POINTSTREAK 1	PREDATOR MISSILE
POINTSTREAK 2	REAPER
POINTSTREAK 3	JUGGERNAUT
DEATH STREAK	REVENGE

FALLEN

Size Classification:	Medium
Terrain Classification:	Mixed
Engagement Profile:	Mixed
Conflict Between:	Spetsnaz and Delta

TEAM DEATHMATCH

1
2
3
4
5
6
7

DEMOLITION

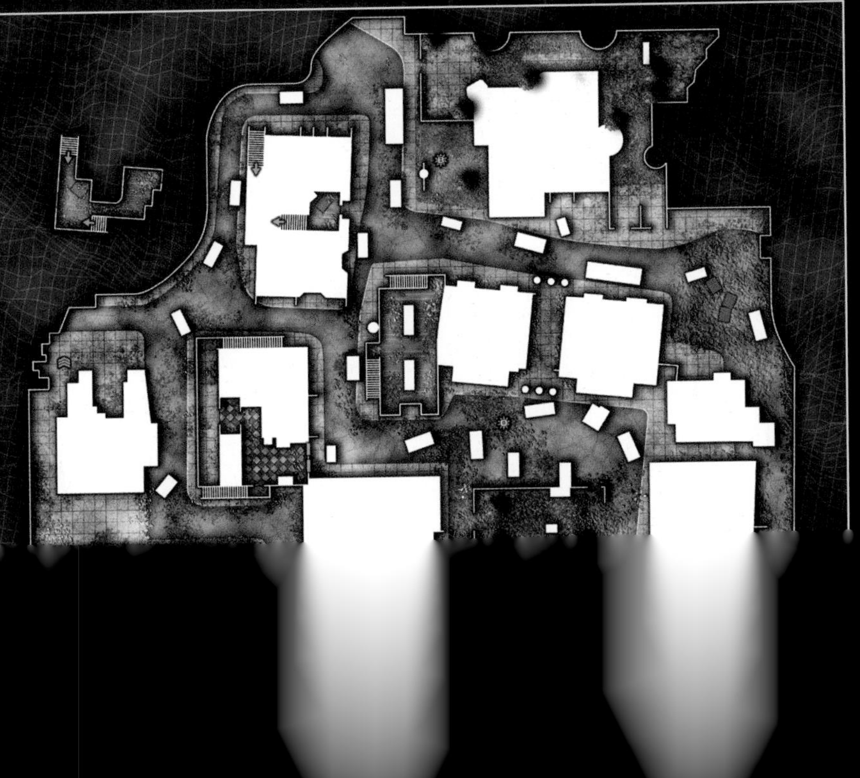

The derelict remains of a Russian town, Fallen is a demanding, mixed map with heavy cover and strong connectivity between all parts of the level. You need to be very alert and aware of your surroundings at all times. Enemies can sneak up on you from multiple directions in most parts of the map.

The southern courtyard and the street just north of it tend to be hotspots, due to their central location and connections to all outer sections. Be careful when you travel through them. The buildings in the west and south have good overwatch positions to different areas of the level. However, none have perfect line of sight, and you're very vulnerable to a stealthy intruder or a well-placed grenade. So, be careful about posting up in any one building for too long.

You can access a raised rooftop in the center of the map via the north or the south. It has great line of sight to the middle of the map. But it also provides no cover from the railings at the building's edges, and it's exposed to fire from multiple directions. Use the rooftop, but don't linger there!

KEY

	Team Spawn Points
	Bomb–Search & Destroy / Sabotage Modes
A B	Search & Destroy / Demolition Plant Site
A B C	Domination Flags
	CTF Flags
	Headquarters Point
	Ladder
	Sabotage Plant Destinations
	Arrows are color-coded to match the levels to which they lead

DOMINATION

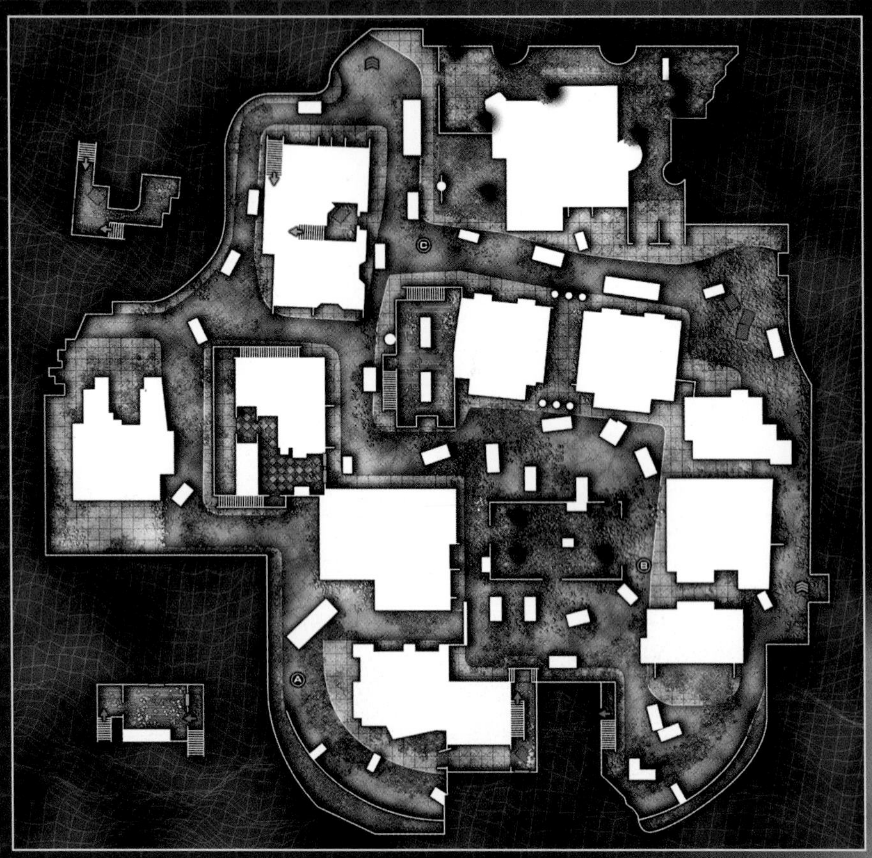

HEADQUARTERS

CAPTURE THE FLAG

SEARCH & DESTROY

LOADOUT SUGGESTION

SOLDAT

Set up in the buildings and block off chokepoints with your silenced LMG. Guard your back with your Equipment and streaks.

PRIMARY WEAPON	MK46	
ATTACHMENT	SILENCER	
PROFICIENCY	KICK	
SECONDARY WEAPON	FIVE SEVEN	
ATTACHMENT	EXTENDED MAGS	
EQUIPMENT		
LETHAL	BOUNCING BETTY	
TACTICAL	PORTABLE RADAR	
PERK 1	EXTREME CONDITIONING	
PERK 2	BLAST SHIELD	
PERK 3	SITREP	
STRIKE PACKAGE	SUPPORT	
POINTSTREAK 1	SAM TURRET	
POINTSTREAK 2	ADVANCED UAV	
POINTSTREAK 3	ESCORT AIRDROP	
DEATH STREAK	JUICED	

OUTPOST

Size Classification:	Large
Terrain Classification:	Mixed
Engagement Profile:	Mixed
Conflict Between:	Spetsnaz and Delta

TEAM DEATHMATCH

1

2

3

4

5

6

DEMOLITION

A sprawling Russian compound in Siberia, Outpost is a large map with a heavy urban combat component. The abundant warehouses and significant amounts of cover scattered around the level set the tone. Two narrow chokepoints around a large comm tower in the center of the map sharply divide Outpost into eastern and western halves, creating killing lanes. Be careful when you use these chokepoints to pass from one side to the other.

As with the other large maps, objective modes demand fast movement and possibly Tactical Insertions to traverse the level quickly. Don't let haste make you reckless. Move swiftly, stop when you approach dangerous areas, and sweep them carefully.

Almost all of the buildings on this level make good control points. But with the size of the level, it's possible to bypass many of them entirely. Watch your main map when UAVs are up, and communicate with your team to stay updated on enemy team locations. Despite the map's size, medium- and even short-range weaponry can enjoy success if you're smart about your movement and engagement choices.

DOMINATION

HEADQUARTERS

KEY

	Team Spawn Points
	Bomb–Search & Destroy / Sabotage Modes
A B	Search & Destroy / Demolition Plant Site
A B C	Domination Flags
	CTF Flags
	Headquarters Point
	Ladder
	Sabotage Plant Destinations
	Arrows are color-coded to match the levels to which they lead

SEARCH & DESTROY

FROSTBITE 3.0

Mix up your weapons as you move through the map. Dominate CQC with your Striker, while your stable and accurate G36C gives you solid ranged firepower.

PRIMARY WEAPON	STRIKER	
ATTACHMENT	EXTENDED MAGS	
PROFICIENCY	RANGE	
SECONDARY WEAPON	G36C	
ATTACHMENT	RED DOT SIGHT	
EQUIPMENT		
LETHAL	BOUNCING BETTY	
TACTICAL	PORTABLE RADAR	
PERK 1	SCAVENGER	
PERK 2	OVERKILL	
PERK 3	SITREP	
STRIKE PACKAGE	ASSAULT	
POINTSTREAK 1	PREDATOR MISSILE	
POINTSTREAK 2	REAPER	
POINTSTREAK 3	OSPREY GUNNER	
DEATH STREAK	FINAL STAND	

INTERCHANGE

Size Classification:	Large
Terrain Classification:	Open
Engagement Profile:	Long Range
Conflict Between:	Spetsnaz and Delta

TEAM DEATHMATCH

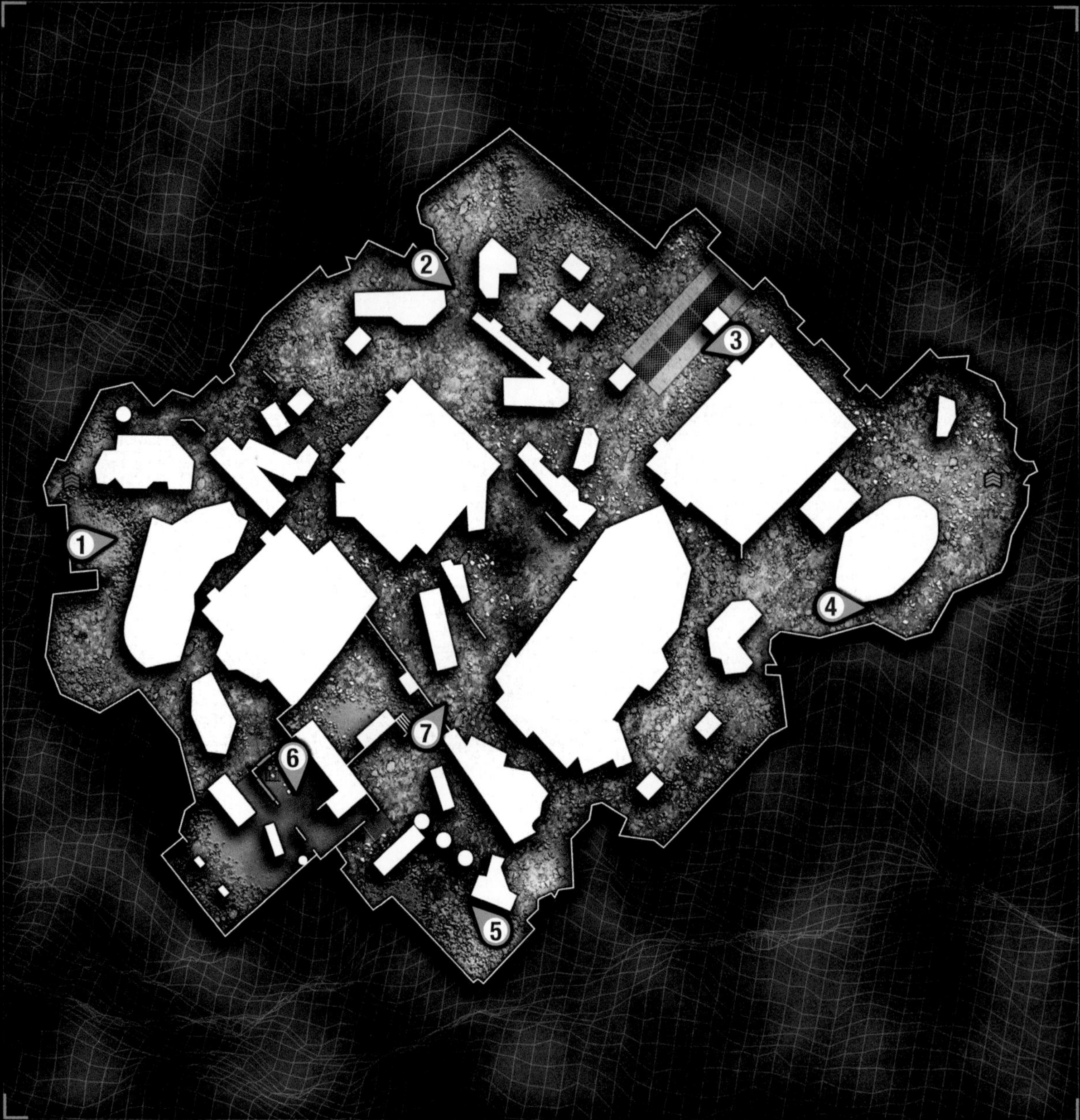

1
2
3
4
5
6
7

1

2

3

4

5

6

7

SABOTAGE

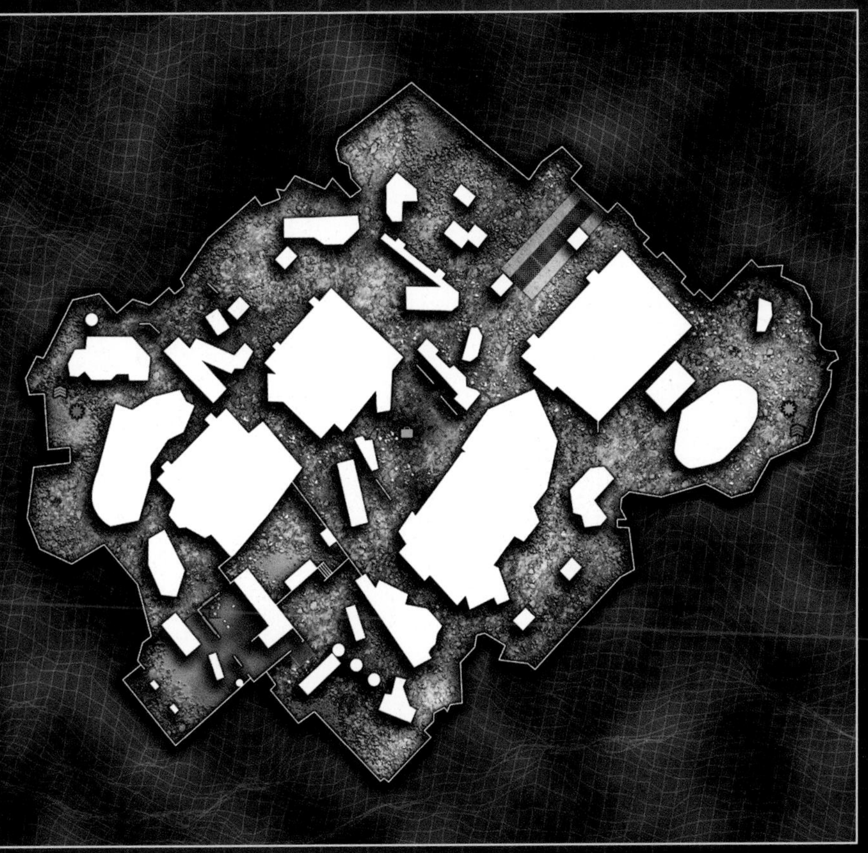

DEMOLITION

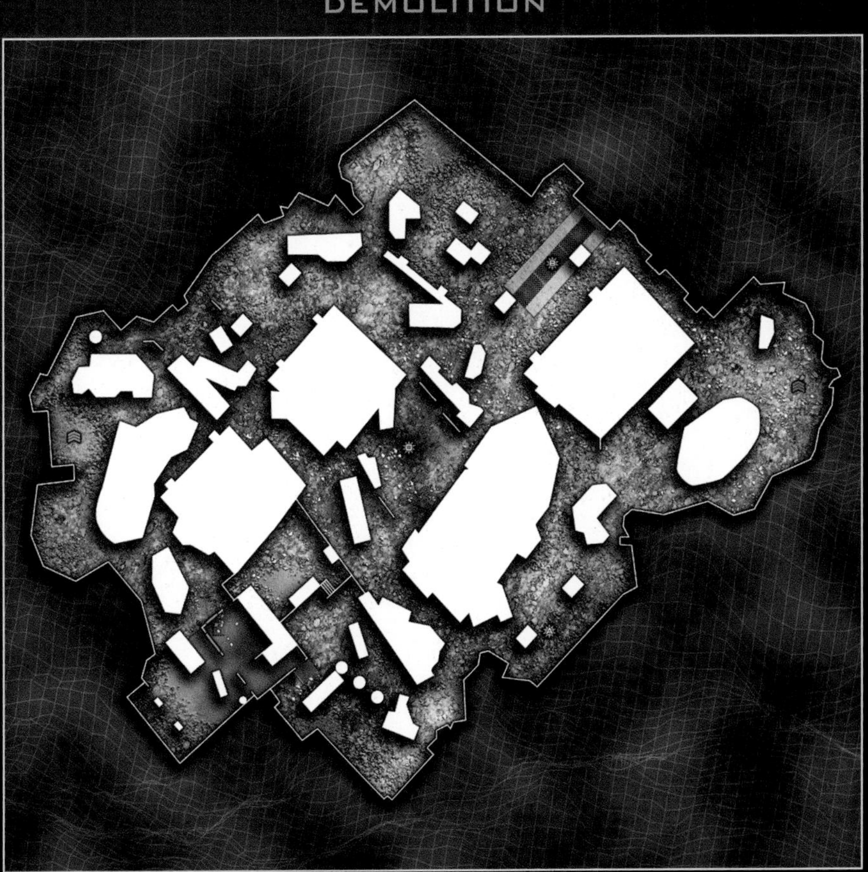

Interchange is set beneath the intersection of several large freeways. Blasted out by the war, the rubble beneath the interchange has created a large, very open killing field. Interchange is the largest open map in the game, so expect snipers! As with other large maps, this is also a good home for light machine guns and assault rifles with ranged setups. Unlike the other large maps, Interchange is wide open. Consequently, shorter-ranged weapons have a much harder time competing, even with careful movement.

Objective modes are especially brutal on this level. There is so little cover on the approach that you can expect long-range firefights to pop up constantly. Thankfully, slight elevation changes and some large vehicle wrecks provide hard cover in the level's center. This gives you some route choices to different parts of the map.

DOMINATION

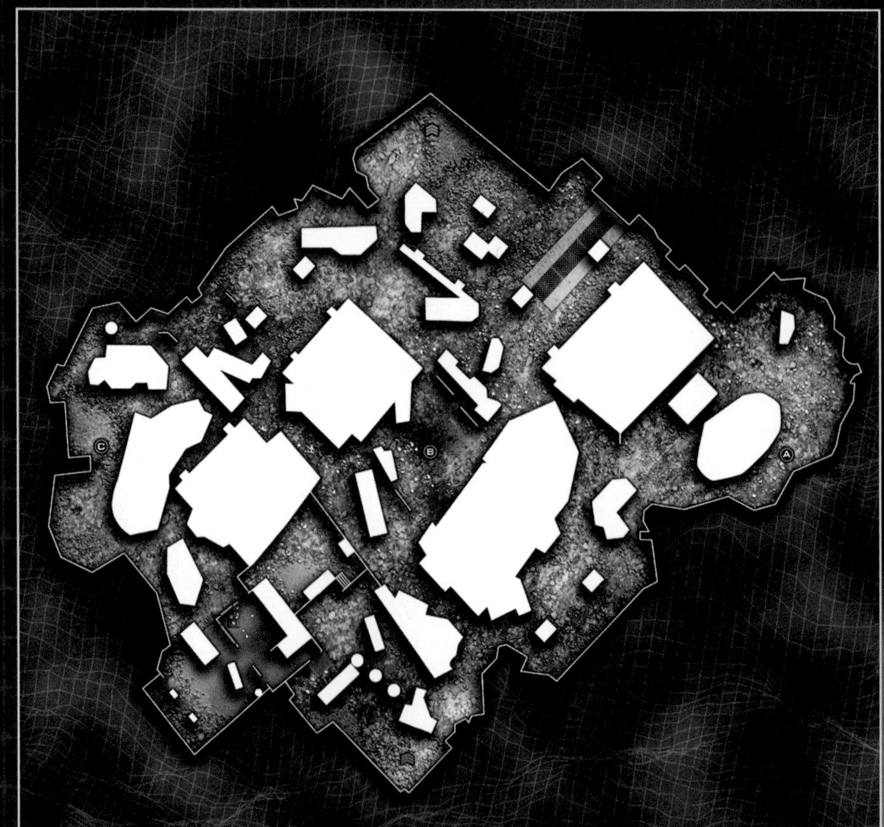

HEADQUARTERS

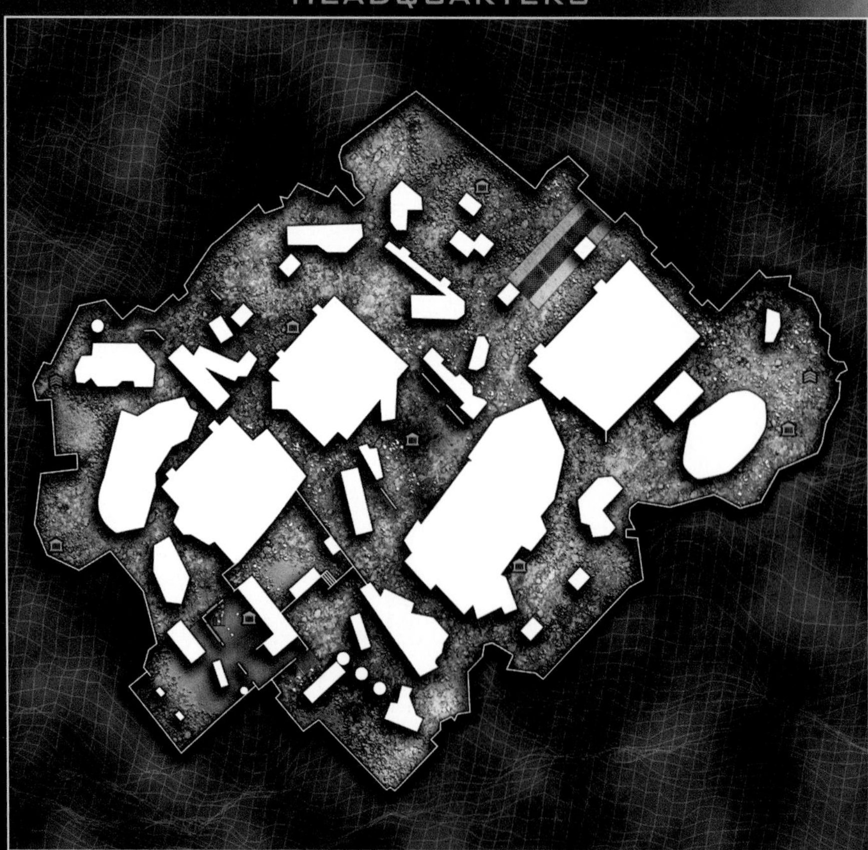

KEY

	Team Spawn Points
	Bomb–Search & Destroy / Sabotage Modes
A B	Search & Destroy / Demolition Plant Site
A B C	Domination Flags
	CTF Flags
	Headquarters Point
	Ladder
	Sabotage Plant Destinations
	Arrows are color-coded to match the levels to which they lead

CAPTURE THE FLAG

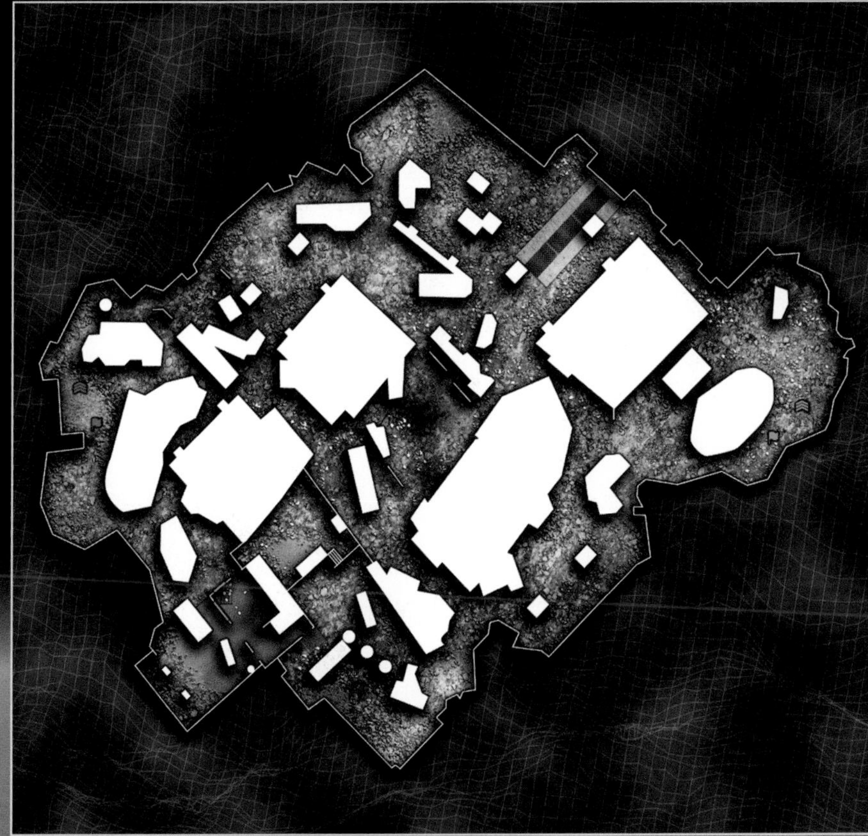

SEARCH & DESTROY

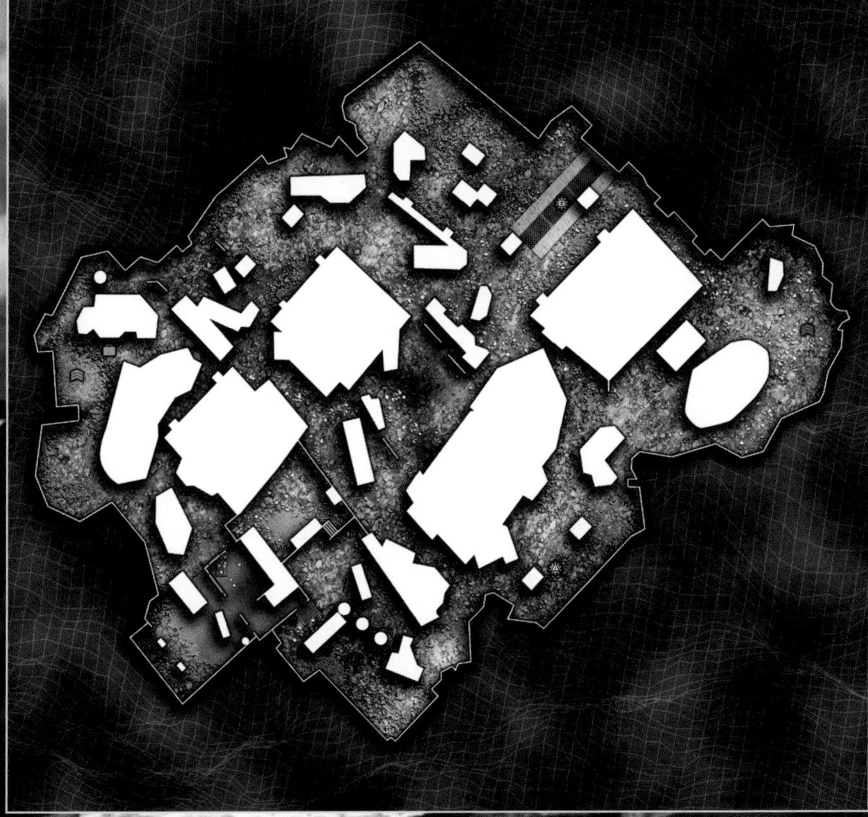

LOADOUT SUGGESTION

PRO SNIPER

A pure and clean sniper build, keep your distance, pick off targets, and stay mobile to avoid detection.

PRIMARY WEAPON	L118A	
ATTACHMENT	VARIABLE ZOOM SCOPE	
PROFICIENCY	SPEED	
SECONDARY WEAPON	FMG9	
ATTACHMENT	EXTENDED MAGS	
EQUIPMENT		
LETHAL	FRAG	
TACTICAL	FLASH GRENADE	
PERK 1	EXTREME CONDITIONING	
PERK 2	ASSASSIN	
PERK 3	MARKSMAN	
STRIKE PACKAGE	ASSAULT	
POINTSTREAK 1	PREDATOR MISSILE	
POINTSTREAK 2	REAPER	
POINTSTREAK 3	AC-130	
DEATH STREAK	FINAL STAND	

UNDERGROUND

Size Classification:	Medium
Terrain Classification:	Urban
Engagement Profile:	CQC
Conflict Between:	Spetsnaz and SAS

TEAM DEATHMATCH

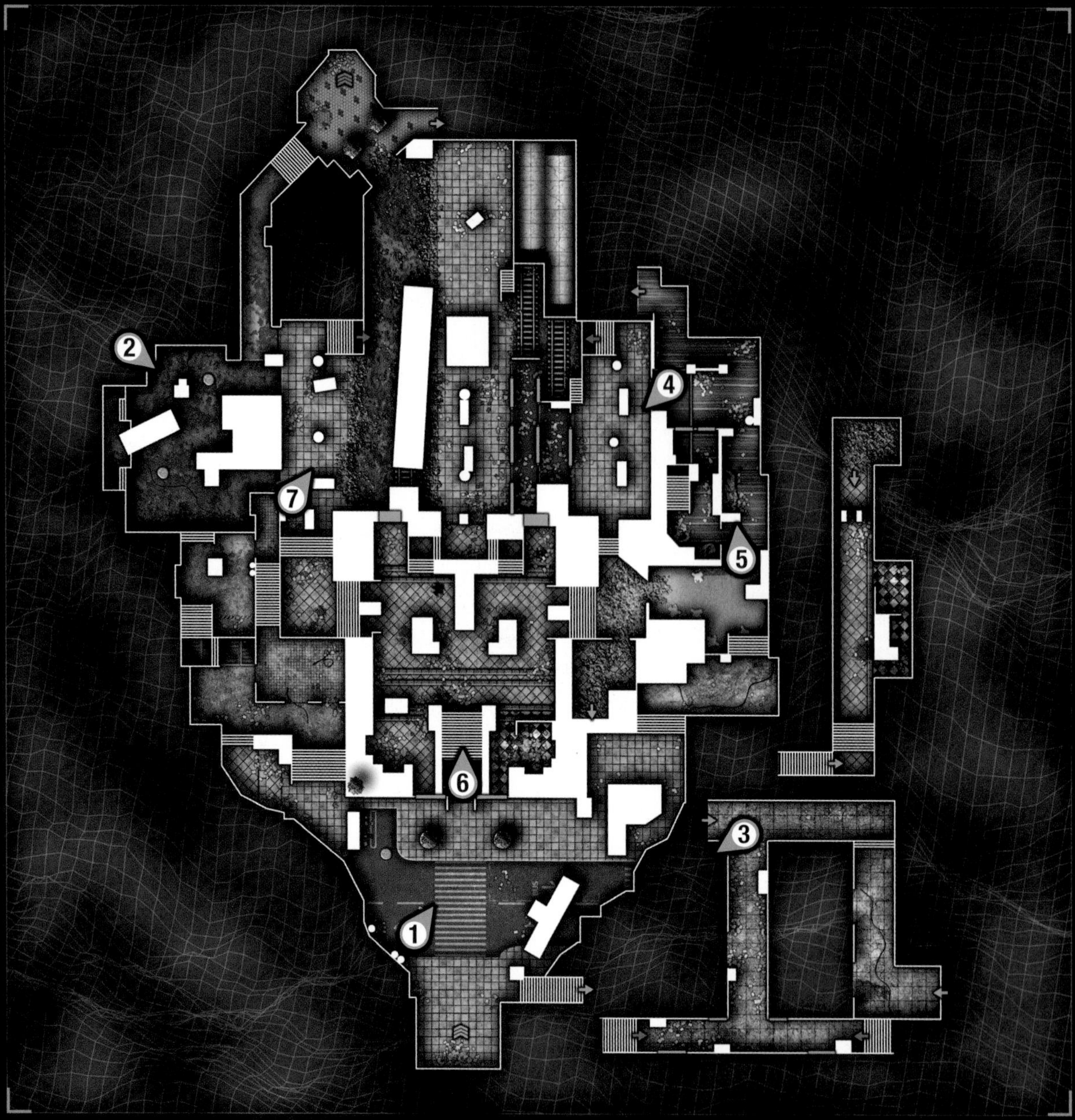

3

4

5

6

7

SABOTAGE

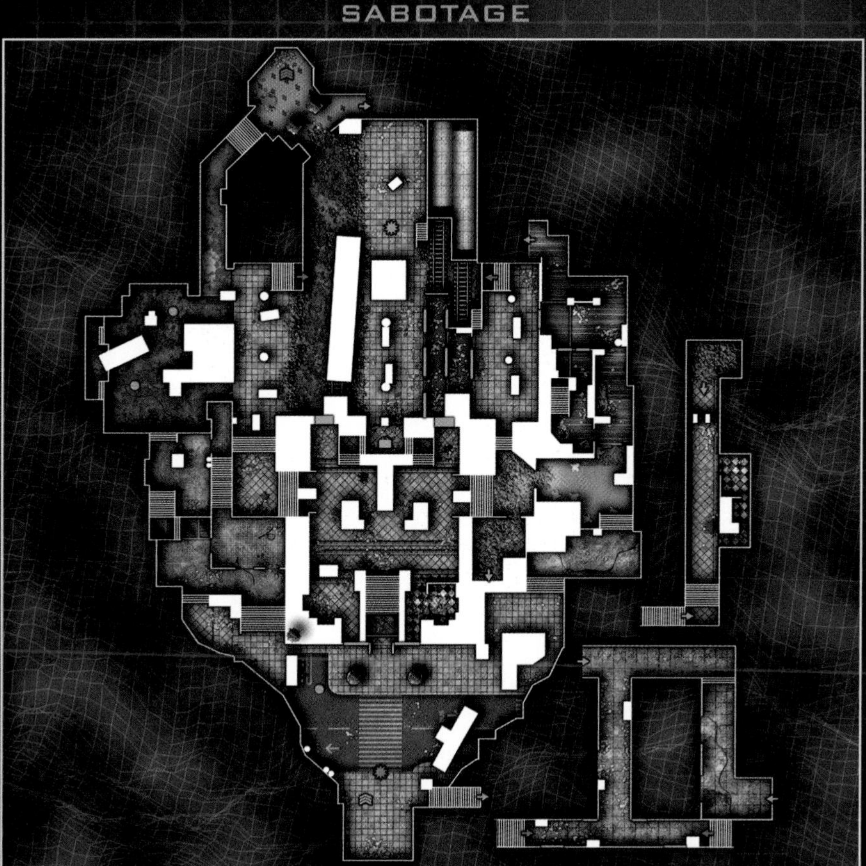

DEMOLITION

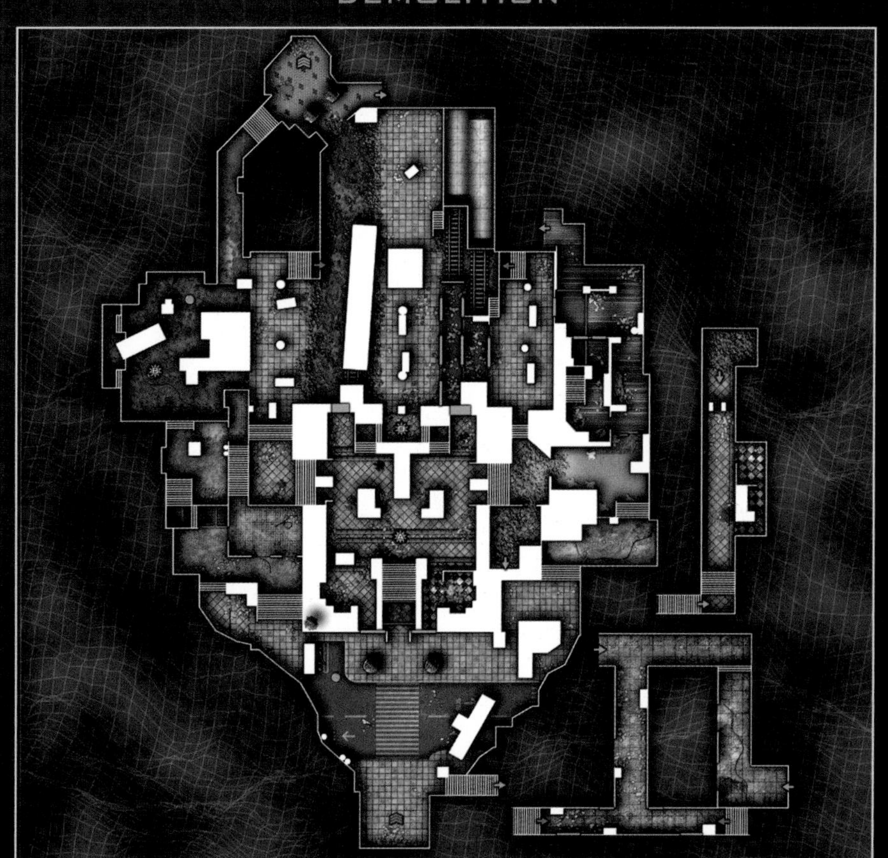

Set in a London subway station, Underground is similar to Arkaden as a mid-sized level with strong connectivity throughout the map. However, it's a bit larger from end to end. The wreckage of multiple trains just outside the subway station to the south dominates the map's center. Meanwhile, blocked sightlines separate the map's north and south ends, thanks to a raised walkway.

The eastern side has several lengthy hallways that are dangerous to traverse due to their linear nature and limited cover. The western side is largely open. Cutting through the center at any part of this map is tricky. Many routes lead in and out of the middle, and you can expect to run into enemies no matter which path you take.

CQC weaponry can do well here, provided you stick to the chokepoints and corners. If you're careful about your movement, blocked sightlines protect you from most long-range harassment.

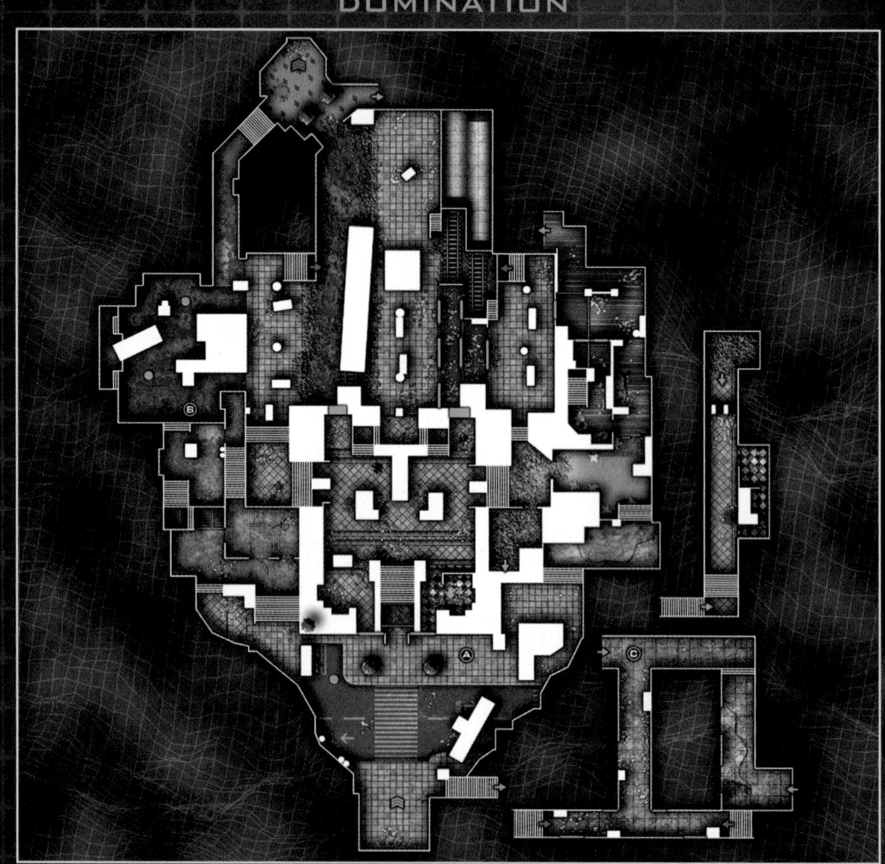

HEADQUARTERS

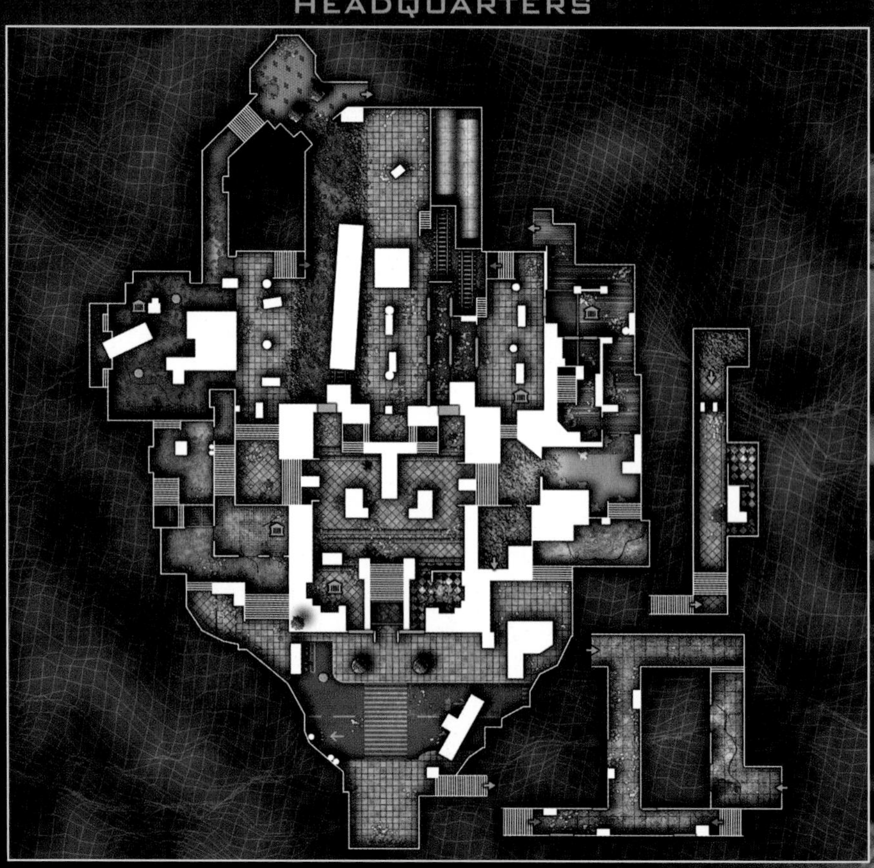

KEY

	Team Spawn Points
	Bomb–Search & Destroy / Sabotage Modes
A B	Search & Destroy / Demolition Plant Site
A B C	Domination Flags
	CTF Flags
	Headquarters Point
	Ladder
	Sabotage Plant Destinations
	Arrows are color-coded to match the levels to which they lead

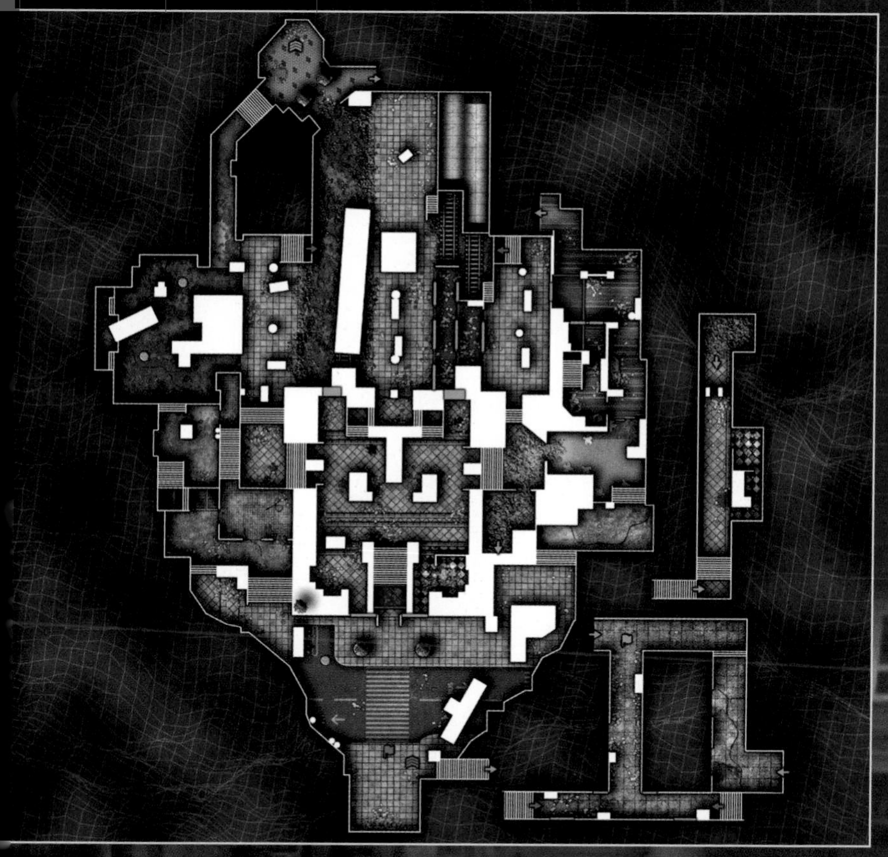

SEARCH & DESTROY

DIGITAL SOLDIER

An efficient close- to mid-range build, use your Hardline-fueled Support streaks for constant recon and enemy radar denial, while you track down enemies via Sitrep.

PRIMARY WEAPON	UMP45
ATTACHMENT	RED DOT SIGHT
PROFICIENCY	RANGE
SECONDARY WEAPON	USP .45
ATTACHMENT	EXTENDED MAGS
EQUIPMENT	
LETHAL	SEMTEX
TACTICAL	EMP GRENADE
PERK 1	SLIGHT OF HAND
PERK 2	HARDLINE
PERK 3	SITREP
STRIKE PACKAGE	SUPPORT
POINTSTREAK 1	UAV
POINTSTREAK 2	COUNTER UAV
POINTSTREAK 3	SAM TURRET
DEATH STREAK	DEAD MAN'S HAND

MISSION

Size Classification:	Medium
Terrain Classification:	Open
Engagement Profile:	Mixed
Conflict Between:	Africa Militia and PMC

TEAM DEATHMATCH

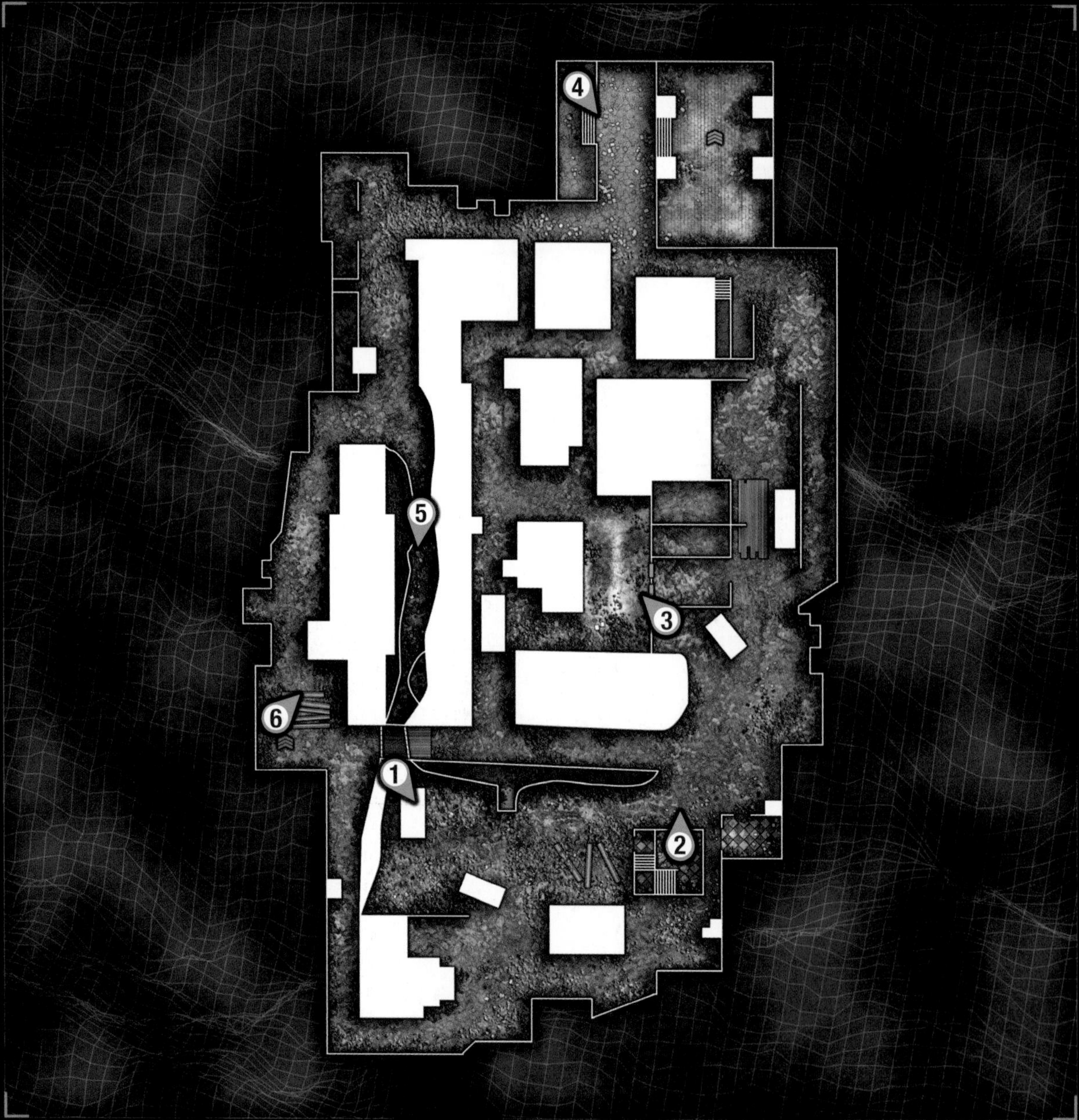

3

4

5

6

SABOTAGE

DEMOLITION

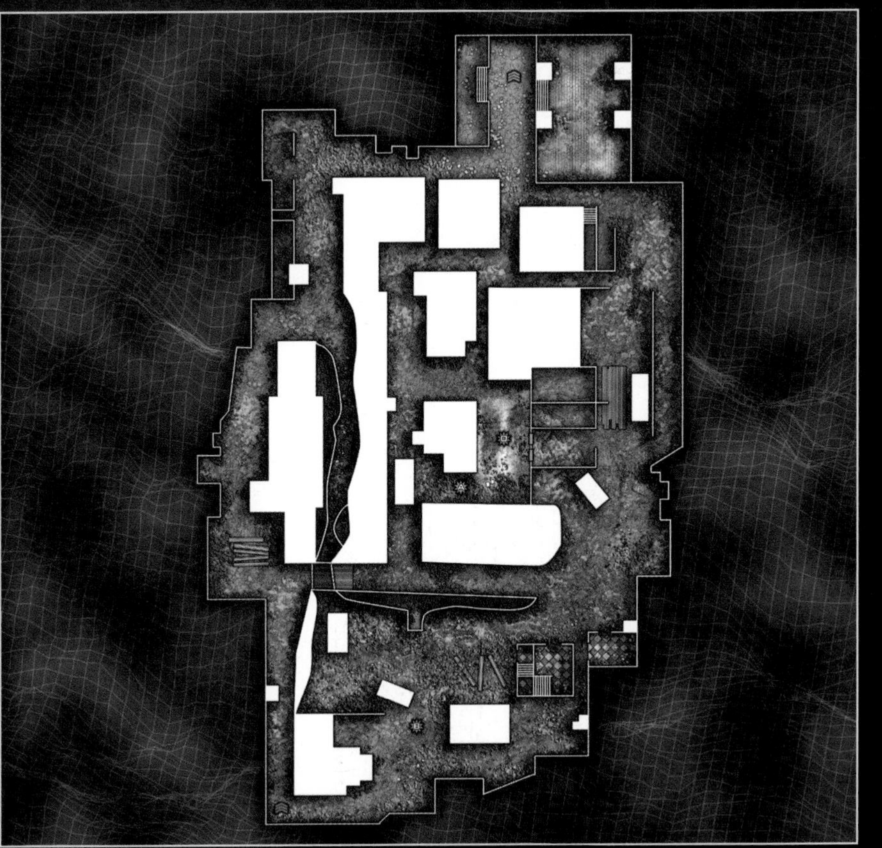

An African colonial settlement, Mission is a small map with highly unusual terrain. A large trench runs down the west side of the map, and a sheer cliff at the edge of the buildings drops into a basin at the extreme south. Accordingly, the level is split into a northeast section, the southern basin, and a far-western channel that can go either down the trench to the basin, or up through a few small huts to the cliff area. The map's center hosts several nasty 90-degree blind turns that can put you face to face with an enemy with little warning.

The raised areas that overlook parts of the map below them to the south and east are dominant positions. Try to control the center of the level whenever you can, blocking access to the alleys with Equipment or teammate coverage. Objective modes can be brutal on this level; a team locking down the center can put you in a very unpleasant spawning situation.

DOMINATION

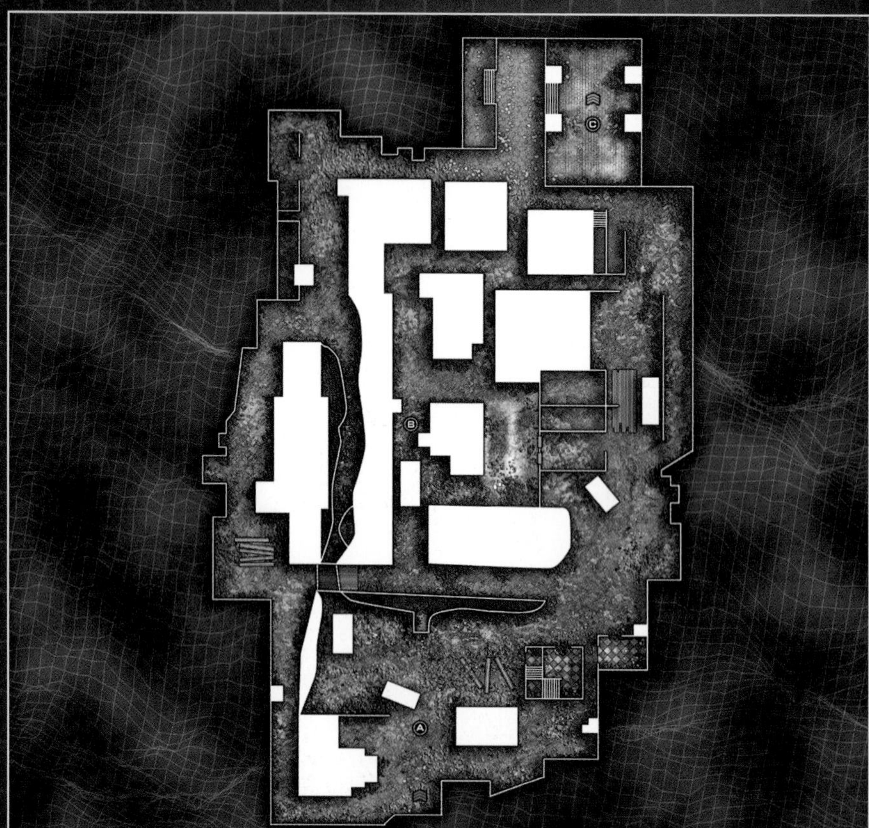

HEADQUARTERS

KEY

	Team Spawn Points
	Bomb–Search & Destroy / Sabotage Modes
A B	Search & Destroy / Demolition Plant Site
A B C	Domination Flags
	CTF Flags
	Headquarters Point
	Ladder
	Sabotage Plant Destinations
	Arrows are color-coded to match the levels to which they lead

CAPTURE THE FLAG

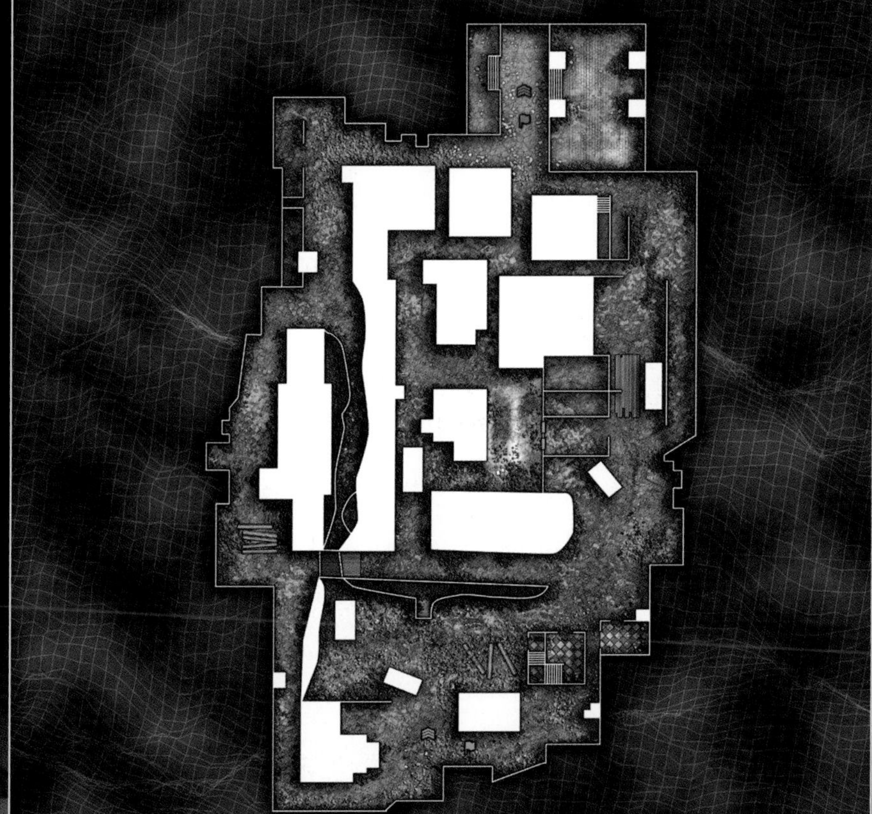

SEARCH & DESTROY

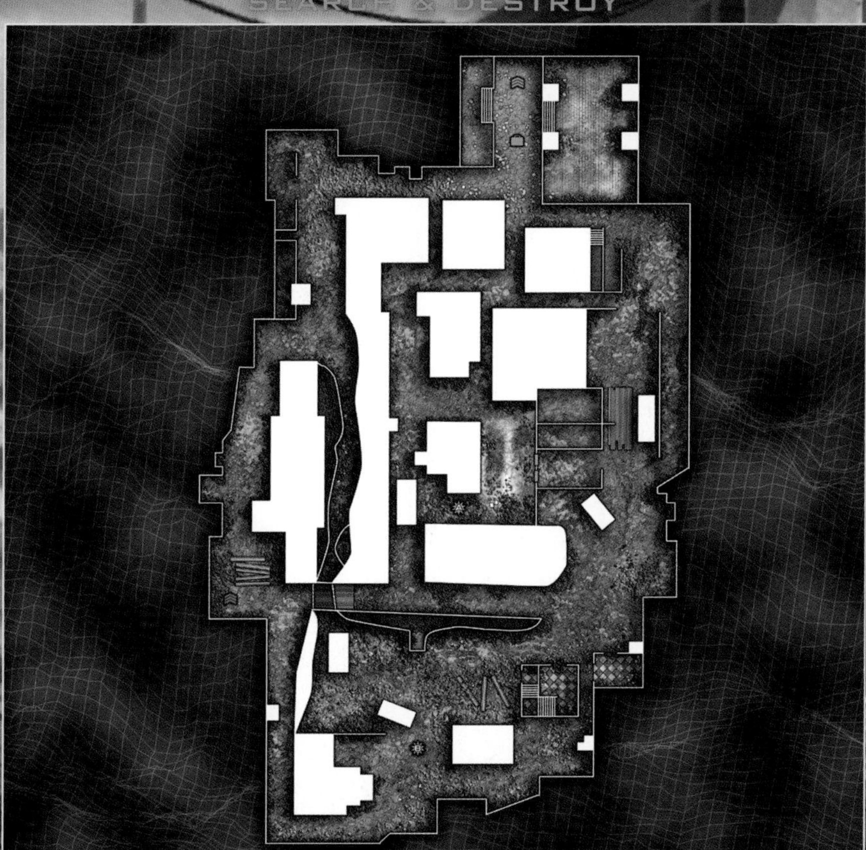

LOADOUT SUGGESTION

DOUBLE TAP

An SMG build meant to use ADS, rather than the usual hip-fire. Abuse your mobility and the ultra-fast swap to your pistol to finish damaged targets.

PRIMARY WEAPON	PM-9	
ATTACHMENT	RED DOT SIGHT	
PROFICIENCY	FOCUS	
SECONDARY WEAPON	FIVE SEVEN	
ATTACHMENT	TACTICAL KNIFE	
EQUIPMENT		
LETHAL	THROWING KNIFE	
TACTICAL	CONCUSSION GRENADE	
PERK 1	SLIGHT OF HAND	
PERK 2	QUICKDRAW	
PERK 3	STALKER	
STRIKE PACKAGE	ASSAULT	
POINTSTREAK 1	PREDATOR MISSILE	
POINTSTREAK 2	ATTACK HELICOPTER	
POINTSTREAK 3	AH-6 OVERWATCH	
DEATH STREAK	HOLLOW POINTS	

GAME MODES

WAGE WAR IN A VARIETY OF TACTICAL ENGAGEMENTS.

STANDARD MODES

FREE-FOR-ALL

EVERY MAN FOR HIMSELF. FIRST PLAYER TO REACH THE TARGET SCORE WINS.

FFA is a challenging game mode, pitting you against every other player in a race to reach the target score. Note that because only a single player can top out in FFA, kill/death ratio matters less here than it does in TDM for victory—you can potentially have more deaths than kills and still win. This doesn't mean that suicidal play is a good idea. But it does mean that aggressive play can win a match just as defensive play can.

With that said, the stock FFA strategy is to take a stealthy build and post up in a defensible area, taking down anyone who comes into 'your' part of the map.

TEAM DEATHMATCH

ORGANIZED CHAOS. FIRST TEAM TO REACH THE TARGET SCORE WINS.

TDM is the most basic of all teamplay modes. It features you and your teammates, and a bunch of enemy targets to shoot. Good TDM strategy means moving with your teammates, but not *too* close to them. Cover each other, and lock down the enemy team near their spawn location.

Communication is vital in this mode. You need to know where dangerous enemy campers or snipers are, if you're being flanked, and where the enemy team is spawning. Because you don't have to worry about objectives focusing the action on a particular area, it's entirely viable to lock down a defensible spot as a team, or simply to roam the level as a pack, hunting the opposition as they appear.

SEARCH AND DESTROY

ONE BOMB, TWO TARGETS. TWO TEAMS SWAP OFFENSE AND DEFENSE. FIRST TEAM TO ELIMINATE THE OPPOSING TEAM, DETONATE THE BOMB, OR DEFUSE THE BOMB, WINS.

With no respawns mid-round, Search and Destroy is an intense, tactical game mode. Stealth, communication, and carefully organized aggression are the keys to victory in this mode. Hunting down the enemy team is just as viable as planting the bomb. Choosing the best course of action means responding intelligently to the situation as teammates and enemies go down in combat.

On offense or defense, killing the enemy team is possible; meanwhile, dealing with the bomb depends on the situation. Planting the bomb can force the enemy out of hiding, but it can also get the planter killed by campers if you aren't careful. Unlike Demolition, you must defuse the bomb where it's planted on the target, so choose the plant location carefully for best possible coverage.

SABOTAGE

ONE BOMB, ONE TARGET FOR EACH TEAM. BLOW UP THE TARGET TO WIN.

Sabotage is a unique mode, with a single bomb placed in the middle of the map. Either team can pick it up and attempt to plant it at the enemy team's target location. Sabotage is unusual in that there is just a single round: the first team to successfully plant and detonate the bomb wins immediately. As a result, the difficulty of nailing a plant and winning depends heavily on which side you spawn. On any given map, some sides are considerably easier than others.

Be wary of bomb campers on all maps, particularly in public games. You can expect a lot of players to cover the bomb wherever it drops and not move to pick it up or go for a plant. Successfully planting and defending the plant typically requires a combination of smoke, tactical equipment, and a well-timed barrage of Assault Pointstreaks to cover the bomb location.

DOMINATION

THREE FLAGS ON THREE CONTROL POINTS. OWN A POINT TO EARN POINTS. REACH THE SCORE LIMIT TO WIN.

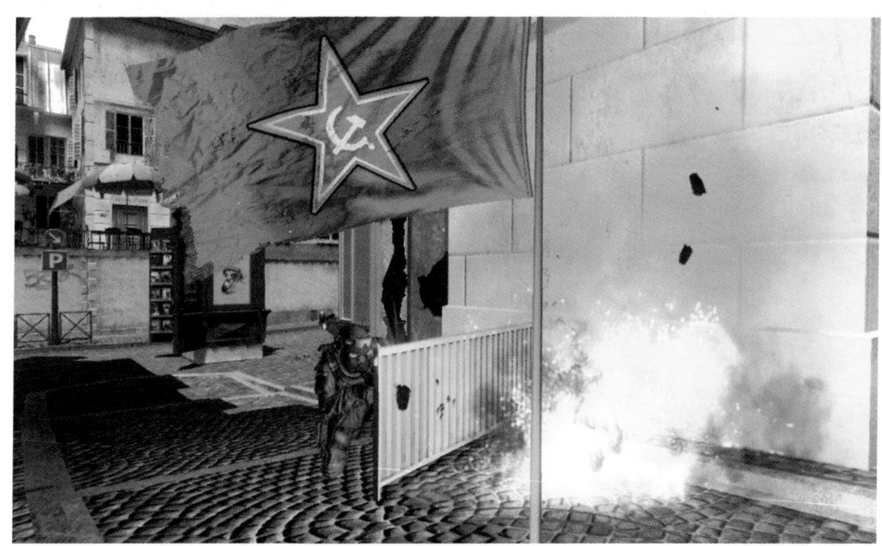

Domination is one of the most popular game modes outside Team Deathmatch. With three focal points for conflict on every map, Domination has seesaw battles that push back and forth (and sometimes flip), creating a constantly shifting battlefield.

Winning in Domination is a matter of securing two points and locking the enemy team at their spawn by the third point. Ideally, you secure the two points that are easiest to defend, and prevent the enemy team from ever moving off their home point. Be wary of capturing the third flag if you have two on lockdown. If the enemy team's last flag is taken—or your team pushes into their territory too strongly—the entire enemy team can respawn elsewhere on the level, usually resulting in quick flag swaps.

HEADQUARTERS

CONTROL RANDOMLY SHIFTING HEADQUARTERS LOCATIONS TO SCORE POINTS. REACH THE SCORE LIMIT TO WIN.

Headquarters tests your team heavily. It requires locating the HQ point, capturing it, and then defending it to squeeze as many points out of it as possible before it shuts down and a new HQ point appears. When your team controls an HQ point, any teammate who falls in battle has a long respawn point. Thus, headquarters are typically defended by less than a full squad, and they usually fall apart piecemeal as defenders succumb.

When the current HQ is shutting down, mobility and speed are very important. Start moving away from the current HQ point toward a central location in order to reach the next HQ spawn quickly. Once an HQ is secured, it's a good idea on most maps to immediately vacate the premises and cover the HQ from a distance. Otherwise, you can open yourself up to grenade and explosive spam.

CAPTURE THE FLAG

TWO FLAGS, TWO BASES. CAPTURE THE ENEMY FLAG WITH YOUR FLAG AT HOME. REACH THE CAPTURE LIMIT TO WIN.

Capture the Flag requires an organized team to do well, with appointed defenders, flag runners, and midfield support. Typically, two players on defense is sufficient, with the remainder on offense or patrolling the midfield for the enemy team. Flag runners should use fast, stealthy builds. Naturally, defenders can use defensive equipment and Pointstreaks. Players on patrol should use builds well suited for the map you're playing.

CTF has a short respawn delay, so be careful about reckless play. You can leave your team down a few men for a few crucial seconds when the enemy team makes a push for your flag. Your flag *must* be at your base to score a capture. If your flag runner ends up at home with the enemy flag, leave one defender with him and send the rest of your team to recover your flag. Only one or two players trying to recover their flag can rarely break a dedicated flag-carrier defense.

DEMOLITION

OFFENSE AND DEFENSE WITH TWO BOMB SITES. EVERY OFFENSIVE PLAYER HAS A BOMB. DETONATE BOTH BOMB SITES OR DEFEND THEM UNTIL THE TIME EXPIRES TO WIN A ROUND.

Demolition is a mix of Search & Destroy and Sabotage. Every player on offense is armed with a bomb, and defusing a bomb does *not* end the round. Instead, defense needs to hold out until the time runs down, while offense needs to destroy *both* bomb sites.

Winning in Demolition is a matter of team coordination. Choose the *correct* bomb site and push with all or almost all of the team to destroy it. On almost every map, one of the two bomb sites is easier to tackle: hit the *harder* site first, so that the second plant is easier to secure. Even in public games, once the first bomb site is destroyed, you can expect the entire enemy team to hole up around the second site. If you've left the harder site for last, you have a much more difficult task.

NEW MODES

KILL CONFIRMED

TEAM DEATHMATCH WITH A TWIST. KILLS DROP DOG TAGS. CAPTURE ENEMY TAGS FOR KILLS; SAVE FRIENDLY TAGS TO DENY KILLS.

Kill Confirmed plays out like TDM in most respects, but the addition of the dropping dog tags creates 'hotspots' all over the map. A common scenario is a few players meeting each other in firefight. One side goes down, then the other side goes down before they can secure all of the tags, and repeat. Soon you have a nice pile of tags in one part of the map, and both teams are rushing to capture or save tags as fast as they can.

Because this creates new focal points for conflict all over the map on any level, playing well in Kill Confirmed means knowing every level cold. You need to know where the enemy is likely to approach any given hotspot. A perfectly valid and nasty tactic is to camp out in an area and down a few targets. Then, instead of picking up the tags, wait for the enemy team to send more players to recover them. Down them as well, and *then* capture all of the tags at once. Be watchful for this common tactic when you're heading for tags: the area may be under the watchful eye of a nearby camper.

TEAM DEFENDER

SCORE ONE KILL AT THE START OF THE ROUND TO ACQUIRE THE FLAG. HOLD THE FLAG TO DOUBLE KILL POINTS FOR TEAMMATES. SECURE THE FLAG TO EARN THE BONUS FOR YOUR TEAM.

Team Defender is a fast-paced, highly mobile TDM mode, where teams struggle to control a single flag. Holding the flag doubles the points your team gains, allowing you to quickly pull an insurmountable lead. However, your flag carrier is highlighted on the enemy team's HUD at all times. Although holing up in an area and protecting your flag carrier is smart play, there's no way to hide from the enemy team. Expect constant assaults!

Team Defender is an interesting mode, because it forces conflict all over the map, in areas that even Headquarters doesn't send you. Get used to fighting in strange places!

SPECIAL MODES

OUTSIDE NORMAL OPERATING PROCEDURES.

The 'normal' game modes are bundled into a variety of playlists. They're typically played in 6v6 matches with standard settings. Outside these modes, there are many other ways to play *Modern Warfare 3* multiplayer.

First, you can customize almost any setting you can think of for private matches. Want a throwing-knives arena on Dome? Headshots-only duel on Interchange? Go for it! There are also special playlists that modify the number of players. Ground War can have 18 or more players in a match, while Team Tactical pares that down to 8 players for intense, small-scale combat.

There are also Mercenary playlists for players not in parties, to ensure fair lone-wolf teams. Hardcore playlists disable the HUD, lower health, and turn on team damage for extremely challenging tactical combat. Additionally, Infinity Ward can update playlists down the road, changing up which modes appear, and adding, changing, or tweaking modes.

CHALLENGE CHARTS

ASSAULT RIFLE CHALLENGES

CHALLENGE DESCRIPTION	TITLE	TARGET 1	TARGET 2	TARGET 3	TARGET 4	TARGET 5	TARGET 6	TARGET 7	TARGET 8	XP 1	XP 2	XP 3	XP 4	XP 5	XP 6	XP 7	XP 8
M4A1 CHALLENGES																	
Get N kills with this weapon.	Marksman	10	25	75	150	300	500	750	1000	250	1000	2000	5000	10000	10000	10000	10000
Get N headshots with this weapon.	Expert	5	15	30	75	150	250	350	500	500	1000	2500	5000	10000	10000	10000	10000
Get N kills while looking through the Red Dot Sight attached to this weapon.	Attachment: Reflex Sight	60	—	—	—	—	—	—	—	1000	—	—	—	—	—	—	—
Get N kills with the Silencer attached to this weapon.	Attachment: Silencer	15	—	—	—	—	—	—	—	750	—	—	—	—	—	—	—
Get N kills with the attached Grenade Launcher.	Attachment: Grenade Launcher	20	—	—	—	—	—	—	—	750	—	—	—	—	—	—	—
Get N kills while looking through the ACOG Sight attached to this weapon.	Attachment: ACOG	20	—	—	—	—	—	—	—	750	—	—	—	—	—	—	—
Get N kills with the Heartbeat Sensor attached to this weapon.	Attachment: Heartbeat Sensor	40	—	—	—	—	—	—	—	1000	—	—	—	—	—	—	—
Get N kills with the Hybrid Sights attached to this weapon.	Attachment: Hybrid Sights	40	—	—	—	—	—	—	—	1000	—	—	—	—	—	—	—
Get N kills with the attached Shotgun.	Attachment: Shotgun	40	—	—	—	—	—	—	—	1000	—	—	—	—	—	—	—
Get N kills while looking through the Holographic Sight attached to this weapon.	Attachment: Holographic Sight	40	—	—	—	—	—	—	—	1000	—	—	—	—	—	—	—
Get N kills using the Extended Mags attachment.	Attachment: Extended Mags	40	—	—	—	—	—	—	—	1000	—	—	—	—	—	—	—
Get N kills while looking through the Thermal Scope attached to this weapon.	Attachment: Thermal	40	—	—	—	—	—	—	—	1000	—	—	—	—	—	—	—
Achieve maximum weapon proficiency with this weapon.	M4A1: Mastery	10	—	—	—	—	—	—	—	10000	—	—	—	—	—	—	—
TYPE 95 CHALLENGES																	
Get N kills with this weapon.	Marksman	10	25	75	150	300	500	750	1000	250	1000	2000	5000	10000	10000	10000	10000
Get N headshots with this weapon.	Expert	5	15	30	75	150	250	350	500	500	1000	2500	5000	10000	10000	10000	10000
Get N kills while looking through the Red Dot Sight attached to this weapon.	Attachment: Reflex Sight	60	—	—	—	—	—	—	—	1000	—	—	—	—	—	—	—
Get N kills with the Silencer attached to this weapon.	Attachment: Silencer	15	—	—	—	—	—	—	—	750	—	—	—	—	—	—	—
Get N kills with the attached Grenade Launcher.	Attachment: Grenade Launcher	20	—	—	—	—	—	—	—	750	—	—	—	—	—	—	—
Get N kills while looking through the ACOG Sight attached to this weapon.	Attachment: ACOG	20	—	—	—	—	—	—	—	750	—	—	—	—	—	—	—
Get N kills using the Rapid Fire attachment.	Attachment: Rapid Fire	40	—	—	—	—	—	—	—	1000	—	—	—	—	—	—	—
Get N kills with the Heartbeat Sensor attached to this weapon.	Attachment: Heartbeat Sensor	40	—	—	—	—	—	—	—	1000	—	—	—	—	—	—	—
Get N kills with the Hybrid Sights attached to this weapon.	Attachment: Hybrid Sights	40	—	—	—	—	—	—	—	1000	—	—	—	—	—	—	—

CHALLENGE DESCRIPTION	TITLE	TARGET 1	TARGET 2	TARGET 3	TARGET 4	TARGET 5	TARGET 6	TARGET 7	TARGET 8	XP 1	XP 2	XP 3	XP 4	XP 5	XP 6	XP 7	XP 8
Get N kills with the attached Shotgun.	Attachment: Shotgun	40	—	—	—	—	—	—	—	1000	—	—	—	—	—	—	—
Get N kills while looking through the Holographic Sight attached to this weapon.	Attachment: Holographic Sight	40	—	—	—	—	—	—	—	1000	—	—	—	—	—	—	—
Get N kills using the Extended Mags attachment.	Attachment: Extended Mags	40	—	—	—	—	—	—	—	1000	—	—	—	—	—	—	—
Get N kills while looking through the Thermal Scope attached to this weapon.	Attachment: Thermal	40	—	—	—	—	—	—	—	1000	—	—	—	—	—	—	—
Achieve maximum weapon proficiency with this weapon.	Type 95: Mastery	11	—	—	—	—	—	—	—	10000	—	—	—	—	—	—	—
SCAR-L CHALLENGES																	
Get N kills with this weapon.	Marksman	10	25	75	150	300	500	750	1000	250	1000	2000	5000	10000	10000	10000	10000
Get N headshots with this weapon.	Expert	5	15	30	75	150	250	350	500	500	1000	2500	5000	10000	10000	10000	10000
Get N kills while looking through the Red Dot Sight attached to this weapon.	Attachment: Reflex Sight	60	—	—	—	—	—	—	—	1000	—	—	—	—	—	—	—
Get N kills with the Silencer attached to this weapon.	Attachment: Silencer	15	—	—	—	—	—	—	—	750	—	—	—	—	—	—	—
Get N kills with the attached Grenade Launcher.	Attachment: Grenade Launcher	20	—	—	—	—	—	—	—	750	—	—	—	—	—	—	—
Get N kills while looking through the ACOG Sight attached to this weapon.	Attachment: ACOG	20	—	—	—	—	—	—	—	750	—	—	—	—	—	—	—
Get N kills with the Heartbeat Sensor attached to this weapon.	Attachment: Heartbeat Sensor	40	—	—	—	—	—	—	—	1000	—	—	—	—	—	—	—
Get N kills with the Hybrid Sights attached to this weapon.	Attachment: Hybrid Sights	40	—	—	—	—	—	—	—	1000	—	—	—	—	—	—	—
Get N kills with the attached Shotgun.	Attachment: Shotgun	40	—	—	—	—	—	—	—	1000	—	—	—	—	—	—	—
Get N kills while looking through the Holographic Sight attached to this weapon.	Attachment: Holographic Sight	40	—	—	—	—	—	—	—	1000	—	—	—	—	—	—	—
Get N kills using the Extended Mags attachment.	Attachment: Extended Mags	40	—	—	—	—	—	—	—	1000	—	—	—	—	—	—	—
Get N kills while looking through the Thermal Scope attached to this weapon.	Attachment: Thermal	40	—	—	—	—	—	—	—	1000	—	—	—	—	—	—	—
Achieve maximum weapon proficiency with this weapon.	SCAR-L: Mastery	10	—	—	—	—	—	—	—	10000	—	—	—	—	—	—	—
G36C CHALLENGES																	
Get N kills with this weapon.	Marksman	10	25	75	150	300	500	750	1000	250	1000	2000	5000	10000	10000	10000	10000
Get N headshots with this weapon.	Expert	5	15	30	75	150	250	350	500	500	1000	2500	5000	10000	10000	10000	10000
Get N kills while looking through the Red Dot Sight attached to this weapon.	Attachment: Reflex Sight	60	—	—	—	—	—	—	—	1000	—	—	—	—	—	—	—
Get N kills with the Silencer attached to this weapon.	Attachment: Silencer	15	—	—	—	—	—	—	—	750	—	—	—	—	—	—	—
Get N kills with the attached Grenade Launcher.	Attachment: Grenade Launcher	20	—	—	—	—	—	—	—	750	—	—	—	—	—	—	—
Get N kills while looking through the ACOG Sight attached to this weapon.	Attachment: ACOG	20	—	—	—	—	—	—	—	750	—	—	—	—	—	—	—
Get N kills with the Heartbeat Sensor attached to this weapon.	Attachment: Heartbeat Sensor	40	—	—	—	—	—	—	—	1000	—	—	—	—	—	—	—

CHALLENGE DESCRIPTION	TITLE	TARGET 1	TARGET 2	TARGET 3	TARGET 4	TARGET 5	TARGET 6	TARGET 7	TARGET 8	XP 1	XP 2	XP 3	XP 4	XP 5	XP 6	XP 7	XP 8
G36C CHALLENGES																	
Get N kills with the Hybrid Sights attached to this weapon.	Attachment: Hybrid Sights	40	—	—	—	—	—	—	—	1000	—	—	—	—	—	—	—
Get N kills with the attached Shotgun.	Attachment: Shotgun	40	—	—	—	—	—	—	—	1000	—	—	—	—	—	—	—
Get N kills while looking through the Holographic Sight attached to this weapon.	Attachment: Holographic Sight	40	—	—	—	—	—	—	—	1000	—	—	—	—	—	—	—
Get N kills using the Extended Mags attachment.	Attachment: Extended Mags	40	—	—	—	—	—	—	—	1000	—	—	—	—	—	—	—
Get N kills while looking through the Thermal Scope attached to this weapon.	Attachment: Thermal	40	—	—	—	—	—	—	—	1000	—	—	—	—	—	—	—
Achieve maximum weapon proficiency with this weapon.	G36C: Mastery	10	—	—	—	—	—	—	—	10000	—	—	—	—	—	—	—
MK 14 CHALLENGES																	
Get N kills with this weapon.	Marksman	10	25	75	150	300	500	750	1000	250	1000	2000	5000	10000	10000	10000	10000
Get N headshots with this weapon.	Expert	5	15	30	75	150	250	350	500	500	1000	2500	5000	10000	10000	10000	10000
Get N kills while looking through the Red Dot Sight attached to this weapon.	Attachment: Reflex Sight	60	—	—	—	—	—	—	—	1000	—	—	—	—	—	—	—
Get N kills with the Silencer attached to this weapon.	Attachment: Silencer	15	—	—	—	—	—	—	—	750	—	—	—	—	—	—	—
Get N kills with the attached Grenade Launcher.	Attachment: Grenade Launcher	20	—	—	—	—	—	—	—	750	—	—	—	—	—	—	—
Get N kills while looking through the ACOG Sight attached to this weapon.	Attachment: ACOG	20	—	—	—	—	—	—	—	750	—	—	—	—	—	—	—
Get N kills using the Rapid Fire attachment.	Attachment: Rapid Fire	40	—	—	—	—	—	—	—	1000	—	—	—	—	—	—	—
Get N kills with the Heartbeat Sensor attached to this weapon.	Attachment: Heartbeat Sensor	40	—	—	—	—	—	—	—	1000	—	—	—	—	—	—	—
Get N kills with the Hybrid Sights attached to this weapon.	Attachment: Hybrid Sights	40	—	—	—	—	—	—	—	1000	—	—	—	—	—	—	—
Get N kills with the attached Shotgun.	Attachment: Shotgun	40	—	—	—	—	—	—	—	1000	—	—	—	—	—	—	—
Get N kills while looking through the Holographic Sight attached to this weapon.	Attachment: Holographic Sight	40	—	—	—	—	—	—	—	1000	—	—	—	—	—	—	—
Get N kills using the Extended Mags attachment.	Attachment: Extended Mags	40	—	—	—	—	—	—	—	1000	—	—	—	—	—	—	—
Get N kills while looking through the Thermal Scope attached to this weapon.	Attachment: Thermal	40	—	—	—	—	—	—	—	1000	—	—	—	—	—	—	—
Achieve maximum weapon proficiency with this weapon.	MK14: Mastery	11	—	—	—	—	—	—	—	10000	—	—	—	—	—	—	—
M16A4 CHALLENGES																	
Get N kills with this weapon.	Marksman	10	25	75	150	300	500	750	1000	250	1000	2000	5000	10000	10000	10000	10000
Get N headshots with this weapon.	Expert	5	15	30	75	150	250	350	500	500	1000	2500	5000	10000	10000	10000	10000
Get N kills while looking through the Red Dot Sight attached to this weapon.	Attachment: Reflex Sight	60	—	—	—	—	—	—	—	1000	—	—	—	—	—	—	—
Get N kills with the Silencer attached to this weapon.	Attachment: Silencer	15	—	—	—	—	—	—	—	750	—	—	—	—	—	—	—
Get N kills with the attached Grenade Launcher.	Attachment: Grenade Launcher	20	—	—	—	—	—	—	—	750	—	—	—	—	—	—	—

Get N kills while looking through the ACOG Sight attached to this weapon.	Attachment: ACOG	20	—	—	—	—	—	—	—	750	—	—	—	—	—	—	—
Get N kills using the Rapid Fire attachment.	Attachment: Rapid Fire	40	—	—	—	—	—	—	—	1000	—	—	—	—	—	—	—
Get N kills with the Heartbeat Sensor attached to this weapon.	Attachment: Heartbeat Sensor	40	—	—	—	—	—	—	—	1000	—	—	—	—	—	—	—
Get N kills with the Hybrid Sights attached to this weapon.	Attachment: Hybrid Sights	40	—	—	—	—	—	—	—	1000	—	—	—	—	—	—	—
Get N kills with the attached Shotgun.	Attachment: Shotgun	40	—	—	—	—	—	—	—	1000	—	—	—	—	—	—	—
Get N kills while looking through the Holographic Sight attached to this weapon.	Attachment: Holographic Sight	40	—	—	—	—	—	—	—	1000	—	—	—	—	—	—	—
Get N kills using the Extended Mags attachment.	Attachment: Extended Mags	40	—	—	—	—	—	—	—	1000	—	—	—	—	—	—	—
Get N kills while looking through the Thermal Scope attached to this weapon.	Attachment: Thermal	40	—	—	—	—	—	—	—	1000	—	—	—	—	—	—	—
Achieve maximum weapon proficiency with this weapon.	M16A4: Mastery	11	—	—	—	—	—	—	—	10000	—	—	—	—	—	—	—

ACR 6.8 CHALLENGES

Get N kills with this weapon.	Marksman	10	25	75	150	300	500	750	1000	250	1000	2000	5000	10000	10000	10000	10000
Get N headshots with this weapon.	Expert	5	15	30	75	150	250	350	500	500	1000	2500	5000	10000	10000	10000	10000
Get N kills while looking through the Red Dot Sight attached to this weapon.	Attachment: Reflex Sight	60	—	—	—	—	—	—	—	1000	—	—	—	—	—	—	—
Get N kills with the Silencer attached to this weapon.	Attachment: Silencer	15	—	—	—	—	—	—	—	750	—	—	—	—	—	—	—
Get N kills with the attached Grenade Launcher.	Attachment: Grenade Launcher	20	—	—	—	—	—	—	—	750	—	—	—	—	—	—	—
Get N kills while looking through the ACOG Sight attached to this weapon.	Attachment: ACOG	20	—	—	—	—	—	—	—	750	—	—	—	—	—	—	—
Get N kills with the Heartbeat Sensor attached to this weapon.	Attachment: Heartbeat Sensor	40	—	—	—	—	—	—	—	1000	—	—	—	—	—	—	—
Get N kills with the Hybrid Sights attached to this weapon.	Attachment: Hybrid Sights	40	—	—	—	—	—	—	—	1000	—	—	—	—	—	—	—
Get N kills with the attached Shotgun.	Attachment: Shotgun	40	—	—	—	—	—	—	—	1000	—	—	—	—	—	—	—
Get N kills while looking through the Holographic Sight attached to this weapon.	Attachment: Holographic Sight	40	—	—	—	—	—	—	—	1000	—	—	—	—	—	—	—
Get N kills using the Extended Mags attachment.	Attachment: Extended Mags	40	—	—	—	—	—	—	—	1000	—	—	—	—	—	—	—
Get N kills while looking through the Thermal Scope attached to this weapon.	Attachment: Thermal	40	—	—	—	—	—	—	—	1000	—	—	—	—	—	—	—
Achieve maximum weapon proficiency with this weapon.	ACR 6.8: Mastery	10	—	—	—	—	—	—	—	10000	—	—	—	—	—	—	—

FAD CHALLENGES

Get N kills with this weapon.	Marksman	10	25	75	150	300	500	750	1000	250	1000	2000	5000	10000	10000	10000	10000
Get N headshots with this weapon.	Expert	5	15	30	75	150	250	350	500	500	1000	2500	5000	10000	10000	10000	10000
Get N kills while looking through the Red Dot Sight attached to this weapon.	Attachment: Reflex Sight	60	—	—	—	—	—	—	—	1000	—	—	—	—	—	—	—

CHALLENGE DESCRIPTION	TITLE	TARGET 1	TARGET 2	TARGET 3	TARGET 4	TARGET 5	TARGET 6	TARGET 7	TARGET 8	XP 1	XP 2	XP 3	XP 4	XP 5	XP 6	XP 7	XP 8
FAD CHALLENGES (continued)																	
Get N kills with the Silencer attached to this weapon.	Attachment: Silencer	15	—	—	—	—	—	—	—	750	—	—	—	—	—	—	—
Get N kills with the attached Grenade Launcher.	Attachment: Grenade Launcher	20	—	—	—	—	—	—	—	750	—	—	—	—	—	—	—
Get N kills while looking through the ACOG Sight attached to this weapon.	Attachment: ACOG	20	—	—	—	—	—	—	—	750	—	—	—	—	—	—	—
Get N kills with the Heartbeat Sensor attached to this weapon.	Attachment: Heartbeat Sensor	40	—	—	—	—	—	—	—	1000	—	—	—	—	—	—	—
Get N kills with the Hybrid Sights attached to this weapon.	Attachment: Hybrid Sights	40	—	—	—	—	—	—	—	1000	—	—	—	—	—	—	—
Get N kills with the attached Shotgun.	Attachment: Shotgun	40	—	—	—	—	—	—	—	1000	—	—	—	—	—	—	—
Get N kills while looking through the Holographic Sight attached to this weapon.	Attachment: Holographic Sight	40	—	—	—	—	—	—	—	1000	—	—	—	—	—	—	—
Get N kills using the Extended Mags attachment.	Attachment: Extended Mags	40	—	—	—	—	—	—	—	1000	—	—	—	—	—	—	—
Get N kills while looking through the Thermal Scope attached to this weapon.	Attachment: Thermal	40	—	—	—	—	—	—	—	1000	—	—	—	—	—	—	—
Achieve maximum weapon proficiency with this weapon.	FAD: Mastery	10	—	—	—	—	—	—	—	10000	—	—	—	—	—	—	—
AK-47 CHALLENGES																	
Get N kills with this weapon.	Marksman	10	25	75	150	300	500	750	1000	250	1000	2000	5000	10000	10000	10000	10000
Get N headshots with this weapon.	Expert	5	15	30	75	150	250	350	500	500	1000	2500	5000	10000	10000	10000	10000
Get N kills while looking through the Red Dot Sight attached to this weapon.	Attachment: Reflex Sight	60	—	—	—	—	—	—	—	1000	—	—	—	—	—	—	—
Get N kills with the Silencer attached to this weapon.	Attachment: Silencer	15	—	—	—	—	—	—	—	750	—	—	—	—	—	—	—
Get N kills with the attached Grenade Launcher.	Attachment: Grenade Launcher	20	—	—	—	—	—	—	—	750	—	—	—	—	—	—	—
Get N kills while looking through the ACOG Sight attached to this weapon.	Attachment: ACOG	20	—	—	—	—	—	—	—	750	—	—	—	—	—	—	—
Get N kills with the Heartbeat Sensor attached to this weapon.	Attachment: Heartbeat Sensor	40	—	—	—	—	—	—	—	1000	—	—	—	—	—	—	—
Get N kills with the Hybrid Sights attached to this weapon.	Attachment: Hybrid Sights	40	—	—	—	—	—	—	—	1000	—	—	—	—	—	—	—
Get N kills with the attached Shotgun.	Attachment: Shotgun	40	—	—	—	—	—	—	—	1000	—	—	—	—	—	—	—
Get N kills while looking through the Holographic Sight attached to this weapon.	Attachment: Holographic Sight	40	—	—	—	—	—	—	—	1000	—	—	—	—	—	—	—
Get N kills using the Extended Mags attachment.	Attachment: Extended Mags	40	—	—	—	—	—	—	—	1000	—	—	—	—	—	—	—
Get N kills while looking through the Thermal Scope attached to this weapon.	Attachment: Thermal	40	—	—	—	—	—	—	—	1000	—	—	—	—	—	—	—
Achieve maximum weapon proficiency with this weapon.	AK-47: Mastery	10	—	—	—	—	—	—	—	10000	—	—	—	—	—	—	—
CM901 CHALLENGES																	
Get N kills with this weapon.	Marksman	10	25	75	150	300	500	750	1000	250	1000	2000	5000	10000	10000	10000	10000
Get N headshots with this weapon.	Expert	5	15	30	75	150	250	350	500	500	1000	2500	5000	10000	10000	10000	10000

CHALLENGE DESCRIPTION	TITLE	TARGET 1	TARGET 2	TARGET 3	TARGET 4	TARGET 5	TARGET 6	TARGET 7	TARGET 8	XP 1	XP 2	XP 3	XP 4	XP 5	XP 6	XP 7	XP 8
Get N kills while looking through the Red Dot Sight attached to this weapon.	Attachment: Reflex Sight	60	—	—	—	—	—	—	—	1000	—	—	—	—	—	—	—
Get N kills with the Silencer attached to this weapon.	Attachment: Silencer	15	—	—	—	—	—	—	—	750	—	—	—	—	—	—	—
Get N kills with the attached Grenade Launcher.	Attachment: Grenade Launcher	20	—	—	—	—	—	—	—	750	—	—	—	—	—	—	—
Get N kills while looking through the ACOG Sight attached to this weapon.	Attachment: ACOG	20	—	—	—	—	—	—	—	750	—	—	—	—	—	—	—
Get N kills with the Heartbeat Sensor attached to this weapon.	Attachment: Heartbeat Sensor	40	—	—	—	—	—	—	—	1000	—	—	—	—	—	—	—
Get N kills with the Hybrid Sights attached to this weapon.	Attachment: Hybrid Sights	40	—	—	—	—	—	—	—	1000	—	—	—	—	—	—	—
Get N kills with the attached Shotgun.	Attachment: Shotgun	40	—	—	—	—	—	—	—	1000	—	—	—	—	—	—	—
Get N kills while looking through the Holographic Sight attached to this weapon.	Attachment: Holographic Sight	40	—	—	—	—	—	—	—	1000	—	—	—	—	—	—	—
Get N kills using the Extended Mags attachment.	Attachment: Extended Mags	40	—	—	—	—	—	—	—	1000	—	—	—	—	—	—	—
Get N kills while looking through the Thermal Scope attached to this weapon.	Attachment: Thermal	40	—	—	—	—	—	—	—	1000	—	—	—	—	—	—	—
Achieve maximum weapon proficiency with this weapon.	CM901: Mastery	10	—	—	—	—	—	—	—	10000	—	—	—	—	—	—	—

SUBMACHINE GUN CHALLENGES

CHALLENGE DESCRIPTION	TITLE	TARGET 1	TARGET 2	TARGET 3	TARGET 4	TARGET 5	TARGET 6	TARGET 7	TARGET 8	XP 1	XP 2	XP 3	XP 4	XP 5	XP 6	XP 7	XP 8
MP5 CHALLENGES																	
Get N kills with this weapon.	Marksman	10	25	75	150	300	500	750	1000	500	1000	2000	5000	10000	10000	10000	10000
Get N headshots with this weapon.	Expert	5	15	30	75	150	250	350	500	500	1000	2500	5000	10000	10000	10000	10000
Get N kills while looking through the Red Dot Sight attached to this weapon.	Attachment: Reflex Sight	60	—	—	—	—	—	—	—	1000	—	—	—	—	—	—	—
Get N kills with the Silencer attached to this weapon.	Attachment: Silencer	60	—	—	—	—	—	—	—	1000	—	—	—	—	—	—	—
Get N kills using the Rapid Fire attachment.	Attachment: Rapid Fire	30	—	—	—	—	—	—	—	1000	—	—	—	—	—	—	—
Get N kills while looking through the ACOG Sight attached to this weapon.	Attachment: ACOG	20	—	—	—	—	—	—	—	750	—	—	—	—	—	—	—
Get N kills with the HAMR Scope attached to this weapon.	Attachment: HAMR Sight	40	—	—	—	—	—	—	—	1000	—	—	—	—	—	—	—
Get N kills while looking through the Holographic Sight attached to this weapon.	Attachment: Holographic Sight	20	—	—	—	—	—	—	—	750	—	—	—	—	—	—	—
Get N kills using the Extended Mags attachment.	Attachment: Extended Mags	40	—	—	—	—	—	—	—	1000	—	—	—	—	—	—	—
Get N kills while looking through the Thermal Scope attached to this weapon.	Attachment: Thermal	40	—	—	—	—	—	—	—	1000	—	—	—	—	—	—	—
Achieve maximum weapon proficiency with this weapon.	MP5: Mastery	8	—	—	—	—	—	—	—	10000	—	—	—	—	—	—	—

CHALLENGE DESCRIPTION	TITLE	TARGET 1	TARGET 2	TARGET 3	TARGET 4	TARGET 5	TARGET 6	TARGET 7	TARGET 8	XP 1	XP 2	XP 3	XP 4	XP 5	XP 6	XP 7	XP 8
UMP45 CHALLENGES																	
Get N kills with this weapon.	Marksman	10	25	75	150	300	500	750	1000	500	1000	2000	5000	10000	10000	10000	10000
Get N headshots with this weapon.	Expert	5	15	30	75	150	250	350	500	500	1000	2500	5000	10000	10000	10000	10000
Get N kills while looking through the Red Dot Sight attached to this weapon.	Attachment: Reflex Sight	60	—	—	—	—	—	—	—	1000	—	—	—	—	—	—	—
Get N kills with the Silencer attached to this weapon.	Attachment: Silencer	60	—	—	—	—	—	—	—	1000	—	—	—	—	—	—	—
Get N kills using the Rapid Fire attachment.	Attachment: Rapid Fire	30	—	—	—	—	—	—	—	1000	—	—	—	—	—	—	—
Get N kills while looking through the ACOG Sight attached to this weapon.	Attachment: ACOG	20	—	—	—	—	—	—	—	750	—	—	—	—	—	—	—
Get N kills with the HAMR Scope attached to this weapon.	Attachment: HAMR Sight	40	—	—	—	—	—	—	—	1000	—	—	—	—	—	—	—
Get N kills while looking through the Holographic Sight attached to this weapon.	Attachment: Holographic Sight	20	—	—	—	—	—	—	—	750	—	—	—	—	—	—	—
Get N kills using the Extended Mags attachment.	Attachment: Extended Mags	40	—	—	—	—	—	—	—	1000	—	—	—	—	—	—	—
Get N kills while looking through the Thermal Scope attached to this weapon.	Attachment: Thermal	40	—	—	—	—	—	—	—	1000	—	—	—	—	—	—	—
Achieve maximum weapon proficiency with this weapon.	UMP45: Mastery	8	—	—	—	—	—	—	—	10000	—	—	—	—	—	—	—
PP90M1 CHALLENGES																	
Get N kills with this weapon.	Marksman	10	25	75	150	300	500	750	1000	500	1000	2000	5000	10000	10000	10000	10000
Get N headshots with this weapon.	Expert	5	15	30	75	150	250	350	500	500	1000	2500	5000	10000	10000	10000	10000
Get N kills while looking through the Red Dot Sight attached to this weapon.	Attachment: Reflex Sight	60	—	—	—	—	—	—	—	1000	—	—	—	—	—	—	—
Get N kills with the Silencer attached to this weapon.	Attachment: Silencer	60	—	—	—	—	—	—	—	1000	—	—	—	—	—	—	—
Get N kills using the Rapid Fire attachment.	Attachment: Rapid Fire	30	—	—	—	—	—	—	—	1000	—	—	—	—	—	—	—
Get N kills while looking through the ACOG Sight attached to this weapon.	Attachment: ACOG	20	—	—	—	—	—	—	—	750	—	—	—	—	—	—	—
Get N kills with the HAMR Scope attached to this weapon.	Attachment: HAMR Sight	40	—	—	—	—	—	—	—	1000	—	—	—	—	—	—	—
Get N kills while looking through the Holographic Sight attached to this weapon.	Attachment: Holographic Sight	20	—	—	—	—	—	—	—	750	—	—	—	—	—	—	—
Get N kills using the Extended Mags attachment.	Attachment: Extended Mags	40	—	—	—	—	—	—	—	1000	—	—	—	—	—	—	—
Get N kills while looking through the Thermal Scope attached to this weapon.	Attachment: Thermal	40	—	—	—	—	—	—	—	1000	—	—	—	—	—	—	—
Achieve maximum weapon proficiency with this weapon.	PP90M1: Mastery	8	—	—	—	—	—	—	—	10000	—	—	—	—	—	—	—
P90 CHALLENGES																	
Get N kills with this weapon.	Marksman	10	25	75	150	300	500	750	1000	500	1000	2000	5000	10000	10000	10000	10000
Get N headshots with this weapon.	Expert	5	15	30	75	150	250	350	500	500	1000	2500	5000	10000	10000	10000	10000
Get N kills while looking through the Red Dot Sight attached to this weapon.	Attachment: Reflex Sight	60	—	—	—	—	—	—	—	1000	—	—	—	—	—	—	—

CHALLENGE DESCRIPTION	TITLE	TARGET 1	TARGET 2	TARGET 3	TARGET 4	TARGET 5	TARGET 6	TARGET 7	TARGET 8	XP 1	XP 2	XP 3	XP 4	XP 5	XP 6	XP 7	XP 8
Get N kills with the Silencer attached to this weapon.	Attachment: Silencer	60	—	—	—	—	—	—	—	1000	—	—	—	—	—	—	—
Get N kills using the Rapid Fire attachment.	Attachment: Rapid Fire	30	—	—	—	—	—	—	—	1000	—	—	—	—	—	—	—
Get N kills while looking through the ACOG Sight attached to this weapon.	Attachment: ACOG	20	—	—	—	—	—	—	—	750	—	—	—	—	—	—	—
Get N kills with the HAMR Scope attached to this weapon.	Attachment: HAMR Sight	40	—	—	—	—	—	—	—	1000	—	—	—	—	—	—	—
Get N kills while looking through the Holographic Sight attached to this weapon.	Attachment: Holographic Sight	20	—	—	—	—	—	—	—	750	—	—	—	—	—	—	—
Get N kills using the Extended Mags attachment.	Attachment: Extended Mags	40	—	—	—	—	—	—	—	1000	—	—	—	—	—	—	—
Get N kills while looking through the Thermal Scope attached to this weapon.	Attachment: Thermal	40	—	—	—	—	—	—	—	1000	—	—	—	—	—	—	—
Achieve maximum weapon proficiency with this weapon.	P90: Mastery	8	—	—	—	—	—	—	—	10000	—	—	—	—	—	—	—
PM-9 CHALLENGES																	
Get N kills with this weapon.	Marksman	10	25	75	150	300	500	750	1000	500	1000	2000	5000	10000	10000	10000	10000
Get N headshots with this weapon.	Expert	5	15	30	75	150	250	350	500	500	1000	2500	5000	10000	10000	10000	10000
Get N kills while looking through the Red Dot Sight attached to this weapon.	Attachment: Reflex Sight	60	—	—	—	—	—	—	—	1000	—	—	—	—	—	—	—
Get N kills with the Silencer attached to this weapon.	Attachment: Silencer	60	—	—	—	—	—	—	—	1000	—	—	—	—	—	—	—
Get N kills using the Rapid Fire attachment.	Attachment: Rapid Fire	30	—	—	—	—	—	—	—	1000	—	—	—	—	—	—	—
Get N kills while looking through the ACOG Sight attached to this weapon.	Attachment: ACOG	20	—	—	—	—	—	—	—	750	—	—	—	—	—	—	—
Get N kills with the HAMR Scope attached to this weapon.	Attachment: HAMR Sight	40	—	—	—	—	—	—	—	1000	—	—	—	—	—	—	—
Get N kills while looking through the Holographic Sight attached to this weapon.	Attachment: Holographic Sight	20	—	—	—	—	—	—	—	750	—	—	—	—	—	—	—
Get N kills using the Extended Mags attachment.	Attachment: Extended Mags	40	—	—	—	—	—	—	—	1000	—	—	—	—	—	—	—
Get N kills while looking through the Thermal Scope attached to this weapon.	Attachment: Thermal	40	—	—	—	—	—	—	—	1000	—	—	—	—	—	—	—
Achieve maximum weapon proficiency with this weapon.	PM-9: Mastery	8	—	—	—	—	—	—	—	10000	—	—	—	—	—	—	—
MP7 CHALLENGES																	
Get N kills with this weapon.	Marksman	10	25	75	150	300	500	750	1000	500	1000	2000	5000	10000	10000	10000	10000
Get N headshots with this weapon.	Expert	5	15	30	75	150	250	350	500	500	1000	2500	5000	10000	10000	10000	10000
Get N kills while looking through the Red Dot Sight attached to this weapon.	Attachment: Reflex Sight	60	—	—	—	—	—	—	—	1000	—	—	—	—	—	—	—
Get N kills with the Silencer attached to this weapon.	Attachment: Silencer	60	—	—	—	—	—	—	—	1000	—	—	—	—	—	—	—
Get N kills using the Rapid Fire attachment.	Attachment: Rapid Fire	30	—	—	—	—	—	—	—	1000	—	—	—	—	—	—	—
Get N kills while looking through the ACOG Sight attached to this weapon.	Attachment: ACOG	20	—	—	—	—	—	—	—	750	—	—	—	—	—	—	—

CHALLENGE DESCRIPTION	TITLE	TARGET 1	TARGET 2	TARGET 3	TARGET 4	TARGET 5	TARGET 6	TARGET 7	TARGET 8	XP 1	XP 2	XP 3	XP 4	XP 5	XP 6	XP 7	XP 8
MP7 CHALLENGES (continued)																	
Get N kills with the HAMR Scope attached to this weapon.	Attachment: HAMR Sight	40	—	—	—	—	—	—	—	1000	—	—	—	—	—	—	—
Get N kills while looking through the Holographic Sight attached to this weapon.	Attachment: Holographic Sight	20	—	—	—	—	—	—	—	750	—	—	—	—	—	—	—
Get N kills using the Extended Mags attachment.	Attachment: Extended Mags	40	—	—	—	—	—	—	—	1000	—	—	—	—	—	—	—
Get N kills while looking through the Thermal Scope attached to this weapon.	Attachment: Thermal	40	—	—	—	—	—	—	—	1000	—	—	—	—	—	—	—
Achieve maximum weapon proficiency with this weapon.	MP7: Mastery	8	—	—	—	—	—	—	—	10000	—	—	—	—	—	—	—

SHOTGUN CHALLENGES

CHALLENGE DESCRIPTION	TITLE	TARGET 1	TARGET 2	TARGET 3	TARGET 4	TARGET 5	TARGET 6	TARGET 7	TARGET 8	XP 1	XP 2	XP 3	XP 4	XP 5	XP 6	XP 7	XP 8
SPAS-12 CHALLENGES																	
Get N kills with this weapon.	Marksman	10	25	75	150	250	400	500	1000	500	1000	2500	5000	10000	10000	10000	10000
Get N headshots with this weapon.	Expert	5	10	20	40	100	200	350	500	500	1000	2500	5000	10000	10000	10000	10000
Get N kills using the Grip attachment.	Attachment: Grip	20	—	—	—	—	—	—	—	750	—	—	—	—	—	—	—
Get N kills with the Silencer attached to this weapon.	Attachment: Silencer	15	—	—	—	—	—	—	—	750	—	—	—	—	—	—	—
Get N kills while looking through the Red Dot Sight attached to this weapon.	Attachment: Reflex Sight	60	—	—	—	—	—	—	—	1000	—	—	—	—	—	—	—
Get N kills while looking through the Holographic Sight attached to this weapon.	Attachment: Holographic Sight	40	—	—	—	—	—	—	—	1000	—	—	—	—	—	—	—
Get N kills using the Extended Mags attachment.	Attachment: Extended Mags	40	—	—	—	—	—	—	—	1000	—	—	—	—	—	—	—
Achieve maximum weapon proficiency with this weapon.	SPAS-12: Mastery	5	—	—	—	—	—	—	—	10000	—	—	—	—	—	—	—
KSG 12 CHALLENGES																	
Get N kills with this weapon.	Marksman	10	25	75	150	250	400	500	1000	500	1000	2500	5000	10000	10000	10000	10000
Get N headshots with this weapon.	Expert	5	10	20	40	100	200	350	500	500	1000	2500	5000	10000	10000	10000	10000
Get N kills using the Grip attachment.	Attachment: Grip	20	—	—	—	—	—	—	—	750	—	—	—	—	—	—	—
Get N kills with the Silencer attached to this weapon.	Attachment: Silencer	15	—	—	—	—	—	—	—	750	—	—	—	—	—	—	—
Get N kills while looking through the Red Dot Sight attached to this weapon.	Attachment: Reflex Sight	60	—	—	—	—	—	—	—	1000	—	—	—	—	—	—	—
Get N kills while looking through the Holographic Sight attached to this weapon.	Attachment: Holographic Sight	40	—	—	—	—	—	—	—	1000	—	—	—	—	—	—	—
Get N kills using the Extended Mags attachment.	Attachment: Extended Mags	40	—	—	—	—	—	—	—	1000	—	—	—	—	—	—	—
Achieve maximum weapon proficiency with this weapon.	KSG 12: Mastery	5	—	—	—	—	—	—	—	10000	—	—	—	—	—	—	—

CHALLENGE DESCRIPTION	TITLE	TARGET 1	TARGET 2	TARGET 3	TARGET 4	TARGET 5	TARGET 6	TARGET 7	TARGET 8	XP 1	XP 2	XP 3	XP 4	XP 5	XP 6	XP 7	XP 8
AA12 CHALLENGES																	
Get N kills with this weapon.	Marksman	10	25	75	150	250	400	500	1000	500	1000	2500	5000	10000	10000	10000	10000
Get N headshots with this weapon.	Expert	5	10	20	40	100	200	350	500	500	1000	2500	5000	10000	10000	10000	10000
Get N kills using the Grip attachment.	Attachment: Grip	20	—	—	—	—	—	—	—	750	—	—	—	—	—	—	—
Get N kills with the Silencer attached to this weapon.	Attachment: Silencer	15	—	—	—	—	—	—	—	750	—	—	—	—	—	—	—
Get N kills while looking through the Red Dot Sight attached to this weapon.	Attachment: Reflex Sight	60	—	—	—	—	—	—	—	1000	—	—	—	—	—	—	—
Get N kills while looking through the Holographic Sight attached to this weapon.	Attachment: Holographic Sight	40	—	—	—	—	—	—	—	1000	—	—	—	—	—	—	—
Get N kills using the Extended Mags attachment.	Attachment: Extended Mags	40	—	—	—	—	—	—	—	1000	—	—	—	—	—	—	—
Achieve maximum weapon proficiency with this weapon.	AA-12: Mastery	5	—	—	—	—	—	—	—	10000	—	—	—	—	—	—	—
STRIKER CHALLENGES																	
Get N kills with this weapon.	Marksman	10	25	75	150	250	400	500	1000	500	1000	2500	5000	10000	10000	10000	10000
Get N headshots with this weapon.	Expert	5	10	20	40	100	200	350	500	500	1000	2500	5000	10000	10000	10000	10000
Get N kills using the Grip attachment.	Attachment: Grip	20	—	—	—	—	—	—	—	750	—	—	—	—	—	—	—
Get N kills with the Silencer attached to this weapon.	Attachment: Silencer	15	—	—	—	—	—	—	—	750	—	—	—	—	—	—	—
Get N kills while looking through the Red Dot Sight attached to this weapon.	Attachment: Reflex Sight	60	—	—	—	—	—	—	—	1000	—	—	—	—	—	—	—
Get N kills while looking through the Holographic Sight attached to this weapon.	Attachment: Holographic Sight	40	—	—	—	—	—	—	—	1000	—	—	—	—	—	—	—
Get N kills using the Extended Mags attachment.	Attachment: Extended Mags	40	—	—	—	—	—	—	—	1000	—	—	—	—	—	—	—
Achieve maximum weapon proficiency with this weapon.	Striker: Mastery	5	—	—	—	—	—	—	—	10000	—	—	—	—	—	—	—
USAS 12 CHALLENGES																	
Get N kills with this weapon.	Marksman	10	50	300	1000	2500	—	—	—	500	1500	10000	10000	10000	—	—	—
Get N headshots with this weapon.	Expert	5	10	20	40	100	200	350	500	500	1000	2500	5000	10000	10000	10000	10000
Get N kills using the Grip attachment.	Attachment: Grip	20	—	—	—	—	—	—	—	750	—	—	—	—	—	—	—
Get N kills with the Silencer attached to this weapon.	Attachment: Silencer	15	—	—	—	—	—	—	—	750	—	—	—	—	—	—	—
Get N kills while looking through the Red Dot Sight attached to this weapon.	Attachment: Reflex Sight	60	—	—	—	—	—	—	—	1000	—	—	—	—	—	—	—
Get N kills while looking through the Holographic Sight attached to this weapon.	Attachment: Holographic Sight	40	—	—	—	—	—	—	—	1000	—	—	—	—	—	—	—
Get N kills using the Extended Mags attachment.	Attachment: Extended Mags	40	—	—	—	—	—	—	—	1000	—	—	—	—	—	—	—
Achieve maximum weapon proficiency with this weapon.	USAS 12: Mastery	5	—	—	—	—	—	—	—	10000	—	—	—	—	—	—	—
MODEL 1887 CHALLENGES																	
Get N kills with this weapon.	Marksman	10	50	300	1000	2500	—	—	—	500	1500	10000	10000	10000	—	—	—
Get N headshots with this weapon.	Expert	5	10	20	40	100	200	350	500	500	1000	2500	5000	10000	10000	10000	10000

CHALLENGE DESCRIPTION	TITLE	TARGET 1	TARGET 2	TARGET 3	TARGET 4	TARGET 5	TARGET 6	TARGET 7	TARGET 8	XP 1	XP 2	XP 3	XP 4	XP 5	XP 6	XP 7	XP 8
L86 LSW CHALLENGES																	
Get N kills with this weapon.	Marksman	10	25	75	150	300	500	750	1000	500	1000	2000	5000	10000	10000	10000	10000
Get N headshots with this weapon.	Expert	5	15	30	75	150	250	350	500	500	1000	2500	5000	10000	10000	10000	10000
Get N kills while looking through the Red Dot Sight attached to this weapon.	Attachment: Reflex Sight	60	—	—	—	—	—	—	—	1000	—	—	—	—	—	—	—
Get N kills with the Silencer attached to this weapon.	Attachment: Silencer	15	—	—	—	—	—	—	—	750	—	—	—	—	—	—	—
Get N kills using the Grip attachment.	Attachment: Grip	60	—	—	—	—	—	—	—	1000	—	—	—	—	—	—	—
Get N kills while looking through the ACOG Sight attached to this weapon.	Attachment: ACOG	20	—	—	—	—	—	—	—	750	—	—	—	—	—	—	—
Get N kills using the Rapid Fire attachment.	Attachment: Rapid Fire	40	—	—	—	—	—	—	—	1000	—	—	—	—	—	—	—
Get N kills with the Heartbeat Sensor attached to this weapon.	Attachment: Heartbeat Sensor	40	—	—	—	—	—	—	—	1000	—	—	—	—	—	—	—
Get N kills while looking through the Holographic Sight attached to this weapon.	Attachment: Holographic Sight	40	—	—	—	—	—	—	—	1000	—	—	—	—	—	—	—
Get N kills using the Extended Mags attachment.	Attachment: Extended Mags	40	—	—	—	—	—	—	—	1000	—	—	—	—	—	—	—
Get N kills while looking through the Thermal Scope attached to this weapon.	Attachment: Thermal	40	—	—	—	—	—	—	—	1000	—	—	—	—	—	—	—
Achieve maximum weapon proficiency with this weapon.	L86 LSW: Mastery	9	—	—	—	—	—	—	—	10000	—	—	—	—	—	—	—
MG36 CHALLENGES																	
Get N kills with this weapon.	Marksman	10	25	75	150	300	500	750	1000	500	1000	2000	5000	10000	10000	10000	10000
Get N headshots with this weapon.	Expert	5	15	30	75	150	250	350	500	500	1000	2500	5000	10000	10000	10000	10000
Get N kills while looking through the Red Dot Sight attached to this weapon.	Attachment: Reflex Sight	60	—	—	—	—	—	—	—	1000	—	—	—	—	—	—	—
Get N kills with the Silencer attached to this weapon.	Attachment: Silencer	15	—	—	—	—	—	—	—	750	—	—	—	—	—	—	—
Get N kills using the Grip attachment.	Attachment: Grip	60	—	—	—	—	—	—	—	1000	—	—	—	—	—	—	—
Get N kills while looking through the ACOG Sight attached to this weapon.	Attachment: ACOG	20	—	—	—	—	—	—	—	750	—	—	—	—	—	—	—
Get N kills using the Rapid Fire attachment.	Attachment: Rapid Fire	40	—	—	—	—	—	—	—	1000	—	—	—	—	—	—	—
Get N kills with the Heartbeat Sensor attached to this weapon.	Attachment: Heartbeat Sensor	40	—	—	—	—	—	—	—	1000	—	—	—	—	—	—	—
Get N kills while looking through the Holographic Sight attached to this weapon.	Attachment: Holographic Sight	40	—	—	—	—	—	—	—	1000	—	—	—	—	—	—	—
Get N kills using the Extended Mags attachment.	Attachment: Extended Mags	40	—	—	—	—	—	—	—	1000	—	—	—	—	—	—	—
Get N kills while looking through the Thermal Scope attached to this weapon.	Attachment: Thermal	40	—	—	—	—	—	—	—	1000	—	—	—	—	—	—	—
Achieve maximum weapon proficiency with this weapon.	MG36: Mastery	9	—	—	—	—	—	—	—	10000	—	—	—	—	—	—	—

CHALLENGE DESCRIPTION	TITLE	TARGET 1	TARGET 2	TARGET 3	TARGET 4	TARGET 5	TARGET 6	TARGET 7	TARGET 8	XP 1	XP 2	XP 3	XP 4	XP 5	XP 6	XP 7	XP 8
MK46 CHALLENGES																	
Get N kills with this weapon.	Marksman	10	25	75	150	300	500	750	1000	500	1000	2000	5000	10000	10000	10000	10000
Get N headshots with this weapon.	Expert	5	15	30	75	150	250	350	500	500	1000	2500	5000	10000	10000	10000	10000
Get N kills while looking through the Red Dot Sight attached to this weapon.	Attachment: Reflex Sight	60	—	—	—	—	—	—	—	1000	—	—	—	—	—	—	—
Get N kills with the Silencer attached to this weapon.	Attachment: Silencer	15	—	—	—	—	—	—	—	750	—	—	—	—	—	—	—
Get N kills using the Grip attachment.	Attachment: Grip	60	—	—	—	—	—	—	—	1000	—	—	—	—	—	—	—
Get N kills while looking through the ACOG Sight attached to this weapon.	Attachment: ACOG	20	—	—	—	—	—	—	—	750	—	—	—	—	—	—	—
Get N kills using the Rapid Fire attachment.	Attachment: Rapid Fire	40	—	—	—	—	—	—	—	1000	—	—	—	—	—	—	—
Get N kills with the Heartbeat Sensor attached to this weapon.	Attachment: Heartbeat Sensor	40	—	—	—	—	—	—	—	1000	—	—	—	—	—	—	—
Get N kills while looking through the Holographic Sight attached to this weapon.	Attachment: Holographic Sight	40	—	—	—	—	—	—	—	1000	—	—	—	—	—	—	—
Get N kills using the Extended Mags attachment.	Attachment: Extended Mags	40	—	—	—	—	—	—	—	1000	—	—	—	—	—	—	—
Get N kills while looking through the Thermal Scope attached to this weapon.	Attachment: Thermal	40	—	—	—	—	—	—	—	1000	—	—	—	—	—	—	—
Achieve maximum weapon proficiency with this weapon.	MK46: Mastery	9	—	—	—	—	—	—	—	10000	—	—	—	—	—	—	—
PKP PECHENEG CHALLENGES																	
Get N kills with this weapon.	Marksman	10	25	75	150	300	500	750	1000	500	1000	2000	5000	10000	10000	10000	10000
Get N headshots with this weapon.	Expert	5	15	30	75	150	250	350	500	500	1000	2500	5000	10000	10000	10000	10000
Get N kills while looking through the Red Dot Sight attached to this weapon.	Attachment: Reflex Sight	60	—	—	—	—	—	—	—	1000	—	—	—	—	—	—	—
Get N kills with the Silencer attached to this weapon.	Attachment: Silencer	15	—	—	—	—	—	—	—	750	—	—	—	—	—	—	—
Get N kills using the Grip attachment.	Attachment: Grip	60	—	—	—	—	—	—	—	1000	—	—	—	—	—	—	—
Get N kills while looking through the ACOG Sight attached to this weapon.	Attachment: ACOG	20	—	—	—	—	—	—	—	750	—	—	—	—	—	—	—
Get N kills using the Rapid Fire attachment.	Attachment: Rapid Fire	40	—	—	—	—	—	—	—	1000	—	—	—	—	—	—	—
Get N kills while looking through the Holographic Sight attached to this weapon.	Attachment: Holographic Sight	40	—	—	—	—	—	—	—	1000	—	—	—	—	—	—	—
Get N kills using the Extended Mags attachment.	Attachment: Extended Mags	40	—	—	—	—	—	—	—	1000	—	—	—	—	—	—	—
Get N kills while looking through the Thermal Scope attached to this weapon.	Attachment: Thermal	40	—	—	—	—	—	—	—	1000	—	—	—	—	—	—	—
Achieve maximum weapon proficiency with this weapon.	PKP Pecheneg: Mastery	8	—	—	—	—	—	—	—	10000	—	—	—	—	—	—	—

CHALLENGE DESCRIPTION	TITLE	TARGET 1	TARGET 2	TARGET 3	TARGET 4	TARGET 5	TARGET 6	TARGET 7	TARGET 8	XP 1	XP 2	XP 3	XP 4	XP 5	XP 6	XP 7	XP 8
M60E4 CHALLENGES																	
Get N kills with this weapon.	Marksman	10	25	75	150	300	500	750	1000	500	1000	2000	5000	10000	10000	10000	10000
Get N headshots with this weapon.	Expert	5	15	30	75	150	250	350	500	500	1000	2500	5000	10000	10000	10000	10000
Get N kills while looking through the Red Dot Sight attached to this weapon.	Attachment: Reflex Sight	60	—	—	—	—	—	—	—	1000	—	—	—	—	—	—	—
Get N kills with the Silencer attached to this weapon.	Attachment: Silencer	15	—	—	—	—	—	—	—	750	—	—	—	—	—	—	—
Get N kills using the Grip attachment.	Attachment: Grip	60	—	—	—	—	—	—	—	1000	—	—	—	—	—	—	—
Get N kills while looking through the ACOG Sight attached to this weapon.	Attachment: ACOG	20	—	—	—	—	—	—	—	750	—	—	—	—	—	—	—
Get N kills using the Rapid Fire attachment.	Attachment: Rapid Fire	40	—	—	—	—	—	—	—	1000	—	—	—	—	—	—	—
Get N kills while looking through the Holographic Sight attached to this weapon.	Attachment: Holographic Sight	40	—	—	—	—	—	—	—	1000	—	—	—	—	—	—	—
Get N kills using the Extended Mags attachment.	Attachment: Extended Mags	40	—	—	—	—	—	—	—	1000	—	—	—	—	—	—	—
Get N kills while looking through the Thermal Scope attached to this weapon.	Attachment: Thermal	40	—	—	—	—	—	—	—	1000	—	—	—	—	—	—	—
Achieve maximum weapon proficiency with this weapon.	M60E4: Mastery	8	—	—	—	—	—	—	—	10000	—	—	—	—	—	—	—

SNIPER CHALLENGES

CHALLENGE DESCRIPTION	TITLE	TARGET 1	TARGET 2	TARGET 3	TARGET 4	TARGET 5	TARGET 6	TARGET 7	TARGET 8	XP 1	XP 2	XP 3	XP 4	XP 5	XP 6	XP 7	XP 8
MSR CHALLENGES																	
Get N kills with this weapon.	Marksman	10	25	75	150	300	500	750	1000	250	1000	2000	5000	10000	10000	10000	10000
Get N headshots with this weapon.	Expert	5	15	30	75	150	250	350	500	500	1000	2500	5000	10000	10000	10000	10000
Get N kills while looking through the ACOG Sight attached to this weapon.	Attachment: ACOG	20	—	—	—	—	—	—	—	750	—	—	—	—	—	—	—
Get N kills with the Silencer attached to this weapon.	Attachment: Silencer	15	—	—	—	—	—	—	—	750	—	—	—	—	—	—	—
Get N kills while looking through the Thermal Scope attached to this weapon.	Attachment: Thermal	40	—	—	—	—	—	—	—	1000	—	—	—	—	—	—	—
Get N kills using the Extended Mags attachment.	Attachment: Extended Mags	40	—	—	—	—	—	—	—	1000	—	—	—	—	—	—	—
Get N kills with the Heartbeat Sensor attached to this weapon.	Attachment: Heartbeat Sensor	40	—	—	—	—	—	—	—	1000	—	—	—	—	—	—	—
Get N kills while looking through the Variable Zoom Scope attached to this weapon.	Attachment: Variable Zoom Scope	40	—	—	—	—	—	—	—	1000	—	—	—	—	—	—	—
Achieve maximum weapon proficiency with this weapon.	MSR: Mastery	6	—	—	—	—	—	—	—	10000	—	—	—	—	—	—	—
L118A CHALLENGES																	
Get N kills with this weapon.	Marksman	10	25	75	150	300	500	750	1000	250	1000	2000	5000	10000	10000	10000	10000
Get N headshots with this weapon.	Expert	5	15	30	75	150	250	350	500	500	1000	2500	5000	10000	10000	10000	10000
Get N kills while looking through the ACOG Sight attached to this weapon.	Attachment: ACOG	20	—	—	—	—	—	—	—	750	—	—	—	—	—	—	—

CHALLENGE DESCRIPTION	TITLE	TARGET 1	TARGET 2	TARGET 3	TARGET 4	TARGET 5	TARGET 6	TARGET 7	TARGET 8	XP 1	XP 2	XP 3	XP 4	XP 5	XP 6	XP 7	XP 8
Get N kills with the Silencer attached to this weapon.	Attachment: Silencer	15	—	—	—	—	—	—	—	750	—	—	—	—	—	—	—
Get N kills while looking through the Thermal Scope attached to this weapon.	Attachment: Thermal	40	—	—	—	—	—	—	—	1000	—	—	—	—	—	—	—
Get N kills using the Extended Mags attachment.	Attachment: Extended Mags	40	—	—	—	—	—	—	—	1000	—	—	—	—	—	—	—
Get N kills with the Heartbeat Sensor attached to this weapon.	Attachment: Heartbeat Sensor	40	—	—	—	—	—	—	—	1000	—	—	—	—	—	—	—
Get N kills while looking through the Variable Zoom Scope attached to this weapon.	Attachment: Variable Zoom Scope	40	—	—	—	—	—	—	—	1000	—	—	—	—	—	—	—
Achieve maximum weapon proficiency with this weapon.	L118A: Mastery	6	—	—	—	—	—	—	—	10000	—	—	—	—	—	—	—
BARRETT .50CAL CHALLENGES																	
Get N kills with this weapon.	Marksman	10	25	75	150	300	500	750	1000	250	1000	2000	5000	10000	10000	10000	10000
Get N headshots with this weapon.	Expert	5	15	30	75	150	250	350	500	500	1000	2500	5000	10000	10000	10000	10000
Get N kills while looking through the ACOG Sight attached to this weapon.	Attachment: ACOG	20	—	—	—	—	—	—	—	750	—	—	—	—	—	—	—
Get N kills with the Silencer attached to this weapon.	Attachment: Silencer	15	—	—	—	—	—	—	—	750	—	—	—	—	—	—	—
Get N kills while looking through the Thermal Scope attached to this weapon.	Attachment: Thermal	40	—	—	—	—	—	—	—	1000	—	—	—	—	—	—	—
Get N kills using the Extended Mags attachment.	Attachment: Extended Mags	40	—	—	—	—	—	—	—	1000	—	—	—	—	—	—	—
Get N kills with the Heartbeat Sensor attached to this weapon.	Attachment: Heartbeat Sensor	40	—	—	—	—	—	—	—	1000	—	—	—	—	—	—	—
Get N kills while looking through the Variable Zoom Scope attached to this weapon.	Attachment: Variable Zoom Scope	40	—	—	—	—	—	—	—	1000	—	—	—	—	—	—	—
Achieve maximum weapon proficiency with this weapon.	Barrett .50cal: Mastery	6	—	—	—	—	—	—	—	10000	—	—	—	—	—	—	—
RSASS CHALLENGES																	
Get N kills with this weapon.	Marksman	10	25	75	150	300	500	750	1000	250	1000	2000	5000	10000	10000	10000	10000
Get N headshots with this weapon.	Expert	5	15	30	75	150	250	350	500	500	1000	2500	5000	10000	10000	10000	10000
Get N kills while looking through the ACOG Sight attached to this weapon.	Attachment: ACOG	20	—	—	—	—	—	—	—	750	—	—	—	—	—	—	—
Get N kills with the Silencer attached to this weapon.	Attachment: Silencer	15	—	—	—	—	—	—	—	750	—	—	—	—	—	—	—
Get N kills while looking through the Thermal Scope attached to this weapon.	Attachment: Thermal	40	—	—	—	—	—	—	—	1000	—	—	—	—	—	—	—
Get N kills using the Extended Mags attachment.	Attachment: Extended Mags	40	—	—	—	—	—	—	—	1000	—	—	—	—	—	—	—
Get N kills with the Heartbeat Sensor attached to this weapon.	Attachment: Heartbeat Sensor	40	—	—	—	—	—	—	—	1000	—	—	—	—	—	—	—
Get N kills while looking through the Variable Zoom Scope attached to this weapon.	Attachment: Variable Zoom Scope	40	—	—	—	—	—	—	—	1000	—	—	—	—	—	—	—
Achieve maximum weapon proficiency with this weapon.	RSASS: Mastery	6	—	—	—	—	—	—	—	10000	—	—	—	—	—	—	—

CHALLENGE DESCRIPTION	TITLE	TARGET 1	TARGET 2	TARGET 3	TARGET 4	TARGET 5	TARGET 6	TARGET 7	TARGET 8	XP 1	XP 2	XP 3	XP 4	XP 5	XP 6	XP 7	XP 8
DRAGUNOV CHALLENGES																	
Get N kills with this weapon.	Marksman	10	25	75	150	300	500	750	1000	250	1000	2000	5000	10000	10000	10000	10000
Get N headshots with this weapon.	Expert	5	15	30	75	150	250	350	500	500	1000	2500	5000	10000	10000	10000	10000
Get N kills while looking through the ACOG Sight attached to this weapon.	Attachment: ACOG	20	—	—	—	—	—	—	—	750	—	—	—	—	—	—	—
Get N kills with the Silencer attached to this weapon.	Attachment: Silencer	15	—	—	—	—	—	—	—	750	—	—	—	—	—	—	—
Get N kills while looking through the Thermal Scope attached to this weapon.	Attachment: Thermal	40	—	—	—	—	—	—	—	1000	—	—	—	—	—	—	—
Get N kills using the Extended Mags attachment.	Attachment: Extended Mags	40	—	—	—	—	—	—	—	1000	—	—	—	—	—	—	—
Get N kills with the Heartbeat Sensor attached to this weapon.	Attachment: Heartbeat Sensor	40	—	—	—	—	—	—	—	1000	—	—	—	—	—	—	—
Get N kills while looking through the Variable Zoom Scope attached to this weapon.	Attachment: Variable Zoom Scope	40	—	—	—	—	—	—	—	1000	—	—	—	—	—	—	—
Achieve maximum weapon proficiency with this weapon.	Dragunov: Mastery	6	—	—	—	—	—	—	—	10000	—	—	—	—	—	—	—
AS50 CHALLENGES																	
Get N kills with this weapon.	Marksman	10	25	75	150	300	500	750	1000	250	1000	2000	5000	10000	10000	10000	10000
Get N headshots with this weapon.	Expert	5	15	30	75	150	250	350	500	500	1000	2500	5000	10000	10000	10000	10000
Get N kills while looking through the ACOG Sight attached to this weapon.	Attachment: ACOG	20	—	—	—	—	—	—	—	750	—	—	—	—	—	—	—
Get N kills with the Silencer attached to this weapon.	Attachment: Silencer	15	—	—	—	—	—	—	—	750	—	—	—	—	—	—	—
Get N kills while looking through the Thermal Scope attached to this weapon.	Attachment: Thermal	40	—	—	—	—	—	—	—	1000	—	—	—	—	—	—	—
Get N kills using the Extended Mags attachment.	Attachment: Extended Mags	40	—	—	—	—	—	—	—	1000	—	—	—	—	—	—	—
Get N kills with the Heartbeat Sensor attached to this weapon.	Attachment: Heartbeat Sensor	40	—	—	—	—	—	—	—	1000	—	—	—	—	—	—	—
Get N kills while looking through the Variable Zoom Scope attached to this weapon.	Attachment: Variable Zoom Scope	40	—	—	—	—	—	—	—	1000	—	—	—	—	—	—	—
Achieve maximum weapon proficiency with this weapon.	AS50: Mastery	6	—	—	—	—	—	—	—	10000	—	—	—	—	—	—	—

MACHINE PISTOL CHALLENGES

CHALLENGE DESCRIPTION	TITLE	TARGET 1	TARGET 2	TARGET 3	TARGET 4	TARGET 5	TARGET 6	TARGET 7	TARGET 8	XP 1	XP 2	XP 3	XP 4	XP 5	XP 6	XP 7	XP 8
FMG9 CHALLENGES																	
Get N kills with this weapon.	Marksman	10	25	50	75	100	150	300	1000	500	1000	1500	2000	2500	3500	10000	10000
Get N headshots with this weapon.	Expert	5	15	30	75	150	250	350	500	500	1000	2500	5000	10000	10000	10000	10000
Get N kills with the Silencer attached to this weapon.	Attachment: Silencer	40	—	—	—	—	—	—	—	1000	—	—	—	—	—	—	—
Get N kills using Akimbo.	Attachment: Akimbo	40	—	—	—	—	—	—	—	1000	—	—	—	—	—	—	—

CHALLENGE DESCRIPTION	TITLE	TARGET 1	TARGET 2	TARGET 3	TARGET 4	TARGET 5	TARGET 6	TARGET 7	TARGET 8	XP 1	XP 2	XP 3	XP 4	XP 5	XP 6	XP 7	XP 8
Get N kills while looking through the Red Dot Sight attached to this weapon.	Attachment: Reflex Sight	40	—	—	—	—	—	—	—	1000	—	—	—	—	—	—	—
Get N kills while looking through the Holographic Sight attached to this weapon.	Attachment: Holographic Sight	40	—	—	—	—	—	—	—	1000	—	—	—	—	—	—	—
Get N kills using the Extended Mags attachment.	Attachment: Extended Mags	40	—	—	—	—	—	—	—	1000	—	—	—	—	—	—	—
Achieve maximum weapon proficiency with this weapon.	FMG9: Mastery	5	—	—	—	—	—	—	—	10000	—	—	—	—	—	—	—
G18 CHALLENGES																	
Get N kills with this weapon.	Marksman	10	25	50	75	100	150	300	1000	500	1000	1500	2000	2500	3500	10000	10000
Get N headshots with this weapon.	Expert	5	15	30	75	150	250	350	500	500	1000	2500	5000	10000	10000	10000	10000
Get N kills with the Silencer attached to this weapon.	Attachment: Silencer	40	—	—	—	—	—	—	—	1000	—	—	—	—	—	—	—
Get N kills using Akimbo.	Attachment: Akimbo	40	—	—	—	—	—	—	—	1000	—	—	—	—	—	—	—
Get N kills while looking through the Red Dot Sight attached to this weapon.	Attachment: Reflex Sight	40	—	—	—	—	—	—	—	1000	—	—	—	—	—	—	—
Get N kills while looking through the Holographic Sight attached to this weapon.	Attachment: Holographic Sight	40	—	—	—	—	—	—	—	1000	—	—	—	—	—	—	—
Get N kills using the Extended Mags attachment.	Attachment: Extended Mags	40	—	—	—	—	—	—	—	1000	—	—	—	—	—	—	—
Achieve maximum weapon proficiency with this weapon.	G18: Mastery	5	—	—	—	—	—	—	—	10000	—	—	—	—	—	—	—
SKORPION CHALLENGES																	
Get N kills with this weapon.	Marksman	10	25	50	75	100	150	300	1000	500	1000	1500	2000	2500	3500	10000	10000
Get N headshots with this weapon.	Expert	5	15	30	75	150	250	350	500	500	1000	2500	5000	10000	10000	10000	10000
Get N kills with the Silencer attached to this weapon.	Attachment: Silencer	40	—	—	—	—	—	—	—	1000	—	—	—	—	—	—	—
Get N kills using Akimbo.	Attachment: Akimbo	40	—	—	—	—	—	—	—	1000	—	—	—	—	—	—	—
Get N kills while looking through the Red Dot Sight attached to this weapon.	Attachment: Reflex Sight	40	—	—	—	—	—	—	—	1000	—	—	—	—	—	—	—
Get N kills while looking through the Holographic Sight attached to this weapon.	Attachment: Holographic Sight	40	—	—	—	—	—	—	—	1000	—	—	—	—	—	—	—
Get N kills using the Extended Mags attachment.	Attachment: Extended Mags	40	—	—	—	—	—	—	—	1000	—	—	—	—	—	—	—
Achieve maximum weapon proficiency with this weapon.	Skorpion: Mastery	5	—	—	—	—	—	—	—	10000	—	—	—	—	—	—	—
MP9 CHALLENGES																	
Get N kills with this weapon.	Marksman	10	25	50	75	100	150	300	1000	500	1000	1500	2000	2500	3500	10000	10000
Get N headshots with this weapon.	Expert	5	15	30	75	150	250	350	500	500	1000	2500	5000	10000	10000	10000	10000
Get N kills with the Silencer attached to this weapon.	Attachment: Silencer	40	—	—	—	—	—	—	—	1000	—	—	—	—	—	—	—
Get N kills using Akimbo.	Attachment: Akimbo	40	—	—	—	—	—	—	—	1000	—	—	—	—	—	—	—
Get N kills while looking																	

CHALLENGE DESCRIPTION	TITLE	TARGET 1	TARGET 2	TARGET 3	TARGET 4	TARGET 5	TARGET 6	TARGET 7	TARGET 8	XP 1	XP 2	XP 3	XP 4	XP 5	XP 6	XP 7	XP 8
MP9 CHALLENGES (continued)																	
Get N kills while looking through the Holographic Sight attached to this weapon.	Attachment: Holographic Sight	40	—	—	—	—	—	—	—	1000	—	—	—	—	—	—	—
Get N kills using the Extended Mags attachment.	Attachment: Extended Mags	40	—	—	—	—	—	—	—	1000	—	—	—	—	—	—	—
Achieve maximum weapon proficiency with this weapon.	MP9: Mastery	5	—	—	—	—	—	—	—	10000	—	—	—	—	—	—	—

HANDGUN CHALLENGES

CHALLENGE DESCRIPTION	TITLE	TARGET 1	TARGET 2	TARGET 3	TARGET 4	TARGET 5	TARGET 6	TARGET 7	TARGET 8	XP 1	XP 2	XP 3	XP 4	XP 5	XP 6	XP 7	XP 8
USP .45 CHALLENGES																	
Get N kills with this weapon.	Marksman	10	25	50	75	100	150	300	1000	500	1000	1500	2000	2500	3500	10000	10000
Get N headshots with this weapon.	Expert	5	15	30	75	150	250	350	500	500	1000	2500	5000	10000	10000	10000	10000
Get N kills with the Silencer attached to this weapon.	Attachment: Silencer	40	—	—	—	—	—	—	—	1000	—	—	—	—	—	—	—
Get N kills using Akimbo.	Attachment: Akimbo	40	—	—	—	—	—	—	—	1000	—	—	—	—	—	—	—
Get N kills using the Tactical Knife.	Attachment: Tactical	40	—	—	—	—	—	—	—	1000	—	—	—	—	—	—	—
Get N kills using the Extended Mags attachment.	Attachment: Extended Mags	40	—	—	—	—	—	—	—	1000	—	—	—	—	—	—	—
Achieve maximum weapon proficiency with this weapon.	USP .45: Mastery	4	—	—	—	—	—	—	—	10000	—	—	—	—	—	—	—
MP412 CHALLENGES																	
Get N kills with this weapon.	Marksman	10	25	50	75	100	150	300	1000	500	1000	1500	2000	2500	3500	10000	10000
Get N headshots with this weapon.	Expert	5	15	30	75	150	250	350	500	500	1000	2500	5000	10000	10000	10000	10000
Get N kills using Akimbo.	Attachment: Akimbo	40	—	—	—	—	—	—	—	1000	—	—	—	—	—	—	—
Get N kills using the Tactical Knife.	Attachment: Tactical	40	—	—	—	—	—	—	—	1000	—	—	—	—	—	—	—
Achieve maximum weapon proficiency with this weapon.	MP412: Mastery	2	—	—	—	—	—	—	—	10000	—	—	—	—	—	—	—
.44 MAGNUM CHALLENGES																	
Get N kills with this weapon.	Marksman	10	25	50	75	100	150	300	1000	500	1000	1500	2000	2500	3500	10000	10000
Get N headshots with this weapon.	Expert	5	15	30	75	150	250	350	500	500	1000	2500	5000	10000	10000	10000	10000
Get N kills using Akimbo.	Attachment: Akimbo	40	—	—	—	—	—	—	—	1000	—	—	—	—	—	—	—
Get N kills using the Tactical Knife.	Attachment: Tactical	40	—	—	—	—	—	—	—	1000	—	—	—	—	—	—	—
Achieve maximum weapon proficiency with this weapon.	.44 Magnum: Mastery	2	—	—	—	—	—	—	—	10000	—	—	—	—	—	—	—
DESERT EAGLE CHALLENGES																	
Get N kills with this weapon.	Marksman	10	50	100	300	1000	2500			500	1500	2500	10000	10000	10000		
Get N headshots with this weapon.	Expert	5	15	30	75	150	250	350	500	500	1000	2500	5000	10000	10000	10000	10000
Get N kills using Akimbo.	Attachment: Akimbo	40	—	—	—	—	—	—	—	1000	—	—	—	—	—	—	—
Get N kills using the Tactical Knife.	Attachment: Tactical	40	—	—	—	—	—	—	—	1000	—	—	—	—	—	—	—
Achieve maximum weapon proficiency with this weapon.	Desert Eagle: Mastery	2	—	—	—	—	—	—	—	10000	—	—	—	—	—	—	—

CHALLENGE DESCRIPTION	TITLE	TARGET 1	TARGET 2	TARGET 3	TARGET 4	TARGET 5	TARGET 6	TARGET 7	TARGET 8	XP 1	XP 2	XP 3	XP 4	XP 5	XP 6	XP 7	XP 8
P99 CHALLENGES																	
Get N kills with this weapon.	Marksman	10	25	50	75	100	150	300	1000	500	1000	1500	2000	2500	3500	10000	10000
Get N headshots with this weapon.	Expert	5	15	30	75	150	250	350	500	500	1000	2500	5000	10000	10000	10000	10000
Get N kills with the Silencer attached to this weapon.	Attachment: Silencer	40	—	—	—	—	—	—	—	1000	—	—	—	—	—	—	—
Get N kills using Akimbo.	Attachment: Akimbo	40	—	—	—	—	—	—	—	1000	—	—	—	—	—	—	—
Get N kills using the Tactical Knife.	Attachment: Tactical	40	—	—	—	—	—	—	—	1000	—	—	—	—	—	—	—
Get N kills using the Extended Mags attachment.	Attachment: Extended Mags	40	—	—	—	—	—	—	—	1000	—	—	—	—	—	—	—
Achieve maximum weapon proficiency with this weapon.	P99: Mastery	4	—	—	—	—	—	—	—	10000	—	—	—	—	—	—	—
FIVE SEVEN CHALLENGES																	
Get N kills with this weapon.	Marksman	10	25	50	75	100	150	300	1000	500	1000	1500	2000	2500	3500	10000	10000
Get N headshots with this weapon.	Expert	5	15	30	75	150	250	350	500	500	1000	2500	5000	10000	10000	10000	10000
Get N kills with the Silencer attached to this weapon.	Attachment: Silencer	40	—	—	—	—	—	—	—	1000	—	—	—	—	—	—	—
Get N kills using Akimbo.	Attachment: Akimbo	40	—	—	—	—	—	—	—	1000	—	—	—	—	—	—	—
Get N kills using the Tactical Knife.	Attachment: Tactical	40	—	—	—	—	—	—	—	1000	—	—	—	—	—	—	—
Get N kills using the Extended Mags attachment.	Attachment: Extended Mags	40	—	—	—	—	—	—	—	1000	—	—	—	—	—	—	—
Achieve maximum weapon proficiency with this weapon.	Five Seven: Mastery	4	—	—	—	—	—	—	—	10000	—	—	—	—	—	—	—

LAUNCHER CHALLENGES

CHALLENGE DESCRIPTION	TITLE	TARGET 1	TARGET 2	TARGET 3	TARGET 4	TARGET 5	TARGET 6	TARGET 7	TARGET 8	XP 1	XP 2	XP 3	XP 4	XP 5	XP 6	XP 7	XP 8
SMAW CHALLENGES																	
Get N kills with this weapon.	Marksman	10	25	75	150	300	500	800	1200	250	1000	2000	5000	10000	10000	10000	10000
M320 GLM CHALLENGES																	
Get N kills with this weapon.	Marksman	10	25	75	150	300	500	800	1200	250	1000	2000	5000	10000	10000	10000	10000
STINGER CHALLENGES																	
Shoot down N helicopters with this weapon.	Marksman	3	8	15	25	40	60	100	250	250	1000	2000	5000	10000	10000	10000	10000
JAVELIN CHALLENGES																	
Get N kills with this weapon.	Marksman	10	25	75	150	300	500	800	1200	250	1000	2000	5000	10000	10000	10000	10000
RPG CHALLENGES																	
Get N kills with this weapon.	Marksman	10	25	75	150	300	500	800	1200	250	1000	2000	5000	10000	10000	10000	10000
XM25 CHALLENGES																	
Get N kills with this weapon.	Marksman	10	25	75	150	300	500	800	1200	250	1000	2000	5000	10000	10000	10000	10000

RIOT SHIELD CHALLENGES

CHALLENGE DESCRIPTION	TITLE	TARGET 1	TARGET 2	TARGET 3	XP 1	XP 2	XP 3
Kill N enemies with the shield melee attack.	Shield Veteran	2	5	15	500	1000	2500
Get a 3 kill streak with the Riot Shield without dying.	Smasher	1	—	—	500	—	—
Crush an enemy from behind.	Back-Smasher	1	—	—	500	—	—
Absorb N damage with your Riot Shield.	Sponge	1000	10000	50000	500	1000	2500
Deflect N bullets with your Riot Shield.	Bullet Proof	1000	10000	50000	500	1000	2500
Deflect N explosions with your Riot Shield.	Unbreakable	10	50	100	500	1000	2500

EQUIPMENT CHALLENGES

CHALLENGE DESCRIPTION	TITLE	TARGET 1	TARGET 2	TARGET 3	XP 1	XP 2	XP 3
Kill N enemies with grenades.	**Frag-tastic**	**10**	**25**	**50**	**500**	**2500**	**5000**
Stick N players with a Semtex grenade.	Plastered	5	15	30	500	2500	5000
Kill N players with a Throwing Knife.	Carnie	5	15	30	500	2500	5000
Kill N enemies with claymores.	Tick ... Boom	5	15	30	500	2500	5000
Kill N enemies by using C4.	Plastic Surgery	5	15	30	500	2500	5000
Kill N enemies with Bouncing Betties.	My Bouncy Lady	5	15	30	500	2500	5000
Hurt an enemy then finish them with a Throwing Knife.	It's Personal!	1	—	—	1000	—	—
Kill someone with a Throwing Knife while flashed or stunned.	Did you see that?	1	—	—	1000	—	—

SPECIAL EQUIPMENT CHALLENGES

CHALLENGE DESCRIPTION	TITLE	TARGET 1	TARGET 2	TARGET 3	XP 1	XP 2	XP 3
Stop N enemy projectiles with the Trophy System.	No Boom For You	10	25	50	500	2500	5000
Flash N enemies.	Indecent Exposure	10	25	50	500	2500	5000
Kill N enemies inside your Smoke screen.	Smoke 'em If You Got 'em	10	25	50	500	2500	5000
Stun N enemies.	A Little Concussed	10	25	50	500	2500	5000
EMP N enemies.	On The Pulse	10	25	50	500	2500	5000
Kill an enemy within 5 seconds of tactically inserting, N times.	Jack-in-the-Box	10	25	50	500	2500	5000
Kill N enemies within the proximity of your Scrambler.	Scram!	10	25	50	500	2500	5000
Kill N enemies within the proximity of your Portable Radar.	Zero Latency	10	25	50	500	2500	5000
Prevent 25 Tactical Insertions.	Dark Bringer	25	—	—	1000	—	—
Kill 25 players that spawn using Tactical Insertion.	Tactical Deletion	25	—	—	1000	—	—

SNIPER CHALLENGES: GHILLIE SUIT

CHALLENGE DESCRIPTION	TITLE	TARGET 1	TARGET 2	TARGET 3	XP 1	XP 2	XP 3
Get N one-shot kills with sniper rifles.	Ghillie in the Mist	50	100	200	1000	2500	5000

PROFICIENCY CHALLENGES

CHALLENGE DESCRIPTION	TITLE	TARGET 1	TARGET 2	TARGET 3	TARGET 4	TARGET 5	TARGET 6	XP 1	XP 2	XP 3	XP 4	XP 5	XP 6
Use Kick Proficiency to kill N enemies while aiming down sights.	**Kick-Stop**	**15**	**30**	**60**	**120**	**300**	**750**	**500**	**1000**	**2500**	**5000**	**10000**	**10000**
Kill N enemies through a surface using the Impact Proficiency.	X-Ray Vision	15	30	60	120	300	750	500	1000	2500	5000	10000	10000
Use Attachments Proficiency to kill N enemies while using a weapon with two attachments.	Bling Bling	15	30	60	120	300	750	500	1000	2500	5000	10000	10000
Use Focus Proficiency to kill N enemies that just shot you.	Unshakeable	15	30	60	120	300	750	500	1000	2500	5000	10000	10000
Use Breath Proficiency to kill N enemies while aiming down sights.	Hold It Right There	15	30	60	120	300	750	500	1000	2500	5000	10000	10000
Use Stability Proficiency to kill N enemies while aiming down sights.	Swayless	15	30	60	120	300	750	500	1000	2500	5000	10000	10000
Use Range Proficiency to kill N enemies.	Long-ish Shot	15	30	60	120	300	750	500	1000	2500	5000	10000	10000
Use Melee Proficiency to kill N enemies with melee.	Cold Steel	15	30	60	120	300	750	500	1000	2500	5000	10000	10000
Kill N enemies while using the Speed Proficiency.	Speed Kills	15	30	60	120	300	750	500	1000	2500	5000	10000	10000
Use Damage Proficiency to kill N enemies.	More Damage	15	30	60	120	300	750	500	1000	2500	5000	10000	10000

BOOT CAMP CHALLENGES

CHALLENGE DESCRIPTION	TITLE	TARGET 1	TARGET 2	TARGET 3	XP 1	XP 2	XP 3
Fall 30 feet or more to your death.	**Goodbye**	**1**	**—**	**—**	**500**	**—**	**—**
Fall 15 feet or more and survive.	Base Jump	1	—	—	750	—	—
Shoot down an enemy helicopter.	Flyswatter	1	—	—	1000	—	—
Destroy a car.	Vandalism	1	—	—	750	—	—
Kill N enemies while you are crouching.	Crouch Shot	5	15	30	500	1000	2500
Kill N enemies while you are prone.	Prone Shot	5	15	30	500	1000	2500
Get N assists.	Point Guard	5	15	30	500	1000	2500
Destroy N enemy equipment.	Backdraft	2	5	15	500	1000	2500

OPERATIONS CHALLENGES

CHALLENGE DESCRIPTION	TITLE	TARGET 1	TARGET 2	TARGET 3	XP 1	XP 2	XP 3
Place first, second or third in N Free-for-all matches.	**Free-for-all Victor**	**3**	**5**	**10**	**500**	**1000**	**2500**
Win N Team Deathmatch matches.	Team Player	5	15	30	500	1000	2500
Win N Search And Destroy matches.	Search And Destroy Victor	5	15	30	500	1000	2500
Play Team Deathmatch and get the top score overall.	MVP Team Deathmatch	1	—	—	1000	—	—
Win N Hardcore Team Deathmatch game(s).	Hardcore Team Player	1	5	15	500	1000	2500
Win N Sabotage matches.	Sabotage Victor	5	20	50	500	1000	2500
Win a Team Hardcore match with the top score.	MVP Team Hardcore	1	—	—	1000	—	—
Kill a bomb carrier in Sabotage or Search and Destroy.	Bomb Down	1	—	—	1000	—	—
Kill N enemies while they are defusing a bomb.	Bomb Defender	3	10	—	500	1000	—
Kill N enemies while they are planting a bomb.	Bomb Prevention	3	10	—	500	1000	—
Defuse N bombs.	Defuser	2	10	—	500	1000	—
Be the last man standing in Search and Destroy.	Last Man Standing	1	—	—	1000	—	—
Plant N bombs.	Saboteur	2	10	—	500	1000	—

PRECISION CHALLENGES

CHALLENGE DESCRIPTION	TITLE	TARGET 1	TARGET 2	TARGET 3	XP 1	XP 2	XP 3
Fire an entire Assault Rifle magazine into your enemies without missing.	**The Surgical**	**1**	**—**	**—**	**2000**	**—**	**—**
Fire an entire SMG magazine into your enemies without missing.	Mach 5	1	—	—	2000	—	—
Fire an entire LMG magazine into your enemies without missing.	Dictator	1	—	—	2000	—	—
Fire an entire Sniper magazine into your enemies without missing.	Perfectionist	1	—	—	2000	—	—
Kill N enemies with a headshot while using an assault rifle.	Assault Expert	5	25	50	2000	5000	10000
Kill N enemies with headshots while using a submachine gun.	SMG Expert	5	25	50	2000	5000	10000
Kill N enemies with headshots while using a light machine gun.	LMG Expert	5	25	50	2000	5000	10000
Kill 2 or more enemies with a single RPG shot, N times.	Multi-RPG	5	25	50	2000	5000	10000
Kill 2 or more enemies with a single claymore, N times.	Claymore	5	25	50	2000	5000	10000
Kill 2 or more enemies with a single frag grenade, N times.	Multi-frag	5	25	50	2000	5000	10000
Kill 2 or more enemies with a single C4 pack, N times.	Multi-C4	5	25	50	2000	5000	10000
Kill 2 or more enemies with a single sniper rifle bullet.	Collateral Damage	1	—	—	2000	—	—
Play an entire full-length match without dying.	Flawless	1	—	—	2000	—	—
Kill 10 enemies in a single match without dying.	Fearless	1	—	—	2000	—	—
Kill multiple enemies with a Semtex stuck to one of them.	Group Hug	1	—	—	2000	—	—
Get 3 longshots in one life.	NBK	1	—	—	2000	—	—
Headshot 2+ enemies with 1 bullet.	All Pro	1	—	—	2000	—	—
Get a 2 kill streak with bullets while in mid-air.	Airborne	1	—	—	2000	—	—

DOMINANCE CHALLENGES

CHALLENGE DESCRIPTION	TITLE	TARGET 1	XP 1
Kill the entire enemy team within 10 seconds.	Omnicide!	1	5000
Get all 3 of your Pointstreak rewards within 20 seconds.	Wargasm	1	3500
Kill the top player 3 times in a row.	The Bigger they are...	1	2500
Kill the top player 5 times in a row.	...The Harder They Fall	1	5000
Kill 10 enemies with a single Pointstreak.	Crab Meat	1	7500
Kill an enemy before they earn a 10 or higher Pointstreak reward.	The Denier	1	5000
Kill 5 enemies with a single airstrike.	Carpet Bomb	1	5000
Kill 6 enemies with a single Stealth Bomber.	Red Carpet	1	5000

CHALLENGE DESCRIPTION	TITLE	TARGET 1	XP 1
Kill 5 enemies with a single Predator Missile.	Grim Reaper	1	5000
Call in a UAV 3 times in a single match.	No Secrets	1	2500
Counter the enemy's UAV 3 times in a single match.	Sunblock	1	2500
Call in an airstrike 2 times in a single match.	Afterburner	1	2500
Call in an Attack Helicopter 2 times in a single match.	Air Superiority	1	2500
Get a 5 kill streak while on a mounted machine gun.	MG Master	1	2500
Get a 3 melee kill streak without dying.	Slasher	1	3500

CHALLENGE DESCRIPTION	TITLE	TARGET 1	TARGET 2	XP 1	XP 2
Get a Payback in the game winning killcam.	Money Shot!	1	—	3500	—
Get Payback N times while in Final Stand.	Robin Hood	5	25	3500	10000
Get Payback N times with Frag Grenades.	Bang for your Buck	5	25	3500	10000
Get a Payback that sticks to the victim.	Overdraft	1	—	3500	—
Get a Payback with a Throwing Knife.	ATM	1	—	3500	—

CHALLENGE DESCRIPTION	TITLE	TARGET 1	TARGET 2	XP 1	XP 2
Get Payback N times with Semtex.	Time Is Money	5	25	3500	10000
Get Payback N times with C4.	I'm Rich!	5	25	3500	10000
Get a Payback with a Claymore.	Break the Bank	1	—	3500	—
Get Payback N times with headshots.	Blood Money	5	25	3500	10000
Get hurt by an enemy but survive and backstab them.	Never Forget	1	—	3500	—

VETERAN CHALLENGES

CHALLENGE DESCRIPTION	TITLE	TARGET 1	TARGET 2	TARGET 3	TARGET 4	XP 1	XP 2	XP 3	XP 4
Kill N enemies with the knife melee attack.	**Knife Veteran**	**10**	**50**	**100**	**250**	**2500**	**5000**	**10000**	**5000**
Kill N enemies while in Final Stand.	Final Stand Veteran	5	15	50	100	2500	5000	10000	5000
Kill N enemies while using a silenced weapon.	Stealth Veteran	10	25	50	1000	2500	5000	10000	5000
Kill N enemies still dazed by a stun grenade.	Stun Veteran	20	75	150	300	2500	5000	10000	5000
Kill N enemies dazed by a flashbang.	Flashbang Veteran	20	75	150	300	2500	5000	10000	5000

ELITE CHALLENGES

CHALLENGE DESCRIPTION	TITLE	TARGET 1	TARGET 2	TARGET 3	XP 1	XP 2	XP 3
Get a 3 or more kill streak while near death. (Screen flashing red)	The Brink	1	—	—	4500	—	—
Hurt an enemy with a primary weapon, then finish them off with a pistol.	Fast Swap	1	—	—	4500	—	—
Play an entire match of any game type with a 5:1 kill / death ratio.	Star Player	1	—	—	4500	—	—
Kill an enemy by using bullet penetration to shoot an explosive device through a wall.	How the ?	1	—	—	4500	—	—
Kill an enemy by setting off chain reactions of explosives.	Dominos	1	—	—	4500	—	—
Kill N enemies with cooked grenades.	Master Chef	5	10	20	2500	5000	10000
Get 5 health regenerations from enemy damage in a row, without dying.	Invincible	1	—	—	4500	—	—
Survive for 5 consecutive minutes.	Survivalist	1	—	—	4500	—	—
Kill N enemies by shooting a claymore.	Counter-Claymore	3	10	20	2500	5000	10000
Kill N enemies by shooting C4.	Counter-C4	3	10	20	2500	5000	10000
Kill 3 enemies while you are the only surviving member of your team.	Enemy of the State	1	—	—	4500	—	—
Kill an enemy by sticking Semtex to a teammate.	The Resourceful	1	—	—	4500	—	—
Get a knife kill when all of your ammo is empty.	The Survivor	1	—	—	4500	—	—

HUMILIATION CHALLENGES

CHALLENGE DESCRIPTION	TITLE	TARGET 1	TARGET 2	XP 1	XP 2
Kill N enemies with thrown back grenades.	Hot Potato	5	10	3000	5000
Kill N enemies by destroying cars.	Car Bomb	5	10	3000	5000
Stab an enemy in the back with your knife.	Backstabber	1	—	3000	—
Kill 1 enemy while being stunned by a stun grenade.	Slow But Sure	1	—	3000	—
Kill yourself and 1 enemy by cooking a grenade without throwing it.	Misery Loves Company	1	—	3000	—
Kill an enemy with a rifle-mounted grenade launcher without detonation. (Direct impact)	Ouch	1	—	3000	—
Kill the same enemy 5 times in a single match.	Rival	1	—	3000	—
Kill an enemy, pick up his weapon, then kill him again with his own weapon.	Cruelty	1	—	3000	—
Finish an enemy off by hitting					

CHALLENGE DESCRIPTION	TITLE	TARGET 1	TARGET 2	XP 1	XP 2
Finish an enemy off by hitting them with a stun grenade. (Direct impact)	Think Fast Stun	1	—	3000	—
Finish an enemy off by hitting them with a flashbang. (Direct impact)	Think Fast Flash	1	—	3000	—
Kill 1 enemy by shooting their own explosive.	Return To Sender	1	—	3000	—
Kill an enemy while you are still dazed by a flashbang.	Blindfire	1	—	3000	—
Kill an enemy that is in mid-air.	Hard Landing	1	—	3000	—
Kill every member of the enemy team (at least 4 enemies) without dying.	Extreme Cruelty	1	—	3000	—
Kill every member of the enemy team. (4 enemy minimum)	Tango Down	1	—	3000	—
Kill the #1 player on the enemy team 10 times in a single match.	Counter-MVP	1	—	3000	—

CHALLENGE DESCRIPTION	TITLE	TARGET 1	TARGET 2	TARGET 3	XP 1	XP 2	XP 3
Get a Game Winning Killcam by dropping a crate on the enemy.	Droppin' Crates	1	—	—	2500	—	—
Get a Game Winning Killcam with a Sentry Gun.	Absentee Killer	1	—	—	2500	—	—
Get a Predator Missile kill in the Game Winning Killcam.	Drone Killer	1	—	—	2500	—	—
Get a Game Winning Killcam with a Precision Airstrike.	Finishing Touch	1	—	—	2500	—	—
Get a Game Winning Killcam with an Attack Helicopter.	OG	1	—	—	2500	—	—
Get a Game Winning Killcam with a Pave Low.	Transformer	1	—	—	2500	—	—
Get a Game Winning Killcam with a Stealth Bomber.	Techno Killer	1	—	—	2500	—	—
Get a Game Winning Killcam with an AC-130.	Death From Above	1	—	—	2500	—	—
Get the match winning kill N time(s).	The Edge	5	10	20	2500	5000	10000
Get a Throwing Knife kill in Game Winning Killcam.	Unbelievable	1	—	—	2500	—	—
Get a Riot Shield melee kill in Game Winning Killcam.	Owned	1	—	—	2500	—	—
Stick a Semtex to the enemy in a Game Winning Killcam.	Stickman	1	—	—	2500	—	—
Get a Final Stand kill in Game Winning Killcam.	Last Resort	1	—	—	2500	—	—

PERK CHALLENGES: STANDARD

CHALLENGE DESCRIPTION	TITLE	TARGET 1	TARGET 2	TARGET 3	TARGET 4	TARGET 5	TARGET 6	XP 1	XP 2	XP 3	XP 4	XP 5	XP 6
Sprint N miles using Extreme Conditioning.	Extreme Conditioning Pro	5280	26400	52800	105600	211200	422400	500	1000	2500	5000	10000	10000
Get N kills using Sleight of Hand.	Sleight of Hand Pro	15	30	60	120	300	750	500	1000	2500	5000	10000	10000
Resupply N times while using Scavenger.	Scavenger Pro	10	25	50	100	250	500	500	1000	2500	5000	10000	10000
Destroy N enemy Pointstreak rewards using Blind Eye.	Blind Eye Pro	3	10	20	40	100	250	500	1000	2500	5000	10000	10000
Paint N enemies using Recon.	Recon Pro	15	30	60	120	300	750	500	1000	2500	5000	10000	10000
Get N Pointstreaks while using Hardline.	Hardline Pro	10	20	40	80	200	500	500	1000	2500	5000	10000	10000
Get N kills while enemy UAV is up and using Assassin.	Assassin Pro	2	5	10	20	50	100	500	1000	2500	5000	10000	10000
Get N kills within a few seconds of aiming down your sights while using Quickdraw.	Quickdraw Pro	10	20	40	80	200	500	500	1000	2500	5000	10000	10000
Get N kills with your second primary weapon.	Overkill Pro	15	30	60	120	300	750	500	1000	2500	5000	10000	10000
Survive N explosions while using Blast Shield.	Blast Shield Pro	2	5	10	20	50	100	500	1000	2500	5000	10000	10000
Get N kills while holding breath and using Marksman.	Marksman Pro	5	10	25	50	125	250	500	1000	2500	5000	10000	10000
Destroy N enemy devices while using SitRep.	SitRep Pro	5	10	25	50	125	250	500	1000	2500	5000	10000	10000
Get N hipfire kills using Steady Aim.	Steady Aim Pro	15	30	60	120	300	750	500	1000	2500	5000	10000	10000
Get N close range kills using Dead Silence.	Dead Silence Pro	5	10	25	50	125	250	500	1000	2500	5000	10000	10000
Get N kills while aiming down sights and using Stalker.	Stalker Pro	15	30	60	120	300	750	500	1000	2500	5000	10000	10000

PERK CHALLENGES: PRO

CHALLENGE DESCRIPTION	TITLE	TARGET 1	TARGET 2	TARGET 3	TARGET 4	TARGET 5	TARGET 6	XP 1	XP 2	XP 3	XP 4	XP 5	XP 6
Mantle N objects while using Extreme Conditioning Pro.	Parkour	3	10	20	40	100	250	500	1000	2500	5000	10000	10000
Get N kills shortly after swapping weapons while using Sleight of Hand Pro.	High Noon	15	30	60	120	300	750	500	1000	2500	5000	10000	10000
Get N kills while using Scavenger Pro.	Hoarding Ammo	15	30	60	120	300	750	500	1000	2500	5000	10000	10000
Destroy N enemy Pointstreak rewards by locking on while using Blind Eye Pro.	Restricted Airspace	3	10	20	40	100	250	500	1000	2500	5000	10000	10000
Paint N enemies with bullet damage using Recon Pro.	Paintball Gun	15	30	60	120	300	750	500	1000	2500	5000	10000	10000
Get N assists to count as kills using Hardline Pro.	And One!	10	20	40	80	200	500	500	1000	2500	5000	10000	10000
Get N kills while enemy CUAV or EMP is active and using Assassin Pro.	Surprise!	2	5	10	20	50	100	500	1000	2500	5000	10000	10000
Get N kills with your offhand weapon using Quick Draw Pro.	Bringing The Boom	10	20	40	80	200	500	500	1000	2500	5000	10000	10000
Get N kills with your second primary weapon with an attachment while using Overkill Pro.	Overkiller	15	30	60	120	300	750	500	1000	2500	5000	10000	10000
Get N kills shortly after being flashed or	Can't Phase Me	2	5	10	20	50	100	500	1000	2500	5000	10000	10000

CHALLENGE DESCRIPTION	TITLE	TARGET 1	TARGET 2	TARGET 3	TARGET 4	TARGET 5	TARGET 6	XP 1	XP 2	XP 3	XP 4	XP 5	XP 6
Get N long distance kills while using Marksman Pro.	CQC Not For Me	2	5	10	20	50	100	500	1000	2500	5000	10000	10000
Get N kills while using SitRep Pro.	I Heard That	15	30	60	120	300	750	500	1000	2500	5000	10000	10000
Get N kills shortly after sprinting while using Steady Aim Pro.	Runner's High	10	20	40	80	200	500	500	1000	2500	5000	10000	10000
Fall N times that would have normally caused you damage while using Dead Silence Pro.	Featherweight	2	5	10	20	50	100	500	1000	2500	5000	10000	10000
Trip N enemy explosives and survive while using Stalker Pro.	Trip Delayed	2	5	10	20	50	100	500	1000	2500	5000	10000	10000

PRESTIGE CHALLENGES

CHALLENGE DESCRIPTION	TITLE	TARGET 1	TARGET 2	TARGET 3	TARGET 4	TARGET 5	TARGET 6	TARGET 7	TARGET 8	XP 1	XP 2	XP 3	XP 4	XP 5	XP 6	XP 7	XP 8
Prestige for the first time.	Prestige	1	2	3	4	5	6	7	8	0	0	0	0	0	0	0	0
Reach Maximum Prestige.	Prestige: Max	1	—	—	—	—	—	—	—	0	—	—	—	—	—	—	—
M4A1 CHALLENGES																	
Get N kills with this weapon.	Prestige: Marksman	500	1000	2500	—	—	—	—	—	10000	10000	10000	—	—	—	—	—
Get N headshots with this weapon.	Prestige: Expert	250	500	1000	—	—	—	—	—	10000	10000	10000	—	—	—	—	—
TYPE 95 CHALLENGES																	
Get N kills with this weapon.	Prestige: Marksman	500	1000	2500	—	—	—	—	—	10000	10000	10000	—	—	—	—	—
Get N headshots with this weapon.	Prestige: Expert	250	500	1000	—	—	—	—	—	10000	10000	10000	—	—	—	—	—
SCAR-L CHALLENGES																	
Get N kills with this weapon.	Prestige: Marksman	500	1000	2500	—	—	—	—	—	10000	10000	10000	—	—	—	—	—
Get N headshots with this weapon.	Prestige: Expert	250	500	1000	—	—	—	—	—	10000	10000	10000	—	—	—	—	—
G36C CHALLENGES																	
Get N kills with this weapon.	Prestige: Marksman	500	1000	2500	—	—	—	—	—	10000	10000	10000	—	—	—	—	—
Get N headshots with this weapon.	Prestige: Expert	250	500	1000	—	—	—	—	—	10000	10000	10000	—	—	—	—	—
MK 14 CHALLENGES																	
Get N kills with this weapon.	Prestige: Marksman	500	1000	2500	—	—	—	—	—	10000	10000	10000	—	—	—	—	—
Get N headshots with this weapon.	Prestige: Expert	250	500	1000	—	—	—	—	—	10000	10000	10000	—	—	—	—	—
M16A4 CHALLENGES																	
Get N kills with this weapon.	Prestige: Marksman	500	1000	2500	—	—	—	—	—	10000	10000	10000	—	—	—	—	—
Get N headshots with this weapon.	Prestige: Expert	250	500	1000	—	—	—	—	—	10000	10000	10000	—	—	—	—	—
ACR 6.8 CHALLENGES																	
Get N kills with this weapon.	Prestige: Marksman	500	1000	2500	—	—	—	—	—	10000	10000	10000	—	—	—	—	—
Get N headshots with this weapon.	Prestige: Expert	250	500	1000	—	—	—	—	—	10000	10000	10000	—	—	—	—	—
FAD CHALLENGES																	
Get N kills with this weapon.	Prestige: Marksman	500	1000	2500	—	—	—	—	—	10000	10000	10000	—	—	—	—	—
Get N headshots with this weapon.	Prestige: Expert	250	500	1000	—	—	—	—	—	10000	10000	10000	—	—	—	—	—
AK-47 CHALLENGES																	
Get N kills with this weapon.	Prestige: Marksman	500	1000	2500	—	—	—	—	—	10000	10000	10000	—	—	—	—	—
Get N headshots with this weapon.	Prestige: Expert	250	500	1000	—	—	—	—	—	10000	10000	10000	—	—	—	—	—
CM901 CHALLENGES																	
Get N kills with this weapon.	Prestige: Marksman	500	1000	2500	—	—	—	—	—	10000	10000	10000	—	—	—	—	—
Get N headshots with this weapon.	Prestige: Expert	250	500	1000	—	—	—	—	—	10000	10000	10000	—	—	—	—	—

CHALLENGE DESCRIPTION	TITLE	TARGET 1	TARGET 2	TARGET 3	TARGET 4	TARGET 5	TARGET 6	TARGET 7	TARGET 8	XP 1	XP 2	XP 3	XP 4	XP 5	XP 6	XP 7	XP 8
MP5 CHALLENGES																	
Get N kills with this weapon.	Prestige: Marksman	500	1000	2500	—	—	—	—	—	10000	10000	10000	—	—	—	—	—
Get N headshots with this weapon.	Prestige: Expert	250	500	1000	—	—	—	—	—	10000	10000	10000	—	—	—	—	—
UMP45 CHALLENGES																	
Get N kills with this weapon.	Prestige: Marksman	500	1000	2500	—	—	—	—	—	10000	10000	10000	—	—	—	—	—
Get N headshots with this weapon.	Prestige: Expert	250	500	1000	—	—	—	—	—	10000	10000	10000	—	—	—	—	—
PP90M1 CHALLENGES																	
Get N kills with this weapon.	Prestige: Marksman	500	1000	2500	—	—	—	—	—	10000	10000	10000	—	—	—	—	—
Get N headshots with this weapon.	Prestige: Expert	250	500	1000	—	—	—	—	—	10000	10000	10000	—	—	—	—	—
P90 CHALLENGES																	
Get N kills with this weapon.	Prestige: Marksman	500	1000	2500	—	—	—	—	—	10000	10000	10000	—	—	—	—	—
Get N headshots with this weapon.	Prestige: Expert	250	500	1000	—	—	—	—	—	10000	10000	10000	—	—	—	—	—
PM-9 CHALLENGES																	
Get N kills with this weapon.	Prestige: Marksman	500	1000	2500	—	—	—	—	—	10000	10000	10000	—	—	—	—	—
Get N headshots with this weapon.	Prestige: Expert	250	500	1000	—	—	—	—	—	10000	10000	10000	—	—	—	—	—
MP7 CHALLENGES																	
Get N kills with this weapon.	Prestige: Marksman	500	1000	2500	—	—	—	—	—	10000	10000	10000	—	—	—	—	—
Get N headshots with this weapon.	Prestige: Expert	250	500	1000	—	—	—	—	—	10000	10000	10000	—	—	—	—	—
L86 LSW CHALLENGES																	
Get N kills with this weapon.	Prestige: Marksman	500	1000	2500	—	—	—	—	—	10000	10000	10000	—	—	—	—	—
Get N headshots with this weapon.	Prestige: Expert	250	500	1000	—	—	—	—	—	10000	10000	10000	—	—	—	—	—
MG36 CHALLENGES																	
Get N kills with this weapon.	Prestige: Marksman	500	1000	2500	—	—	—	—	—	10000	10000	10000	—	—	—	—	—
Get N headshots with this weapon.	Prestige: Expert	250	500	1000	—	—	—	—	—	10000	10000	10000	—	—	—	—	—
MK46 CHALLENGES																	
Get N kills with this weapon.	Prestige: Marksman	500	1000	2500	—	—	—	—	—	10000	10000	10000	—	—	—	—	—
Get N headshots with this weapon.	Prestige: Expert	250	500	1000	—	—	—	—	—	10000	10000	10000	—	—	—	—	—
PKP PECHENEG CHALLENGES																	
Get N kills with this weapon.	Prestige: Marksman	500	1000	2500	—	—	—	—	—	10000	10000	10000	—	—	—	—	—
Get N headshots with this weapon.	Prestige: Expert	250	500	1000	—	—	—	—	—	10000	10000	10000	—	—	—	—	—
M60E4 CHALLENGES																	
Get N kills with this weapon.	Prestige: Marksman	500	1000	2500	—	—	—	—	—	10000	10000	10000	—	—	—	—	—
Get N headshots with this weapon.	Prestige: Expert	250	500	1000	—	—	—	—	—	10000	10000	10000	—	—	—	—	—
MSR CHALLENGES																	
Get N kills with this weapon.	Prestige: Marksman	500	1000	2500	—	—	—	—	—	10000	10000	10000	—	—	—	—	—
Get N headshots with this weapon.	Prestige: Expert	250	500	1000	—	—	—	—	—	10000	10000	10000	—	—	—	—	—
L118A CHALLENGES																	
Get N kills with this weapon.	Prestige: Marksman	500	1000	2500	—	—	—	—	—	10000	10000	10000	—	—	—	—	—
Get N headshots with this weapon.	Prestige: Expert	250	500	1000	—	—	—	—	—	10000	10000	10000	—	—	—	—	—
BARRETT .50CAL CHALLENGES																	
Get N kills with this weapon.	Prestige: Marksman	500	1000	2500	—	—	—	—	—	10000	10000	10000	—	—	—	—	—
Get N headshots with this weapon.	Prestige: Expert	250	500	1000	—	—	—	—	—	10000	10000	10000	—	—	—	—	—

CHALLENGE DESCRIPTION	TITLE	TARGET 1	TARGET 2	TARGET 3	TARGET 4	TARGET 5	TARGET 6	TARGET 7	TARGET 8	XP 1	XP 2	XP 3	XP 4	XP 5	XP 6	XP 7	XP 8
RSASS CHALLENGES																	
Get N kills with this weapon.	Prestige: Marksman	500	1000	2500	—	—	—	—	—	10000	10000	10000	—	—	—	—	—
Get N headshots with this weapon.	Prestige: Expert	250	500	1000	—	—	—	—	—	10000	10000	10000	—	—	—	—	—
DRAGUNOV CHALLENGES																	
Get N kills with this weapon.	Prestige: Marksman	500	1000	2500	—	—	—	—	—	10000	10000	10000	—	—	—	—	—
Get N headshots with this weapon.	Prestige: Expert	250	500	1000	—	—	—	—	—	10000	10000	10000	—	—	—	—	—
AS50 CHALLENGES																	
Get N kills with this weapon.	Prestige: Marksman	500	1000	2500	—	—	—	—	—	10000	10000	10000	—	—	—	—	—
Get N headshots with this weapon.	Prestige: Expert	250	500	1000	—	—	—	—	—	10000	10000	10000	—	—	—	—	—
SPAS-12 CHALLENGES																	
Get N kills with this weapon.	Prestige: Marksman	500	1000	2500	—	—	—	—	—	10000	10000	10000	—	—	—	—	—
Get N headshots with this weapon.	Prestige: Expert	250	500	1000	—	—	—	—	—	10000	10000	10000	—	—	—	—	—
KSG 12 CHALLENGES																	
Get N kills with this weapon.	Prestige: Marksman	500	1000	2500	—	—	—	—	—	10000	10000	10000	—	—	—	—	—
Get N headshots with this weapon.	Prestige: Expert	250	500	1000	—	—	—	—	—	10000	10000	10000	—	—	—	—	—
AA12 CHALLENGES																	
Get N kills with this weapon.	Prestige: Marksman	500	1000	2500	—	—	—	—	—	10000	10000	10000	—	—	—	—	—
Get N headshots with this weapon.	Prestige: Expert	250	500	1000	—	—	—	—	—	10000	10000	10000	—	—	—	—	—
STRIKER CHALLENGES																	
Get N kills with this weapon.	Prestige: Marksman	500	1000	2500	—	—	—	—	—	10000	10000	10000	—	—	—	—	—
Get N headshots with this weapon.	Prestige: Expert	250	500	1000	—	—	—	—	—	10000	10000	10000	—	—	—	—	—
USAS 12 CHALLENGES																	
Get N kills with this weapon.	Prestige: Marksman	500	1000	2500	—	—	—	—	—	10000	10000	10000	—	—	—	—	—
Get N headshots with this weapon.	Prestige: Expert	250	500	1000	—	—	—	—	—	10000	10000	10000	—	—	—	—	—
MODEL 1887 CHALLENGES																	
Get N kills with this weapon.	Prestige: Marksman	500	1000	2500	—	—	—	—	—	10000	10000	10000	—	—	—	—	—
Get N headshots with this weapon.	Prestige: Expert	250	500	1000	—	—	—	—	—	10000	10000	10000	—	—	—	—	—
FMG9 CHALLENGES																	
Get N kills with this weapon.	Prestige: Marksman	500	1000	2500	—	—	—	—	—	10000	10000	10000	—	—	—	—	—
Get N headshots with this weapon.	Prestige: Expert	250	500	1000	—	—	—	—	—	10000	10000	10000	—	—	—	—	—
G18 CHALLENGES																	
Get N kills with this weapon.	Prestige: Marksman	500	1000	2500	—	—	—	—	—	10000	10000	10000	—	—	—	—	—
Get N headshots with this weapon.	Prestige: Expert	250	500	1000	—	—	—	—	—	10000	10000	10000	—	—	—	—	—
SKORPION CHALLENGES																	
Get N kills with this weapon.	Prestige: Marksman	500	1000	2500	—	—	—	—	—	10000	10000	10000	—	—	—	—	—
Get N headshots with this weapon.	Prestige: Expert	250	500	1000	—	—	—	—	—	10000	10000	10000	—	—	—	—	—
MP9 CHALLENGES																	
Get N kills with this weapon.	Prestige: Marksman	500	1000	2500	—	—	—	—	—	10000	10000	10000	—	—	—	—	—
Get N headshots with this weapon.	Prestige: Expert	250	500	1000	—	—	—	—	—	10000	10000	10000	—	—	—	—	—
USP .45 CHALLENGES																	
Get N kills with this weapon.	Prestige: Marksman	500	1000	2500	—	—	—	—	—	10000	10000	10000	—	—	—	—	—
Get N headshots with this weapon.	Prestige: Expert	250	500	1000	—	—	—	—	—	10000	10000	10000	—	—	—	—	—

CHALLENGE DESCRIPTION	TITLE	TARGET 1	TARGET 2	TARGET 3	TARGET 4	TARGET 5	TARGET 6	TARGET 7	TARGET 8	XP 1	XP 2	XP 3	XP 4	XP 5	XP 6	XP 7	XP 8
MP412 CHALLENGES																	
Get N kills with this weapon.	Prestige: Marksman	500	1000	2500	—	—	—	—	—	10000	10000	10000	—	—	—	—	—
Get N headshots with this weapon.	Prestige: Expert	250	500	1000	—	—	—	—	—	10000	10000	10000	—	—	—	—	—
.44 MAGNUM CHALLENGES																	
Get N kills with this weapon.	Prestige: Marksman	500	1000	2500	—	—	—	—	—	10000	10000	10000	—	—	—	—	—
Get N headshots with this weapon.	Prestige: Expert	250	500	1000	—	—	—	—	—	10000	10000	10000	—	—	—	—	—
DESERT EAGLE CHALLENGES																	
Get N kills with this weapon.	Prestige: Marksman	500	1000	2500	—	—	—	—	—	10000	10000	10000	—	—	—	—	—
Get N headshots with this weapon.	Prestige: Expert	250	500	1000	—	—	—	—	—	10000	10000	10000	—	—	—	—	—
P99 CHALLENGES																	
Get N kills with this weapon.	Prestige: Marksman	500	1000	2500	—	—	—	—	—	10000	10000	10000	—	—	—	—	—
Get N headshots with this weapon.	Prestige: Expert	250	500	1000	—	—	—	—	—	10000	10000	10000	—	—	—	—	—
FIVE SEVEN CHALLENGES																	
Get N kills with this weapon.	Prestige: Marksman	500	1000	2500	—	—	—	—	—	10000	10000	10000	—	—	—	—	—
Get N headshots with this weapon.	Prestige: Expert	250	500	1000	—	—	—	—	—	10000	10000	10000	—	—	—	—	—
SMAW CHALLENGES																	
Get N kills with this weapon.	Prestige: Marksman	500	1000	2500	—	—	—	—	—	10000	10000	10000	—	—	—	—	—
Get N Multi-Kills with this weapon.	Prestige: Expert	250	500	1000	—	—	—	—	—	10000	10000	10000	—	—	—	—	—
M320 GLM CHALLENGES																	
Get N kills with this weapon.	Prestige: Marksman	500	1000	2500	—	—	—	—	—	10000	10000	10000	—	—	—	—	—
Get N Multi-Kills with this weapon.	Prestige: Expert	250	500	1000	—	—	—	—	—	10000	10000	10000	—	—	—	—	—
STINGER CHALLENGES																	
Shoot down N helicopters with this weapon.	Prestige: Marksman	500	1000	2000	5000	—	—	—	—	10000	10000	10000	10000	—	—	—	—
Shoot down N helicopters with this weapon.	Prestige: Expert	250	500	1000	—	—	—	—	—	10000	10000	10000	—	—	—	—	—
JAVELIN CHALLENGES																	
Get N kills with this weapon.	Prestige: Marksman	500	1000	2500	—	—	—	—	—	10000	10000	10000	—	—	—	—	—
Get N Multi-Kills with this weapon.	Prestige: Expert	250	500	1000	—	—	—	—	—	10000	10000	10000	—	—	—	—	—
RPG CHALLENGES																	
Get N kills with this weapon.	Prestige: Marksman	500	1000	2500	—	—	—	—	—	10000	10000	10000	—	—	—	—	—
Get N Multi-Kills with this weapon.	Prestige: Expert	250	500	1000	—	—	—	—	—	10000	10000	10000	—	—	—	—	—
XM25 CHALLENGES																	
Get N kills with this weapon.	Prestige: Marksman	500	1000	2500	—	—	—	—	—	10000	10000	10000	—	—	—	—	—
Get N Multi-Kills with this weapon.	Prestige: Expert	250	500	1000	—	—	—	—	—	10000	10000	10000	—	—	—	—	—

CHALLENGE DESCRIPTION	TITLE	TARGET 1	TARGET 2	TARGET 3	TARGET 4	TARGET 5	TARGET 6	TARGET 7	TARGET 8	XP 1	XP 2	XP 3	XP 4	XP 5	XP 6	XP 7	XP 8
Call in N Assault UAVs.	Exposed	5	15	30	75	150	250	350	500	500	1000	2500	5000	10000	10000	10000	10000
Call in N Care Packages.	Air Mail	5	15	30	75	150	250	350	500	500	1000	2500	5000	10000	10000	10000	10000
Call in N Predator Missiles.	Air To Ground	5	15	30	75	150	250	350	500	500	1000	2500	5000	10000	10000	10000	10000
Call in N I.M.S.	Smart Mine	5	15	30	75	150	250	350	500	500	1000	2500	5000	10000	10000	10000	10000
Call in N Sentry Guns.	Automated Protection	5	15	30	75	150	250	350	500	500	1000	2500	5000	10000	10000	10000	10000
Call in N Precision Airstrikes.	Makin' It Rain	5	15	30	75	150	250	350	500	500	1000	2500	5000	10000	10000	10000	10000
Call in N Attack Helicopters.	Aerial Assault	5	15	30	75	150	250	350	500	500	1000	2500	5000	10000	10000	10000	10000
Call in N Strafe Runs.	Birds Of A Feather...	3	8	15	25	40	60	100	250	250	1000	2000	5000	10000	10000	10000	10000
Call in N AH-6 Overwatches.	Walkin' The Attack Dog	3	8	15	25	40	60	100	250	250	1000	2000	5000	10000	10000	10000	10000
Call in N Reapers.	Reaping The Rewards	3	8	15	25	40	60	100	250	250	1000	2000	5000	10000	10000	10000	10000
Call in N Assault Drones.	Careful, He Bites	3	8	15	25	40	60	100	250	250	1000	2000	5000	10000	10000	10000	10000
Call in N Pave Lows.	21 Ton Giant	3	8	15	25	40	60	100	250	250	1000	2000	5000	10000	10000	10000	10000
Call in N AC-130s.	Raining Death	3	8	15	25	40	60	100	250	250	1000	2000	5000	10000	10000	10000	10000
Call in N Juggernauts.	Monster	3	8	15	25	40	60	100	250	250	1000	2000	5000	10000	10000	10000	10000
Call in N Osprey Gunners.	Generosity	3	8	15	25	40	60	100	250	250	1000	2000	5000	10000	10000	10000	10000
Call in N Assault Pointstreak Rewards.	Assault Master	10	25	50	75	100	150	300	1000	500	1000	1500	2000	2500	3500	10000	10000

POINTSTREAK CHALLENGES: KILLS

CHALLENGE DESCRIPTION	TITLE	TARGET 1	TARGET 2	TARGET 3	TARGET 4	XP 1	XP 2	XP 3	XP 4
Kill an enemy by dropping a crate on them.	Heads Up!	1	—	—	—	2500	—	—	—
Get N kills with a Sentry Gun.	Look! No hands!	50	250	500	1000	2500	5000	10000	10000
Get N kills with a Predator Missile.	Predator	50	250	500	1000	2500	5000	10000	10000
Get N kills with a Precision Airstrike.	Carpet bomber	50	250	500	1000	2500	5000	10000	10000
Kill N enemies by calling in Attack Helicopters.	Aerial Assault Veteran	50	250	500	1000	2500	5000	10000	10000
Get N kills with a Pave Low.	Jolly Green Giant	50	250	500	1000	2500	5000	10000	10000
Get N kills with a Stealth Bomber.	The Spirit	50	250	500	1000	2500	5000	10000	10000
Get N kills with an AC-130.	Spectre	50	250	500	1000	2500	5000	10000	10000

POINTSTREAK CHALLENGES: SPECIALIST

CHALLENGE DESCRIPTION	TITLE	TARGET 1	TARGET 2	TARGET 3	TARGET 4	TARGET 5	TARGET 6	TARGET 7	TARGET 8	XP 1	XP 2	XP 3	XP 4	XP 5	XP 6	XP 7	XP 8
Earn Extreme Conditioning N times.	Why Walk?	5	15	30	75	150	250	350	500	500	1000	2500	5000	10000	10000	10000	10000
Earn Sleight Of Hand N times.	Magician	5	15	30	75	150	250	350	500	500	1000	2500	5000	10000	10000	10000	10000
Earn Scavenger N times.	Hoarder	5	15	30	75	150	250	350	500	500	1000	2500	5000	10000	10000	10000	10000
Earn Blind Eye N times.	Transparent	5	15	30	75	150	250	350	500	500	1000	2500	5000	10000	10000	10000	10000
Earn Recon N times.	Paintballer	5	15	30	75	150	250	350	500	500	1000	2500	5000	10000	10000	10000	10000
Earn Hardline N times.	Just One More	5	15	30	75	150	250	350	500	500	1000	2500	5000	10000	10000	10000	10000
Earn Assassin N times.	Hidden In Plain Sight	5	15	30	75	150	250	350	500	500	1000	2500	5000	10000	10000	10000	10000
Earn Quick Draw N times.	Cowboy	5	15	30	75	150	250	350	500	500	1000	2500	5000	10000	10000	10000	10000
Earn Blast Shield N times.	That Tickles	5	15	30	75	150	250	350	500	500	1000	2500	5000	10000	10000	10000	10000
Earn SitRep N times.	No Surprises	5	15	30	75	150	250	350	500	500	1000	2500	5000	10000	10000	10000	10000
Earn Markman N times.	Sniping Connoisseur	5	15	30	75	150	250	350	500	500	1000	2500	5000	10000	10000	10000	10000
Earn Steady Aim N times.	Why Aim?	5	15	30	75	150	250	350	500	500	1000	2500	5000	10000	10000	10000	10000
Earn Dead Silence N times.	Ninja Vanish	5	15	30	75	150	250	350	500	500	1000	2500	5000	10000	10000	10000	10000

CHALLENGE DESCRIPTION	TITLE	TARGET 1	TARGET 2	TARGET 3	TARGET 4	TARGET 5	TARGET 6	TARGET 7	TARGET 8	XP 1	XP 2	XP 3	XP 4	XP 5	XP 6	XP 7	XP 8
Earn Stalker N times.	Peeping Tom	5	15	30	75	150	250	350	500	500	1000	2500	5000	10000	10000	10000	10000
Earn the All Perks Bonus N times.	OMA	3	8	15	25	40	60	100	250	250	1000	2000	5000	10000	10000	10000	10000
Earn N Specialist Pointstreak Rewards.	Specialist Master	15	30	60	120	300	750	1000	1500	500	1000	2500	5000	10000	10000	10000	10000

POINTSTREAK CHALLENGES: SUPPORT

CHALLENGE DESCRIPTION	TITLE	TARGET 1	TARGET 2	TARGET 3	TARGET 4	TARGET 5	TARGET 6	TARGET 7	TARGET 8	XP 1	XP 2	XP 3	XP 4	XP 5	XP 6	XP 7	XP 8
Call in N Support UAVs.	Eye In The Sky	5	15	30	75	150	250	350	500	500	1000	2500	5000	10000	10000	10000	10000
Call in N Counter-UAVs.	Interference	5	15	30	75	150	250	350	500	500	1000	2500	5000	10000	10000	10000	10000
Call in N Ballistic Vests.	Well Protected	5	15	30	75	150	250	350	500	500	1000	2500	5000	10000	10000	10000	10000
Call in N Airdrop Traps.	Scare Package	5	15	30	75	150	250	350	500	500	1000	2500	5000	10000	10000	10000	10000
Call in N SAM Turrets.	Keeping 'em Down	5	15	30	75	150	250	350	500	500	1000	2500	5000	10000	10000	10000	10000
Call in N Recon Drones.	Mosquito	5	15	30	75	150	250	350	500	500	1000	2500	5000	10000	10000	10000	10000
Call in N Advanced UAVs.	Above And Beyond	5	15	30	75	150	250	350	500	500	1000	2500	5000	10000	10000	10000	10000
Call in N Remote Sentry Guns.	Remote Support	5	15	30	75	150	250	350	500	500	1000	2500	5000	10000	10000	10000	10000
Call in N Stealth Bombers.	Lead Curtain	3	8	15	25	40	60	100	250	250	1000	2000	5000	10000	10000	10000	10000
Call in N EMPs.	Blackout	3	8	15	25	40	60	100	250	250	1000	2000	5000	10000	10000	10000	10000
Call in N Juggernaut Recons.	Bullet Proof Monster	3	8	15	25	40	60	100	250	250	1000	2000	5000	10000	10000	10000	10000
Call in N Escort Airdrops.	Santa Claus With A Gun	3	8	15	25	40	60	100	250	250	1000	2000	5000	10000	10000	10000	10000
Call in N Support Pointstreak Rewards.	Support Master	10	25	50	75	100	150	300	1000	500	1000	1500	2000	2500	3500	10000	10000

SECRET CHALLENGES

CHALLENGE DESCRIPTION	TITLE	TARGET 1	TARGET 2	TARGET 3	TARGET 4	TARGET 5	TARGET 6	TARGET 7	TARGET 8	XP 1	XP 2	XP 3	XP 4	XP 5	XP 6	XP 7	XP 8
Get killed by an enemy M.O.A.B.	Fallout Shelter	1	—	—	—	—	—	—	—	1500	—	—	—	—	—	—	—
Killed by an infected...	Infected	1	—	—	—	—	—	—	—	1000	—	—	—	—	—	—	—
Transmission complete.	Transfer	1	—	—	—	—	—	—	—	1000	—	—	—	—	—	—	—
Kill 3 different people with 3 different weapons in one life.	Renaissance Man	1	—	—	—	—	—	—	—	1000	—	—	—	—	—	—	—
Get a 10 Pointstreak with 0 Pointstreaks selected.	The Loner	1	—	—	—	—	—	—	—	2500	—	—	—	—	—	—	—
Get a 7-8-9 Pointstreak.	6 Fears 7	1	—	—	—	—	—	—	—	1500	—	—	—	—	—	—	—
Get 1 kill with a Martyrdom Death Streak.	Martyr	1	—	—	—	—	—	—	—	1000	—	—	—	—	—	—	—
Survive Final Stand.	Living Dead	1	—	—	—	—	—	—	—	1000	—	—	—	—	—	—	—
Get 3 kills in one life with your secondary weapon.	Sidekick	1	—	—	—	—	—	—	—	1000	—	—	—	—	—	—	—
Get 1 kill with C4 while in Final Stand.	Click Click Boom	1	—	—	—	—	—	—	—	1000	—	—	—	—	—	—	—
Hijack N crates.	Hijacker	10	50	200	—	—	—	—	—	2500	5000	10000	—	—	—	—	—
Kill an enemy cooking a Frag Grenade.	Martyrdoh!	1	—	—	—	—	—	—	—	1000	—	—	—	—	—	—	—
Avenge a fallen teammate.	...with a Vengance.	1	—	—	—	—	—	—	—	1000	—	—	—	—	—	—	—
Call in N M.O.A.B.s.	Mother Of All Bombs	2	5	15	25	40	60	100	250	2500	5000	10000	10000	10000	10000	10000	10000

LEVEL UNLOCKS

WEAPONS

PRIMARY WEAPONS

Level	AR	SMG	LMG	Sniper	Shotgun
4	M4A1, M16A4	MP5, UMP45	L86 LSW, MG36	Barrett .50CAL, L118A	USAS 12, KSG 12
6	SCAR-L	—	—	—	—
8	—	—	—	—	SPAS-12
12	—	—	—	Dragunov	—
14	—	—	PKP Pecheneg	—	—
18	CM901	—	—	—	—
21	—	—	—	AS50	—
26	—	—	—	—	AA-12
28	—	PP90M1	—	—	—
32	Type 95	—	—	—	—
38	—	P90	—	—	—
42	G36C	—	—	—	—
43	—	—	—	RSASS	—
48	—	—	—	—	Striker
50	ACR 6.8	—	—	—	—
54	—	—	MK46	—	—
56	—	PM-9	—	—	—
60	MK14	—	—	—	—
62	—	—	—	—	Model 1887
66	—	—	—	MSR	—
68	AK-47	—	—	—	—
72	—	—	M60E4	—	—
74	—	MP7	—	—	—
78	FAD	—	—	—	—

SECONDARY WEAPONS

Level	Machine Pistol	Handgun	Launcher
4	FMG9	USP .45	SMAW
10	—	P99	—
16	MP9	—	—
24	—	—	Javelin
29	—	MP412	—
36	Skorpion	—	—
40	—	—	Stinger
46	—	.44 Magnum	—
52	—	—	XM25
58	—	Five Seven	—
64	—	—	M320 GLM
70	G18	—	—
76	—	Desert Eagle	—
80	—	—	RPG-7

EQUIPMENT

LETHAL

Level	Lethal
4	Frag, Semtex
5	Throwing Knife
37	Bouncing Betty
53	Claymore
69	C4

TACTICAL

Level	Tactical
4	Flash Grenade, Concussion Grenade
13	Scrambler
21	EMP Grenade
29	Smoke Grenade
45	Trophy System
61	Tactical Insertion
77	Portable Radar

PERKS

PERK 1

Level	Perk 1
4	Recon, Sleight of Hand
11	Blind Eye
22	Extreme Conditioning
38	Scavenger

PERK 2

Level	Perk 2
4	Quickdraw, Blast Shield
15	Hardline
27	Assassin
47	Overkill

PERK 3

Level	Perk 3
4	Marksman, Stalker
19	Sitrep
30	Steady Aim
55	Dead Silence

STREAKS

Pointstreaks are not unlocked at specific levels (beyond the basic streaks awarded at Level 5).

LEVEL 5 UNLOCKS

Assault	UAV, Predator, Attack Helicopter
Support	UAV, SAM Turret, Advanced UAV

At certain levels you receive a Pointstreak unlock point that can be used to unlock a Pointstreak reward of your choice from the Assault or Support lists.

POINTSTREAK POINT UNLOCK LEVELS

8	32	60
11	36	64
14	38	66
18	42	68
21	44	74
26	50	76
30	54	80

SPECIAL

Level	Unlock
4	Riot Shield
19	Specialist Strike Package

WEAPON UNLOCKS

CAMOUFLAGE GALLERY

You can acquire camouflage for all of your primary weapons by leveling them up. There are a few minor differences for when each weapon class earns a particular camouflage. Take a look at this gallery to see how the camouflage looks when applied to a weapon.

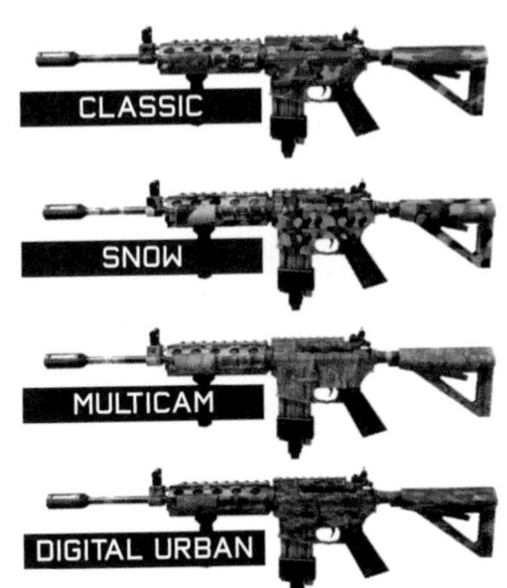

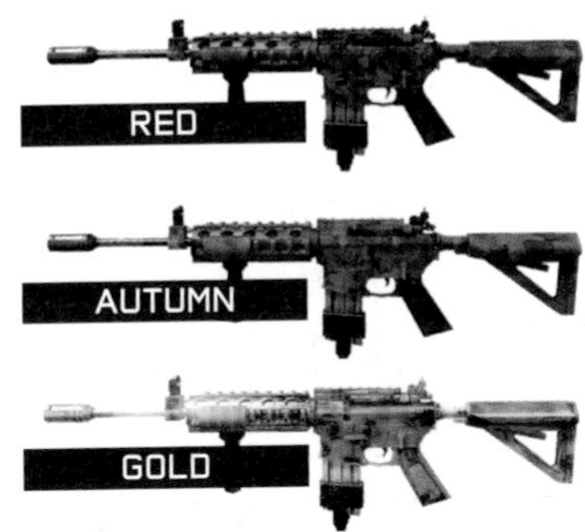

ASSAULT RIFLE UNLOCKS

Level	AR Camo	AR Proficiencies	AR Attachments
2	—	—	Red Dot Sight
3	Classic	—	—
4	—	Kick	—
5	Snow	—	Silencer
6	Multicam	—	—
8	Digital Urban	—	Grenade Launcher
9	—	Impact	—
10	Hex	—	—
11	—	—	ACOG Scope
12	—	Attachments	—
13	Choco	—	Heartbeat Sensor
16	—	Focus	—
17	—	—	Hybrid Sight
18	Snake	—	—
20	—	—	Shotgun
22	—	Breath	—
23	—	—	Holographic Sight
24	Blue	—	—
26	—	—	Extended Mags
27	Red	—	—
28	—	Stability	—
29	—	—	Thermal
30	Autumn	—	—
31	Gold	—	—

SUBMACHINE GUN UNLOCKS

Level	SMG Camo	SMG Proficiencies	SMG Attachments
2	—	—	Red Dot Sight
3	Classic	—	—
4	—	Kick	—
5	—	—	Silencer
6	Snow	—	—
7	Multicam	—	—
8	Digital Urban	Range	—
9	—	—	—
10	Hex	—	—
11	—	—	Rapid Fire
12	—	Attachments	—
14	Choco	—	—
15	—	Focus	—
16	—	—	ACOG Scope
18	Snake	—	—
19	—	—	HAMR Scope
21	—	Melee	—
22	—	—	Holographic Sight
23	—	—	—
24	—	—	Extended Mags
25	Blue	—	—
26	—	—	Thermal
27	Red	—	—
28	—	Stability	—
29	Autumn	—	—
30	—	—	—
31	Gold	—	—

LIGHT MACHINE GUN UNLOCKS

Level	LMG Camo	LMG Proficiencies	LMG Attachments
2	—	—	Red Dot Sight
3	Classic	—	—
4	—	Kick	—
5	Snow	—	Silencer
6	Multicam	—	—
7	—	—	—
8	Digital Urban	—	Grip
9	—	Impact	—
10	Hex	—	—
11	—	—	ACOG Scope
12	—	Attachments	—
13	Choco	—	—
14	—	—	Rapid Fire
16	—	Focus	—
18	Snake	—	—
20	—	—	Heartbeat Sensor
21	—	Speed	—
22	—	—	Holographic Sight
23	Blue	—	—
25	—	—	Extended Mags
26	Red	—	—
27	—	—	Thermal
28	—	Stability	—
29	Autumn	—	—
30	—	—	—
31	Gold	—	—

SNIPER RIFLE UNLOCKS

Level	Sniper Camo	Sniper Proficiencies	Sniper Attachments
2	—	—	ACOG Scope
3	Classic	—	—
4	—	Kick	—
5	—	—	Silencer
6	Snow	—	—
8	Multicam	—	—
10	—	Impact	—
11	Digital Urban	—	—
13	—	Attachments	Extended Mags
14	—	—	—
15	—	—	Heartbeat Sensor
16	Hex	—	—
18	—	Focus	—
19	—	—	Thermal
20	Choco	—	—
22	—	—	Variable Zoom Scope
23	Snake	—	—
24	—	Speed	—
25	Blue	—	—
26	Red	—	—
28	—	Stability	—
29	Autumn	—	—
31	Gold	—	—

SHOTGUN UNLOCKS

Level	Shotgun Camo	Shotgun Proficiencies	Shotgun Attachments
2	—	—	Grip
3	Classic	—	—
4	—	Kick	—
5	—	—	Silencer
6	Snow	—	—
7	Multicam	—	—
9	—	Focus	—
10	Digital Urban	—	—
11	Hex	—	—
12	—	—	Red Dot Sight
13	Choco	—	—
14	—	Attachments	—
17	—	—	Holographic Sight
18	Snake	—	—
19	—	Melee	—
21	Blue	—	—
23	—	Range	—
26	—	—	Extended Mags
27	Red	—	—
28	—	Damage	—
29	Autumn	—	—
30	—	—	—
31	Gold	—	—

RIOT SHIELD UNLOCKS

Level	Riot Shield Proficiencies
5	Melee
10	Speed

MACHINE PISTOL UNLOCKS

Level	MP Attachments
2	Silencer
5	Akimbo
7	Holographic Sight
8	Red Dot Sight
10	Extended Mags

HANDGUN UNLOCKS

Level	Handgun Attachments
2	Silencer
5	Akimbo
7	Tactical Knife
10	Extended Mags

EXTRAS

CALLSIGN

Your Callsign is simply your username with an attached Emblem icon and a background Title. You can earn Titles and Emblems by completing a variety of challenges, with some basic ones unlocked immediately. You can also quickly unlock the ability to set a Clan Tag, giving you the ability to fully customize your Callsign.

Your full Callsign only shows up to enemies who watch Killcams from your point of view, which can be viewed in the lobby by any player.

CHALLENGES AND ACCOLADES

There are dozens of Challenges to tackle in *Modern Warfare 3*. The vast majority just award bonus experience, allowing you to rank up faster and unlock new items.

A handful of Challenges are tied to the perks, and completing them unlocks the Pro version of that specific perk.

Finally, there are Prestige Challenges that carry over when you Prestige, allowing you to gain some bonus experience to speed up your second (and subsequent) Prestige runs.

ACCOLADES

Accolades are awards earned after a match for specific behavior: longest distance sprinted, most time prone, least kills from behind, and so on.

Accolades don't provide any gameplay bonuses. They are only a running tally of *how you play*. By comparing your Accolades with those of your friends, you can see who is aggressive, who is defensive, and who has the dubious honor of earning 'special' Accolades awarded for particularly poor (or amusing) performances.

PRESTIGE MODE

When you reach level 80, you face a choice. You can remain at level 80 with all of your unlocked items, *or* you can give it all up for a shiny new icon and a bit of glory. Entering Prestige mode resets your level to 1 and removes all of your acquired items, though you do retain your Clan Tag and ability to use Custom Classes.

This also earns you a Prestige Point. You can spend these points to purchase certain special rewards, including special titles and emblems, bonus double-XP time, extra custom classes, or the ability to retain one (and only one) unlocked item into future Prestige runs.

At the end of the road—tenth Prestige—you also gain the ability to reset all of your stats, fully cleaning your slate to begin anew. Feel like gaining 800 levels? Get to work, soldier!

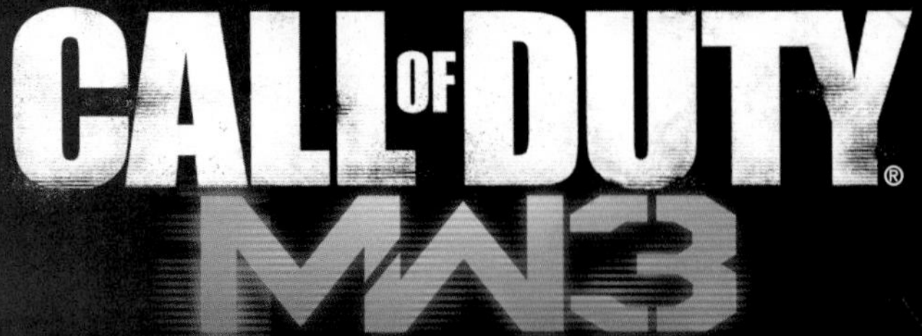

OFFICIAL STRATEGY GUIDE

Written by Michael Owen, Phillip Marcus, Jason Fox, Arthur Davis, and Michael Fry
Maps illustrated by Rich Hunsinger

DK/BradyGames, a division of Penguin Group (USA) Inc.
800 East 96th Street, 3rd Floor
Indianapolis, IN 46240

ISBN 10: 0-7440-1347-X

ISBN 13 EAN: 978-0-7440-1347-4

Printing Code: The rightmost double-digit number is the year of the book's printing; the rightmost single-digit number is the number of the book's printing. For example, 11-1 shows that the first printing of the book occurred in 2011.

14 13 12 11 4 3 2 1

Printed in the USA.

BRADYGAMES STAFF

Global Strategy Guide Publisher
MIKE DEGLER

Digital and Trade Category Publisher
BRIAN SALIBA

Editor-In-Chief
H. LEIGH DAVIS

Licensing Manager
CHRISTIAN SUMNER

Operations Manager
STACEY BEHELER

CREDITS

Title Manager
TIM FITZPATRICK

Development Editor, LE
JENNIFER SIMS

Book Designer
TIM AMRHEIN

Designer, LE
DAN CAPARO

Production Designer
WIL CRUZ

Copy Editor
HEIDI NEWMAN

ACKNOWLEDGMENTS

BradyGAMES sincerely thanks everyone at Infinity Ward, Sledgehammer Games, and Activision for their incredible support and hospitality. A thousand thanks to Pete Blumel, Andy Dohr, Richard Kriegler and John Wasilczyk—your time, effort, and generous participation made this guide possible! Very special thanks to Mike Mejia, Sahara Martinez, Karen Starr, Marcus Iremonger, Bret Robbins, Michael Condrey, Derek Racca, Vince Fennel, Adrienne "Rizzo" Arrasmith, John Banayan, and Daniel Shaffer for your tireless assistance all the way down to the wire—thank you!

Michael Owen: It's a great privilege to work on the guide for such a highly-anticipated game as *Call of Duty: Modern Warfare 3*. It's even better when you have a great team helping to put it all together. Big thanks to Phillip Marcus for being a consummate professional as my authoring partner, and to Rich Hunsinger for creating some amazing maps. I couldn't have gotten through the Special Operations without help from Arthur Davis, Michael Fry, and Jason Fox.

I'd like to extend thanks to Leigh Davis for giving me this opportunity. The biggest of thanks goes to Tim Fitzpatrick for taking in all of the content, mixing it all together, and creating this masterpiece. Thank you to Tim Amrhein and Wil Cruz for designing this beautiful guide.

A huge thanks must go out to everyone at Infinity Ward for all the great assistance. Thanks to Pete Blumel and Andy Dohr for getting us what we needed, to Joe for all the great Special Operations information, and to Cheng and Norbert for the Survival mode strategy.

Last, but definitely not least, I thank my lovely wife, Michelle, for picking up the slack at home and putting up with me through this busy time.

Phillip Marcus: In the span of just a few years, *Modern Warfare* went from a hit to a superstar, and for me personally, it has become one of my very favorite online games. Working on the multiplayer has been a real pleasure, and I hope this guide helps you have just a little bit more fun.

As always, a book of this size is the work of many people, with contributions from even more. A tip of the hat to Tim Fitzpatrick, for helming a grueling march to the finish, Pete Blumel at Infinity Ward for welcoming our whole crazy crew onsite with good grace, and Jordan Hirsh for answering my constant nitpicky queries on all aspects of the game. The multiplayer design team, level designers, and programmers at IW all played a role as well, answering questions and offering advice that helped shape and refine this guide.

Respect to our awesome on-site team: Rich Hunsinger, Michael Fry, Arthur Davis, and Michael Owen. Rich's maps are the ones you're ogling in this book, and the Sea Snipers team (consisting of Army and Navy vets—sorry, Air Force) helped test and retest all aspects of MP. Michael, of course, handled that *other* part of the game, the epic campaign!

Finally, very special thanks to my good friend Jason Fox, who has not only been my battle brother since the first *Modern Warfare*, but has also assisted with his programming expertise on numerous crucial tasks. Jason was invaluable in handling the level of weapon detail we were able to share in this guide.

Oh, and you Evilgamer fans? You rock!

And while I know the ladies never read these, I love you Daphne!

Rich Hunsinger: Big thanks to everyone at Infinity Ward for their support, especially Pete Blumel, Andy Dohr, Jordan Hirsh, and Greta Gravrisheff. They helped make our stay as productive as possible; thanks everyone! Thanks to Chief and Grunt for their hard work on this project. It couldn't have been done without you, boys! Thank you to all of the Sea Snipers, and especially my wife for enduring our 11th anniversary alone while I was working on this guide. Happy anniversary, baby girl!

CPL Arthur "Tony" Davis: I would like to thank God, my family and friends, the Sea Snipers, and the 89th Trans, both here and in Iraq. I'd like to thank Infinity Ward for their incredible hospitality toward us. I'll never forget this and hope to work with you guys again.

Michael Fry: I'd like to thank the wonderful folks of Infinity Ward, who truly rolled out the red carpet—especially Jordan Hirsh, who endured my many screams of frustration, as his skilled development team knew all the great hiding spots. I'm glad you had headphones on hand in your office. I'd also like to thank my two sons, Mao Shinoda and Cody Fry—you boys help me stay young; and my fellow Sea Sniper Brethren—I'm sure we're going to log many hours in this latest addition to the *Call of Duty* family. And finally, thanks to Brian and Nicholas Gawlik, who've continued being my willing online victims through and through!

Jason Fox: Another year, another *Call of Duty* guide—and this one was the most enjoyable to create yet. Thanks again to Phil for bringing me along and cracking the union-boss whip during the trip. Big thanks to Jordan Hirsh for getting us the data we needed and accompanying us for the extended hours creating this guide. As with previous guides, I have to thank my wife and son for letting me do these crazy things and for putting up with my gaming addiction.